Describing the World

ENTERPRISE

MODEL

PATTERNS

The UML Version

DAVID C. HAY

Published by:
Technics Publications, LLC
Post Office Box 161
Bradley Beach, NJ 07720 U.S.A.
www.technicspub.com

Edited by Carol Lehn
Cover design by Mark Brye
Origami globe designed by Tomako Fusé and folded by Robert Hay

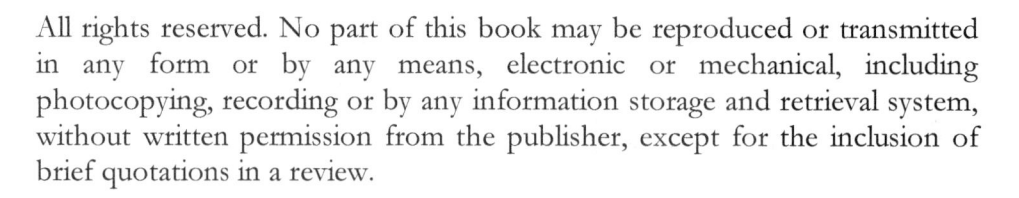

All rights reserved. No part of this book may be reproduced or transmitted in any form or by any means, electronic or mechanical, including photocopying, recording or by any information storage and retrieval system, without written permission from the publisher, except for the inclusion of brief quotations in a review.

The author and publisher have taken care in the preparation of this book, but make no expressed or implied warranty of any kind and assume no responsibility for errors or omissions. No liability is assumed for incidental or consequential damages in connection with or arising out of the use of the information or programs contained herein.

All trade and product names are trademarks, registered trademarks, or service marks of their respective companies, and are the property of their respective holders and should be treated as such.

This book is printed on acid-free paper.

Copyright © 2011 by David C. Hay

ISBN, print ed.   978-1-9355040-5-4
First Printing 2011
Second Printing 2012

Library of Congress Control Number: 2010932253

ATTENTION SCHOOLS AND BUSINESSES: Technics Publications books are available at quantity discounts with bulk purchase for educational, business, or sales promotional use. For information, please write to Technics Publications, PO Box 161, Bradley Beach, NJ 07090, or email Steve Hoberman, President of Technics Publications, at me@stevehoberman.com

Dedicated to my children,

Pamela and Bob

My inspiration and my teachers

Contents at a Glance

PART ONE: Introduction 31
Chapter 1: Data modeling's promise . . . and failure 33
Chapter 2: About Conventions 41
Chapter 3: About This Book 75

PART TWO: Level 1 - The Generic Enterprise Model 81
Chapter 4 : People and Organizations (Who) 83
Chapter 5: Geographic Locations (Where) 107
Chapter 6: Assets (What) 129
Chapter 7: Activities (How) 153
Chapter 8: Timing (When) 173

PART THREE: Level 0 - A Template and Metadata 181
Chapter 9: The Template 183
Chapter 10: Documents and Other Information Resources 207
Chapter 11: Accounting 221

PART FOUR: Level 2 - Within an Organization 237
Chapter 12: Facilities 241
Chapter 13: Human Resources 263
Chapter 14: Marketing and Communications 287
Chapter 15: Contracts 301
Chapter 16: Manufacturing 313
Chapter 17: The Laboratory 337

PART FIVE: Level 3 - Some Industry-Specific Examples 357
Chapter 18: Criminal Justice 361
Chapter 19: Microbiology 377
Chapter 20: Banking 389
Chapter 21: Oil Field Production 417
Chapter 22: Highway Maintenance 437

Contents

Foreword 15
Preface 17
Acknowledgements 27

PART ONE: Introduction 31

Chapter 1: Data modeling's promise . . . and failure 33
Business vs. Systems Issues 34
Fundamentals of the Business 37
Clarity 38
The Response: This Book 38
In Summary 39

Chapter 2: About Conventions 41
Notation Conventions 42
   UML on the Prowl 42
   Your Author Surrenders 43
   Warning to Data Modelers 45
   Warning to UML Modelers 46
   A Peace Offering 47
   The Notation 47
      Entity Classes (and Objects) 47
      Sub-types and Super-types 48
      Attributes 49
      Relationships 51
      Unique Identifiers 54
Aesthetic Conventions 56
   Straighten Lines 57
   Starry Skies Orientation 59
   Limit Number of (Highlighted) Boxes 61
   Follow Accepted Graphic Design Principles 62
Architectural Conventions 64
   About Abstraction 70
In Summary 73

Chapter 3: About This Book **75**
Levels of Abstraction 75
The Organization of the Book 78

PART TWO: Level 1 - The Generic Enterprise Model **81**

Chapter 4: People and Organizations (Who) **83**
Parties 85
Party Relationships 87
Party Identifiers and Names 89
    Constraints 95
Party Characteristics 98
Derived Characteristics 103
Characteristics and Party Types 105
Summary 106

Chapter 5: Geographic Locations (Where) **107**
Geographic Location 107
Geographic Location Relationships 110
Geographic Names 112
Geographic Identifiers 115
Geographic Location Characteristics 119
Derived Characteristics 122
Characteristics and Geographic Location Types 124
Geographic Roles 125
Summary 127

Chapter 6: Assets (What) **129**
About Assets 129
Assets, Asset Types, and Asset Specifications 131
Asset Structures 136
Naming and Identifying Assets 140
Describing Assets 143
Derived Characteristics 148
Asset Roles 150
Summary 151

Chapter 7: Activities (How) 153
Defining Activities 153
Naming and Identifying Activities 157
Dividing up Activities 159
    Approach 1 – Steps and Projects 159
    Approach 2 – Activity Structures 161
Activity Characteristics 163
Derived Characteristics 165
Events 168
Activity Roles 170
Summary 171

Chapter 8: Timing (When) 173
Capturing Time with Attributes 173
Capturing Time with Entity Classes 174
Summary 179

PART THREE: Level 0 - A Template and Metadata 181

Chapter 9: The Template 183
Thing and Thing Type 183
Things and the Enterprise Model 188
Thing Relationship 191
Thing Names and Identifiers 193
Thing Characteristics 197
    Derived Characteristics 200
Thing Characteristic Constraints 202
Thing Role 203
A Word about Language 205
Summary 206

Chapter 10: Documents and other Information Resources . 207
Information Resources 207
Information Resource Relationships 210
Concepts 211
    Information Resources and Concepts 213
Distribution 215

x Enterprise Model Patterns

Dispositions 216
Summary 219

Chapter 11: Accounting 221
Accounts 221
   Rolling up Accounts 225
Accounting Transactions 227
Accounting Transaction Rules 230
Connections to the Real World 233
   Cost Center Assignments 233
   Transaction Assignments 235
Summary 236

PART Four: Level 2 - Within an Organization 237

Chapter 12: Facilities 241
Parties and Facilities 241
   Addresses 243
Geographic Locations and Facilities 246
   The Direct Approach (U.S. Version) 247
   The Abstract (International) Approach 251
Activities and Facilities 255
Assets and Facilities 257
   Asset Types and Specification Locations 260
Summary 261

Chapter 13: Human Resources 263
Employment 263
   Position Assignments 265
   Hiring 269
Education and Certification 270
   Certification Requirements 271
   Obtaining Certification 275
Benefits 276
Payday! 279
   Accounting Implications 283

Contents   xi

Chapter 14: Marketing and Communications 287
About Communications 287
    Communication Role 289
    Communications Among Sites 291
    Communication Procedures 292
Advertising and Information Resource 295
    Communication in Context 296
    Events 299
Summary 300

Chapter 15: Contracts 301
Contracts 302
    Contract Costs 305
    Employment as a Contract 307
Delivering Against a Contract 307
    Contract Roles 310
Summary 312

Chapter 16: Manufacturing 313
The Manufacturing Process 313
    Routing Steps 313
    Work Orders 315
        Production Work Orders 315
    Dependence 317
    Maintenance Work Orders 323
Material Usage 325
    Asset Specification Structure 325
    Material Usage Costs 326
        Material Movement 326
        Asset Structure 329
        Utilizing Equipment 329
        Adjustments 330
Labor Usage 331
    Standard Labor Cost 331
    Actual Labor Cost 332
    Accounting for Manufacturing Costs 334

Summary **336**

Chapter 17: The Laboratory **337**
Samples **337**
Laboratory Tests **340**
    Sampling in Context 342
The Laboratory Model in Context **345**
Observations **347**
    Actual Observations 347
    Expected Observations 349
Parameters and Characteristics.. **351**
    Derived Parameters 353
Summary **355**

PART FIVE: Level 3 - Some Industry-Specific Examples ... 357
The Examples **358**
A Word of Advice—and an Invitation **359**

Chapter 18: Criminal Justice **361**
Cases **362**
    Evidence and Status..365
    Linking to the Enterprise Model 366
    Events..367
People and Organizations **369**
    Characteristics and Categories..371
    Employment...373
    Roles 373
Summary **376**

Chapter 19: Microbiology **377**
Basic Chemistry **377**
Biochemistry.. **379**
    What Life is Made of...379
    How Life is Organized 381
Composition... **382**
Physical Structures **384**
Packaged Products **386**

Contents **xiii**

Summary 387

Chapter 20: Banking 389
Instruments and Instrument Specifications 390
   About Financial Instruments 391
   Instrument Characteristics..393
      Characteristic Values 396
   Instrument Categories 397
   Marketing Relationships 397
      Instrument Components 398
      Agreements 400
   Roles 402
   Delivering Against Instruments..404
   Geography and Currency...407
   Guidance Facility 409
Banking and the Enterprise Model **411**
   Agreements and Asset Types 411
   Roles and Activities 413
Summary – An Issue..415

Chapter 21: Oil Field Production...417
Facilities...**417**
   Surface Facilities 418
   Completions 422
   Purposes and Products 425
Well Assemblies **428**
   Well Assemblies in Facilities 431
   Well Assembly Structure..432
   Well Assembly Characteristics 434

Chapter 22: Highway Maintenance 437
Paths...**437**
   Complex Paths 444
   Locating Nodes Geographically 444
Grade Separated Crossings **448**
Flows..**450**
Physical Assets **453**

A Final Word About Identifiers 457
Summary 458
Glossary 459
Bibliography 523
Index 529

Foreword

Recently, there was a lovely movie about a young writer/blogger who set out to learn the art of French cooking. She set out to cook each of the recipes in Julia Child's famous *Mastering the Art of French Cooking* in a year. In the end, this blogger not only taught herself the intricacies of French cuisine, but she learned important insights about French culture and a whole new way of thinking, as well.

This movie, which was based on a bestselling novel, revived interest in Julia Child and led to a reprinting of Child's most famous book. It also led my wife to pull out her treasured copy of Child's work and order a new copy, because her book was almost unusable—it had been literally "loved to death". On page after page, there were stains: stains of gravy, stains of wine and stains of butter. For contrast, there were bits of flour and pinches of salt, as well—and the pages that contained her favorite recipes were torn, and in many cases, held together with faded Scotch tape.

When people ask me to describe a data model pattern book by Dave Hay, I point to the Julia Child experience. Dave's data model pattern books are not intended to be read cover to cover in one sitting, or even in a week or a month. No, they are meant to be used. It might seem to trivialize Dave's work by comparing it to a cookbook, since the term "cookbook" has come to mean a non-thinking, step by step approach to something. But great cookbooks, as any great chef will tell you, represent anything but a trivial step-by-step approach. Rather, they are an attempt to provide, by way of a narrative and illustrations, something nearly impossible to share—experiences and a specific model of thinking about the world.

In this book, you will find on nearly every page an example of a way of "doing data modeling" that is the result of having been the disciple of one of the pioneering data modelers, Richard Barker, and then personally applying that training to literally hundreds of real-world projects. There are a number of ways one can teach a complex subject like data modeling-- Dave has chosen to use examples.

My advice is to read Dave's introduction and then scan the rest of the book, stopping to absorb those models that interest you. Then, after you have a sense of the nature of scope of the work, select a model or two that seems particularly important and analyze it in detail. The more you do this, the more impressed you will be with Dave's way of thinking and diagramming the real world.

If you are new to classical data modeling (if, for example, you come to this book because you saw that it used UML), don't put it down because it doesn't follow all of the conventions that you have been taught. What Dave has done is to translate one of the most significant bodies of data modeling knowledge, expressed in classical Entity-Relationship Diagrams (ERDs), into your language to make it easier for you to access, just as Julia Child adapted (transliterated) a French cookbook, begun by her co-authors, into real English without losing the nuances.

In the end, the success of this book will be in whether you use it to solve real world problems. Being an author means that you often don't know if anyone is reading what you wrote, or even if they read it they understand it. Occasionally, Dave will worry whether his writing is making a difference—I can tell you that it does. Indeed, I have people around the world with well worn copies of Dave's other books on their desks and in their code. Like Julia Child, Dave Hay has influenced a generation of data modelers both here and abroad. I'm pleased that Dave asked me to write this foreword. I wish you *bon appétit*.

Ken Orr

President and Founder of Ken Orr Associates

Preface

Any modeler trying to describe a business in graphic terms comes up with the same problems that faced map makers throughout the centuries. How does one represent a large, multi-dimensional topic on a flat piece of paper? First, you have to understand the domain you are trying to represent. This means you have to begin by gathering an incredible amount of detailed information. Then you have to render a multi-dimensional view in two dimensions. Even at that, however, you can only show a relatively small part of the information you have gathered. The most important decisions to be made in creating any map are to determine *which parts* to show. This means both the level of detail chosen and the details selected.

These are precisely the kinds of decisions that face a data modeler attempting to represent a business as comprehensively as possible, but with the right amount of detail to address a particular set of business problems.

Maps – Geographic Descriptions of the World

Map makers over the centuries faced their own challenges in trying to produce drawings to describe the physical world.

The effort, of course, was initially limited by how much of the world the original mapmakers knew. The earliest maps preserved for us are on clay tablets, created by the Babylonians in about 2300 BCE. By definition, these described a couple of square miles, at best. Cartography advanced in ancient Greece, giving us, among other things, the concept of a spherical Earth by the time of Aristotle, in 350 BCE.[1] In each case, however, a map could only describe the part of the world known to the map makers—that is, Europe, Northern Africa, and some of Asia

As the rest of the world was explored, the assignment was then to collect the millions of points required to draw maps describing it. The map shown in Figure Pre-1 shows Martin Waldseemüller's 1507 world map.

---

[1] J. S. Aber. 2008. "Brief History of Maps and Cartography". Emporia State University. http://academic.emporia.edu/aberjame/map/h_map/h_map.htm.

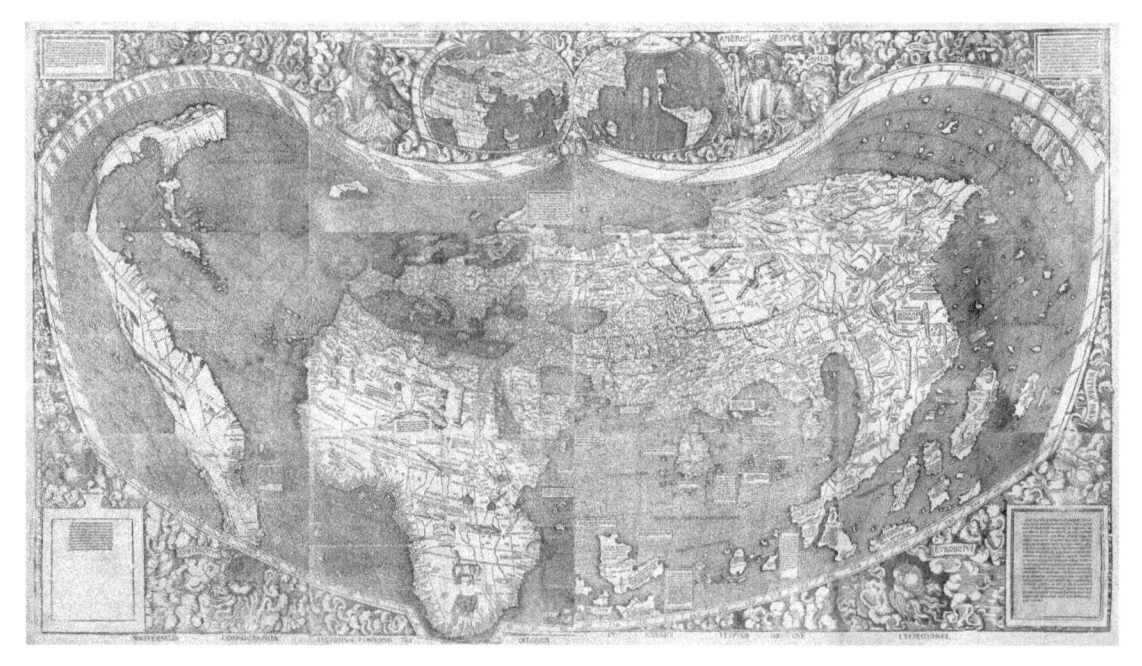

Figure Pre- 1: The First Map of America - 1507

This was the first map ever to portray the American continents, but, as you can see, there were still a *lot* of missing points. This map was based on notes from Columbus and Amerigo Vespucci[2], and it was Waldseemüller who, based on Vespucci's notes, first called the new continent "America"[♥][♣].

Forgetting the sheer number of points involved, producing maps of this new, enlarged, world also turn out to be difficult, because it was not easy even to identify the points. Determining latitude from the stars was straightforward enough, but the *longitude* of a point, in the ocean or in a remote land, could be determined also by examining the positions of the stars visible—but you also had to know the positions of the same stars—*at the same time*—in another part of the world! This required accurate clocks. Unfortunately, before the 18th century, clocks were not precise or stable enough for the task. In the 17th century, the astronomer Galileo discovered

---

[2]   Martin Waldseemüler. 1507. *Universalis cosmographia secundum Ptholomaei traditionem et Americi Vespucii alioru[m]que lustrationes*. In the collection of the Library of Congress Geography and Map Division Washington, D.C. Can be viewed at: http://www.loc.gov/rr/geogmap/waldexh.html

[♥]   In type too small to read on this reproduction, alas. But it is there in the original.

[♣]   For an excellent overview of the history and implications of this map (and more detailed presentations of it), see Toby Lester. 2009. *The Fourth Part of the World*. (New York: Free Press).

that the orbits of moons around Jupiter could be used as a kind of clock, but holding a telescope still enough on a moving ship was problematic.[3] Then, in response to a prize set out by a parliamentary committee in 1714, John Harrison set out to invent a clock precise enough and stable enough to keep time on board a rocking ship. He finally succeeded in 1759.[4]

So it wasn't until the late 1700s that the data were even available to create a moderately accurate map of the world.

In the 20th century, aerial photography--and ultimately satellite images--allowed for the creation of maps that were based on photographs. This was *much* easier, and made for much more accurate maps. More significantly, it allowed map makers to begin with larger structures and then fill in the details, instead of having to meticulously build up the structures from surveyed points.

Take note, however, that any map—as with any model of "reality"—must be but an approximation. Selection of both the level of detail required and the details to be included is a function of the purpose of the map. By definition, trying to map an immense, three-dimensional domain on a flat piece of paper—even in modern times—cannot be done without leaving off a *lot* of detail. A US Geological Survey (or UK Ordinance Survey) map has a different set of details than a common road map or a guide to a shopping center. A measure of the skill of a map maker is the ability to understand its purposes and to select the correct details to satisfy those purposes.

It was only in the 21st century that Google Corporation combined satellite maps with the technology of the World-wide Web to allow *anyone* to consult a map of nearly *any* part of the world—at *any* scale.

As with the advent of printed maps in the 15th century, 21st century technology revolutionized the ability to manipulate and use them.

Think about it: With a few key strokes, you can dynamically choose both the scale of a map and the details to portray. It is for the viewer to choose to view all of the United States, the San Francisco Bay area (Figure Pre-2) or a neighborhood in San Francisco (Figure Pre-3). It is now for the viewer to realize which scale he wants to see—or if he wants something in between.

---

[3]   J. S. Aber. 2008. "Brief History of Maps and Cartography". Emporia State University. http://academic.emporia.edu/aberjame/map/h_map/h_map.htm.

[4]   David Sobel. 1995. *Longitude: The True Story of a Lone Genius Who Solved the Greatest Scientific Problem of His Time* New York: Penguin Books

xx Enterprise Model Patterns

And the annotations? Do you want to show restaurants? Hotels? Tourist attractions? You decide.

Selecting level of detail? Choosing the details? Data modeling has the same problem.

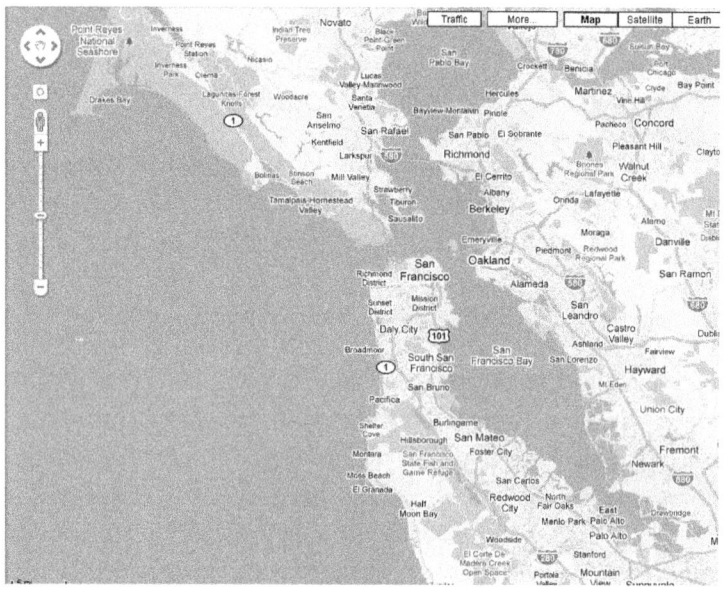

Figure Pre-2: San Francisco Bay Area, USA - 2010[5]

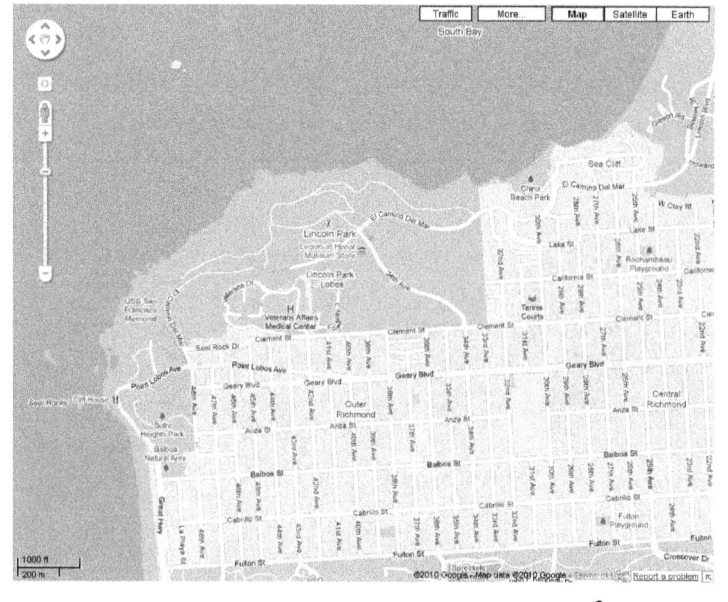

Figure Pre-3: San Francisco, USA – 2010[6]

---

[5] Map copyright © 2010 Google.

Data Modeling – Business Descriptions of the World

As with maps of the Earth, the first maps of companies' data were limited in "area". They were simply descriptions of the individual files used by the earliest programs. In effect, documentation of the files' layouts were maps. Moreover, there were separate files for every computer application program. That's a lot of unconnected maps.

In the 1960s, Charles Bachman created one of the first ***database management systems***[*], Integrated Data Store (IDS), which later became the IBM product, IDMS.[7] For the first time, a company could consider a complete set of data as a whole unit. There was little guidance, however, as to how to organize data, and none whatsoever as to how to document that organization.

Then, in 1970, Dr. Codd described his ***relational theory*** as a technique for organizing data into simple sets of rows and columns.[8] Specifically, a table was called a ***relation*** consisting of ***rows*** described by a fixed set of ***attributes*** as columns. There was no logical relationship (and no sequence implied) between rows, nor between attributes. This offered considerable advantage by reducing the complexity of the resulting data structures. Among other things, it also introduced the discipline of "normalization" that allowed one to take large quantities of data and infer structures from them.

Over the next decade or so, commercial database system products were introduced that were designed with the relational theory in mind.

In 1976, Dr. Peter Chen addressed the documentation issue with his invention of ***data modeling***, describing the domain of a system with boxes representing ***entity types***, circles representing ***attributes***, and lines connected to rhombi representing ***relationships***.[9] (Figure Pre-4 shows an example of this.) An entity type box

---

[6] Map copyright © 2010. Google.

[*] All terms in ***bold faced italics*** are specialized words that will also be defined in **Appendix A: Glossary**.

[7] Wikipedia. 2010. "Charles Bachman". Retrieved October 15, 2010 from http://en.wikipedia.org/wiki/Charles_Bachman

[8] Edward F. Codd. 1970. "A Relational Model of Data for Large Shared Data Banks." *Communications of the ACM* 13, No. 6 (June).

[9] Peter Chen. 1976. "The Entity-Relationship Approach to Logical Data Base Design." *The Q.E.D. Monograph Series: Data Management*. Wellesley, MA: Q.E.D. Information Sciences, Inc. This is based on his articles, "The Entity-Relationship Model: Towards a

represented something of interest. Relationships were depicted by rhombi[♠] between the boxes. An attribute in a circle, attached to an entity type box, represented a characteristic of that entity type.

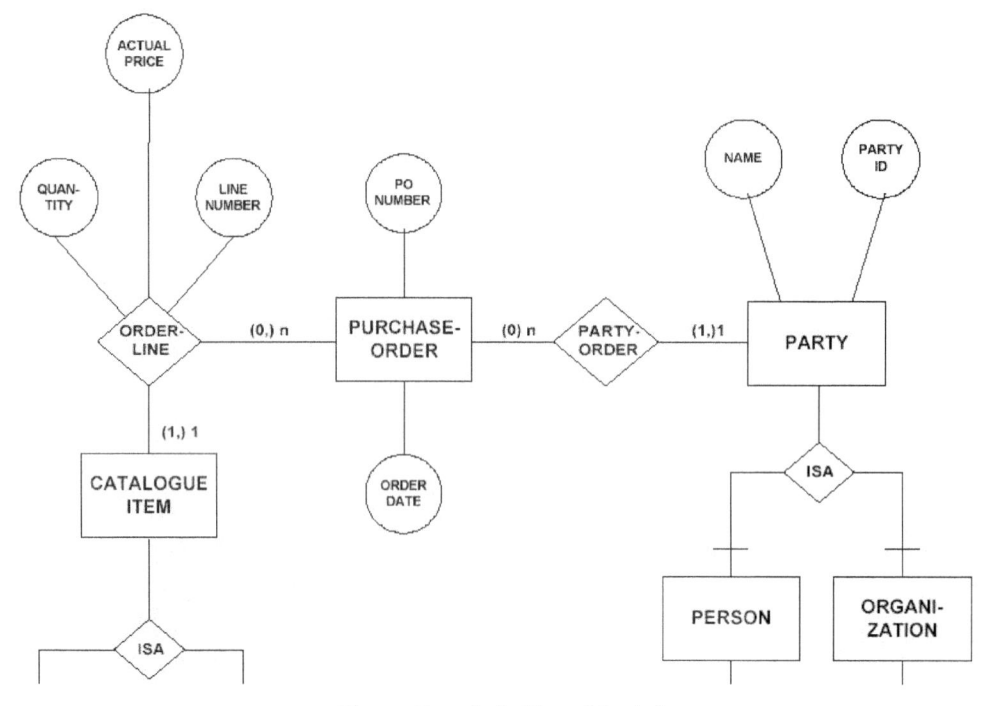

Figure Pre-4: A Chen Model

This was an early "map" of data. It was followed by other notations with similar structure, including ***Information Engineering***,[10] and ***Barker/Ellis***.[11] (Figure Pre-5 shows the same model as an Information Engineering diagram. Figure Pre-6 shows a Barker/Ellis version of the same model.) Regardless of the particular notation, instead of building structures through the detailed normalization process, it was

---

Unified View of Data", *ACM Transactions on Database Systems*, Vol. 1, No 1, (March 1976), 9-36.

[♠] Plural of "rhombus". Ok, "diamond shapes".

[10] James Martin and Clive Finkelstein. 1981. *Information Engineering*. Technical Report, (2 volumes) Carnforth, UK: Savant Institute

[11] Richard. Barker. 1990. *CASE*Method: Entity Relationship Modeling*. Wokingham, England: Addison-Wesley.

possible to begin with major structures, and then fill in the details describing attributes and relationships.[12]

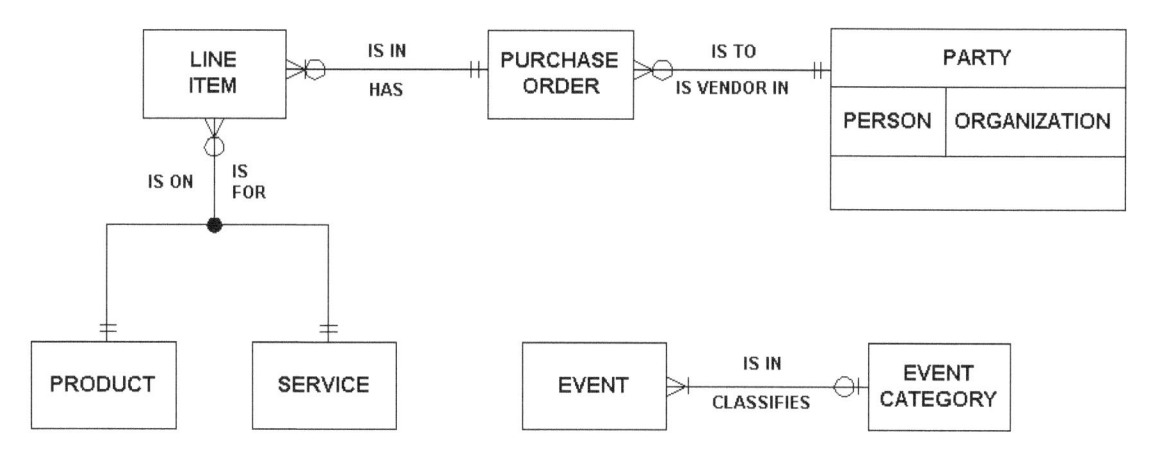

Figure Pre-5: An Information Engineering Diagram

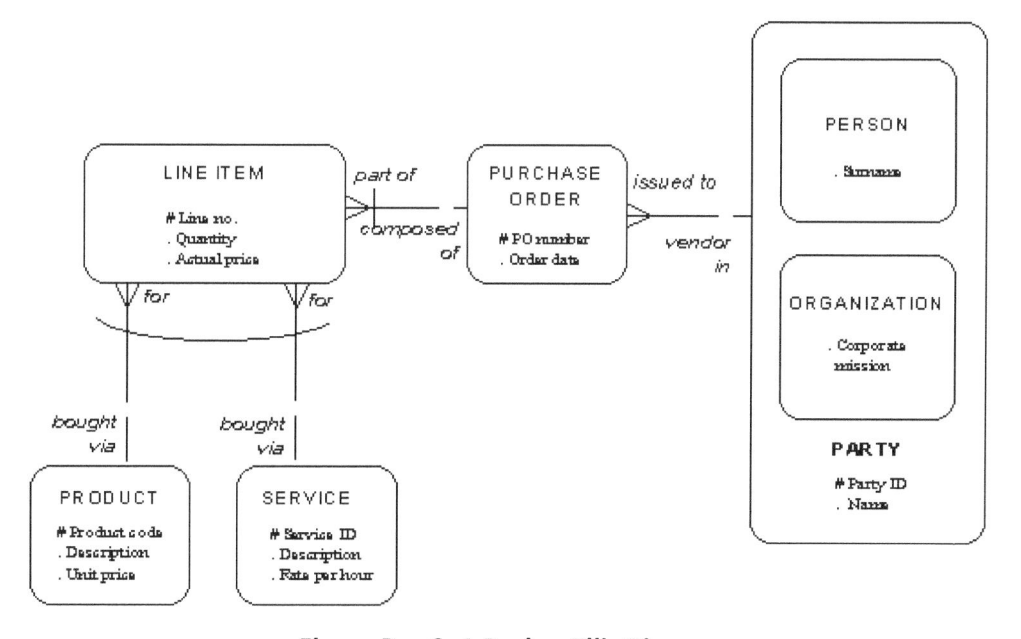

Figure Pre-6: A Barker-Ellis Diagram

Note that the relationship names are different. In Information Engineering, the only guidance for relationship names is that they be "verb phrases". Messrs. Barker and Ellis took a much more disciplined approach to naming relationships. The

---

[12] David C. Hay. 2003. *Requirements Analysis: From Business Views to Architecture*. Upper Saddle River, NJ: Prentice Hall PTR. Appendix B.

Barker/Ellis approach will be carried into the way we address UML. It is further described in Chapter 2.

Notations notwithstanding, the assignment is still one of exploring enough of the conceptual world (and having the proper organizational insights) to be able to show it clearly in a data model. As with the 16th and 17th century explorers, the trick was to figure out what the continents in business data space really looked like. Normalization allowed you to infer structures from the points of data, but it was not until Dr. Chen invented data modeling that people could begin by asking what the continents were (the entity types) *prior to* filling in the detailed points (the attributes).

Nevertheless, even modelers who focused on entity types could get lost in those details without ever getting a picture of the whole problem in context. Even data models tended to get bogged down with too much detail to make them useful.

It was not until 1995 that your author published a book describing certain "shapes" of patterns that recurred in almost every company, as well as in government agencies.[13] These patterns greatly reduced the amount of time required to create a company's architectural data model. Using these patterns, however, only worked if the data modeler was thinking more abstractly about the domain in question. The question remains, however: How abstract should you go?

Again, no model (as with no map) can describe an entire situation both in the abstract and in detail. Graeme Simsion, as part of his doctoral thesis, asked a group of well-respected modelers how to address a particular situation that he described. As it happens, nearly every resulting model was different. A significant issue turned out to be one of the level of abstraction that the modeler began with. Those who began with the same general level came out with similar models. Those who were either more concrete or more abstract came up with different models.[14]

This book addresses the question of "level of abstraction" head on. It is organized approximately from the most abstract to the most concrete. (Ok, the sequence is "Level 1", then "Level 0", then "Level 2" and "Level 3", but you get the idea.) These are patterns, not definitive final models, but the book should provide guidance not only as to what a finished model might look like, but also what level of abstraction to take in the first place.

---

[13] David C. Hay. 1995. *Data Model Patterns: Conventions of Thought.* (New York: Dorset House).

[14] Graeme Simsion. 2007. *Data Modeling: Theory and Practice.* (Bradley Beach, NJ).

Unfortunately, there is no "Google Data Models" tool that allows us dynamically to zoom in and out of the models' abstraction layers. (as shown in Figure Pre-7). But it is to be hoped that perhaps this book will provide a guide to what such a tool might look like.

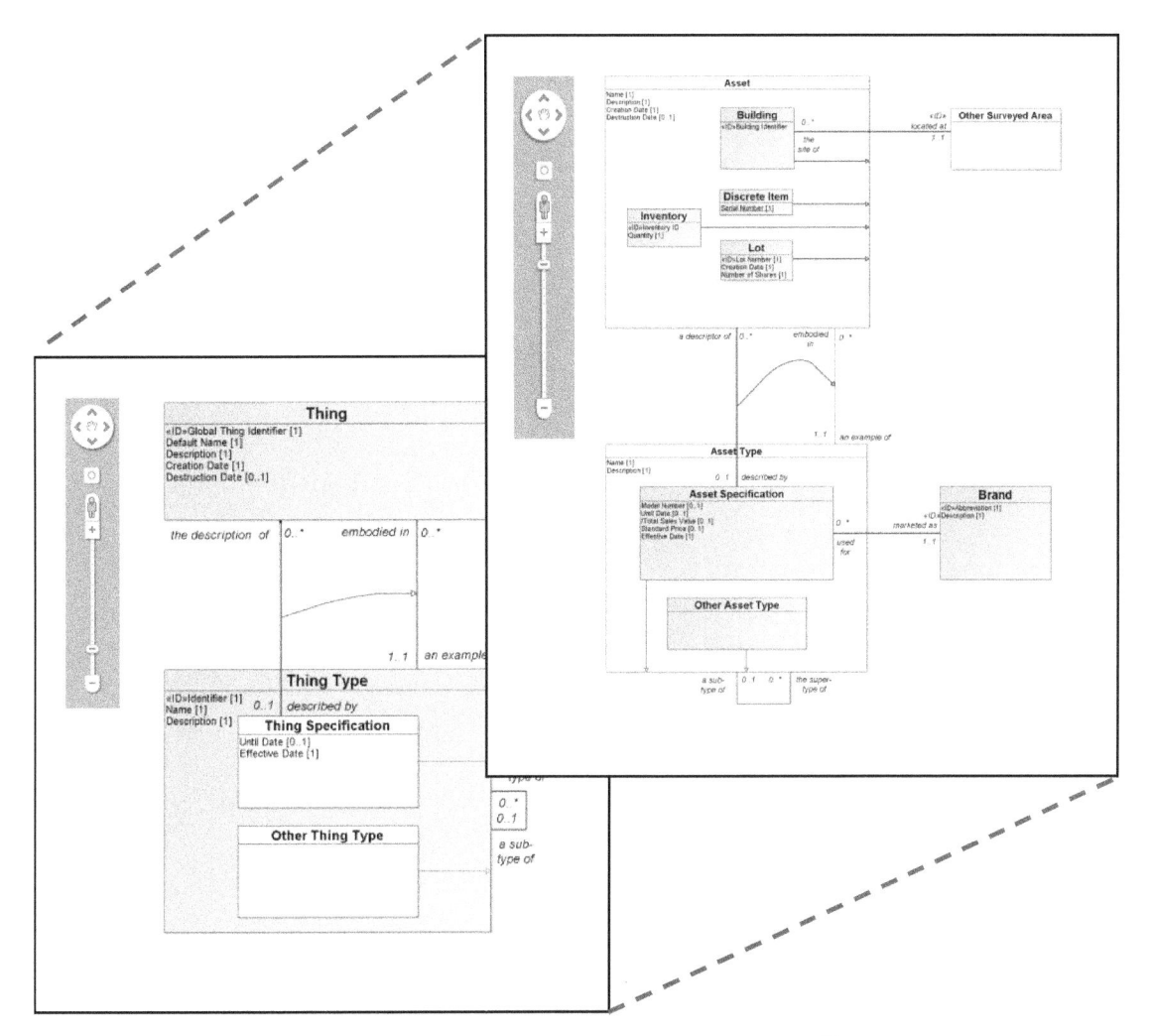

Figure Pre-7: Zooming in a Data Model[15]

The "globe" featured on the cover of this book was folded by Robert Hay, using 28 square pieces of paper from a design by Tomako Fusé. This is an example of the Japanese art of **origami**. It uses the simple principles of folding pieces of paper to form amazing figures. In this case, multiple pieces were used, but in fact, there are probably thousands of designs (patterns, if you will), for flowers, birds, dinosaurs, et

---

[15] Scroll bar Copyright 2010, Google.

cetera[*], that can be created using but a single piece of paper. Origami is an example of how understanding the basic geometry of something as simple as a piece of paper can provide incredible power for creating new "worlds".

---

[*] ...with an emphasis on the *et cetera*...

Acknowledgements

No project this large is the accomplishment of one person. Your author has been blessed over the years with many generous colleagues and friends, all of whom have contributed to this book.

I must begin with my teachers, the people who, over the years have provided insights, arguments and intellectual stimulation for all that you see here: Mike Lynott, my long-term friend and colleague, who taught me data modeling in the first place; Cliff Longman, who, among other things provided the origin for many of the patterns in this book, but who also in later years introduced me to Kalido, a revolutionary way to look at data warehousing; Richard Barker and Harry Ellis, who introduced the world to the idea of creating data models that business people could read and understand; Ken Orr, a fellow philosopher whose long telephone conversations with me made me realize that education really is a continuous process; Matthew West and Chris Partridge, two ontologists whose completely different way of looking at data modeling provided many subtle insights into what I have been doing; Tom Redman, who's original approach to involving management in the issues of data quality stimulated my thinking greatly.

And of course I must express my ongoing gratitude to Bob Seiner, who's Data Administration Newsletter have provided an outlet for my thoughts for many years, now.

My decision to use UML as the notation came from my three-year participation in the Object Management Group's project to develop an industry metadata standard. It was called the "Information Management Metamodel" (IMM) project. I was responsible for the metamodels of entity/relationship modeling and relational modeling. Since these were to be "platform-independent" models, I expected to use the Richard Barker / Harry Ellis notation I was used to. I was so surrounded with UML people, however, that I decided to give UML a try. As it happens, I was able to do it! That inspired me to use UML for this book.

I want to give particular thanks to Harsh Sharma (who was Chairman of the effort), as well as Jim Logan, Kenn Hussy, and Pete Rivett for their assistance in leading me through the wilds of UML.

In the Spring of 2009, Ron Murray of the Library of Congress called me to discuss data modeling. Our of those conversations came an invitation to present this model as part of their ongoing series of presentations, "Library of Congress's Digital

Future and You". In particular, the Library is in the business of cataloguing "Information Resources", so that part of the presentation was of particular interest to them. My thanks to Ron for the invitation and to Barbara Tillet for her introduction to me of different ways to approach the problem of describing these intangible resources.

Thanks to my work with the Object Management Group, I was introduced to the graphics management tool, MagicDraw, by NoMagic, Inc. of Dallas, Texas. Because it is a truly comprehensive tool addressing all aspects of the UML notation, my first assignment was figuring out how to turn off the large number of parts that were not useful to me. Then I had to figure out how to implement some of the quirky non-standard practices I needed for my strange approach to UML.

My congratulations to the NoMagic people for their skill at guiding me through both assignments. Their technical support staff both in the U.S. and in Kaunas, Lithuania was never baffled by any of my questions and was very effective at quickly and concisely answering them. This was far more effective than any other technical support organization I have ever dealt with. Their task was made easier, of course, by the fact that the underlying structure of the tool is completely coherent. It is easily the best tool for manipulating model graphics I have used—for any notation. My congratulations (and thanks) to Gary Duncanson, President, and his development staff for an outstanding product.

Thanks of course go to my clients who provided the raw materials both for the generic models and for the industry-specific ones. Confidentiality practice prevents me from naming them, but you know who you are.

This book is not exactly light reading, so I am particularly grateful to the colleagues who were willing to read at least parts of it and provide their guidance and editing.

- Roland Berg
- David Eddy
- Cliff Longman
- Mike Lynott
- Chris Partridge
- Gabriel Tanase
- Matthew West

My particular appreciation goes to Steve Hoberman, a long-time data modeling colleague, whose relatively new venture, Technics Publications, was the perfect publisher for this book. He has shown considerable patience as I discovered that a book like this, which starts by being 95% complete (I'd been working on it for four years before I actually sat down to write it) can take *forever*. It is nice having someone knowledgeable in the data modeling world to be the final editor. And my thanks also go to Carol Lehn-Dodson who did a masterful job of editing the copy.

And of course none of this could be done without the love and support of my family—Jola, my wife who made all of this possible, Pamela, my very talented opera singer daughter who's artistic sense always inspires me, and Bob, my son, a most clever fellow who teaches young people how to succeed in their college careers. The origami globe on the cover of this book was thanks to all three of them: Jola found the original model, Pamela encouraged me to use it with the Technics layout, and Bob did the incredible job of folding it so that it actually looks like a globe.

By extension, I must also thank Paul, Pamela's husband, for his support of her and me as well, and Lauren, Bob's wife, who, in addition to being a data modeler herself, recently presented us with Audrey, my first granddaughter.

A Note About the 2d Printing

You may have noticed, as you examined this book that there are nearly 700 pages. This includes some 220 diagrams describing perhaps several thousand entity classes. It pains your author to admit that there were some mistakes made. Actually, only 6 of the drawings had consequential errors, but another 9 had inconsequential ones.

More sad to me as an author is the fact that the text also had errors in it. In some cases it was carelessness in referring to an entity class, and in others it was typographical. But, yes, there were some sentences in there that were not entirely clear. I am my own worst critic when I write a book, and I just couldn't stand to let these things be.

The good thing about this book's "publish on demand" approach, is that I could correct these and not leave the publisher with hundreds of older copies. So, I happily submit this to my newer readers, as the "new, improved" version.

(The errors aren't *so* egregious that readers of the 1st printing should storm the gates. Besides, that means they have the "Collector's Edition".)

PART ONE

INTRODUCTION

This introductory part to the book contains three chapters:

The first, "Data Modeling's Promise . . . and Failure", describes the objectives of data modeling in the requirements analysis domain: communication, discipline, and identification of fundamental structures. It then goes on to show how these are hindered by three tendencies of data modeling practitioners: orientation towards systems issues, failure to reveal fundamental structures, and confusing and unclear drawings. Finally, it describes how this book will address those issues.

The second chapter, "About Conventions", describes the three sets of approaches to standardization relevant to the data modeling world:

- **Notation** – The sets of symbols to be used. There have been some half dozen or more sets of notation in the industry since Dr. Chen invented the data modeling approach. For reasons explained here, the book will make use of the Unified Modeling Language, developed by the Object Management Group.

- **Aesthetics** – Since models are fundamentally communications tools, certain aesthetic principles must be followed if they are to be successful.

- **Architecture** – The subject of the book is standard architectural structures to be used to describe standard business situations.

The third chapter, "About this Book", describes first, the levels of abstraction to be addressed by the book, and then the sequence in which those levels will be described.

CHAPTER 1

Data modeling's promise . . . and failure

Data modeling serves three purposes in the systems analysis process. First, as a graphic technique, it should aid in communication between analysts and the ultimate users of the systems they will specify, and then between analysts and those who will design and build systems for those users.

Second, as a structured technique, it imposes discipline on the specification of problems, ensuring that the results are logically coherent. Syntactic, aesthetic, and semantic standards can provide this discipline to the modeling process.

Third, creation of a data model is supposed to focus the user's, the analyst's, and the designer's attention on things that are most fundamental to the nature of the business. The technique promises to lead to the development of stable, robust, and reliable information systems, so that normal changes in the business will not affect system structure. Moreover, data models promise to be useful as the basis for discussions among all three sets of players (users, analysts, and designers) about the future of information systems development.

Alas, data modeling has not always kept these promises. If it is not used effectively, the technique neither improves communication, imposes discipline, nor even effectively represents the enterprise.

Herein lies the purpose of this book. It is intended to describe an approach to data modeling which can restore those promises.

Data modeling, as currently practiced, suffers from three problems:

- Diagrams are too oriented towards systems issues, such as database and systems design.
- Diagrams do not represent the fundamental nature of the organizations they are supposed to describe.

- Diagrams are not clear to outsiders: they are often confusing and difficult to read.

Business vs. Systems Issues

A picture of the structure of a body of data looks different, depending on its purpose. If it is for the purpose of representing the structure of a real, physical database, it describes the tables that constitute that data base. If it is an "object model" describing the classes of data to be used or produced by an object-oriented program, it is about the pieces of program code that manipulate those data. In both cases, these are models of technology, as seen by designers of artifacts using that technology.

In the years since 1995, when your author's first *Data Model Patterns* book[16] was published, data modeling has become much more prevalent in the information technology industry. The problem with that is that the definition of the term has become associated more strongly with modeling database design than with modeling business. It has been acknowledged that there are several kinds of data modeling—"conceptual", "logical", and "physical"—but there is limited agreement as to what each of these terms mean.[17]

In 1987, John Zachman first laid out his "Framework for Enterprise Architecture", and described the world along two dimensions. Across the top, he laid out the domains as covering "what" (data), "how" (activities and functions), "who" (people and organizations), "where" (locations), "when" (events and schedules), and "why" (enterprise motivation). Both of your author's books on requirements analysis[18] and on metadata[19] were organized to address all of these domains. This book, on the other hand is primarily concerned with "what" (data), although the other domains come into play occasionally.

---

[16] David C. Hay. 1995. *Data Model Patterns: Conventions of Thought*. (New York: Dorset House).

[17] Danette McGilvray (with David Hay). 2008. "Data Model Comparison" in McGilvray, D., *Executing Data Quality Projects: Ten Steps to Quality Data and Trusted Information*. (Boston: Morgan Kaufmann Publishers): 48-49.

[18] David C. Hay. 2003. *Requirements Analysis: From Business Views to Architecture*. (Upper Saddle River, NJ: Prentice Hall PTR).

[19] David C. Hay. 2006. *Data Model Patterns: A Metadata Map*. Boston: Morgan Kaufmann.

Data modeling's promise and failure   35

More significant was Mr. Zachman's recognition that various players in any systems development effort have completely different perspectives on the problem.

- **Planner's View** – This is the view of the CEO and other top executives. It is concerned with what the enterprise is about. At this level, it is typically drawn as a ***context model***. This is a sketch of the primary things of concern to an enterprise. It consists of pairs of major categories (represented as ***entity classes***), connected by ***many-to-many relationships***. This is also called by some "conceptual", "subject", or "environmental" model.

- **Business Owner's View** – This is the perspective of the people who run the day-to-day activities of the enterprise. The important thing to capture here is the ***semantics*** of the enterprise. Since this is about ***language***, there is no modeling notation per se, although the conceptual notations described for the architect's view (below) can be used. Because it is linguistic, it is more often represented in structured text of various forms. Traditionally, this has included simple compilation of a glossary, but more recently, the ***semantic languages*** of the ***Resource Description Framework*** (***RDF***) and the ***Web Ontology Language*** (***OWL***) have appeared in an attempt to capture an organization's use of language.[20] [21] It is also addressed by techniques described in the Object Management Group's "Semantics of Business Vocabulary and Business Rules".[22]

Even without graphics, these approaches can be used to produce a ***semantic model*** of the enterprise.

- **Architect's view**♣ – The architect is the person who distills a wide range of business owners' views of the business (and the corresponding semantics) to arrive at a single view of the underlying nature of the enterprise.♥ Each

---

[20] D. Allemang, and, Jim Hendler. 2009. *Semantic Web for the Working Ontologist: Effective Modeling in RDFS and OWL.* (Boston: Morgan Kaufmann).

[21] David.C. Hay. 2008. "Semantics, Ontology, and Data Modeling", *Cutter Report on Business Intelligence, Vol. 6, No. 7.* June 1, 2008.

[22] Object Management Group. 2008. *Semantics of Business Vocabulary and Business Rules.* OMG Available Specification formal/2008-01-02. http://www.omg.org/spec/SBVR/1.0/

♣ Your author's approach to naming the different perspectives of the Zachman framework differ a bit from Mr. Zachman's original. These differences are discussed in detail in: Hay, D.C. 2003. *Requirements Analysis: From Business Views to Architecture.* (Upper Saddle River, NJ: Prentice Hall PTR):5-6.

♥ This is analogous to the experience of the ancient blind men who encountered an elephant. One, feeling its leg, likened it to a tree. Another, feeling its tail, likened it to a piece of rope. Another, feeling its ear, likened it to a palm frond. And yet another,

box in the model of this view (***entity class***) represents the definition of something of fundamental significance to the enterprise. Annotated lines between the boxes represent ***one-to-many relationships*** between entity classes. Attributes are collected and available, although they may or may not be displayed.

Names reflect the underlying semantics of the organization, integrating the details from the semantic model described above. The model is intended to serve as a vehicle for conversation between the modeler and the business. This is a subset of the "ontology" that would represent the extent of the enterprise's semantics.

Along with this model is documentation of issues, problems, and requests for help from the business. It is these issues, et cetera. that are the motivation to develop new systems, procedures, or other tools to improve the operation of the business.

The model from this perspective is the subject of this book. Your author's name for it is the ***conceptual model*** of the enterprise. This is also called by some the "logical" or "platform independent" model. In the context of this Framework, it should be called the ***architectural model***.

- **Designer's view** – The designer is the person who applies technology to address the issues, problem, et cetera, in terms of the architecture represented by the conceptual model. This model is organized in terms required for manipulation by a particular data management technology. This includes relational tables and columns, XML Schema tags, object-oriented classes, and so forth. It should reflect the structures of the conceptual model, but it is constrained by the technology involved.

  This is called by some the "logical", "physical", "technology specific", or "vendor independent" model.

- **Builder's view** – This is the perspective of the person well versed in the technology involved, who has the job of implementing the Designer's designs. In the data domain, the Builder's View is not so much of a data model as of a schematic of how data are physically stored in a database. This is in terms of disk drives, "tablespaces", and the like.

- **Functioning system view** – This is both the beginning and the end of the system development process. Analysis begins by understanding the nature

---

feeling its trunk, likened it to a hose. These are the business owners' views. It is the architect's job to describe the elephant.

of the current system, and implementation ends with people, systems, databases, and procedures in place. This is not the subject of a model, *per se*.

Note that the first three perspectives above are concerned solely with describing the *business*. The description of issues, problems, and requests for help may be in terms of current system inadequacies, but even these should not determine what system solution may be built. It is those holding the designers', builders', and functioning system views that are concerned with current and updated technology.

This book is solely concerned with the architect's view. It attempts to show fundamental structures that could apply to any company or government agency.

Fundamentals of the Business

Even if the model is created to be independent of data processing technology, it can still fall into a different trap: if a model is too concrete, it will be inflexible and difficult to change.

If you choose to build a new system, you want it to reflect the true requirements of your business — not simply to reproduce the techniques and technology now in use. The reason for making the investment in the first place is that you want to *change the way things are done*, without changing the *nature* of your enterprise.

A data model can help do this if it reflects that nature. The object is to present what is *unchanging* in an enterprise. It is intended to portray the things of significance—the things of *fundamental* significance—about which the company wishes to hold information. If the model succeeds, the things represented are unlikely to change greatly as the business changes. What technology does is to improve the operational aspects of the business. Technology whose architecture is based on what is fundamental to the business will be more robust, stable, and flexible than that which is based only on current operational structures.

Unfortunately, what most people see in the course of their work (and consequently tell systems analysts about) is not this unchanging nature at all, but merely instances of phenomena that appear now. Since the information an analyst gathers is usually expressed in terms of current practices, distinguishing between what is essential to a business and what is merely an accident of current technology is not always easy. The essential facts are the things that "go without saying" — so they don't get said. These facts don't get described or explained — or reflected in new systems.

The elements of a business portrayed in many data models reflect this difficulty. Model diagrams are often dominated by references to the objects that represent the particular way things are done now. This may be anything from a paper form used to the system currently carrying out significant processes. A careless analyst may interpret transient things to be things of importance. The resulting model will then reflect only those things that are important to *current* business practices.

A purchasing agent, for example, might describe the company's purchasing system (with special emphasis on its shortcomings), but not the essential facts about a purchase order. To build a new system based solely on the structure (and failings) of an existing system is to fail to take advantage of technological opportunities.

Clarity

As typically produced, data model diagrams can be less than inviting. While the use of graphics is supposed to make the ideas presented more accessible, the use of graphics without regard for aesthetic principles has the opposite effect. A mass of symbols with no shape or organization aids neither in the understanding of an organization nor in the planning of its future system development efforts: There are so many boxes and lines! Where do I start? What is really going on here? How can I use this?

Defining a set of symbols to represent data structures is not enough. It is necessary to add a method for *organizing* those symbols, so that the viewer of the model can deal with the drawing as a whole. It is also necessary to apply some aesthetic standards to the drawings, in order to ensure that meaning encoded in the symbols can be accessible to the viewer.

The Response: This Book

This book presents a set of model patterns that describe any enterprise or government agency from a business point of view. In terms of the Zachman Framework, it takes the architect's view, consolidating numerous detailed perspectives. It addresses this view from various levels of abstraction, from the most arcane to the very particular. But at all levels, it is describing the logic of a domain of interest, not the technology that might be appropriate to serve it.

At all levels of abstraction, it is attempting to identify fundamental structures. This includes not only the abstract elements that form the framework at abstraction levels 0 and 1, but even in the department-specific model of level 2, it is fundamental concepts that are being described. In those models, the concepts are so fundamental that they apply pretty much to anyone. In the industry examples, the concepts are specific to the industry, but they are fundamental concepts in that industry, at least.

In Chapter 2, this book describes your author's reluctant journey to the use of the Unified Modeling Language (UML). Initially, he resisted because the notation itself seemed to interfere with the objective of producing clear models. He also resisted because the notation seemed excessively oriented towards object-oriented design. He is convinced now, however, that by following the aesthetic conventions described in that chapter, the drawings should be clear and, if not exactly pretty, at least they will be useable for communications. Moreover, by understanding the differences in point of view between object-oriented design and entity/relationship modeling, these differences can be dealt with.

So, onward with UML! (Well, this version, anyway.)

In Summary

Both discipline and communications in our models can be improved, and the fundamental structures of business can be better represented. Moreover, we can make better use of each other's work. What is needed is standardization of our approach to the modeling process. This does not simply mean using a common system of notation, although that would certainly help. What it means, rather, is standardization in *the way we think about* business situations, and in the way we organize our presentations of them. This book is about that kind of standardization. It identifies common approaches to modeling common situations, which can then be applied to a variety of businesses and government agencies. This standardization can make models both easier to read and more descriptive of what is fundamental to an enterprise.

Note that "standardizing the way we think" is not meant to imply rigid thought control. Quite the opposite is the case. The conventions presented here do not represent the final models of *any* real company or agency. Rather they are *starting points*. They are ways of looking at business situations which should allow an analyst to quickly come to terms with the most important aspects of a situation. Having done so, the analyst is expected to apply creativity and imagination to develop a model to precisely describe the situation at hand.

The purpose of this book is to describe a generic enterprise data model—at various levels of abstraction--which meets the following objectives:

- Serve as a graphic vehicle for improving *communication* between analysts and the people of the organization being analyzed, as well as between the analysts and the designers of the systems to be built to serve that organization.

- By virtue of a disciplined approach, be logically coherent.

- Focus the user's, the analyst's, and the designer's attention on things that are most fundamental to the nature of the business.

The ultimate objective, after all, is to use the model as the basis for development of stable, robust, and reliable information systems, so that normal changes in the business will not affect them.

The response of this book is to present an enterprise model of a generic organization's data architecture that is independent of technology, descriptive of fundamental concepts, and clearly presented.

CHAPTER 2

About Conventions

Use of diagramming conventions greatly improves communications among analysts, and it provides discipline to the analytical work. With the conventions establishing a framework, entire categories of decisions do not have to be made. Only in recent years has the data modeling field been mature enough to begin establishing conventions; but it has not been easy. While much has been written about the syntax and grammar of data modeling, precious little has been written about the other elements that make up good modeling standards. In fact, three levels of convention apply to data modeling:

- **Notational conventions**. These define syntax: the symbols used in the models. In data modeling, the symbols include at least those portraying the classes of things significant to the enterprise (***entity classes***), and those for the relationships among them. Relationship symbols include those for ***cardinality*** (the "one" and "many" in a "one-to-many" relationship) and ***optionality*** (whether or not an occurrence of one entity class must have an occurrence of the other entity class). These conventions may also include the structure of phrases used to name relationships and entity classes. Syntactic conventions are the subject of most data modeling books.
- **Aesthetic conventions**. These concern the overall appearance and organization of a drawing. This includes such things as relative positions of different categories of entity classes on the page, use of lines, and general graphic design principles. These have traditionally *not* been addressed in the literature.
- **Architectural conventions**. These have to do with the grouping of entity classes according to their meaning. These are the primary subject of this book.[*]

---

[*] In *Data Model Patterns: Conventions of Thought*, these were called "semantic conventions". The underlying concepts haven't changed, but the term "semantics" has taken on a wider meaning than is understood here. These conventions are more disciplined and are

The three kinds of conventions in data modeling warrant further discussion.

Notation Conventions

A disproportionately large amount of the text written about data modeling concerns notation—the symbols used in models to express their meaning. Half a dozen notations have developed over the past thirty-five years, each with its own adherents[♥]. Each notation is promoted with a passionate energy that borders on the religious. In your author's opinion, this comes at least in part from the fact that it is hard to learn data modeling, and each of us has invariably done so in a particular context, usually with a particular tool. Because each notation (and the tool) has its shortcomings, each of us has had to come up with ways of working around those shortcomings. Then, if we've been at it long enough, those workarounds become an integral part of the way we think about problems.

UML on the Prowl

Your author has been as passionate a defender as anyone of his favorite notation, the one developed by Harry Ellis and Richard Barker in the early 1980s. This is relatively simple in its symbols and was originally designed to address the modeling of a business' semantics. It is for this reason that your author's professional experience has been entirely oriented toward semantic and architectural modeling.

He has been equally as passionate in his criticisms of the **Unified Modeling Language** (**UML**). UML was originally designed to support object-oriented modelers in their program *design*. It was never intended as a vehicle for representing *business architecture*.

The problem is that UML has all but taken over the data modeling world. This is for two reasons:

- The Unified Modeling Language is designed to be all-encompassing. Whatever its initial limitations, the ability to define ***stereotypes*** as a way of

---

  represented by the "architect's view" in the Architecture Framework, so this seems a more precise way to refer to them.

[♥] For an extensive summary of the various notations available, check out: David C. Hay. *Requirements Analysis: from Business Views to Architecture.* (Upper Saddle River, NJ: Prentice Hall PTR, 2003): 343-387.

adding to the notation has made it possible to use the notation in areas for which it was not originally intended.
- Because of the pervasiveness of object-oriented development, a lot of people who would not otherwise have been involved in modeling data have learned to do so as they have mastered the ***class models*** of UML. This has introduced them to the data world "from the back door", so to speak. This means that the public at large, who doesn't know any other approaches, has come to believe that UML and data modeling are the same things.

Unfortunately, none of this has addressed the fundamental problem: UML was designed to support program design, and design is typically concerned with specific problems. Designers are typically not expected to understand the underlying nature of the enterprise that provides the context for those problems.

As it happens, many users of the traditional data modeling notations take a similarly narrow approach. They often design databases to address specific problems without understanding the underlying nature of the enterprise that provides the context for those problems.

What is needed is a book that can be illuminating to both groups.

Your Author Surrenders

The objective of this book is to present an approach to modeling that emphasizes the semantics and architecture of a business or government agency, without respect to the design of either software or a database. As such, it represents the specialized use of a notation—whatever notation is chosen. For this reason, choice of the notation itself is not as important as even your author once thought it was.

He recently spent over two years working with the Object Management Group to develop a new standard called the ***Information Management Metamodel*** (***IMM***). Because he was responsible for the platform-independent part of the metamodel, he was inclined to use the Barker/Ellis. notation to present the underlying concepts of the domain of interest. He preferred it because of the simplicity of its symbols and its semantic orientation.

As an experiment, however, he decided to dive in to determine whether this so called *Unified* Modeling Language was unified enough to be used to create a conceptual model of the semantics of a domain of interest. Here's what he discovered:

It can be done!

It can be done with UML "class" models—but only if the approach is constrained in the following ways:

- **Not all classes are of interest**. UML allows *anything* to be a class, including classes of technological objects, such as cursors and windows and pieces of program code. For an architectural business model, however, only classes of things of significance to the business (people, physical assets, et cetera) are acceptable. In this context, these are called ***entity classes***♣.
- **Not all of the UML notation elements are of use**. Only the symbols for classes, attributes, associations, roles, and "exclusive or" constraints are used. Symbols for visibility, composition, and association direction are not used.
- **The naming convention for roles (association ends) is significantly different**. As in the object-oriented world, a ***role*** is a ***property*** of a class, but it is a *preposition* describing a ***predicate*** including a second (object) class. In the object-oriented world, a role is a *path*, describing how a program might navigate from the first class to the second. In this view, a role is not a *structure*. A role name, then, is a noun that simply labels the object class for navigation purposes. (This will be described in more detail below.)

Oh, and to the entity/relationship modelers out there, a role name isn't just any *verb* either. The implicit verb in the sentences formed is "to be". The preposition is the part of speech that connotes "relationship-ness" in a sentence. Think of Grover's words on the children's program "Sesame Street".♥

♣ When Dr. Peter Chen invented data modeling in the early 1970s, he carefully distinguished "entities" (things of interest) from "entity types" (classes of things). His drawings were all about the relationships between entity types. Examples of each entity type would be described as entities, and the distinction between them and entity types was made clear. Over the years, however, data modelers became careless and described their boxes (incorrectly) as referring to "entities". Then when object-orientation came into flower, the object-oriented people would chide data modelers for not knowing the difference between "objects" and "classes". But in fact, they had understood the distinction for over twenty years. They were just lazy. So, with the interest of clarifying the distinctions between object-orientation and data modeling, the classes previously referred to as "entity types" will henceforth be called "entity classes". An instance of an entity class will be called "an instance of an entity class". An "entity class" in object oriented terms, is a kind of "class".

♥ For more on this, see: David C. Hay, "Prepositions, Not Verbs or Nouns," *The Data Administration Newsletter* (May 1, 2010). http://www.tdan.com/view-articles/13276.

- **Sub-type boxes are shown inside super-type boxes**. For the sake of making the graphics of a drawing more compact, and for conveying the fact that an instance of a sub-type really *is* an instance of its super-type, sub-type boxes are shown *inside* super-type boxes, *rather than* being strung out alongside them. To clarify that this is a generalization (sub-type/super-type) relationship, the lines denoting generalization are maintained. (This is a departure not only from the UML approach, but also from many implementations of the Information Engineering notation as well.)
- **Names may include spaces**. For the sake of making the overall drawing more accessible to non-technical people, multi-word entity class names, attribute names, and relationship names include spaces.

Because in 2010 books sold better when they were about UML than when they were about data modeling, your author decided to take the plunge and use UML for this book. He does so with concern that the resulting models may be misinterpreted, so he will proceed with the following warnings:

Warning to Data Modelers

Learning a new notation is difficult. All the more so when the notation reflects a completely different world-view than you are used to. UML comes from that different world view. Instead of focusing on data as an asset, to be collected, used, and cared for, UML reflects the object-oriented concerns with programs, where data are used to help organize them. You will see that while the concepts you want to manipulate are there, they are in a different form than you are used to.

As an example, instead of using graphic symbols to represent optionality and cardinality so they can be *seen*, UML uses combinations of numbers and characters so that information describing optionality and cardinality must be *read*. This makes the models a bit less intuitive to data modelers (and their audiences) than they would be otherwise.

And the boxes have *square* corners instead of *round* ones!

While in this book no effort has been spared to make the presentation of models as accessible to all as possible, the combination of the cardinality notation plus the square-cornered entity classes with lines across them make UML model pretty formidable-looking.

As it happens, however, as long as aesthetic conventions are followed (See the next section.), the notational quirks are not significant when it comes to presenting the overall concepts involved.

You can adjust. Your author did.

It is also the case that relationship names (role names, actually—half a relationship) follow a convention that you may not be used to. This comes not from UML, but from your author's experience with the Barker/Ellis entity/relationship approach. The role names are *not verbs*. They are prepositions. The objective here is to use these role names to create structured sentences that make important assertions about the enterprise. The implied verb is always "to be", appearing in the resulting sentence as "may be" or "must be". The sentences are easier and more forceful to read, though, than would be the case with typical names, so it is important to learn at least how to read this naming convention.

If you recognize that what is being modeled here really is the architecture of a domain of interest, described using natural language semantics—and the resultant view is not constrained by technology (like database performance issues), then you should find it easy to adjust. The whole purpose of this approach, after all, is to be able to present models to audiences who have no experience with data modeling. If business executives can master this, you can too.

Warning to UML Modelers

While this looks like UML, as described earlier, it is not what it appears to be. Yes, the definitions of **class**, **attribute**, and **association** are consistent with what you know. A semantic model, however, represents a unique way of looking at those classes, attributes, and associations. The constraints described earlier mean that the *meaning* of the overall model may not be quite what you expect.

First of all the domain of this model is more restrictive than you are used to. Only business classes are represented here. Only a relatively small sub-set of the UML notation is used, and that is used in ways that may look out of place, at first.

It is also the case that role names follow a convention that you may not be used to. In the world of object-oriented design, a relationship is a *path*—to be navigated from one class to another. The label on the far end reveals to the program the entity class at that end. In entity/relationship modeling, a relationship is a *structure* describing how two classes are related to each other. The objective here, however, is to use these role names to create structured sentences that make important assertions about the enterprise. Instead of nouns, the role names are prepositions. This allows for direct creation of sentences that are easier and more forceful to read than would be the case with UML nouns. Thus, it is important to learn at least how to read roles using this naming convention.

If you recognize that what is being modeled here really is the architecture of a domain of interest, described using natural language semantics—and the resultant view is not constrained by technology (like Java Namespaces), then you should find it easy to adjust. The whole purpose of this approach, after all, is to be able to present models to audiences who have no experience with data modeling. If business executives can master this, you can too.

A Peace Offering

Think of this book as a peace offering across the great divide that has kept object modelers and data modelers apart over the last two decades. The patterns described in this book should be just as useful as input to object-oriented system design as they are as input to relational database design. This is so, even though they are not directly about either.

The Notation

Entity Classes (and Objects)

An *entity class* is the definition of a thing of significance about which the organization wishes to hold (which is to say, collect, maintain, and use) information. This may be a tangible thing like a product or customer, or it may be an intangible thing like a transaction or a role.

In the sample model shown in Figure 2-1, entity classes are represented by rectangles. **Organization**, **Person**, **Purchase Order**, **Catalogue Item**, and **Product** are all entity classes.

In the language of object-orientation, an *object* is an *occurrence* of an entity. The models described here do not show individual objects (say, purchase order 3245-A). The object-oriented term for entity class is *class* (as in a "class of objects"), but in this book, since only classes of interest to the enterprise are of interest, "entity class" is used exclusively.

Henceforth, unless otherwise stated, references to an entity class will be to an instance (object) that constitutes a *representative occurrence* of that entity class. For example, in our sample model, to speak of the entity class **Purchase Order** is to speak of a representative purchase order. For this reason, all entity class names are singular. The text of this book will show the names of entity classes in **Capitalized Bold Face**, and plural forms will be used as appropriate in the sentences formed from relationships.

48 Enterprise Model Patterns

NOTE: Unlike in standard UML, spaces will be permitted in entity class names. The purpose of an architectural model, after all, is to be the basis for discussions with non-technical people.[*]

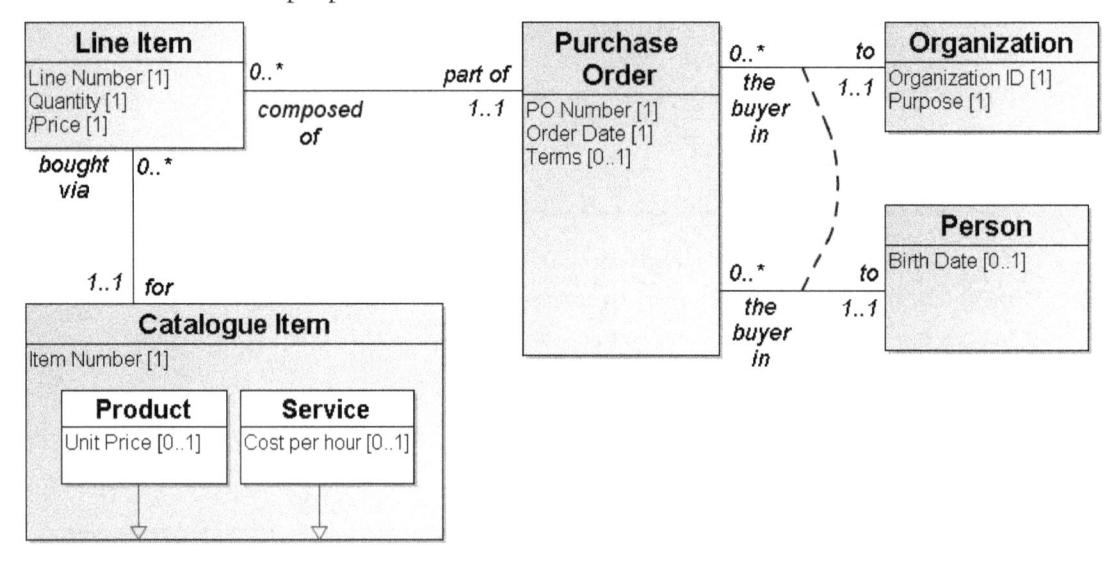

Figure 2-1: A Sample Model

Sub-types and Super-types

A ***sub-type*** of an entity class is the definition of a subset of the objects that the ***super-type*** entity class describes. Any attributes or relationships that are properties of a super-type are ***inherited by*** each sub-type. Any attributes or relationships of a particular sub-type are not inherited by any other sub-type, nor are they properties of the super-type.

Both UML and some versions of Information Engineering notations show sub-types as boxes next to their super-type boxes. This can take up a lot of space on a diagram. Moreover, if the hierarchy is relatively deep, it is not easy to see that an attribute of—or a relationship to—a super-type is in fact also an attribute of—or a relationship to—each of its sub-types, however deep in the hierarchy.

The approach to UML taken in this book shows sub-types as rectangles *within* the rectangles of their super-types. In addition to making the drawings much more compact, it means that an attribute of a super-type (even if it is several levels away) clearly *is* an attribute of each sub-type.

---

[*] Not only is "PurchaseOrder" discouraging, it is tough to "wrap", as shown in the Figure.

For example, in Figure 2-1, **Catalogue Item** is a super-type, while **Product** and **Service** are sub-types. Each **Catalogue Item** must be *either* a **Product** or a **Service**. Conversely, each **Product** must also be a **Catalogue Item** and each **Service** must also be a **Catalogue Item**.

Both **Product** and **Service** inherit from **Catalogue Item** both the attribute Item Number and the relationship, "Each **Line Item** must be *for* one and only one **Catalogue Item**." That is, "Each **Line Item** must be *for* either one and only one **Product** or one and only one **Service**." The attribute of **Service** (Cost per Hour) is *not* an attribute of **Product**. Similarly, the attribute of **Product** (Unit Price) is *not* an attribute of **Service**.

In another wing of UML, the "box-in-box" convention is also used, but that is not relevant to a class model. To clarify the meaning for people accustomed to relationship lines between super- and sub-types, however, these are retained even as the boxes are nested.

Attributes

An ***attribute*** is a discrete, atomic piece of information that identifies, describes, classifies, or measures an entity class The *values* of a set of attributes of an entity class describe instances of that entity class. If an entity class is the definition of a thing of significance about which an enterprise wishes to hold information, then an attribute defines one kind of information held.

The data model diagram may or may not show the attributes. Even if not shown, they should be documented as part of the overall deliverable that is the model. UML allows representation of the attributes as text in the entity class box, but does not require this, and does not use separate symbols for them as is done in other methods.[23]

An attribute's ***cardinality*** is shown by the expression [<min>...<max>], describing the minimum cardinality (is the attribute ***optional*** or ***mandatory***?) and the maximum cardinality (can the attribute have more than one value?). For example, in **Purchase Order**, "Terms" is optional, as shown by "[0..1]", but PO Number and Order Date are required, as shown by "[1..1]".

---

[23] For example, see P. Chen. 1976. "The Entity-relationship Model — Toward a Unified View of Data," *ACM Transactions on Database Systems*, 1,(1).

Note that in a relational world, the maximum cardinality for an attribute must always be "1". Since multi-valued attributes are prohibited, there can never be more than one value. Thus, the only two values available are:

- [0..1] – The attribute is optional.
- [1] – The attribute is mandatory.* (Note that "[1]" is an abbreviation for "[1..1]")

In this book, attributes with cardinality are shown when the entity class is first introduced. In subsequent drawings that portray the entity class they usually are not shown.

An attribute's *data type* describes the format of the attribute. It is important to document the data type of each attribute as part of the materials supporting the model. The data types of interest in a conceptual model such as this are:

- String – alphanumeric text
- Number – a real number, such as "3542.35"
- Integer – a number without a fractional part, such as "42"
- Date – a point in time positioned in terms of the calendar, such as "April 24, 1914"
- Date Time – a point in time to the level of detail of the clock, such as "April 24, 1914, 23:45"
- Boolean – with values only of "true" or "false".

In this book, *data types* are discussed explicitly in some discussions about entity class characteristics, and in a real model for a client, they must be included as part of the documentation, but they are not shown on the model diagrams.

As described previously, an attribute of a super-type is also an attribute of every sub-type, but an attribute specified for a sub-type is not known to any other sub-type. The sub-type is said to *inherit* the attribute from the super-type. In the example (Figure 2-1), **Description** (an attribute of **Catalogue Item**) is also an attribute of both **Product** and **Service**. Unit Price (an attribute of **Product**), however, is not an attribute of **Service**.

Note that \Price has an initial slash character. This means that values for the attribute would not be stored in a database, but rather derived as necessary from the

---

* This same notation is used to designate the cardinality of relationships, below.

values of other attributes. In this case, **\Price** is defined as being equal to **Line Item** Quantity times either the **Product** Unit Price or the **Service** Cost per Hour– depending on which kind of **Catalogue Item** was referred to by this **Line Item**. (See "Relationships", next.)

Note that in an architectural model such as this one, there is no indication as to whether the calculation is done when data are entered into a database or when they are retrieved. The actual encoding of such attributes is the domain of the *designer*, not the *data modeler*.

In the text of this book, attribute names will always be shown in **Calibri** type face.

Relationships

The model in Figure 2-1 shows ***relationships*** between the entity classes as annotated lines. "Relationship" here corresponds to the UML concept of ***association***. The name of each half of the relationship corresponds to UML's concept of ***role***, but it has a very different meaning.

It is the names assigned to each end of the relationship that describe the *architecture* of the model. The naming conventions represent a much more disciplined approach than is usually taken in either entity/relationship modeling or conventional UML. This is important, because to capture the architecture of an organization, you have to go to the heart of what its entity classes and the relationships between them *mean*. To simply say "a **Purchase Order** *has* zero, one, or many **Line Items**" (as often done by data modelers) does not convey the true nature of the relationship between **Purchase Order** and **Line Item**. Neither does naming the role something like "order line item" (as is done by a UML modeler).

Fundamentally, an architectural data model consists of a set of assertions about the nature of the enterprise. These assertions are contained in the role names. A more rigorous approach would allow one to say that "each **Purchase Order** *(is) composed of* one or more **Line Items**." Note that the implied verb is always "is", although this is always elaborated to express optionality by being either "may be" or "must be".

In the approach used here, the annotation of relationships showing optionality and cardinality for roles is identical to that used for attributes. As you've just seen, each relationship can be read as two structured sentences. (See Figure 2-2.)

52 Enterprise Model Patterns

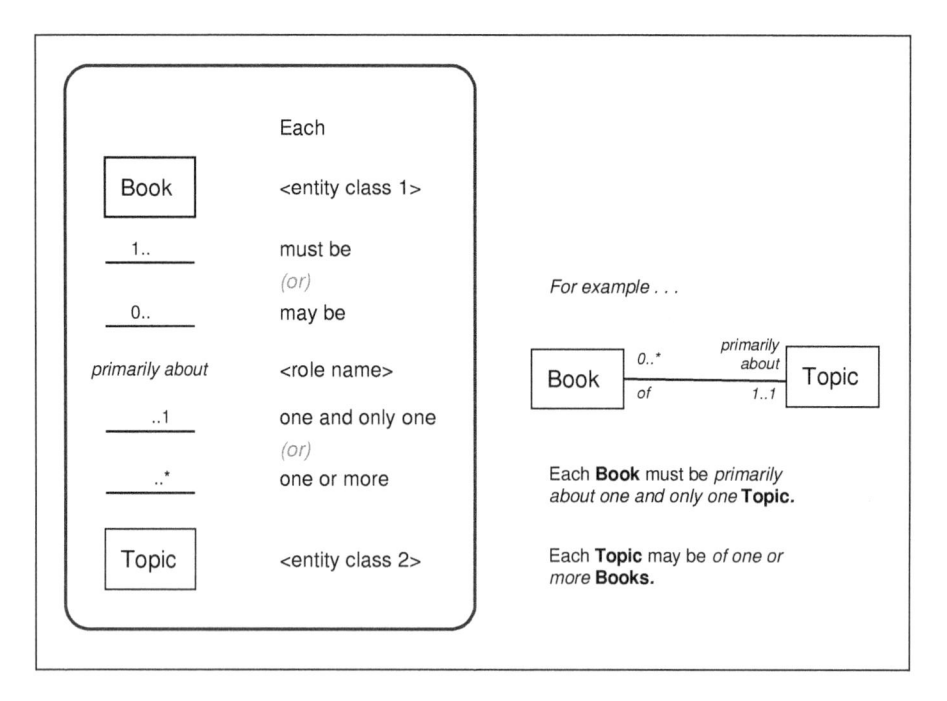

Figure 2-2: How to Read a Data Model

In the example in Figure 2-1, reproduced as Figure 2-3, below, the line between **Line Item** and **Catalogue Item** can be read as these two sentences:

- Each **Catalogue Item** may be *bought via* one or more **Line Items**.

- Each **Line Item** must be[♥] *for* one and only one **Catalogue Item** (which must be <u>either</u> one **Product** <u>or</u> one **Service**.

This structure (and the names required by it) consists of strong assertions, so the person signing off on the model is in a position to judge whether they are true or not.

These are questions of fact that can only be confirmed by a subject-matter expert in the organization being modeled. But the subject-matter expert cannot answer the question if it isn't asked in terms of a concrete relationship sentence.

For example, is this sentence true?

- Each **Purchase Order** <u>may be</u> *composed of* one or more **Line Items**

♥ For relationships, since the maximum and minimum cardinalities are separated in the descriptive sentences, they are kept separate in the notation. For attributes, since maximum cardinality must be "1", the abbreviated form is acceptable.

About Conventions 53

Could a **Purchase Order** have *no* **Line Items**? This statement asserts that this is possible (*"may be"*). If it is not possible in your organization, the notation should be "1..*", not "0..*".

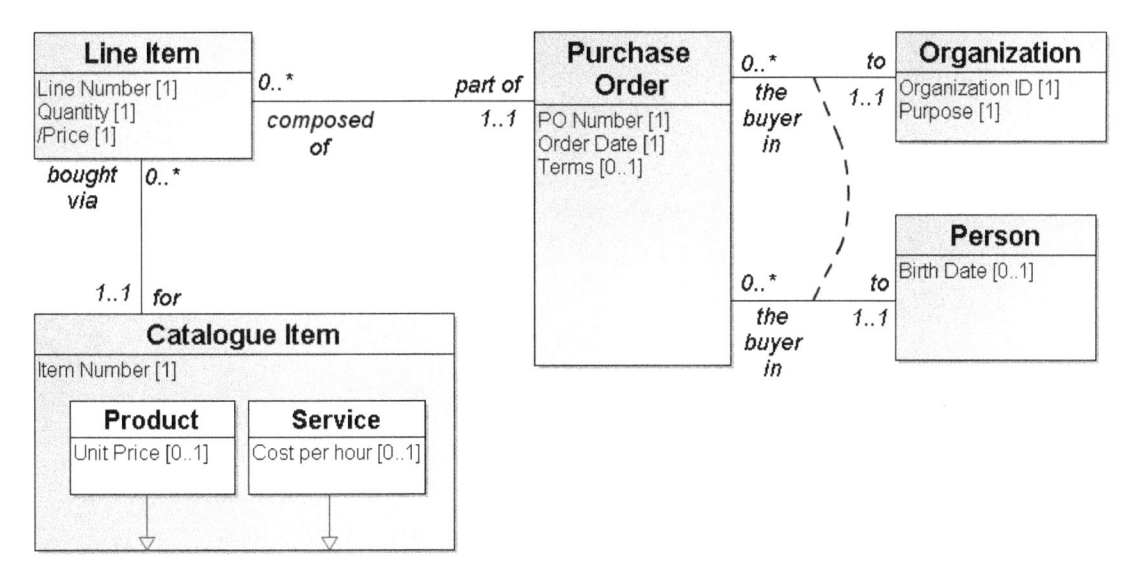

Figure 2-3: The Sample Model, Again

Note that the effect of the sub-/super-type structure is to say that each **Line Item** must be either *for* one and only one **Product** or *for* one and only one **Service**. An alternative way to present the same idea is with a ***mutually exclusive*** ("***XOR***") ***constraint***. This is shown in the Figure as:

- Each **Purchase Order** must be either *to* one **Organization** or *to* one **Person**.

Going in the other direction, these relationships assert that:

- Each **Organization** may be the *buyer in* one **Purchase Order**, and
- Each **Person** may be the *buyer in* one **Purchase Order**.

The dashed line between the relationships from **Purchase Order** to **Person** and from **Purchase Order** to **Organization** denotes mutual exclusivity. In UML, the notion of "constraint" is widely used, which in that context, would require the dashed line to be labeled "{xor}". Since, in the context of this book, this is the only UML constraint that will be used, it will not be labeled. In the entity/relationship world, this constraint is sometimes referred to as an ***arc***, since that is usually its form. Because of constraints in the graphic tool used for this book, its "arc-ness" sometimes gets tested, but you will get the idea.*

To summarize, the facts described in data model relationships are: (1) whether the existence of one occurrence of one entity class *requires* at least one occurrence of another, and (2) whether an occurrence of one entity class affects *multiple* occurrences of another, or just one occurrence.

The text in this book will show role names in *italics*. By convention, the relationship name and the cardinality notations are placed next to the 2nd (object) entity class, next to the relevant cardinality/optionality labels. They will always be positioned so that the relationship sentences can be read in a clock-wise direction.

Unique Identifiers

In an entity/relationship model, it is important to be able to identify the attributes and/or relationships in an entity class whose values can uniquely identify instances of that entity class. It may be as simple as a **Catalogue Item's** "Item Number", or it could be a combination of a **Line Item's** "Line Number" and its association with a single purchase order.

UML, in its original form, does not recognize the notion of natural unique identifiers for classes. In the object-oriented world, all objects within classes are already identified by the ultimate surrogate key, the ***Object Identifier*** (***OID***). Thus, there is no requirement to label either attributes or relationships as being required to identify instances of a class. In the world of data modeling, however, it is necessary to identify the attributes and/or relationships that uniquely identify instances of entity classes.

Fortunately, UML can be modified by adding symbols. In this case, the concept of ***unique identifier*** can be added to the notation as a "stereotype". A ***stereotype*** is a piece of notation added to UML to describe something that was not part of the original UML specification. For the purposes of this book, the symbol **<<ID>>** is a stereotype appearing next to either attributes or roles that participate in a unique identification of the entity class. The unique identifier may be any combination of attributes of the entity class and roles that the entity class is playing with respect to other entity classes.

---

* Of course, in many entity/relationship modeling tools, the 'exclusive or' constraint is not supported at all. Score a point for UML!

For example, Figure 2-4 shows that instances of **Organization** may be uniquely identified by the value in the attribute **Organization ID**. Similarly,

- instances of **Person** can be identified by the attribute **Person ID**,

- instances of **Purchase Order** are identified by the attribute **Purchase Order Number**, and

- instances of **Catalogue Item** (whether they be of a **Product** or a **Service**) are identified by the attribute **Item Number**.

Note that in Figure 2-4, each of these identifying attributes is flagged by the stereotype *<<ID>>*.

Instances of **Line Item**, on the other hand are identified by a combination of the attribute Line Number and the relationship "must be *part of* one and only one **Purchase Order**". Note that the stereotype symbol (<<ID>>) appears not only next to the attribute Line Number, but also above the relationship name *part of*.*

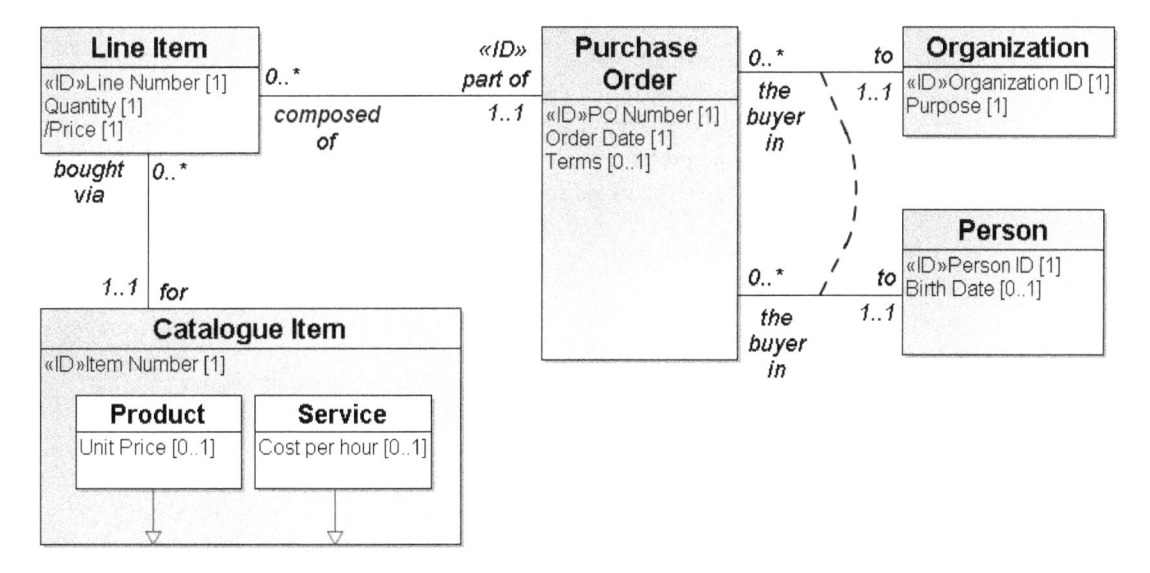

Figure 2-4: Sample With Unique Identifiers

---

* Until now, to denote that an attribute or a relationship is part of an entity class's unique identifier, it was necessary to add the stereotype <<ID>> as described here. As of this writing, however, the Object Management Group is in the process of approving a property ({isID}) to serve that purpose. This book still uses the older approach, but the reader is encouraged to learn to use the newer one.

Aesthetic Conventions

A second kind of convention applies to the *aesthetics* of an architectural model. In many data models, entity classes are positioned randomly on a page. Perhaps some effort is made to minimize the crossing of lines, but otherwise there is no pattern to the arrangement of entity classes. Because a data model is fundamentally a vehicle of communication with people who may be unfamiliar with the notion of data modeling itself, it is important that the aesthetics of data modeling follow basic principles of graphic design. These include, among others:

- ***Straighten Lines:*** Modify the dimensions of entity class boxes so that all relationship lines are *straight*. While it is desirable for them not to cross, this is less critical than ensuring that there are no "elbows". Each elbow in a line appears to be an additional symbol on the page. This appears to the viewer as yet another thing to have to understand.♦ Also, having to navigate a line with many bends from one side of the drawing to the other makes it extremely difficult to understand what it means.

- ***"Starry Skies" Orientation:*** Orient the entity class boxes so that the "many" end of each relationship is either toward the top or the left side of the drawing. This tends to aggregate the "reference" entity classes—the ones that represent tangible things—towards the lower right, and the "transaction" entity classes towards the upper left.

  It's true that there are some heretics that would do that upside-down. But as long as it is done consistently throughout the organization, that's ok.

- ***Limit Number of (highlighted) Boxes:*** Limit each subject area to a master diagram on A4 (or 8.5" X 11") paper, with no more than 10-15 entity classes. Then present the subject area as a succession of diagrams beginning with just a couple of entity classes and adding a few on each next page. On each page, only the entity classes added in that step are highlighted (with a different color, for example). The older, un-highlighted, part of the model can be in a less emphatic font with dimmer lines. You can judge for yourself how effective this can be, as I've used the "build-up" technique described here throughout the book.

- ***Follow Accepted Graphic Design Principles:*** Follow the practices of good layout – align the edges of boxes, et cetera.

♦ …the understanding of which is hard, since they don't actually mean anything.

Straighten Lines

Figure 2-5 shows an example of a data model arranged randomly. Note that there are no crossing lines, but that does not prevent it from being quite difficult to understand. It appears to be about a laboratory, but that's as far as the casual observer could be expected to go. Perhaps if the person viewing it were thoroughly versed in laboratory principles—and patient in navigating all the lines—it would be understandable. To anyone else, however, it is quite hopeless.

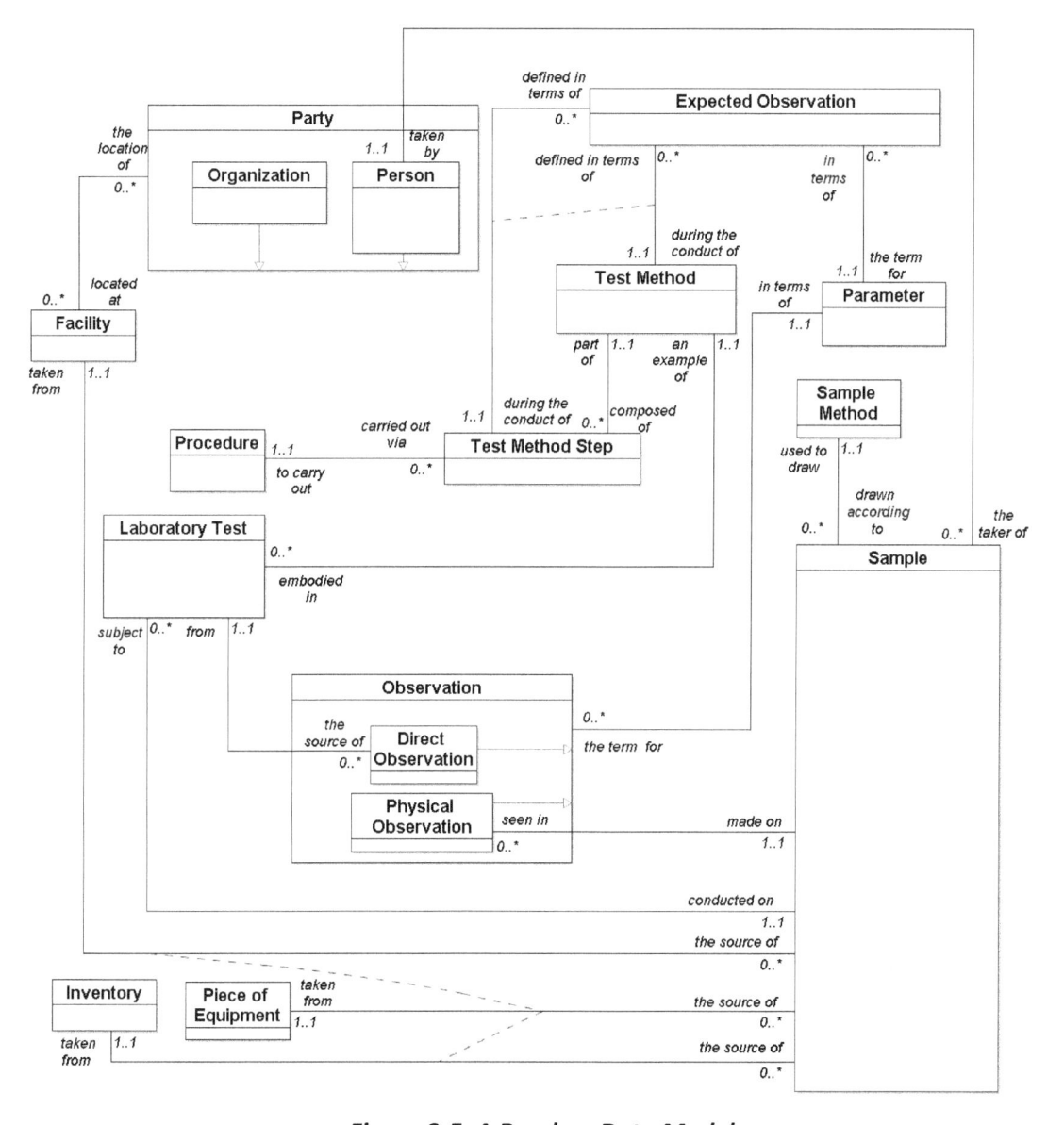

Figure 2-5: A Random Data Model

58 Enterprise Model Patterns

Figure 2-6 shows a somewhat neater version of the same model. In this case, all relationships are shown with direct, straight lines. This means no "elbows" to distract the eye. It is easier to see exactly how things are connected together. And even though there is one instance of crossed lines, because all lines are seen to be straight, this adds no ambiguity; the crossing is inconsequential. Here you see that **Observation** seems to be at the center, surrounded by the elements that describe it—**Laboratory Test**, **Sample**, **Parameter**, and so forth.

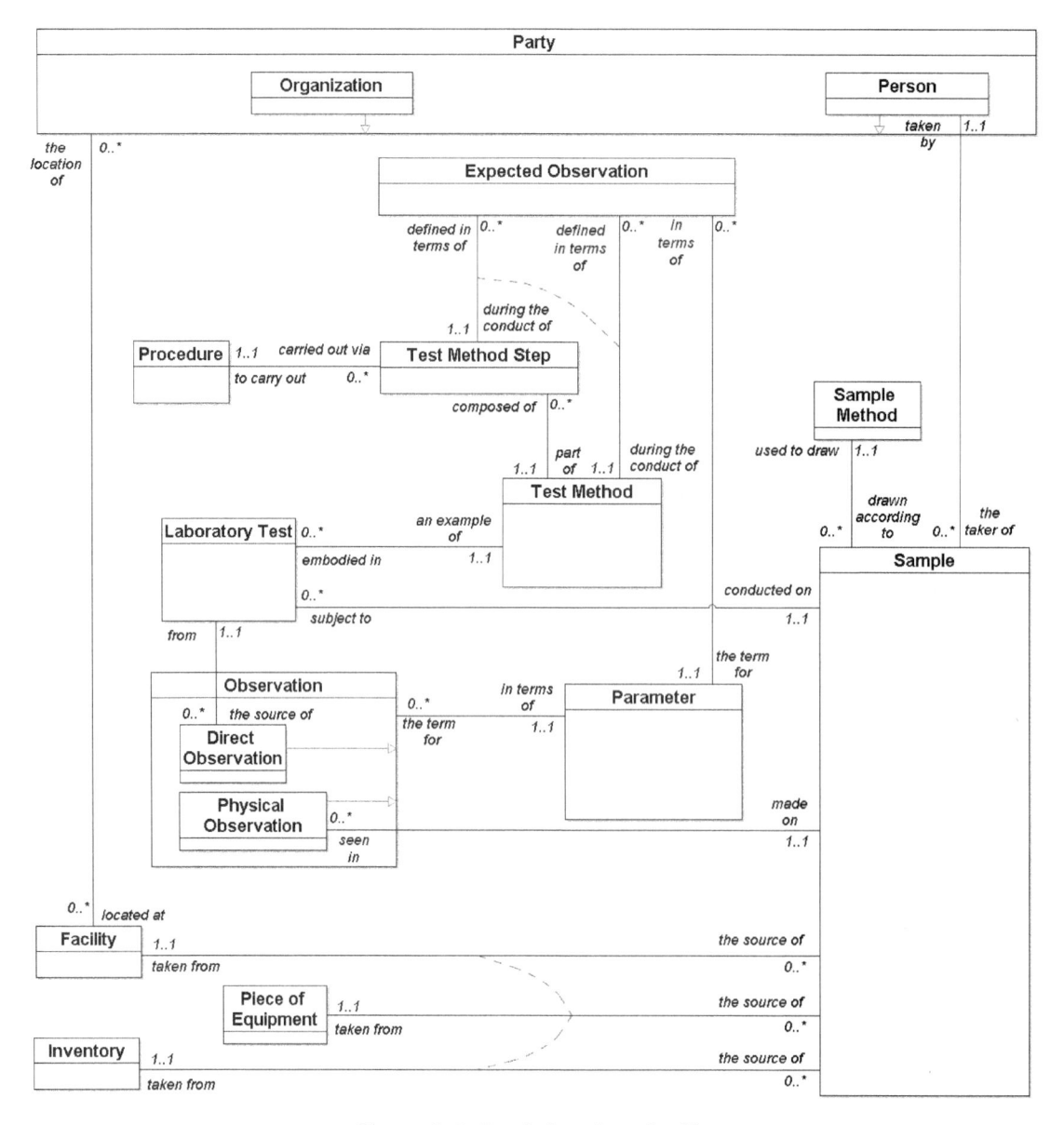

Figure 2-6: Straightening the Lines

The observations apparently come from **Laboratory Tests** and **Samples**. Now, we're beginning to get a sense of what the model is about.

Role names have themselves become more consistent, as well. In each case, the role name assertion sentence is read in a clockwise direction. Thus, "each **Expected Observation** must be *during the conduct of* one and only one **Test Method**", while "each **Test Method** may be *defined in terms of* one or more **Expected Observations**".

Starry Skies Orientation

Figure 2-7 shows the same model organized according to the ***starry skies*** positional conventions that will be adopted in this book. That is, the asterisks (the "many" side of the relationships) are always to the left or toward the top of the diagram.

This has the effect of putting entity classes representing tangible objects (such as **Party**) in the lower right area of the diagram, and putting those representing the less tangible roles, interactions, and transactions (such as **Observation**) in the upper left.

Note that even without prior knowledge of the laboratory, you can see that the focus of the diagram is **Laboratory Test** *conducted on* **Sample**, and the results describing each **Sample** (**Observations**). Some entity classes describe the context of the model: **Test Method, Person, Organization, Piece of Equipment**, and **Inventory**. With that context, you can now begin to dig further: A **Direct Observation** seems to come *from* a **Laboratory Test** *conducted on* a **Sample**, while a **Physical Observation** is *made on* a **Sample** directly.

Now, by simply looking at the diagram, you don't have to be a laboratory technician to understand that apparently some **Observations** are **Physical Observations** *made on* the **Sample**. (What color is the sample? What is its consistency?) Other **Observations** involve conducting a **Laboratory Test** (according to a **Test Method**) on a **Sample** and taking **Direct Measurements**. In either case, an **Observation** must be *in terms of* one **Parameter**.

This approach has several benefits: First, with different kinds of entity classes in appropriate positions in the drawing, someone who has never seen it will still be able to get an idea of what the model is about. From its overall organization, even the most casual observer can get some sense of both its subject matter and contents.

60 Enterprise Model Patterns

A second benefit of following a positional convention is that it makes patterns easier to see. For example, the structure of **Observation** (*from a* **Laboratory Test**, *in terms of* a **Parameter**) is parallel to the structure of **Expected Observation** (*during conduct of* a **Test Method** or a **Test Method Step**, and *in terms of* a **Parameter**). The comparison of actual and expected observations will be an important part of the quality control procedures in the laboratory.

These patterns become candidates for consolidation of entity classes, as we shall see in subsequent chapters. The laboratory example shown in Figure 2-7 is itself an example of a recurring pattern.

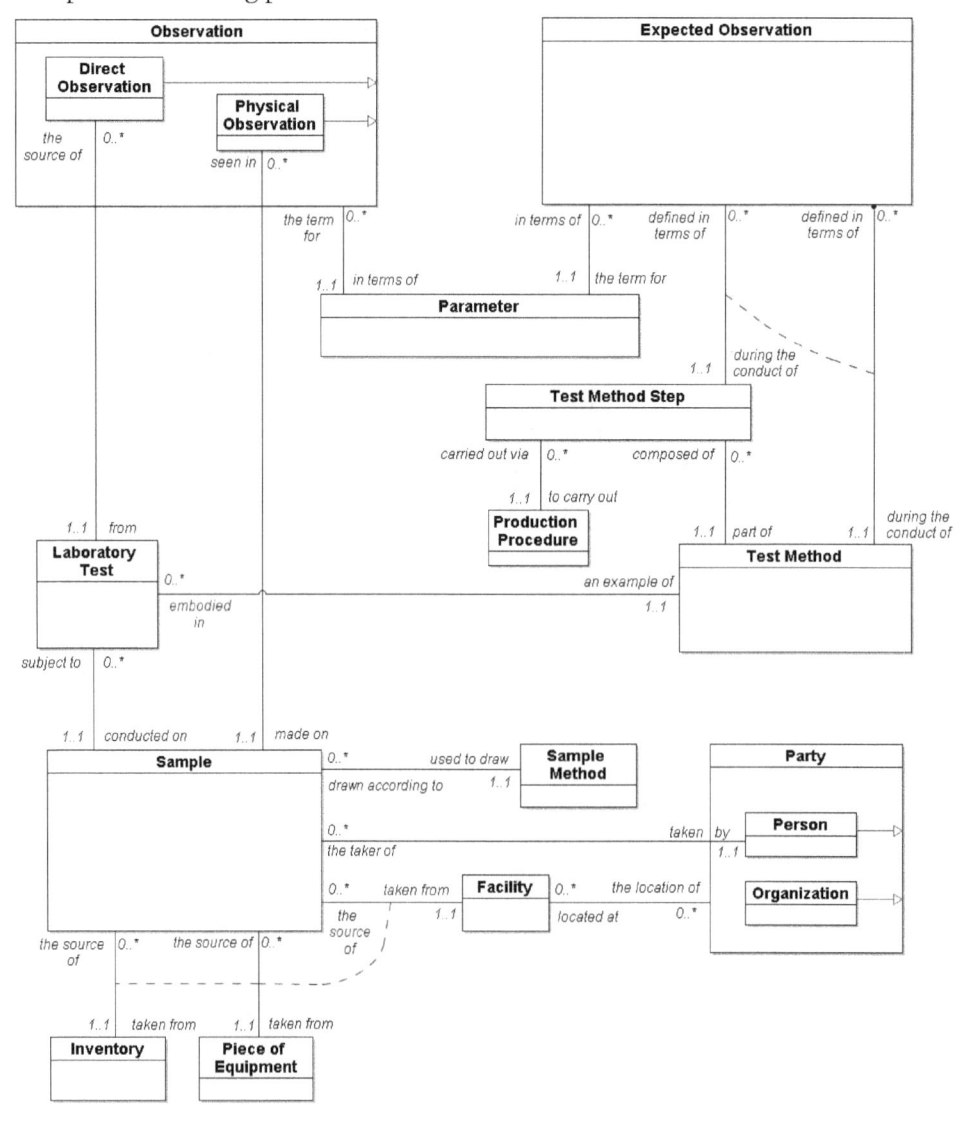

Figure 2-7: An Orderly Data Model

You may have come into this chapter not knowing anything about laboratory procedures, but by noting the positions of entity classes in a diagram, you (it is to be hoped) learned something about them. If you are interested in learning more about this subject, check out Chapter 16 of this book for more details. ♣

Conventions about the position of entity classes on a page are less well articulated in either the data modeling or the object-oriented development industries (and certainly less frequently followed) than conventions about syntax. Among those who do follow such conventions, some will argue that the asterisks should be toward the bottom and to the right. While this policy is clearly heresy to your author♣, it does at least impose the required consistency, and he will grudgingly admit that it does no harm if everyone follows it.

Limit Number of (Highlighted) Boxes

There are 13 boxes (17 if you include sub-types) in Figure 2-7. That is a typical number for a subject area model, and is acceptable at the end of a chapter to let people understand how the subject area fits together. However…

Under no circumstances should a subject area try to squeeze more than 15 (maximum 20, but only if it is otherwise aesthetically perfect) boxes into the space of an A4♥ piece of paper. If you get close to that number, you probably have two (or more?) subject areas, and these should be in separate drawings.

In addition, the model should not be presented as a single drawing. Begin with a drawing that has between one and three entity classes and their relationships. Highlight those entity classes and relationships. The second drawing will have exactly those entity classes and relationships (without highlighting) plus between one and four more. The new entity classes and attributes will then be highlighted. This process continues until you have the complete subject area—with only the one to four entity classes and relationships added in the last step highlighted.

---

* This is the only data modeling book you will find that is presumptuous enough to expect that the reader unfamiliar with these subjects will, in fact, learn something about not only laboratory procedures, but also criminal justice, microbiology, banking, oil production, and highway maintenance. The data models in Part Five will teach you about these subjects.

♣ So far in his experience, all "upside-down" models have been done by Canadians. Hmm…

♥ That's (approximately) 8.5" by 11" for the Yanks.

This is in response to insights first published in a paper by G.A. Miller in 1956.[24] He conducted a series of experiments and concluded that there is a fundamental limit to the number of "things" people can hold in their active memory. Specifically, it is 7±2 concepts. Proof of this is in the experience of older Americans responding to the growth of telephone numbers in the United States. Some years ago, an area code was an "object" that everyone understood Each city had one, with maybe one to three for the suburban areas. You pretty much "knew" what everyone's area code was, plus you knew that the second digit would be a 0 or a 1. To learn a 7-digit telephone number, then, was not difficult for most of us. In recent years, however, the shortage of telephone numbers meant that more area codes were added. Originally they were geographic, so that different sections of the city got new area codes. But people objected to having to change area codes so frequently, so the policy was then changed so that only new subscribers got new area codes.

This meant that, even for a local call, you had to dial all 10 digits. This also meant that you now had to remember 10 digits. As Dr. Miller could have predicted, this is *very difficult*. "Speed dialing" was invented in the nick of time.

The implication of this principle in presentations is simple. On any slide, limit the number of "things" (bullet points, graphic objects, et cetera) to 7±2. A slide with fewer than 5 things appears too simplistic, while a slide with more than 9 is too complicated.

The implication for presenting data models is simple. If you must have 15-20 objects on a slide, make the group fade into the background; the entire set of things you've seen already is effectively one concept. Then highlight the three or four entity classes that are the subject of the current part of the presentation.

Follow Accepted Graphic Design Principles

This is a matter of aesthetic tidiness. Figures 2-8 and 2-9 show elements of these.

- If one side of two or three boxes are approximately in line with each other—line them up. For example, check out **Laboratory Test** and **Observation** in the two diagrams. Also **Sample** with both **Laboratory Test** and **Observation**.

---

[24] G. A. Miller. 1956. "The Magical Number Seven, Plus or Minus Two: Some Limits on Our Capacity for Processing Information," *The Psychological Review*, 63:2 (March 1956), 81–97.

About Conventions

- If you have several sub-types in a super-type, and it is reasonable to do so, make them the same size. (Yes, there are exceptional circumstances, sometimes.) Also put reasonable space around them. In the examples, see **Observation's** sub-types: **Direct Observation** and **Physical Observation**.

- The constraints described in the previous sections will make it impossible to completely eliminate crossed lines, but at least keep them to a minimum.

- If at all possible, don't let lines cross relationship names. See *subject to*, *from*, and *the source of* in the two figures.

- Be sure that the relationships can be read in a clockwise direction. In the examples: "Each **Laboratory Test** must be *conducted on* one and only one **Sample**." "Each **Sample** may be *subject to* one or more **Laboratory Tests**."

- Indeed, if a relationship name is next to a sub-type, either wrap it so it entirely fits inside the super-type box, add a space or so between words so the super-type border can go between words, or simply narrow the space between the super-type and sub-type boundaries and put the relationship name outside. In the examples, "each **Sample** may be *seen in* one or more **Physical Observations**.

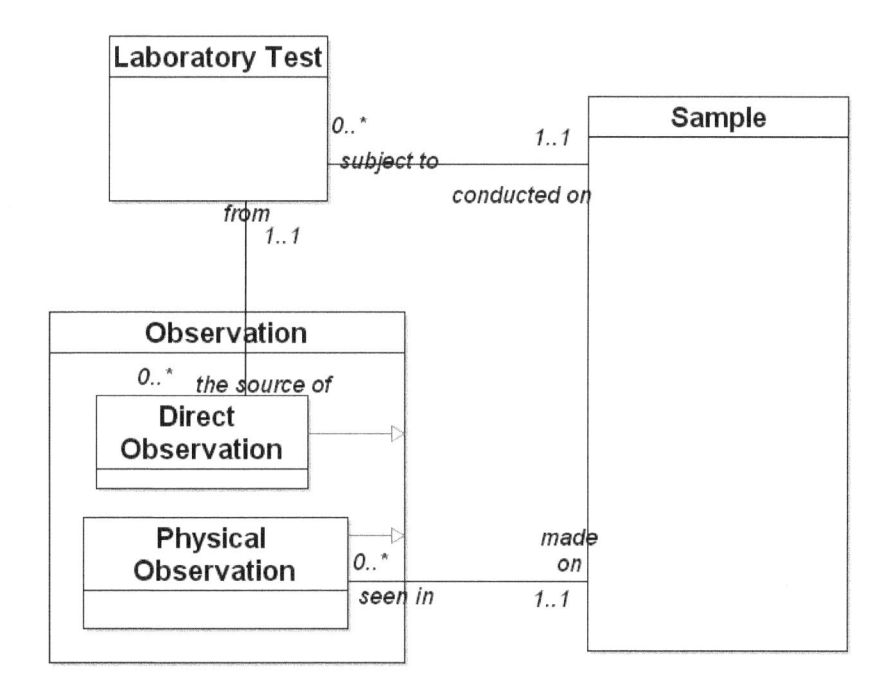

Figure 2-8: Ugly Drawing

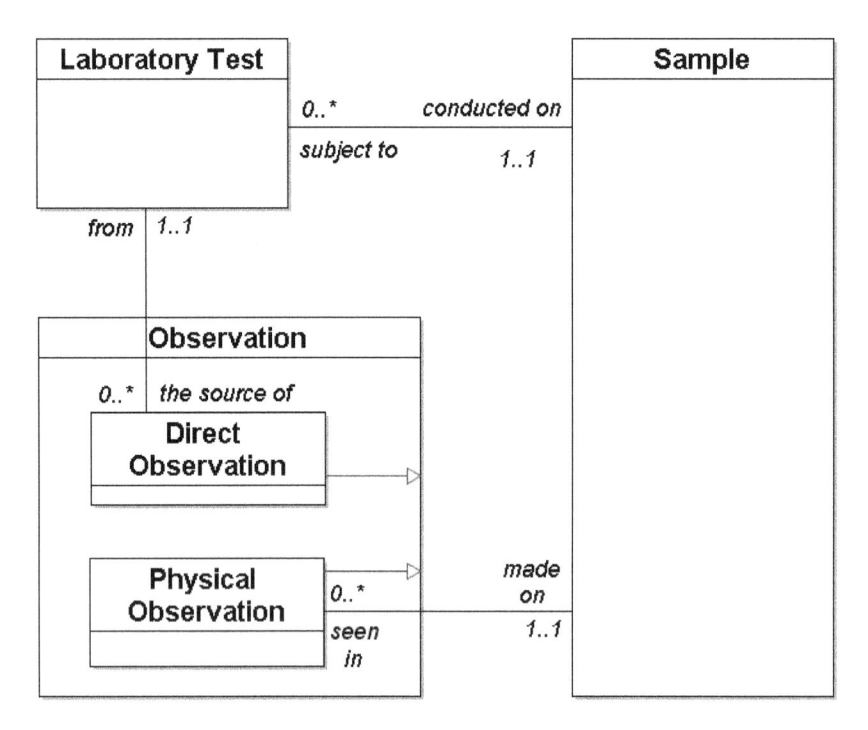

Figure 2-9: Pretty Drawing

Architectural Conventions

The third level of convention — the subject of this book — consists of modeling similar business situations in similar ways. Using common shapes for common phenomena can address both of data modeling's problems: familiar shapes make models easier to read, at least by fellow analysts familiar with the conventions; and shapes used in common by many enterprises are more likely to describe things that are fundamental to each enterprise.

In the author's original book, your author called these "semantic conventions", to emphasize the fact that these are concerned with the structure of the business things recognized by the people who do the work in a company or government agency. Since then, work has been done by groups such as the Business Rules Group and the Object Management Group to refine the capture of business rules, and, in particular, the capture and articulation of the semantics of an organization. The insight here was the refinement of the distinction between two of the perspectives described by John Zachman in *The Zachman Framework*: the

Business Owner's View[25] (in his updated version, called the *Executive Leader's View*[26]); and what he originally called the *Designer's View*, but now calls the *Architect's View*.

It turns out to be the Executive Leaders' views where the *language* of the business is captured. This is the view concerned with **semantics**—theory of *meaning*. This is the study of the signification of signs or symbols, as opposed to the study of their formal relations (called **syntactics**).[27]. Here we deal with the issue that different parts of the same organization use the same words and phrases to mean different things. An analysis of language must address all of the nuances of those differences.

The architect's view, on the other hand, is concerned with bringing together all of the disparate Executive Leader's Views into a single, coherent description of the true nature of the organization—the view of which all the Executive Leader's views are a subset. The view is still concerned with semantics to be sure, but the language used is a sub-set of the set of all business terms used in the organization.

In preparing an architectural model, modelers are always advised to use the language of the business wherever possible. But if a term has multiple definitions, don't use that term. Find a term for each of the defined concepts. Use a conventional, natural language term for each concept, but don't use the controversial term. (See Chapter 22, with its model of a highway department that cannot use the word "road".)

In keeping with that principle, and because of the broad (and not always precisely defined) use of the word "semantics", your author has decided not to use it in this book. The model presented here is indeed at the level of the architect's view, not the semantic view.

At the business level, pharmaceutical clinical research, nuclear power generation, chemical manufacturing, news gathering, and government regulation all exhibit similar patterns in their data models. While each model is different, clearly they are all constructed from a common set of structures.♣ The fundamental aspects of

---

[25] John Zachman. 1987. "A framework for information systems architecture," *IBM Systems Journal*, Vol. 26, No. 3. (IBM Publication G321-5298)

[26] John Zachman and Stan Lock *The Zachman Framework*™,, http://zachmaninternational.com/index.php/home-article/13#maincol.

[27] G. Kemmerling. 2002. *Philosophical Dictionary*. http://www.philosophypages.com/dy/s4.htm#sems.

♣ We could call them "mental blocks", but in the interest of good taste we won't…

66 Enterprise Model Patterns

creating an organization, buying raw materials and supplies, manufacturing and selling products, and testing materials in a laboratory — are not as different from company to company as one might imagine.

For example, a **Company** may be *composed of* one or more **Divisions**, each of which may be *composed of* one or more **Departments**, each of which may be *composed of* one or more **Groups**. Figure 2-10 shows this. This is all well and good, but what if the company decides to re-organize? A new organizational unit—**Section**—has been added between **Department** and **Division**, such that each **Department** now is *part of one* or more **Sections**—except that some **Departments** still will report directly to **Division**.

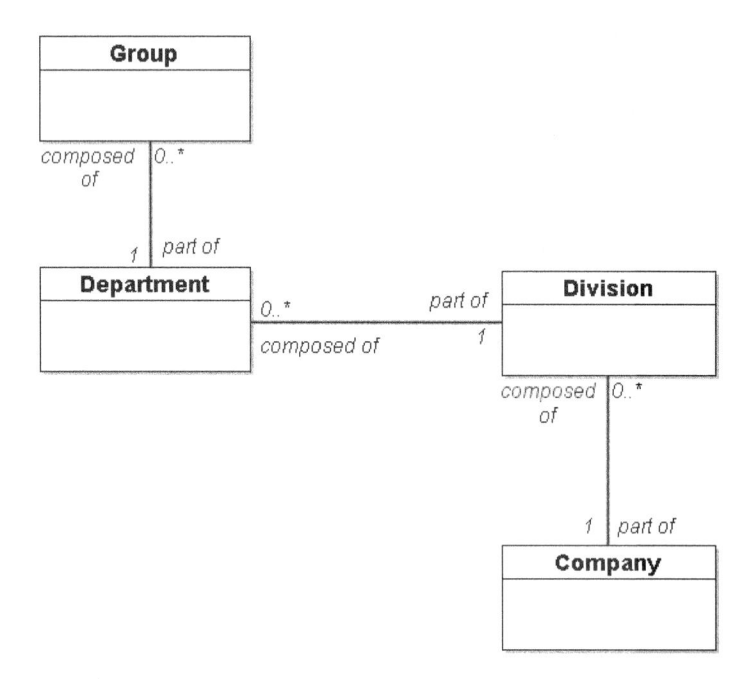

Figure 2-10: One Model of Organizations

This could have serious implications not just for the data model, but also for all of the databases derived from this model.

As it happens, these entity classes are but specific examples of a more general concept, **Organization**. Figure 2-11 shows a much simpler model, where each **Organization** may be *composed of* one or more other **Organizations** (and each **Organization** may be *part of* one and only one other **Organization**). Each **Organization**, in turn, must be *an example of* one and only one **Organization Type**, which defines (in data) if it is a "division", "group", or whatever.

The model in Figure 2-11 encompasses all the meaning of Figure 2-10, but it has fewer components, and it leaves room for the company to define new groupings sometime in the future. In addition, the entity can now encompass other organizations not considered before. These might include work crews, labor unions, and professional societies.

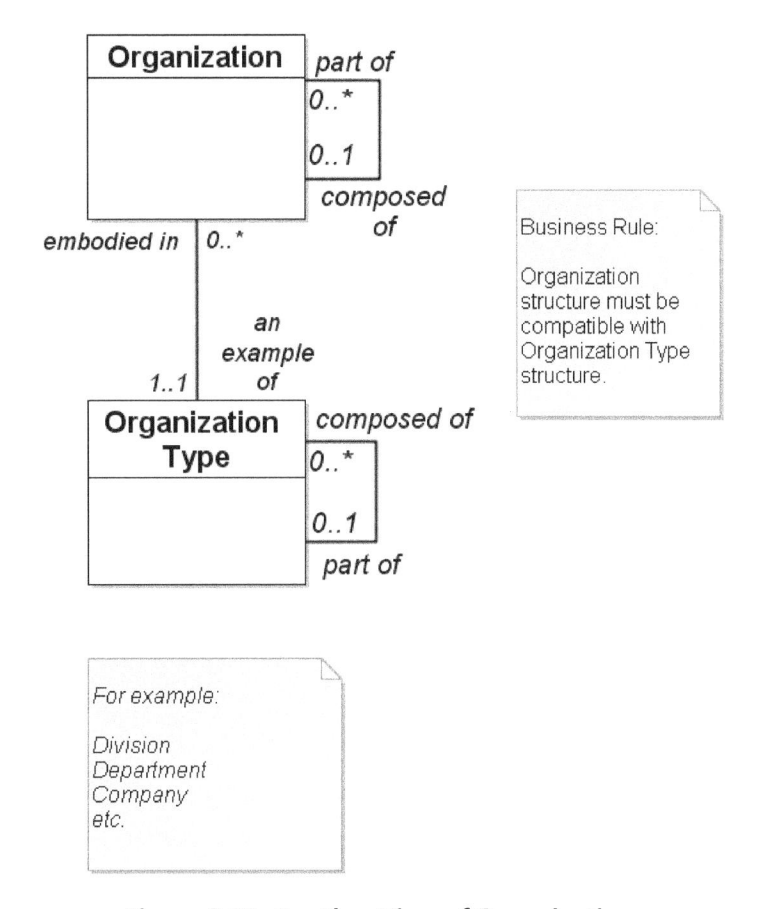

Figure 2-11: Another View of Organizations

Understand that one consequence of this approach is that certain ***business rules*** that are inherent in the version that is Figure 2-10 disappear in Figure 2-11. For example, it is no longer possible to guarantee that only **Departments** are *part of* **Groups** and **Groups** are only *composed of* **Departments**. Figure 2-11 does allow one to make such assertions as relationships between **Organization Types**. That is, you can assert that, in principle, "Group" is *part of* one and only one "Division". But nothing in the model prevents the "Marketing Division" from being a component of the "Sales Group". The business rule that the **Organization** structure must be consistent with the **Organization Type** structure must be asserted (and enforced) outside the model.

So, the benefit of robustness that comes from more abstract structures comes at the cost of not being able to describe business rules directly. Recognize, however, that data structures should not change frequently, and achieving data structures that do not change is one of our objectives here. Business rules, on the other hand, change more frequently, so it is desirable to uncouple them from the data structure and manage them separately.

Note that the closer you get to identifying what is basic to a particular business, the closer you are to identifying what is basic to businesses in general: different businesses will have similar fundamental data structures. In the example here, nearly any company may embrace the notion of an organization, while the more specific references to "Department" or "Group" do not apply as generally.

At the deeper level of architectural conventions, certain data modeling situations recur in different *parts* of the business. Things are classified, things have structure, and people play roles in activities. These, too, are patterns that are useful to the data modeler.

The organization of product structure information, for example, is the same, no matter who needs it. Whether a manufacturer is describing what it puts into a product, a maintenance department is describing what is necessary to fix it, or a regulatory agency is describing what should *not* be in a food or medicine, the data structure for *composition* is the same. Moreover, the idea of structure can be adapted to situations not involving products at all — project critical paths, reporting relationships, and so forth. (Chapter Six discusses this particular pattern in more detail.)

This means that we can develop a vocabulary of common business situations and natural structures, with a data model corresponding to each element in the vocabulary. These models constitute architectural conventions to guide us in building our company models. These "conventions of thought" can help us understand *what the models mean*.

To be sure, various companies and government agencies differ from each other. They provide different products and services, and they operate on different scales. They also differ significantly in their operating procedures and organizational structures.

While these variations dramatically color the appearance and experience of the company, they can be made to reside in the *contents* of data, rather than in the *structure* of that data. For example, in Figure 2-11, if a new **Organization Type** (say, "Section") were added after a system had been built from this model, the simple creation of an occurrence of **Organization Type** and appropriate modifications to **Organization Type Structure** would do the trick. As previously described, to do the same thing with the model in Figure 2-10, however, would require major database surgery to create the new entity (table) and to link it properly to the others.

This isn't to say that all company models should be identical. Companies also differ in the emphasis placed on different aspects of the business. Where the model of one area may be detailed and sophisticated for one business or government agency, it may be greatly simplified for another. Even in these cases, however, while the complexity of the models may indeed differ, the overall data organizations should be similar.

Taking this approach to data modeling has several advantages:

1. It makes the task of building a new model easier, since you now have but to modify and blend existing structures (and to find meaningful examples of them), rather than creating new ones from scratch.
2. Where models reflect conventions, they are easier to read, since the same kinds of things will tend to take the same shape in all diagrams.
3. This, in turn, makes it possible to highlight those things which are genuinely unique about a particular enterprise.
4. It helps reduce or eliminate gross modeling errors, since the basic elements of a model are already defined.
5. Relatively few entity classes describe many specific aspects of a situation. This will result in a system with fewer tables to maintain, simplifying it and making it more reliable.

This book sets out to describe these architectural conventions, and to identify their common model elements. In addition to describing these conventions, it also presents the issues involved in adapting them to specific situations. It is intended to provide guidance both in making models easier to read, and in making them more representative of the fundamental nature of an enterprise. It hopes to restore the promise of data modeling as a useful technique by establishing conventions which, if followed, will lead the analyst to better discipline and clearer models.

About Abstraction

The book in your hands builds extensively on your author's original book on this subject, *Data Model Patterns: Conventions of Thought*.[28] During the years since publication of that book in 1995, your author has had the opportunity to develop many models for many different industries. In each case, having the patterns in his toolkit meant that he could go into a company in an industry he'd never seen before (except, perhaps, as a consumer) and in short order, understand the business better than many people who worked there.

The same year *Data Model Patterns* was published, Eric Gamma, Richard Helm, Ralph Johnson, and John Vlissides published *Design Patterns: Elements of Reusable Object-oriented Software*.[29] Where *Data Model Patterns* had dealt with patterns in business structures, this book addressed patterns in software.

Since then, several books have come out elaborating on the models in the author's original book: *The Data Model Resource Book: A Library of Logical Data and Data Warehouse Model*, by Len Silverston, Bill Inmon, and Kent Graziano presented a similar, but different set of patterns.[30] *Analysis Patterns: Reusable Object Models* by Martin Fowler took a more object-oriented approach.[31]

Mr. Silverston updated his *Data Model Resource Book* in a second edition. This was initially published by him in two volumes: one describes patterns that cross industries,[32] and one describing patterns specific to selected industries.[33]

---

[28] David C. Hay. 1995. *Data Model Patterns: Conventions of Thought*. (New York: Dorset House).

[29] Eric Gamma, Richard Helm, Ralph Johnson, and John Vlissides. 1995. *Design Patterns: Elements of Reusable Object-Oriented Software*. (Reading, MA: Addison-Wesley Publishing Company).

[30] Len Silverston, Bill Inmon, and Ken Graziano. 1997. *The Data Model Resource Book: A Library of Logical Data Models and Data Warehouse Designs*. (New York: John Wiley & Sons).

[31] Martin Fowler 1997. *Analysis Patterns*. (Reading, MA: Addison-Wesley).

[32] Len Silverston. 2001. *The Data Model Resource Book, Volume 1: A library of Universal Data Models for All Enterprises*. (New York: John Wiley & Sons).

[33] Len Silverston. 2001. *The Data Model Resource Book, Volume 2: A library of Universal Data Models by Industry Types*. (New York: John Wiley & Sons).

Subsequently, a third volume was written with Paul Agnew to describe more atomic and general purpose patterns that appear as components in the larger patterns.[34]

Clearly using data model patterns has become a respectable technique for building a data architecture.

Figure 2-12 shows how the principle works in the patterns field arrange themselves, both in terms of level of abstraction and their bias towards technological issues.

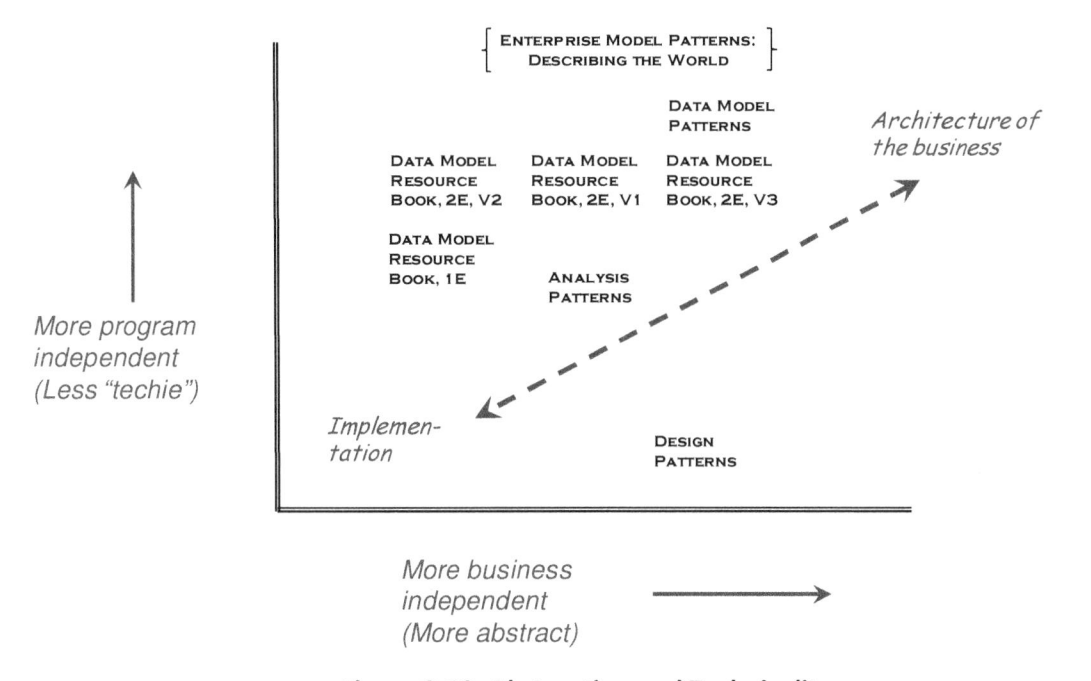

Figure 2-12: Abstraction and Technicality

The most technologically specific, of course, is *Design Patterns*. Its intention was specifically to describe patterns of object-oriented program code. As such, it is completely independent of any business issues, since it isn't about the semantics of business at all, but it is deeply enmeshed in object-oriented technology.

Mr. Fowler's *Analysis Patterns* is moderately business independent, although a large part of it is about the details of modeling accounting. It also is oriented towards the implementation of structures using object-orientation, which makes it less technologically independent than your author's *Data Model Patterns*.

---

[34] Len Silverston, and Paul Agnew. 2009. *The Data Model Resource Book, Volume 3: Universal Patterns for Data Modeling*. (Indianapolis, IN: Wiley Publishing, Inc.).

The first version of *The Data Model Resource Book* ("1E" in the Figure) was specifically oriented towards support of the building of a data warehouse. This led to some technological bias. Its models also tended to be on the concrete side, to address specific business problems.

The second version of *The Data Model Resource Book* is relatively free of technological biases. Even though the book is not about designing a relational database, though, the author does have extensive experience in relational database design, which provides a slight bias towards relational thinking.

This book, *Enterprise Model Patterns* is more technologically independent than the books that have gone before, largely because it has made the definition of attributes into a "data" rather than a "data structure" issue. (See the **…Characteristic** entity classes described in Parts Two and Three of this book.) That is, this book is more abstract than the relatively concrete examples that show up in Volumes 1 and 2 of *The Data Model Resource Book* (designated as "2E,V1" and "2E,V2" on the chart). *Data Model Resource Book, Volume 3*, however, is entirely made up of highly abstract model components. Many of those also show up in *Enterprise Model Patterns*, albeit in a different form.

One thing that has become clear from these and other works is that, while patterns offer specific guidance for addressing particular modeling problems, there is considerable latitude available in producing models for real businesses and government agencies. When your author wrote the original book he didn't think about it, but picked a level of abstraction that seemed the right balance between creating a model that would be general-purpose, and using a language that would be generally understandable. So, "Party" is an abstraction of "Person" and "Organization", and "Asset" is an abstraction encompassing any physical thing. By and large, however, the language ("Geographic Location", "Activity", et cetera) was recognizable.

This turned out to be more abstract than some liked, and not nearly abstract enough for others. This suggests that perhaps it was a good level.

Graeme Simsion, in his Doctoral Thesis, published as *Data Modeling Theory and Practice*,[35] gave a modeling problem to several experts in the field and discovered that each produced a different model in response to it. While this was a startling finding among people who believed they were producing "true" models of a generic

---

[35] Graeme Simsion. 2007. *Data Modeling Theory and Practice*. (Bradley Beach, NJ: Technics Publications).

business, it turned out that many differences came down to one thing: the *level of abstraction* taken in viewing the problem.

In Summary

In any industry, a convention is a kind of standard practice to guide a practitioner in carrying out his or her work. In the data industry, three categories of conventions are relevant to this discussion:

- Notation conventions
- Aesthetic Conventions
- Architectural Conventions

Notation conventions refer to the syntax of a model. This consists of the set of symbols (boxes, circles, lines, et cetera) that carry structural meaning in the model. These are the symbols that describe classes of things of significance, attributes of those things, and relationships among them. Various sets of notations have been created since Dr. Peter Chen originally invented data modeling, and everyone seems to have a favorite. Because each has advantages and disadvantages, there has been little agreement as to which is "best". That, among other things, seems to depend on its purpose.

For the purposes of this book—describing an organization's fundamental architecture—your author has always favored that of Harry Ellis and Richard Barker, developed in the early 1980s. Based on recent experiences, however, he is willing to produce this book using a highly constrained version of the Unified Modeling Language, or UML. This will be unfamiliar to the traditional data modeling audience, and his particular way of using UML will also be unfamiliar to the UML community.

We'll see how that goes…

Because a data model is fundamentally a vehicle of communication with people who may be unfamiliar with the notion of data modeling itself, it is important that the *aesthetics* of data modeling follow basic principles of graphic design.

Architectural conventions are, of course, the subject of the entire book. What is the best set of standard model structures to represent standard business situations? Over the last 15 years, several books have been written on the subject; and while they all are similar in many ways, they differ in the degree of abstraction, as well as in the degree of technological independence.

As for technological independence, the use of UML here suggests a bias towards object-oriented technology. Based on the history of UML, this is understandable. Note, however, that the whole point of this exercise is to show that UML can be used to represent technologically independent models, and that is the intent of the book. Do recognize the relational bias of your author, however: there are constraints on the model derived from relational theory. Any databases derived without change from this model will be in fifth normal form.

This book has set out to address "level of abstraction" head on by presenting more than one, even as it maintains complete technological independence. At one end are very abstract representations of the nature of knowledge, and at the other are specific examples of models of particular industry-specific problems

CHAPTER 3

About This Book

What are these "levels of abstraction" referred to above? How does one use this book to learn more about them?

Levels of Abstraction

This book is organized in terms of several specifically defined *Levels of Abstraction*. Figure 3-1 shows the structure in graphic form.

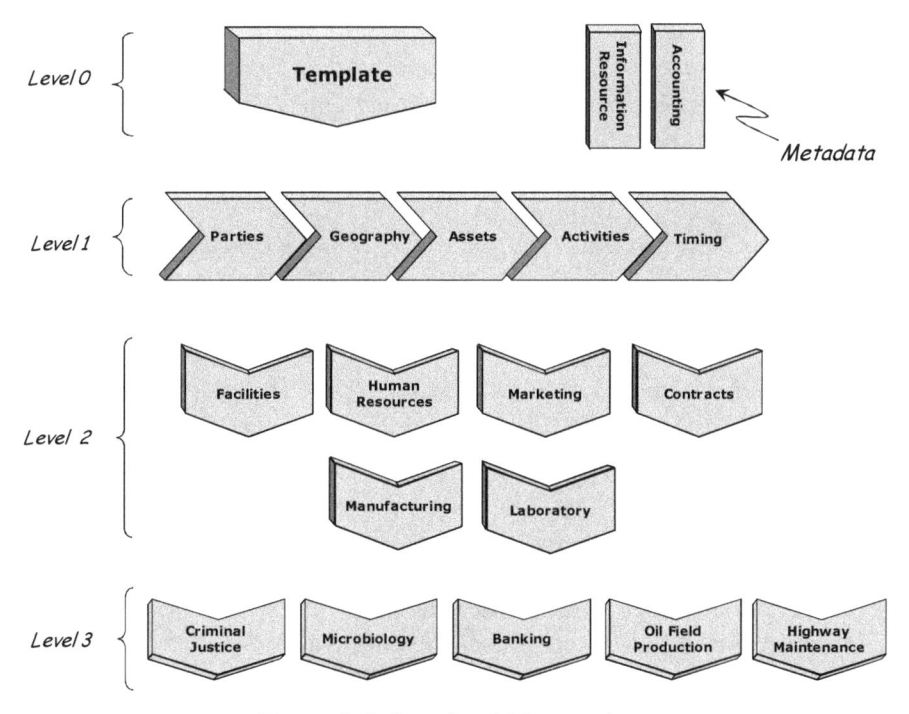

Figure 3-1: Levels of Abstraction

The levels covered are the following:

Level 0 is first a generic, low-level pattern. This is the most abstract model that makes any sense. Among other things, it is directly the basis for the enterprise models in Level 1.

At right angles to this scheme, two categories of ***metadata*** are relevant to enterprise-oriented models. The term "metadata" refers to the data that are used to describe other data. Typically, these are such things as entity and attribute names, but it can encompass much more. Normally, it is the model itself that constitutes metadata. A different kind of metadata, however, is a model whose elements refer to elements of a different model. In this case, there are in fact two modeling domains that are metadata in this sense—referring to part of the basic enterprise model. These are:

- ***Information Assets***, including books, documents, video recordings, and the like – these are significant because they may allude to or otherwise refer to anything in the enterprise. A document, for example, may have a logical connection to literally *anything* else in the data model. To model information assets is to model what is approximately a model of the business.
- ***Accounting*** – (well, double-entry bookkeeping, at least) is itself a modeling language that has been used for modeling organizations for many centuries longer than data modeling. As such, the elements of accounting may refer to anything also being represented by the business model. To model accounting is to model a model of the business.

For the purposes of this book, metadata are discussed in the context of Abstraction Level 0. The remaining levels are the following:

- ***Level 1*** is a model of an enterprise in general, but still in fundamental terms. It is the first level less abstract than the 0 level. Models at this level can be the starting point for modeling any enterprise—be it a company or a government agency. It has four primary components, plus one. The *primary* components are:

    People and Organizations – the parties that both populate and constitute the environment of the enterprise.

    Geography – places on the Earth where everything takes place.

    Physical Assets – the physical "stuff" of the world. This includes products, raw materials, equipment and furniture, buildings, and the like.

Activities – what the enterprise does, described either as fundamental functions or as transformative processes. This also includes descriptions of the events that cause activities to take place.

Time – when do things happen? Modeling time is fundamentally different from modeling everything else.

- *Level 2* consists of models of functional areas within an organization. These are specific to a functional area, but they are still patterns, in that they could be expected to apply to that functional area in many organizations. While there may be many, those included here include:

    Facilities – A facility is a geographic location with a purpose, where people and organizations use physical assets to perform activities to achieve objectives.

    Human Resources – "Employee" is not a thing of significance. This is a role played by a **Person** when *employed by* an **Organization**. The fact of **Employment** is complex, involving training, position assignments, and benefits, among other issues.

    Marketing and Communications – What a company does as it carries out its business is *communicate* with the outside world. This turns out to be much more complicated to model than most people realize.

    Contracts – A contract is an agreement between two or more people and/or organizations obligating some of them to supply activities and/or physical assets to the others—typically in exchange for a monetary payment.

    Manufacturing – This part of the model is based extensively on the model of physical assets, but it is a bit more specialized. It does not go into as much detail, however, as did *Data Model Patterns; Conventions of Thought*.

    The Laboratory – This concerns the gathering of data via structured technologies and procedures.

Throughout the model, people and organizations play **roles**. Examples of this are collected and discussed separately here.

- *Level 3* consists of models specific to various industries. Note that this section does not present a complete model of an oil producer or a bank. Most of the components of all companies will follow the generic patterns of Levels 1 and 2. But each industry has one or more areas that call for more specialized models. These are the models that make banking different from highway administration or pharmaceutical research. Here are included some examples of addressing an industry in more detailed concrete terms—but in each case relating the model to levels 1 and 2.

Four approaches characterize these variations:

Change names. The model for *criminal justice* is very similar to the enterprise model of Level 1. It is only that the names of nearly all of the entity classes are different.

Elaborate sub-types. *Micro-biology* takes the entity class (physical) **Asset Specification** all the way to **Protein** and **Deoxyribonucleic Acid**.

Modify selected concepts. *Banking* turns the conventional structure of contracts on its head by asserting that an instance of an ordered **Product Specification** is itself another contract, here called an **Account**. (The underlying problem is that, in this case, a "Product" is *not* a physical asset.)

Add specialized details. Interesting examples are the structure of an oil well and of a highway interchange—all linked to concepts from the Level 1 enterprise model.

But even these models are patterns within the industry to show what all companies within that industry share.

The Organization of the Book

The remainder of this book is fundamentally a collection of model diagrams. It is organized in terms of the levels of abstraction just described. The remaining Parts of the book describe:

- **Part Two: Abstraction Level One: The Enterprise Model** – This section focuses on the five primary components of any corporate, enterprise-wide conceptual model: people and organizations, geography, physical assets, activities, and time.
- **Part Three: Abstraction Level Zero: A Template and Metadata** – Based on the patterns observed in Part Two, this section describes the Level Zero template that is common to the four primary components of the Level One model. It also describes the two flavors of metadata that are needed in the business model: information resources and accounting.

- **Part Four: Abstraction Level Two: Within an Organization** – This section addresses more specialized models to deal with common problems within most enterprises: contracts, facilities management, marketing and communications, logistics, and (for some companies) laboratory management.
- **Part Five**: **Abstraction Level Three: Industry Models** – This section covers the elements that make certain industries unique. In each case, a company in that industry can use the Level One Enterprise Model for most of its requirements. There are only a few specialized areas of interest. Examples of these are described within this section.

About "levels" of abstraction:

To talk about "level" of abstraction is to use a metaphor. This metaphor suggests that somehow that more abstract things are "higher" than less abstract things. A common expression for the generalized overview model is that it is from the "30 thousand foot level". The idea here is that the higher you go, the less detail you see. It could be argued therefore that the most concrete models should be at "level 0" and the most abstract ones should have a higher number. The problem with that is that we don't really know how high a number that should be. Should the "thing/thing type" model be at level 3? Level 5? The open-endedness of that scheme makes it unworkable as a metaphor.

So, your author has decided to recognize that the most abstract model represents a baseline. It will not get more abstract than that. So, the metaphor is reversed. This way, if someone wants to get even more detailed and concrete, levels 4, 5, 6, and beyond are all available. Level 0 is the starting point. Yes, that has the least detail. But rather than thinking in terms of an airplane, think of a mountain. As you go higher and higher you find more and more interesting fauna and flora.

PART TWO

ABSTRACTION LEVEL 1: THE GENERIC ENTERPRISE MODEL

The primary components of a truly general-purpose architectural enterprise model describe the who, where, what, how, and when of the organization. Specifically, as shown in Figure Two-1, the primary components are:

- ***People and Organizations*** – *Who* is involved with the business? These are the heart of any enterprise. The people involved are not only the employees within the organization, but customers, agents, and others with whom the organization comes in contact. Organizations of interest include the enterprise itself and its own internal departments, as well as customers, competitors, government agencies, and the like. Commonly, people and organizations are collectively referred to as **Parties**.
- ***Geographic Locations*** – W*here* is business conducted? A geographic location may be either a geographic area (defined as any bounded area on the Earth), a geographic point (used to identify a particular location), or, if you are an oil company for example, a geographic solid (such as an oil reserve). Note that this only describes places on Earth. When we start adding buildings and using these places for something such as homes or office buildings, we are not speaking of **Geographic Locations**, but rather about ***addresses*** and ***facilities***, to be described in Chapter 11.
- ***Assets*** – *What* tangible items are used to carry out the business? These are any physical things that are manipulated, sometimes as products, but also as the means to producing products and services. This includes equipment for

82 Enterprise Model Patterns

manufacturing, oil field equipment, computers, cars and trucks, and the like. It also includes natural gas, cement, and gasoline. Anything tangible falls into this category. (Non-physical assets are treated differently in the discussion about *data resources* in Chapter 10.)

- *Activities* – *How* is the business carried out? This model not only covers services offered, but also projects and any other kinds of activities. In addition, the model describes the *events* that cause activities to happen.
- *Time* – All data is positioned in time, but some more than others. Because time is a different dimension, it has to be addressed differently than the other four areas. There are two ways to approach it:
  - …as *attributes*, primarily for transaction-type entity classes. Every *intersection entity class* (with two or more required relationships) has the equivalent of Effective Date and Until Date as attributes. *Reference entity classes* (those which stand alone, without any required relationships) usually do not, since they are not about events that take place in time, although sometimes it may be appropriate to do so.
  - …as *entity classes*, each representing a time element, such as **Month**, **Quarter**, and **Year**. These are not required for the architectural model, but are useful in design models to support dimensional structures.

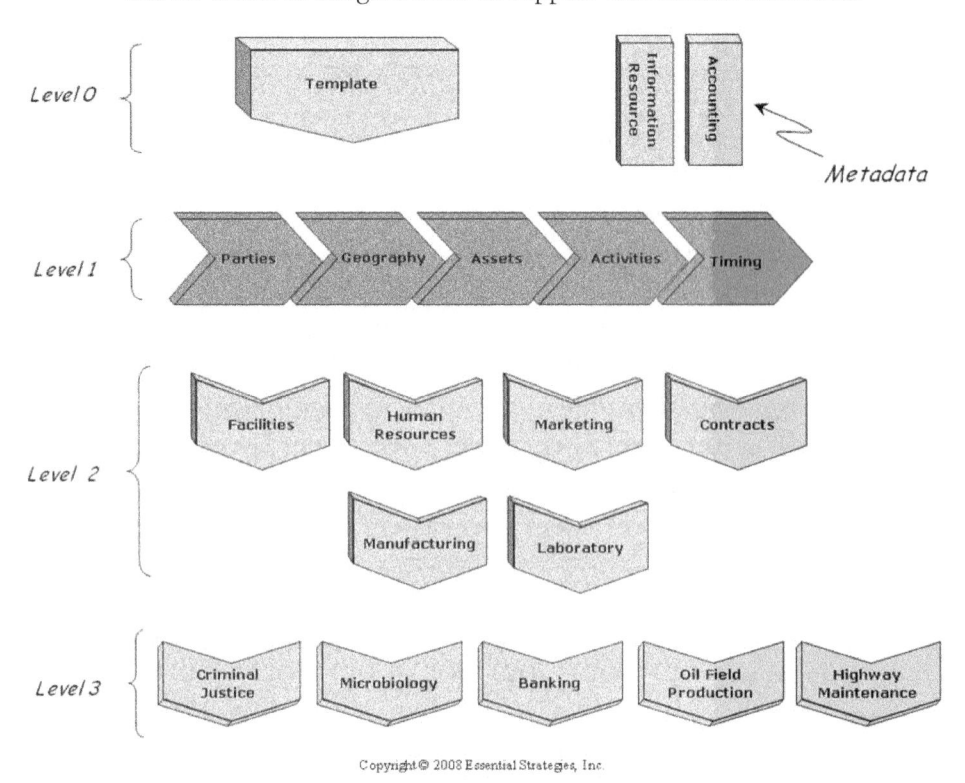

Figure Two-1: The Level 1 Components

CHAPTER 4

People and Organizations (Who)

An enterprise cannot exist without people. Whether one is an employee, a vendor agent, or the president of a company, a **Person** can clearly be assumed to be a "thing of significance" to most companies and government agencies. A few of the things to be known about a *Person*, such as **Name**, or **Birth Date** are attributes of the **Person** entity. Others (more than you might suppose) are not attributes, but relationships to other entities, as we shall see. A *Person* may enroll in one or more courses, for example, or may play a role in one or more activities, and so forth. (More examples of these roles will be shown throughout the book.)

If an enterprise is concerned with people, it must surely also be concerned with aggregations of people. Such an aggregation (called henceforth an *organization*) may be a department, a committee, a vendor, a labor union, or any other collection of people or other organizations. It is described by such attributes as **Purpose, Federal Tax ID**, and so forth.

Figure 4-1 shows entity classes for **Person**, a human being of interest, and **Organization**, a collection of human beings.[*] We'll discuss attributes in detail later on, but here for the sake of argument, **Person** has the attribute **Birth Date**, and **Organization** has the attribute **Purpose**.

Four kinds of **Organization** (sub-types) are shown:

- **Company** – a legally recognized commercial business, which, in the United States, is a corporation, a partnership, or a sole proprietorship.

---

[*] Yes, it is possible to define an organization without specifying the people it contains. The presumption is that even if it is being postulated, it is expected to consist of human beings.

- **Internal Organization** – an organization within the enterprise, such as a department.
- **Government** – the body which is responsible for administration of a geopolitical area, such as a country or a state.
- **Government Agency** – a component of a **Government** usually concerned with regulating a particular area of concern, such as pharmaceuticals, air travel, criminal activities, and so forth.

The sub-types shown here are pretty standard, but every enterprise has its own way of segmenting **Organizations**. **Other Organization** is for any **Organization** not covered by the other categories.* Examples might include labor unions and professional societies, political parties, and the like.

Note that **Person** is described by the attribute **Birth Date** while **Organization** is described solely by the attribute **Purpose**. So far they have no identifying attributes, but these will come next.

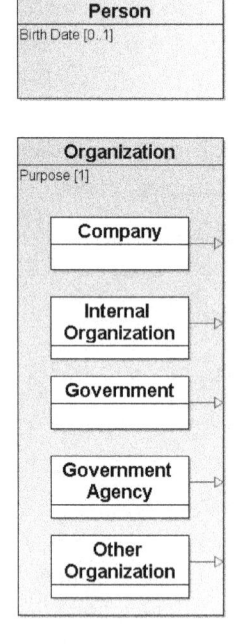

Figure 4-1: People and Organization

---

* Note that according to the data modeling approach being followed in this book, sub-types do not overlap. The same **Organization** may not be both an **Internal Organization** and a **Company**. Note also the constraint that every instance of a super-type must be an instance of only one sub-type. This constraint is finessed by including **Other Organization** for the ones we haven't thought of yet.

Parties

People and organizations share many attributes and relationships to other entities. A corporation is, after all, a legal **Person**. Both people and organizations can be described by **Name** and **Address**, and both may be party to contracts. For this reason, while **Person** and **Organization** are useful entities, so too is the super-set of the two, which we will here call **Party**. This is shown in Figure 4-2.

In this example, **Party** has the common attributes **Global Party Identifier** and **Name**. In Figure 4-1 we saw that **Person** has the attribute **Birth Date**, and **Organization** has the attribute **Purpose**. Now we can see that both **Person** and **Organization** also have **Global Party Identifier** and **Name**.

Of course, **Person** actually has *two* names (plus a middle initial, if you want to get thorough). This could be handled by moving **Name** to **Organization** and giving **Person First Name** and **Last Name**. An alternative is shown here, with the principle **Name** being equivalent to a **Person**'s surname. Names will be treated in a much more comprehensive way, below.[*]

Notice that **Global Party Identifier** is specified as a unique identifier for both **Person** and **Organization**. This is a fairly strong assertion: no **Person** can have the same identifier as any **Organization**. The modeler may, instead, choose to have a separate set of identifiers for **Person** (say, **Person ID**) and for **Organization** (say, **Organization ID**).

The answer to the question of which approach to take is, as they say, beyond the scope of this book. This is, after all, only a "pattern". It is for the reader to apply it appropriately.

Note that in Figure 4-2, each **Party** must be *an example of* exactly one **Party Type**. This is a structure that we'll see again often. In this case, **Party Type** is defined as the definition of a kind of **Party**. That each **Party** must be *an example of* <u>exactly one</u> **Party Type** suggests some overlap with the sub-type structure, where each **Party** must be either a **Person**, a **Company**, a **Government Agency**, and so forth.

---

[*] Henceforth, unless there is reason to display them (as there was here, to make a point), attributes will only be shown in the first figure where the entity class appears. For the sake of clarity, they will not be shown after that.

86 Enterprise Model Patterns

Indeed, **Party Type** does exactly reproduce the sub-type structure. That is, instances of **Party Type** include "`Person`", "`Organization`", "`Company`", and so forth.

The generalization structure of **Party** is further represented by the assertion that "each **Party Type** may be *a super-type of* one or more other **Party Types**". (Alternatively, "each **Party Type** may be *a sub-type of* one and only one other **Party Type**".) For example, "`Company`" is *a sub-type of* "`Organization`".

This redundancy is a bit of a gimmick, but it allows us both to see graphically the principal categories of **Party**, and to make use of them in the formulation of business rules. We will see examples of this later.

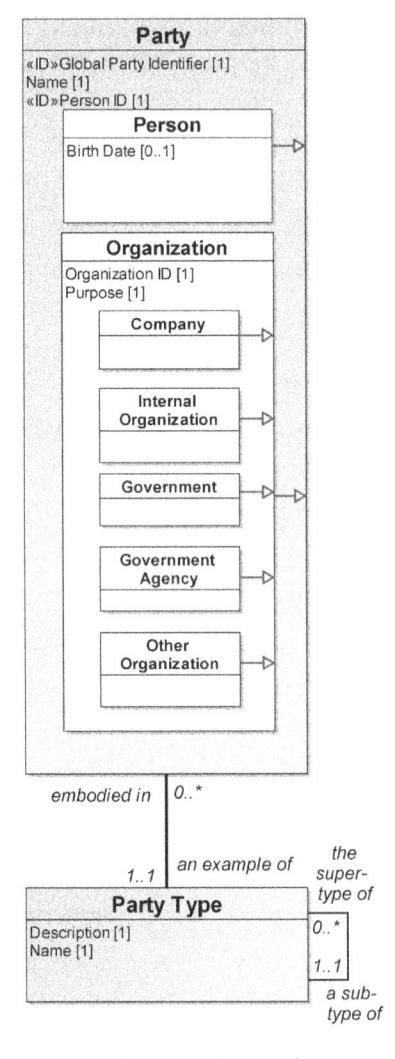

Figure 4-2: Parties

Business Rule

- Instances of **Party Type** must at least include one for each sub-type of **Party** shown. Other, more detailed instances are permitted.

Party Relationships

People are related to each other; people belong to unions and clubs; departments are contained in divisions; companies band together into industrial associations, buying groups, and so forth.

To address this diversity of possible associations among **Parties**, the entity class **Party Relationship** is introduced in Figure 4-3. This allows us to represent *any* relationship between two parties. That is, each **Party Relationship** is defined to be *from* one **Party** and *to* another **Party**.

Thus, a **Party Relationship** *from* **Person** "George Gobel" *to* **Organization** "The Screen Actors' Guild" **Effective Date** "June 18, 1952", **Until Date** "February 24, 1991".—would be *an example of* the **Party Relationship Type**, "Member".

The important attributes of this are the **Effective Date** of the **Party Relationship** and its **Until Date**. Note that each **Party Relationship** must be *an example of* exactly one **Party Relationship Type**, such as "organizational structure", "club membership", "family relationship", and so forth.

Thus, "George Gobel" may go down in history as having been in a relationship (of type "membership"), with "The Screen Actors' Guild", Effective "June 18, 1952", Until "February 24, 1991".

88 Enterprise Model Patterns

Party Relationship
«ID»Relationship Identifier [1]
«ID»Effective Date [1]
Until Date [0..1]
Comment [0..1]

embodied in 0..*
related to 0..* «ID» from 1..1
related from 0..* «ID» to 1..1

an example of 1..1

Party Relationship Type
«ID»Name [1]
Description [1]

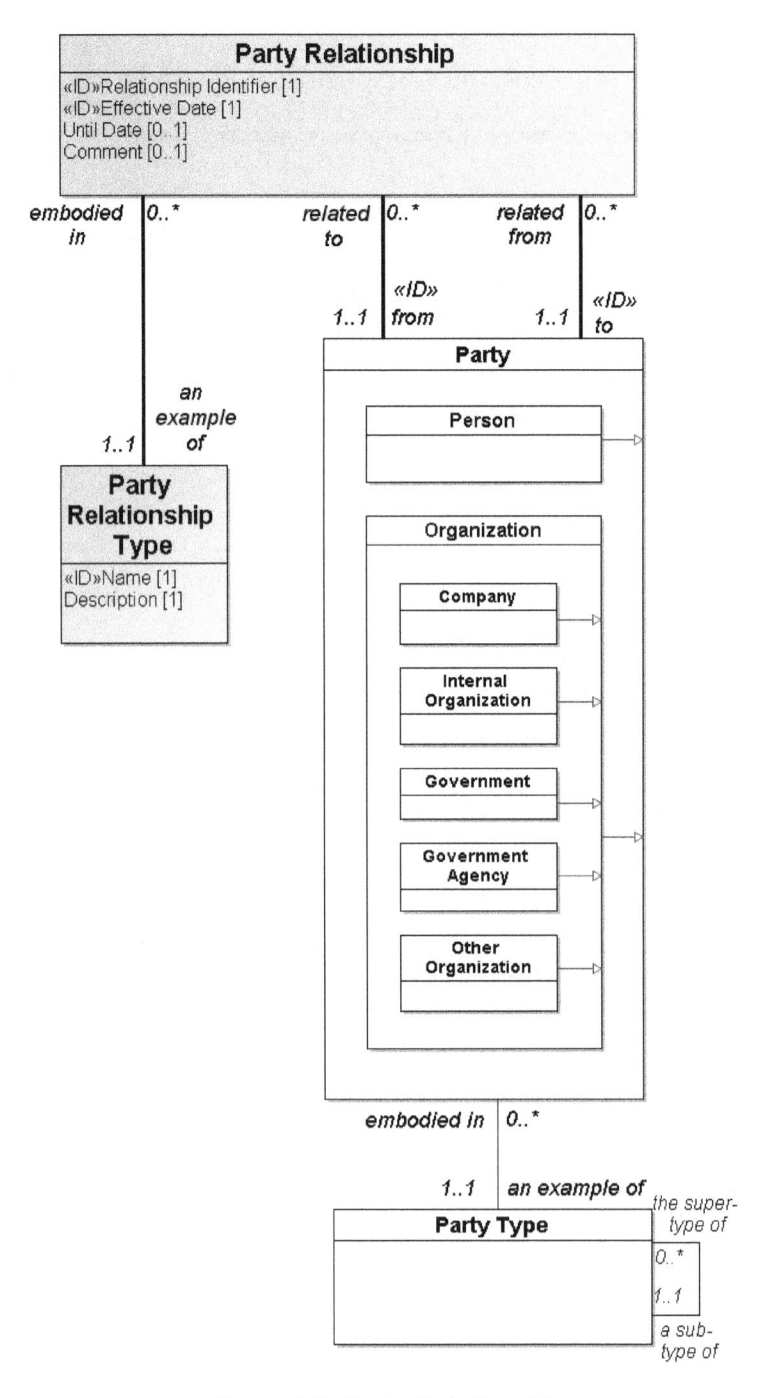

Party
- Person
- Organization
  - Company
  - Internal Organization
  - Government
  - Government Agency
  - Other Organization

embodied in 0..*
1..1 an example of

Party Type
the super-type of 0..*
a sub-type of 1..1

Figure 4-3: Party Relationships

Party Identifiers and Names

Back in Figure 4-2, **Party** is shown with the attribute **Global Party Identifier**, marked with <<ID>> to show that it is a component of the unique identifier for the entity class.[*] This symbol is an extension to UML to show that each instance of an entity class is uniquely identified—at least in part—by the annotated attribute. In this case, it shows that each instance of **Party** has a unique value for **Global Party Identifier**. It is also only a dream today. Many are working on schemes for eliminating duplicate records and neatly being able to identify everyone. It hasn't happened yet. Many systems have a surrogate key that forces uniqueness for all instances of **Party** within the system, but there is no guarantee that in the world there aren't multiple instances of the same **Person** or **Organization** across different systems.

Figure 4-4 shows an alternative approach. This acknowledges that there are lots of identifiers for Persons (`"Social Security Number"`, `"passport number"`, `"employee number"`, and so forth.) and for organizations as well (`"Employer Identification Number"`, `"department number"`, and so forth.) This structure allows us to capture all the possible identifiers in the entity class **Party Identifier** and then to give each a Value as it is evaluated in **Party Identifier Value**. Each of these must be *for* one **Party Identifier** and *assigned to* one **Party**.

The identification of instances of **Party Identifier Value** is via a combination of the attribute **Identifier Value**, and the two relationships:

- Each **Identifier Value** must be *assigned to* one **Party**.
- Each **Identifier Value** must be *for* one **Party Identifier**.

Note the "<<ID>>" symbol next to both the attribute and the role names. This means that `"George Smith"` can have two different values of **Employee ID** (for different **Party Identifiers**). There could be a business rule preventing that, but if the situation exists, it should be captured—and then revealed.

---

[*] See "Unique Identifiers" on Page 65.

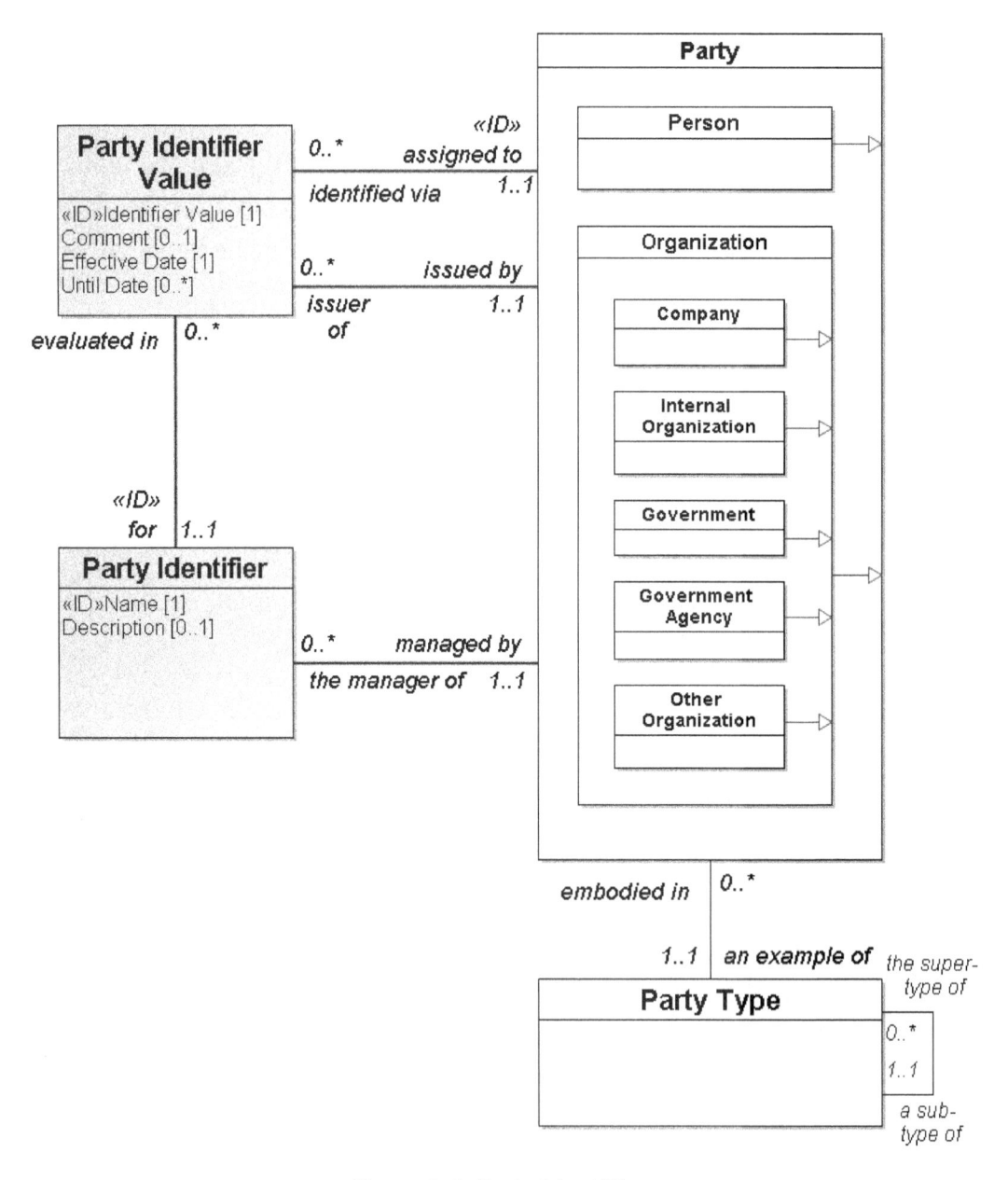

Figure 4-4: Party Identifiers

Tables 4-1 and 4-2 show examples of tables derived from these entity classes. The names of identifying columns are highlighted. In Figure 4-2, the reference to **Party Identifier** matches the value of **Party Identifier** Name shown in Figure 4-1. Note that including the Identifier Value to the unique identifier allows for "George Smith" to have two values for Employee Number at two different times. Without that, "George Smith" could not be employed more than once.

People and Organizations

Table 4-1: Party Identifiers

Name <<ID>>	Description	*managed by*
Social Security Number	Number used to identify individual people who are present or future pensioners.	U.S. Social Security Administration
Employer Identification Number	Number used to identify corporations.	U.S. Social Security Administration
Emp No	Number used to identify individual employees.	a specified Company

Table 4-2: Party Identifier Values

<<ID>> *assigned to* Party	<<ID>> *for* Party Identifier	<<ID>> Identifier Value	*issued by* Party	Effective Date	Until Date
Marlon Brando	Social Security Number	234-99-3122	Social Security Administration	February 4, 1940	July 1, 2004
The Company Company	Employee Identification Number	99-1234567	Social Security Administration	August 4, 1989	--
George Smith	Employee Number	241533	Lockheed Martin	December 15, 2004	December 16, 2004
George Smith	Employee Number	242687	Lockheed Martin	January 24, 2006	August 15, 2009

The Figure also shows that each **Party Identifier** must be *managed by* a **Party**. For example, the concept of the "Social Security Number" is managed by the U.S. Social Security Administration. The "Employee ID" is managed by the company's Human Resources Department. Along the same lines, the actual assignment of an **Identifier** to a **Party** is *issued by* a **Party**, such as an **Internal Organization**, or even the **Party** itself.

Moving from identifying people to the task of identifying data (instances of **Party Identifier Value**, in this case), each instance of **Party Identifier Value** is identified by the combination of the two relationships just described, plus the attribute

Identifier Value. That is, there is only one instance of `"Essential Strategies, Inc."` having an **Employee Identification Number** of `"99-1234-123"`. With this configuration, it is possible for `"Essential Strategies, Inc."` to have another **Employer Identification Number**.

To constrain it so that, for example, `"Essential Strategies, Inc."` may never have more than one **Employer Identification Number**, simply remove the designation of **Identifier Value** as part of the unique identifier. Then, there could be no more than one instance of the combination of **Party** and **Party Identifier**.

Note that each **Party Identifier** must be *managed by* a **Party**. For example, the concept of the `"Social Security Number"` is managed by the U.S. Social Security Administration. The `"Employee ID"` is managed by the company's Human Resources Department. Along the same lines, the actual assignment of a **Party Identifier Value** to a **Party** is itself *issued by* one **Party**, such as an **Internal Organization**, a **Government Agency**, or the **Party** itself.

An obvious attribute for **Party**, as we have seen, is **Name**. Well, not exactly. You can have a name for an organization, but what about people's names? In addition to simple first and last name, what about middle? Or Jr.? What about the title? No, it's more complex than even that. For that matter, companies have official names, nicknames, and stock tickers. And on top of everything else, names change. No, a simple name attribute just won't do.

Figure 4-5 shows that, as with **Party Identifier**, **Party Name** has been pulled out from the **Party** entity class, so that each **Party** may be *labeled by* one or more **Party Names**. That is, each **Party Name** must be *of* one **Party** and (significantly) it must be *of* one **Party Name Type**. This allows a woman, for example to have one **Party Name** that is of **Party Name Type** `"married name"`, and another of **Party Name Type** `"maiden name"`.

Note that each **Party Name** is uniquely identified by both the **Name Text** and the **Party** being named. The name `"David Charles Hay"` can only exist once for the fellow who is the author of this book.

The **Company** `"IBM"` may be *labeled by* the **Name Text** attribute of **Party Name**, `"International Business Machines Corp"`. That **Party Name** is *an example of* **Party Name Type Name** of `"official name"`. IBM is also

People and Organizations 93

labeled by the **Party Name** Name Text, "IBM", where that **Party Name** is *an example of* **Party Name Type** Name of "official abbreviation".

The entity class **Party Name** has attributes Effective Date and Until Date, which allows capture of the history of names. For example, Table 4-3 shows a history of names for the company known since 2000 officially (if redundantly) as "FedEx Express".

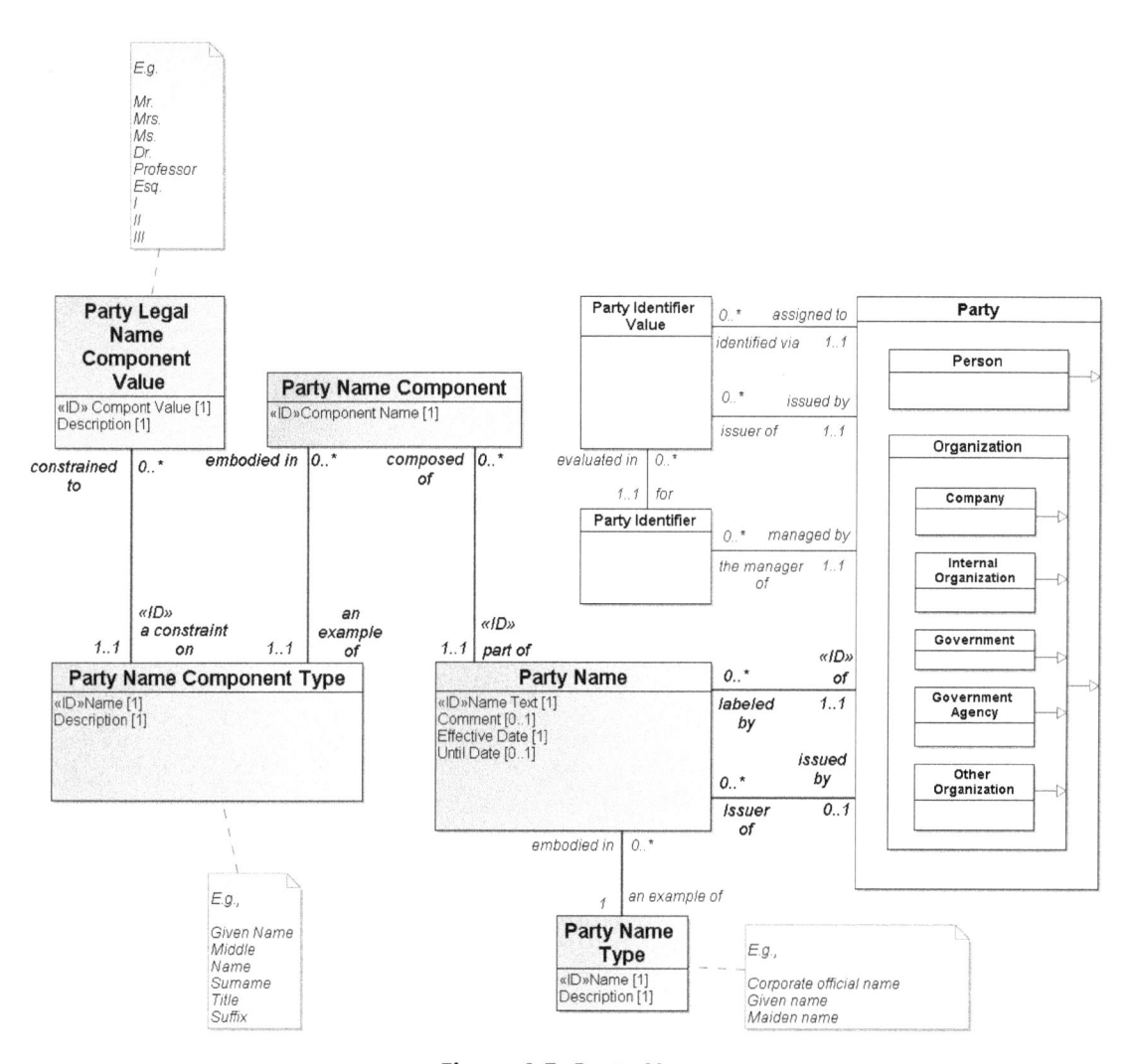

Figure 4-5: Party Names

Table 4-3 The Names of Federal Express

Party	Effective Date	Party Name Text	Party Name Type Name
Federal Express	6/1/96	Fed Ex	Nickname
Federal Express	1/1/98 (became subsidiary of FDX Corp)	Federal Express	Official name
FDX Corp	1/1/2000	Fedex Corp	Official name
Federal Express	1/1/2000	FedEx Express	Official name

Note that while each **Party Name** must be *of* one **Party**, it may also be *issued* by a **Party**. Presumably, in the case of a **Person**, that **Person** is responsible at least for reporting '**e**♥ own name (rare is the organization that requires parents to sign off on someone's name), but in the case of **Organizations**, it could be important who specified the **Party Name**.

The naming problem for people is more complicated than that. As pointed out above, people's names have a complex structure. Each may be *composed of* one or more **Party Name Components**, where each **Party Name Component** must be *an example of* exactly one **Party Name Component Type**, such as `"first name"`, `"last name"`, `"suffix"`, `"title"`, and so forth. Some **Party Name Component Types** are constrained to certain values, though. That is, the Component Name in a **Party Name Component**, if it is an example of **Party Legal Name Component Value** `"Title"`, must then be `"Mr."`, `"Ms."`, `"Dr."`, and so forth.

Figure 4-5 showed annotations with examples of the primary entity types. Table 4-4 shows the example in tabular form.

♥ As a modern man, your author is properly reticent to use "he" to mean "he or she". As a grammarian, however, he also objects to using "their" when only one person is involved. (Although he does acknowledge that this practice goes back at least to the 17th century). He also finds "he or she" to be incredibly clumsy. So, in the interest of conciseness and logical consistency, he hereby proposes the following conventions: *'e* means "he or she"; *h'* means either "him or her" or "his or her".

Remember, you saw it here first.

People and Organizations

Table 4-4: An Example of a Name

Party Name	Party Name Type	Party Name Component Type	Legal Party Name Component Type Value	Party Name Component
Mr. David Charles Hay II	Birth name	Title	Mr. Mrs. Ms. Dr. Professor	Mr.
		Given name	--	David
		Middle name	--	Charles
		Surname	--	Hay
		Suffix	II III IV Esq.	II

Business Rule

- If a **Party Name Role Type** is constrained to one or more **Legal Name Component Values**, then any instance of **Party Name Component** that is an example of that **Party Name Component Type** must have as its Component Name the "value" of one of those **Legal Name Component Values**. (*Translation:* If a **Party Name Component Type** is *constrained to* one or more **Party Legal Name Component Values**, any **Party Name Component** must be *an example of* one of those values.)

Constraints

The structure for identifiers and names has the advantage of being supremely flexible. Any name value can be given to any **Person** or **Organization**. Any identifier value can be given to any **Person** or **Organization**. But only certain kinds of **Party Identifiers** are appropriate for certain kinds of **Parties**, just as only certain **Party Name Types** are appropriate for certain kinds of **Parties**. For example, the **Party Identifier** "Social Security Number" is only appropriate for

Person. The **Party Name Type** `"corporate abbreviation"` is only appropriate for **Company**.

Here is where splitting out **Party Type** becomes useful. Figure 4-6 shows that we can specify that each **Party Identifier** is only appropriate for particular **Party Types**. This is done through specifying a **Party Identifier Assignment** that is *of* a **Party Identifier** and *to* a **Party Type**. That is, for example, one can assert that the **Party Identifier** `"Employer Identification Number"` may only be assigned to a **Party** that is an *example of* the **Party Type** `"Company"`.

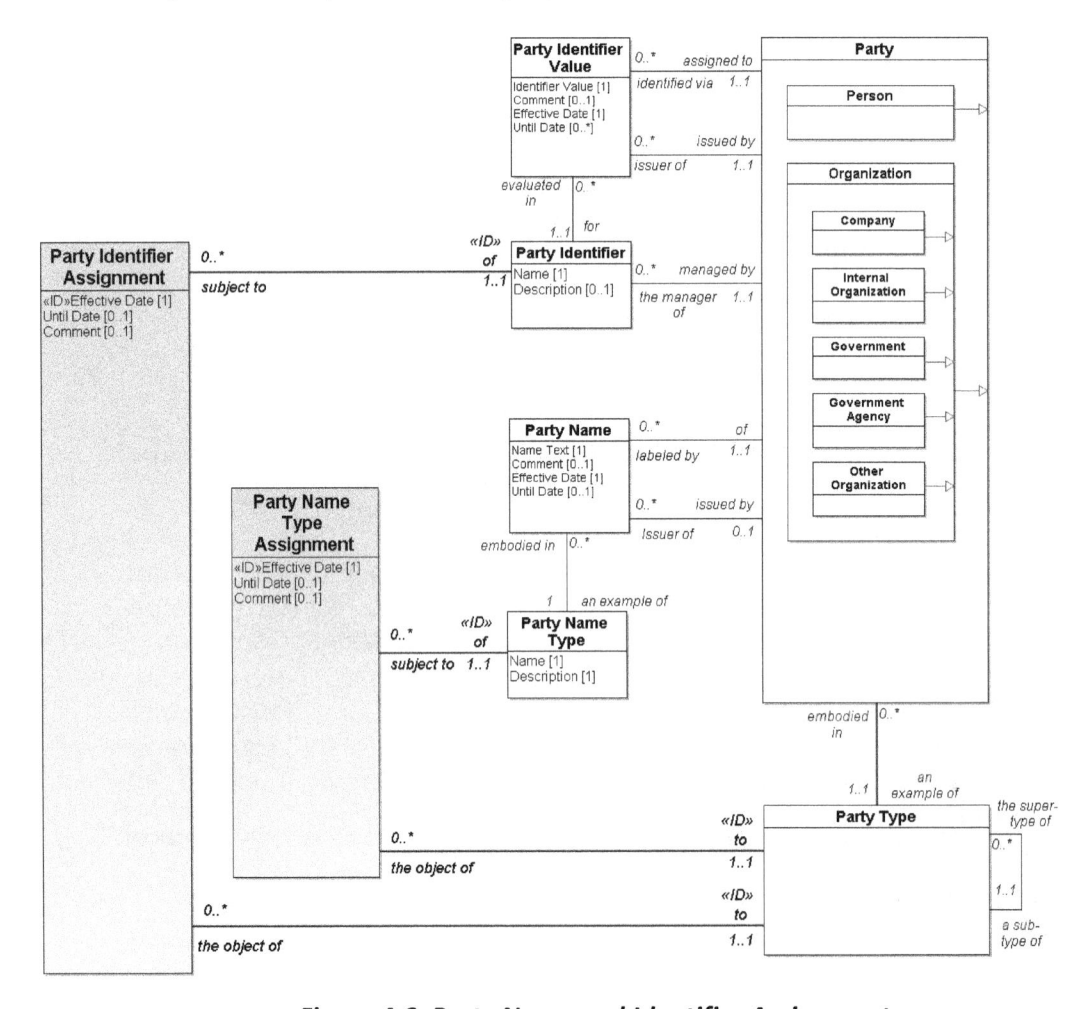

Figure 4-6: Party Name and Identifier Assignments

The same constraint is described by **Party Name Assignment**. **Party Name Types** such as `"married name"` and `"personal name"` can only be *embodied in* **Party Names** *of* **Parties** that are *examples of* the **Party Type** `"Person"`. (Indeed, the **Party Types** `"male person"` and `"female person"` could be added as **Party Types** that are each a sub-type of **Person**, even though they don't appear as sub-types. In that case, the **Party Name Type** `"maiden name"` could be constrained to `"female person"`).

Table 4-5 shows some examples of **Party Name Types** being assigned to **Party Types**.

Table 4-5: Some Party Constraints

<<ID>> *of* **Party Name Type**	<<ID>> *to* **Party Type**
Given Name	Person
Corporate Official Name	Company
Location Name	Government

Note that in a data model, only *the existence of* constraints such as these assignments can be shown. Since they will ultimately be implemented via program code, rather than database structures, the constraints themselves must be specified separately. The constraints are:

Business Rules

- A Party Name Name Text *of* a **Party** may only be *an example of* a **Party Name Type** if a **Party Name Assignment** exists that is *of* that **Party Name Type** and is *to* the **Party Type** that the named **Party** is *an example of*. That is, a **Party** may not be *labeled by* a **Party Name**, unless the **Party Name Type** it is *an example of* is *subject to* a **Party Name Assignment** *to* the **Party Type** *embodied in* the **Party** involved. (***Translation:*** Only certain kinds of **Party Names** can be used for each kind of **Party**.)

- A Party Identifier Value Identifier Value *assigned to* a **Party** may only be *an example of* a **Party Identifier** if a **Party Identifier Assignment** exists that is *of* that **Party Identifier** and is *to* the **Party Type** that the named **Party** is *an example of*. That is, a **Party** may not be *identified via* a **Party Identifier Value** unless the **Party Identifier** it is *for* is subject to a **Party Identifier Assignment** *to* the **Party Type** *embodied in* the **Party** in question. (***Translation:*** Only certain kinds of **Party Identifiers** can be used for each kind of **Party**.)

Party Characteristics

One problem with defining attributes for **Party** is agreeing amongst ourselves as to just what those attributes should be. Traditionally, employee tables have had hundreds of attributes, with the attendant problems of keeping them updated, dealing with history, and linking them to reference data. **Birth Date** seems pretty safe for **Person**, although not all applications will require (or even permit) it. **Gender** was pretty safe in past years, but modern times have made defining the list of legal values (or even making it permanent) a little dodgy. Things like **Height** and **Weight**, of course, won't do either, since they change over time.

On the **Organization** side, there are numerous descriptors that could be added, but they vary greatly from company to company and application to application.

In any real data model, local circumstances will dictate which attributes should be encoded permanently into the data model. For our purposes here, however, in the interest of producing a truly general model, virtually all descriptive **Party** characteristics will be captured not as attributes but as values for the entity class, **Party Characteristic**, as shown in Figure 4-7.

Here, a **Party Characteristic** is a distinguishing trait, quality, or property that can be given one or more values for a **Party**. Indeed, **Party Characteristic Value** is the value *of* a **Party Characteristic** *for* a **Party** (in its attribute **Characteristic Value**, of course). Note that this way of describing properties has several advantages over using attributes for this purpose:

- A **Party** can have multiple values for the same **Party Characteristic** over time (with the time identified).
- A **Party** can have different values for the same **Party Characteristic** as *issued by* different other **Parties**. So the marketing department may classify someone one way, but the sales department (or accounting) may describe the **Person** or **Organization** in completely different terms.
- It is easy to keep track of who set the values.
- Different departments can maintain completely different sets of parameters for describing the same set of people.
- And most significantly, changes to the list of **Party Characteristics** do not require changes to the data structure—either in the model or in the subsequent physical database.

People and Organizations 99

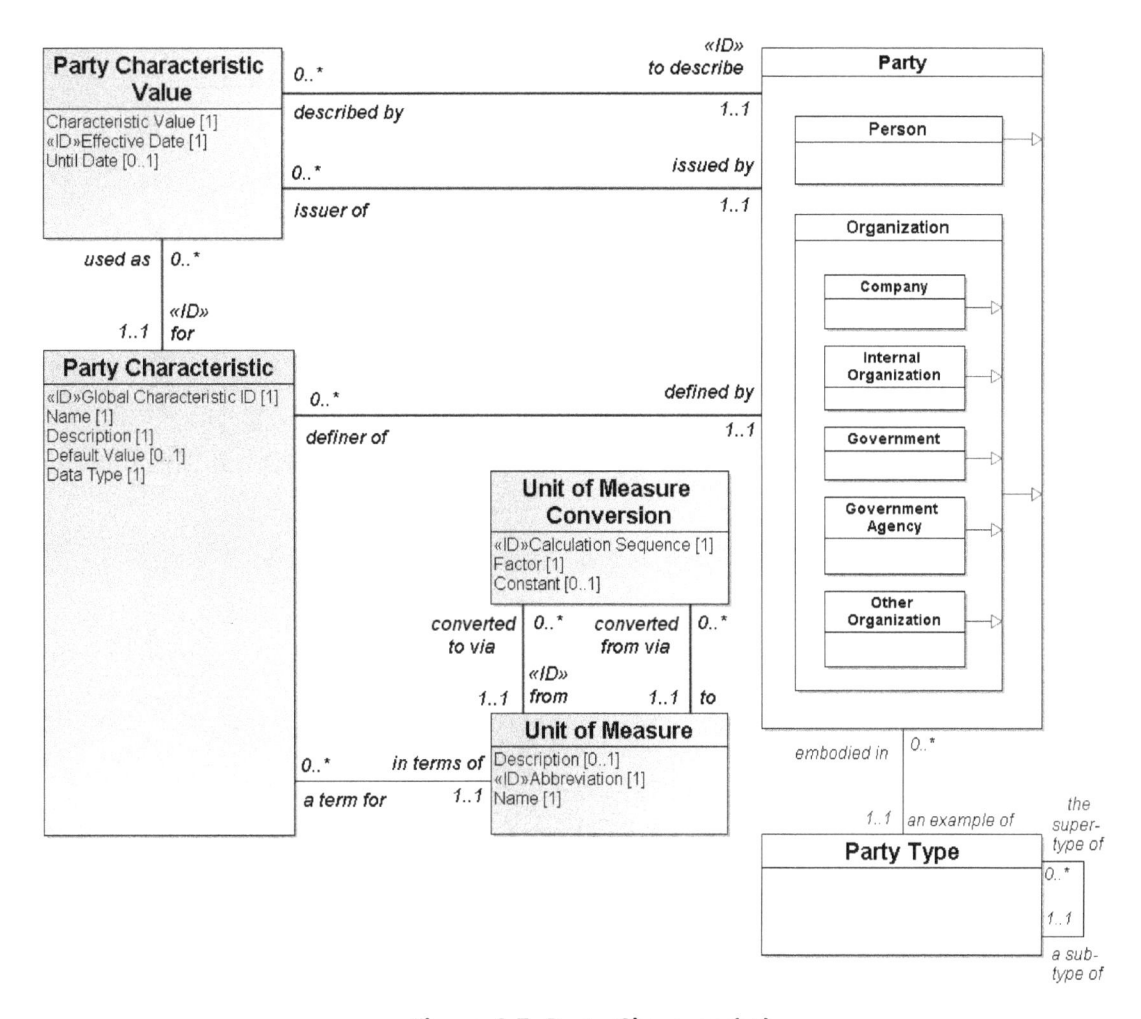

Figure 4-7: Party Characteristics

Each **Party Characteristic** is uniquely identified by a surrogate key **Global Characteristic ID**. Each **Product Characteristic Value** is identified by a combination of the **Party Characteristic** that the **Product Characteristic Value** is *of*, the **Party** that the value is *for*, and the Effective Date of the value. Thus, a single **Party** can have multiple **Party Characteristic Values** *of* the same **Party Characteristic** *over time*.

Figure 4-7 also shows that each **Party Characteristic** must be (recorded) *in terms of* exactly one **Unit of Measure**. A **Unit of Measure** a definite magnitude of a physical quantity, defined and adopted by convention and/or by law, that is used as a standard for measurement of the same physical quantity.[36] Should it be necessary to *report* a **Party Characteristic Value** in terms of a different **Unit of Measure**, the entity class **Unit of Measure Conversion** can be used to, for example, change "pounds" into "kilograms" (via the **Factor** ".4545").

Each instance of a **Party Characteristic** is uniquely identified by its value for the attribute **Global Characteristic ID**. Again, the concept of a global identifier comes into play because of the desirability of having a master list of characteristics defined uniformly across all systems. This may not be practical, of course, so at least a system surrogate identifier will be required.

Tables 4-6 and 4-7 show sample instances of both **Party Characteristics** and **Party Characteristic Values**.

Figure 4-8 elaborates on the nature of these **Party Characteristics**. In fact, there are two principal kinds:

- **Continuous Party Characteristic** – This is a property that is expressed as a real number or a time period. Examples of this include "height", "number of employees", and so forth. In Table 4-6, "Height", "Number of Employees", and "Family Income" are examples of **Continuous Party Characteristic**.
- **Party Category** – This is a property that can only have one of a set of discrete values. Indeed, the model shows that each **Party Category** may be *constrained to* one or more **Legal Party Category Values**. Examples of this include "eye color", "North American Industry Classification System Code", and "Company Income Rank".

---

[36] "Measurement Unit," in *International Vocabulary of Metrology – Basic and General Concepts and Associated Terms, VIM,* 8th ed., (Joint Committee for Guides in Metrology, 2008): 6–7. http://www.bipm.org/utils/common/documents/jcgm/JCGM_200_2008.pdf.

People and Organizations

Table 4-6: Party Characteristic Instances

Global Charac-teristic ID	Name	Description	Default Value	Data Type	*defined by* Party	*in terms of* Unit of Measure
345	Height	Vertical dimension	-	Number	Human Resources	Inches
678	Number of Employees	company population	0	Integer	Marketing Department	Count
942	Family income	Amount of money received by family each year	-	Number (Money)	Marketing Department	Dollars
10567	Eye color	Hue of a person's eyes	-	String	Medical department	-
11234	Company Income rank	Category of family income, relative to national averages	-	String	Standard and Poors	-
2413	NAICS code	North American Industry Classification System code	-	Integer	U.S. Census Bureau	-

Table 4-7: Party Characteristic Value Instances

<<ID>> for Party Charact-eristic	<<ID>> *to describe* Party	Characteristic Value	Effective Date	Until Date	*issued by* Party
Height	John Smith	68	January 16, 2008	August 24, 1010	John Smith
Number of Employees	IBM Corporate HQ	320	July 18, 2009		IBM Human Resources Dept
Family Income	Saunders Family	75,241	January 1, 2004	December 31, 2004	George Sanders
Eye color	Frank Sinatra	blue	December 12, 1915	May 14, 1998	http://sinatra.com♥
NAICS Code	Apple Computer, Inc.	334111 (Computer manufacturing)	1976		Apple Computer, Inc.
Company Income Rank	IBM	73	March 15, 2003	March 14, 2004	Forbes Magazine

---

♥ This raises a philosophical question. Were Frank Sinatra's blue eyes *issued* by Natalie. and Anthony Sinatra, or are we here only concerned with the source of the information? The answer depends upon the purpose of the model. In general, a system can only record where it got information, but it is incumbent upon the company to ensure that the source of data is as close to its creator as possible. It is to be hoped that someone at Sinatra.com actually looked at "old blue eyes" and recorded the result.

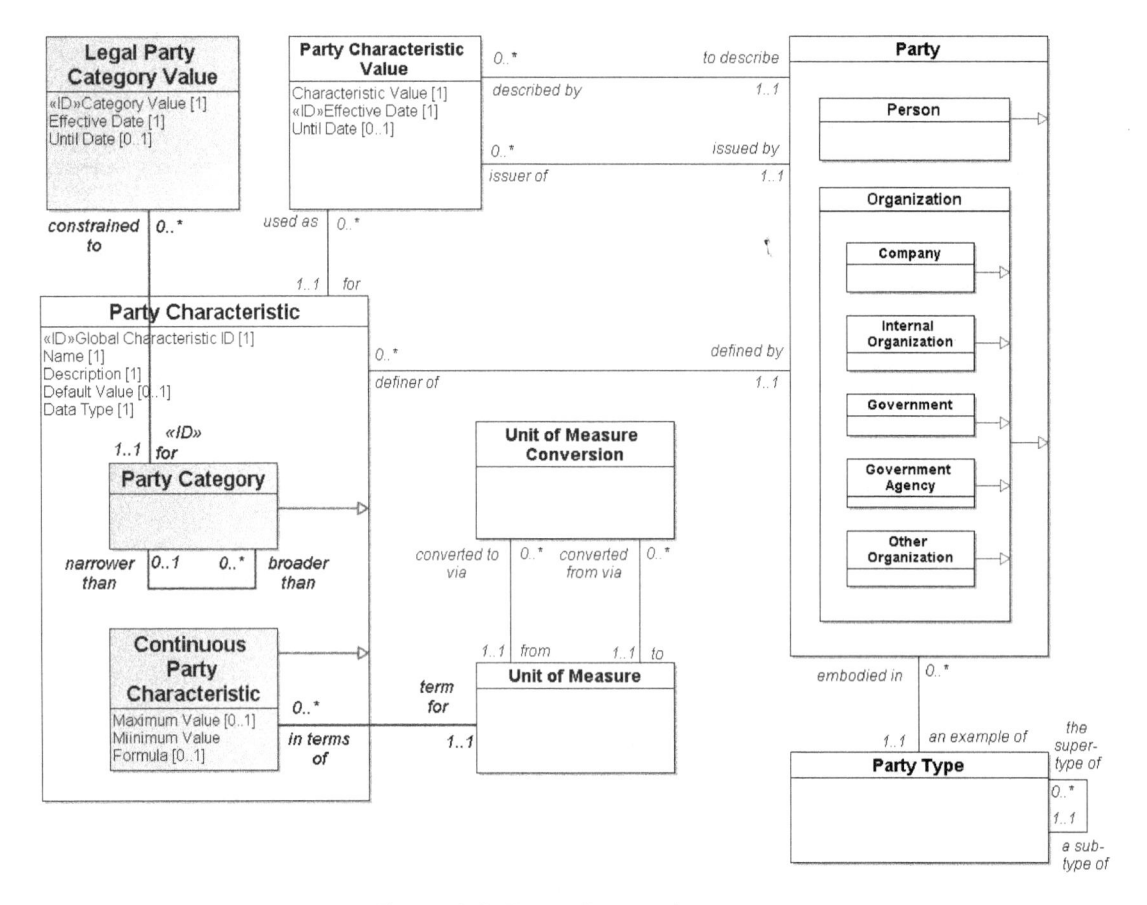

Figure 4-8: Party Categories

For example, "annual income" would be an example of a **Continuous Party Characteristic**. If appropriate, a **Maximum Value** or a **Minimum Value** could be specified for the **Continuous Party Characteristic** to constrain the **Characteristic Value** of all **Party Characteristic Values** *of* this **Party Characteristic**.

"Income level", on the other hand, would be an example of a **Party Category**, with, say, **Legal Party Category Values** of "Less than $25,000", "$25,000 to $50,000", "$50,000 to $100,000", and "Over $100,000".

Business Rules

- If a **Party Characteristic Value** is *of* a **Party Category**, the Characteristic Value of that **Party Characteristic Value** must equal the Category Value of a **Legal Party Category Value** (if any exist) that is *for* the **Party Category** involved. (*Translation:* a **Party Characteristic Value** for a **Party Category** must conform to the constraints on that **Party Category**.)

- If a **Party Characteristic Value** is *of* a **Continuous Party Characteristic**, and if values are given for Minimum Value and/or Maximum Value, the Characteristic Value of that **Party Characteristic Value** must be greater than the Minimum Value and/or less than the Maximum Value specified. (*Translation:* A **Party Characteristic Value** for a **Continuous Party Characteristic** must be within any minimum or maximum constraints defined for that **Characteristic**.)

Note that **Unit of Measure** is a *term for* **Continuous Party Characteristic** only. If a **Party Characteristic** is a **Party Category**, then **Unit of Measure** does not apply.

Derived Characteristics

While many **Party Characteristics** are evaluated with data from other sources and stored, some are derived from other **Party Characteristics** (or at least **Continuous Party Characteristics**). For example "age" is derived by subtracting the "birthdate" from the <system date> (today). While formulae can be very complex, the technique called ***Reverse Polish Notation*** is a way of representing them so that they can easily be evaluated.

Given a standard **Formula**, such as A=mx+y, this approach evaluates each variable in turn, from the inside out, until a value is obtained for the entire formula. In this example, you start by postulating m as a positive number. You then process x with the operator multiply. Then you process y with the operator plus. If the formula had been A=m*(x+y), you would have begun with x and y and then incorporated m.

The point is that any formula can be constructed by a succession of variables plus operators.

104 Enterprise Model Patterns

Figure 4-9 shows that a **Party Characteristic Derivation Element** must be *to derive* a **Continuous Party Characteristic**. This in turn may be *the use of* either another **Party Characteristic**, a **System Variable** (like today's date), or a constant.

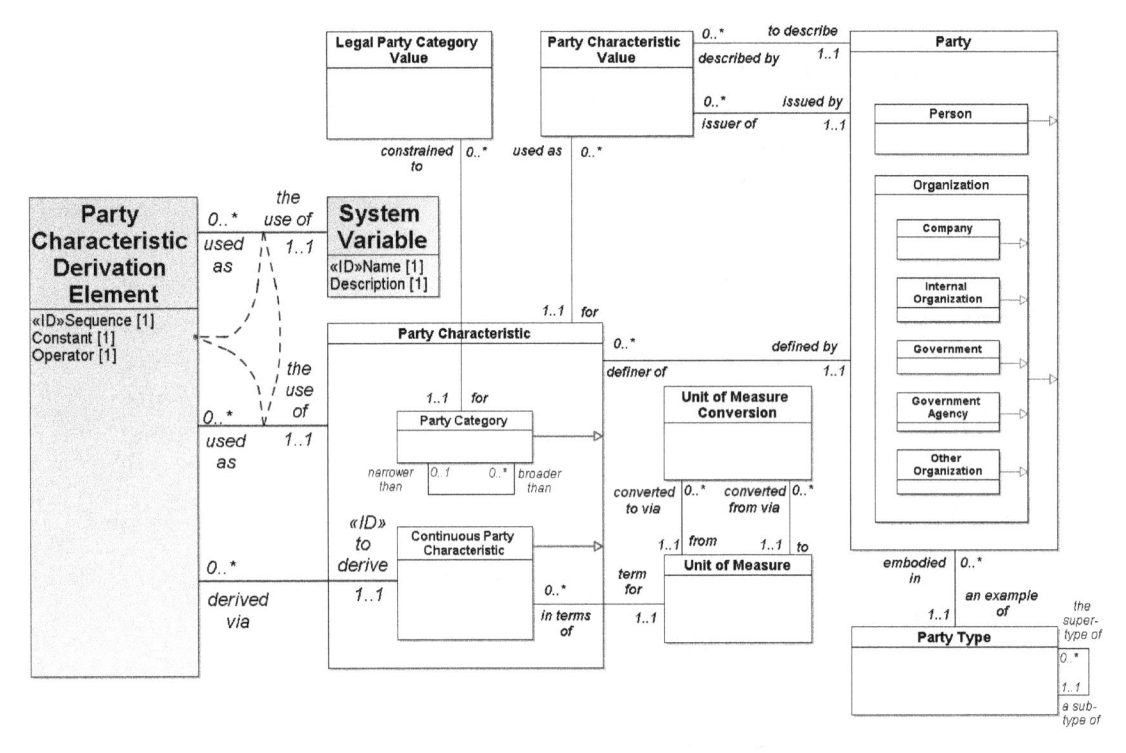

Figure 4-9: Party Characteristic Derivations

For example, to calculate…

```
Age = (system date - birth date) / 365
```

…requires three instances of **Party Characteristic Derivation Element**, as shown in Table 4-8.

Table 4-8: Party Characteristic Derivation Element

to derive **Party Characteristic**	*the use of* **Party Characteristic**	*the use of* **System Variable**	*(the use of)* **Constant**	Operator
Age		system date		Add
Age	birth date			Subtract
Age			365	Divide

Characteristics and Party Types

As with identifiers and names, different **Party Characteristics** are only appropriate for specific **Party Types**. "`Birth date`", for example, may be appropriate only for the **Party Type** "`person`". The **Characteristic** "`annual sales`" is only meaningful for a "`company`", and so forth.

Figure 4-10 shows the entity class **Party Characteristic Assignment**, which is the fact that a particular **Party Characteristic** is only appropriate for a particular **Party Type**.

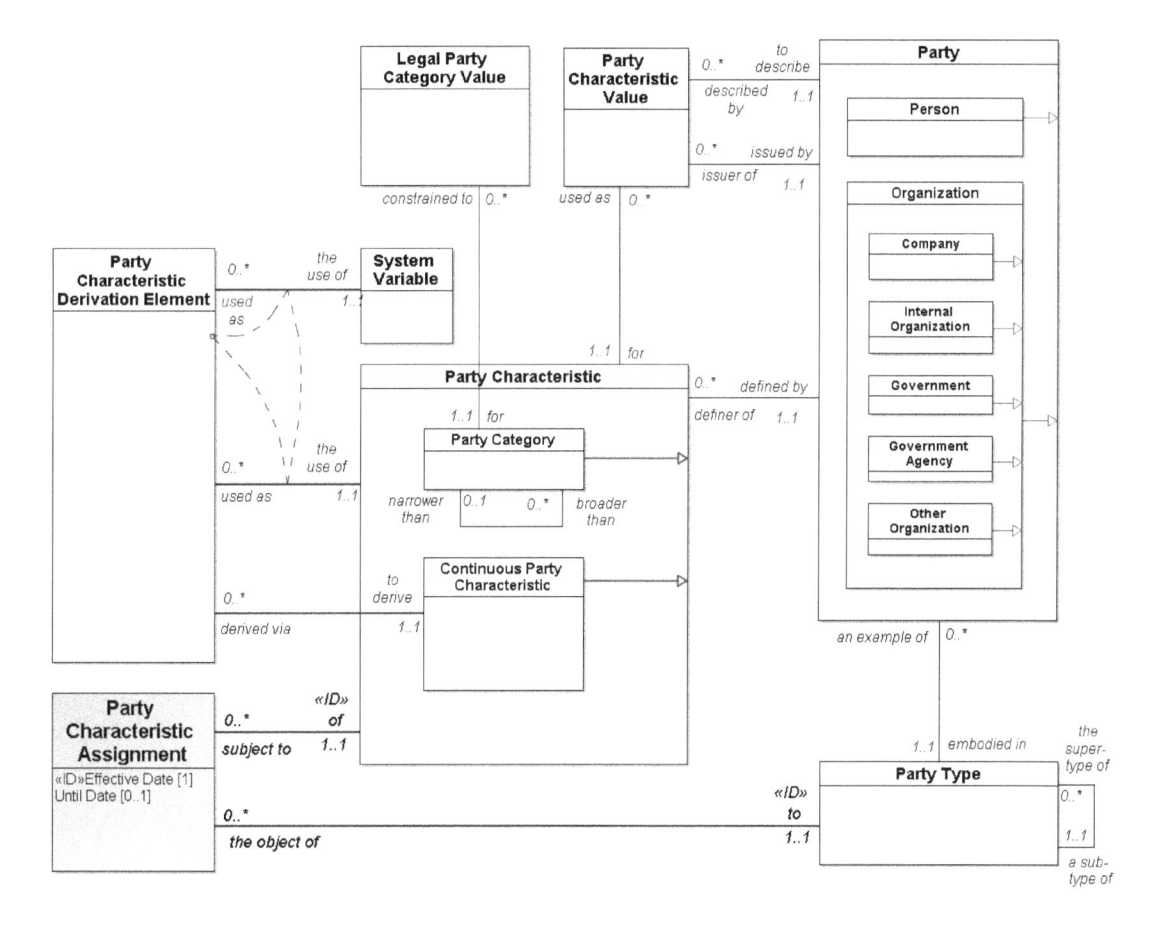

Figure 4-10: Party Characteristic Assignments

Business Rule

- A Party may only be *described by* a Party Characteristic if that Party Characteristic is *subject to* a Party Characteristic Assignment *to* the Party Type that the Party in question is *an example of*. (**Translation:** Party Characteristic Assignments assure that only certain Party Characteristics can describe Parties of a particular Party Type.)

Summary

This chapter concerned the people and organizations that constitute the heart of the enterprise. Without knowing anything about the nature of an organization, it is possible to postulate the existence of the entity classes presented here:

- **Person**, **Organization**, and **Party** – The population of both the organization and its environment.

- **Party Relationships** – The fact that **Parties** are associated with each other.

- **Party Identifiers** and **Party Names** – Along with constraints on how they are applied.

- **Party Characteristics** – All those attributes usually collected for **Person** and **Organization**, described as *data*, instead of *data structure*, so that they are the responsibility of *subject matter experts*, not *data modelers*.

Note that a structure was introduced here that will be repeated throughout the book: the entity class **Party Type** reproduces the sub-type structure of **Party**. So, just as each instance of **Party** must also be an instance of one of its sub-types, so, too, must each instance of **Party** be *an example of* exactly one **Party Type**.

CHAPTER 5

Geographic Locations (Where)

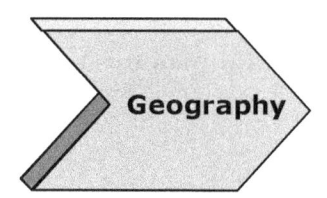

The second primary category in the Enterprise entity/relationship model concerns *geography*. Specifically, where on the Earth[*] are things located? The starting point for the model (as shown in Figure 5-1) is to define **Geographic Location** as an identified place on the earth.

Geographic Location

A **Geographic Location** can be either a:

- **Geographic Area** – a bounded area on the surface of the planet.
- **Geographic Point** – used to define the position of other **Geographic Locations**.
- **Geographic Solid** – such as a defined oil deposit. This also could refer to a mapped volume in space.[Δ]
- **Geographic Lines** – such as the route of a telephone line or a highway.

Note that the most significant sub-type of **Geographic Location** is **Geographic Area**. This encompasses:

- **Geopolitical Area** - A place whose boundaries are defined by law or treaty. These include

---

[*] OK, your author concedes that he is geo-centric. Most people are concerned with locations on the Earth, not on other planets. So that is how this chapter is written. But understand that the logic of the model can easily be extended to cover elsewhere, as well.

[Δ] See previous note…

107

- **Country** – a nation, such as the "United States of America" or "Indonesia".

- **Principal Country Division** – a part of a **country**, defined so that the entire country is divided into such divisions, and they do not overlap. This would include (for example) The commonwealth of "Virginia" (in the "United States"), The province of "Alberta" (in "Canada"), or the state of "Nuevo Leon" (in "Mexico").

- **City** – an incorporated municipality, such as "New York" (USA), "Glasgow" (UK), or "Prague" (Czech Republic).

- **Other Geopolitical Area** – any legal **Geopolitical Area** that is not one of the above—such as "county" in the United States, or "borough" in the United Kingdom.

* **Management Area** – a place whose boundaries are determined by the enterprise or affiliated enterprises. This would include such things as the Sales Department's "Southwestern Sales Region", the U.S. military's "PACCOM" (the Command Center covering the countries of the world surrounding the Pacific Ocean), or the United States Postal Service's **Postal Area "90210"**.

* **Natural Area** – a place whose boundaries are natural phenomena. This could describe something as specific as the boundary of a lake or a continent, or as vague as a wildlife habitat.

* **Other Surveyed Area** – a place (other than a **Geopolitical Area**, **Management Area**, or **Natural Area**) whose boundaries are measured or surveyed. This includes all the lots where houses and buildings are located. In the United States, this is the site of a street (mailing) address. (See Chapter 12 for more about addresses.)

Again, as with **Party Type**, **Geographic Location Type** reproduces the sub-type structure of **Geographic Location**. By definition, the first instances of **Geographic Location Type** must be "Geographic Area", "Geographic Point", "Geographic Solid", and so forth.

The generalization structure of **Geographic Location** is also represented in the relationship showing that each **Geographic Location Type** may be *a super-type of* one or more other **Geographic Location Types**. So **Geopolitical Area** is *a super-type of* **Country**, **City**, and so forth. **Geopolitical Area** may, of course, be *a sub-type of* one and only one **Geographic Area**.

Geographic Locations

Geographic Location
«ID»Global Geographic Identifier [1]
Default Name [1]
Description [1]
Elevation [0..1]

- **Geographic Area**
  - **Management Area**
    - **Postal Area**
      Postal Code [1]
    - **Other Management Area**
  - **Natural Area**
  - **Other Surveyed Area**
    «ID»Street Address [0..1]
    /Country Name [1]
    Principle Country Division Name [1]
  - **Geopolitical Area**
    «ID»Abbreviation [1]
    Formal Name [1]
    Common Name [0..1]
    - **Principal Country Division**
      /Country Name [1]
    - **Country**
      Country Telephone Code [0..1]
    - **City**
      /Principal Country Division Name [1]
      /Country Name [1]
    - **Other Geopolitical Area**
- **Geographic Line**
- **Geographic Solid**
- **Geographic Point**
  Longitude [0..1]
  «ID»Global Geographic Point Identifier
  Lattitude [0..1]
  Elevation [0..1]

embodied in 0..*
1..1 an example of   the super-type of
Geographic Location Type
«ID»Name [1]
Description [1]
0..*
0..1 a sub-type of

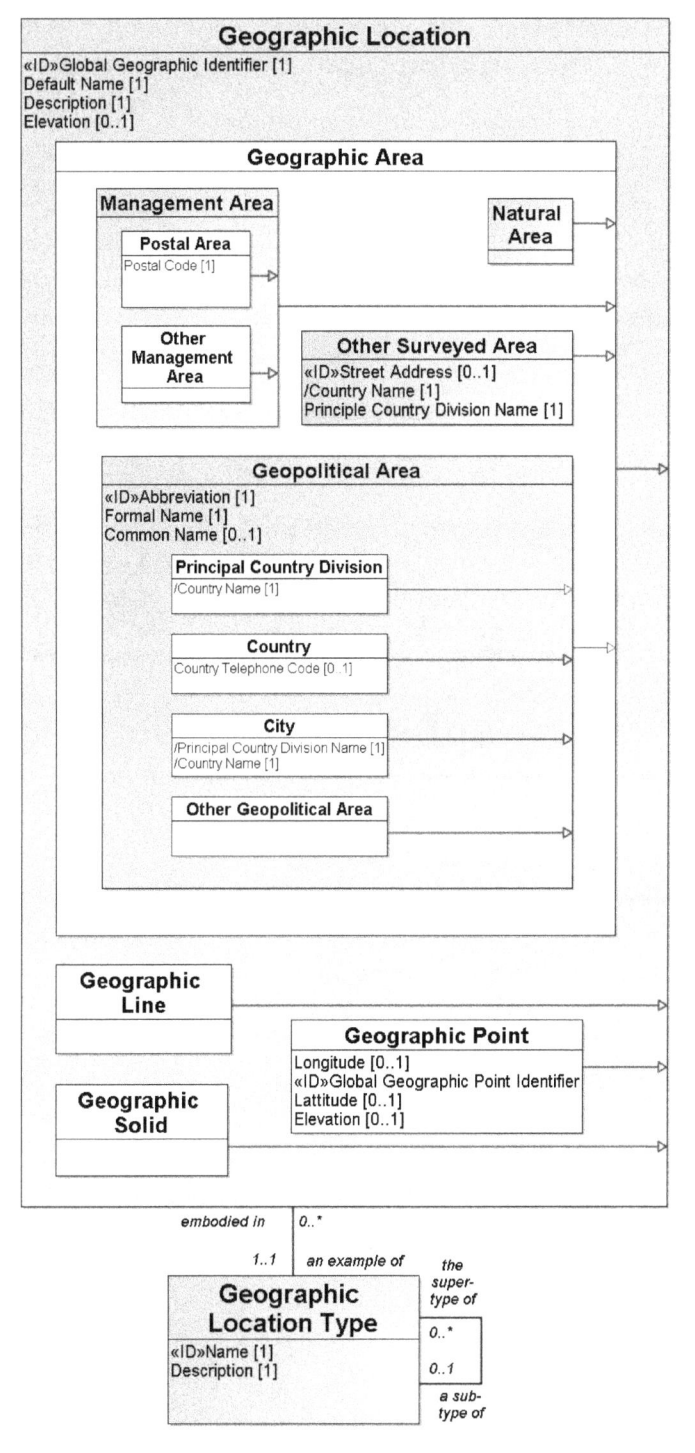

Figure 5-1: Geographic Locations

Geographic Location Types that are not equivalent to sub-types of **Geographic Location** are also permitted, as long as each is *a sub-type of* one other **Geographic Location Type**.

Here you can see the advantage of the **Geographic Location Type**. While the instances that correspond to sub-types of **Geographic Location** are required, you can, for example, add sub-types of **Other Geopolitical Area** as instances of **Geographic Location Type**, without having to expand the model. For example, in the United States, "County" could be entered as *a sub-type of* **Other Geopolitical Area**.

Business Rule

- Instances of **Geographic Location Type** must at least include one for each sub-type of **Geographic Location** shown— "Geographic Area", "Geopolitical Area", et cetera. Other, more detailed instances are also permitted.

Geographic Location Relationships

Geographic Locations are clearly related to each other. At the very least, the boundaries of every **Geographic Area** are defined by the "Latitude", "Longitude" and elevation of a set of **Geographic Points**. In addition, **Countries** are composed of one or more **Principal Country Divisions**. And so forth.

Geographic Location Relationship is shown in Figure 5-2. Note that there are three principle sub-types:

- **Geographic Structure** places "Colorado" in The United States, and "Edinburgh" in Scotland.
- **Geographic Definition** associates a **Geographic Point**—with its "Latitude", "Longitude", and, where necessary, "Elevation"—with a **Geographic Area** or a **Geographic Solid** to define the latter's boundaries.
- **Geographic Overlap** describes the situation where one **Geographic Area** overlaps another, as where a **Postal Area** applies to more than one **City**. Similarly, the "Navaho Indian Reservation" overlaps the states of "Utah", "Arizona", and "New Mexico".

- **Other Geographic Relationship** describes any association between two **Geographic Locations** that is not **Geographic Structure**, **Geographic Definition**, or **Geographic Overlap**.

The first four instances of **Geographic Area Relationship Type** are of course `"Geographic Structure"`, `"Geographic Definition"`, `"Geographic Overlap"`, and `"Other Geographic Relationship"`, but others can be added, in particular as *sub-types of* Other Geographic Relationship.

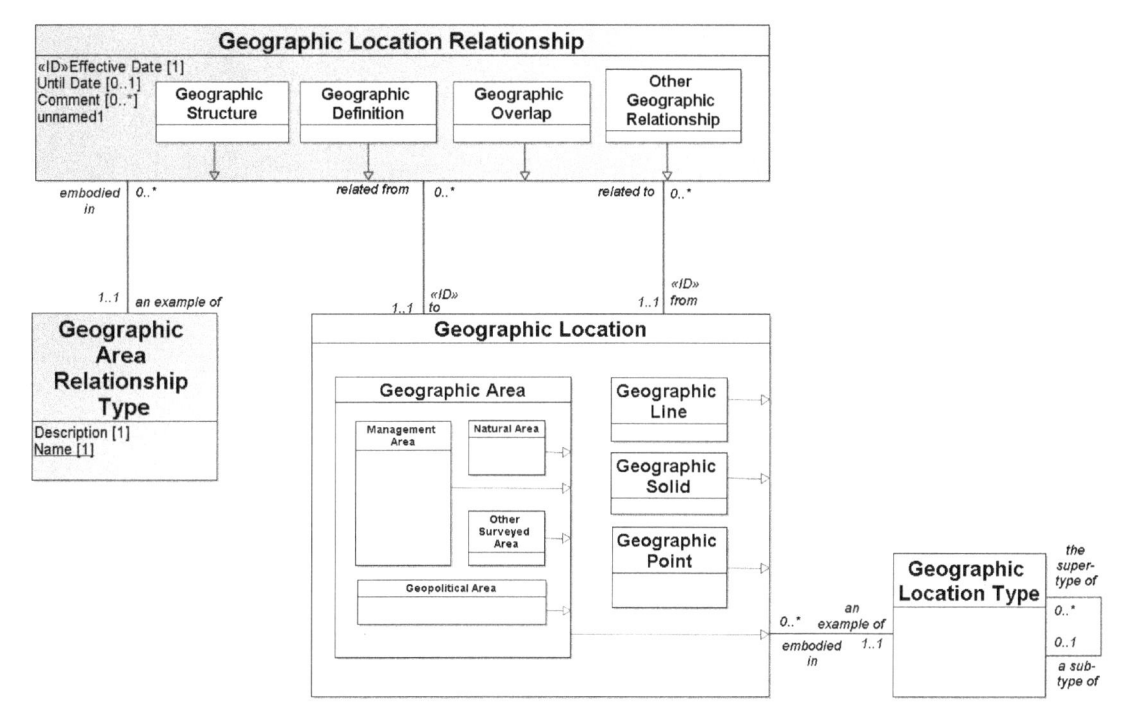

Figure 5-2: Geographic Location Relationships

Figure 5-3 shows how **Geographic Points** can be used for the **Geographic Definition** of one or more **Geopolitical Areas**. Note that there will be an instance of **Geographic Definition** for each use of one **Geographic Point** to define one **Geopolitical Area**. In this example, the U.S. **State**, `"Colorado"` [♣], is defined by four **Geographic Points** (latitude/ longitude): `"41.00/-109.05"`, `"41.00/-102.05"`, `"37.00/-109.05"`, and `"37.00/-102.05"`. The southwestern corner of `"Colorado"`, `"37.00/-109.05"`, participates in four

---

[♣] The quotation marks around state names may seem excessive, but that follows from the fact that these are *instances* of **Principal Country Division**

Enterprise Model Patterns

Geographic Definitions: one each for "Colorado", "New Mexico", "Arizona", and "Utah".◆

In the northwest corner, **Geographic Point** "41.00/-109.05", participates in only two **Geographic Definitions**, one each for "Colorado" and "Utah", but not for "Wyoming". That one is further east, at longitude "-104.05", but it does not define a boundary of "Colorado". Similarly, other **Geographic Points** along the "Colorado" border, don't participate in the definition of that border: "40.00/-102-05", defining "Nebraska" and "Kansas", and "37.00/-103.00", defining "Oklahoma" and "New Mexico".

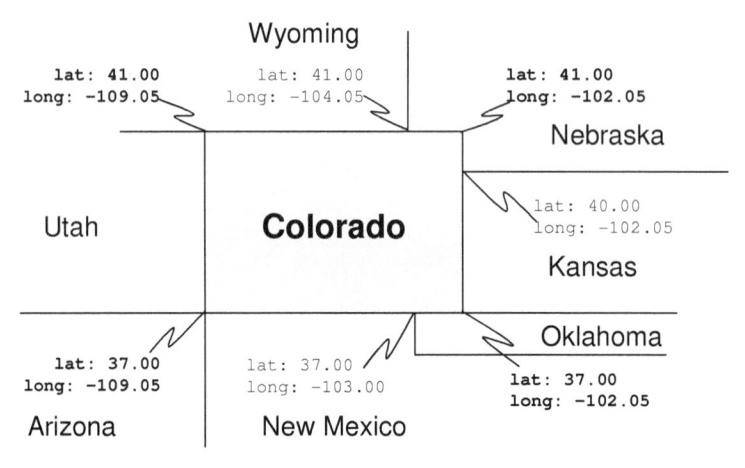

Figure 5-3: Geopolitical Areas and Geographic Points

Geographic Names

As with **Parties**, the variety of **Geographic Location Names** calls for a separate entity class, as shown in Figure 5-4. As an analogy to what was previously seen for **Party**, **Geographic Location** may be *labeled with* one or more **Geographic Location Names**. Each **Geographic Location Name** must be *an example of* one and only one **Geographic Location Name Type**.

◆ This is the only point in the United States where that is true, by the way.

Note that each **Geographic Name** may be specified by a **Party**. For a **Management Area**, the name might be assigned by the company itself (as in a company's designating `"South Central Sales area"` as the name of sales region), or the U.S. Department of Defense designating the countries that surround the Pacific `"USPACCON"`.

In the case of **Surveyed areas** and **Management Areas**—as well as **Geographic Lines** and **Geographic Solids**, the naming of these **Geographic Locations** is at the discretion of each organization sponsoring a model.

In the case of most **Geopolitical Areas**, however, the naming of places is rooted in tradition, and, over the years, coming up with standard names that all can agree to has been trying. For this reason a number of both government and non-government standards organizations have tried to bring some order into this. From these efforts have come a number of **Geographic Name Location Standards**. Most notable for countries is ISO 3116-1, that provides English names along with country codes. (See "Geographic Location Identifiers", below.) The United Nations has standard names in each of the official languages for each country, and so forth. Within the United States, the United States Board on Geographic Names has compiled official names for "physical features" (**Natural Areas**) in the United States.[*] The United States Census Bureau compiles the names of U.S. States, counties, and cities.

What all this points to is the fact that there is a sub-type of **Geographic Name Type** which in Figure 5-4 is shown as **Geographic Location Name Standard**. This is constrained by a set of **Geographic Location Standard Names**. For example, county names in each official language is maintained by the United Nations. That is, "Official United Nations List" (or some such) could be an instance of **Geographic Location Name Standard**, that would be *constrained by* one or more instances of **Geographic Location Standard Name**, such as `"United Kingdom"`, `"les États-Unis d'Amérique"`, `"La République de l'Allemagne"`, `"Kingdom of Saudi Arabia"`, and so forth.

Each **Geographic Area Type**, then, and particularly each **Geographic Name Standard** must be *defined by* one **Organization**. This might be the organization itself, or it could be an outside agency, such as the International Standards Organization, the United Nations, or some other body.

---

[*]   …and Antarctica, of all places.

114 Enterprise Model Patterns

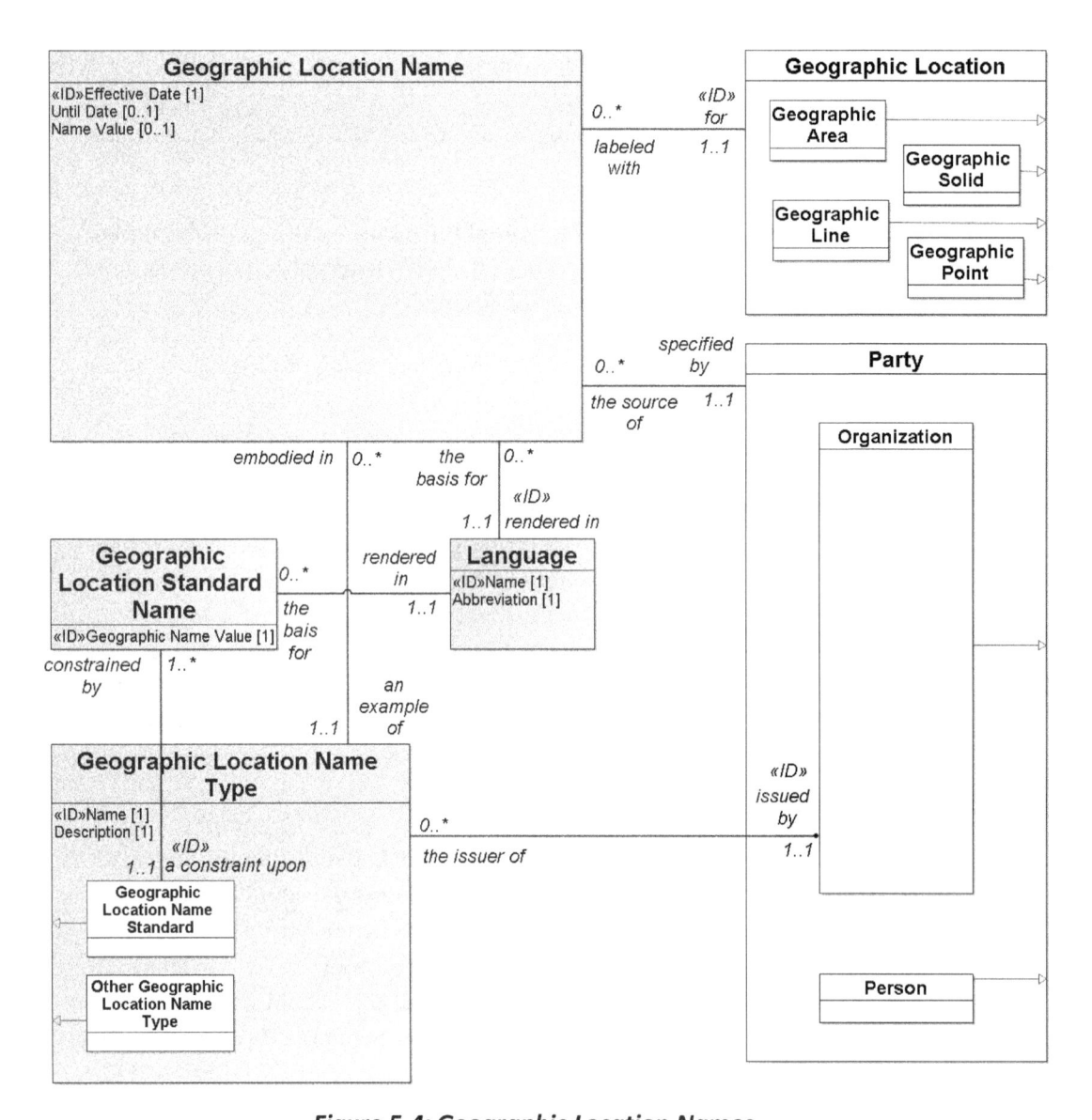

Figure 5-4: Geographic Location Names

Business Rule

- If an instance of a **Geographic Location Name** is *an example of* a **Geographic Location Name Standard**, then the value of the attribute Name Value must be equivalent to the value of Geographic Name Value in one of the **Geographic Standard Names** that is *a constraint upon* that instance of **Geographic Name Standard**. (*Translation*: If a Geographic Location Name is of a kind that has a master list, it must be on that list.)

Note that both each **Geographic Location Name** and each **Geographic Location Standard Name** must be *rendered in* a particular **Language**. Many countries and cities have different names in different languages. For example, the city known to Poles as `"Warszawa"` is known in English as `"Warsaw"`, in French as `"Varsovie"`, and in German as `"Warshau"`. In the examples described two paragraphs ago, `"The United States of America"` and `"The Republic of Germany"` were rendered in French.

Geographic Location Names can change over time. Hence the entity class has the attributes **Effective Date** and **Until Date**. What was once known as `"The Union of South Africa"` had that name from `"May 31, 1910"`, until `"May 31, 1961"`, when it became `"The Republic of South Africa"`. That name was effective `"May 31, 1961"` until the present day. Each instance of **Geographic Location Name**, then, must be unique for every combination of the **Geographic Location** it is *for*, the **Geographic Name Type** it is *an example of*, the **Language** it is *rendered in*, and its value for the attribute **Language**.

Geographic Identifiers

As with **Parties**, there are numerous schemes for identifying **Geographic Locations**. To be sure, a **Geographic Point** can really only be identified by a combination of its attributes, **Latitude**, **Longitude**, and **Elevation**, although these can be described in multiple terms (Is latitude and longitude expressed in "minutes and seconds" or "decimal"? Is elevation in "feet" or "meters"?). To identify countries, ISO 3166 provides both two- and three-letter abbreviations. Alternatively, the International Telecommunications Union uses 2 and 3-digit identifiers for telephone number country codes. States can be identified by name, but there are at least three sets of identifying abbreviations and codes. Typically enterprise sales regions are identified by internal abbreviations. And so forth.

Thus, as with **Party**, while there is in principle a global identifier for **Geographic Location** (whose implementation is not an industry standard yet, but which we can postulate as a kind of place holder), there are enough different potential identifiers for **Geographic Locations** to warrant creating the entity class **Geographic Location Identifier Value**, as shown in Figure 5-5.

That is, each **Geographic Location** may be *identified via* one or more **Geographic Location Identifier Values**, each of which must be *for* exactly one **Geographic Location Identifier Type**.

116 Enterprise Model Patterns

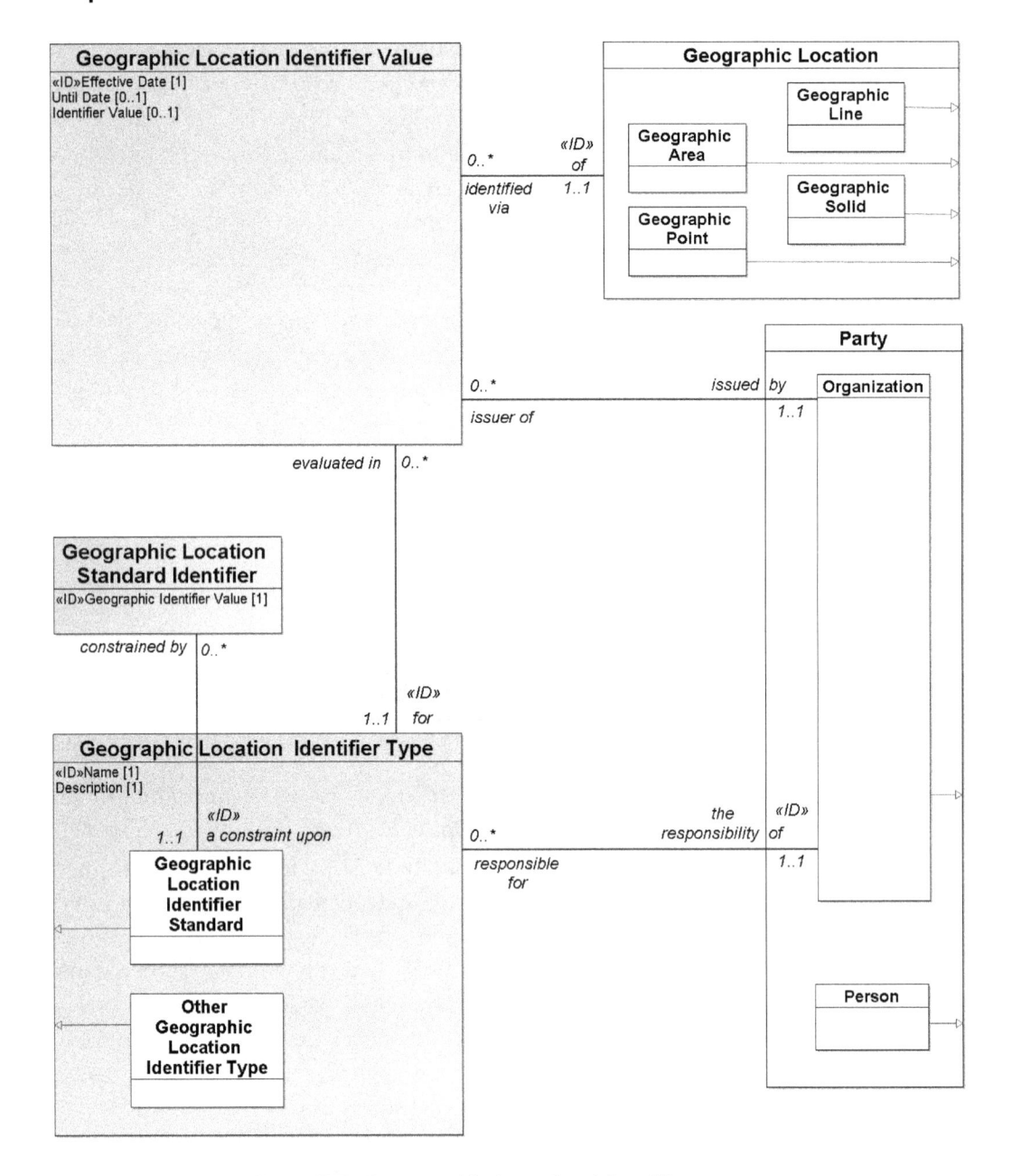

Figure 5-5: Geographic Location Identifiers

A **Geographic Location Identifier Value**, then, is the fact that a particular instance of **Geographic Location** is identified via a particular **Geographic Location Identifier Type**.

A **Geographic Location Identifier Type** is the name of a kind of identifier. It may be a **Geographic Location Identifier Standard**, which a scheme of identifiers defined by an external organization, such as the set of country codes defined by the International Standards Organization (ISO) or the one from The International Olympic Coordinating Committee).

A **Geographic Identifier Standard** is the name of an identifier (such as a code or abbreviation) *issued by* an **Organization** that is from a standards board or agency. **Geographic Name Standard** comes into play because many (such as ISO standard 3166-1[37]) describe both names and identifying codes for each **Country**. (...*issued by* an **Organization** that is a standards board or agency, such as International Standards Organization (ISO) (Standard 3166-1 for country codes), or the United States Board on Geographic Names.)

Alternatively, the **Geographic Location Identifier Type** may be an **Other Geographic Location Identifier Type**—any other classification of identifiers specified by the organization being modeled. This could be `"Oil Field Identifiers"`, `"Survey numbers"`, or any other organization that invented a system of identifying a specific kind of **Geographic Location**.

Each instance of **Geographic Location Identifier Value** is uniquely identified by the **Geographic Location** being identified, the **Geographic Location Corporate Identifier Type** or the **Geographic Name Standard** involved, and the attribute **Effective Date**. This means that while a business rule may constrain the `"United Kingdom"` to have only one `"Telephone Country Code"` at a time (it happens to be `"44"`), in general, any **Geographic Location** may be identified by multiple values of **Geographic Location Identifier Value**, that is *an example of* one **Geographic Location Identifier Type**, over time.

Business Rule

- If an instance of a Geographic Location Identifier is an example of a **Geographic Location Identifier Standard**, then the value of the attribute Name Value must be equivalent to the value of Geographic Name Value in one of the **Geographic Standard Names** that is a constraint upon that instance of **Geographic Name Standard**. (*Translation*: If a **Geographic Location Identifier** is of a kind that has a master list, it must be on that list.)

---

[37] International Standards Organization. 2006. "Codes for the representation of names of countries and their subdivisions -- Part 1: Country codes.", *ISO 3166-1*.
http://www.commondatahub.com/live/geography/country/iso_3166_country_codes?gclid=CNOHjr7mi6MCFdVb2godeUMXew.

118 Enterprise Model Patterns

As with **Parties**, both names and identifiers of **Geographic Locations** apply differently to different **Geographic Location Types**. Each **Geographic Location Type** usually can have its **Geographic Locations** identified by **Geographic Location Identifier Values** that are *examples of* a particular **Geographic Location Identifier Type**. For example a **Geographic Location** that is a "U.S. State" may be *identified via* either a **Geographic Location Identifier Value** that is *an example of* either the **Geographic Location Identifier Type**, "Standard Abbreviation", or "Old Abbreviation". A **Geographic Location** that is a "Country" may be *identified via* either a **Geographic Location Identifier Value** that is *an example of* either the **Geographic Location Identifier Type**, "ISO 3166-1 Code", or "IOC Abbreviation".

Table 5-1 shows some sample instances of **Geographic Identifier Constraints**, which is depicted in Figure 5-6.

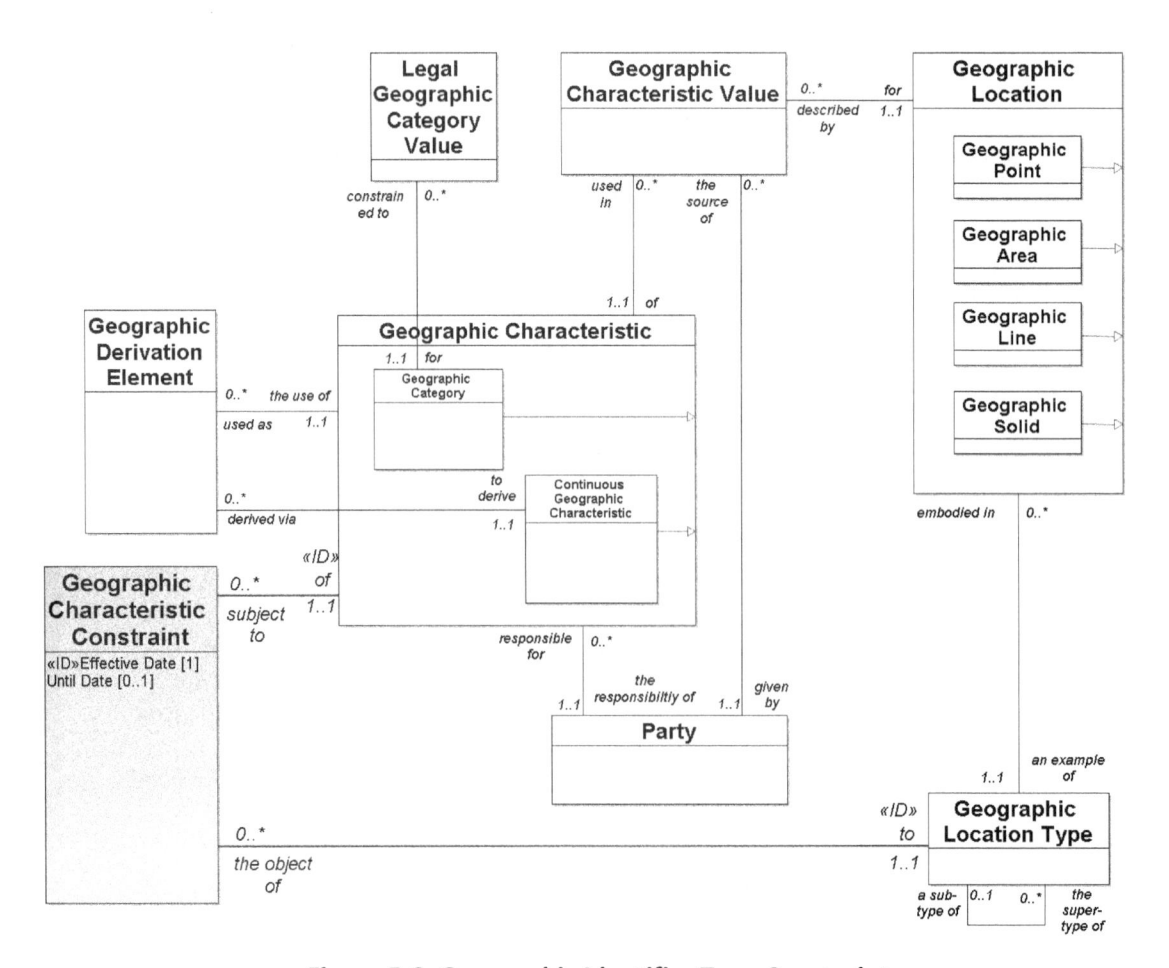

Figure 5-6: Geographic Identifier Type Constraints

Geographic Locations

Table 5-1: Geographic Identifier Constraints

Geographic Location Type	Geographic Location Identifier Type	*the responsibility of*
U.S. State (Sub-type of Principle Country Division)	U.S. State official abbreviations	U.S. Postal Service
Canadian Province	Canadian Provincial abbreviations	Post Canada
Country	ISO 3166-1	International Standards Association
Telephone Country Code	ICC Standard	International Telecommunications Union
U.S. County (by state)	County registry	State constitutions
Oil fields (by company)	Well Number	The oil company

Business Rule

- A **Geographic Location** may not be *identified via* a Geographic Location Identifier Value unless the **Geographic Location Identifier Type** the value is *an example of* is *a term for* a **Geographic Identifier Constraint** on the **Geographic Location Type** *embodied in* the **Geographic Location** in question. (***Translation:*** Only certain **Geographic Identifier Types** can be given values for **Geographic Locations** that are *examples of* each **Geographic Location Type**.)

Geographic Location Characteristics

The advent of Geographic Information Systems has exploded the amount of data people want to collect about **Geographic Locations**. Whether it is ***demographic data***, such as population or average income, or ***physical data***, such as average annual rainfall, the amount and variety of data to be collected go way beyond anything that could be captured in simple attributes.

To accommodate this, Figure 5-7 shows the entity class **Geographic Characteristic**, which is a distinguishing trait, quality, or property that can be given a value for a **Geographic Location**. A **Geographic Characteristic Value**, then, is the value *of* a **Geographic Characteristic** *for* a particular **Geographic Location**. The Characteristic Value of the **Geographic Characteristic Value**, then, is *in terms of* the **Unit of Measure** that is the *term for* the **Geographic Location Characteristic** that it is the **Geographic Characteristic Value** *of*.

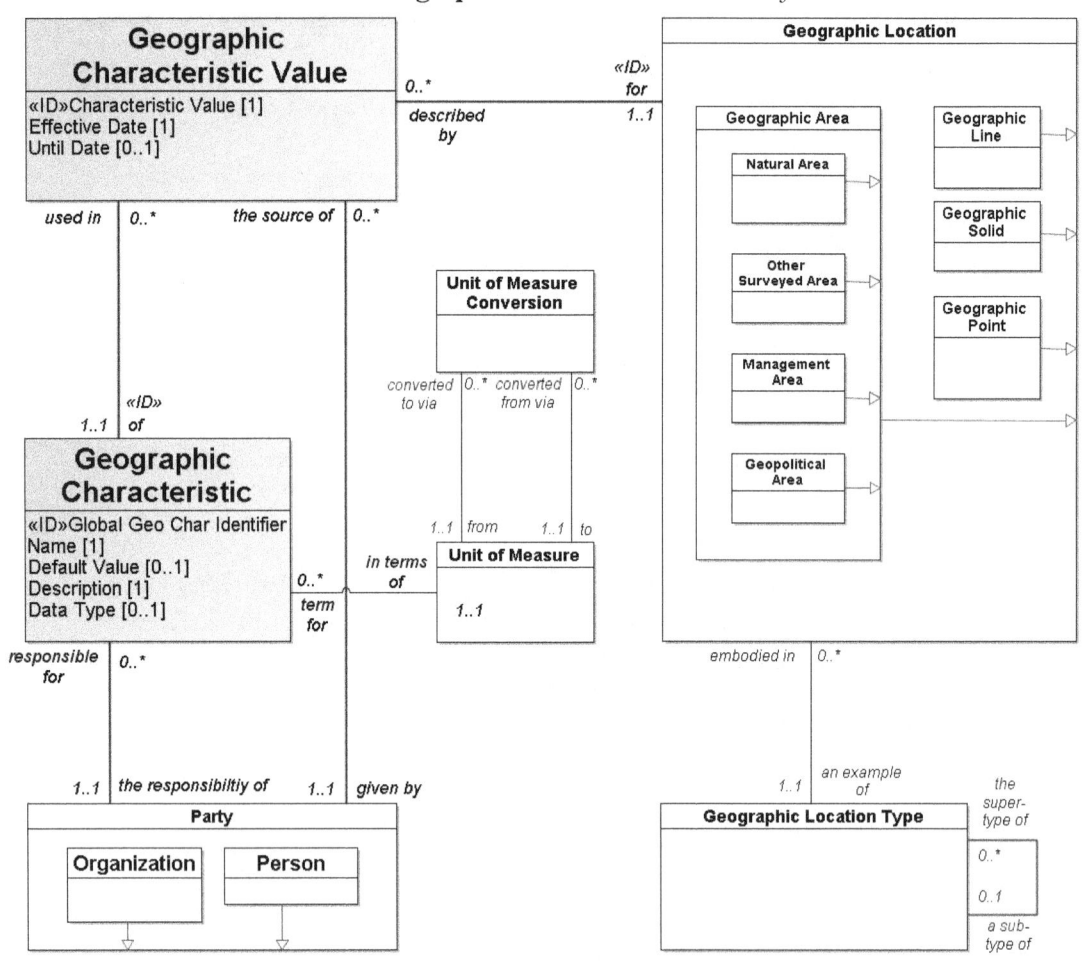

Figure 5-7: Geographic Characteristics

Note that, as with **Party Characteristics**, described previously, this way of describing properties has several advantages over using attributes for this purpose:

- A **Geographic Location** can have multiple values for the same **Geographic Characteristic** over time. Each **Geographic Characteristic Value** is identified as to its **Effective Date** and **Until Date**.
- A **Geographic Location** can have different values for the same **Geographic Characteristic** as *given by* different **Parties**. So the marketing department may classify the location one way, but the sales department (or accounting) may describe the location in completely different terms.

- It is easy to keep track of who set the values.
- Different departments can be *responsible for* completely different sets of characteristics for describing the same set of **Geographic Locations**.

Figure 5-8 shows that there are, in fact, two kinds of **Geographic Location Characteristics:**

- **Continuous Geographic Characteristic** is a property that is expressed as a real number or a time period. The **Characteristic Value** of a **Geographic Characteristic Value** that is *of* an instance of **Continuous Geographic Characteristic** may be constrained to fall between values of its attributes **Minimum Value** and **Maximum Value**. Examples of **Continuous Geographic Characteristic** may include "population", "average income", and so forth.
- **Geographic Category** is a property that can only have one of a set of discrete values. Indeed, the model shows that each **Geographic Category** may be *constrained to* one or more **Legal Geographic Category Values**. Examples of this include "climate", "state bird", and so forth.

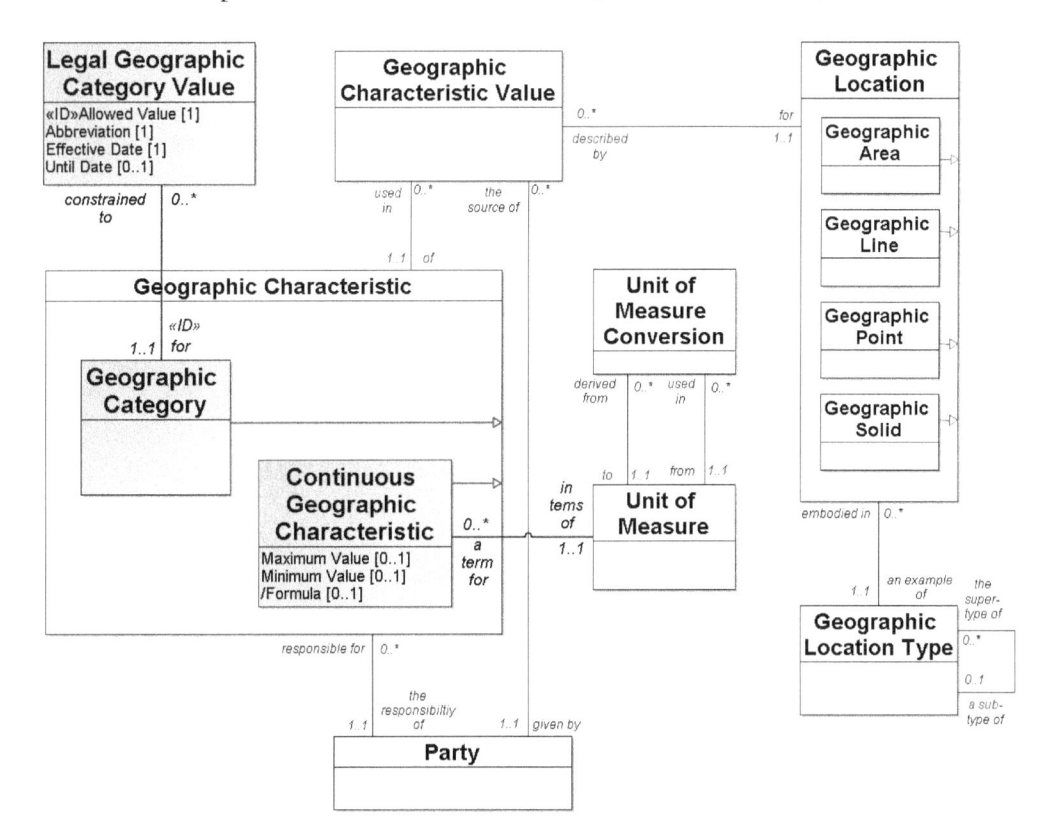

Figure 5-8: Geographic Categories

Business Rules

- If a Geographic Characteristic Value is *of* a Geographic Category, the Characteristic Value of that Geographic Characteristic Value must equal the Category Value of a Legal Geographic Category Value (if any exist) that is *for* the Geographic Category involved. *(Translation:* a Geographic Characteristic Value for a Geographic Category must be one of the values available for that Geographic Category.)

- If a **Geographic Characteristic Value** is *of* a **Continuous Geographic Characteristic**, and if values are given for Minimum Value and/or Maximum Value, the Characteristic Value of that **Geographic Characteristic Value** must be greater than the Minimum Value and/or less than the Maximum Value specified. *(Translation:* A **Geographic Characteristic Value** for a **Continuous Geographic Characteristic** must be within any minimum and maximum constraints defined for that **Characteristic**.)

Note that the Unit of Measure is only the *term for* **Continuous Geographic Characteristic**, not **Geographic Category**.

Derived Characteristics

While many **Geographic Characteristics** are evaluated with data from other sources and stored, some are derived from other **Geographic Characteristics**. For example, building height may be calculated from the tangent of the site angle times the distance from the observer to the building. While formulae can be very complex, the technique called ***Reverse Polish Notation***, described previously for derived **Party Characteristics**, is a way of representing them so that they can easily be evaluated.

Again, given a standard **Formula**, such as $A=mx+y$, this approach evaluates each variable in turn, from the outside in, until a value is obtained for the entire formula. In this example, you start by postulating m as a positive number. You then process x with the operator `multiply`. You then process y with the operator `plus`. If the formula had been $A=m*(x+y)$, you would have begun with x and y and then incorporated m.

Geographic Locations

The point is that any formula can be constructed by a succession of variables plus operators.

Figure 5-9 shows that a **Geographic Derivation Element** must be *to derive* a **Continuous Geographic Characteristic**. It, in turn, may be *the use of* either another **Geographic Characteristic**, a **System Variable** (like today's date), or a constant.

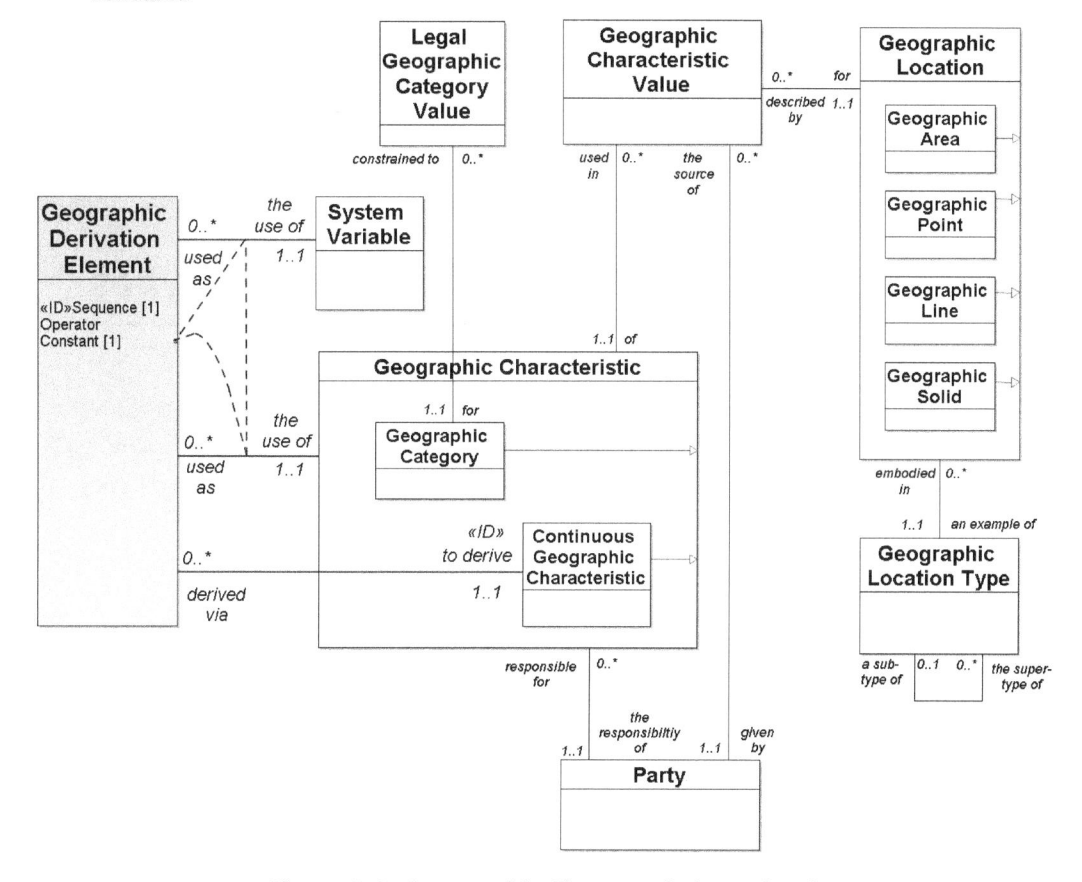

Figure 5-9: Geographic Characteristic Derivations

For example, to calculate building height with the formula:

```
Building height = Tangent(sight angle) * horizontal distance.
```

Two **Geographic Derivation Elements** are required, as shown in Table 5-2.

For a more ambitious example, the distance between two points on the earth can be computed from their latitude and longitude, based on a collection of formulae developed by Thadeus Vincenty.[38]

Table 5-2: Calculating Building Height

to derive **Geographic Location Characteristic**	the use of **Geographic Location Characteristic**	the use of **System Variable**	the use of **Constant**	Operator
Building Height	Sight Angle			Tangent
Building Height	Horizontal Distance			Multiply

Characteristics and Geographic Location Types

As with identifiers and names, different **Geographic Location Characteristics** are only appropriate for specific **Geographic Location Types**. `"Population"`, for example, is typically only appropriate for the **Geographic Location Type** `"geopolitical area"`. `"Predominant species"` is only meaningful for a `"natural area"`, and so forth.

Figure 5-10 shows the entity class **Geographic Location Characteristic Assignment** that is the fact that a particular **Geographic Location Characteristic** is only appropriate for a particular **Geographic Location Type**.

Business Rule

- A Geographic Location may only be *described by* a Geographic Characteristic if that Geographic Characteristic is *subject to* a Geographic Characteristic Assignment *to* the Geographic Location Type that the Geographic Location in question is *an example of*. (**Translation:** The entity class Geographic Characteristic Assignment assures that each Geographic Characteristic Value is of a Geographic Characteristic that is appropriate for the Geographic Location Type.)

---

[38] Thadeus Vincenty, "Direct and Inverse Solutions of Geodesics on the Ellipsoid with Application of Nested Equations", *Survey Review*, Directorate of Overseas Surveys of the Ministry of Overseas Development. April (1975). http://www.movable-type.co.uk/scripts/latlong-vincenty.html (accessed May 17, 2010).

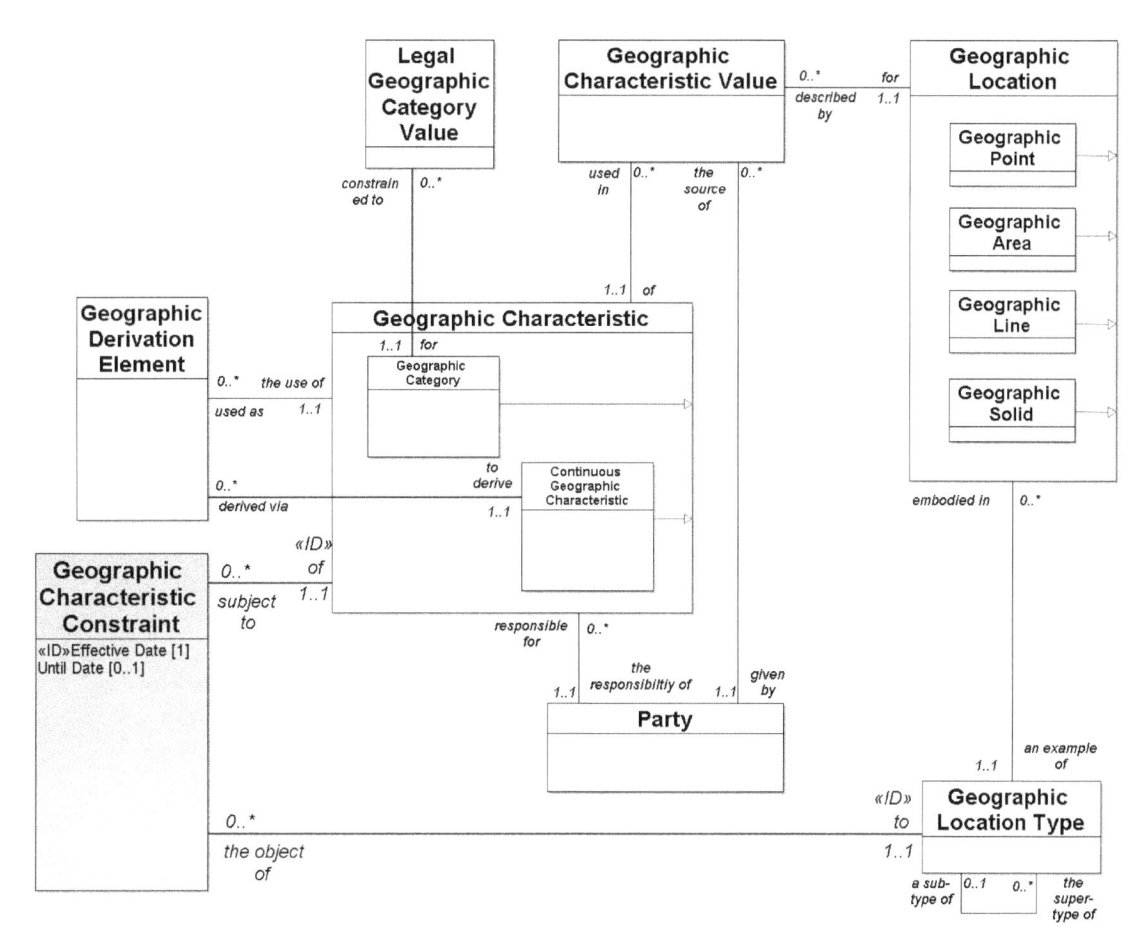

Figure 5-10: More Geographic Constraints

Geographic Roles

In thinking about **Geopolitical Areas**, it is important to recognize that thus far, the model has only described the physical aspects of geography. The land area of "California" is, in this model, a **Geopolitical Area**. The "Government of California", on the other hand, is an **Organization**—specifically, a **Government**. To be sure, the "Government of California" plays an important **Geographic Role** in the **Principle Country Division** (State) that is the land area of California. In particular, it is the *holder of* a **Jurisdiction** over it as a **Geopolitical Area**.

As Figure 5-11 shows, any **Party** may be *player of* one or more **Geographic Roles** *for* a **Geographic Location**. The nature of that role is determined by its

126 Enterprise Model Patterns

Geographic Role Type, the definition of a category of such roles. By definition, the first **Geographic Role Type** must be "`jurisdiction`", as we have seen, but certainly others are possible: "`inspector`", "`marketing manager`", and so forth.

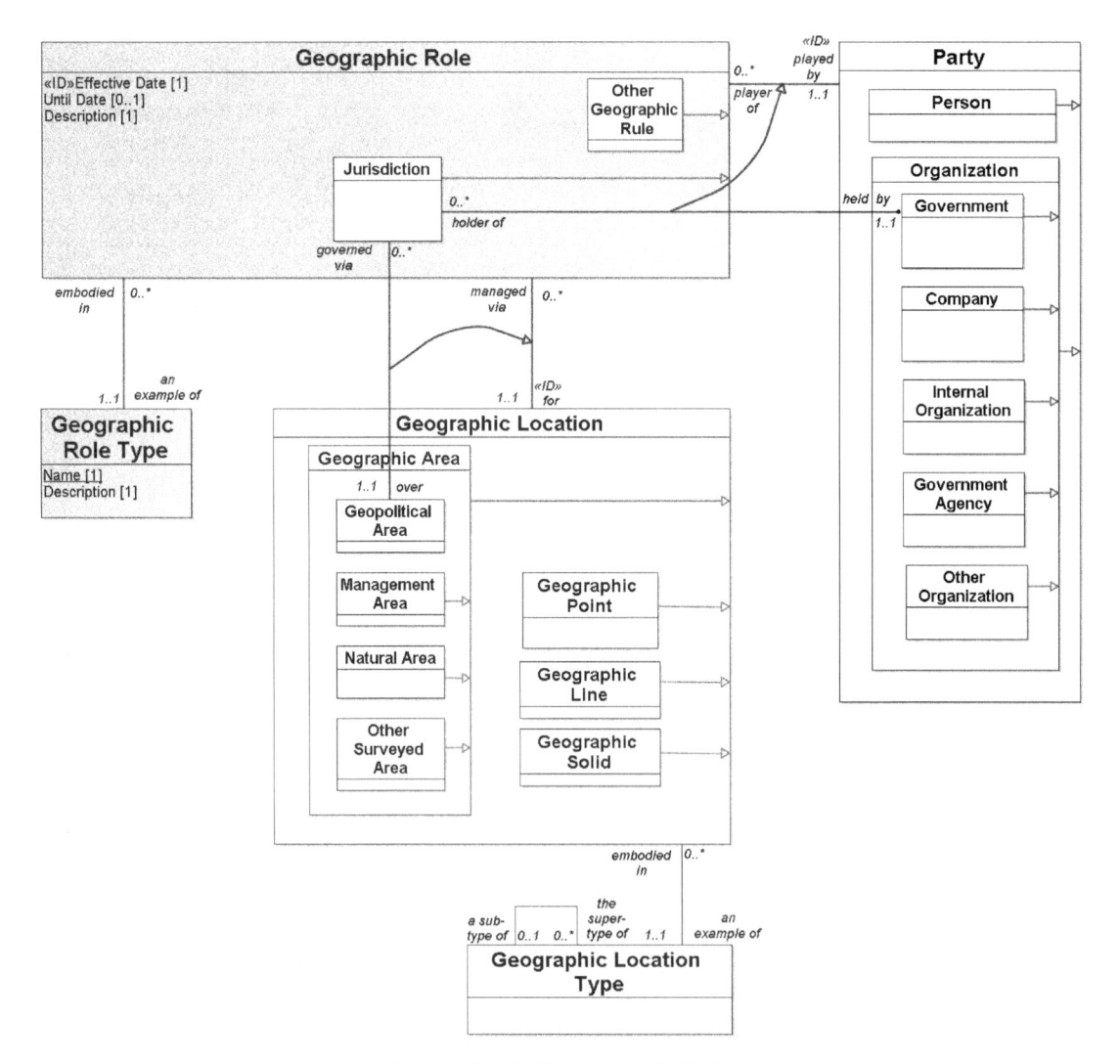

Figure 5-11: Geographic Roles

Note, by the way, that the relationship "*held by/ holder of*" between **Jurisdiction** and **Government** is, in fact, a *sub-type of* the relationship "*played by/ player of*" between the entity class's super-types **Geographic Role** and **Party**. Similarly, the relationship "*over / governed via*" between **Jurisdiction** and **Geopolitical Area** is, in fact, a sub-type of the relationship "*for / managed via*" between the super-types **Geographic Role** and **Geographic Location**. This generalization relationship is as real as it is between entity classes, even though most CASE tools and their notations do not recognize it. (In fact, UML does.)

Summary

This chapter described how to locate the enterprise in the world. This is *not* about the addresses of factories, warehouses, and offices. That will be discussed in detail in Chapter 12, below, which describes addresses and, in particular, the physical addresses that are *facilities*.

Here the focus was on **Geographic Location** - a defined place on the Earth. In keeping with our Junior High geometry, this may be a:

- **Geographic Area** – A bounded two-dimensional space (or as two-dimensional as you can get on the surface of a sphere). This includes:

  - **Geopolitical Area** – A Geographic Area whose boundaries are defined by law or treaty.

  - **Management Area** – A Geographic Area whose boundaries are defined by a private or governmental organization for management purposes.

  - **Natural Area** – A Geographic Area whose boundaries are based on natural phenomena.

  - **Other Surveyed Area** – A Geographic Area, other than the three just mentioned, whose boundaries are defined by measuring them explicitly.

- **Geographic Point** – A specific point, defined by its latitude, longitude, and (optionally) elevation.

- **Geographic Solid** – A bounded three-dimensional space. Among other things, this can describe an oil or gas reservoir or a particular area in space.

- **Geographic Line** – A two-dimensional line, useful for describing telephone lines or highways.

As with **Parties**, there were the following four categories of information collected to describe **Geographic Locations:**

- **Geographic Location Relationships** – The fact that one **Geographic Location** is associated in some way with another. This could be a **Geographic Point** serving to define a boundary for a **Geographic Area** or **Geographic Solid**, one **Geographic Area** being adjacent to another, one

Geographic Area overlapping another, or one **Geographic Area** encompassing another.

- **Geographic Location Identifiers** and **Geographic Names**, along with constraints defining which kinds of either could be used for **Geographic Locations** that are *examples of* a particular **Geographic Location Type**.

- **Geographic Location Characteristics** – What might otherwise be attributes of **Geographic Location**, rendered as instances of an entity class, so they can be the responsibility of a subject matter expert instead of the responsibility of the data modeler.

- **Geographic Location Roles** – The fact that a **Person** or **Organization** plays a defined part in the care of a **Geographic Location**.

CHAPTER 6

Assets (What)

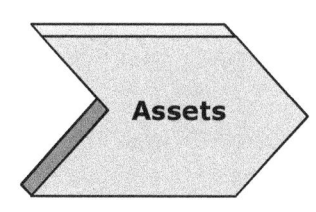

An **Asset Account**, in the financial world, keeps track of the value of an enterprise's assets. But what is an asset? According to Merriam Webster, an asset is "an item of value owned"[39]. Most of the assets everyone is familiar with are *Physical* **Assets**, those that have a presence in the world, like buildings, computers, office supplies, and the like. These include the products we make and consume, the equipment used to make and transport those products, the raw materials that are required to make them, and the buildings and other structures that house them and their construction activities.

An *Abstract* **Asset**, on the other hand, has no physical presence. This could be a bank account, shares of stock, or a computer program. This is discussed later, in Chapter 10 "Documents and Other Information Resources". under "Data Resource". Here we are concerned with physical assets only.

This part of the Enterprise model defines an "asset" as "any physical thing". While these are usually represented in the financial systems as "asset accounts", for our purposes here, financial assets are different, and they will be addressed later, in Chapter 11. Here, we are only concerned with physical things. We will presume that by definition, if we are interested in them, they have value.

About Assets

Figure 6-1 shows our starting point with **Asset**. An **Asset** could be your author's laptop computer (with a serial number, used to prepare this book), a particular

---

[39] Merriam-Webster. 2008. "The Merriam-Webster Online Dictionary.", *http://www.merriam-webster.com/dictionary/asset* (accessed October 22).

building, an identified quantity of natural gas, or any other physical thing. Note in the model that, fundamentally, there are four principal kinds of **Asset:**

- A **Discrete Item** is a single physical item that is uniquely identifiable. Your author's microwave oven, with **Serial Number** "XD-3245-A" is an example of this. A **Discrete Item** must be an instance of one of the following:
    - ✓ **Manufacturing Equipment Item** – a device (**Discrete Item**) that is used in the production of other Assets.
    - ✓ **Vehicle** – a **Discrete Item** used to carry people and or goods from one place to another.
    - ✓ **Measurement Instrument** – a **Discrete Item** used in a laboratory to determine values for characteristics of materials.
    - ✓ **Computer / Communication Equipment** – a **Discrete Item** used to process or transmit information.
    - ✓ **Other Discrete Item** – a **Discrete Item** that is not listed here.
- An **Inventory** is a collection or a quantity of the **Asset** that can only be identified in bulk. There are two basic kinds of **Inventory**:
    - ✓ **Material** – a liquid, powdered, or gaseous substance, which can only be described in terms of weight or volume. Examples of this are diatomatious earth and crude oil.
    - ✓ **Spare Part** – a physical item that is too small to keep track of individually. This includes such things as nuts and bolts.
- A **Lot** is a quantity of inventory that is uniquely identified with a **Lot Number**. In pharmaceutical and chemical manufacturing, typically the output of each production run is given a lot number, which is kept track of as the quantity of material is then subdivided to be used or sold.
- A **Building** is a permanent enclosure, such as a house, an office building, a factory, or a warehouse. (Typically this is located in an identified **Surveyed Area**, with a **Street Address**).

Assets 131

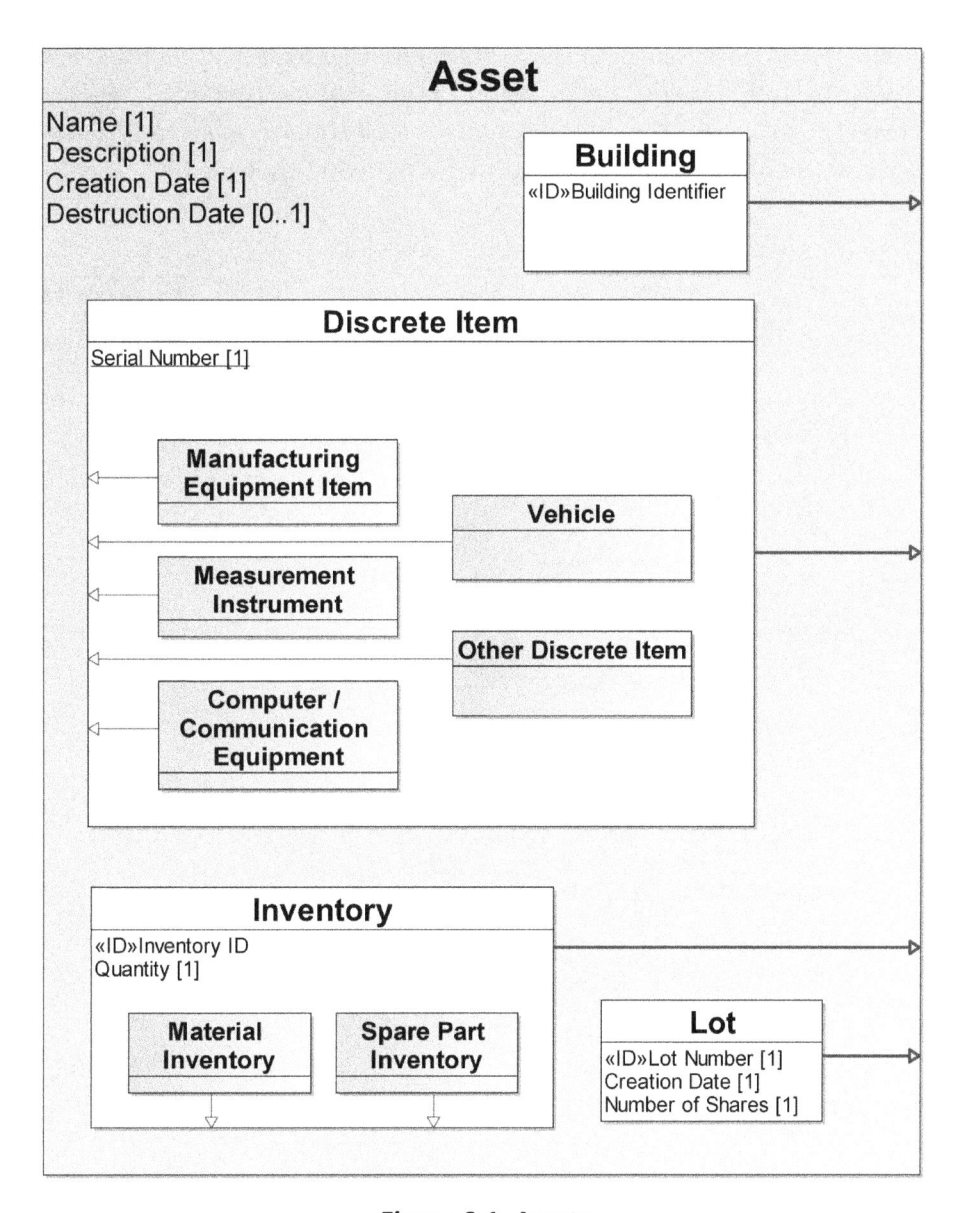

Figure 6-1: Assets

Assets, Asset Types, and Asset Specifications

Analogous to the treatment of **Party** and **Geographic Location**, in the **Asset** section of the model, each **Asset** is shown in Figure 6-2 to be *an example of* a single **Asset Type**. As in the other sections, the initial set of **Asset Types** reproduces the set of sub-types of **Asset**: **Inventory**, **Discrete Item**, **Lot**, and **Building**.

132 Enterprise Model Patterns

For example, in one gasoline station, you could have an **Inventory** with a Quantity of "300" gallons, *described by* an **Asset Type** with a Name of "gasoline". Alternatively, in your office, you might have an **Inventory** with a Quantity of "4000", *described by* an **Asset Type** with a Name of "#10 Envelopes".

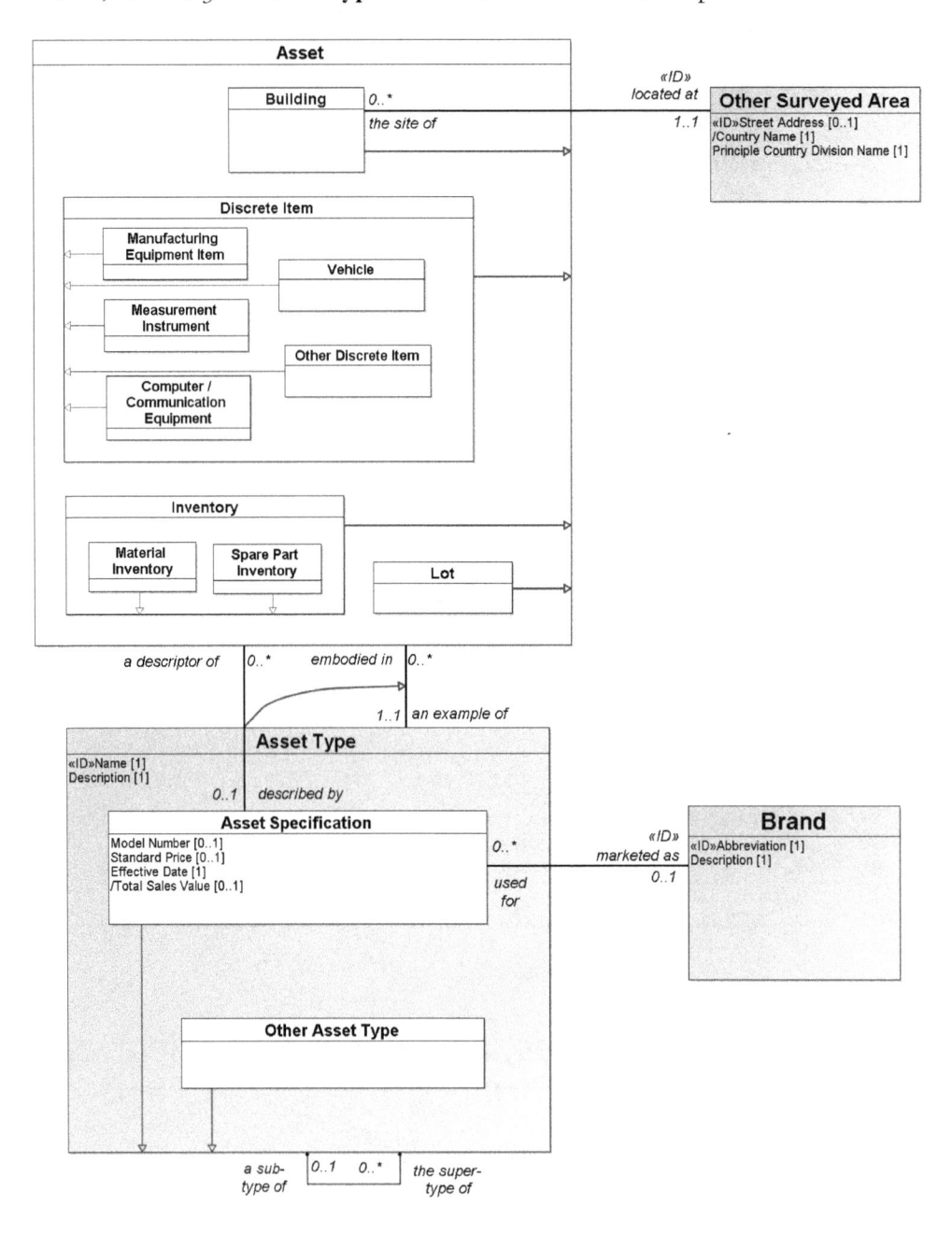

Figure 6-2: Asset Specifications

Asset Type provides a set of fundamental categories for assets. This covers the whole range of classifications of physical things that the company might be concerned with. As with other "Types", it begins by reproducing the sub-types of **Asset**, such as "Discrete Item", "Building", and "Vehicle". These in turn can then be elaborate upon as further sub-types, such as, for example, "Office Building" that is *a sub-type of* "Building", or "Desktop Computer" that is *a sub-type of* "Computer / Communication Equipment". This is shown by the explicit relationship portrayed in Figure 6-2 as "each **Asset Type** may be *the super-type of* one or more (other) **Asset Types**".

Table 6-1 shows a list of possible *sub-type (instances) of* **Asset Type**. Note that in each case, the **Asset Type** may only be *a sub-type of* one other **Asset Type.**

Table 6-1: Asset Types

Name	a sub-type of
Manufacturing Equipment Item	Discrete Item
Lathe	Manufacturing Equipment Item
Measurement Instrument	Discrete Item
Tachometer	Measurement Instrument
Vehicle	Discrete Item
Truck	Vehicle
Pickup Truck	Truck
Tractor Trailer	Truck
Electronic device	Discrete Item
Communications device	Electronic Device
Wi-Fi Router	Communications Device
Computer	Electronic Device
Laptop Computer	Computer
Desktop Computer	Computer

In a departure from the models for **Party** and **Geographic Area,** in addition to specifying an **Asset** as *an example of* an **Asset Type**, an **Asset** may also be *described by* a more detailed **Asset Specification**. This is the catalogue entry that defines the basic characteristics of the kind of **Asset** in detail. An **Asset Specification** is an **Asset Type** that describes an **Asset** sufficiently to offer it for sale. Instances are typically identified by a Model Number. This is shown in Figure 6-2. So, as an alternative to simply saying that your author's 1990 Acura Integra (with a particular vehicle identification number) is *an example of* an `"Automobile"`, you can say that it is *described by* the **Asset Specification** for a `"1990 Acura Integra"`.

In addition, each **Asset Specification** may be *marketed as* a **Brand**.

This means that the simple categorizations described above are in fact *examples of* **Other Asset Type**. The more detailed alternative sub-type of **Asset Type**, then, is **Asset Specification**. For example, a specific instance of **Asset Type** could be the **Asset Specification** that is *a descriptor of* your author's laptop computer—specifically, "Lenovo ThinkPad T43 computer", with a **Model Number** of "2687-D8U". This model was introduced on "September 15, 2005" (its **Effective Date**), and it is supposed that sales might have been discontinued on "August 16, 2007" (its **Until Date**).

Note that to specify the **Asset Specification** for the "1990 Acura Integra" does not invalidate the assertion that it is an "automobile". In the diagram, we have explicitly added the relationship that asserts that one **Asset Type** (in this case, the **Asset Description** for the "1990 Acura Integra") may be *a sub-type of* an (other) **Asset Type** (in this case "Automobile".)

Note also the interesting UML feature that allows us to assert that the very relationship, "each **Asset** may be *described by* one and only one **Asset Specification**", is itself a sub-type of the relationship "each **Asset** must be *an example of* one and only one **Asset Type**.

That each **Asset** is *an example of* any **Asset Type**, may be at any level of specificity. Moreover, if it is *described by* an **Asset Description**, that **Asset Description** should be designated as *a sub-type of* an **Other Asset Type** at the lowest level of specificity. Note, however, that the model does not require that. The **Asset Descriptions** themselves can be classified as coarsely or as finely as desired. This model gives the data manager choices as to how deeply to categorize anything.

Table 6-2 shows examples of this for both a laptop computer and a desktop computer. In it, "*This* Lenovo ThinkPad Computer, (S/N: 987423A3)" is simply described as being *an example of* the **Other Asset Type** "Laptop Computer", while "*That* Lenovo ThinkPad T61 Computer, (S/N: 24072F09)" and "*That* Lenovo IdeaCentre K23, (S/N: 3987534E87)" are each *described by* their respective **Asset Descriptions**. Note, however, that the data manager chose to classify the "…ThinkPad…" as a sub-type of the **Other Asset Type** "Laptop computer", implying the hierarchy of sub-types all the way to **Discrete Item**, while the data manager chose to classify the "…IdeaCenter…" simply as a **Discrete Item**, ignoring the lower levels of categorization.

Table 6-2: Asset Types and Descriptions

Asset	*an example of* Other Asset Type	*described by* Asset Description	Asset Description Model Number	*sub-type of* Asset Type
This Lenovo ThinkPad Computer, (S/N: 987423A3)	Laptop Computer			Computer / Communication Equipment
				Discrete Item
That Lenovo ThinkPad T61 Computer, (S/N: 24072F09)		Lenovo ThinkPad T61 Computer,	2687-D8U	Laptop Computer
				Computer / Communication Equipment
				Discrete Item

Note that this model does not provide the ability to classify an **Asset** into multiple categories "horizontally". An **Asset** is *an example of* one and only one (direct) **Asset Type**. It *inherits* classification into more general types, but that is all. To classify the computer into other categories (say "black things" or "portable things") you must use one or more **Asset Characteristic Values** to classify it into multiple **Asset Categories**. This part of the model is described below (page 143), in "Describing Assets"..

There are fundamentally two kinds of **Asset Specification:**

- **Specified Material**—Liquid, powdered, or gaseous substance, which can only be described in terms of weight or volume. As an **Asset Specification**, this could describe a particular grade of sand, or a grade of crude oil. The characteristics that constitute this specification will be described below.
- **Product Model**, an item that can be counted or viewed individually.
    - **Vehicle** – a **Piece of Equipment** that is a device for transporting people and goods from one place to another.[♣]

[♣] One entertaining thing about writing a book like this is coming up with definitions for things that "everybody knows". But do they?

- **Other Piece of Equipment** – a **Piece of Equipment** that is not a **Manufacturing Equipment Item**, a **Measurement Instrument**, a **Computer/communications Equipment Item**, or a **Vehicle.**
- **Other Product Model** – a **Product Model** that is not a manufactured device, such as a foodstuff. It could also be something like a `"Standard House Plan JX-364"`, describing a specification for a kind of mass-produced house.

A **Product Model** usually *marketed as* a **Brand**. In some cases **Specified Materials** may carry a **Brand** name as well. This is a combination of a name plus visual artifacts that convey a particular image. A brand may be owned by one company, but it may be sold from one to another.

Asset Structures

Anyone familiar with manufacturing knows that products are composed of sub-assemblies, which ultimately are composed of parts and materials. Similarly, anyone in the chemical business knows that materials are composed of other materials. In the data model, the concept of one **Asset** being a component of another **Asset** is called **Asset Structure**. Specifically, as shown in Figure 6-3, each **Asset Structure** must be *the use of* one **Asset** …*in* one other **Asset**. To accommodate different kinds of **Asset Structure**, each must be *an example of* one and only one **Asset Structure Type**.

Similarly, each **Asset Type** may have a design structure before any examples of it are built. That is, it may be *composed of* one or more **Asset Type Structures**, each of which must be *the use of* another **Asset Type**. Going in the other direction, each **Asset Type** may be *part of* one or more **Asset Type Structures**, each of which must be *the use in* another **Asset Type**.

For the most part **Asset Type Structures** apply only to **Asset Specifications**, but it is possible to make general assertions about **Other Asset Types**: An `"Automobile"` consists of 4 `"Wheels"`, 1 `"chassis"`, 1 `"engine"`, et cetera.

Ideally, each **Asset Structure** that is *the use in* a particular **Asset** is directly *based on* the **Asset Type Structure** of the **Asset Type** that is *embodied in* that **Asset**. This may not be the case, however, so each **Asset Structure** may be *based on* one and only one **Asset Type Structure** –the one that is *the use in* the **Asset Type** that is *embodied in* the **Asset** just mentioned. The actual structure of an **Asset** may be different from the structure of its **Asset Type**.

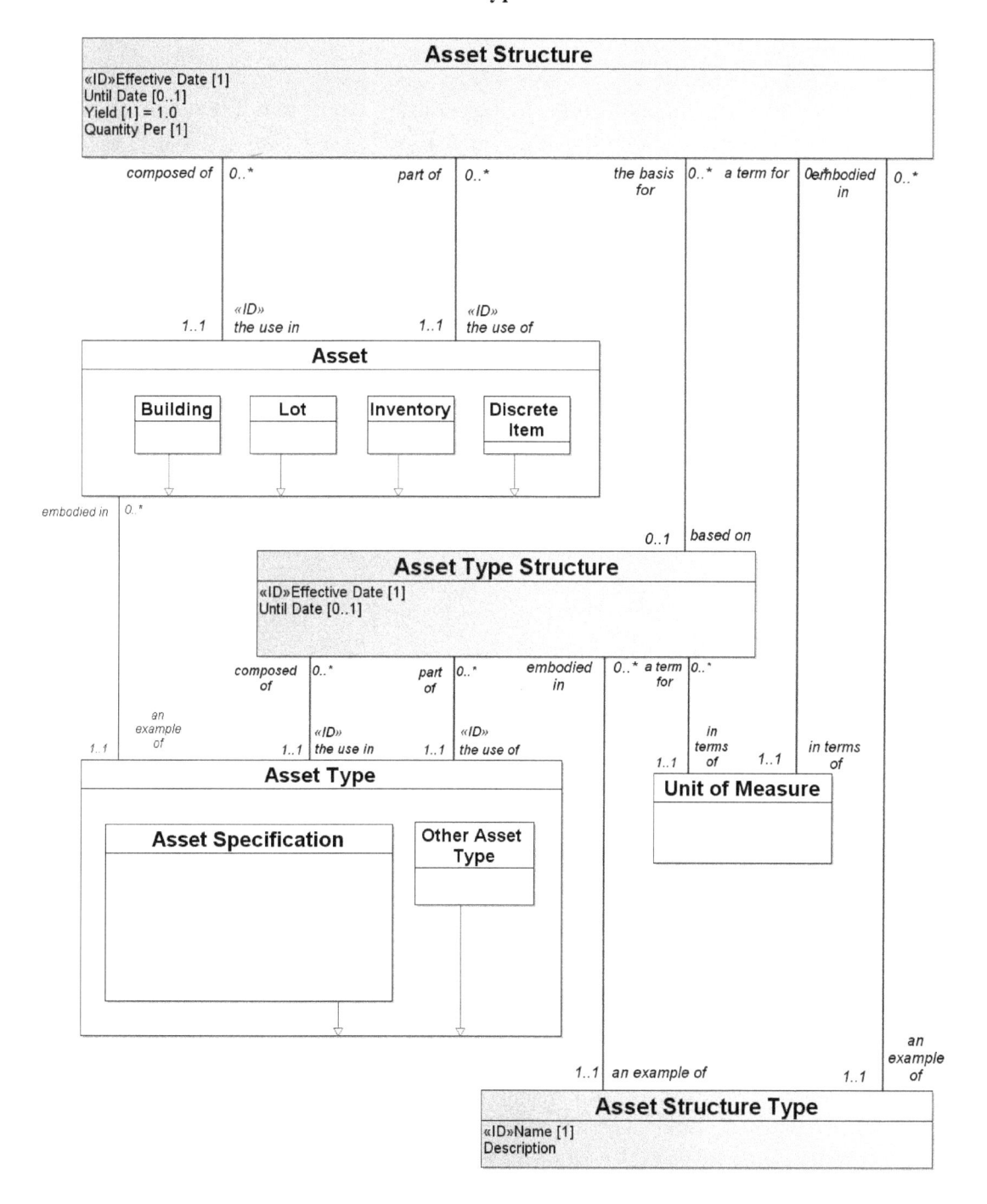

Figure 6-3: Asset Structures

138 Enterprise Model Patterns

Figure 6-4 shows an example of an **Asset Specification** (`"Bicycle, Model 235-A"`) and its component **Asset Specifications** (`"Frame 25-G, Crank and Chain Assembly, Model 72"`), and so forth. Each line connecting two of the **Asset Specifications** is an instance of an **Asset Specification Structure**. For example, one says that producing a `"Bicycle, Model 235-A"` requires a `"Back Wheel 24-A"`. Note that the value of **Quantity Per** in that case is `"1"`.

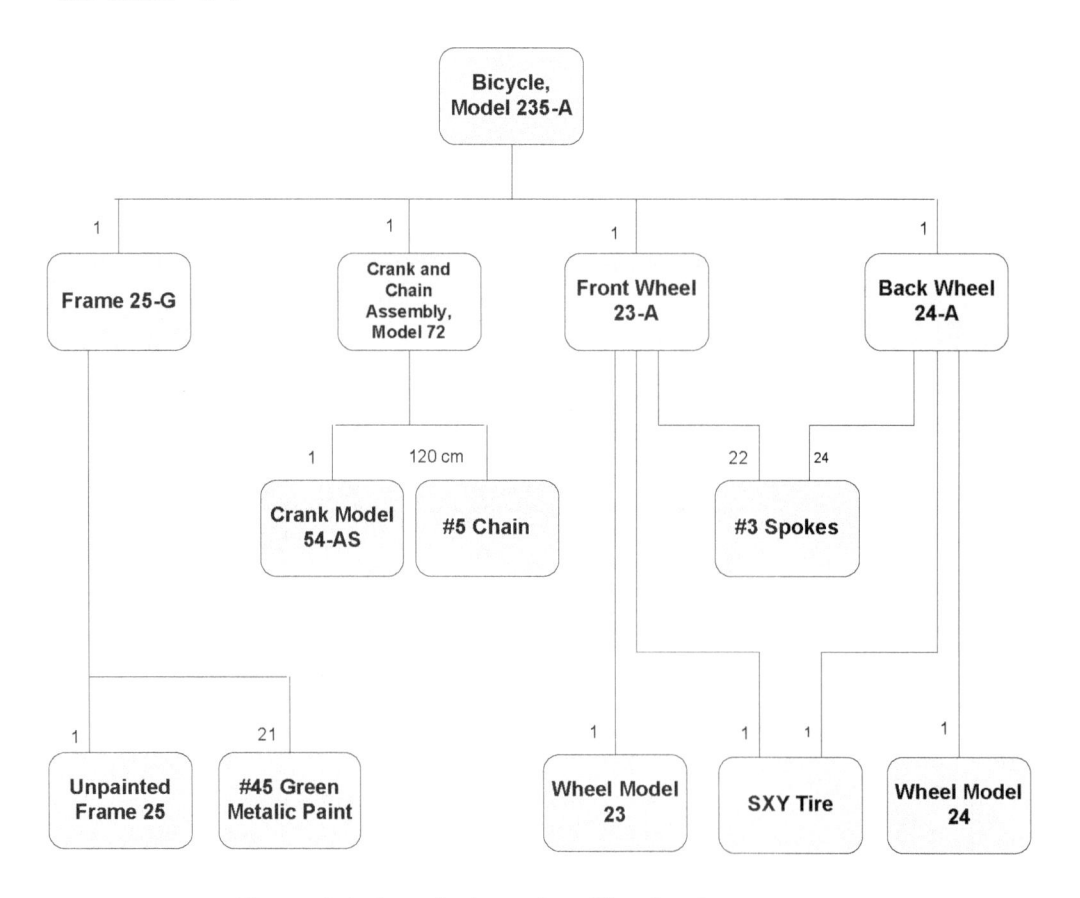

Figure 6-4: Sample Asset Specification Structures

To produce a `"Back Wheel 24-A"`, in turn, will require 24 `"#3 Spokes"`. The value of **Quantity Per** in this case is `"24"`. Note that to produce a `"Front Wheel 23-A"` also requires `"#3 Spokes"`, but only `"22"` of them. This is a ***network structure***, as evidenced by the fact that a lower level node can have more than one higher level node. This is as opposed to a ***hierarchical structure***, which is

Assets **139**

constrained such that each node can have only one higher level node. The latter is sometimes referred to metaphorically, as a tree structure.

You can see that the two entity classes **Asset Type** (shown in Figure 6-4 as boxes) and **Asset Type Structure** (shown in the Figure 6-4 as lines) are sufficient to specify an assembly of unlimited complexity. The product structure configuration is one of the most powerful (and one of the oldest) in data modeling.

Of course, keeping track of exactly how your author's bicycle was built requires an analogous model configuration, this one captured by **Assets** and **Asset Structures**. As described above, it is desirable for each **Asset Structure** to be *based on* a corresponding **Asset Type Structure**, although, in the real world, this doesn't always happen.

A table derived from the bicycle structure shown in Figure 6-4 might look like Table 6-3.

Table 6-3: Table of Structures

the use in **Asset Specification**	*the use of* **Asset Specification**	**Asset Specification Relationship Quantity per**	**Unit of Measure Abbreviation**
Bicycle, Model 235-A	Frame 25-G	1	Ea
Bicycle, Model 235-A	Crank and Chain Assembly, Model 72	1	Ea
Bicycle, Model 235-A	Front Wheel 23-A	1	Ea
Bicycle, Model 235-A …	Back Wheel 24-A	1	Ea
Crank and Chain Assembly, Model 72	Crank Model 54-AS	1	Ea
Crank and Chain Assembly, Model 72 …	#5 Chain	120	CM
Front Wheel 23-A	#3 Spokes	22	Ea
Front Wheel 23-A	SXY Tire	1	Ea
Front Wheel 23-A	Wheel Model 23	1	Ea
Back Wheel 24-A	#3 Spokes	24	Ea
Back Wheel 24-A	SXY Tire	1	Ea
Back Wheel 24-A	Wheel Model 24	1	Ea

At the **Asset Type** level, manufactured products typically have a brand name and model number. Chemicals may have brand name, as well as a chemical name.

Naming and Identifying Assets

Virtually all assets as specified certainly have at least one identifying code, and often they have a name. The latter may be a variation on the model name, a nickname (as for one's favorite automobile) or some other name. Often, **Asset** instances will have only one name, but there are enough examples of multiple names for an asset that this must be accounted for. In most cases, they will have only one identifier, but sometimes there will be more than one. For these reasons, and in the interest of flexibility, in this model we will establish the same multiple identifier and name type structure that we've seen for **Party** and **Geographic Location**.

Figure 6-5 shows that both an **Asset Type** and an **Asset** may be *labeled by* one or more **Asset Names**. Each **Asset Name**, in turn must be *an example of* one **Asset Name Type**. **Asset Name Types** include `"trade name"`, `"generic name"`, `"advertising name"`, and so forth.

Similarly, both **Asset Types** and **Assets** each may be *identified via* one or more **Asset Identifier Values**, each of which must be *of* a particular **Asset Identifier Type**. **Asset Identifier Types** include such things as a `"U.S. Vehicle Identification Number (VIN)"` (for cars and trucks), a company `"asset identifier"` for personal computers and terminals, a `"Universal Product Code (UPC)"` for groceries, and so forth. For example, the **Asset Type** with the **Default Name** `"Canon Pixma ChromaLife 100 Twin Pack ink cartridges"` can be *identified via* (among others) the **Asset Identifier Value** with the **Identifier Value** of `"13803 04440"`. This is *for* the **Asset Identifier Type** with the **Name** of `"Universal Product Code (UPC)"`.

Note that the `"Vehicle Identification Number (VIN)"` in the previous example applies only to vehicles (that is, instances of **Assets** that are *specified by* **Asset Types** that are *examples of* the **Asset Type** "vehicle"). Similarly, `"trade name"` only applies to certain **Asset Types**.

Assets 141

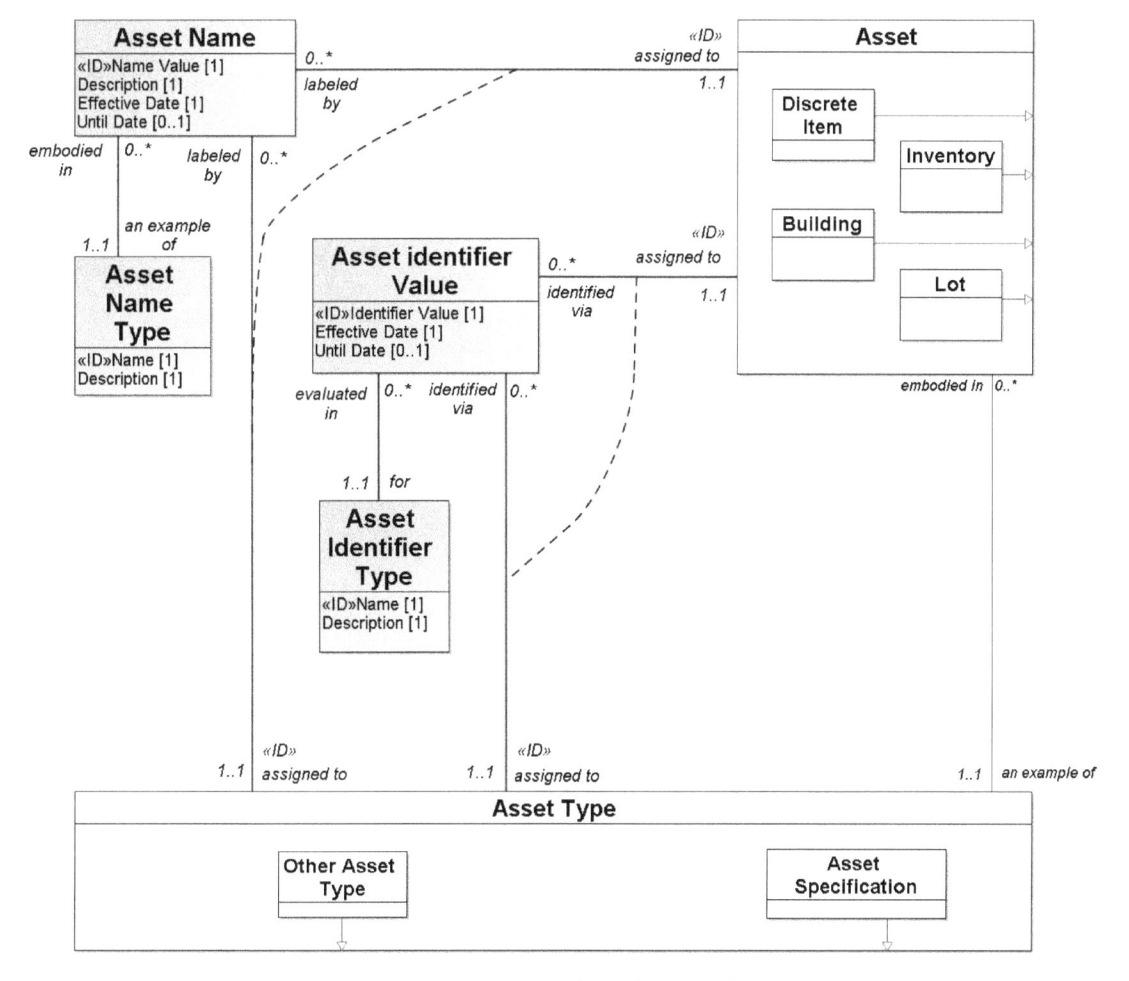

Figure 6-5: Asset Identifiers and Names

Figure 6-6 shows that only certain **Asset Identifier Types** and **Asset Name Types** may appropriately be used for specified **Asset Types** or **Assets**.

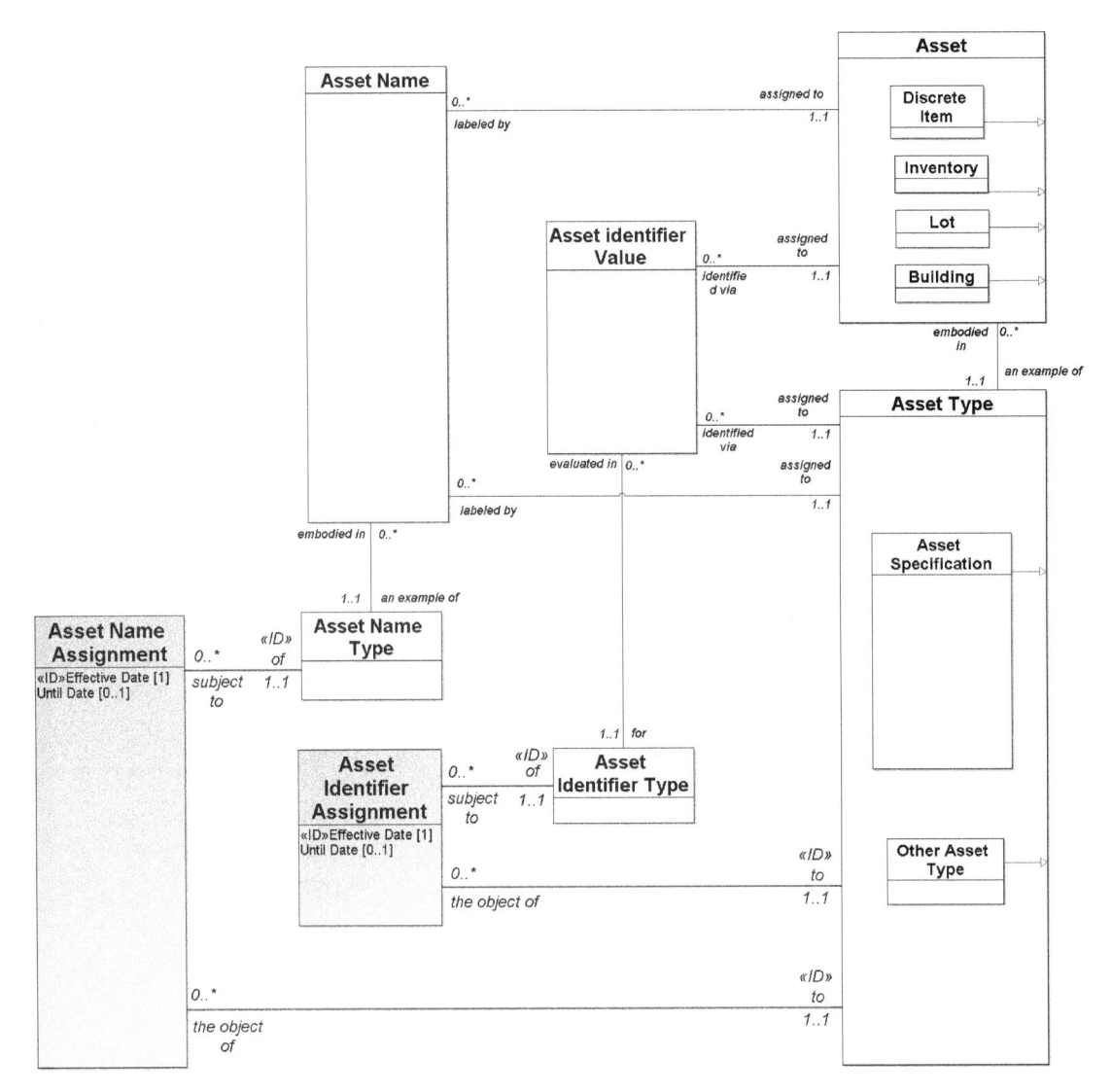

Figure 6-6: Some Asset Assignments

Assets **143**

Business Rules

- An **Asset Name** Name Value may be *assigned to* an **Asset** only if an **Asset Name Assignment** exists that is *of* the **Asset Name Type** that is *embodied in* that **Asset Name**, and is *to* the **Asset Type** that the named **Asset** (via either an **Asset** or an **Asset Type**) is *an example of*. That is, an **Asset** may not be *labeled by* an **Asset Name**, unless the **Asset Name Type**, it is *an example of,* is *subject to* an **Asset Name Assignment** *to* the **Asset Type** *embodied in* the **Asset** involved. *(Translation: Asset Name Assignment* assures that each **Asset Name** is appropriate for the **Asset Type** involved.)

- An **Asset Identifier Value** Identifier Value *assigned to* an **Asset** only if an **Asset Identifier Assignment** exists that is *of* that **Asset Identifier** and is *to* the **Asset Type** that the named **Asset** (via either an **Asset** or an **Asset Type**) is *an example of*. That is, an **Asset** may not be *identified via* an **Asset Identifier Value** unless the **Asset Identifier** it is *for* is subject to an **Asset Identifier Assignment** *to* the **Asset Type** *embodied in* the **Asset** in question. (*Translation:* **Asset Identifier Assignment** assures that each **Asset Identifier Value** is appropriate for the **Asset Type** involved.)

Describing Assets

In principle, every instance of an entity class is described by the same set of attributes. Occasionally, an instance might have a null value for one or two attributes, but this should not be common. What about the case, however, where there are a myriad of different kinds of **Asset Specifications**, and these are of a wide variety of different products—each of which could be described by a completely different set of attributes? An Apple iPod is a very different product from an HP Personal Computer, and both of these are different from a GE Refrigerator. We could extend the sub-type structure of **Asset Specification**, but it would quickly become insurmountably complex. This is most often a concern when the organization is defining the characteristics of an **Asset Specification**, but it is also useful in the description of generic **Other Asset Types** as well. Begin with the

144 Enterprise Model Patterns

basic characteristics that will be present in any "Laptop computer", and then refine them for a particular specified model.

Fortunately, since we have set up **Asset Type** to record as complex a sub-type structure as necessary, the problem is easily solved. First, define an **Asset Characteristic** as a distinguishing trait, quality, or property that can be given a value for either an **Asset Specification** or an **Other Asset Type**. This entity class is shown in Figure 6-7.

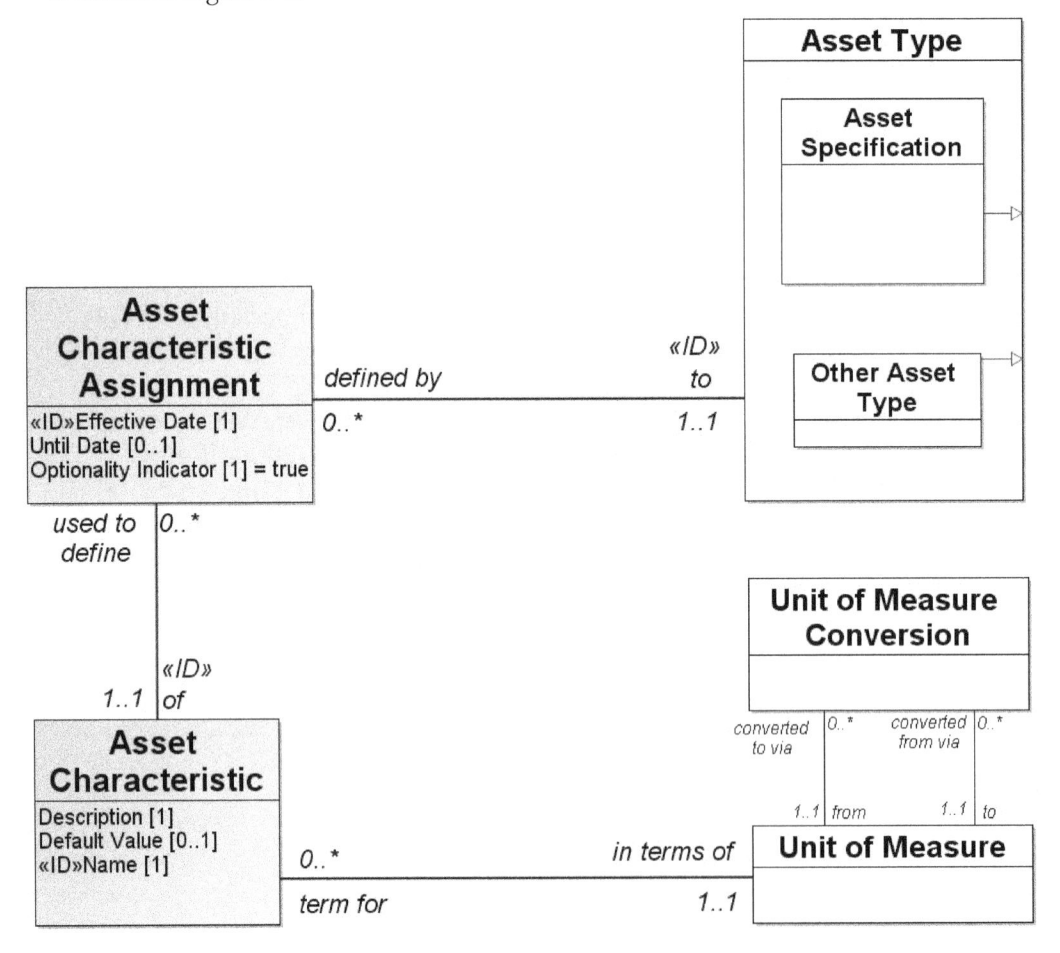

Figure 6-7: Asset Characteristics

Some of the characteristics used to describe a particular model or instance of a product are defined for all instances of an **Asset Type**. That is, your author's computer has `"memory size"` as an **Asset Characteristic** because it is a `"laptop computer"`. If it were a `"home generator"`, it would be described by `"voltage"`, `"output wattage"`, and so forth. Figure 6-7 shows that an **Asset Characteristic Assignment** is the assignment *of* one **Asset**

Characteristic to one **Asset Type**. For example, it could be the assignment *of* `"output wattage"` *to* `"home generator"`.

Table 6-4 shows a set of sample **Asset Characteristic Assignments**.

Alternatively, an **Asset Characteristic** may be *used to define* an **Asset Specification** as well. It could be the *assignment of* "output wattage" *to* the "Westinghouse Model 241 home generator".

That is, each **Asset Characteristic Assignment** must be *of* one and only one **Asset Characteristic** either *to* one and only one **Asset Type**.

Table 6-4 shows a sample set of **Asset Characteristic Assignments**.

Table 6-4: Asset Characteristic Assignments

Asset Type	Asset Specification	Asset Characteristic	Unit of Measure
Laptop Computer		Disk Space	Giga Bytes
Laptop Computer	Lenovo Model T61	Color of Cover	(none)
Wireless Router		Range	Feet
Home Generator		Output power	Watts
Home Generator		Electrical Tension	Volts
Refrigerator		Volume	Cubic Feet

Of course, each **Asset Characteristic** must be described in terms of a **Unit of Measure**. A basic **Unit of Measure** will be recorded for each **Asset Characteristic**, but if values are to be reported in a different one, **Unit of Measure Conversion** contains the **Factor** and, if necessary, a **Constant** required to convert one to another. For example, the **Asset Characteristic** `"range"` of the **Asset Type** `"wireless router"` could be recorded in terms of the **Unit of Measure** `"feet"`. But if a value has to be reported in `"meters"`, the **Unit of Measure Conversion** *from* `"feet"` to `"meters"` would have a **Factor** with the value `".3048"`.

In the case of **Asset Specifications**, multiple **Asset Characteristic Assignments** can provide for optional alternatives. The **Optionality Indicator**, an attribute of **Asset Characteristic Assignment**, determines whether values for corresponding **Asset Characteristic Values** are required (**Optionality Indicator** = `"false"`)

146 Enterprise Model Patterns

or not(Optionality Indicator = true)".[*] If **Asset Characteristic Assignment** has the effect of assigning attributes to **Asset Type** and **Asset Specification**, how do we provide values for these **Asset Characteristics?**

The answer is in Figure 6-8. A**sset Characteristic Value** must be *of* one **Asset Characteristic** and it must be *to describe* either one **Asset** or one **Asset Type**. In the case of **Assets**, the **Asset Characteristic Value** is the actual value of the **Asset Characteristic**.

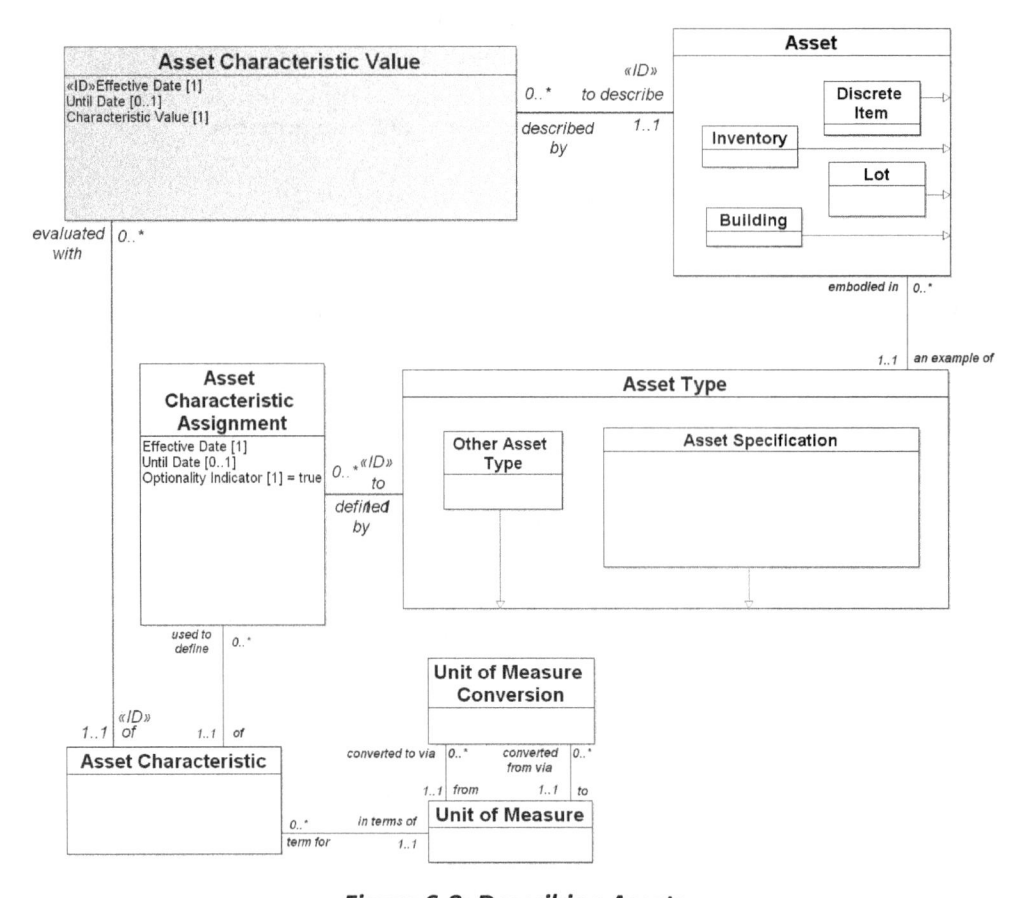

Figure 6-8: Describing Assets

Table 6-5 shows examples of both options and actual values.

---

[*] In Figure 6-6, the attribute Optionality Indicator [1] has the additional annotation "=true", meaning that the default value for that attribute is "true. This is a UML convention.

Table 6-5: Asset Characteristic Values

Asset Specification	Asset Characteristic	Asset	Asset Characteristic Value	Asset Characteristic Value Type
Lenovo ThinkPad T43	Disk Space		75 GB	Option
Lenovo ThinkPad T43	Disk Space		100 GB	Option
Lenovo ThinkPad T43	Disk Space		125 GB	Option
Lenovo ThinkPad T43	Disk Space	DH's ThinkPad	125 GB	Actual

Business Rule

- If an **Asset Characteristic Value** is *of* an **Asset Category**, the Characteristic Value of that **Asset Characteristic Value** must equal the Category Value of an **Asset Category Legal Value** (if any exist) that is *for* the **Asset Category** involved. *(Translation:* For **Asset Categories**, any **Asset Characteristic Value** must be the same as one of the available **Asset Category Legal Values**.)

As shown in Figure 6-9, **Asset Characteristics** are, in fact, of two kinds: a **Continuous Asset Characteristic** is one whose values are either real numbers, simple text, or dates. They can be constrained with a **Minimum Value** and/or a **Maximum Value**. "Ambient temperature", for example, or "output power" are examples of these. An **Asset Category** is a characteristic that can only take one of a discrete list of values. "Color" and "number of doors" (for a car) are examples of these. In defining an **Asset Category**, it is also possible to define the set of **Asset Category Legal Values** that constrain it.

148 Enterprise Model Patterns

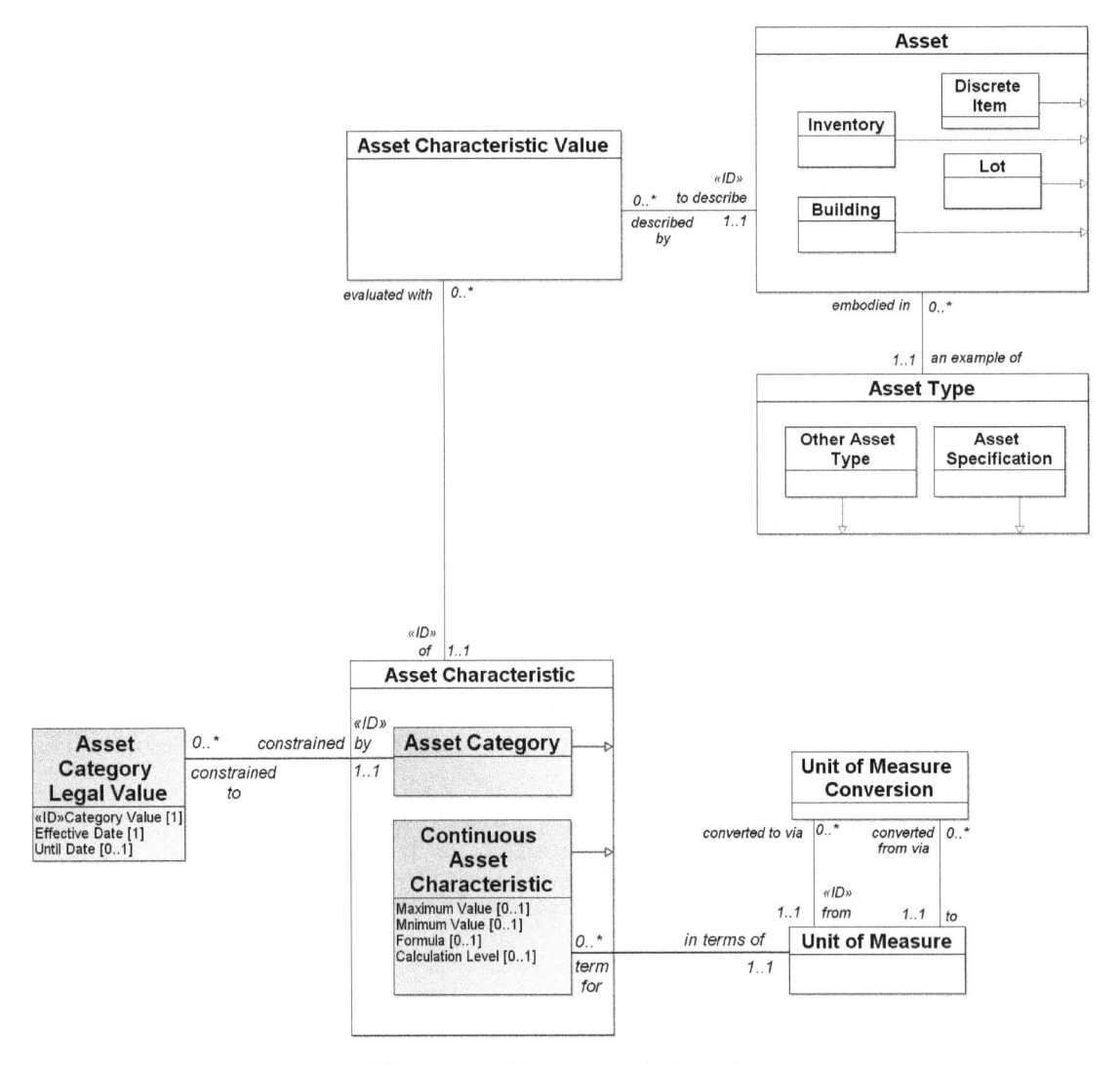

Figure 6-9: Characteristic Details

Derived Characteristics

While many **Asset Characteristics** are evaluated with data from other sources and then stored, some are derived from other **Asset Characteristics**. For example "volume" may be calculated by multiplying "height" times "width" times "depth". While formulae can be very complex, the technique called ***Reverse Polish Notation***, as previously described for derived **Party Characteristics**, is a way of representing them so that they can easily be evaluated.

Again, given a standard **Formula**, such as A=mx+y, this approach evaluates each variable in turn, from the outside in, until a value is obtained for the entire formula. In this example, you start by postulating m as a positive number. You then process x with the operator multiply. You then process y with the operator plus. If the formula had been A=m*(x+y), you would have begun with x and y and then incorporated m.

The point is that any formula can be constructed by a succession of variables plus operators.

Figure 6-10 shows that an **Asset Derivation Element** must be *to derive* a **Continuous Asset Characteristic**. It, in turn, may be *the use of* either another **Asset Characteristic**, a **System Variable** (like today's date), or a **Constant**. Table 6-6 shows how the formula power = voltage * current would be represented as two instances of **Asset Derivation Element**.

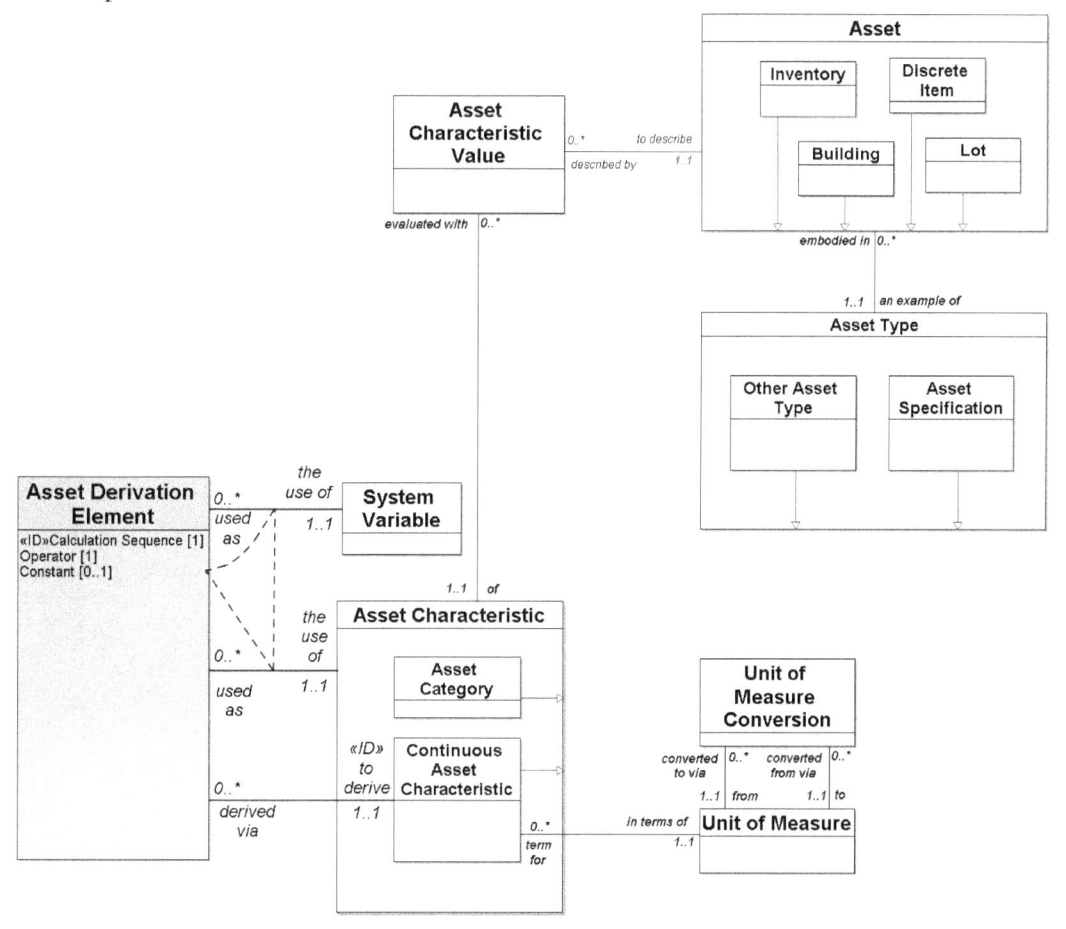

Figure 6-10: Derived Characteristics

Enterprise Model Patterns

Table 6-6: Sample Asset Derivation Elements

to derive Asset Characteristic	the use of Asset Characteristic	the use of System Variable	(the use of) Constant	Operator
Power	Voltage			Add
Power	Current			Multiply

Asset Roles

Assets don't exist outside the environment of the organization. Various **Parties** (both individual **Persons** and **Organizations**) have important roles to play in the acquisition, manufacture, and distribution of both **Asset** instances and **Asset Types**. Figure 6-11 shows **Asset Role**, each of which is the fact that a particular **Party** is somehow involved with either a particular **Asset Type** or **Asset i**nstance. That is, each **Asset Role** must be *played by* one **Party** and be *for* either one **Asset** instance or one **Asset Type**.

This version of the model focuses on assets that are purchased, with primary sub-types being **Wholesaler**, **Retailer**, and **Manufacturer**. Different organizations may have other priorities, so **Other Asset Role** could be broken out into different categories.

As with other parts of the model, **Asset Role Type** encapsulates the sub-type structure shown. The first instances of **Asset Role Type** must be `"wholesaler"`, `"retailer"`, `"manufacturer"`, and `"other asset role type"`, with the ability to make the latter a *super-type* of **Asset Role Types** yet to be added.

Assets **151**

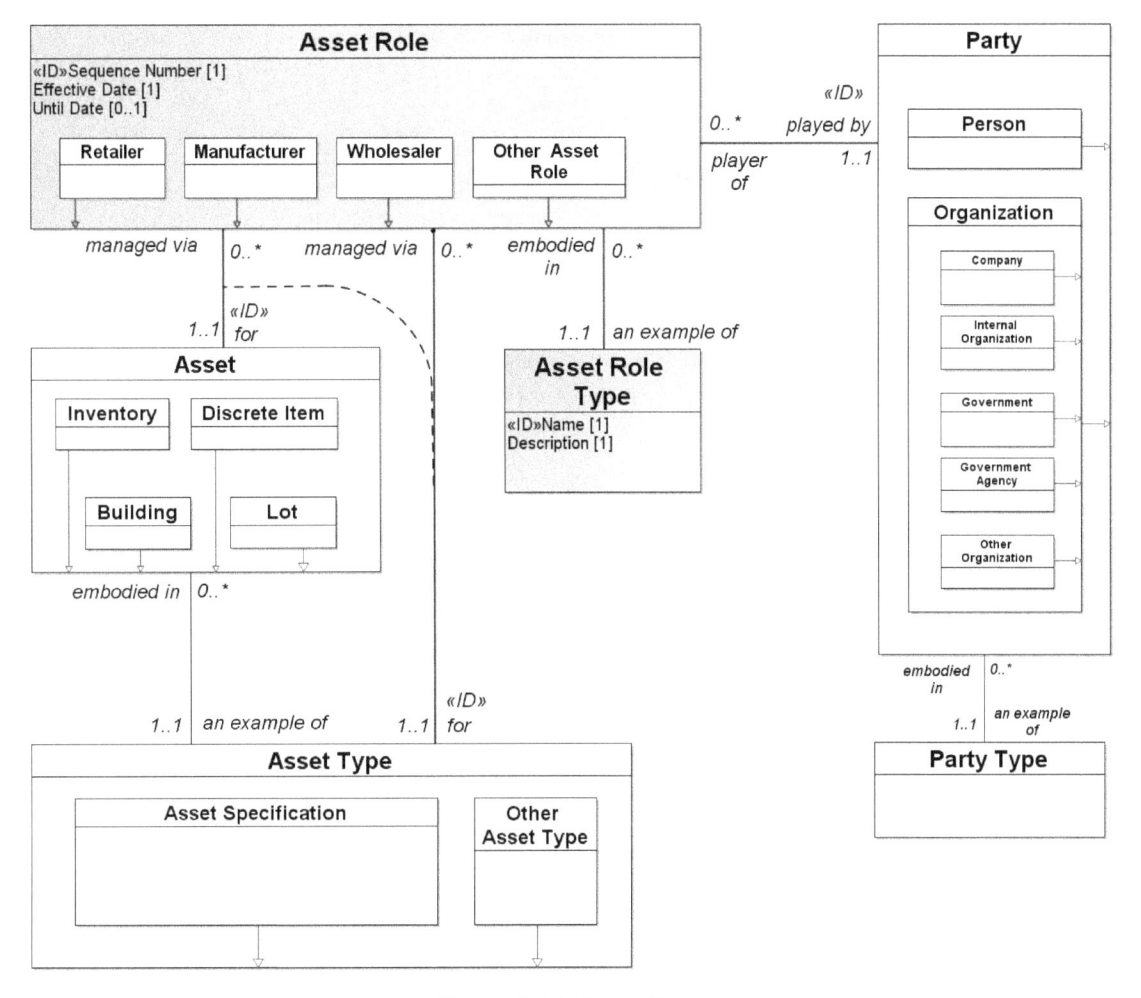

Figure 6-11: Asset Roles

Summary

An **Asset** is an item of value to the enterprise. Of concern in this chapter are ***physical assets***, those with physical presence in the world. These include such things as buildings, pieces of equipments, products, raw material, and office supplies. A (physical) asset is any substance.

An **Asset** is *an example of* one and only one **Asset Type**. This must be either an **Asset Specification** or an **Other Asset Type**. An **Other Asset Type** is a generic category, such as `"vehicle"` or `"air conditioner"`. An **Asset Specification** is a defined item for sale, as described in a catalogue entry. Each **Asset Type** (such as the **Other Asset Type**, `"Automobile"`, may be *the super-*

type of one or more other **Asset Types**, such as "Ford Focus", and "Acura MDX".

Each **Asset Type** is a fundamental classification of **Assets**. If an asset is identified as being *an example of* a more detailed **Asset Type**, such as "Acura MDX", it does also inherit its presence in a more general **Asset Type**, such as "Vehicle" and "Automobile".

An **Asset Type** may be *composed of* one or more **Asset Type Structures**, identifying its designed component assets. Some of these may be optional alternatives. An **Asset** is similarly *composed of* one or more **Asset Structures** that are *the* actual *use of* specific **Assets**. Here, the actual components selected are identified.

An **Asset Type** may be *defined by* the set of **Asset Characteristics** that provide the structure for describing it. This is analogous to the specific set of attributes that might describe an **Asset Type**. For example, the **Asset Type** "Laptop Computer" is *defined by* the **Asset Characteristics** "width", "disk space", "memory", et cetera. An actual instance of an **Asset**, then, is described by **Asset Characteristic Values** of each of these **Asset Characteristics**.

Some **Asset Characteristics** can be derived from others, and the chapter described the use of ***reverse Polish notation*** to accomplish this.

And **Parties** can be *players of* various kinds of **Asset Roles**, such as **Retailer**, **Wholesaler**, **Manufacturer**, or **Other Role**.

CHAPTER 7

Activities (How)

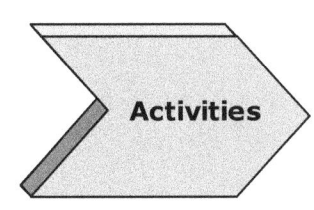

A company must do something. A manufacturing company must make its products and maintain its equipment. If a company provides services for hire, those services are the activities of the company. A major task of any organization, then, is the planning, scheduling, and recording of actions taken, procedures followed, and services rendered. This chapter will model these actions, procedures, and services.

Understand, by the way, that when we model actions as entity classes here, it is not the same thing as modeling actions as functions or procedures. Rather than using the model to describe the nature of what is being done, we are recognizing that activities, procedures, and services are themselves things of significance to the business, and they are related as things to other things—just like the **People**, **Organizations**, **Geographic Locations**, and **Assets** discussed in the last three chapters.

That is, our concern here is not to describe the activities themselves, but to identify the data required to describe them. Activities are described better and in more detail in data flow diagrams and other kinds of process models. Here we are simply identifying them as things of significance to the enterprise and their relationships to other enterprise things.

Defining Activities

Figure 7-1 shows **Activity**—an action taken. An **Activity** must be one of the following:

- A **Production Step** – An **Activity** undertaken at a particular time to manufacture a quantity of an **Asset** . It is *the implementation of* a **Procedure** that is *used in* a **Routing Step**. (See Chapter 16.)

- A **Maintenance Task** - An **Activity** *authorized by* a **Maintenance Work Order** *to fix, install, or replace* a **Discrete Item**, such as a **Piece of Equipment**. (See Chapter 16.)

- A **Cleaning Activity** – The removal of dirt or debris from a **Facility**. (See Chapter 16)

- A **Laboratory Test** – A collection of **Procedures** that is the use of a **Measuring Instrument** to determine a numerical value of an **Asset Characteristic** of a **Sample** material. (See Chapter 17)

- A **Communication** - An **Activity** that is the transmission of information between one or more representatives of the enterprise with representatives of other organizations. (See Chapter 14)

- An **Other Activity** – Any **Activity** that is not one of those above.

Examples of an **Activity** could include `"Fabricate a run of 15 20" x 40 sheets (on January 23, 2009)"`, `"Sweep the floors of Warehouse A (on 9/14/2009)"`, and so forth.

As with **Assets**, it is necessary to distinguish *examples* of services or procedures from *fundamental categories* of them. The former is here called an **Activity**, and the latter is an **Activity Type**.

Figure 7-1 shows that, as with **Party, Geographic Location**, and **Asset**, each **Activity** must be *an example of* an **Activity Type**, while each **Activity Type** may be *embodied in* one or more actual **Activities**. Also, as with the other sections of the Enterprise Model, **Activity Type** begins as an itemization of the sub-types of **Activity**. Thus, the first five instances are `"Production Step"`, `"Maintenance Task"`, `"Cleaning Activity"`, `"Laboratory Test"`, and `"Communication"`. As before, each of these may be *the super-type of* one or more other **Activity Types** not shown on the drawing.

Other **Activity Types** may be specified as well, as long as each is *a sub-type of* one of those three.

Activities

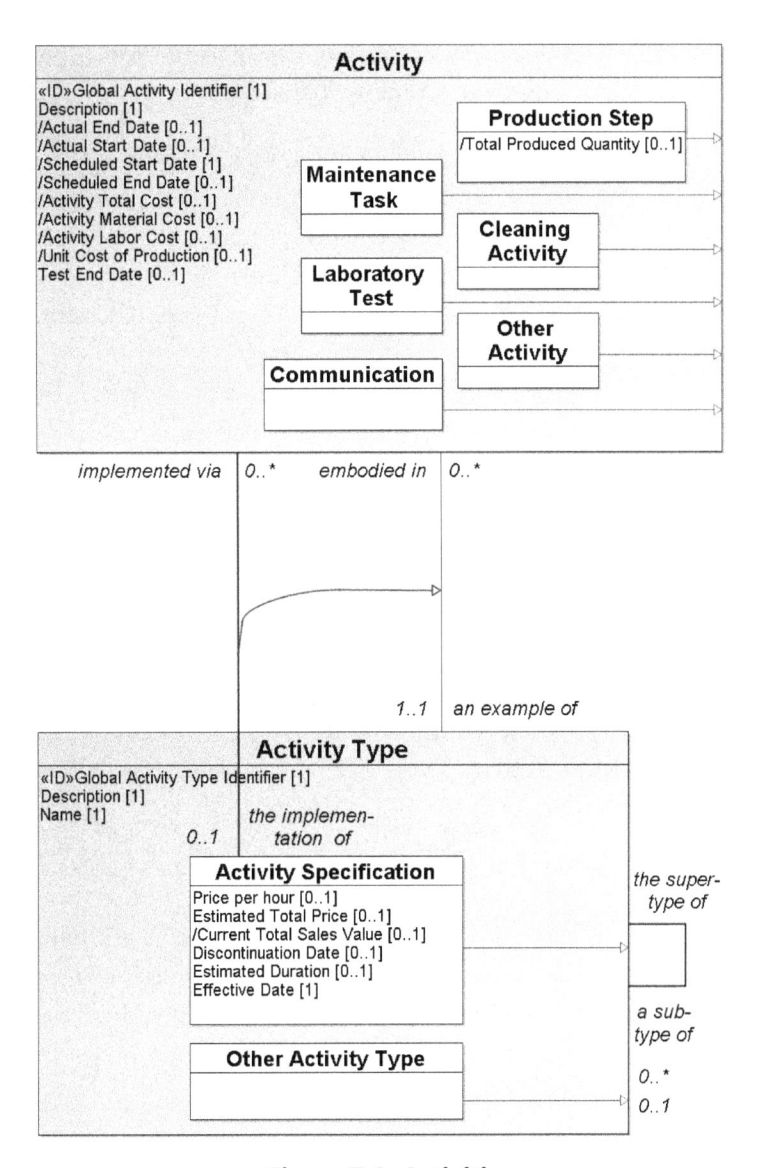

Figure 7-1: Activities

As with **Asset**, his part of the model adds something not in the **Party** and **Geographic Area** sections. Rather than simply classifying it, an **Activity Specification** is a more detailed kind of **Activity Type**, that provides a detailed description of how to carry out the activity. Thus, as shown in Figure 7-1, in addition to being required to be *an example of* one of its sub-types, an **Activity** may be also *the implementation of* a more detailed **Activity Specification.** An **Activity Specification** is an **Activity Type** that specifically describes an **Activity** sufficiently to offer it for sale.

156 Enterprise Model Patterns

As with **Asset**, the general categories of **Activity** shown as sub-types above are each *an example of* one and only one **Other Activity Type.**

Table 7-1 shows three sample **Activity Types**. One, "Sweep Garage on (January 9, 2010)" is simply categorized as being *an example of* the **Other Activity Type**, "Garage Cleaning". This, in turn, is *a sub-type of* the **Other Activity Type**, "Cleaning Activity". "Cleaning Activity" is an **Other Activity Type** that is a reproduction of the sub-type **Cleaning Activity.** The second **Activity**, "Sanitize Laboratory 72 on (April 19, 2010)" begins by being *the implementation of* the **Activity Description**, "Laboratory Sanitation Procedure". This, in turn, is *a sub-type of* the **Other Activity Type**, "Laboratory Cleanup", which in turn is *a sub-type of* "Cleaning Activity", which indeed is the **Other Activity Type** that **Activity** "Sanitize Laboratory 72 on (April 19, 2010)" must be *an example of*.

Similarly, "Assemble Framis on September 15, 2003" begins by being *the implementation of* the **Activity Specification**, "Framis Assembly". This, in turn, is *a sub-type of* the **Other Activity Type**, "Production Step", which indeed is the **Other Activity Type** that "Assemble Framis on September 15, 2003" must be *an example of*.

As you should have inferred by now, all of this is controlled by a business rule.

The decision about the level of specificity to use in assigning **Activity Types** to **Activities** is a matter of judgment—to be exercised by both data managers and the business community being served by the model and its resulting databases.

Table 7-1: Activity Type Structure

Activity	*an example of* **Other Activity Type**	*the implementation of* **Activity Specification**	**Activity Specification** Activity Number	*sub-type of* **Activity Type**
Sweep Garage on January 9, 2010	Garage Cleaning			Cleaning Activity
Sanitize Laboratory 72 on April 19, 2010		Laboratory Sanitation Procedure	Procedure 721-A	Laboratory Cleanup
				Cleaning Activity
Assemble Framis on September 15, 2003		Framis Assembly	Procedure 8234-A	Sub-assembly process
				Production Step

Note that attributes of **Activity** can place it either in future or actual time (**Scheduled Start Date, Actual Start Date**, and so forth.). The corresponding attribute of **Activity Specification** can only be in the future: **Estimated Duration**. The date the **Activity Specification** itself was created and discontinued are also shown as **Effective Date** and **Discontinue Date**.

Naming and Identifying Activities

Both the naming and the identification of activities depend completely on the organization. Within a manufacturing operation, the list of tasks is typically described by a single name and a single code. If this is the case, attributes **Name** and **Code** for both **Activity Type** and **Activity** might be appropriate. In the case where **Activity Types** represent services for sale, however, the structure shown in Figure 7-2 would be more appropriate.

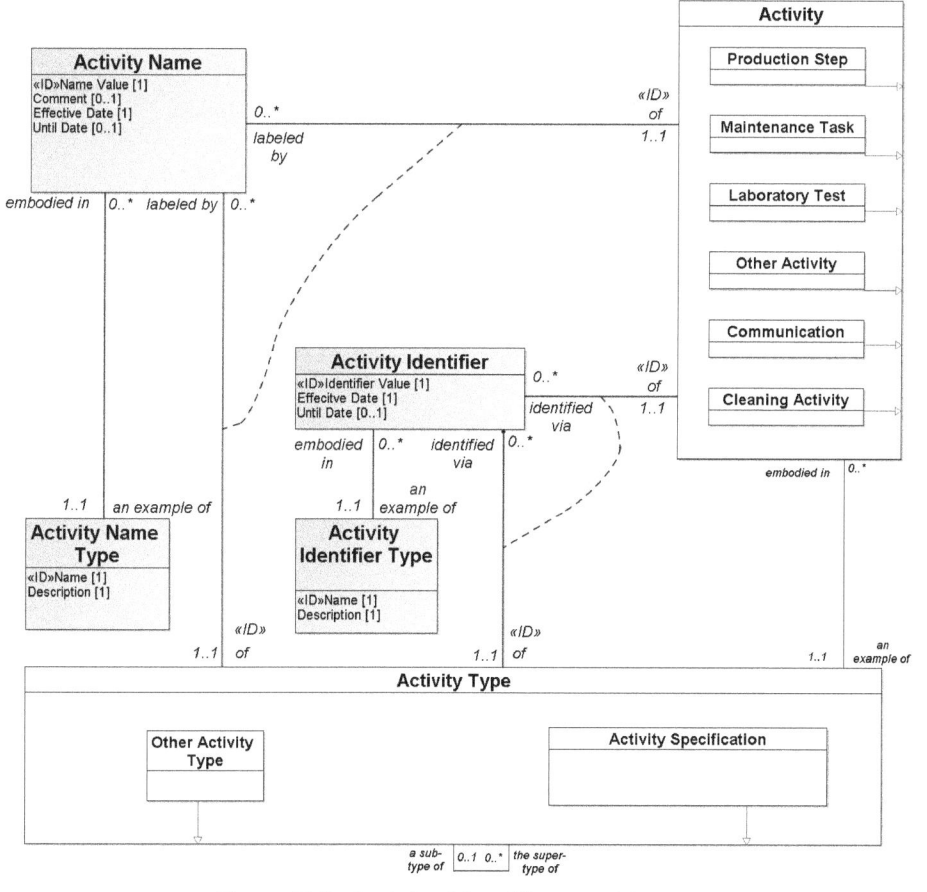

Figure 7-2: Activity Identifiers and Names

158 Enterprise Model Patterns

This permits an **Activity** or an **Activity Type** to be *labeled by* one or more **Activity Names**, depending on circumstances. Here, each **Activity Name** must be *an example of* exactly one **Activity Name Type**.

Similarly, it allows an **Activity** or an **Activity Type** to be *identified via* one or more **Activity Identifiers**.

As with **Party**, **Geographic Location** and **Asset**, not every kind of identifier is appropriate for every kind of **Party**, **Geographic Location**, or **Asset**. Neither is every kind of name appropriate for every kind of **Activity**.

For this reason, in Figure 7-3, **Activity Name Assignment** is appropriate for **Activity Names** that are *an example of* a particular **Activity Name Type** to be *of* any **Activity** that is *an example of* (indirectly, at least) a particular **Activity Type**.

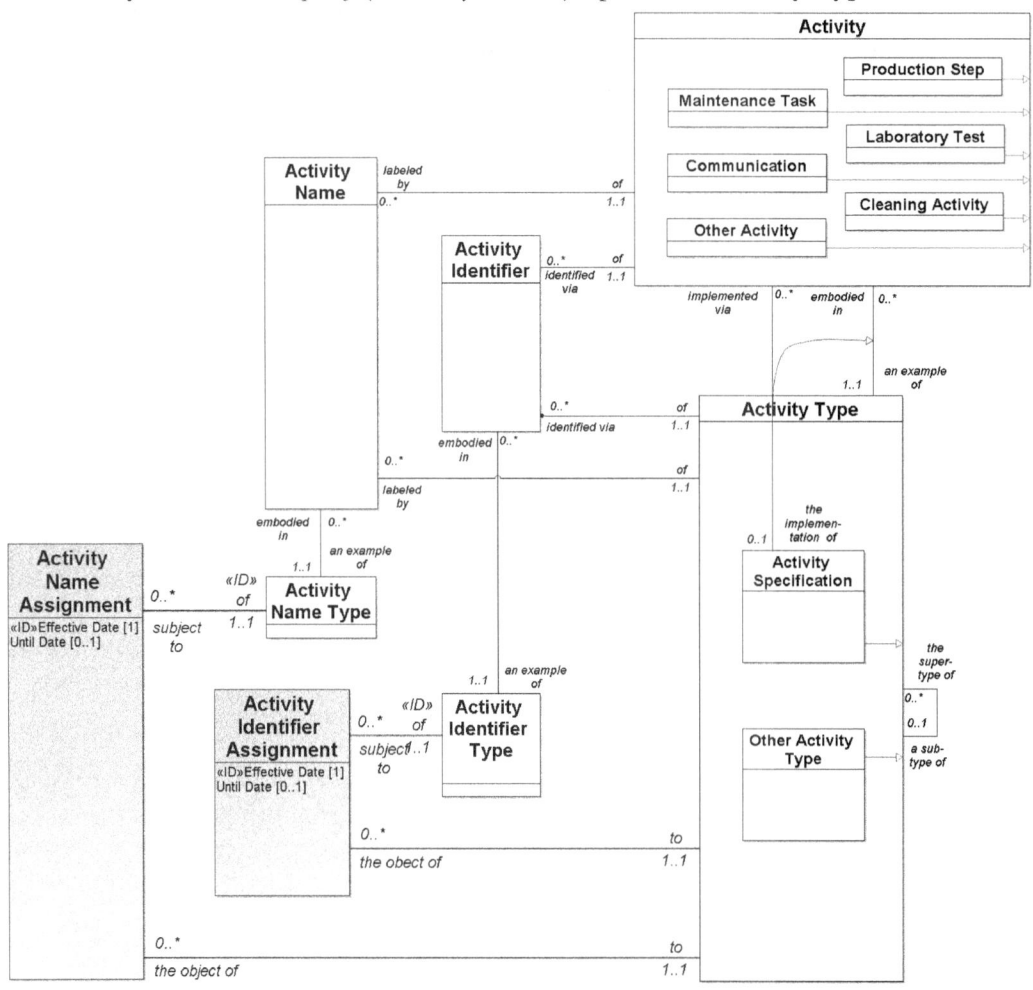

Figure 7-3: Some Activity Constraints

That is, an **Activity Name** that is *an example of* a particular **Activity Name Type** may be *constrained to* **Activities** or **Activity Specifications** that are (directly or indirectly) *an example of* a specified **Activity Type**.

Similarly, **Activity Identifier Assignment** is the fact that **Activity Identifiers** that are *an example of* a particular **Activity Identifier Type** may be applied to **Activities** or **Activity Specifications** that are (directly or indirectly) *an example of* a specified **Activity Type**.

Dividing up Activities

At least two approaches can be taken to organizing activities:

- Explicitly describe pieces of **Activities** as **Activity Steps** and collections of **Activities** as **Projects** (or whatever you want to call them).
- Treat all **Activities** homogenously, and simply recognize that any **Activity** (or **Activity Specification**, for that matter) may be associated with another **Activity** (or **Activity Specification**).

Approach 1 – Steps and Projects

Figure 7-4 shows the first approach. This approach treats an **Activity** as a larger chunk of work, composed of **Activity Steps**. Figure 7-4 adds **Activity Step** and **Activity Specification Step** to show this at both levels. An **Activity Step** is a subdivision of an **Activity** that is the execution of a particular task. An **Activity Specification Step** is a component of an **Activity Specification** that describes how part of the **Activity Specification** is to be carried out.

The constraints on the relationships and the recursive relationships allow us to say:

- Each **Activity** may be *composed of* one or more **Activity Steps**.
- Similarly, each **Activity Specification** may be *composed of* one or more **Specification Steps**.

Implicit in this approach is the idea that an **Activity** or an **Activity Step** may not be *part of* more than one **Activity**.

Also in this approach is the notion that a larger, more complex activity may be called a **Project**. This is different from an **Activity** in that it typically involves many more people, resources, and time. In terms of the constraint shown in Figure 7-4,

Enterprise Model Patterns

- Each **Activity** may *part of* one and only one **Project**.

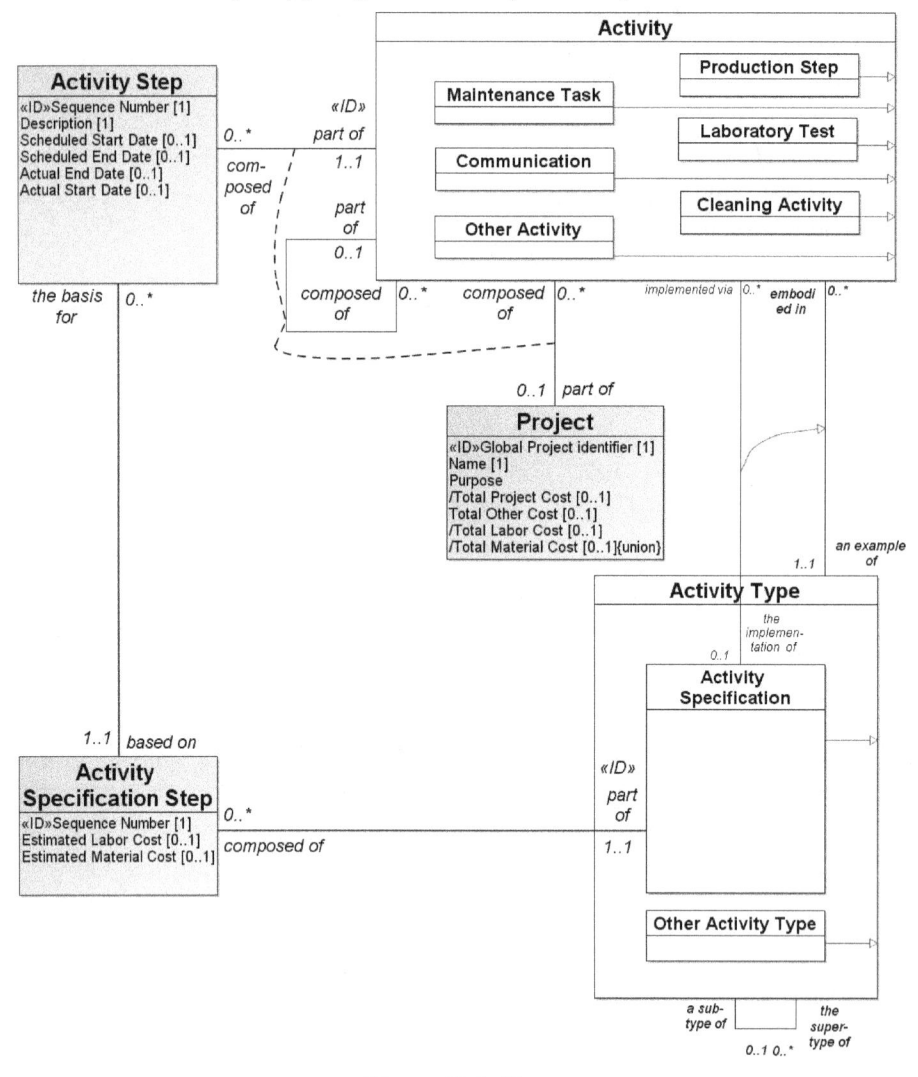

Figure 7-4: Steps

The model doesn't show this, but it is possible that a **Project** is described in a **Project Specification**, but it is rare for projects to be standardized. If you have that in your organization, the model can be easily expanded.[*]

---

[*] Of course, some organizations have "Programs" in addition to (or instead of) "Projects". All that is intended here is to show that some really big activities are qualitatively different from other activities. This is only a pattern, and the reader is encouraged to adjust the language as necessary.

The sequence of steps described by this recursive structure, by convention, is referred to as a ***work breakdown structure***. This is described more fully in the discussion of the next approach.

Approach 2 – Activity Structures

A more general approach is shown in Figure 7-5. Here an **Activity Structure** is *the use of* a particular **Activity** *in* another **Activity**. Of particular significance is the subtype, **Work Breakdown Structure** to describe one **Activity**'s being *part of* one or more other **Activity**.

Similarly, an **Activity Type Structure** is *the use of* a particular **Activity Type** *in* another **Activity Type**. In particular, this allows a **Work Breakdown Type Structure** to describe one **Activity Type** as being *part of* one or more other **Activity Types**.

Note that this approach permits an **Activity** to be *the use in (part of)* more than one other **Activity**. Each **Activity Specification** has a similar structure.

Another kind of **Activity Structure** (and **Activity Type Structure**) is **Activity Dependence** and **Activity Type Dependence**. Figure 7-6 is a kind of ***Program Evaluation and Review Technique (PERT)*** chart, showing the sequence required for a set of **Activities**. Each line is an **Activity** (either **Specification** or **Instance**). Each circle where lines meet is an **Activity Dependence (and Activity Type Dependence)**. For example, the Figure 7-6 asserts that both activity "TT" and activity "UU" must be complete before either activity "VV" or "WW" can take place.

Table 7-2 shows sample individual instances of the dependencies shown in Figure 7-6. Note that the structure is the same for specifications and instances. Each row in the table corresponds to an instance of **Activity Dependence**. Thus, each **Activity Dependence** (shown in Figure 7-5) must be *of* one **Activity** and *on* another **Activity**.

162 Enterprise Model Patterns

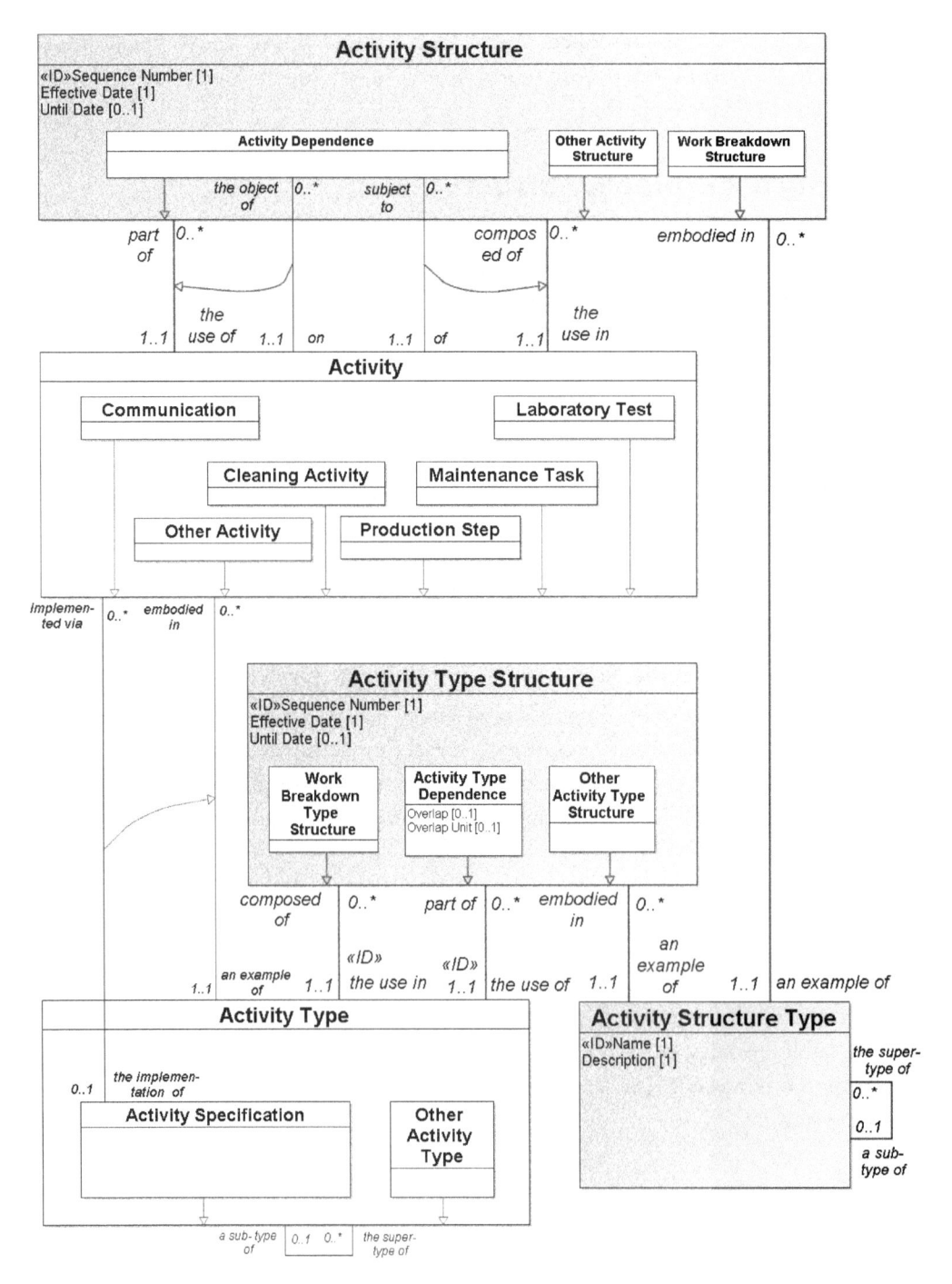

Figure 7-5: Activity Structures

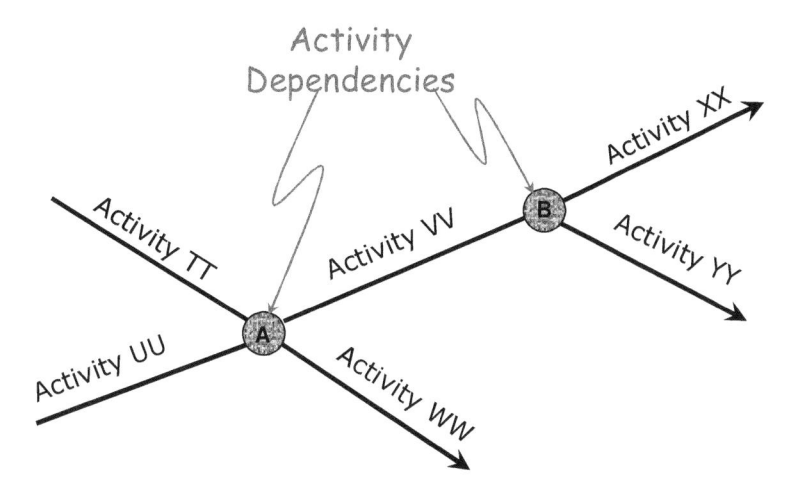

Figure 7-6: Activity Dependencies

Table 7-2: Activity Dependencies

Activity Dependency	predecessor in	successor in
A-1	Activity TT	Activity WW
A-2	Activity TT	Activity VV
A-3	Activity UU	Activity WW
A-4	Activity UU	Activity VV
B-1	Activity VV	Activity XX
B-2	Activity VV	Activity YY

Activity Characteristics

As we saw in Figure 7-1, both **Activity Type** and **Activity** have a larger number of explicit attributes that have not been seen anywhere else in this model. This has to do with placement of **Activities** in time, as well as the use of this entity class for deriving costs. (That will be described in more detail in Chapter 16, on the subject of manufacturing.) Because these are reasonably permanent and universal characteristics of activities, it is reasonable to include them as attributes. There are, however, other characteristics of activities, such as operating conditions and constraints, that are not so stable.

Examples might include `difficulty rating` for a surgical procedure, `clean room indicator` and `ambient temperature` for a precision manufacturing process, and so forth.

164 Enterprise Model Patterns

Fortunately, since we have set up **Activity Type** to record as complex a sub-type structure as necessary, the problem is easily solved. First, define an **Activity Characteristic** as a distinguishing trait, quality, or property that can be given a value for either an **Activity** or an **Activity Type**. Such characteristics are more typically defined for **Activity Specifications** that it is for **Other Activity Type**, but the latter is not out of the question, so the model accounts for it. This entity class, **Activity Characteristic**, is shown in Figure 7-7.

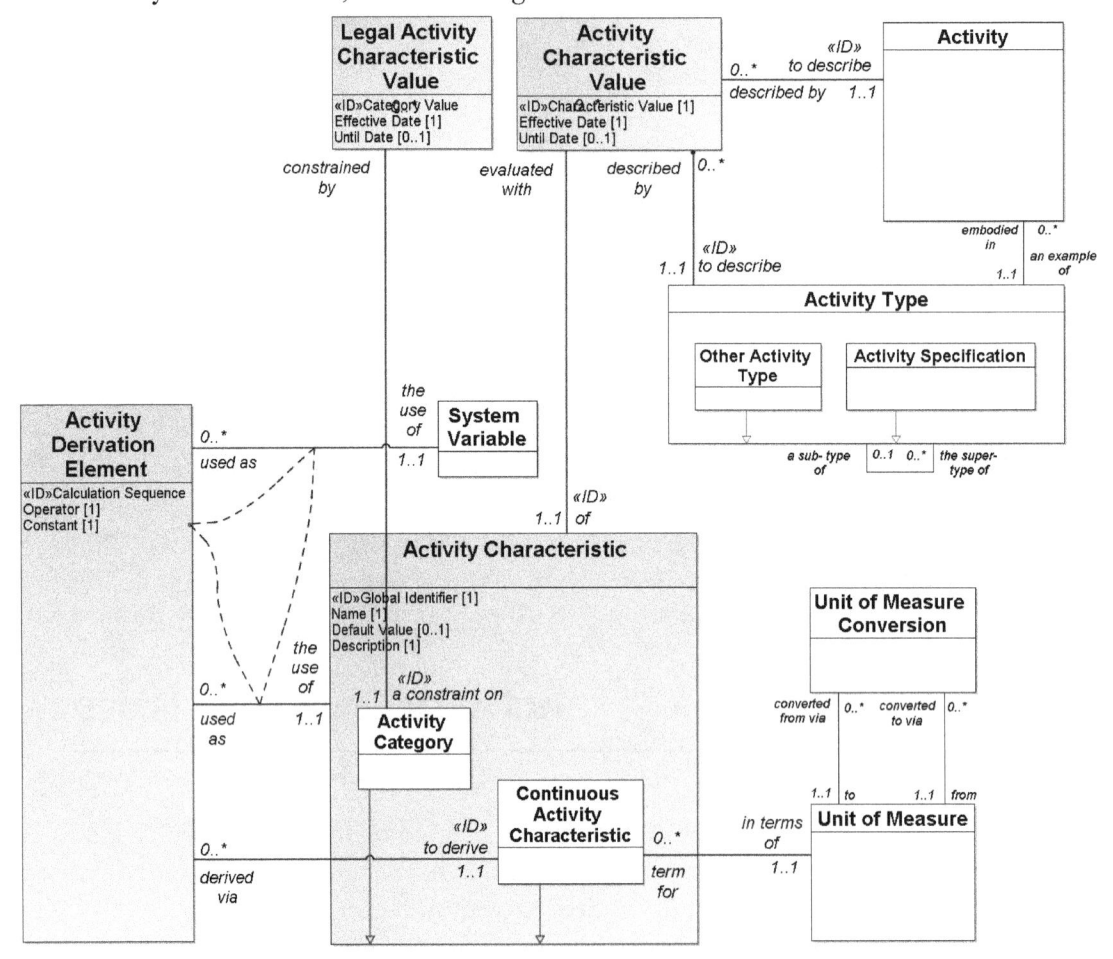

Figure 7-7: Describing Activities

As was the case in the previous chapters, an **Activity Characteristic** must be either a **Continuous Characteristic** (whose value can be any real number, piece of text, or point in time), or an **Activity Category** (also known as a "Discrete Characteristic"), whose value must be selected from a list of **Legal Activity Characteristic Values**. Note the following Business Rules:

Activity Characteristic Value is the fact that a particular **Activity Characteristic** is *evaluated with* a Characteristic Value *to describe* a particular **Activity** (or **Activity Specification**), during a specified time period.

Of course, each **Continuous Activity Characteristic** must be described in terms of a **Unit of Measure**. A basic **Unit of Measure** will be recorded for each **Activity Characteristic**, but if values are to be reported in a different one, **Unit of Measure Conversion** contains the Factor and, if necessary, a Constant to convert one to another. For example, the **Activity Characteristic** "ambient temperature" of the **Activity Specification** "tend greenhouse" could be recorded in terms of the **Unit of Measure** degrees "Fahrenheit". But if a value has to be reported in degrees "Celsius", the **Unit of Measure Conversion** *from* "Fahrenheit" to "Celsius" would have a "Factor" with the value of ".5555" and a Constant with the value of "-17.776". To go from "Celsius" to "Fahrenheit" requires a Factor of "1.8" and a Constant of "+32".

Business Rules

- If an **Activity Characteristic Value** is *of* an **Activity Category**, the Characteristic Value of that **Activity Characteristic Value** must equal the Category Value of a **Legal Activity Category Value** (if any exist) that is *for* the **Activity Category** involved. *(Translation:* An **Activity Characteristic Value** for an **Activity Category** must conform to the constraints on that **Activity Category**.)

- If an **Activity Characteristic Value** is *of* a **Continuous Activity Characteristic**, and if values are given for Minimum Value and/or Maximum Value, the Characteristic Value of that **Activity Characteristic Value** must be greater than the Minimum Value and/or less than the Maximum Value specified. *(Translation:* An **Activity Characteristic Value** for a **Continuous Activity Characteristic** must be within any minimum or maximum constraints defined for that **Characteristic**.)

Derived Characteristics

Note that Figure 7-7 also shows **Activity Derivation Element**. As with the previous sections of the enterprise model, some **Activity Characteristics** (specifically some **Continuous Activity Characteristics**) may be derived from other **Activity Characteristics**.

For example, the "Actual Duration" of an **Activity** is derived by subtracting the **Actual End Date** from the **Actual Start Date**. This is shown using the ***Reverse Polish Notation*** approach in Table 7-3.

There, to calculate "Actual Duration" for an instance of **Activity**, the first element is "Actual End Date", and the **Operator** is "add". Thus, the "Actual End Date" *of* the **Activity Characteristic Value** *to describe* the **Activity** involved is added to the registry. The second element is "Actual Start Date", with the **Operator** "subtract". Thus, the "Actual Start Date" *of* the **Activity Characteristic Value** *to describe* the **Activity** involved is subtracted from the registry. The registry now contains the calculated value for "Actual Duration".

Table 7-3: Activity Derivation Elements

to derive **Characteristic**	the use of **Characteristic**	the use of **System Variable**	(the use of) **Constant**	Operator
Actual Duration	Actual End Date			Add
Actual Duration	Actual Start Date			Subtract

As with identifiers and names, if an **Activity Characteristic Value** is *to describe* an **Activity Specification**, it is probably only appropriate for specific **Activity Types**. Similarly, if an **Activity Characteristic Value** is *to describe* an **Activity**, it is probably only appropriate for specific **Activity Specifications**.

For example, the **Continuous Activity Characteristic** "Actual Press Speed" recorded for the **Activity** "Produce 4' by 6' Aluminum Sheets" is only appropriate for the **Activity Type** "Run Presses". Similarly, the **Continuous Activity Characteristic** "Drip Rate", recorded for the **Activity Specification** "Water Bushes" is only appropriate for **Activity Type** "Garden Maintenance".

Figure 7-8 shows the entity class **Activity Characteristic Assignment**—the fact that a particular **Activity Characteristic** is only appropriate for a particular **Activity Type** or a particular **Activity Specification**.

Activities 167

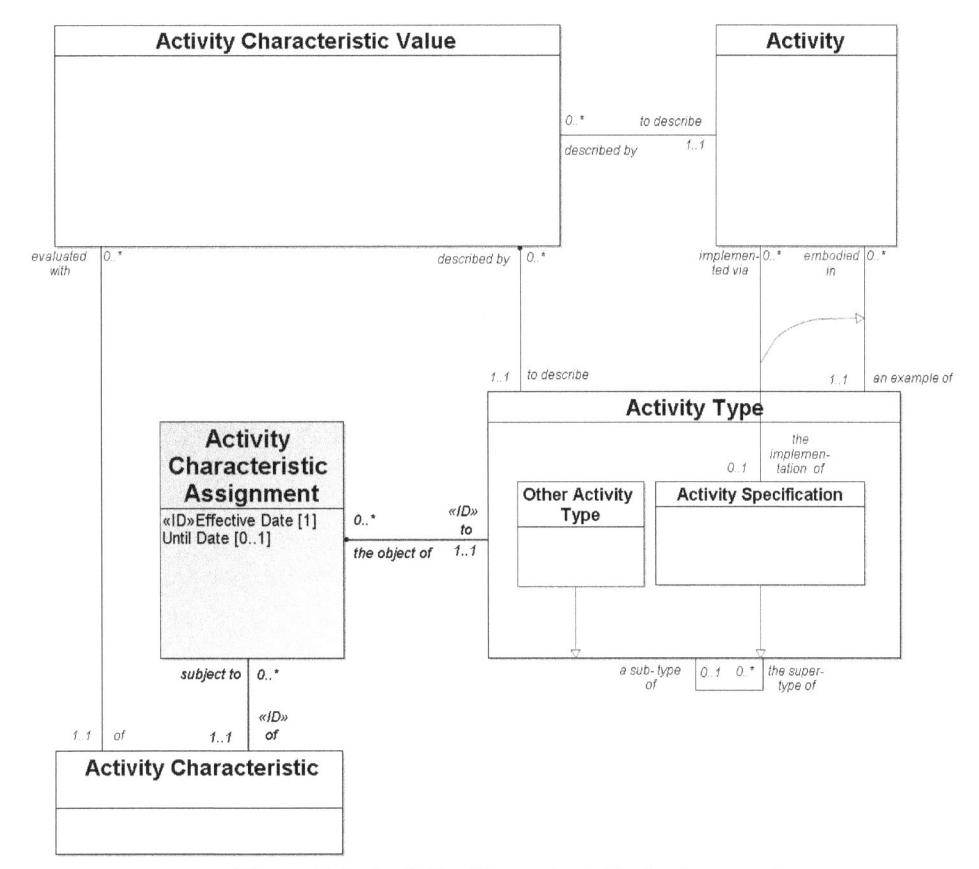

Figure 7-8: Activity Characteristic Assignments

Business Rules

- An Activity may only be *described by* an Activity Characteristic Value *for* an Activity Characteristic if that Activity Characteristic is *subject to* an Activity Characteristic Assignment *to* the Activity Specification that is *the specification of* the Activity in question. (**Translation**: Activity Characteristic Assignment assures that any Activity Characteristic Value that describes an Activity is appropriate for the Activity Specification that the Activity is *the implementation of*.)

- An Activity Specification may only be *described by* an Activity Characteristic Value *for* an Activity Characteristic if that Activity Characteristic is *subject to* an Activity Characteristic Assignment *to* the Activity Type that is *embodied in* the Activity in question. (**Translation**: Activity Characteristic Assignment assures that any Activity Characteristic Value that describes an Activity Specification is appropriate for the Activity Type that the Activity Specification is *an example of*.)

Events

If an activity describes something happening over time, an **Event** is something that happens at a single point in time.

An event is something that happens, either within the organization, under its control (an **Internal Event**), or out in the world, outside its control (an **External Event**). An **Event** causes **Activities** to be performed.

For example, **External Events** might be a particular customer's decision to buy a particular kind of suit, or the arrival of a shipment of towels. As shown in Figure 7-9, an **Event** may be *the cause of* one or more **Triggers**, each of which must in turn be *the cause of* one or more **Activities**, such as processing that sale or receiving that shipment. For example, an **Event** might be a customer's decision on June 18, 2007 to buy a suit. This, in turn, could have been *the cause of* four **Triggers**, each *of* an **Activity**:

- Helping the customer select a suit.
- Processing of the sale.
- Processing a credit card.
- Wrap and provide the suit.

Each of these subsequent **Activities** may then be *the cause of* one or more **Internal Events**. Thus, an **External Event** can trigger one or more **Activities**, each of which plays the part of an **Internal Event**, which in turn triggers more **Activities**, and so forth.

In advance, it is possible to define an **Event Specification**, such as a hypothetical customer's decision to buy a suit. The **Event Specification**, then, would include specification of the **Trigger Specifications** expected, and the **Activity Specifications** expected to be triggered by them. That is, each **Event Specification** may be *the normal cause of* one or more **Trigger Specifications**, each of which must be *the normal cause of* an **Activity Specification**. An **Activity Specification** may then be *the standard cause of* more **Activity Specifications**.

Ideally, each actual **Trigger** is *described by* a **Trigger Specification** although the actual response to an **Event** may not be according to specifications.

Activities **169**

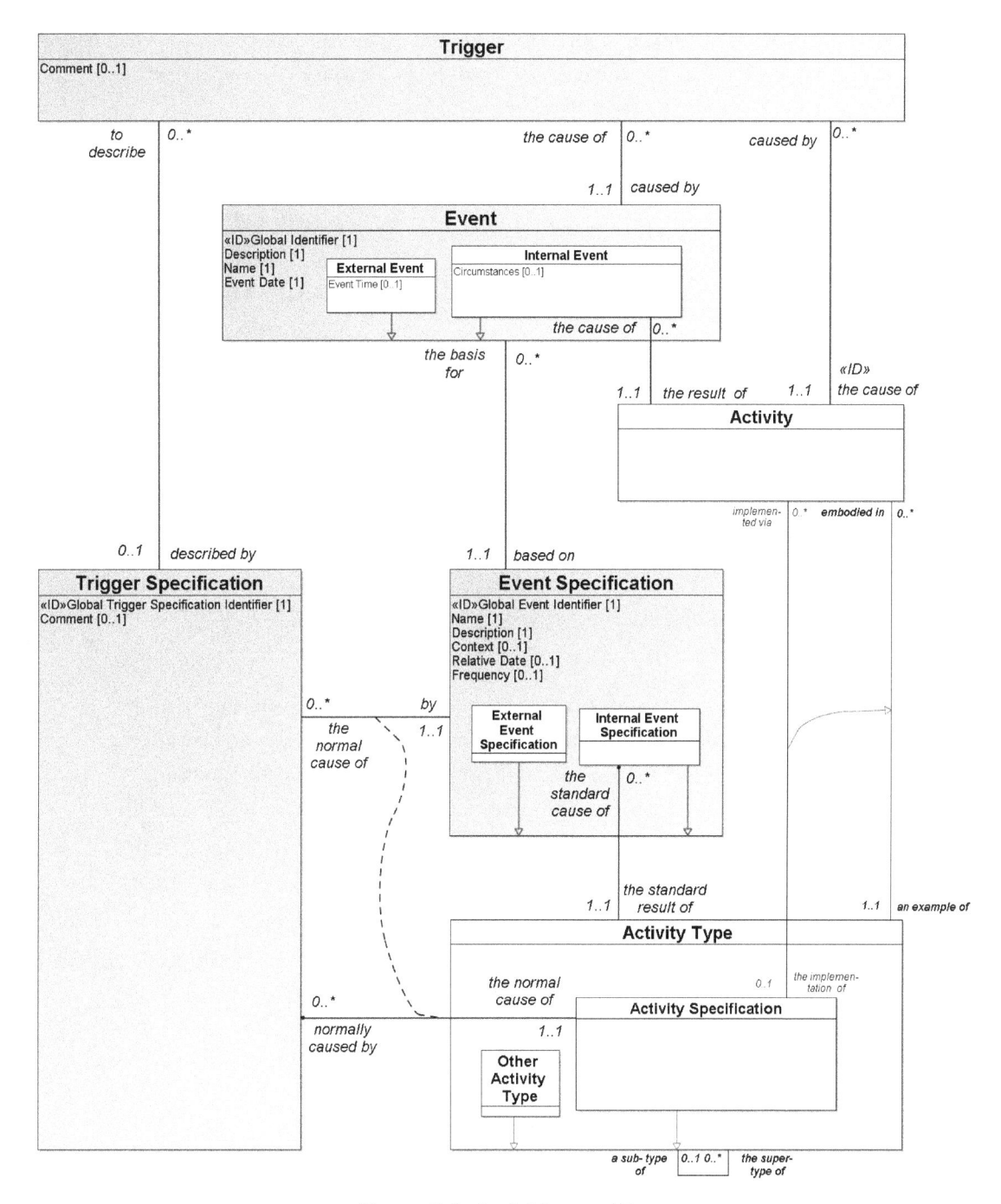

Figure 7-9: Activities and Events

Note the distinction between an **Internal Event** (or **Internal Event Specification**) and an **External Event** (or **External Event Specification**): An **External Event** is something that happens in the world—outside the company's control. An **Internal**

Event is *the result of* an **Activity** itself. Either kind of **Event** may be *the cause of* one or more **Triggers**, each of which is *the cause of* an **Activity**. A corresponding behavior is true of the **Event Specification**.

Specifically, an **External Event Specification** could be `"A Person asks for a job."` This would be *the normal cause of* a **Trigger Specification** *of* an **Activity Specification**. In this example, this would, in turn, be *the standard cause of* an **Internal Event Specification** that is *the normal cause of* (for example) two **Trigger Specification**s: one would be *the normal cause of* the **Activity Specification** `"provide job application to fill out"`; and the other would be `"Review resume"`. With this set of specifications in place, an actual **External Event**, `"Charlie Sheen applies for a job"`, can trigger actual **Activities** and **Internal Events** patterned after the specifications just described.

Activity Roles

People and organizations play various kinds of roles in carrying out activities (as shown in Figure 7-10):

- If the **Activity** is a **Communication**, then the **Activity Role** sub-type of a **Communication Role** determines whether the **Party** `"originated"`, `"received"`, or simply `"participated in"` the communication.
- If the **Activity** is a **Production Step**, that is producer of an asset, then the **Activity Role** may be a **Direct Action**, recording the actual **Hours Worked** on the **Production Step** between the **Effective Date** and the **Until Date** of the **Activity Role**.
- Regardless of the kind of **Activity** that is involved, a **Person** (less commonly, an **Organization**) can play a **Management** role.
- Of course there are **Other Activity Roles** available as well.

Activities 171

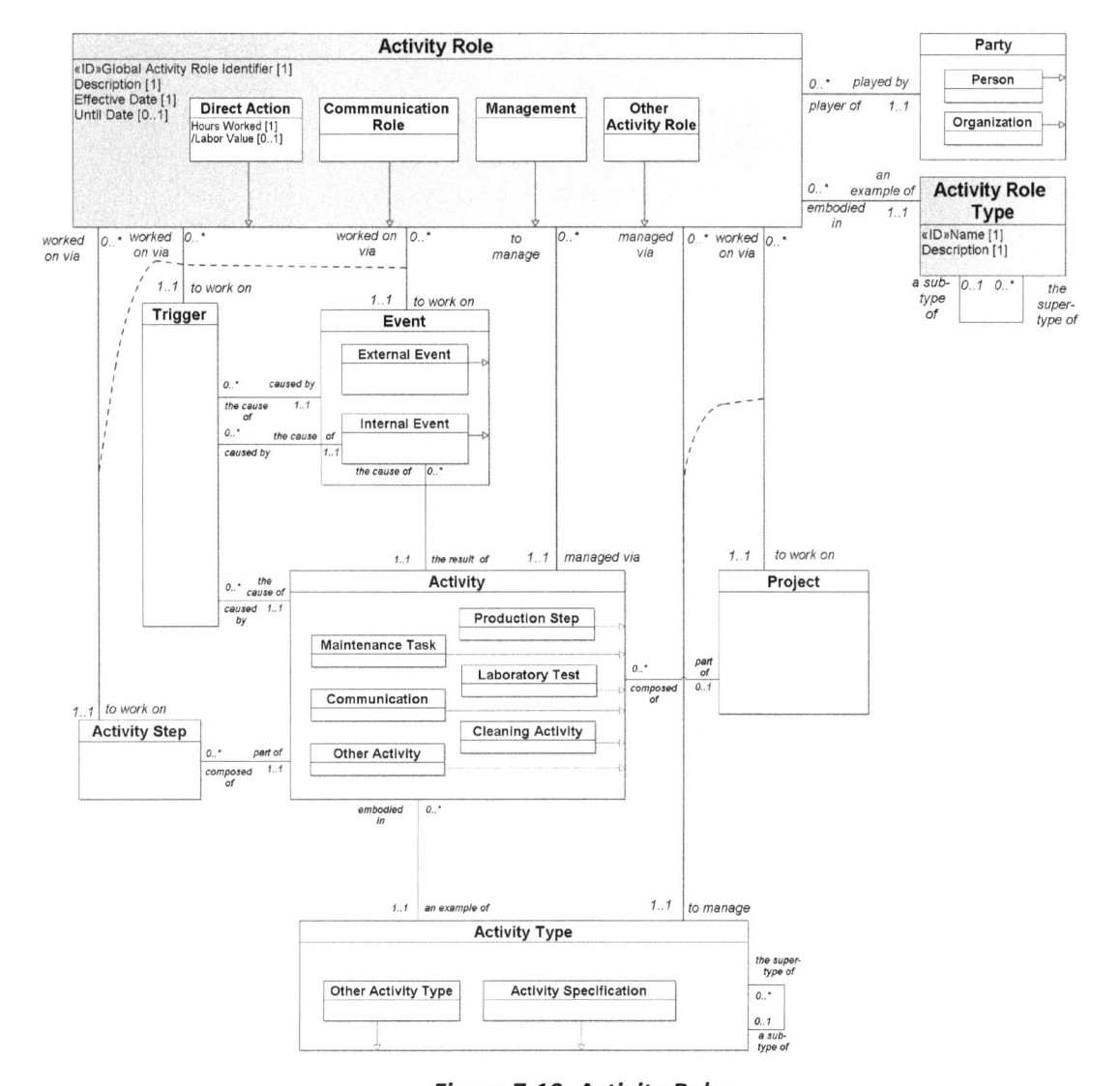

Figure 7-10: Activity Roles

Summary

Unlike the categories seen so far in this Enterprise Model, only **Activities** take place in time. In a similar structure to that of **Assets**, **Other Activity Type** is a fundamental category, and **Activity Specification** lays out a description of what an actual **Activity** is expected to involve. Here, however, the **Activity Specification** lays out the expected time and cost of the effort, while the actual activity ultimately describes the actual start and end dates involved.

Activity Structure includes not just component **Activities** (**Work Breakdown Structure**), but **Activity Dependence** as well. That is, not only is it important to know that the "Assemble bicycle" requires the **Activity** "Add front wheel to frame" and the **Activity** "Assemble front wheel from hub, spokes and rim", it is also important to know that the **Activity** "Assemble front wheel from hub, spokes and rim" must come *before* the **Activity** "Add front wheel to frame". The sequence of steps in dependency order is often called a ***Program Evaluation and Review Technique (PERT) chart***.

Note that both the work breakdown structure and the PERT chart can be described both for an **Activity Specification** (what is supposed to happen, and in what order), and for the **Activity** itself (what actually happened).

The structure of **Activities** and **Activity Specification** can be described in terms solely of big and small **Activities** (each **Activity (Specification)** may be *composed of* one or more **Activity (Specification) Structures** each of which must be *the use of* another **Activity (Structure)**. Alternatively, some medium-sized **Activity (Specification)s** may be *composed of* one or more **Activity Steps**.

As with **Parties**, **Geographic Areas**, and **Assets**, each **Activity Type** and/or **Activity** may be *subject to* one or more **Activity Characteristic Assignments**, each *to* one **Activity Characteristic**. An **Activity Characteristic** is a distinguishing trait, quality, or property that can be given a value for either an **Activity Specification** or an **Activity**. An **Activity**, then may be *given* one or more **Activity Characteristic Values**, each of which must be *of* an **Activity Characteristic**.

As with the other **…Characteristics**, some may be derived from others. This is represented using the ***Reverse Polish Notation***.

CHAPTER 8

Timing (When)

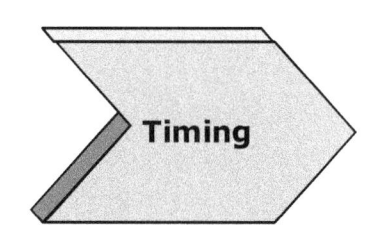

Capturing the time dimension in a data model is either very straight-forward or very tricky, depending on your point of view. In most cases, an entity/relationship model that is simply representing the structure of a business—for an operational data store or a data warehouse—time can be handled well with attributes of the transactions.

Capturing Time with Attributes

Figure 8-1 shows **Event**, whose instances are located in points of time via the attribute **Event Date**. It also shows **Activity**, which has two sets of locations in time—**Scheduled** and **Actual**. The attributes **Scheduled Start Date** and **Scheduled End Date** show when the activity is *expected* to happen, and the attributes **Actual Start Date** and **Actual End Date** show when it *actually* happened.

In support of efforts to build "dimensional" models, however, it is worth exploring (at least for a bit) the use of entity classes to represent time. The two approaches are described in detail in the next two sections.

174 Enterprise Model Patterns

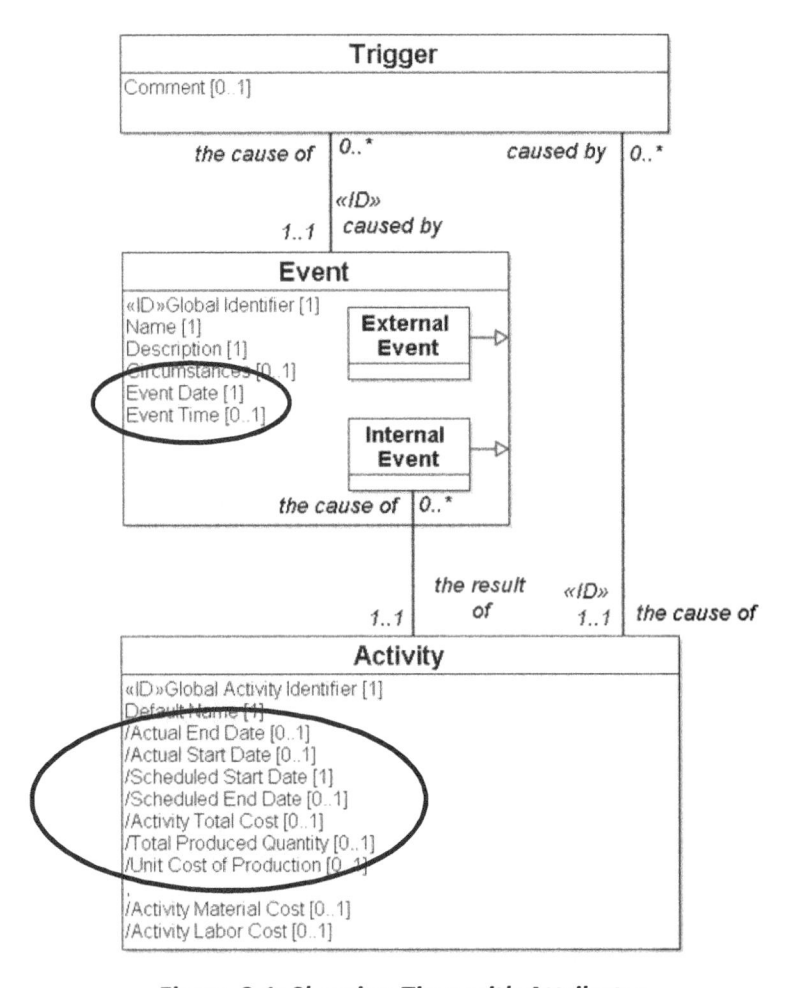

Figure 8-1: Showing Time with Attributes

Capturing Time with Entity Classes

In principle, these attributes could be on every entity class, including such reference entity classes as **Party** and **Asset Specification**. There is a continuum, however, between maintenance of such reference data, which is properly done by data administration, and maintenance of the data that are central to operations, which is properly done by the business people responsible for the data. In the latter case, it is appropriate to make the effective dates visible. In the former case, this is less important (although behind the scenes, this information should, in fact, be kept).

Timing

In the context of a data warehousing environment, when data are extracted to be placed in **data marts**, typically organized around a **fact** table, with one or more dimensions, Time becomes a thing of significance in its own right.

In the central data warehouse, a shipment is associated with a line item, which links it to, on one hand, the **Asset Specification** being supplied, and on the other hand, the **Parties** doing the shipping and receiving the shipment. These are dimensions in the dimensional data base. The analyst can retrieve shipments by product and by customer fairly easily. But what about time? What if a customer wants to know what was shipped in July, 2007?

The query could use a Boolean expression, but all other queries work by navigating the dimensional paths. An orderly universe requires that the time dimension be treated the same way as the who, what, where, and how (even though time really is a completely different dimension).

Figure 8-2 shows **Event**, which takes place at a point in time, and **Activity**, which not only takes place over a duration of time, but can also be represented as taking place over a *future* duration of time. Showing this via attributes is simple enough, but it is, as well, fairly straight-forward to imagine these attributes as relationships pointing to specific instances of **Date**.

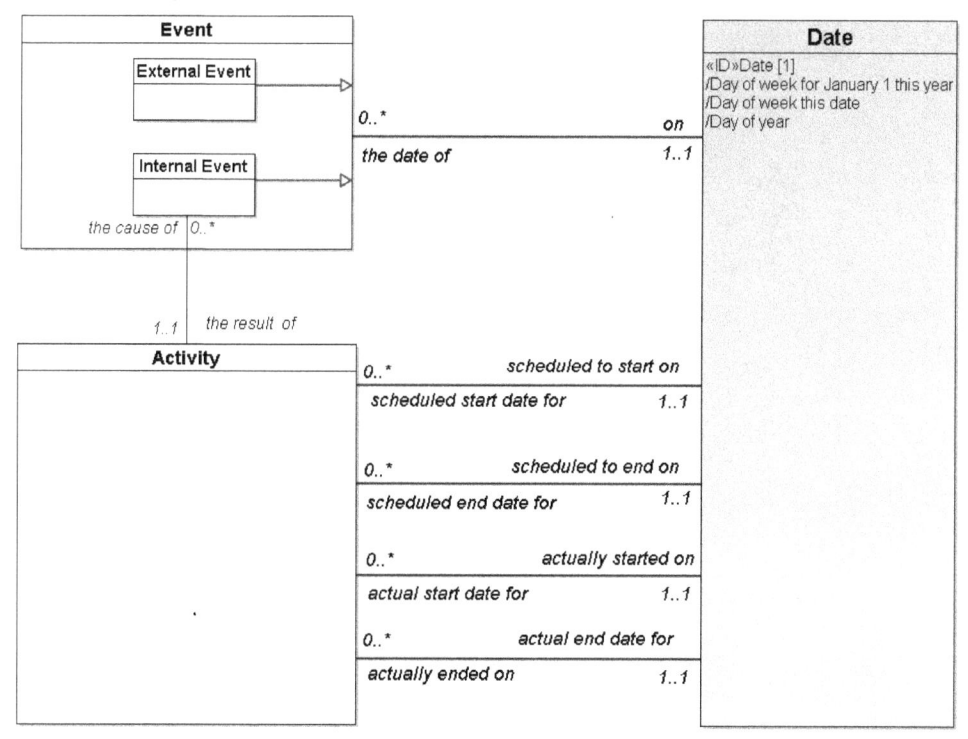

Figure 8-2: Showing Time with Entity Classes

176 Enterprise Model Patterns

In this drawing, each reference to time is rendered as a relationship to **Date**, with its one attribute **Date**. Note that the effect of this is to have each instance represent a particular day, with the month and year attached as reference data. But what is this **Date**? It is, in fact, a fairly complex structure, encompassing **Month, Day,** and **Year**. Again, with the entity class approach, each of these concepts is shown as an entity class in Figure 8-3. Here, an instance of **Day**, such as `"June 7, 1974"` must be *in* a **Day of Month** (`"7"`), a **Month** (`"6"`, indirectly), and a **Year** (`"1974"`). This version of the model makes the assertion that an **Event** is *on* a single **Day**. It does, however, provide the ability to be less specific and assert only that the **Event** was *occurring during* a **Month** (*in* a **Year**), or simply that an **Event** is *occurring during* a **Year**. That is, each **Event** must be either *on* a particular **Day**, *occurring during* a particular **Month**, or *occurring during* a particular **Year**.

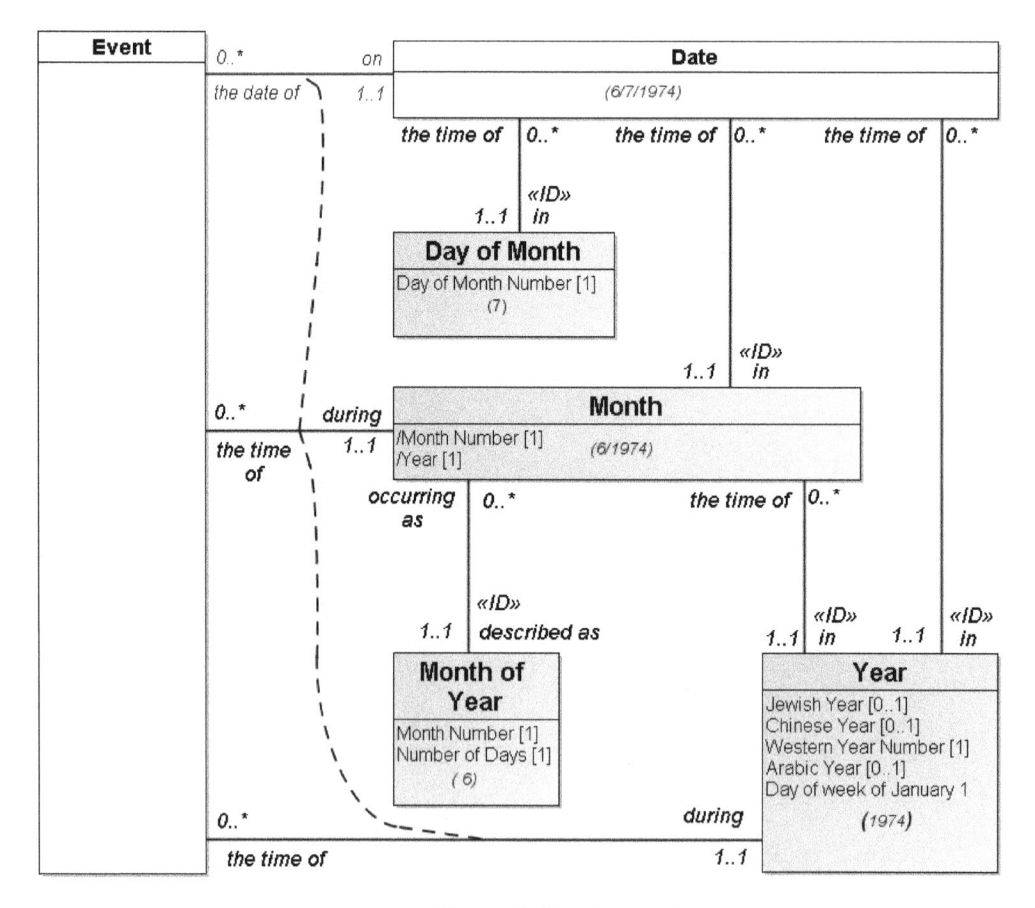

Figure 8-3: A Date

Aside from the absolute positioning of a **Day** in time, the entity classes in Figure 8-4 show information that can be derived from the basic facts:

- **Day of Year** can be calculated based on the **Number of Days** of each month until this point "`(31+28+31+30+31)`", plus the **Day of Month** of this **Day** "`(7)`".
- **Day of Week Day of Week Number** is calculated as

Day of week of January 1

+7*MOD(day of the year,7)*7-1

In the example, "`January 1, 1974`" was a "`Tuesday (2)`", so the day of the week of the 158th day of the year (June 7, 1973) is:

MOD (158,7) = .572428

.572428*7 -1= 3

2+3 = 5 (Friday)♣

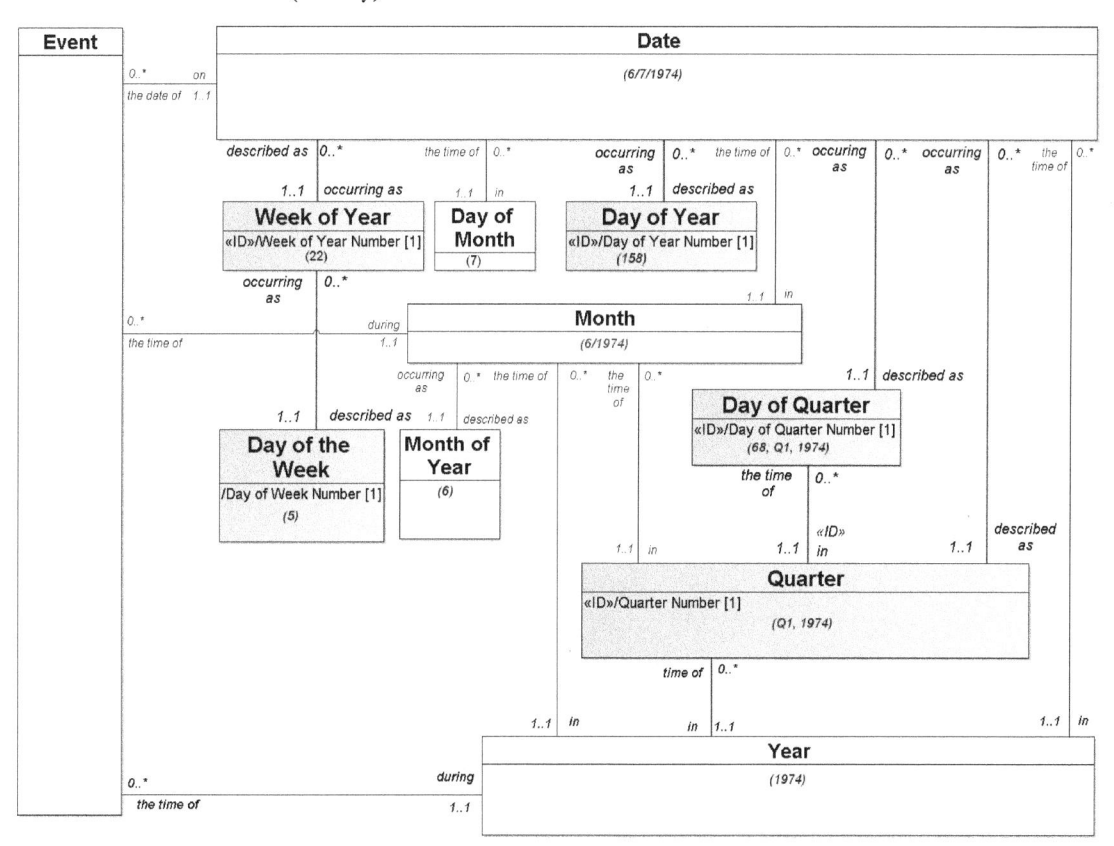

Figure 8-4: Derived Time Elements

♣ Your author did indeed marry his sweetheart on a Friday. You can look it up on http://scphillips.com/cgi-bin/day.cgi

178 Enterprise Model Patterns

Note that it is necessary to infer values from the other entity classes to **Date** and then infer them to **Day of the Week** to do the calculation there.

- **Day of Quarter** is based on the **Day of Month** plus the Number of Days in the month of the **Months** before this one in the **Quarter**. In this case, the lengths of "April (30 days)" and "May (31 days)" are added to "7" to arrive at "68".

Numbering the days of the week and the month are all very well, but what about their names? And the fact that their names are different in every language?

This is handled in Figure 8-5, where each **Day of Week Name** must be *for* a **Day of Week**, each **Month Name** must be *for* one **Month**, and each **Quarter Name** must be *for* one **Quarter**. These are all sub-types of the more general **Time Period Name**, which means that each of them must also be *rendered in* exactly one **Language**.

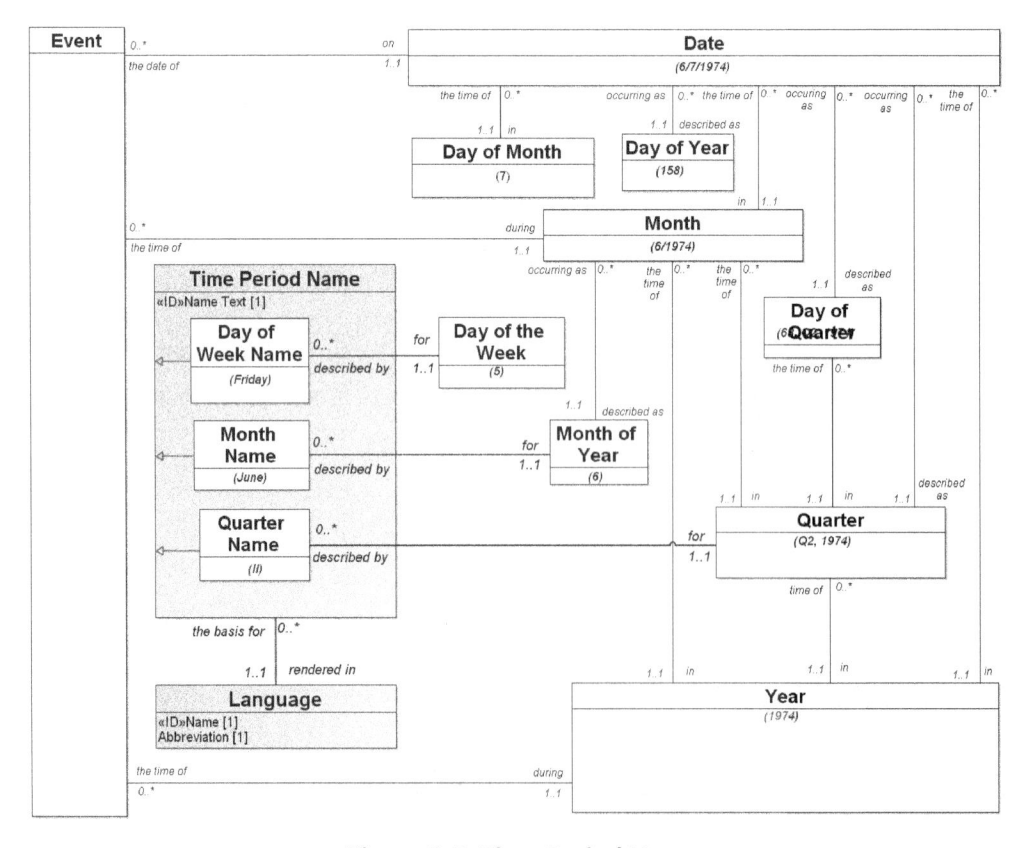

Figure 8-5: Time Period Names

In our example, the English language name for Day of Week "4" is the Day of Week Name "Thursday". The name for Month "6" is "June" in English. The name for Quarter "2" is "II".

Summary

Time is treated in data modeling in two ways:

- In a *conceptual*, *logical*, or *physical* model, it usually shows up as attributes in transaction entity classes. In the model presented in this book, the attributes are usually limited to the **Effective Date** and **Until Date**, describing the duration when the (usually **Activity**, but not always) was taking place. If it is an **Event**, there would be a **Transaction (or event) Date**, instead.

    In general, dates are not used for reference entities, although sometimes they are included as *metadata* to describe when the information was updated.

- In *dimensional models*, dates and their components are entity classes in their own right. These are not relevant for the Enterprise Model being presented here, but for those who will be implementing dimensional systems, they are included here for interest.

PART THREE

ABSTRACTION LEVEL 0: A TEMPLATE AND METADATA

After reading the first four of five chapters describing the basic Enterprise Model, the reader should have seen some patterns in place. This is not an accident. All four—parties, geographic locations, assets, and activities—reflect a single underlying structure. This underlying structure or template is, effectively, **Level 0 of abstraction**. The components, thing and thing type, structure, identifiers and names, characteristics, and roles—these provide similar structures to all four of these areas.

Part Three presents the template for those areas.

This also seems like a good place to present two "meta" models that are an important part of any company or government agency's Enterprise Model.

This is a bit of a twist on the conventional definition of metadata: *the data that describe the structure and workings of an organization's use of information, and which describe the systems it uses to manage that information.*[40]

It is the first part of this definition that concerns us. Usually, the structure and workings of an organization's use of information is described in terms of entity classes, relational tables, files, and the like. Here, however, we have other things in the organization that are describing the structure of its use of information. There are two parts of the Enterprise Model that themselves refer to the same subjects as the basic Enterprise Model—at all levels of abstraction:

- ***Information Resources*** – This usually is covered under the topic of "document management", but more than documents are involved: in addition

---

[40] David C. Hay,. 2006. *Data Model Patterns: A Metadata Map*. (Boston: Morgan Kaufmann).:

to books, articles, and e-mail notes, it also includes photographs, videos, and sound recordings. All of these have the same basic characteristic—they are all *about something else*. In one sense, their physical manifestations can be inventoried and distributed like physical assets. But their physical form is not what makes them important. What is important is that each can refer to instances of any other entity class in the organization.

This means that the data model of information resources is indeed a meta model of one way information is being used in the organization.

- ***Accounting*** – Accounting (or double-entry bookkeeping, at least) is remarkable because it is itself a modeling language. Indeed, it has been modeling corporations and government agencies for several centuries longer than data modeling has been around. It takes a very different approach than data modelers in that instead of using ***entities*** and ***entity classes*** that represent things in the world, it is concerned with ***accounts*** that represent bits of value to the organization. Instead of concern for data moving from one place to another or to describe things of significance, it is concerned with money. Money is an abstraction that is used to record the movement of value from one place to another.

What this means is that a data model of accounting must therefore be a model of a modeling technique. This has some interesting implications.

This twists the conventional view of metadata, to be sure, but that seems the only way to categorize these two topics that don't fit anywhere else. Figure Three-1 visually captures this discussion.

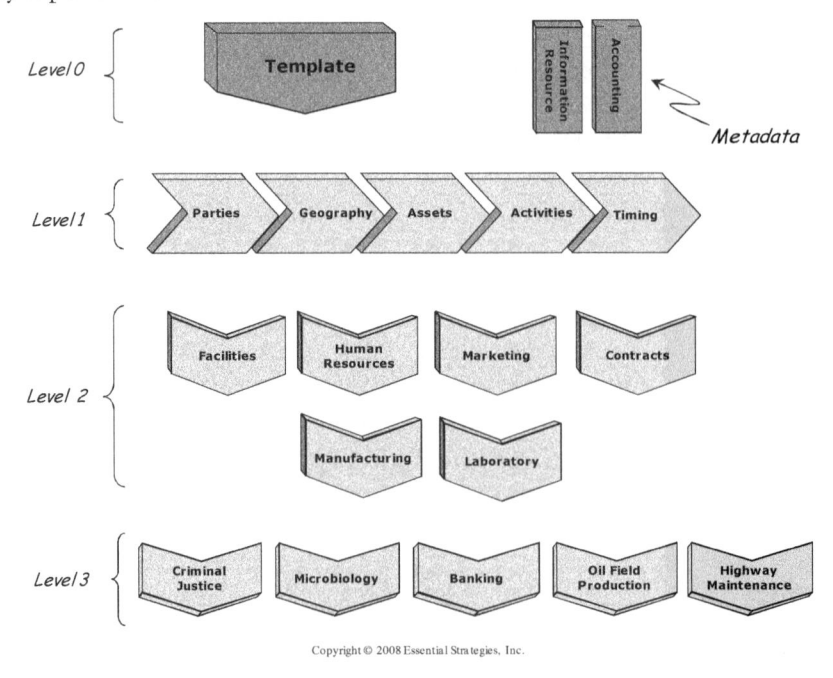

Figure Three-1: The Level 0 Components

CHAPTER 9

The Template

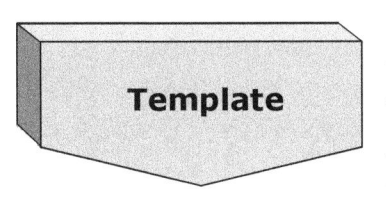

This chapter presents the pattern that was behind the first four models from Section Two: Party, Geographic Location, Asset, and Activity. If they were "Abstraction Level 1", this is one level more abstract, called here, "Abstraction Level 0."

Thing and Thing Type

Thing is a concept so fundamental that it almost defies definition. The third Merriam Webster on-line dictionary definition of **Thing** is first: "a: a separate and distinct individual quality, fact, idea, or usually entity". This is close to what we want. The second definition is narrower than will be used here: "b: the concrete entity as distinguished from its appearances".[41] For the purposes of this model, we are not limited to physical, tangible things. (Physical) **Assets** are tangible. **People** and **Organizations** and **Geographic Locations** have physical aspects, but are not tangible in this sense. **Activities** are clearly not tangible at all. This concept of **Thing** corresponds to the object-oriented community's notion of *object*, but it is constrained to these four kinds of things: **Party** (**Person** or **Organization**), **Geographic Location**, (physical) **Asset**, and **Activity**.

Figure 9-1 shows the basic template model that was the basis for organizing the four first models described in the previous Part of this book.

One attribute of the entity class **Thing** is **Description**. That is a description of this particular instance (such as "Matthew's green Volvo—with a

---

[41] Merriam-Webster. 2010. "Thing – 3.". Merriam-Webster's OnLine Dictionary. *http://www.merriam-webster.com/dictionary/thing*.

183

`Vehicle Identification Number"`). To describe a set of characteristics common to a corresponding set of instances of the **Thing**, each instance of **Thing** must be in addition *an example of* a particular **Thing Type**. A **Thing Type** is the definition of a fundamental category of **Thing** (such as `"Automobile"`). Note that this is a *fundamental* category of **Thing**. Each **Thing** may be *an example of* one and only one **Thing Type**. It may be recalled that in the specific models described in Part Two, the **…Type** entity class encapsulated the sub-types shown for the thing itself. For example, the first instances of **Party Type** listed the sub-types of **Party**—`"Person"`, `"Organization"`, `"Company"`, `"Government Agency"`, and so forth.

It is possible to imagine a large number of sub-types of **Thing Type**, whether it is a **Party Type** `"Company"`, or a **Geographic Location Type** `"Geopolitical Location"`.

In the case of **Asset** and **Activity**, there was a more specific version of **…Type** called **…Specification**. A **Thing Specification** is A **Thing Type** that describes a **Thing** sufficiently to offer it for sale. In Figure 9-1 of this chapter, this is represented by the fact that each **Thing** may also be *described by* one and only one **Thing Specification**. Each **Thing Specification** then may be *a sub-type of* one and only one **Other Thing Type**. Instances of the basic sub-types described above are in fact *an example of* an (**Other**) **Thing Type**. That is, `"Matthew's green Volvo—with a Vehicle Identification Number"` is *described by* the **Thing Specification** `"2009 Volvo Model V70"`, which is *an example of* the **Other Thing Type** `"automobile"`.

This is what would be found in a catalogue offering the **Thing** for sale. Only **Assets** and **Activities** have such **Thing Specifications**. **Parties** and **Geographic Locations** do not. Hence, the **Thing Specification** and **Other Thing Type** do not exist in the **Party** and **Geographic Area** models.

The value of **Thing Specification's** attribute Description might appear in, for example, a catalogue describing it for sale. (Imagine the brochure for the Volvo V70 describing its standard and optional features.)

In the case of **Things** that are **Parties** or **Geographic Areas**, since they are not *described via* **Thing Specifications**, they are a case of directly only being *an example of* one and only one **Thing Type**. For example, each **Party** must be either a `"Person"` or an `"Organization"`, or it could be more specifically, a `"Company"` or a `"Government Agency"`. Similarly, each **Geographic Location** must at least be a `"Geographic Area"`, a `"Geographic Point"`, a `"Geographic Solid"`, or a `"Geographic Line"`. Or it could, more specifically, be a "Geopolitical Area" or a "City". As with the ...**Type** entity classes, each **Thing Type** may be *a super-type* of one or more other **Thing Types.**

```
                          Thing
  «ID»Global Thing Identifier [1]
  Default Name [1]
  Description [1]
  Creation Date [1]
  Destruction Date [0..1]
```

the description of | 0..*   embodied in   0..*

1..1 | an example of

```
                       Thing Type
  «ID»Identifier [1]
  Name [1]          0..1   described by
  Description [1]
                       Thing Specification
                       Until Date [0..1]
                       Effective Date [1]
                                                      the super-
                                                       type of
                                                        0..*
                                                        0..1
                       Other Thing Type              a sub-
                                                     type of
```

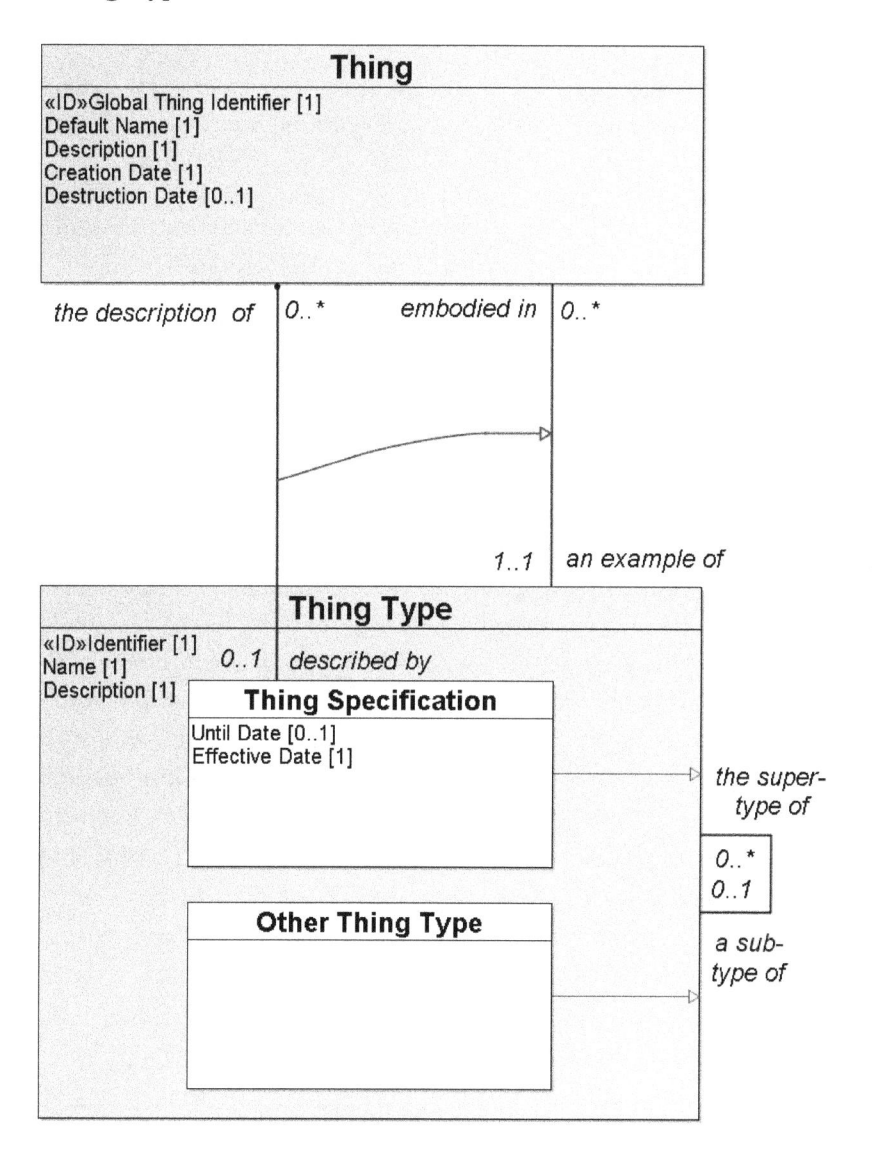

Figure 9-1: Things

In the cases where an **Asset** or an **Activity** may be *described by* an **Asset Specification** or an **Activity Specification**, each of these must be *a sub-type* (either directly or indirectly) of the **Other Asset Type** or **Other Activity Type** that corresponds to the sub-type of the **Asset** or **Activity** involved.

Hence, in the template that is Figure 9-1, each **Thing** must be *example of* one and only one **Thing Type** an may be *described by* one and only one **Thing Specification**, each of which must itself be (directly or indirectly) *a sub-type of* one and only one **Thing Type**.

This model reveals a feature of UML that is not present in other entity/relationship notations. Here we can represent the fact that a ***relationship*** can be a ***sub-type*** of *another relationship!*

This is a template for patterns, so it is two steps removed from what an actual database might look like. Still, the attributes described here are significant to the understanding of the concepts involved.

1. **Thing**
    - **Global Thing Identifier** – a computer-generated surrogate identifier. In most cases, whether it be people and organizations, products, or geography, it is extremely difficult to find natural attributes that can serve as unique identifiers. It is easier to simply assume a surrogate. This could be simply a generated sequence number in the context of a single system installation (just called "ID"), or, in the case of each of the enterprise model topics described here, it could be managed as a "Global" identifier. In this case, steps are made to assure that there is no duplication throughout the enterprise. In some cases, instances of the Thing can be identified in the context of the **Thing Specification** that it is an example of. In the case of **Physical Asset**, for example, it may be appropriate to name the identifying attribute **Serial Number**. Since serial numbers will not be unique across all the kinds of Physical Assets involved, however, this identification should also be combined with the relationship to **Asset Specification**.
    - **Name** – a name applied to this particular instance of **Thing**.
    - **Description** – Text elaborating on the nature of the **Thing**.
    - **Creation Date** – The idea is that there are tangible things described by this template, even though **Party** and **Geographic Location** are not exactly manipulated the same way that tangible **Assets** are. But in any case, there is always the concept of when the **Thing** is created, even if it is only a person's birthday.
    - **Destruction Date** – Again, this is most meaningful for **Assets**, but **Parties** do go out of existence, and **Activities** terminate, so the idea is not without relevance.

2. **Thing Specification**

   - **Thing Specification Identifier** – an identifier assigned to each **Thing (Asset** or **Activity) Specification** In the case of **Assets**, this is usually a **Model Number**, in the context of a **Brand** that it is *marketed by*. The *marketed by* relationship would also be part of the identifier. In the case of an **Activity Specification**, this could be a system-assigned surrogate key in the context of a particular company or system. If it must be unique more generally, a **Global Identifier** may be appropriate.
   - **Default Name** – a name applied to this particular instance of Thing. Note that naming is more sophisticated and subtle than can be conveyed by simple attributes, so the name structures (described for each example in Section One, and shortly in this chapter) are particularly valuable here. But having a **Default** or **Common** name as an attribute is useful.
   - **Description** – Text elaborating on the nature of the **Thing Specification**.
   - **Effective Date** – in principle, the date when the product model or service involved becomes activated. For **Activity Specification** and **Asset Specification**, this is usually the date the specification was approved, although in the case of **Physical Asset Specification** it might also be appropriate to use the date of manufacture.
   - **Until Date** – if the specification is no longer in use, this is the date it was taken out of service.

3. **Thing Type**

   - **Name** – Text identifying a **Thing Type**. Typically, there are relatively few instances of **Thing Type**, so it can be assumed that names are assigned by people and will be kept unique so that they can be used as identifiers.
   - **Description** – Text elaborating on the nature of the **Thing Type**.

Note that the attributes described here are part of the pattern. Actual attribute names (and actual attributes themselves, as well) may be different as the patterns are applied to real situations.

Things and the Enterprise Model

Figure 9-2 shows the **Thing** model expanded to include, as sub-types, references to the enterprise entities described for the enterprise model in Part Two.

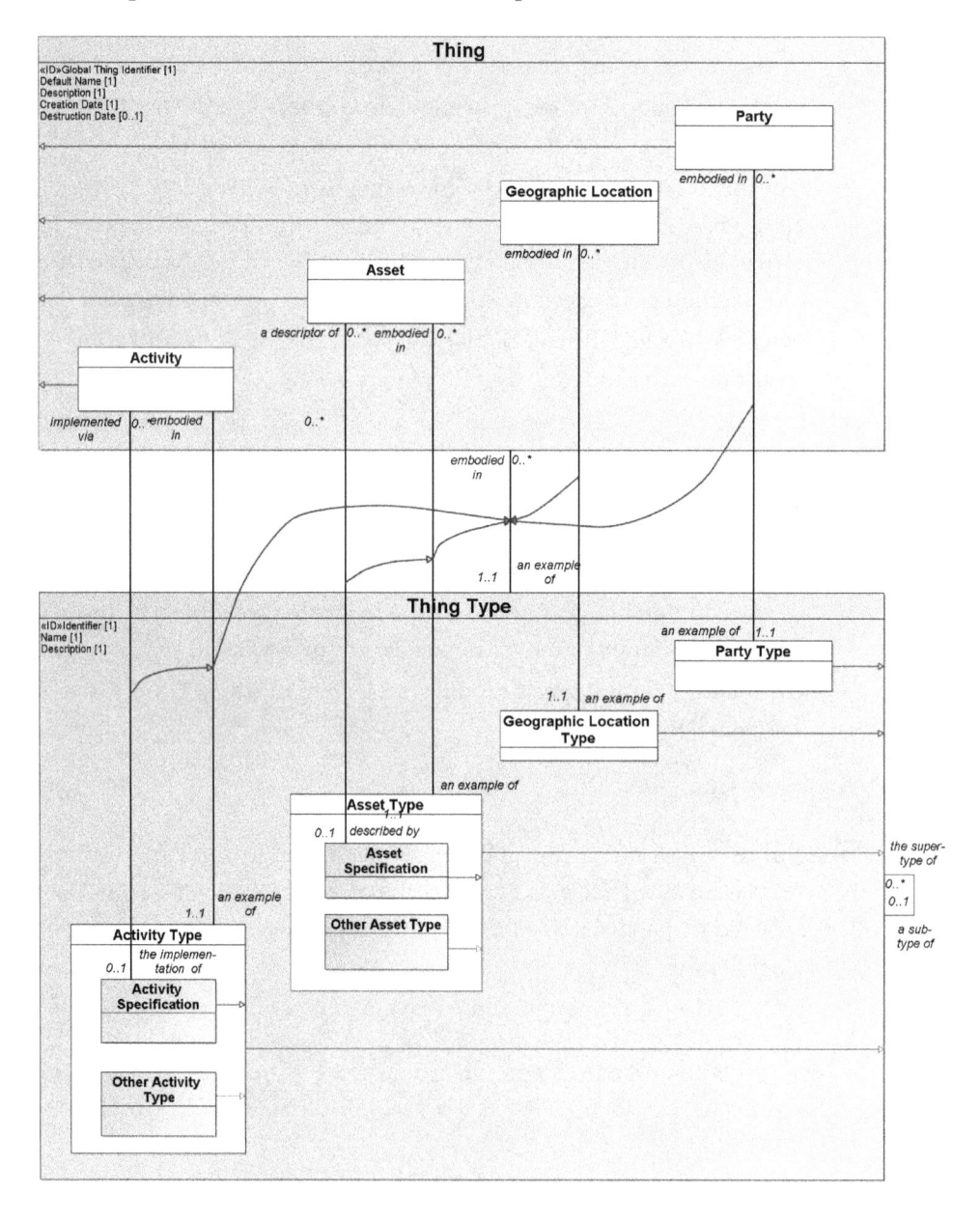

Figure 9- 2: Things and the Enterprise Model

Thing has sub-types to portray:

- Activity
- Asset
- Geographic Location
- Party

The initial instances of **Thing Type** are indeed *embodied in* **Activity Type**, **Geographic Location Type**, **Asset Type**, and **Activity Type**. In the case of more detailed categories they are instances of the more detailed **Asset Specification** and **Activity Specification**.

While the concept of **Thing Specification** is present in the models of **Assets** and **Activities**, it is not in the models of **Geographic Locations** or **Parties**. Since they are usually not specified in advance of coming into existence, neither **Geographic Location** nor **Party** have **Thing Specifications**.*

Thus, **Thing Type** has all sub-types for all four model segments:

- Activity Type
- Asset Type
- Geographic Location Type
- Party Type

Thing Specification has sub-types to portray:

- Activity Specification
- Asset Specification

The detailed relationships between the sub-types are shown in Figure 9-2.

Here, two of the relationships are sub-types of the relationship, "Each **Thing** must be *described by* one **Thing Specification**":

- Each **Asset** must be *described by* one **Asset Specification**.
- Each **Activity** must be *the implementation of* one **Activity Specification**.

---

* Ok, management areas are planned, but it's not as though there is a standard specification to draw upon, so it's not really the same thing as a specification for a computer or standard operating procedure.

That is, to say that a particular **Asset** (say, your author's `"1990 Acura Integra"`) is *described by* an **Asset Specification** (the catalogue entry for a 1990 Acura Integra), is *also* to say that that **Asset** (since it is an example of a **Thing**, after all) is *specified by* a **Thing Specification**. (The catalogue entry is also a **Thing Specification**. Similarly, the fact that the **Activity Specification** `"Instructions for folding an origami crane"` is *embodied in* the **Activity** of folding a crane that your author undertook on July 23, 2010—that fact is a sub-type of the fact that the **Item Specification**, "Instructions for folding an origami crane" is *embodied in* the **Item** that is the folding of a crane that your author undertook on July 23, 2010.

Anomaly

- In Figure 9-1, **Thing Type** had the sub-types **Thing Specification** and **Other Thing Type**. From the Level 1 chapter, it would be reasonable to have **Thing Type** to be divided into **Activity Type, Asset Type, Geographic Location Type**, and **Party Type**. The sub-type **Thing Specification** should similarly be sub-divided into **Activity Specification** and **Asset Specification.**

- But in Figure 9-2, **Activity Specification** is *not* shown as a simple sub-type of **Thing Type**. Instead it is shown as a sub-type of **Activity Type**, as it was in the Level 1 model.

- That is because these are *Patterns*. In creating a real model, you can use either the detailed set of Level 1 models, or the more general Level 0 model (Figure 9-1). In moving between levels of abstraction it is sometimes not enough simply to define sub-types. In this case it was necessary to move an entire sub-type structure across the levels of abstraction.

(The more precise relationships prevent an **Asset** from being *described by* any **Activity Specifications** and an **Activity** from being *the implementation of* any **Asset Specifications**.)

Two other relationships are sub-types of the relationship, "Each **Thing** must be *an example of* one **Thing Type**":

- Each **Geographic Location** must be *an example of* one **Geographic Location Type**.
- Each **Party** must be *an example of* one **Party Type**.

So, if **Geographic Location** "New Jersey" is *an example of* the **Geographic Location Type** "State", then by virtue of it's also being a **Thing** ("New Jersey"), it is also *an example of* the **Thing Type** ("State").

Note that, in Figure 6-1, the following assertions were made:

- Each **Thing** must be *an example of* one **Thing Type**.

  or

- Each **Thing** may be *specified by* one **Thing Specification**,

The corresponding relationships applied to **Asset**, **Asset Type**, and **Asset Specification**, as well as **Activity**, **Activity Type**, and **Activity Specification**

The issue of identification is universal. It is most difficult to address in **Person** and **Physical Asset**. In the case of **Person**, it is well nigh impossible to construct a foolproof **Universal Person Identifier** to guarantee that two people named "John Smith" aren't confused (in a Transportation Security Administration "Do not fly" list, for example). In the case of **Physical Asset**, defining a **Universal Product Code**, to guarantee that all the inventory of a product is accounted for correctly, is also challenging, but still not as much so as defining a **Global Person Identifier**. But government agencies and companies keep trying, and our structure (shown in Figure 9-2) at least provides a way to describe the problem, even if it doesn't provide a solution.

This connection to the specifics of the enterprise model applies to all the other components of each model, but they will not be described in further detail here.

Thing Relationship

As we saw in the specific examples, **Things** are related to other **Things**. Whether it is associations between **Parties**, the overlapping of **Geographic Locations**, **Physical Assets'** product structures, or the **Work Breakdown Structures** of **Activities**, all of our more detailed models made use of the structures present in Figure 9-3:

192 Enterprise Model Patterns

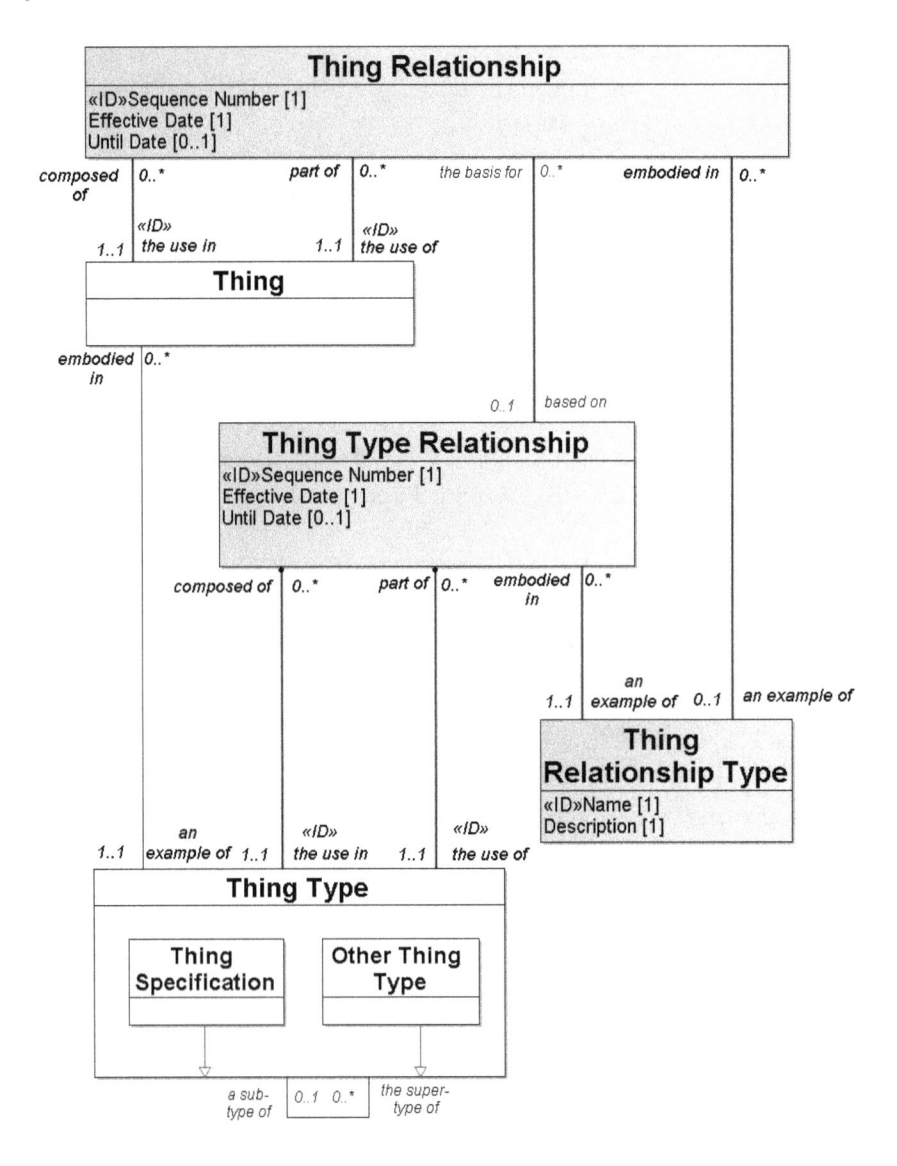

Figure 9-3: Thing Relationships

A **Thing Relationship** is the fact that an actual **Thing** is somehow associated with another actual **Thing**. This could be as a component, as in an **Asset Structure**, a functional relationship, as in an **Activity Dependence**, or another kind of association altogether. At this level, it is the fact that such an association *actually exist*s. A **Thing Type Relationship** is the fact that a **Thing** is specified as having an association with another specified **Thing** as part of its definition. At this level, it is the fact that such an association *can exist*. Both **Thing Relationship** and **Thing Type Structure** are each an *example of* a **Thing Relationship Type**.

Each **Thing Type** may be *composed of* one or more **Thing Type Relationships**, each of which must be *the use of* one other **Thing Type**. Navigating in the other direction, each **Thing Type** may be *part of* one or more **Thing Type Relationships**, each of which must be *the use in* one other **Thing Type**.

Similarly, each **Thing** may be *composed of* one or more **Thing Relationships**, each of which must be *the use of* one other (or the same) **Thing**. Navigating in the other direction, each **Thing** may be *part of* one or more **Thing Relationships**, each of which must be *the use in* one other (or the same) **Thing**.

The nature of either the **Thing Relationship** or the **Thing Type Relationship** is described for the **Thing Relationship Type** that the **Thing (Type) Relationship** is *an example of*.

Ideally, each **Thing Relationship** may be *based on* one **Thing Type Relationship**, but life isn't perfect. The reason **Thing Relationship** exists in the first place is that it cannot be assumed to be inferable from **Thing Type Relationship**.

Thing Names and Identifiers

As we've seen, the problem of how to name **Things** is not unique to any one of our principle categories. To be sure, arriving at names for **Persons** and **Geopolitical Areas** is more complex than naming **Activities** or **Geographic Points**. Still, the problem is widespread enough that it is worth including in our template, as well as in each of the individual topics. The pattern is shown in Figure 9-4. In this model, **Thing Name** is defined to be the application of a piece of text to describe one instance of **Thing** (or, for that matter, a **Thing Specification**). That is, each **Thing Name** must be *to describe* exactly one **Thing** or one **Thing Specification**, and each **Thing Name** must be *an example of* one and only one **Thing Name Type**.

Yes, the same piece of text could describe more than one **Thing**, but it is beyond the scope of this book to elaborate on that. In most cases, the name is not considered an object in its own right, although, as we have seen with **Party Name**, it can have a complex structure.

In this model, each instance of **Thing Name** is uniquely identified by a combination of the Name Text and the **Thing** it is the name of.

The set of **Thing Name Types** depends, of course, on the kind of **Thing** or **Thing Specification** involved—whether it is a **Person's** maiden name, a **Geopolitical Area's** ISO name, or whatever.

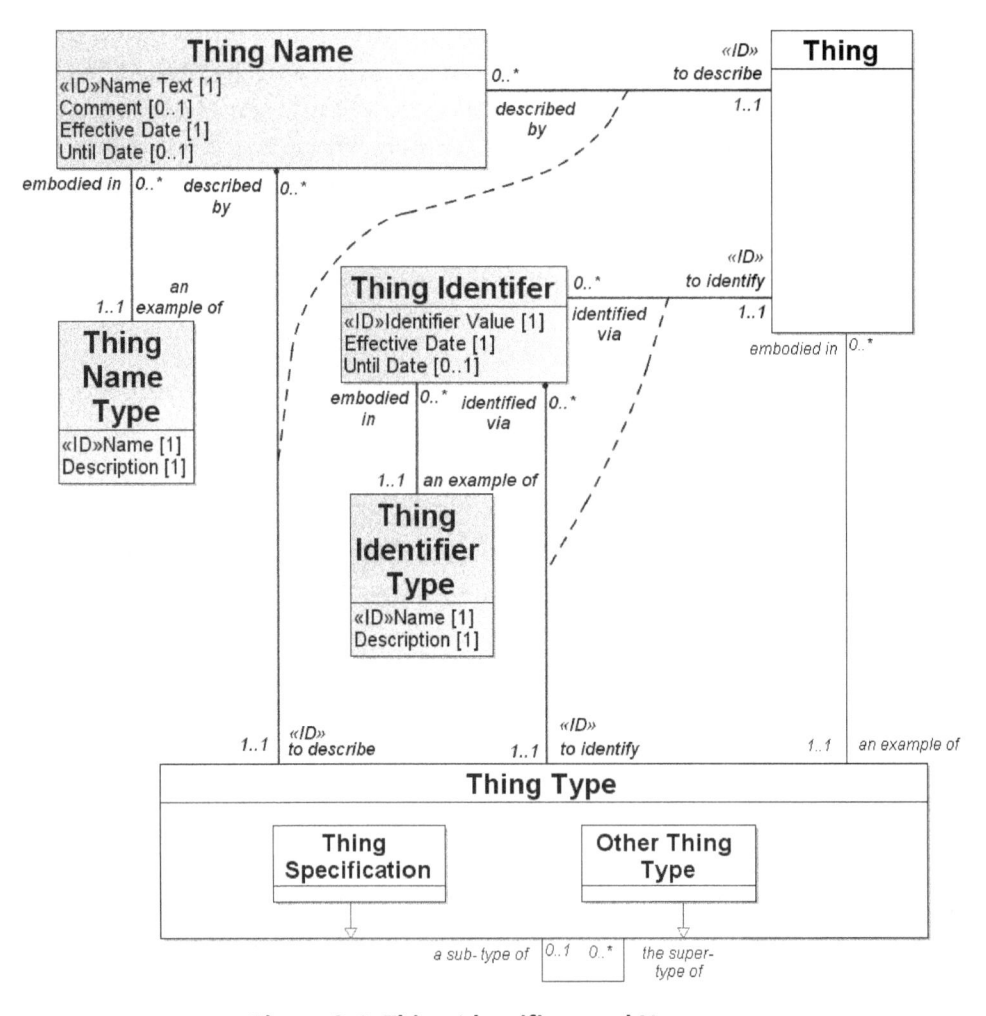

Figure 9-4: Thing Identifiers and Names

This diagram recognizes that each **Thing** and each **Thing Specification** may be *identified by* one or more **Thing Identifiers**, each of which must be *an example of* exactly one **Thing Identifier Type**. Again, the set of **Thing Identifier Types** available depend on the kind of **Thing** or **Thing Specification** involved. For example, **Companies** are identified by "North American Industry Classification System" (NAICS) codes (formerly SIC, or Standard Industrial Classification codes). **People** may be identified by a Passport Number or a Social Security Number.

It is especially true in this model, more than the detailed ones, that it is necessary to specify which kinds of identifiers (**Thing Identifier Type**) and which kinds of names (**Thing Name Type**) are appropriate for **Things** that are *examples of* a particular **Thing Type**. Figure 9-5 shows that a **Thing Identifier Assignment** must be either *of* **Types** of **Thing Names** or *of* **Types** of **Thing Identifiers**. It must then also be either *to* a **Thing Specification** or *to* an **Other Thing Type**. Specifically, a **Thing Identifier Assignment** is defined to be the fact that **Thing Names** that are *examples of* a particular **Thing Name Type** can be used *to describe* **Things** that are *examples of* a particular **Thing Type**.

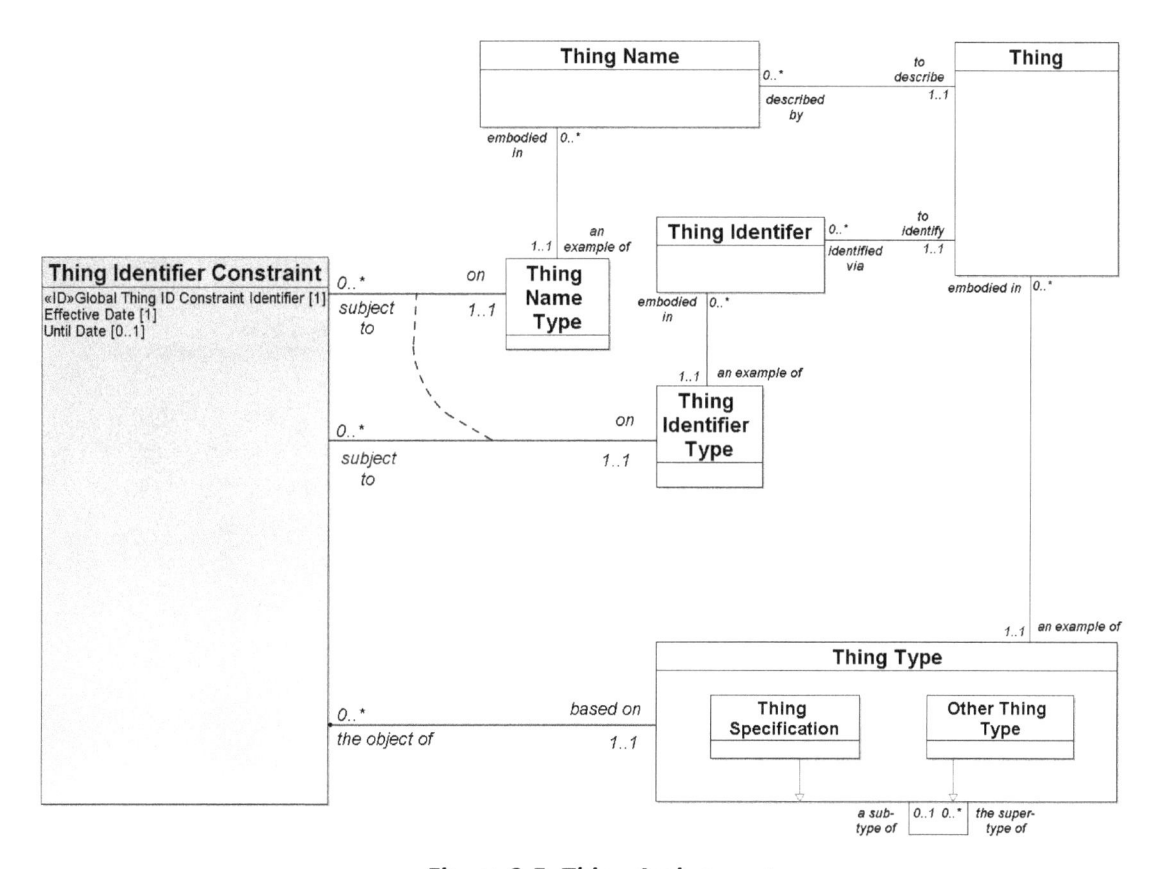

Figure 9-5: Thing Assignment

In other words, each **Thing Name Type** (or each **Thing Identifier Type**) may be *subject to* one or more **Thing Identifier Assignments**, where each **Thing Identifier Constraint** must be *on* a particular **Thing Type**.

That is, each **Thing Identifier Constraint** must be *on* either one **Thing Name Type** or one **Thing Identifier Type**. (Because of the parallel structure, this entity class is doing double duty.)

Business Rules

- A **Thing Name** that is *to describe* a **Thing** may not be specified to be *an example of* a **Thing Name Type**, if that **Thing Name Type** is not *subject to* a **Thing Name Constraint** based on the **Thing Type** that the named **Thing** is *an example of*. (*Translation*: **Thing Name Constraint** provides assurance that a **Thing Name** is appropriate for a particular **Thing**, based on its **Thing Type**.)

- A **Thing Identifier** that is *to identify* a **Thing** may not be specified to be *an example of* a **Thing Identifier Type**, if that **Thing Identifier Type** is not *subject to* a **Thing Identifier Constraint** *based on* the **Thing Type** that the **Thing** is *an example of*. A **Thing Identifier** that is *to identify* a **Thing** may not be specified to be *an example of* a **Thing Identifier Type**, if that **Thing Identifier Type** is not *subject to* a **Thing Identifier Constraint** *based on* the **Thing Type** that the Identifier **Thing Specification** is *an example of*. (*Translation*: **Thing Identifier Constraint** provides assurance that a **Thing Identifier** is appropriate for a particular **Thing Specification**, based on its **Thing Type**.)

For example, if a **Thing** is `"Proctor and Gamble"` (an *example of* the **Thing Type**, `"Party"` / `"Organization"` / `"Company"`), and it is *described by* the **Thing Name** `"PG"`, which is *an example of* a **Thing Name Type**, `"stock ticker"`, then **Thing Name Type** `"stock ticker"` must be *subject to* a **Thing Identifier Assignment** that is *based on* the **Thing Type** `"Party"` or `"Organization"` or `"Company"`. That is, it could have a name that is appropriate to any **Party**, one that is appropriate to any `"Organization"`, or, as is more likely, one that is appropriate to any `"Company"`.

As another example, if a Thing Specification is `"Lenovo Laptop Computer T43"` (an example of the **Thing Type** `"Laptop Computer"`), and it is *identified by* the **Thing Identifier** `"2687-DBU"`, that is *an example of* **Thing Identifier Type** `"Computer Model Type"`, then that **Thing Identifier Type** must be *subject to* a **Thing Identifier Assignment** that is *based on* the **Thing Type** `"Laptop Computer"`.

Again, this model by itself does not represent business rules, but it does provide the terms for expressing them.

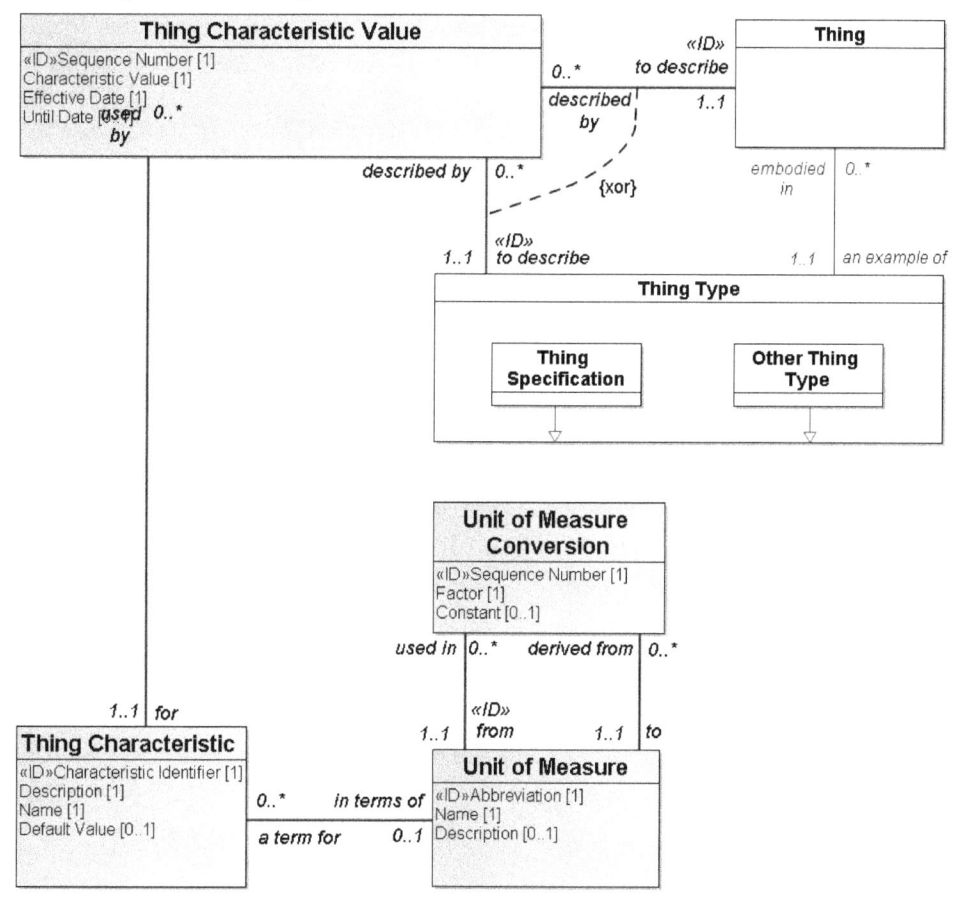

Thing Characteristics

Because this model is the ultimate abstraction, **Thing Type** and **Thing** do not have any inherent attributes beyond the identifiers, names, and descriptions portrayed earlier. Their more concrete embodiments, **Party Type** and **Party**, **Geographic Location Type** and **Geographic Location**, et cetera, also only have a few. At either level of abstraction, the most flexible approach to attributes is *not* to include them in the entity classes directly.

Figure 9-6 shows the template for **Thing Characteristic**—defined here as a variable, attribute, or parameter whose values would describe instances of **Thing Type** (including **Thing Specification**) or **Thing**. Each **Thing Characteristic Value**, then, is the fact that a particular **Thing Type** or **Thing** is described by a value of a particular **Thing Characteristic**.

Figure 9-6: Thing Characteristics

That is, each **Thing Characteristic Value** must be *for* exactly one **Thing Characteristic**, and must be either *to describe* exactly one **Thing** or *to describe* exactly one **Thing Type**.

As we saw in the detailed chapters, the variety of attributes of a **Thing Type**, (such as a "`Volvo V70`") is handled by **Characteristic** entity classes. (This is where the "`Volvo's off-black leather seating`" and "`dark TrimLine trim`" would be described as Characteristic Values (attributes of **Thing Characteristic Value**) of the **Thing Characteristics** (that is **Asset Characteristics**) "`seat color`" and "`trim`", respectively. This will be described further on in this chapter.

Note that each **Thing Characteristic** may be *recorded in terms of* one and only one **Unit of Measure**. (Note also that not all **Characteristics** have a **Unit of Measure**.) Because people may want to see **Thing Characteristics** expressed in various units of measure, however, the entity class **Unit of Measure Conversion** provides the Factor and, if necessary the Constant necessary to do such a conversion *from* one **Unit of Measure** *to* another **Unit of Measure**.

There are, in fact, two kinds of **Thing Characteristics**, as shown in Figure 9-7. Specifically, each **Thing Characteristic** must be either a **Thing Category**, which can only take one of a discrete list of values, or a **Continuous Thing Characteristic**, which can take as a value any real value, text, or date.

A **Continuous Thing Characteristic** may be constrained to a Minimum Value and/or a Maximum Value.

Note that each **Thing Characteristic** must be recorded *in terms of* one and only one **Unit of Measure**. Because people may want to see **Thing Characteristics** expressed in various units of measure, though, the entity class **Unit of Measure Conversion** provides the Factor and, if necessary the Constant necessary to do such a conversion *from* one **Unit of Measure** *to* another **Unit of Measure**.

Note that **Unit of Measure** is only *a term for* one or more **Continuous Thing Characteristics**.

There are in fact two kinds of **Thing Characteristics**, as shown in Figure 9-7. Specifically, each **Thing Characteristic** must be either a **Thing Category**, which can only take one of a discrete list of values, or a **Continuous Thing Characteristic**, which can take as a value any real value, text, or date.

A **Continuous Thing Characteristic** may be constraint to a **Minimum Value** and/or a **Maximum Value**.

Each **Thing Category** may be *constrained by* one or more **Thing Category Legal Values**. That is, there (usually) exists a list of **Thing Category Legal Values** that are the only values that the **Thing Category** can take. Indeed, the value in a **Thing Characteristic Value** *of* a **Thing Characteristic** must be the Value of one of the **Thing Category Legal Values** that is *a constraint on* the **Thing Characteristic** (actually, the **Thing Category**) involved.

Note also that **Thing Categories** may be organized hierarchically. That is, each **Thing Category** may be *broader than* one or more other **Thing Categories**, and it may also be *narrower than* one other **Thing Category**.

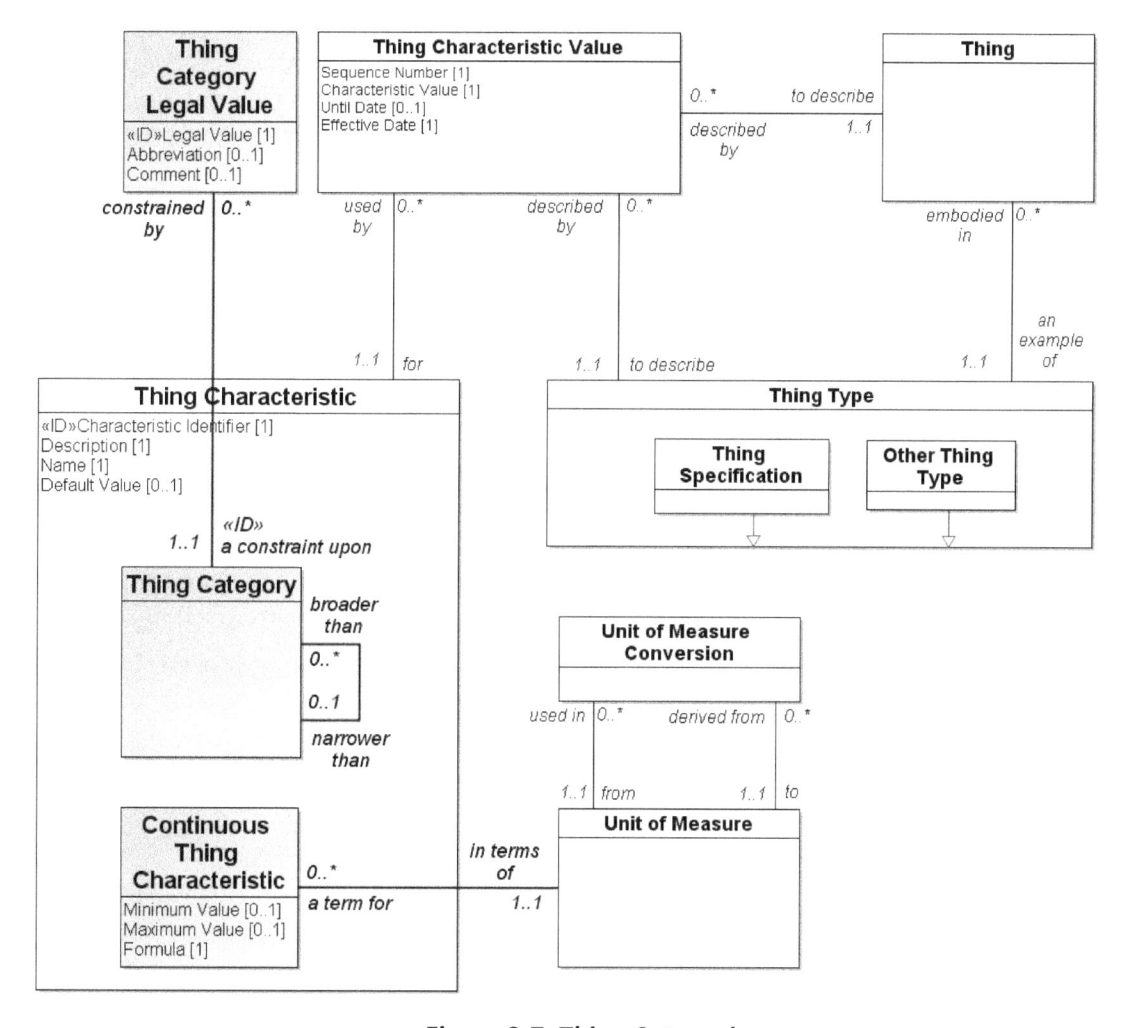

Figure 9-7: Thing Categories

Business Rules

- If **Thing Characteristic Value** is *of* a **Thing Category**, and if that **Thing Category** is *constrained by* one or more **Thing Category Legal Values**, then the Characteristic Value of any **Characteristic Value** must be the Legal Value of one of the **Thing Category Legal Values** of the **Thing Category**. (*Translation:* The value of a **Thing Category** must meet any constraints defined for the category—it must be one of the **Thing Category Legal Values** for that **Thing Category**—if there are any.)

- If **Thing Characteristic Value** is *of* a **Continuous Thing Characteristics**, and if the attributes Minimum Value and/or Maximum Value are given, the **Characteristic Value** must be *greater than* any specified Minimum Value and less than any specified Maximum Value. (*Translation:* The value of a **Thing Continuous Characteristic** must meet any **Thing Characteristic's** constraints (minimum and maximum value)—if there are any.)

Derived Characteristics

It is common for **Thing Characteristics** to be simply entered and stored. Sometimes, however, it is useful to be able to describe a characteristic that is derived from others. The mechanism for doing this is the **Thing Derivation Element**, shown in Figure 9-8. Here, each **Thing Derivation Element** is the fact that a particular **Thing Characteristic** is calculated from either another **Thing Characteristic**, a **System Variable** (typically `"system date"`), or a **Constant**.

Where appropriate, as described in each of the detailed chapters, the **Formula** for the derivation is shown as an attribute of **Continuous Thing Characteristic**. This is actually carried out, however, by parsing the formula into a set of operations, in the style of reverse Polish notation. That is, all formulae consist of a sequence of steps where each is an operation on a variable, where the variable may be either another **Thing Characteristic,** a **Constant**, or a **System Value**.

For example, the formula:

```
Degrees Celsius = (Degrees Fahrenheit-32) * .55556
```

...is represented by three lines in Table 9-1. To perform the calculation:

The calculation engine begins by recording "Degrees Fahrenheit". By definition, the Operation for the first variable is always "Add".

The calculation engine then subtracts the value of another Constant, ("32"), from the result in step 2 and replaces it with the result.

The calculation engine then multiplies the value of a Constant (".55556") times the result of step 1 and replaces it with the result ("37.78").

That is the resulting value of "Degrees Celsius".

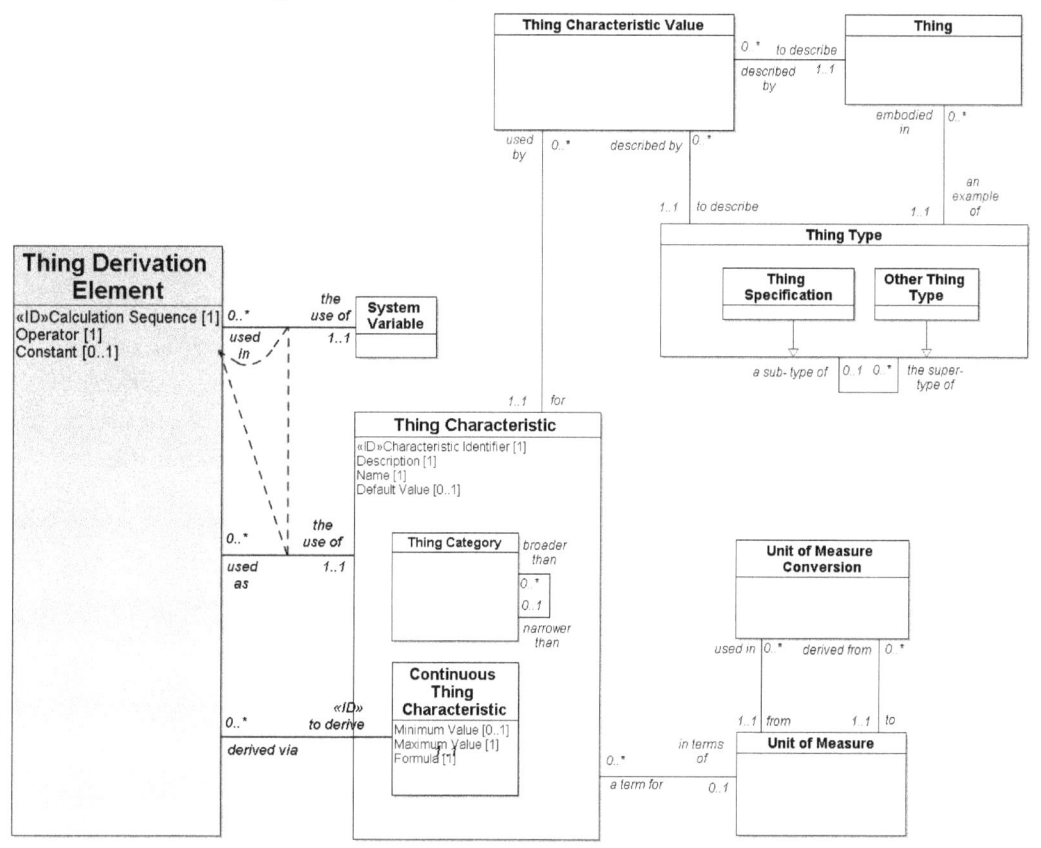

Figure 9-8: Thing Characteristic Derivations

Table 9-1: Example of Reverse Polish Notation

to derive Thing Characteristic	the use of Thing Characteristic	(the use of) Constant	Operator
Degrees Celsius	Degrees Fahrenheit		Add
Degrees Celsius		32	Subtract
Degrees Celsius		.55556	Multiply

Note that calculations are executed from the inner-most parentheses out.

Thing Characteristic Constraints

So far the model has shown complete freedom to describe a **Thing** with values of any **Characteristics** imaginable. In point of fact, only certain characteristics are appropriate to *examples of* each **Thing Type**, depending on what kind of thing it is. If you are talking about an **Asset** or an **Activity**, then certain **Characteristics** are identified as part of the **Thing** (**Asset** or **Activity**) **Specification**. In specifying a telephone **Service**, characteristics such as `"communication speed"`, `"monthly cost"`, and `"per minute cost"` might be appropriate. That is, a **Thing Specification** is *defined by* one or more **Thing Characteristic Assignments**, each of which is *in terms of* a particular **Thing Characteristic**. The model of this is shown in Figure 9-9.

A **Thing Characteristic Assignment** is, from one perspective, the fact that **Thing Characteristic Values** *for* a particular **Thing Characteristic** may be *to describe* **Things** that are either *described by* a particular **Thing Specification** or (directly or indirectly) *an example of* a particular (**Other**)**Thing Type**. From a different perspective, it also can describe the fact that **Thing Characteristic Values** *for* a particular **Thing Characteristic** may be *to describe* **Things** that are *an example of* a particular **Thing Type**.

In the case of **Party** or **Geographic Location**, there is no **Party Specification** or **Geographic Location Specification**, so it is the **Thing** (**Party** or **Geographic Location**) **Type** that determines which **Thing Characteristics** are appropriate. Indeed, even with **Assets** and **Activities** there may be constraints on appropriate **Thing Characteristics** at the **Thing Type** level.

For example, `"disk space"` is an appropriate **Thing Characteristic** of the **Thing Type** laptop computers. `"Fingerprint pad indicator"`, on the other hand is only appropriate for **Thing Specification** `"ThinkPad T43"`. The **Thing Specification** `"ThinkPad T43"` can then have a **Thing Characteristic Value** of `"160"` (gigabytes) for the **Thing Characteristic** `"disk space"`. The **Thing** `"Dave Hay's ThinkPad T43"` then has a value of `"no"` for the **Thing Characteristic** `"Fingerprint pad indicator"`.

The sub-types of **Thing Characteristic** are discussed in more detail in each of the chapters of Section One.

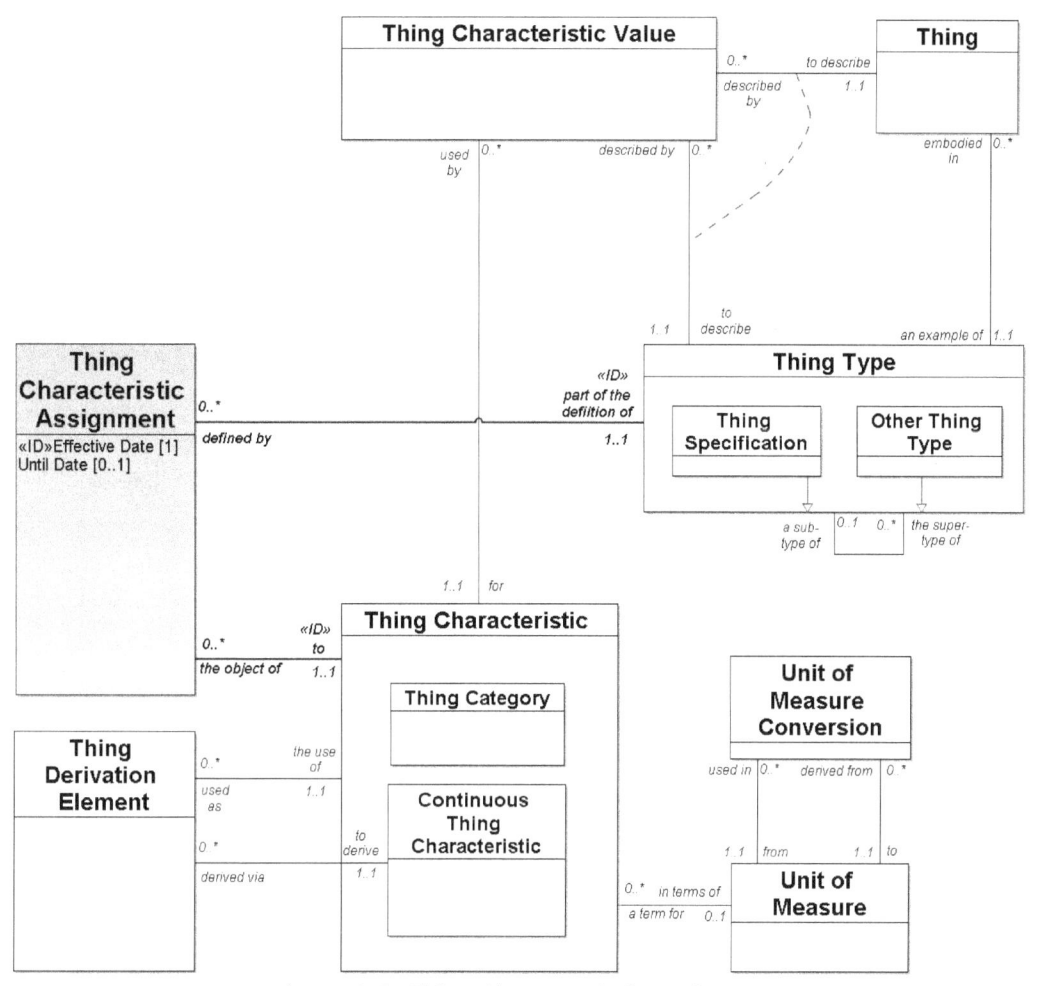

Figure 9-9: Thing Characteristic Assignments

Thing Role

While **Party** is itself an example of **Thing**, in this Chapter, it has a special part to play. In the management of all the data about **Things** (including people) there are people responsible for that management. This is true both at the data level (maintaining **Thing Characteristics** and their use in defining **Thing Types** and **Thing Specifications**) and at the level of maintaining data about the **Things** themselves.

The first case, Figure 9-10, shows that a single **Party** may be the *definer of* one or more **Thing Characteristics** and/or one or more **Thing Characteristic Assignments**.

204 Enterprise Model Patterns

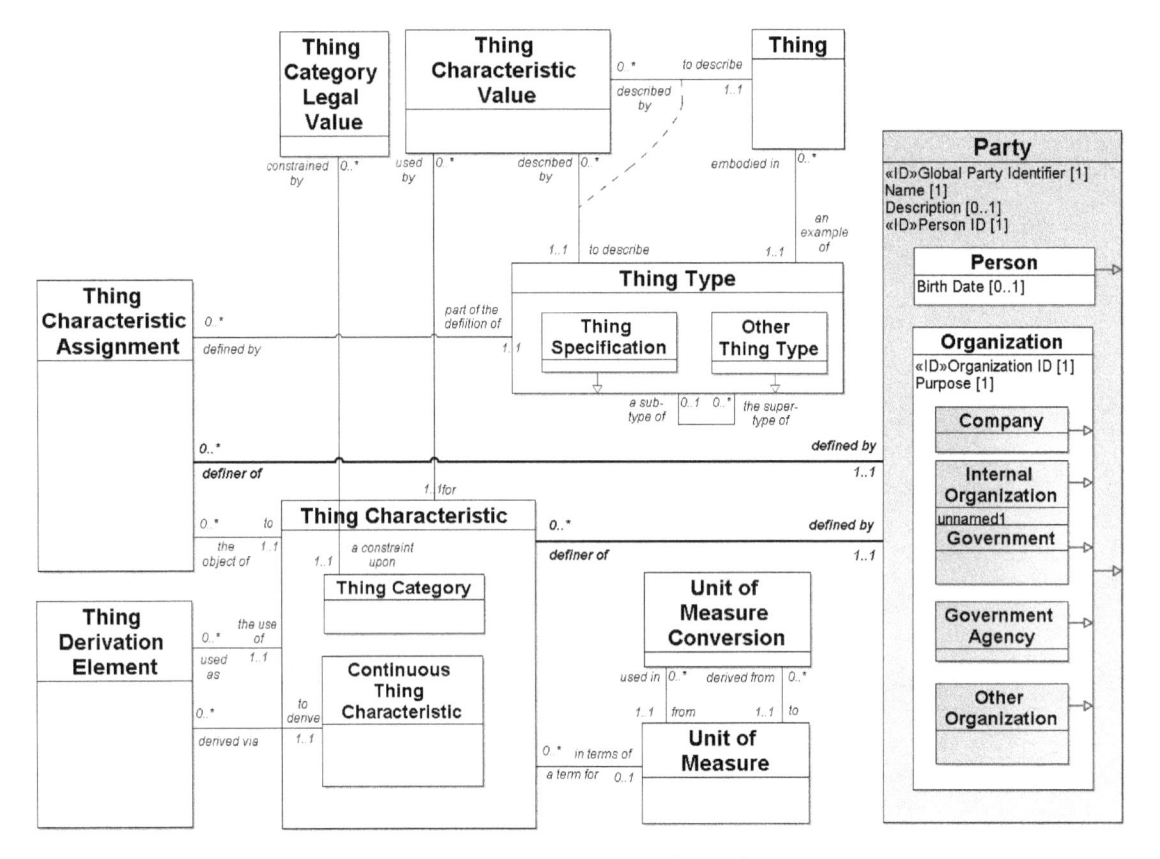

Figure 9-10: Thing Meta-roles

The second case is represented in Figure 9-11, where a **Thing Role** must be *to manage* either one and only one **Thing Type** or one and only one **Thing**. The nature of the **Thing Role** is determined by the **Thing Role Type** the **Thing Role** is *an example of*.

Note the difference between roles as shown in the last two figures. A **Thing Management Role** can be any role required for a real instance of the **Thing** or for defining **Thing Types** over time. A given **Thing Type** or **Thing** may be *managed via* one or more **Thing Roles** either of different **Thing Role Types** or of the same **Thing Role Type** over time.

If either of these assertions turns out not to be true, of course, "Characteristic Definition" can be included as a **Thing Role Type**, and these can become simply instances of **Thing Role**.

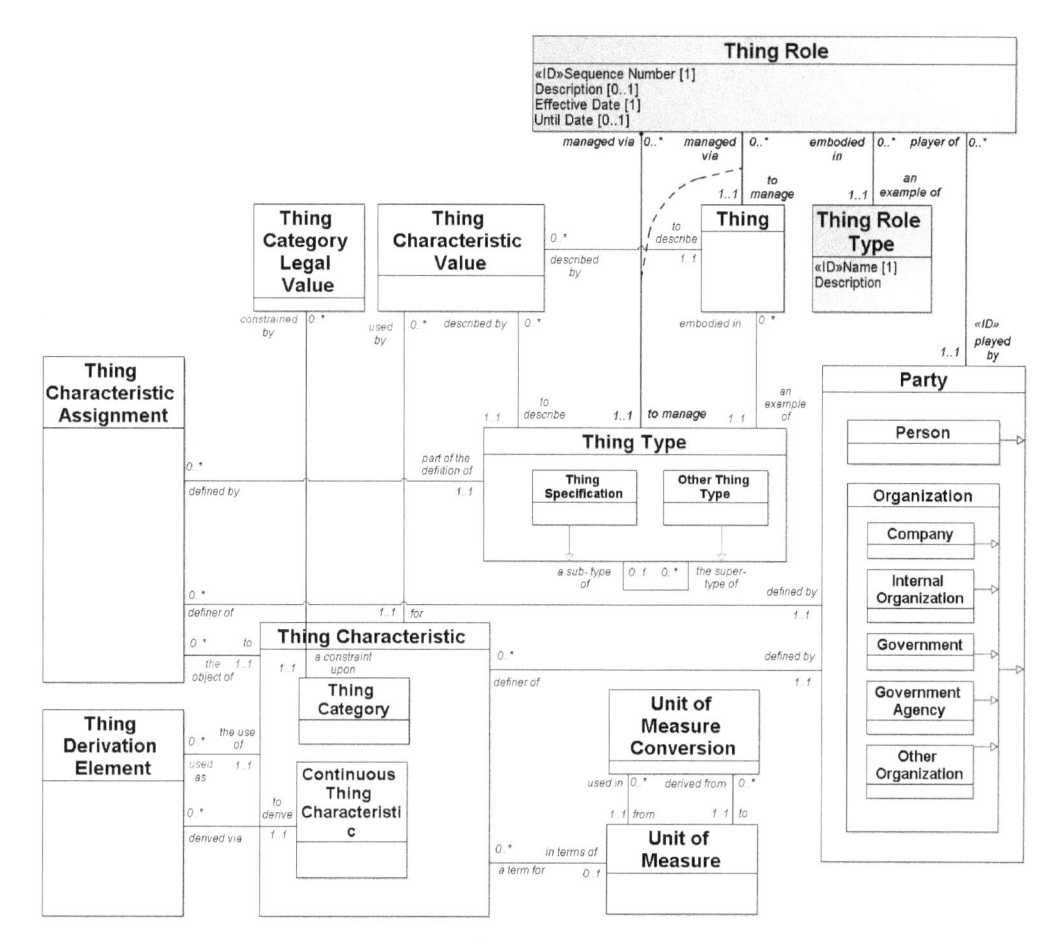

Figure 9-11: Thing Management Roles

A Word about Language

The reader will have noticed variations in the way terms for what is ostensibly the same thing vary from context to context. The structure names for those that are sub-types of other relationships are a good example of this. Indeed the variations in the names of entity classes themselves also show this.

That is an indication of how this model is a living thing. On the one hand, names of things are extremely important. But on the other hand, recognizing subtle differences in names is equally important.

At a particular level of abstraction, there is an appropriate language to use. At another level, the language may well be different. This is to be expected. Indeed, the names of entity classes in this book are by no means sacred either. The modeler is obligated to use, as much as possible, the language of h' audience.

With one exception: In every company, there is invariably the one word or phrase that is critical to the business the company is in. This is the word that everyone uses. The problem is that no one can define it. Or rather everyone defines it. There is no single definition.

Don't include that word in your model. Instead, for each of the concepts represented, find a clear term to describe that concept.

For example, in an oil refinery, the word was "stream". Everyone in the refinery was concerned with streams of fluid. The problem was that to some, it meant the fact that something could be transmitted from one processing unit to another processing unit. To others, it meant that a particular material, such as "Grade 1 Kerosene" could be transmitted from the one unit to the other. To yet others, it meant that, for example, on January 15, 2009, 3000 gallons of "Grade 1 Kerosene" were in fact transmitted from the first unit to the second unit.

The word "stream" could not be used in the data model.*

Summary

The very structure of this chapter parallels the structure of the four principal chapters for Level 1:

- The distinction between the specification of something, the fundamental categories it falls into, and the thing itself.
- The fact that everything is made up of components and otherwise associated with similar things.
- The notion that names, identifiers, and other characteristics should be maintained separately by subject-matter experts, not made part of the structure of a model.
- An approach to representing the derivation of characteristics from other characteristics.
- The fact that, with the possible exception of **Parties** themselves, the managers of each thing can be identified.♦

---

* In fact, the terms modeled turned out to be "fluid path", "material assignment", and "movement".

♦ Ok, as a married person and a parent, perhaps your author should not rule out the possibility of **Persons** having a **Role** to play in the life of other **Persons**. But that sort of sociology is beyond the scope of this book.

CHAPTER 10

Documents and other Information Resources

Documents are problematic. On one level, the media can be managed like any other physical asset. They are located somewhere, they move from place to place, and so on. But documents (and videos, and web pages, among others) are unique in that they refer to other parts of the enterprise. This means that the model of documents must connect to everything else in the Enterprise Model. In one sense, a document is nothing other than a query to retrieve information about an aspect of the enterprise. As such, a query itself is not the appropriate subject of the model of the data being queried.

In some business settings, however, the resulting reports are themselves things of significance to be managed.

A "New Drug Application", for example, is a document encompassing massive quantities of research information that are retrieved from the systems doing clinical research. The document itself, however, is significant in its own right because it is the transmission of the document to the Food and Drug Administration that is a critical part of the process of acquiring approval to sell a particular pharmaceutical. The document is also significant, however, because it is *about* all aspects of the business of clinical research.

That is, the existence of an information resource is itself a thing of significance. To address this kind of thing of significance, however, requires us to look at it as an example of metadata, referring to all the elements in the rest of the model.

Information Resources

An **Information Resource** is any collection of concepts expressed in a form that can be communicated to others. Among other things, it can be the contents of a document as just described, it can be a photograph or a video recording, or it can be a piece of computer software. This is the knowledge managed by *knowledge management* efforts. Figure 10-1 shows **Information Resource Definition** (a set of articulated concepts) and **Information Resource Instance** (a representation of those concepts in a particular **Medium**).[*] The latter may be in a **Physical Copy** (for example, a paper copy) or in an **Electronic Copy** (sent by, for example, electronic mail).

Figure 10-1 also shows the sub-types of **Information Resource Definition**. A **Document** is the contents and structure of a book, an e-mail, a formal written report, or any other collection of textual and graphic language that describes one or more concepts. While a **Document** may *contain* photographs, the photographs themselves would be considered **Information Resource Definitions** (**Images**) in their own right. These might be still photographs (**Still Images**) or videos (**Moving Images**).

Document, **Image**, and **Other Information Resource** are clearly the principal sub-types of **Information Resource Definition**. As before, **Information Resource Type** redundantly captures the sub-types of **Information Resource Definitions**, but it can also include more detailed ones. "Other Information Resource Definition", for example, might be *a super-type of* "Sound Recording" and/or *a super-type of* "Computer Program".

The best example of the distinction between an **Information Resource Definition** and an **Information Resource Instance** is that between what old-timers remember as a card catalogue card and a physical copy of a book. Even if in the form of a computer database, a library card catalogue describes the *title* of each book, along with a summary of its contents and a catalogue number to classify it. Each *copy* of a book is then given an "Accession Number" (usually written on the book), which is recorded in acquisition files, along with the date purchased, and so forth.

This distinction is more esoteric if one is dealing with an e-mail message or a photograph. Typically, we only have a record of the **Information Resource Instance**, and are not concerned with its essential definition. But if you send an electronic copy of a picture of your granddaughter to your aunt in Philadelphia—

---

[*] You should recognize that these correspond to the **Thing** and **Thing Specification** of the previous chapter.

who then passes it to another relative—the fact that these are now three copies of a single image is significant. The information about the underlying image may be kept with the original, but it is important to realize that in its "original-ness", it is serving both as a first copy and as well as the definition of its contents.♣

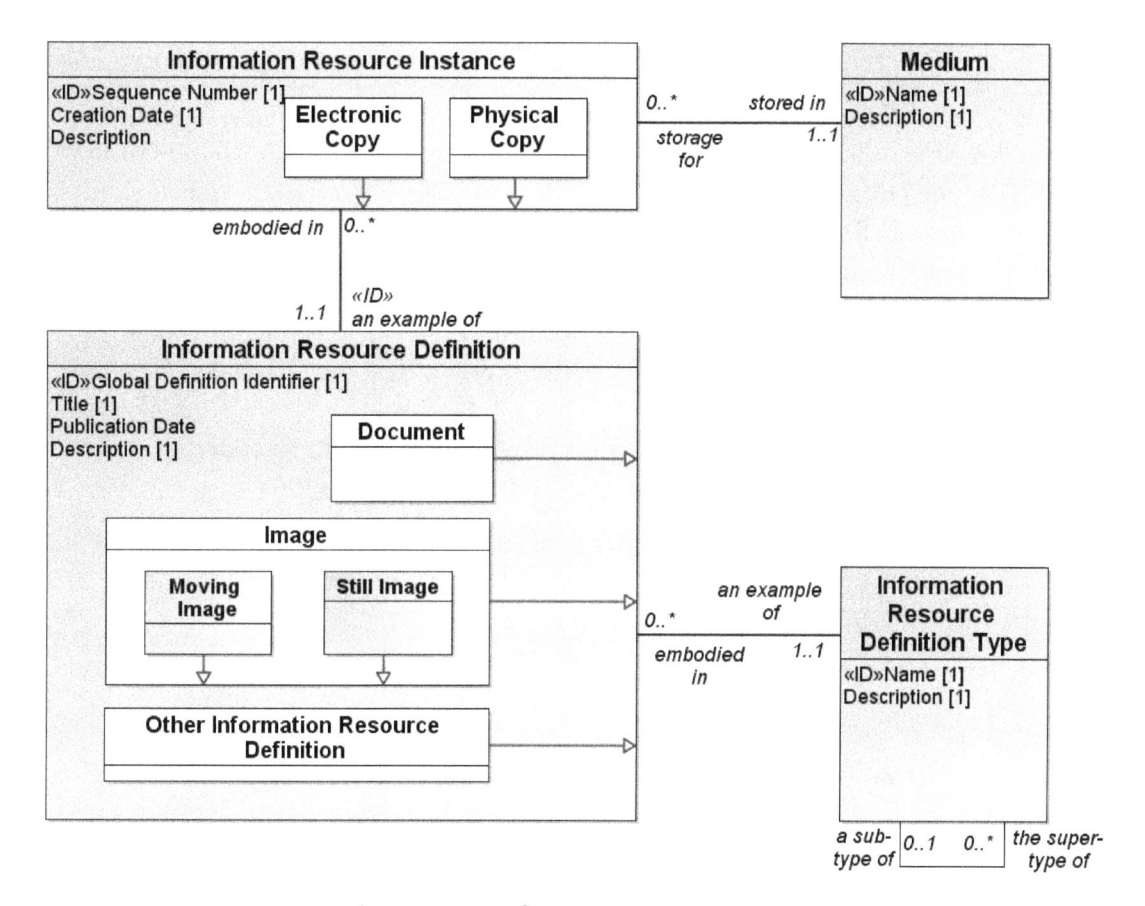

Figure 10-1: Information Resources

Each **Information Resource Instance** is also noteworthy because it must be stored in a **Medium**. This is " a means of effecting or conveying something: as ... a substance regarded as the means of transmission of a force or effect".[42]

♣   Back in ancient times (say, 10 years ago), every photograph began with a negative on a piece of film. This was clearly different from the print copies made from it. The negative was the original **Information Resource Definition**, and all prints were **Information Resource Instances**. The distinction is no longer as clear, but it remains important.

[42] Merriam Webster. 2010. "Medium". The Merriam Webster OnLine Dictionary. Retrieved 11/16/2010 from http://www.merriam-webster.com/dictionary/medium.

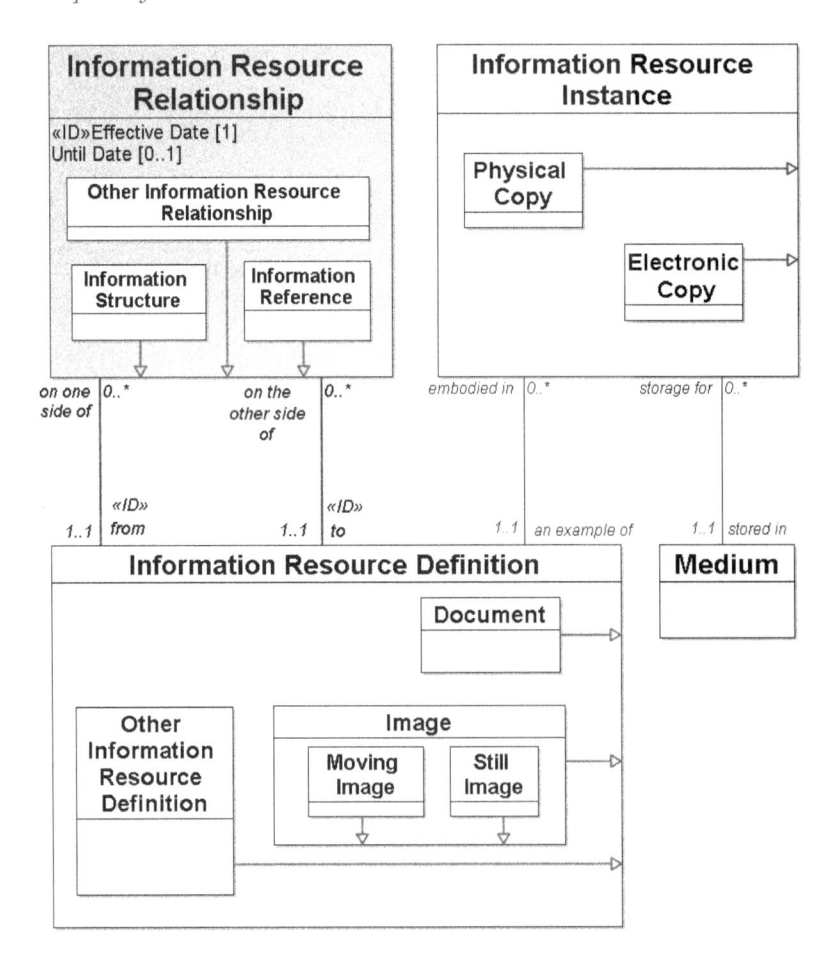

Information Resource Relationships

As mentioned earlier, a book may contain a photograph. It may also consist of chapters. In effect one **Information Resource Definition** is *composed of* one or more others. This is one kind of **Information Resource Relationship**—the fact that one **Information Resource** is in some way associated with others. As with any other relationship entity class, each **Information Resource Relationship** must be *from* one **Information Resource Definition** and *to* another **Information Resource Definition**.

This is portrayed in Figure 10-2. One sub-type of **Information Resource Relationship** is **Information Structure**—the fact that one **Information Resource Instance** is *composed of* at least one other **Information Resource Instance**.

Figure 10-2: Information Resource Relationships

Another kind of **Information Resource Relationship** is **Information Reference**, where one **Information Resource Definition** refers to another, typically in a footnote or an endnote. **Other Information Resource Relationships** are certainly possible as well.

Concepts

If an **Information Resource** is a collection of concepts, it is worthwhile to stop and examine those concepts in our model. Figure 10-3 shows **Concept** as an entity class, where a concept is something that we understand to exist or to be the case. In this context, a **Concept** is an aspect of an enterprise's operations or environment. It may be about something tangible or it may be an abstract idea generalized from particular instances. It is the set of **Concepts** that give meaning to our language.[43]

We can only deal with **Concepts** if we can describe them in language in some way. In particular, the only concepts we can communicate must be *represented by* one or more linguistic **Expressions**. An **Expression** is a collection of **Words**, **Phrases**, or **Sentences** intended to represent meaning. By definition, each of these **Expressions** must be *expressed in* one and only one **Language**.

Each concept, however, can be described by more than one **Expression**. For example, the notion of a place with a purpose, such as an office or a warehouse, can be described as either a "site" or a "facility". By the same token, the same **Expression** can refer to more than one **Concept**. The word "facility", for example, in the oil industry refers to a physical site—a place where oil is removed from the ground or processed—but in the banking industry, a facility is an understanding by the bank that a particular customer will be provided with a specified amount of credit.[♣]

For this reason, we define **Business Term** to mean the use of a particular **Expression** to describe a particular **Concept**.[44]

---

[43] This section is derived from: Object Management Group (OMG). 2008. *Semantics of Business Vocabulary and Business Rules*. OMG Available Specification formal/2008-01-02. Avialable at *http://www.omg.org/spec/SBVR/1.0/PDF/*.

[♣] In an American Restaurant, however, the word has a completely different meaning, as in the phrase, "Waiter, can you direct me to the facilities, please?"

[44] After completion of the first printing, your author realized that "Business Term" could also refer to an entire definition, so that name seemed inadequate. A colleague from the Library of Congress invented the word "Linguification", which would be correct—but perhaps a bit much. Dear Reader, it's your call.

Of course, **Expressions** themselves may be simple or complex. An **Expression Structure** is the fact that a particular **Expression** (such as a **Word**) is *part of* another **Expression** (such as a **Sentence**).

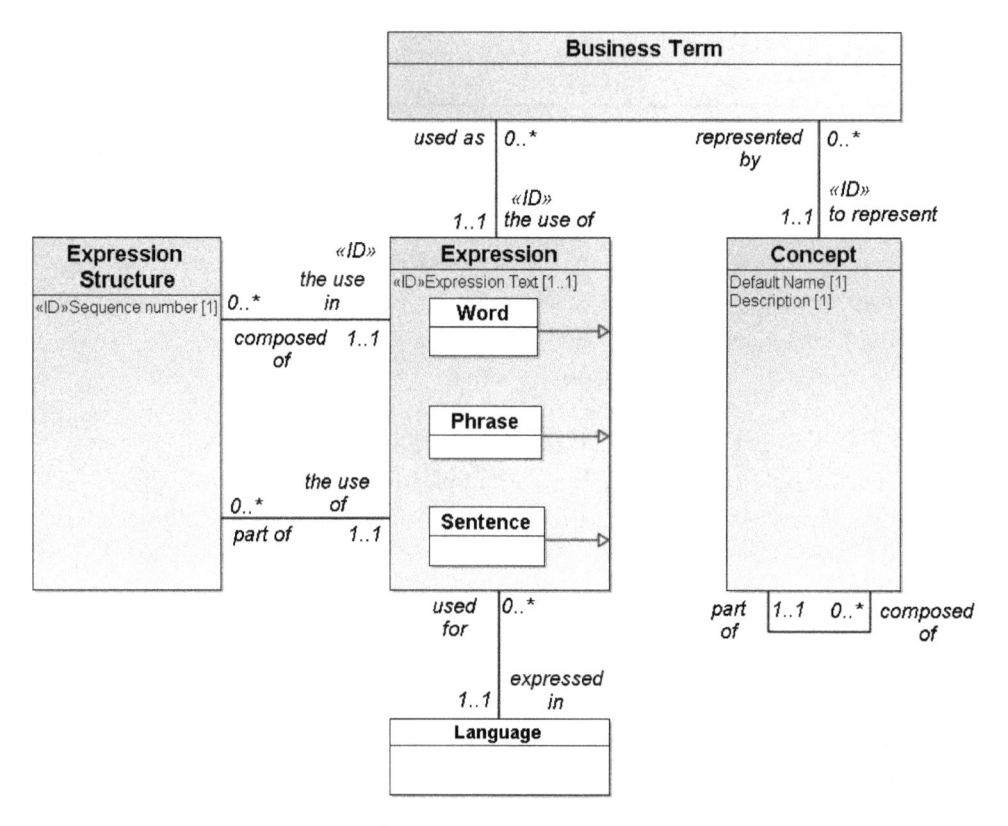

Figure 10-3: Business Terms

This piece of the model is significant, because among the concepts that an **Information Resource** might be concerned with are all those described in this entity/relationship model. Indeed, there are actually two principle kinds of **Concepts** that concern us. Figure 10-4 shows **Modeled Concept**, instances of which (such as **Person**, **Geographic Location**, **Activity**, and the like) constitute the basic vocabulary of the business. Figure 10-4 also shows **Proposition Type** as another kind of **Concept**, which is the template for assertions that can be made about the business. Indeed, one kind of **Proposition Type** is the assertion made by each role (relationship end) in a model's relationships.

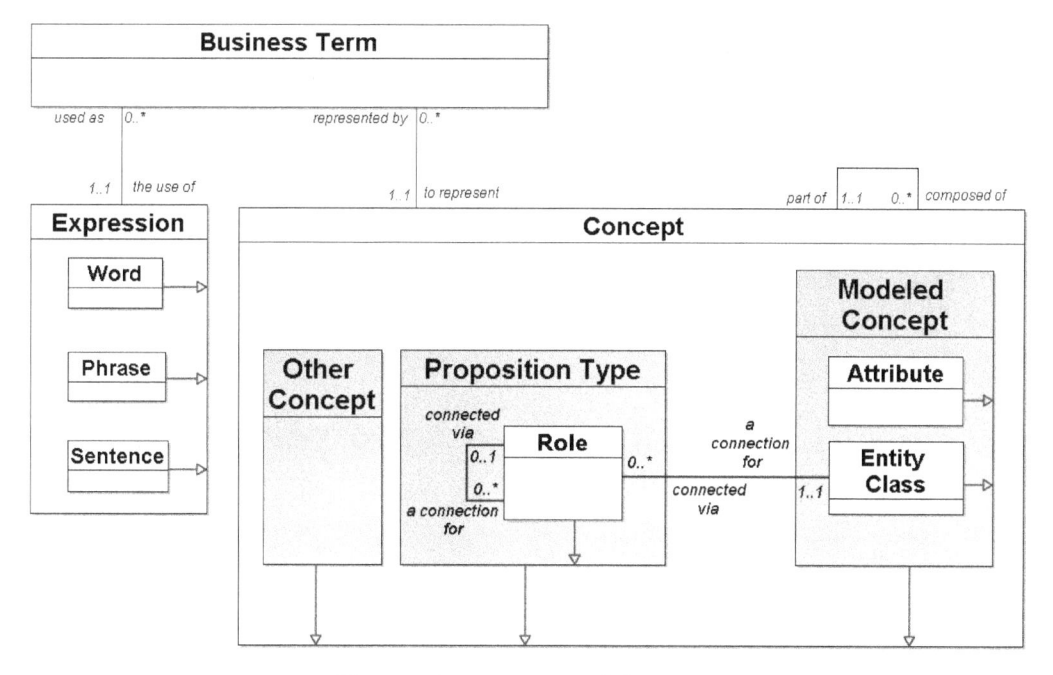

Figure 10-4: Data Model as concepts

Information Resources and Concepts

Ok, now we know something about concepts. You will recall from earlier in the chapter that an *information resource* is any collection of concepts expressed in a form that can be communicated to others.

Figure 10-5 shows how **Information Resource Definitions** are linked to **Business Terms**, and thence to **Concepts** via **Information Resource Elements**.

In Figure 10-5, an **Information Resource Element** is defined as the fact that a particular **Information Resource Definition** is in some way concerned with a particular **Business Term**.

That is, the **Information Resource Definition** may be *composed of* one or more **Information Resource Elements**, each of which must be *the use of* exactly one **Business Term**. As stated previously, each **Business Term**, in turn must be *the use of* one **Expression** *to represent* one **Concept**. Going the other way, each **Business Term** may be *used as* one or more **Information Resource Elements**, each of which must be *part of* one and only one **Information Resource Definition**.

214 Enterprise Model Patterns

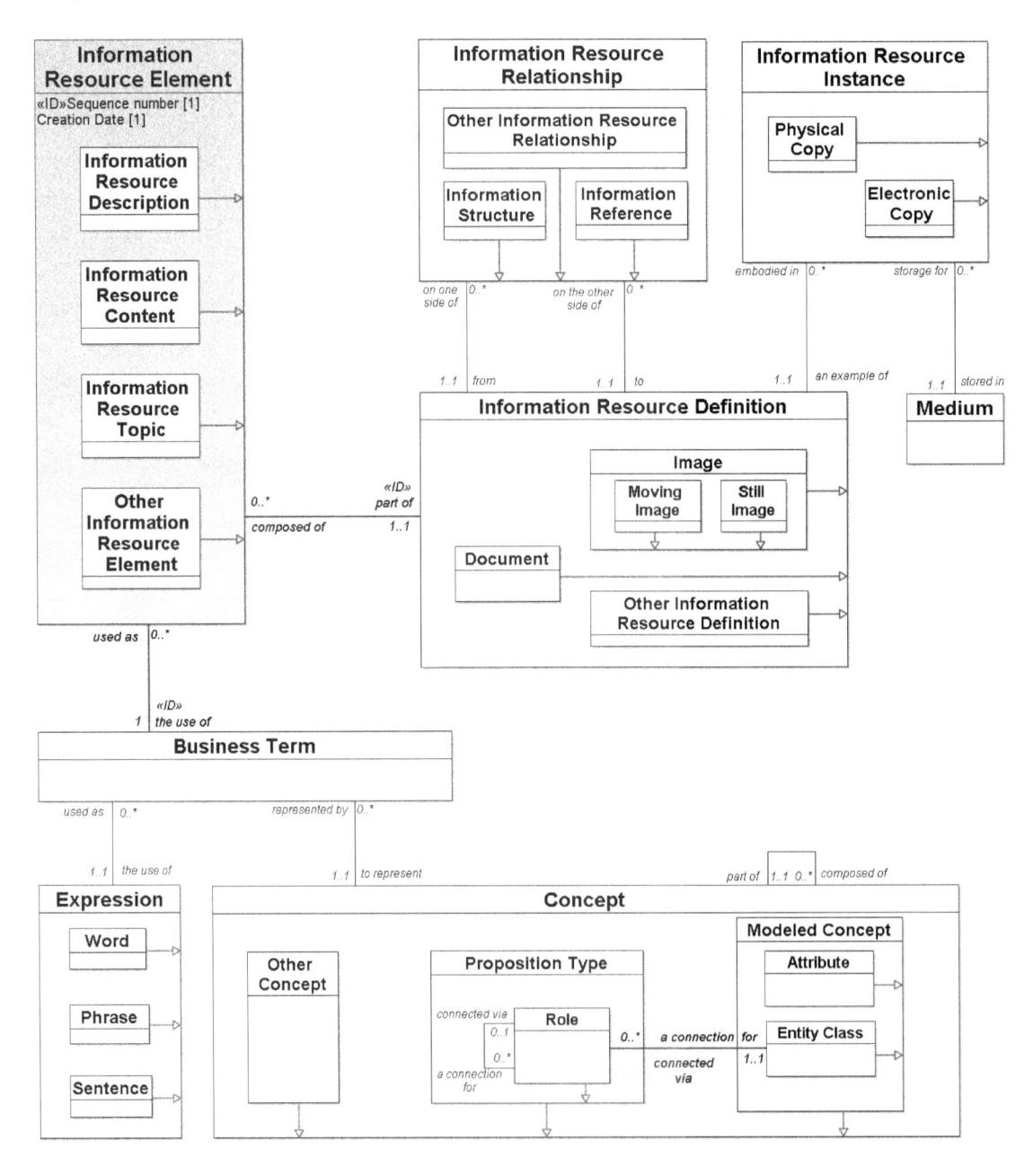

Figure 10-5: Information Resources and Concepts

An **Information Resource Element** must be one of the following:

- An **Information Resource Description** is a brief sentence or two about the **Information Resource Definition**, such as might appear in an advertisement for a book.

- An **Information Resource Topic** is a Word or Phrase (a **Business Term**) describing a category that can be used to locate the **Information Resource Definition**.
- A set of **Information Resource Contents** of a **Document** (if not that of an **Image**) encompasses the collection of **Business Terms** that constitute the words of the **Document**.
- Other **Information Resource Elements** may also be *the use of* one **Business Term** as *part of* one **Information Resource Definition**.

Distribution

The primary difference between an **Information Resource Definition** and an **Information Resource Instance** is that the latter can be *sent* to someone—or many someones. Figure 10-6 shows that each **Information Resource Instance** may be *sent via* one or more **Distributions** each of which must be *to* a **Party**.

Thus, if an electronic mail message may be sent from `"David Hay"` to `"Bob Hay"`, the definition of its contents constitutes an **Information Resource Definition**. One **Electronic Copy** is sent to `"Bob Hay"`, and one **Electronic Copy** is maintained by `"David Hay"`. These represent two **Distributions** of an **Electronic Copy**.

Clearly the world of cyberspace clouds the distinctions here. Traditionally one **Physical Copy** of a magazine might be distributed in succession to several people, while another **Physical Copy** of the same or different magazine could be distributed to a different set of people.

By definition, if an **Electronic Copy** is sent to someone, that is the only destination for that copy. To the extent that a set of people all get copies, each only gets one. Both Bob and David get their own **Electronic Copies** of the e-mail.

Figure 10-6 also shows **Information Resource Role**. Of principal interest, of course, is **Authorship Role**—who wrote or otherwise created the **Information Resource Definition. Other Information Resource Roles** might also be of interest, such as—for a book—`"Illustrator"`, `"Translator"`, `"Editor"`, and so forth. These are instances of **Information Resource Role Type**, where each **Information Resource Role** must be *an example of* one and only one **Information Resource Role Type**. Again, the instances of **Information Resource Role Type** must include `"Authorship Role"` and `"Other

216 Enterprise Model Patterns

`Information Resource Role"`, duplicating the sub-types shown in the diagram.

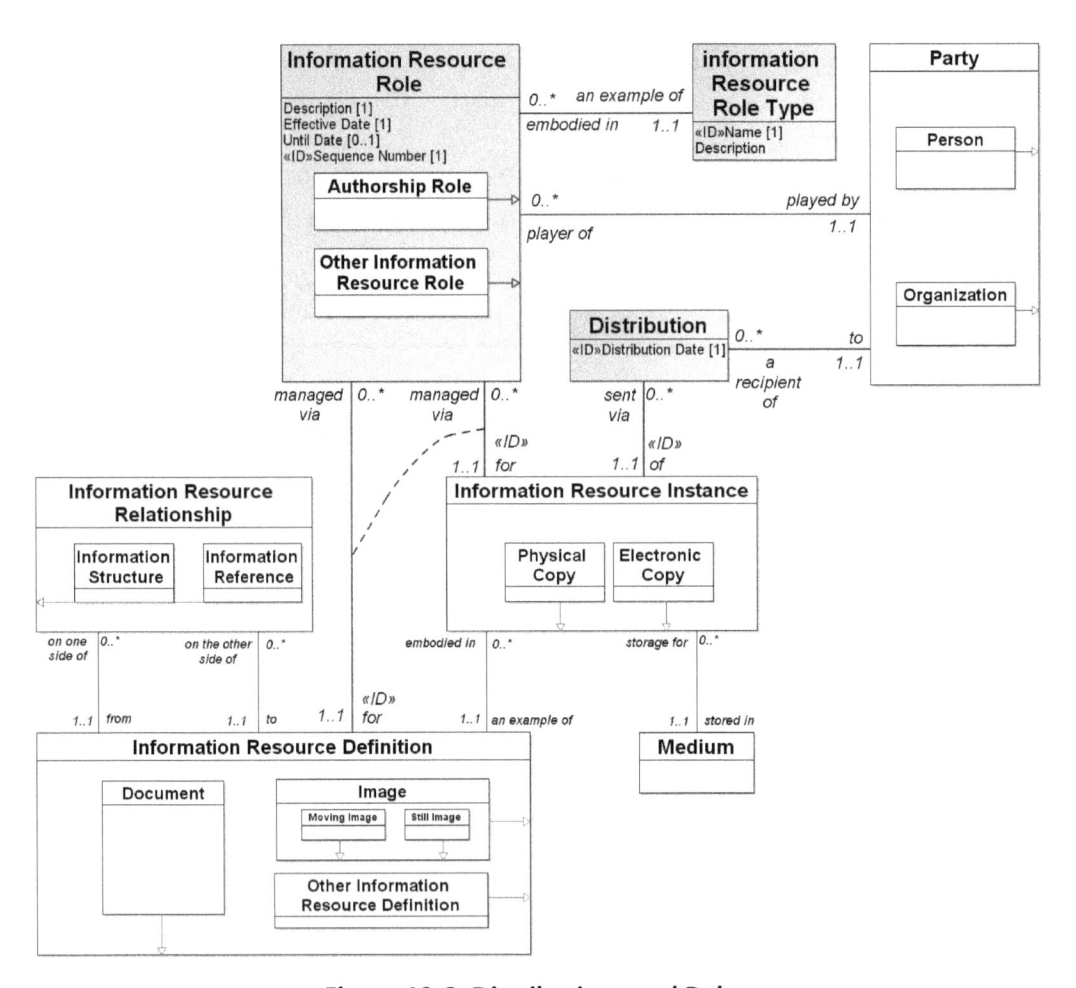

Figure 10-6: Distributions and Roles

Dispositions

In the case of important documents (for a government agency, say, or a bank), there are important rules for archiving and/or destroying them.

Figure 10-7 shows **Disposition Rule**, whose **Description** captures the circumstances under which **Information Resource Instances** (that are *examples of* a particular **Information Resource Definition**) can be destroyed, archived, or otherwise disposed of.

Documents and other Information Resources 217

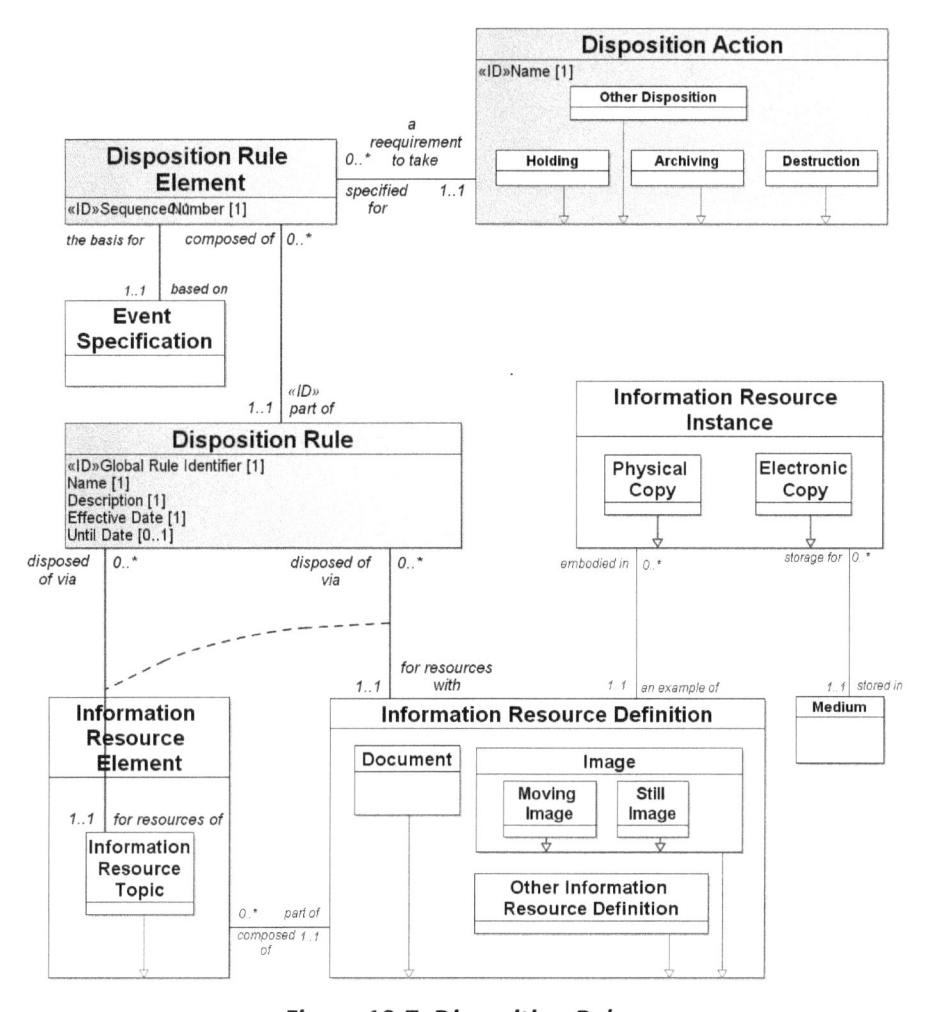

Figure 10-7: Disposition Rules

That is, each **Disposition Rule** may be *composed of* one or more **Disposition Rule Elements**. A **Disposition Rule** *composed of* one or more **Disposition Rule Elements** can describe the entire (theoretical) life cycle of the **Information Resource Definition**. Each **Disposition Rule Element**, among other things, must be *a requirement to take* a particular **Disposition Action**. An instance of **Disposition Action** must be an instance of one of the sub-types of **Holding**, **Archiving**, **Destruction**, or an **Other Disposition**.

A **Disposition Rule Element** may be *based on* an **Event Specification**, such as `"Passage of 6 months"`, `"1 year after last transaction"`, or some such. If it is not *based on* an **Event Specification**, then the **Disposition Action** must be something like `"indefinite hold"`, meaning that the **Information Resource Instances** will never be thrown away.

218 Enterprise Model Patterns

Each **Disposition Rule** must be either *for* all **Information Resource Instances** that are *examples of* a particular **Information Resource Definition** or *for* **Information Resource Instances** that are *examples of* any **Information Resource Definition** that is *described by (composed of)* a particular **Information Resource Topic**. This is represented in Figure 10-7 by the assertion that "each **Disposition Rule** must be either *for resources of* a particular **Information Resource Topic**, or *for resources with* a particular **Information Resource Definition**.

Figure 10-8 shows how actual **Dispositions** are represented. A **Disposition** is the fact that at a point in time, an **Information Resource Instance** was acted upon in a specified way. Each instance of **Disposition**, then, is *of* an **Information Resource**, and *the carrying out of* a **Disposition Action**. It is also *triggered by* an **Event** and is *based on* a **Disposition Rule**.

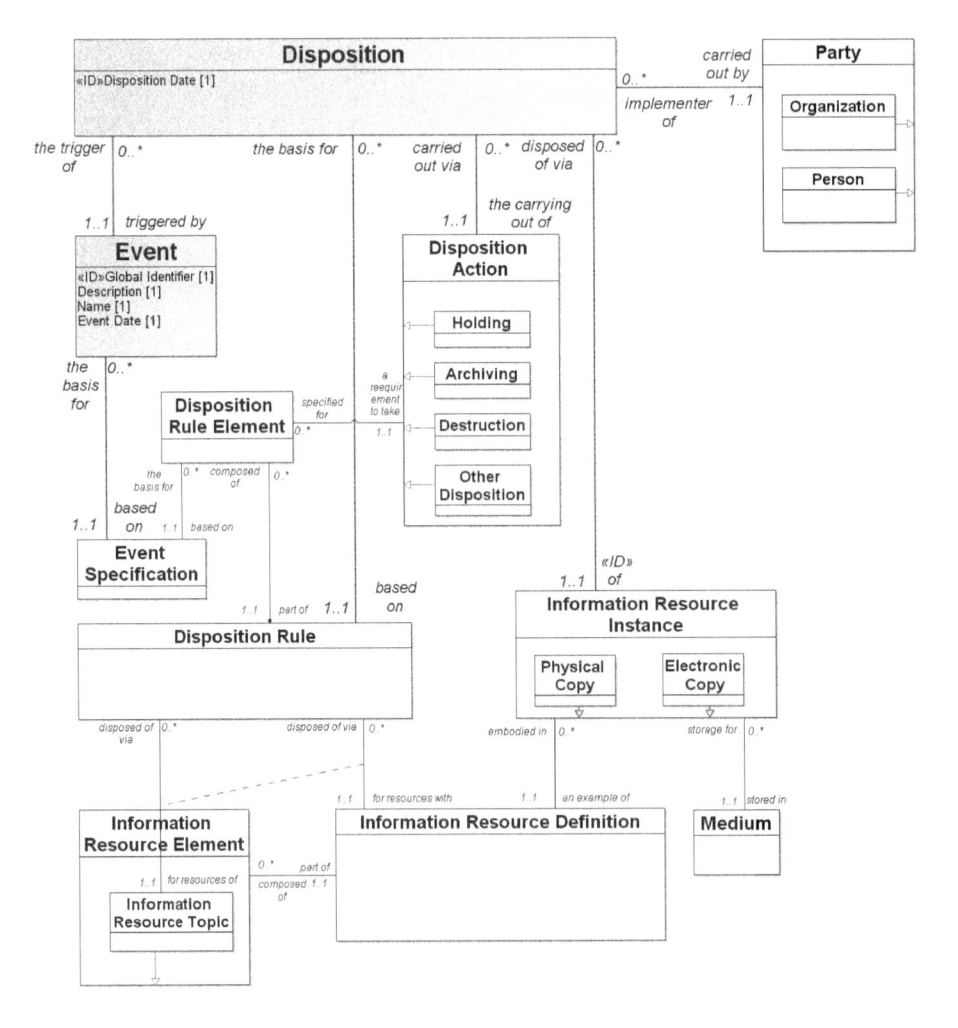

Figure 10-8: Dispositions

Documents and other Information Resources 219

A **Disposition Action** may be **Archiving**, **Destruction**, or **Holding**. Or it may be an **Other Disposition**.

Business Rules

- A **Disposition** *of* an **Information Resource Instance** must be *based on* a **Disposition Rule** that is *for* resources with the **Information Resource Definition** that is *embodied in* the **Information Resource Instance** that the **Disposition** is *of*. *(Translation*: **Disposition** *of* an **Information Resource Instance** must be *based on* a **Disposition Rule** that is *for* the **Information Resource Definition** of that **Information Resource Instance**.)

- The **Event** that was *the trigger of* a **Disposition** *of an* **Information Resource Instance** must be *an example of* the **Event Specification** that was *the basis for* (via a **Disposition Rule Element**) the **Disposition Rule** that was the basis for that **Disposition**. *(Translation:* The **Event** triggering a **Disposition** must be an instance of the **Event Specification** that was specified for a **Disposition Rule**.)

Summary

An **Information Resource** is any collection of concepts expressed in a form that can be communicated to others. It can be, among other things:

- A **Document** – a piece of text that could be a book, an e-mail, a catalogue, or a cable message. This includes virtual documents, such as web sites.

- An **Image** – either a still photograph or a moving picture, either on film or as a digital video. This includes everything from a YouTube video to a major motion picture.

- An **Other Information Resource** – such as, for example, a computer program.

Modeling **Information Resources** is difficult because is in fact a representation of information that is contained in the Enterprise Model. In its role as a query on the model, it would not otherwise be modeled, but often documents, et cetera are in fact important to the business in their own right. So this chapter describes a kind of "meta" model that is in fact itself part of the business model as well.

CHAPTER 11

Accounting

Accounting is itself an abstract model of an organization. It is very good at representing certain kinds of things about the organization's activities and resources. It is in fact *better* at representing certain kinds of situations than is data modeling.

To do a data model of the modeling process called double-entry bookkeeping calls for more abstraction than we've seen so far. Indeed, any accounting transaction journal entry is itself an abstraction. It has been hypothesized that the profound conceptual leap that was Cuneiform writing 6,000 years ago had its start as a means to account for commercial transactions.[45]

This section begins with a model of the basic structure of accounts and transactions, with the corresponding rules for creating debits and credits. Indeed, while the model can show the structures involved, there is a profound set of business rules that apply to these structures, which cannot be shown on the model directly. The structures can be used to design a database, but the rules are implemented by accounting application programs.

Later, this section describes how accounting transactions and cost centers can be linked to the elements of the enterprise data model.

Accounts

The ***general ledger*** is a record of the assets and liabilities of the organization being accounted for, and of the flow of money into or out of the company. This is in the form of a ***chart of accounts***, organizing quantities of money held or owed by the

---

[45] Richard Mattessich. 1998. "Recent insights into Mesopotamian accounting of the 3rd millennium B.C.-successor to token accounting.", *The Accounting Historian's Journal.* http://findarticles.com/p/articles/mi_qa3657/is_199806/ai_n8798263/.

company. This is in terms of things that the enterprise deals with, such as products or personnel. The basic rules and transactions for recording changes to the financial quantities are well-defined by the principles of **double-entry bookkeeping**. At the heart of the system is an **Account**. An account is "a place in which to record particular kinds of effects of the firm's transactions".[46] [*]

Setting up a *chart of accounts* involves defining the **Accounts** and grouping them into **Cost Centers**, where an **Account** is "A place in which to record particular kinds of effects of the firm's transactions,[47] and a **Cost Center** is an element of the organization—usually an **Internal Organization** (such as a department) that is being accounted for.

Each **Account** may be one of three basic kinds, as shown in Figure 11-1:

- **Asset Account** — "any [set of] rights which has value to its owner."[48] That is, the amount of money held by the organization. Occurrences of this type might be `"cash"`, `"accounts receivable"` (amounts owed to the company) or `"equipment"`. An Asset Account may also describe abstractions, such as available labor, which will be discussed in conjunction with labor usage, in Chapter 16.

- **Liability Account** — any amount owed to another party. Examples of this might be `"credit cards"`, `"notes payable"`, or `"employee withholding"`.

- **Equity Account** — the amount of the company's assets contributed or earned by the organization's owners. This is usually either `"owner-held stock"` or `"retained earnings"`. Among the equity accounts are two sub-categories of accounts that have special significance:

Income Account — the assets contributed to the firm by customers in exchange for goods or services. This might be `"professional service revenue"` or `"product sales"`. Each dollar of income represents *an increase in* the organization's equity.

---

[46] M. J. Gordon, and Gordon Shillinglaw. 1969. *Accounting: A Management Approach. Forth Edition.* (Homewood, Illinois: Richard D. Irwin, Inc.): 28.

[*] All descriptions of accounting in this chapter are derived from the Gordon and Shillinglaw book.

[47] *Ibid.*, P. 28.

[48] *Ibid.*, P. 22.

Expense Account — the assets spent by the company to acquire goods and services. This is the money spent for `"hotel"`, `"airfare"`, `"purchase of equipment"`, et cetera. Each dollar of expense represents *a decrease in* the organization's equity.

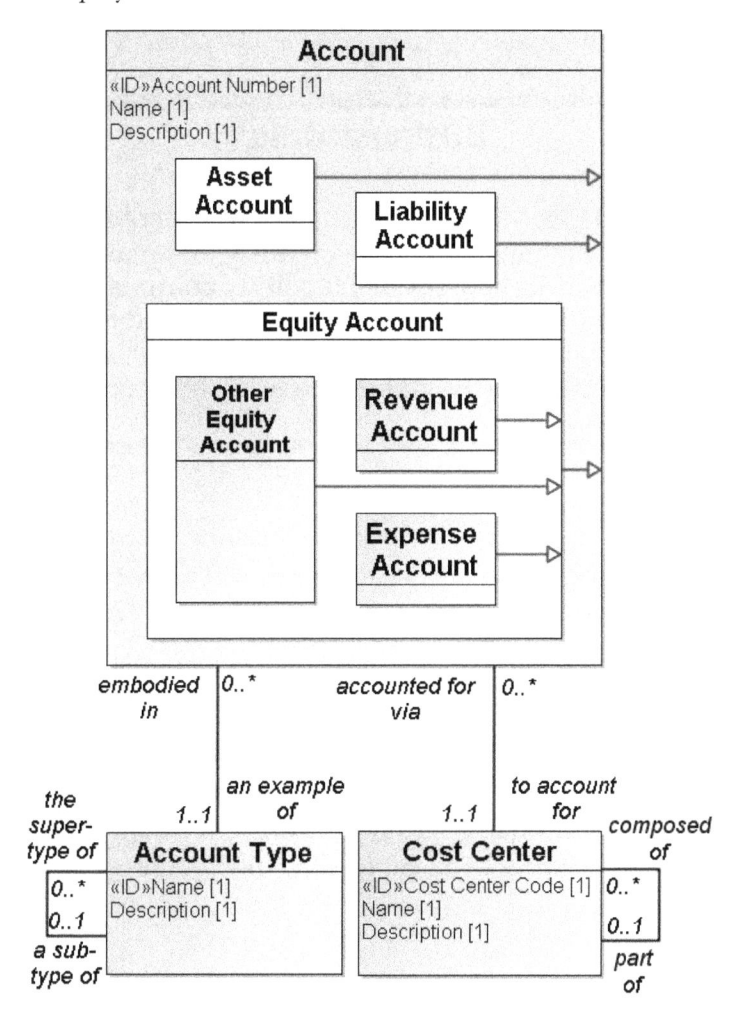

Figure 11-1: Accounts

The **Accounts** other than **Expense Accounts** and **Revenue Accounts** comprise the company's ***balance sheet***. They describe the *value of* the organization at a given point in time, and how much of that value is either owned by the stockholders or owed to others.

Expense Accounts and **Revenue Accounts**, on the other hand, are categories of **Equity Accounts**, but they are not like other **Equity Accounts**. Where other **Accounts** describe the *state* of the organization, **Expense** and **Revenue Accounts**

describe the *flow* of money into and out of the firm. These accounts are the basis for an enterprise's ***income statement***.[*] These **Accounts**, in effect, collect separately the transactions which increment and decrement the **Equity Account** "retained earnings", or its equivalent. They are considered **Equity Accounts** because they represent increases and decreases in equity.

Business Rule

- At all times, the total value represented by the set of **Asset Accounts** (the amount of money held by the organization) must equal the total value represented by the set of **Liability Accounts** (the amount of money obtained via loans) plus the set of **Equity Accounts** (the amount of money contributed by the organization's owners). (***Translation****:* A company's **Assets** must always equal its **Liabilities** plus its **Equities**.)

These accounts and their transactions are held separately, so that they can be reported together as the organization's *income statement*. This is an itemization of the expenses and revenues, along with the contribution to "net earnings" for a given period.

Each **Account** must be *an example of* one **Account Type**. This is a fundamental classification of **Accounts**. As with other parts of the model, the first instances of **Account Type** reproduce the sub-types shown in the figure: **Asset Account**, **Liability Account**, and **Equity Account**. *Sub-types of* **Equity Account** include **Revenue Account**, **Expense Account** and **Other Equity Account** Other **Account Types** can be added, so long as each is *a sub-type of* one and only one other **Account Type**.

There are many **Account Types** that are sub-types *of* these, including such things as **Accounts Receivable**, **Cash**, **Owner's Equity**, et cetera. There are some general principles defined by the accounting industry for the definition of **Account Types**, but the organization has wide latitude in setting up the specific list.

---

[*] "Balance Sheet" and "Income Statement" here refer to structures to be applied to reporting. Particular report designs, of course, correspond to the last chapter's **Information Resource Definitions**. Copies of such reports are then **Information Resource Instances**.

Cost Center[49] is another accounting structure for organizing accounts. Fundamentally, a **Cost Center** is nothing other than a collection of **Accounts** defined for a business purposes. While there are best practices, fundamentally there are no rules about how they are to be defined—other than the assertion that each **Account** must be *to account for* one and only one **Cost Center**. Typically, a **Cost Center** refers to a department or other **Internal Organization**, but it may also refer to any of several other elements of the organization—a **Product Type**, a **Work Center**, or a **Piece Of Equipment**, for example. Which kinds of things are referred to depend on the kind of **Account** it is, as will be discussed in the following section.

Rolling up Accounts

At first glance, it appears that each **Account** may be *composed of* one or more other **Accounts**. Indeed, Figure 11-2 shows that each **Account** may be *composed of* one or more **Account Rollup Structures**, each of which must be *the use of* exactly one other **Account**.

Keeping the integrity of the books, however, requires each **Account** to be *part of* no more than one other **Account**. The same sale, for example, cannot be added into corporate income more than once. This would argue for a single looping relationship showing a hierarchy. The problem with that approach is that there are multiple *ways* to roll up accounts. Each is for a different purpose. Depending on the purpose, the balance on a lower level **Account** might show up in more than one parent **Account**.

Thus, as shown in Figure 11-2, each **Account** may also be *part of* one or more **Account Rollup Structures** (each of which must be *the use in* exactly one other **Account**). An **Account Rollup Structure** is the fact that the money in one **Account** is part of the total money in another **Account**. Note that each **Account Rollup Structure** must also be *part of* one and only one **Roll-up Scheme**. A **Rollup Scheme** is a collection of **Accounts** and **Rollup Structure** instances that collectively represent the financial state of the enterprise. Business rules ensure that it is coherent and that no expense or revenue is double counted. In particular, note that each **Account Rollup Structure** is uniquely identified by the combination of relationships to both *the use of* **Account** and *part of* an **Account Rollup Structure**. For any given **Rollup Structure**, an **Account** can only be *part of* a parent **Account** once.

---

[49] ... or for our British and Canadian colleagues, **Cost Centre**.

226 Enterprise Model Patterns

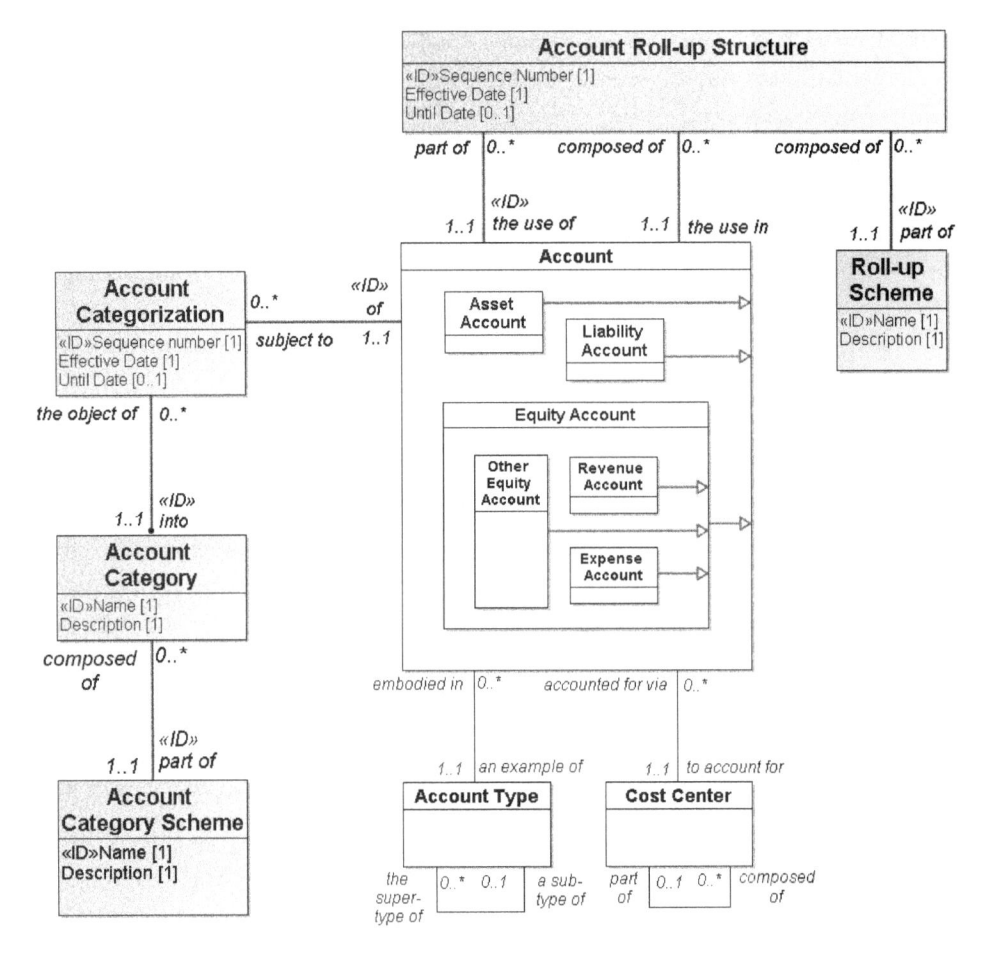

Figure 11-2: Account Structures and Categories

Business Rule

- Each **Account** may be *part of* only one **Account Rollup Structure** that is *part of* a particular **Rollback Scheme**. That is, a **Rollback Scheme** may not be *composed of* more than one **Account Rollup Structure** that is *the use of* a particular **Account**. *(Translation:* For any **Rollback Scheme**, each **Account** may roll up to only one other **Account**.)

For example, in Table 11-1, **Account** `"airline expense"` can be *part of* **Account** `"transportation expense"` only once in the `"daily"` **Roll-up Scheme**. It can, however, be *part of* **Account** `"travel and living expense"` once in the `"monthly"` **Roll-up Scheme**.

Table 11-1: Roll-up Schemes

the use of **Account**	*the use in* **Account**	*part of* **Roll-up Scheme**
Airline expense	Transportation expense	daily
Hotel expense	Lodging expense	daily
Airline expense	Travel and living expense	monthly
Hotel expense	Travel and living expense	monthly

As with **Parties**, **Geographic Locations**, and the like (as described in Part Two), there are many **Account Categories** that **Accounts** can fall into, even though, by definition, an **Account** can only be *part of* one **Cost Center** and may be *an example of* only one **Account Type**. This is shown above in Figure 11-2 by the fact that **Account Categorization** is *of* a particular **Account**, and *into* a particular **Account Category**. That is, each **Account** may be *classified into* as many **Account Categories** as needed, and that classification can change over time. **Account Categories** are organized in terms of **Account Category Schemes.**

Notice, by the way, that each **Cost Center** may be *composed of* one or more other **Cost Centers**. Some companies use this structure, rather than the **Account Roll-up** structure as a way of grouping accounts. Note that overall, the Controller has a lot of freedom in how accounts are defined and grouped.

Just as modelers of data vary in the skill with which they represent an enterprise, so too do modelers of accounts vary in the skill with which they represent an enterprise.

Accounting Transactions

The money that each **Account** is keeping track of is represented by the one or more **Balances** that are *in* each **Account**. Each instance of **Balance** has a Balance Value that was effective on a particular Balance Effective Date. When an instance of an **Account** is created, an initial instance of **Balance** is also created, with a Balance Value of "0".

For each **Accounting Transaction**, two or more **Balances** are updated by creating a new **Balance** with the Balance Value equal to the Balance Value of the previous instance plus the Value of the transaction. This will be described in more detail in the following section.

228 Enterprise Model Patterns

In its most general form, the model of an **Accounting Transaction** looks like that shown in Figure 11-3.

As described earlier, the total amount of an organization's **Assets** must equal the sum of its **Liabilities** and **Equities**. That is, the total resources available to the company must equal the sum of those borrowed plus those contributed or earned by the owners of the organization being accounted for. This is guaranteed by requiring each transaction to be composed of two kinds of **Accounting Entries** — **Debits** and **Credits**. Each **Accounting Transaction** must be *composed of* at least two **Accounting Entries** — which is to say, one or more **Debits** and one or more **Credits**. Each **Accounting Entry** must, in turn, be *to create* one and only one **Balance** *in* an **Account**. **Debits** and **Credits**, in turn, have been cleverly defined to be additions to or subtractions from different kinds of **Accounts**: If you have at least one of each, you will have done the balancing.

Business Rule

- The sum of the "Entry Values" of all **Debit Entries** that are part of a single **Accounting Transaction** must be equal to the sum of the "Entry Values" of all **Debit Entries** that are part of the same transaction. *(Translation:* In any **Accounting Transaction**, the sum of all **Debits** must equal the sum of all **Credits**.)

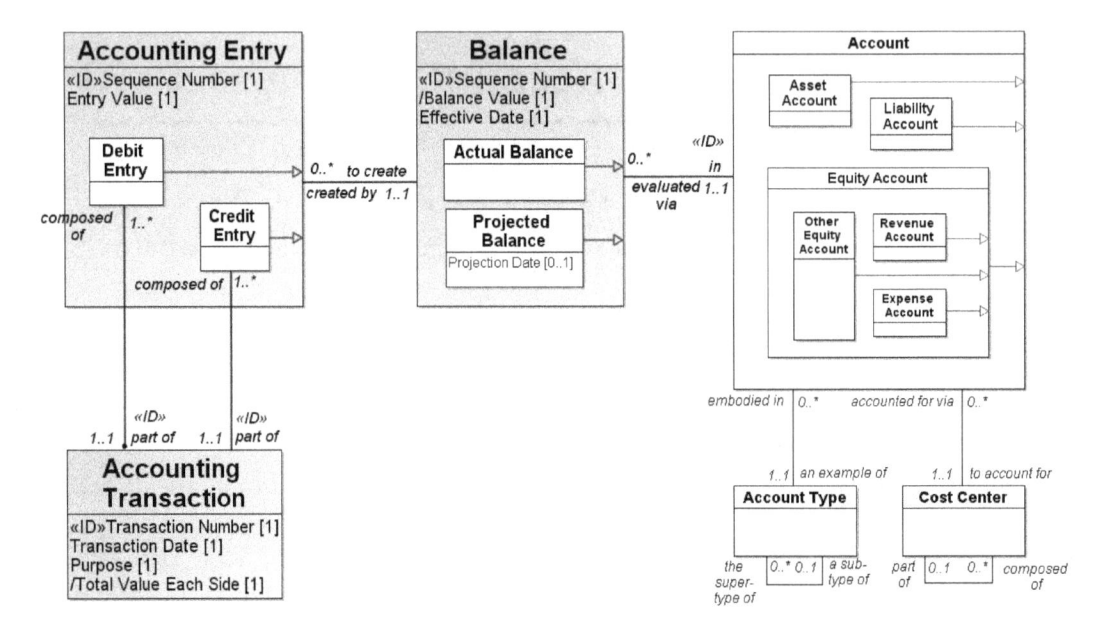

Figure 11-3: Accounting Transactions

Table 11-2 shows how a **Debit** or a **Credit** is either *an increment to* or *a decrement from* (the balance of) an **Account**, depending on what **Account Type** it is.

Table 11-2: Debits and Credits

| Assets || Liabilities || Equity ||
Debit	Credit	Debit	Credit	Debit	Credit
+	-	-	+	-	+

Specifically:

A *debit* must be

- an increment in an **Asset**, or
- a decrement in a **Liability**, or
- a decrement in an **Equity**.

A *credit* must be

- a decrement in an **Asset**, or
- an increment in a **Liability**, or
- an increment in an **Equity**.

For example, a transaction which debits an asset (say, "cash") and credits a liability (say, "short term loans") increases both the asset and the liability. That is, the cash received is equal to the amount borrowed. On the other hand, a transaction that debits one asset (say "raw material inventory") and credits another asset (say, "cash", again) is spending cash in order to add to raw material inventory.

Examples of a set of **Accounting Transactions** are shown in Table 11-3. In the first row, a "cash sale" has the effect of adding to the **Equity Account**, "Revenue" and adding to the **Asset Account**, "Cash", **in** the amount of "$430". That is, the company received "$430" in cash that they credited as "Revenue". This increases the credited **Account** (**Equity**—"Revenue") to a **Balance** of "$6,060". It increases the debited **Account** (**Asset** "Cash") to "$1,024". That is, the money received directly becomes an **Asset**.

In the second row, a sale on credit begins with an "invoice", which also adds to the **Equity Account** "revenue", but in this case, it doesn't increase the **Asset Account** "cash", but rather the **Asset Account** "accounts receivable".

The amount of change in both cases is "$500". The **Balance** for "revenue" goes up again, this time to "$6,560". Note that our assets include not only the money that we hold in cash ("$1,024", from the last transaction), but also the money owed to us (newly incremented to "$1,500"). The total net worth, then, increased from "$2024" to "$2524" ("$1024"+"1500").

Table 11-3: Sample Accounting Transactions

Accounting Transaction Purpose	Account credited	Account debited	Trans-action Value	Cash (Asset Account) Value	Accounts Receivable (Asset Account) Balance Value	Revenue Account Balance Value
(Initial Balance)				594	1000	5630
Cash Sale	Revenue (Equity) +	Cash (Asset) +	430	1024		6060
Invoice	Revenue (Equity) +	Accounts Receivable (Asset) +	500		1500	6560
Payment Receipt	Accounts Receivable (Asset) −	Cash (Asset) +	500	1524	1000	

The third row shows what happens when our customer pays his bill. The **Transaction Type** "payment receipt" credits (subtracts from) the **Asset Account** "accounts receivable" for the "$500" received, and debits (adds to) the **Asset Account** "cash" for the same amount. The **Balance** of "accounts receivable" then returns to the "$1,000" it had before the last transaction, and the **Balance** of cash is now incremented again, this time to "$1,524". Note that our total net worth is unchanged. It is just that the "$2524" is calculated from "$1524" and "$1000", instead of "$1024" and "$1500".

Accounting Transaction Rules

As stated, there are specific rules associated with each **Accounting Transaction Type**. The rules determining which **Accounts** are debited and which are credited

Accounting

are defined for each kind of **Accounting Transaction**, its **Accounting Transaction Type**.;

These rules describe the debits and credits to be created for all **Accounting Transactions** that are *examples of* that **Accounting Transaction Type**. Inferring from the example in Table 11-3, a cash sale always credits (adds to) the **Equity Account** `"revenue"` and debits (adds to) the **Asset Account** `"cash"`.

Figure 11-4 shows how each **Accounting Transaction Type** must be *composed of* one or more **Credit Rules** and one or more **Debit Rules**.

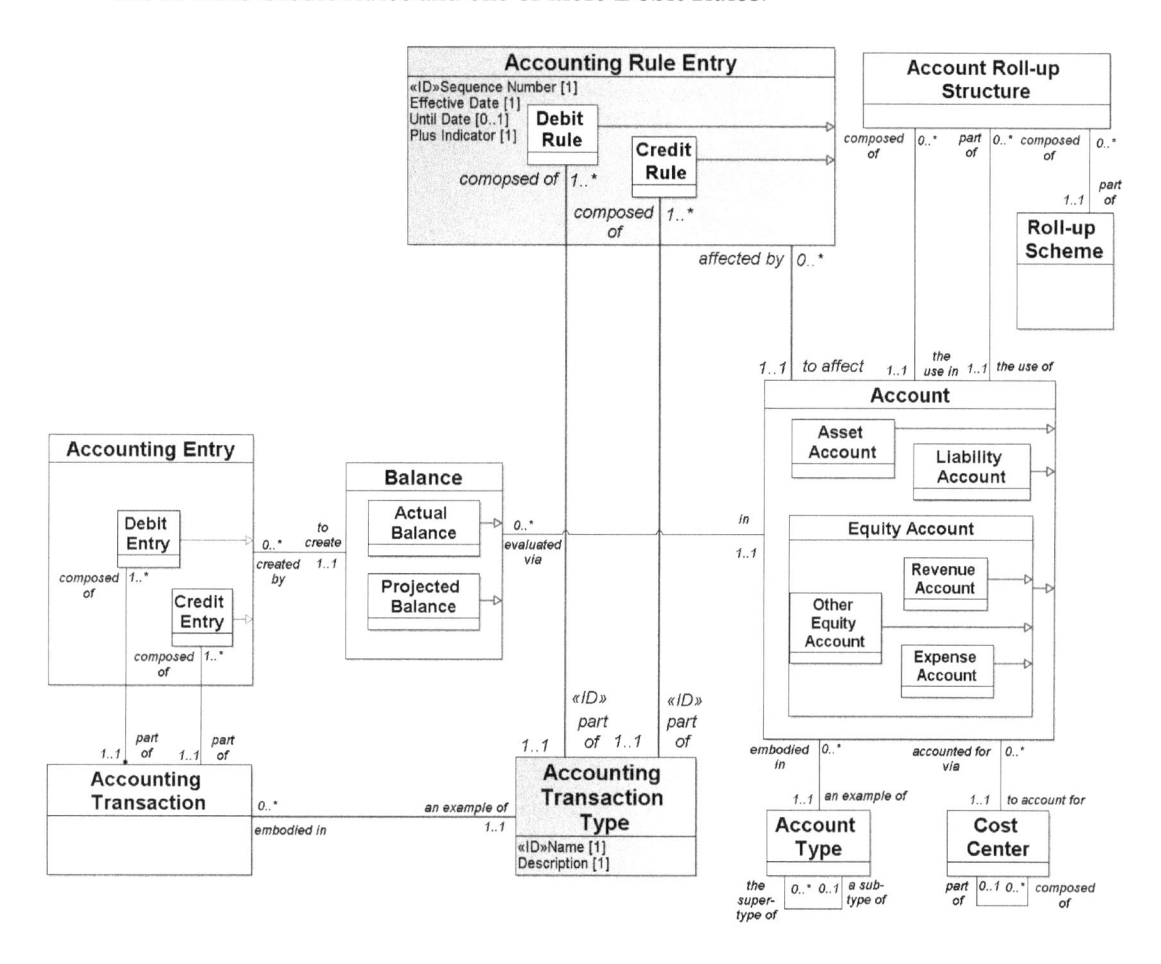

Figure 11-4: Accounting Rule Entries

These are sub-types of **Accounting Rule Entry**, so each has the attribute Plus Indicator. Each then must be *to affect* (add to or subtract from, depending on whether the Plus Indicator is `"true"` or `"false"`, respectively) exactly one **Account**.

232 Enterprise Model Patterns

Note that an **Account** can be *composed of* one or more other **Accounts** as defined by **Account Rollup Structures**. Thus an **Accounting Rule Entry** can be defined at any level of detail in the chart of accounts.

Table 11-4 shows some examples of four **Accounting Transaction Types** and their corresponding **Accounting Rule Entries**.

Table 11-4: Accounting Rules

Accounting Transaction Type	Debit Rule / Account / Account Type	Plus Indicator	Credit Rule / Account / Account Type	Plus Indicator
Invoice	Accounts Receivable (Asset)	"True" (+)	Revenue (Equity)	"True" (+)
Payment Received	Cash on hand (Asset)	"True" (+)	Accounts Receivable (Asset)	"False" (-)
Purchase	Inventory (Asset)	"True" (+)	Accounts Payable (Liability)	"True" (+)
Payment Made	Accounts Payable (Liability)	"False" (-)	Cash on Hand (Asset)	"False" (-)

In the first line, any time an **Accounting Transaction Type** is an "invoice", then

- a **Balance** for the **Asset Account** `"accounts receivable"` must be created by creating a new **Balance**, whose Balance Value is the sum of prior **Balance** instance's Balance Value (The Plus Indicator is `"true"`) and the corresponding **Accounting Entry's** Entry Value.

- In addition, a new **Balance** for the **Equity Account** `"revenue"` must be created by creating a new **Balance**, whose Balance Value is the sum of prior **Balance** instance's Balance Value (The Plus Indicator is also `"true"`) and the corresponding **Accounting Entry's** Entry Value.

That is, any `"Invoice"` adds to `"accounts receivable"` and adds to `"revenue"`.

In the second line, if a payment is received, the `"payment received"` transaction type creates a new, higher **Balance** for the **Asset Account** `"cash on hand"` (via a **Debit Rule**), and a new, smaller **Balance** for the **Asset Account** `"accounts receivable"` (via a **Credit Rule**).

The third line describes a "`purchase`" with a higher **Balance** (via a **Debit Rule**) for the **Asset Account** "`inventory`", and a higher **Balance** (via a **Credit Rule**) to the **Liability Account**, "`accounts payable`".

The fourth line describes a "`payment made`" with a lower **Balance** (via a **Debit Rule**) for the **Account** "`liability`" (or one of its more detailed **Accounts**), and a lower **Balance** (via a **Credit Rule**) to the **Asset**, "`cash on hand`".

Connections to the Real World

The information contained in a chart of accounts purports to describe the entire enterprise—albeit in terms of financial entities and transactions. The enterprise entity/relationship model also purports to describe the entire enterprise, but in terms of the business entities and transactions. Payment of an invoice against a purchase order is a business transaction, linked to the **Parties** involved and the **Assets** and/or **Activities** purchased. It is also a financial transaction, linked to the **Accounts** and **Cost Centers** involved. Clearly, this is a single transaction, so for information systems to be coherent, the two expressions of it must be properly linked. This entails linking **Cost Centers** to the **Internal Organizations** and other enterprise components that are collecting the value of transactions, and linking business transactions to **Accounting Transactions**.

Cost Center Assignments

The concept of **Cost Center** is, in accounting terms, simply a named collection of **Accounts**. Its purpose is to collect money associated with running some part of the business. Usually, a **Cost Center** is a department (an **Internal Organization**), such as "`Data Management`", "`Widget production`", or "`corporate offices`". The linking of the accounting concept **Cost Center** to the real-world concept **Internal Organization** is shown in Figure 11-5.

As described in Chapter Two, **Internal Organization** is a kind of **Organization** (which is a kind of **Party**) that is any departmental entity that has no existence outside the corporation. That is, it is usually called a department. Because a **Cost Center** may be *assigned* one or more **Internal Organizations** and an **Internal Organization** may be *assigned to* multiple **Cost Centers**, the "intersect entity class", **Cost Center Assignment** is the fact that a particular **Cost Center** is used to collect financial information about a particular **Internal Organization**.

234 Enterprise Model Patterns

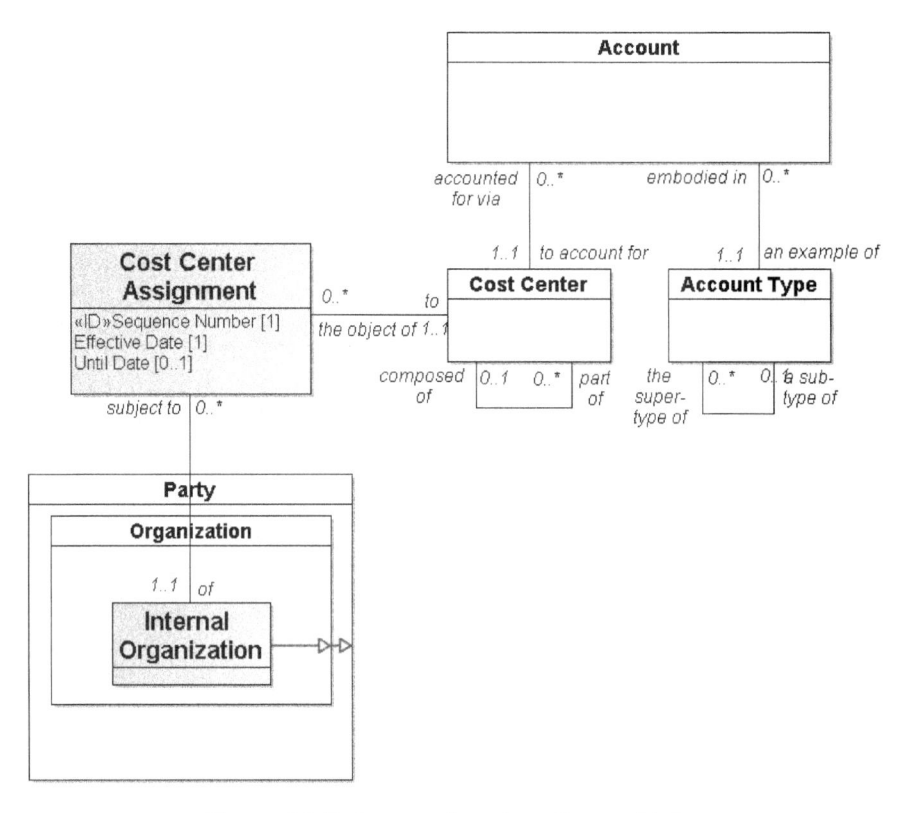

Figure 11-5: Accounting Cost Center Links

There is nothing in the principles of accounting, however, that requires **Cost Centers** to represent internal departments at all. While most **Cost Centers** in most organizations do, in fact, represent such departments, it is also possible to define **Cost Centers** to represent anything the company wants to keep financial track of. For example:

- The part of the Human Resources Department in Austin, as opposed to the part that is in Bakersfield.
- A particular building, as a way to keep track of maintenance expenses.
- A project, or even a large activity that is part of a project.
- And so forth.

Figure 11-6 shows that **Cost Center Assignment** could be extended to link a **Cost Center** to virtually anything else in our enterprise data model.

Transaction Assignments

An **Accounting Transaction** is a reflection of something in the world that happens. The business **Activities** that complete production of a product or make a sale all have attributes associated with them to record costs. This record of costs does not get reflected in the company's books until an appropriate **Accounting Transaction** debits and credits the appropriate **Accounts**.

As we have seen, the specific nature of the transaction is controlled by the **Accounting Transaction Type**, but it is possible to see some of the kinds of transactions in the world that trigger the **Accounting Transactions**. As with **Cost Center Assignments**, it is possible to imagine **Accounting Transaction Assignments** linking **Accounting Transactions** to various events happening in the enterprise.

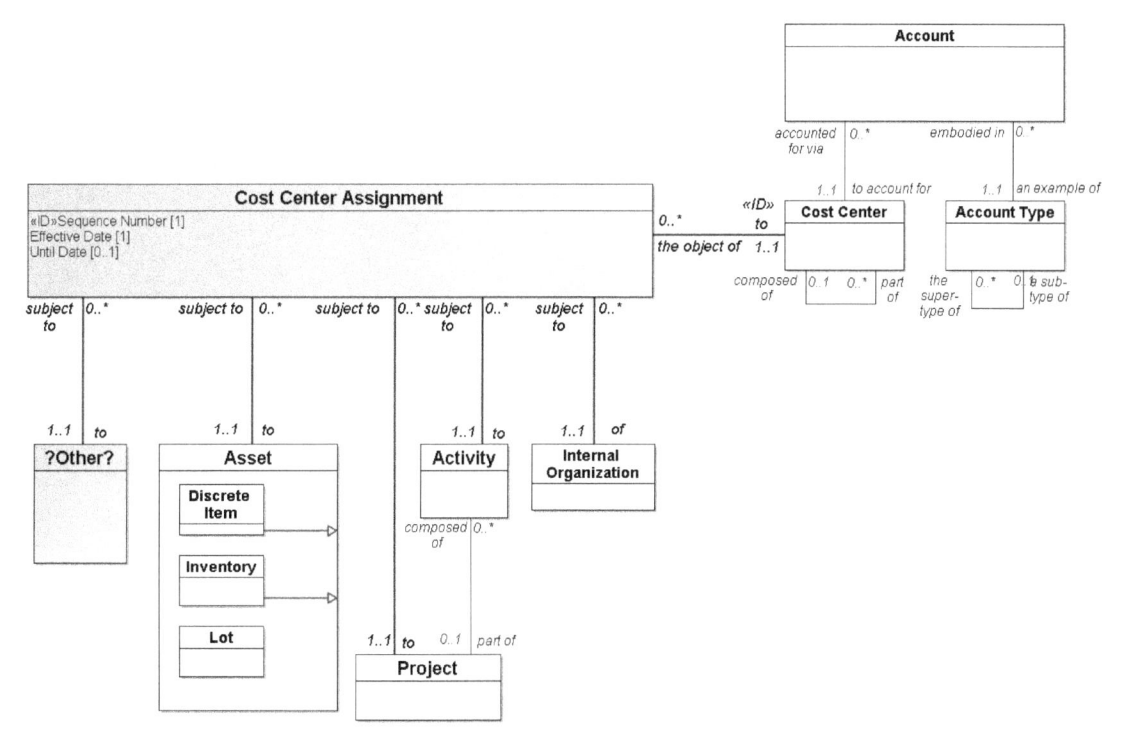

Figure 11-6: More Accounting Cost Center Links

Since the Level 1 enterprise model is primarily about reference data and only describes **Event** in a very constrained way, the kinds of links required for **Accounting Transactions** will have to wait for presentation of the more detailed department models in Section IV.

Summary

Accounting is itself a model of an organization. It is very good at representing certain kinds of things about the organization's activities and resources. It is, in fact, *better* at representing certain kinds of situations than is data modeling.

To do a data model of the modeling process called double-entry bookkeeping calls for more abstraction than we've seen so far. Indeed, any accounting transaction journal entry is itself an abstraction. It has been hypothesized that the profound conceptual leap that was Cuneiform writing 6,000 years ago had its start as a means to account for commercial transactions.[50]

In this chapter, we laid out the raw materials for an accounting system: **Accounts** and **Accounting Transactions**. The chapter provided an introduction to double-entry bookkeeping, as illustrated by the entity/relationship model. It also included the logic for establishing the *rules* that apply to each kind of **Accounting Transaction**.

---

[50] Richard Mattessich,. 1998. "Recent insights into Mesopotamian accounting of the 3rd millennium B.C.-successor to token accounting". *The Accounting Historian's Journal.* http://findarticles.com/p/articles/mi_qa3657/is_199806/ai_n8798263/.

PART FOUR

ABSTRACTION LEVEL 2: WITHIN AN ORGANIZATION

The models we've seen so far can be applied to nearly any corporation or government agency. With proper population of the **Characteristic** and **Characteristic Specification** entities, they truly and accurately could be made to represent any large organization. But is it useful to do so? More significantly, when is it appropriate to be more concrete in your representations.

The parts of the model shown as Level 1 answer five of the six principle questions about the nature of an enterprise: Who (people and organizations)? Where(geography)? What(assets)? How(activities)? And When(time)? Each of these questions could be addressed by a relatively independent section of the model. Moreover, each of these elements describes basic concepts that apply to the enterprise as a whole. A more difficult question is "Why?", since that goes to the heart of what the enterprise does.

To answer this question requires bringing together elements from each of the other sections. It involves mixing parts from the other model components and adding them to address specific issues associated with The various functions of the enterprise. These are still models that can apply generally across enterprises, but they address particular parts of any particular enterprise.

While there are potentially a great number of such specialized models, this chapter will address the following variations (portrayed graphically in Figure Four-1):

238 Enterprise Model Patterns

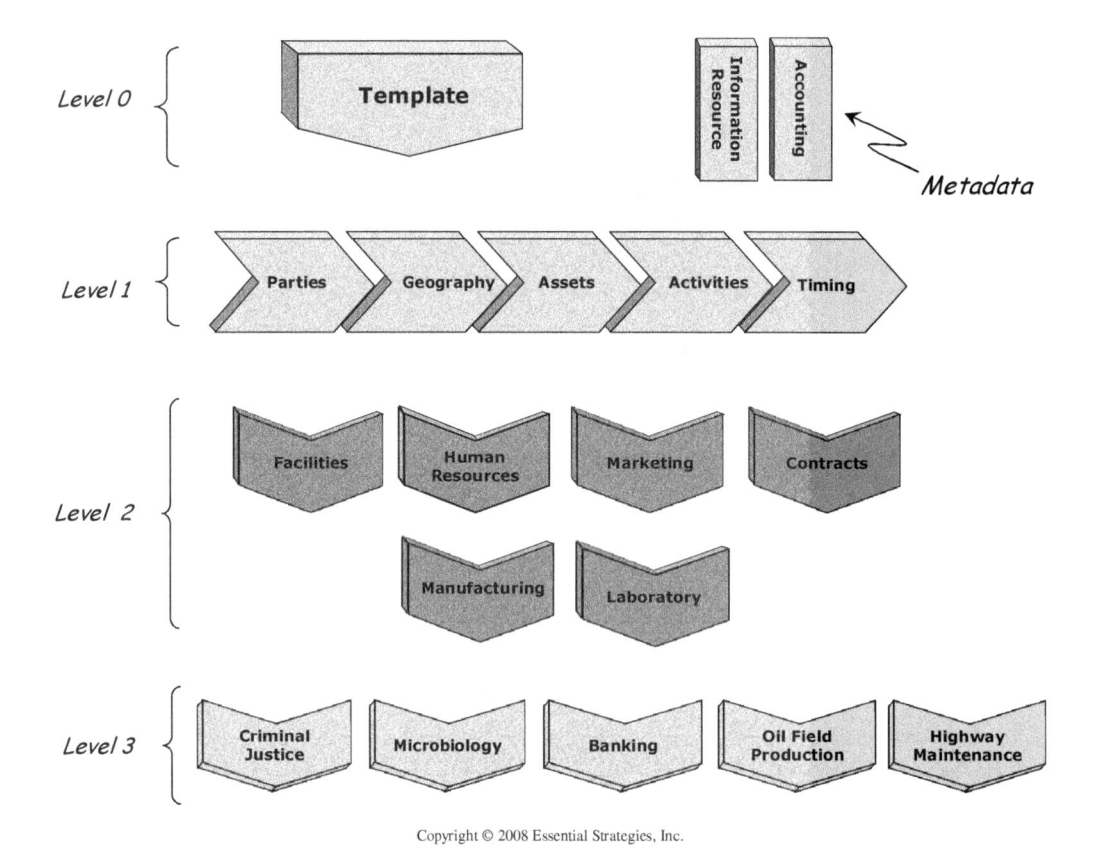

Figure Four-1: The Level 2 Components

1. *Facilities* - a **Facility** is a **Geographic Location** with a purpose, where **Persons** and **Organizations** (**Parties**) make use of **Assets** to carry out **Activities**. Indeed, a facility is simply a (***physical)* Address**. This, coincidentally provides a useful context in which to explore the concept of "address" more generally. This is described in Chapter 12.

2. *Human Resources* – In Chapter 4, care was taken to distinguish between **Parties** (**Persons** and **Organizations**), and the roles that they play. The concept of *employee* was not addressed. This is because people's relationships with their employers is much more complex than can be described in the one or two entity classes shown there. In Chapter 13, this is described in more detail.

3. *Communications and Marketing* – Any enterprise or government agency exists to provide products or services to a marketplace. The first step in that process must be communicating, not only with the marketplace, but also with the world in general. Once the structures for communication have been set up, they can apply also to communications with employees and others within the organization. This is all described in Chapter 14. Note that a

communication is a specialized kind of **Activity**. Part of the "why" of any organization is to work with people.

4. *Contracts* – A **Contract** is an agreement among **Persons** and **Organizations** that imposes an obligation on one or more of them to provide **Activities** and/or **Assets** to the others. From the point of view of any one **Organization**, important contracts are *purchase orders* and *sales orders*. In purchase orders, the **Organization** plays the role of customer, while others play the role of vendor. In sales orders, the **Organization** plays the role of vendor, with the other **Parties** playing the role of customer. Other **Contracts** are used to hire **Persons**, and yet others are for other purposes. With variations, they all have the basic structure described in Chapter 15. The second half of "why" is to provide products and services to customers.

5. *Manufacturing* – This area was covered extensively in the first *Data Model Patterns: Conventions of Thought* book, so it will not be repeated here in as much detail. But the basic structure of work orders, activities, and accounting for material and labor will be described. This is a blending of the concepts behind **Asset** and **Activity**.

6. *The Laboratory* – A Laboratory is a **Facility** (see Chapter 12) that uses various pieces of equipment to gather and analyze data in order to draw conclusions from them. This may include analyses of manufacturing processes, product quality, forensics, or the environment, among others. The formal collection of data supports the collection of some of the **Characteristics** and **Characteristic Specifications** that are described for the enterprise model in Section Two of this book.

The specialization described for each of these functional areas is typically the domain of specific departments. For the most part, however, these functions are done in similar fashion across companies or agencies. The models presented here should be generally applicable.

Human Resources, for example, is concerned with employment, job assignments, qualifications, and so forth. Marketing is concerned with contacting prospects, providing information about products and services offered, and the like. Because these are generally known and used concepts, even though they are more concrete than those described previously, patterns are involved, so it is worthwhile to address a new level of abstraction, called here, "Abstraction Level 2".

CHAPTER 12

Facilities

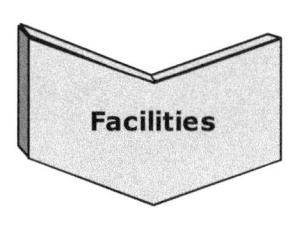

Different industries have very different definitions for the word "facility". In financial institutions, for example, it refers to an internal agreement the bank has reached to extend credit to a particular client. More commonly, however, it refers to a place where work is done, such as a factory or an oil well[♣], and that is the sense in which it is used here.

Synonyms include "physical address", and "site" or "physical site".

For purposes of this model, a **Facility** is defined as a physical address, or "a place with a purpose". This is to distinguish it from **Geographic Location**, which is simply "a place". As shown in Figure 12-1, a **Facility** is *located in* one or more **Geographic Locations**, and *used by* **Parties** *to manufacture, use, or store* **Assets**, in order *to carry out* **Activities**.

Parties and Facilities

It is common for systems to include **Address** as an attribute to describe the location of a **Person**, an **Organization**, or both. This is problematic, though, since many **Parties** have more than one address: home address, shipping address, and office address are common examples. Moreover, two or more **Parties** could be at the same address. For this reason, the address should, in fact, be a separate entity, with an intersect entity to allow for the fact that there is a many-to-many relationship between the two.

[♣] In U.S. restaurants, of course, the term refers to something else altogether.

241

242 Enterprise Model Patterns

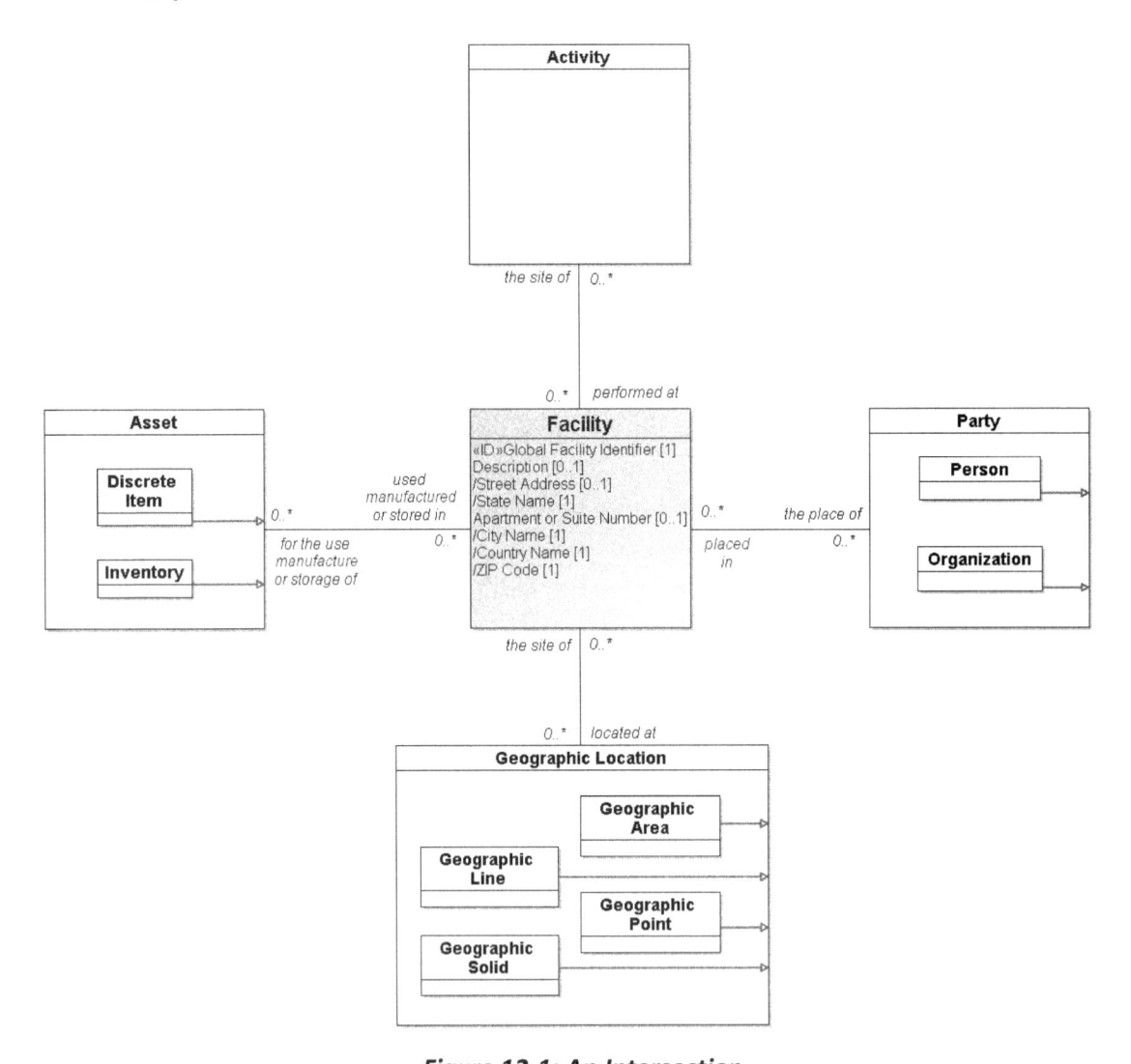

Figure 12-1: An Intersection

In Figure 12-2, the **Address** entity class is shown, with attributes **Street Address**, **/City Name**, **/State Name**, **/Postal Code**, and **/Country Name**. The slash character (/) in front of these attribute names indicates that they are derived from other attributes in the model, as will be shown. **Party Placement** is the intersection entity class that represents the fact that a particular **Party** is located at a particular **Address**. That is, each **Party Placement** must be *of* one and only one **Party** and it must be *at* one and only one **Address**. **Party Placement Type** allows us to enumerate the different kinds of ways a **Party** might need an **Address**. Instances of **Party Placement Type** might include the `"home address"`, `"shipping address"`, or `"office address"`.

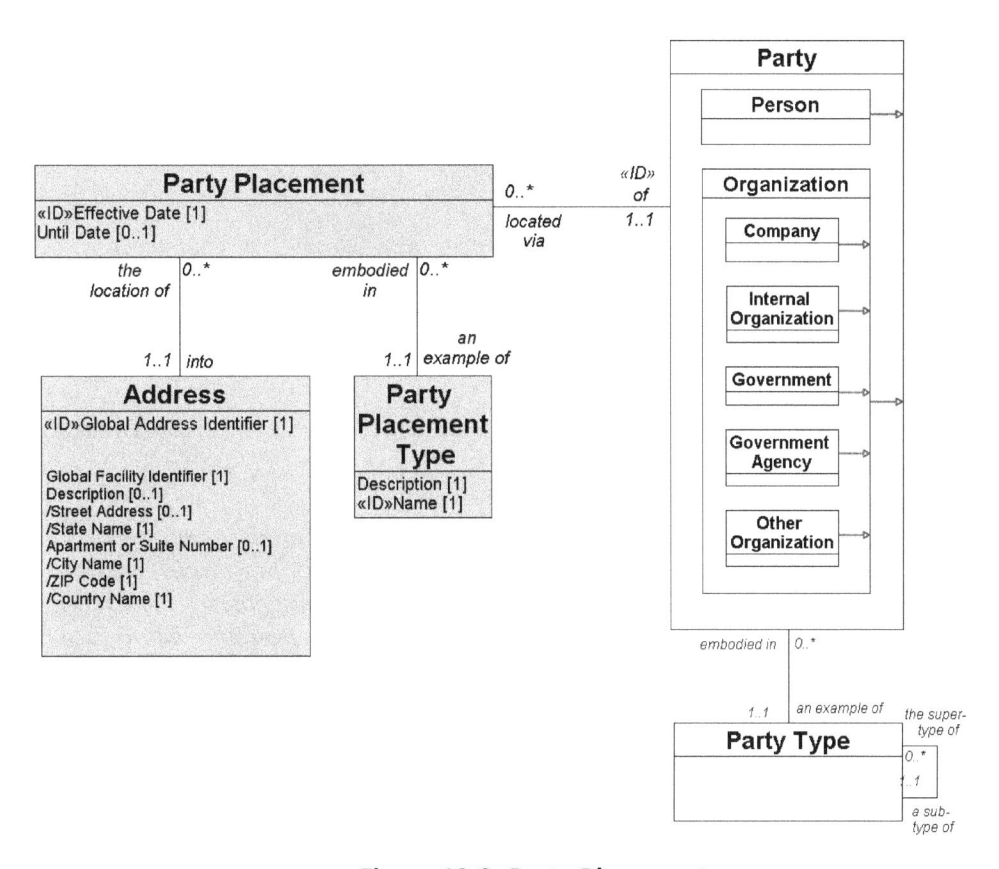

Figure 12-2: Party Placement

Addresses

Figure 12-3 shows that **Address** is a complex entity class. First of all, it shows **Facility** as a kind of **Address**—specifically, this is what may also be called, a *physical address*. This is located at a set of **Geographic Locations**, described by the attributes mentioned previously. It is *located via* structures presented later in this chapter. The figure shows as sub-types various basic kinds of **Facilities** that can occur:

- **Home** – a house or apartment where people live.
- **Office** – a building or part of a building where people carry out their business.
- **Plant** – a collection of one or more buildings and other structures for the purpose of manufacturing or other processing.

- **Warehouse** – a building for the purpose of storing products or materials.

- **Storage Location** – a designated shelf, locker, or other designated space set aside for storage purposes. Usually this is in a warehouse or a manufacturing plant.

- **Work Center** – a part of a plant where specific manufacturing steps take place.

- **Other Facility** – a place with a purpose (and usually building structures) other than those listed above.

Note that each definition characterizes both the kinds of buildings located at the facility, along with its purpose.

Figure 12-3 adds to **Address** the sub-type **Virtual Address**. This encompasses such non-physical addresses as

- **E-Mail Address** – A label for a node on a communications network (usually *the Internet*, but private networks can also have **E-Mail Addresses**) where someone can receive messages from others. The label consists of a specific name concatenated with a *domain name* that describes a portion of the network where the address is located.

- **Telephone Address** – A number on the international telephone network. (That is, a telephone number.)

- **Web Address** – A node on the portion of *the Internet* that is the *World-wide Web*. It is labeled by a *Uniform Record Locator* (*URL*), but is identified by an *Internet Protocol* (*IP*) *Address*.

Note that each **Address** must be *an example of* one and only one **Address Type**. This is like other **…Type** entity classes in that it reproduces the structure of the sub-types of **Address**. The first instances must correspond to the **Address** sub-types: **Facility**, **Virtual Address**, **Office**, **Telephone Address**, et cetera. The structure of the sub-types in **Address** is handled by the relationship that each **Address Type** may be *a sub-type of* one and only one other **Address Type**.

In this case, however, **Facility Type** and **Virtual Address Type** were escalated to sub-type status themselves. This allows for more specific connections with **Facility** and **Virtual Address**. These become useful later on.

Because in some companies a **Work Center** can be moved from one **Plant** or larger **Work Center** to another over time, and because it is difficult to predict exactly what sort of configurations of **Facilities** might occur, Figure 12-3 defines a **Facility Structure** as the fact that one **Facility** is *part of* another at a given time. That is, each **Facility** may be *composed of* one or more other **Facilities**, and each **Facility** (over time, at least) may be *part of* one or more other **Facilities**. To accommodate this many-to-many relationship, **Facility Structure** is defined to be *the presence of* one **Facility** and *the presence in* another **Facility**.

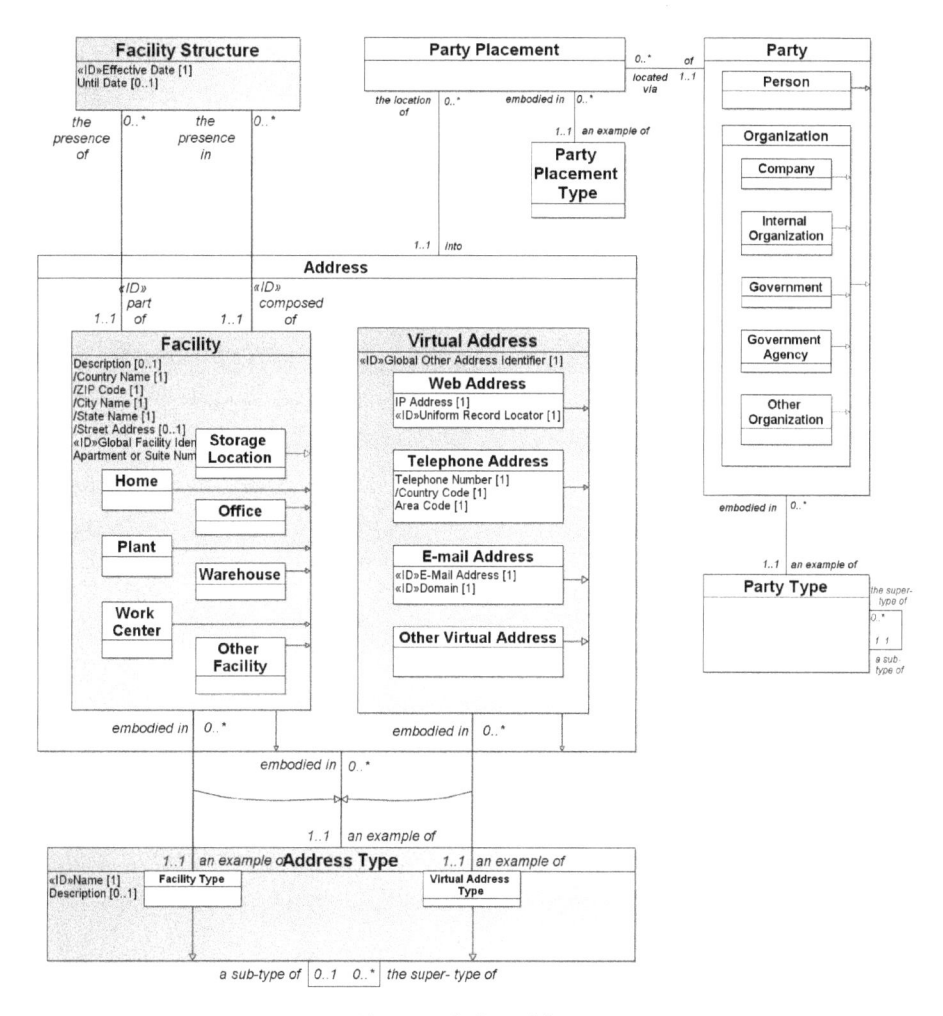

Figure 12-3: Addresses

An alternative would be to replace **Facility Structure** with a simple loop[♣] showing a many-to-one recursive relationship: each **Facility** may be *composed of* one or more **Facilities**; but then each **Facility** may *only* be *part of* one and only one **Facility**.

Note that Figure 12-2 was misleading: The attributes shown only apply to a *physical* **Facility**, not to any **Virtual Address**. Representing the latter in data models has been problematic in the past. On the other hand, if the definition of **Address** is extended here to "a way of locating someone or something", then both these

---

[♣] Known to the modeling trade as a "pig's ear".

Virtual Addresses and physical **Facilities** fall under this definition. Indeed, Merriam-Webster (rather clumsily) defines "address" as "a place where a person or organization may be communicated with"[51]. A **Party**, then, may be *located via* one or more **Party Placements**, each of which must be *in* either a physical address (the **Facility** where it works) or a **Virtual Address** (a **Web Address**, an **E-Mail Address**, or a **Telephone Address**).

As of when this book was written, the three primary sub-types shown represent the complete set of virtual addresses. Next year, of course, there may well be **Other Virtual Addresses** available, as well.♥

Geographic Locations and Facilities

In many applications, addresses are simply stored as one or more attributes in **Party**. As we've already seen, it is greatly beneficial to store them in their own entity class—and ultimately in their own table. Many systems have an important **Address** table.

The attributes of **Facility** shown in Figure 12-3, are representative:

- Description
- /Street Address
- Apartment or Suite
- /City
- /State (The United States version of a **Principal Country Division** Default Name)
- /ZIP Code (The United States version of **Postal Region** Postal Code)
- /Country

---

[51] Merriam-Webster. 2010. "address". *The Merriam-Webster OnLine Dictionary*. *http://merriam-webster.com/dictionary/address* (Viewed 2010).

♥ For purposes of this book, your author is going to pretend that "Twitter Address" has not yet been invented.

Description is not typically used in the United States, but it is popular in the UK. For example, your author's in-laws house outside Glasgow, Scotland is called "The Croft". **Street Address** itself could also simply be a piece of text, but in fact (for the United States, at least) it is an attribute of the **Geographic Location** sub-type **Other Surveyed Area**. In fact, some **Organizations** (such as, in the United States, the Internal Revenue Service or the Central Intelligence Agency) do not have street addresses at all. The **City** and the **ZIP Code** constitute the entire address. **Apartment** or **Suite** is usually a piece of text, but in a more complex **Facility** model, it could point to a smaller **Facility**. **City**, **State**, and **Country** all refer to **Geopolitical Locations**.

Clearly modeling **Address** can be much more complex than the three or four lines of text you see on an envelope would suggest.

This is made more complicated still by the fact that the rules are different in different countries.

So, how flexible must the model be to deal with different countries' approaches both to organizing their land and to constructing addresses? To what extent do we build in a particular approach, and to what extent can we generalize it to make it more flexible?

At what point do we resign ourselves to creating a separate model for each country?

Note the slashes in front of the attribute names in **Address**, denoting that each is derived from somewhere else in the model. As it happens, there are several approaches we can take. First we will present a relatively concrete model reflecting the address structures in the United States. A more abstract model will then follow—which can presumably be adapted to any country.

The Direct Approach (U.S. Version)

The Direct Approach goes on the assumption that every **Address** must have a **Street Address**, and that the location of that **Street Address** is known in advance. These are probably untenable assumptions, but it is useful to follow them through.

To describe the calculated fields requires the invention of a SQL-like language that, in its entirety, is beyond the scope of this book. The stripped down version, however, includes two very important functions, first encountered in a very clever database management system that is now unknown, but which your author first encountered in 1981.[*] The functions address two very important navigation activities:

- INFER-THROUGH(<*role name*>, **<parent entity class name>**, **<attribute name>**
  (WHERE(<*role name*>, **<parent entity class name>**, <attribute name=<"value">>))

  This recognizes that the attributes of a "parent" entity class (the "one" end of a "many-to-one" relationship) are available to the "child" entity. For example, in Formula 1, below, the value for an instance of Street Address in **Other Surveyed Area** is information that can be used to describe any instance of **Facility** that is *located in* that instance of **Other Surveyed Area**.

  The parameters of this function are:

  - **Role name** – the name of the role used to navigate from the subject entity class to the object entity class.

  - **Entity class name** – the name of the object entity class that holds the inferred attribute.

  - **Attribute name** – the name of the attribute being inferred.

  - **WHERE clause** – required for the more complex navigation that will be required when describing the more abstract approach in the next section.

- SUM-THROUGH (<*role name*>, **<child entity class name>**, **<attribute name>**)

  This will be used in a later chapter to allow a summary attribute in a "parent" entity class instance to obtain a sum of the values of all the "child" instances related to that parent. For example, if an **Order** may be *composed of* one or more **Line Items**. The **Order** attribute /Total cost is computed as the sum of the values of the Line Item Cost for all the instances of **Line Item** that are related to this instance of **Order**.

Figure 12-4 shows how a **Facility** in the United States can take its physical mailing address. Thus, its **/Street Address** can be calculated:

---

[*] It was called the "Mitrol Information Management System (MIMS)", produced originally by the Mitrol Corporation (consisting of people from MIT) in the late 1970s. It was owned by the General Electric Corporation for about 5 years, who then sold it to Teamco Systems Innovation in Paris.

1. **Facility /Street Address** =

    INFER-THROUGH (located in, **Other Surveyed Area**, Street Address)

2. **Facility /ZIP Code** =

    INFER-THROUGH (*located in*, **Postal Area**, Postal Code)

3. **Facility /City Name** =

    INFER-THROUGH (*located in*, **City**, Default Name[≈])

4. **Facility /State** =

    INFER-THROUGH (*located in*, **City**, /Principal Country Division Name)

5. **Facility /Country Name** =

    INFER-THROUGH (*located in*, **City**, /Country Name)

Continuing, the following derivations create the attributes of **City**:

6. **City /Principal Country Division Name** =

    INFER-THROUGH (*part of*, **Principal Country Division**, Default Name)

7. **City /Country Name** =

    INFER-THROUGH (*part of*, **Principal Country Division**, /Country Name)

Then, in **Principal Country Division**, you get:

8. **Principal Country Division /Country Name** =

    INFER-THROUGH (*part of*, **Country**, Default Name)

In some cases, an **Other Surveyed Area** may have a **Street Address**, and may not even be in a **City**. Thus, each **Other Surveyed Area** must be either *part of* one **City** or *part of* one **Principal Country Division**. As a result, it has the following attributes:

[≈] "Default Name" is inherited from the super-type **Geographic Area**.

9. **Other Surveyed Area** /Principal Country Division **Name** = INFER-THROUGH(*part of*, **Principal Country Division**, Default Name)

10. **Other Surveyed Area** /Country Name =

    INFER-THROUGH(*part of*, **Principal Country Division**, /Country Name)

Formula 8, above, shows the derivation of **Principal Country Division**, /Country Name.

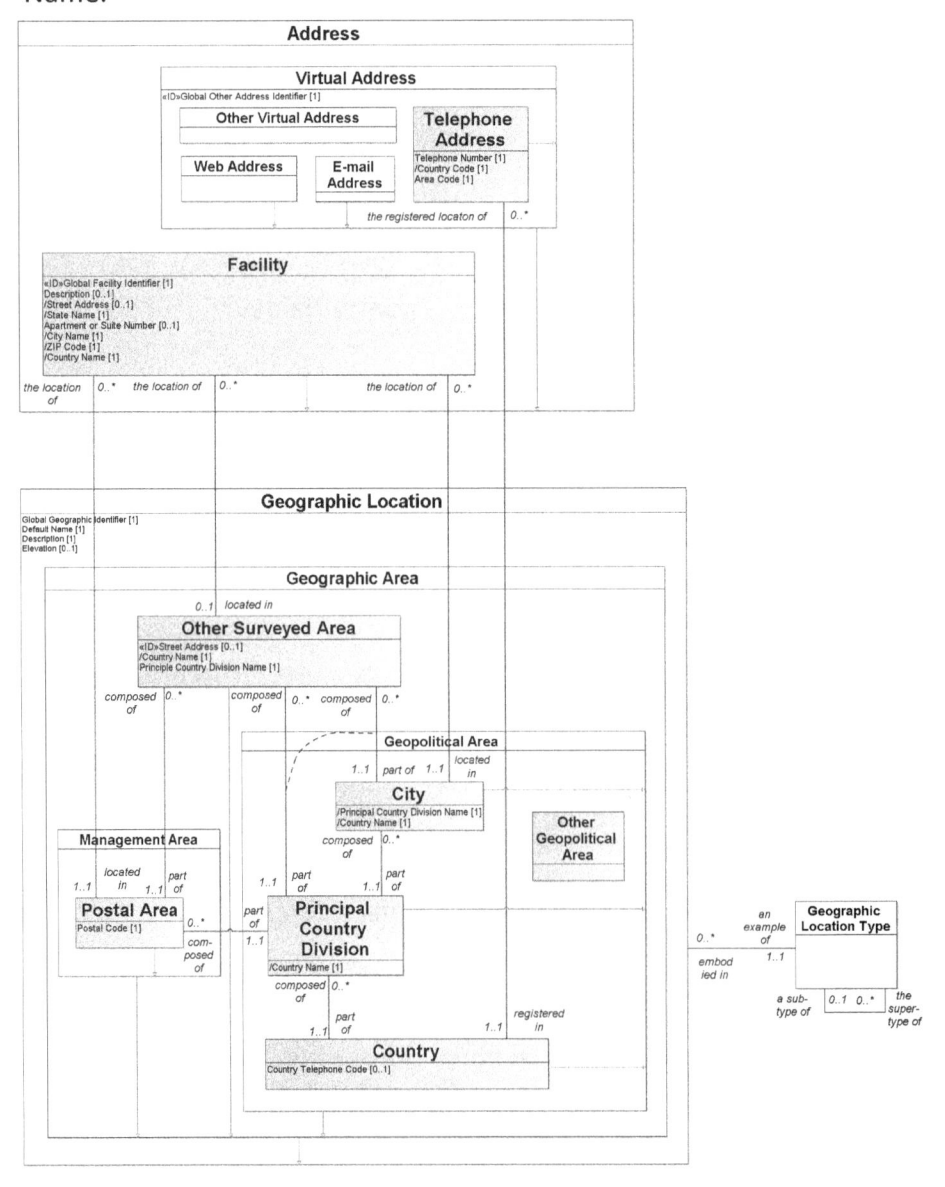

Figure 12-4: The Direct Approach to Locating Addresses

For the most part, it is only physical addresses (**Facilities**) that are connected to **Geographic Areas**. But there are exceptions. Especially in the days of mobile telephones, the **Telephone Address** is clearly an example of a **Virtual Address**. But it does have one link to the Earth in its Country Code. This is derived according to:

11. Telephone Address /Country Code =

    INFER-THROUGH (*registered in*, **Country**, Country Telephone Code)

The Abstract (International) Approach

Note that if the example were of a Canadian **Facility**, the address would have featured a **Province Name** from a **Province**, instead of the State Name shown. In other parts of the world, there might have been references to Village Name or Borough Name.

The problem is that different countries organize the land in different ways. Many of these organizations have evolved over centuries, often making them extremely complex. In many cases the finer points of land organization have been simplified for purposes of mailing addresses, but they are still lurking beneath the surface.

In the more abstract approach shown in Figure 12-5, the inter-geographic location lines are gone. We still have a relationship between **Facility** and **Postal Area** and between **Facility** and **Country**, as well as an (optional) relationship between **Facility** and **Other Surveyed Area**. These relationships should hold up nearly anywhere.

The issue is with all the different organizations of **Geopolitical Areas** that constitute the middle line of the address. In Canada, instead of city, you have municipality and hamlet. You also have province there, instead of state. In the UK, there is no equivalent of state or province that appears on mailing addresses. In every country, though, there are smaller **Geopolitical Areas**, such as county, borough, village, hamlet, and so forth.[*] Aside from the fact that both **State** and **Province** appear in the model, these are subsumed under **Other Geopolitical**

---

[*] As a measure of how strange things can become, your author's home in the United States is in the incorporated place called "The City of Hilshire Village". That bit of nonsense would be problematic except that it is, in fact, entirely contained within the **Postal Area** identified as "ZIP" code 77055, which is itself in the City of Houston, Texas. So, the mailing address simply says "Houston, TX 77055".

252 Enterprise Model Patterns

Areas. Here's where **Geographic Area Type** allows you to add sub-types without having to clutter the diagram.

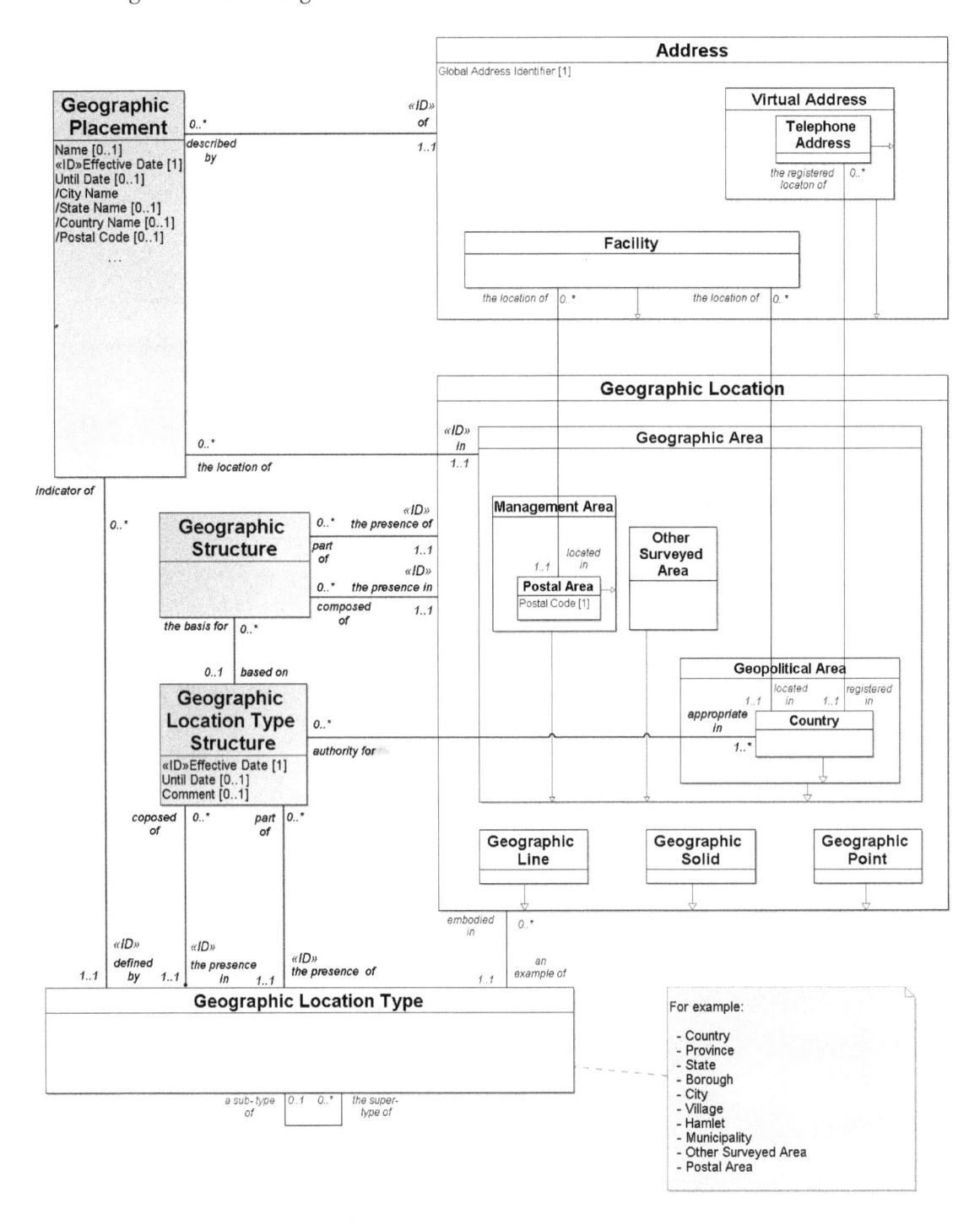

Figure 12-5: The Abstract Version

(Previously we described the UML symbol for "Enumeration", which allows us to list the members of an entity class, instead of its attributes. On this Figure is a more primitive approach to the same thing. The rectangle with the turned down corner is simply a "Note".)

The relationships between particular **Geographic Areas** are defined by instances of **Geographic Structure**, defined as the fact that one particular **Geographic Area** is *part of* another **Geographic Area**. By itself, there are no constraints preventing, for example, the assertion that the State of California is part of the City of New York. (Nor, indeed, even preventing the assertion that the State of New York is part of the City of New York.)

To describe the structures that were previously shown as relationships between subtypes, the entity class **Geographic Location Type Structure** describes the relationship between **Geographic Location Types** for one or more **Countries**. Note that **Geographic Location Type Structure** must be *appropriate in* at least one **Country** but could be *appropriate in* more than one. For example, **Postal Area** is *part of* **State** in the United States and that City is *part of* **State** in both the United States and Mexico. Similarly, **City** is *part of* **Province** in both Canada and France.♣

Note that this is not the same as the relationship showing that each **Geographic Location Type** may be *the sub-type of* one and only one other **Geographic Location Type**. That's the relationship asserting that a **Postal Area** is a *kind of* **Management Area**, not that it is *part of* a **Management Area**.

Note also that each **Geographic Location Structure** *may be* based on a **Geographic Location Type Structure**, but this does not have to be so. In the United States, it is reasonable to assert that **City** is part of **County**. There are at least three notable exceptions, however. New York, Atlanta, and Houston all have part or all of more than one county contained within their borders.

This linking of **Address** to **Geographic Area** is accomplished via the definition of **Geographic Placement**. This is the fact that a particular **Facility** is *located in* a particular **Geographic Location** that is *defined by* a particular **Geographic Location Type**. The unique identifiers for **Geographic Placement** guarantee that

---

♣   Yes, the astute reader will notice that this is a "many-to-many" relationship. Your author is well-known for prohibiting such things in a conceptual model. Please note, however that he has a "meta" rule which says that he may violate any rule 1% of the time—if it does not generate nonsense and makes the diagram more clear. He is invoking that meta-rule here.

each **Address** may be *located in* only one **Geographic Location** *defined by* particular **Geographic Location Type**.

So, if you want to identify the **Address** of, for example `"Gigantic Corporation's Brooklyn Manufacturing Plant"`, you first define a **Geographic Placement** that is *of* `"the Brooklyn Manufacturing Plant"`, and *located in* `"New York City"`.

Note that this **Geographic Placement** is *defined by* the **Geographic Location Type** `"City"`. Other **Geographic Placements** (including one not appearing in a mailing address) appear in Table 12-1. This bit of redundancy is required to infer names, as shown below.

Table 12-1: Geographic Placement

of **Address**	*located in* **Geographic Location**	*defined by* **Geographic Location Type**
Brooklyn Manufacturing Plant	New York City	"City"
Brooklyn Manufacturing Plant	New York State	"State"
Brooklyn Manufacturing Plant	Brooklyn	"Borough" (*sub-type of* "Other Geographic Location")
Brooklyn Manufacturing Plant	United States	"Country"

The assignment now is to derive the attributes that constitute the address for **Facility**. To do this, it will be necessary to create some derived attributes in **Geographic Placement** for the **Facility** attributes to INFER-THROUGH. For example:

12. **Facility** /City Name =

   INFER-THROUGH (*described by*, **Geographic Placement**, /City Name)

Deriving /City Name adds a level of complexity to the problem, since **Address** will have multiple **Geographic Placements** for the multiple components of its mailing address: **City, State, Country,** et cetera /City Name will only be derived for one of those. This means the formula has to add a condition. The following is not official, but it is your author's idea of what that condition might look like:

13. **Geographic Placement,** /City Name =

INFER-THROUGH (*in*, **Geographic Location** **Default** **Name** (WHERE (*defined by*, **Geographic Location Type**, `Name="City"`))

...where `"City"` is an argument that establishes that the **Geographic Location Type** that is *an indicator of* the specified **Geographic Placement** is, in fact, `"City"`.

That is, to retrieve a value for **/City Name** in **Facility**, it is necessary to first identify which of the **Geographic Placement** instances that it is *described by* is the one that is related to a **Geographic Area Type** that is a `"City"`. As shown in Table 12-1, there may be others, such as `"Borough"`, `"County"`, et cetera. Because of the way the unique identifiers are structured, there will be only one.

As a consequence, for the selected **Geographic Placement** instance, the value of /Default Name will be derived from the **Geographic Area** that is a **City**.

One problem with this approach is when we try to derive **Facility /Postal Code**. The logic described here knows how to find the appropriate **Geographic Area** instance, but because of the indirectness, it doesn't know how to find the unique attribute **Postal Area** Postal Code.

The solution for **Postal Areas** is to define the inherited **Default Name** as equivalent to the Postal Code. (This is a further extension of this imaginary programming language.) Hence, in the formula ...

14. **Facility /ZIP Code** =

    INFER-THROUGH (*described by*, **Geographic Placement**, **Default Name**, *defined by*, **Postal Area**)

... the **Default Name** is, in fact, the **Postal Code**.[∇]

Activities and Facilities

Figure 12-6 shows that all aspects of activities take place somewhere:

[∇] For those readers whose home is outside the United States, think of it as a homework assignment to make the abstract model more concrete for your country.

256 Enterprise Model Patterns

Each **Activity Specification** may be *subject to* one or more **Activity Placements** *in* an **Address**. For example, production of `"acetylsalicylic acid"` normally takes place at the Gigantic Corporation's `"Brooklyn Manufacturing Plant"`.

Activity Placement
- «ID»Global Actrivity Placement Identifier [1]
- Effective Date [1]
- Until Date [0..1]

subject to 0..* / subject to 0..* / subject to 0..* / subject to 0..* / the location of 0..*

of 1..1
Event

the basis for 0..*

1..1 of / 1..1 based on 1..1 / of 1..1 in

Activity
- Global Activity Identifier [1]
- Description [1]
- /Actual End Date [0..1]
- /Actual Start Date [0..1]
- /Scheduled Start Date [1]
- /Scheduled End Date [0..1]
- /Activity Total Cost [0..1]
- /Activity Material Cost [0..1]
- /Activity Labor Cost [0..1]
- /Unit Cost of Production [0..1]
- Test End Date [0..1]

Event Specification

Address
- Virtual Address
- Facility

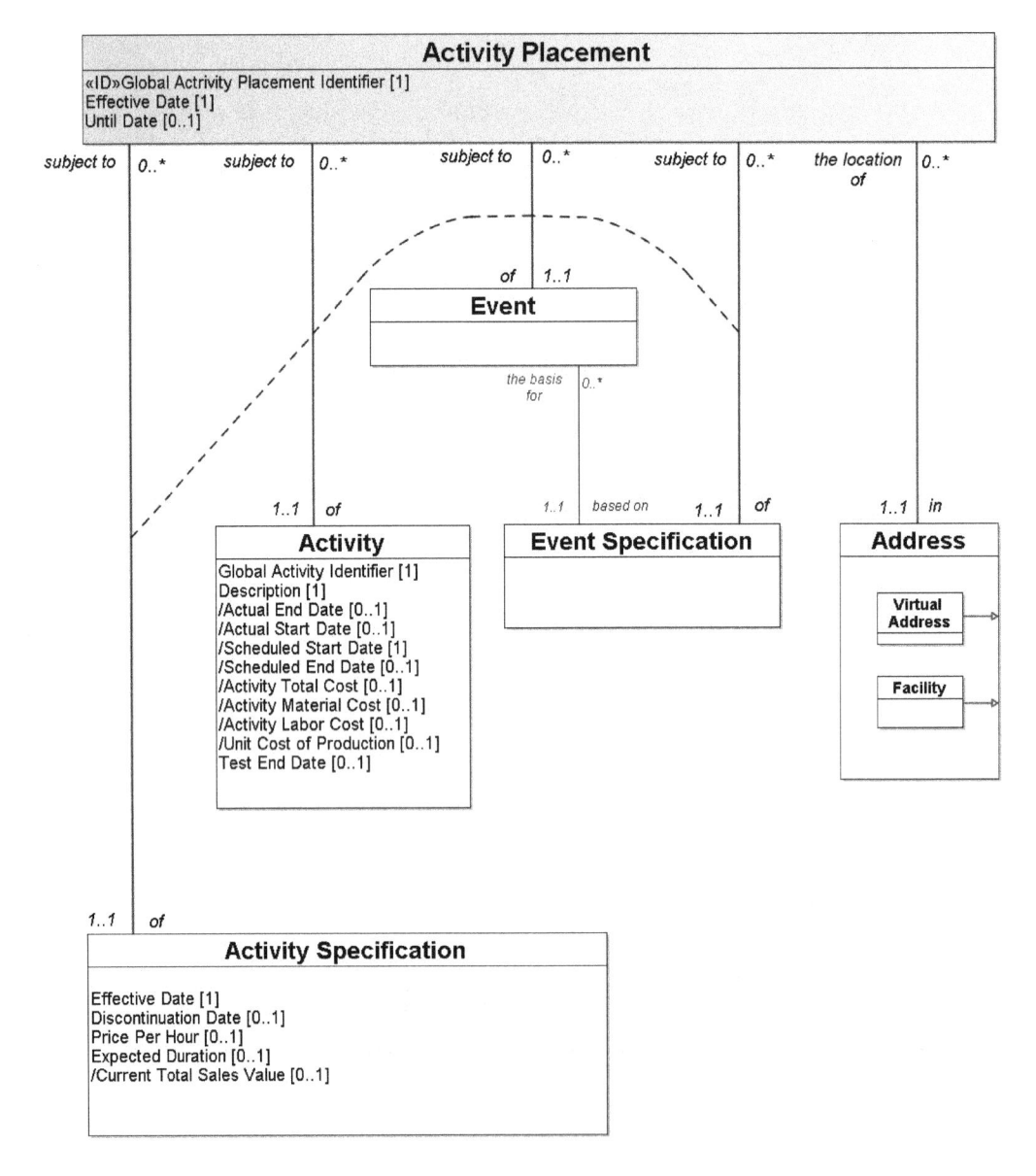

1..1 of

Activity Specification
- Effective Date [1]
- Discontinuation Date [0..1]
- Price Per Hour [0..1]
- Expected Duration [0..1]
- /Current Total Sales Value [0..1]

Figure 12-6: Locating Activities and Events

Each **Activity** may be *subject to* one or more **Activity Placements** *in* an **Address** (either a physical one—a **Facility**—or a **Virtual Address**). For example, `"Production of lot 253 of acetylsalicylic acid"` took place on "June 24, 2004" on "Production line 3" at "Brooklyn Manufacturing Plant".

Events may also be located at a particular **Facility** (Address). Hence the arc across the relationships between **Activity Placement** and the two **Activity...** entity classes, also crosses the **Event...** ones as well. Thus, an **Activity Placement** is defined as the fact that a particular **Activity**, **Activity Specification**, **Event**, or **Event Specification** is *in* a particular **Address**. That is, Each **Activity Placement** must be *of* one **Activity**, or one **Activity Specification**, of one **Event**, or one **Event Specification**.

Note that the rule says that one **Activity Placement** may not be for more than one of these, but since the UML notation only can describe the "XOR" constraint between two at a time, it does not prevent, for example, one **Activity Specification** from being *of* both one **Activity** and one **Event Specification**. For our purposes, however, assume that it does.

Assets and Facilities

It is important to note that a **Facility** is not the same as the building, warehouse, or oil well that occupies it. The building can be torn down and rebuilt and the **Facility** is the same, in terms of its location and purpose. It is also true that in the oil field business, a large piece of equipment that moves from place to place is considered a **Facility** that moves, which is one reason why **Effective Date** and **Until Date** appear in **Geographic Placement** in Figure 12-5.

A reasonable piece of information that people want about an **Asset**, then, is "where is it now?" So, in Figure 12-7, each **Asset** is shown to be *currently at* one and only one **Address**. Note that, while for some companies it may be required to know where everything is, this is not always possible, so the model shows that it *may be* known where the **Asset** is *currently at* ("0..1"). Note also, that **Assets**—such as your mobile (or land-locked) telephone—can be *currently at* a **Virtual Address**—such as your mobile (or land-locked) **Telephone Address**.

It is also possible to make the stronger assertion that any **Asset** may be *used, maintained, or stored* in one (physical) **Facility**.

It is also reasonable to make a stronger assertion about a **Building**—that it must be *located at* a single **Facility**. Note that this is an example of an often unrecognized phenomenon in data modeling—***relationship sub-types***. The relationship "each

258 Enterprise Model Patterns

Building must be *located at* one **Facility** is, in fact, *a sub-type of* the relationship, "each **Asset** must be *currently at* one and only one **Address**".

While available entity/relationship notations do not represent this structure, UML, in fact, does. It represents ***generalization*** (the UML word for a sub-type super-type combination) of relationships with the same arrow it uses to show it for entity classes.

While in the case of a building or a large piece of equipment, there is only one location, in the case of more portable equipment, materials, and other products, the "many to many" relationship between **Asset** and **Facility** requires a more sophisticated approach, as is also shown in Figure 12-7.

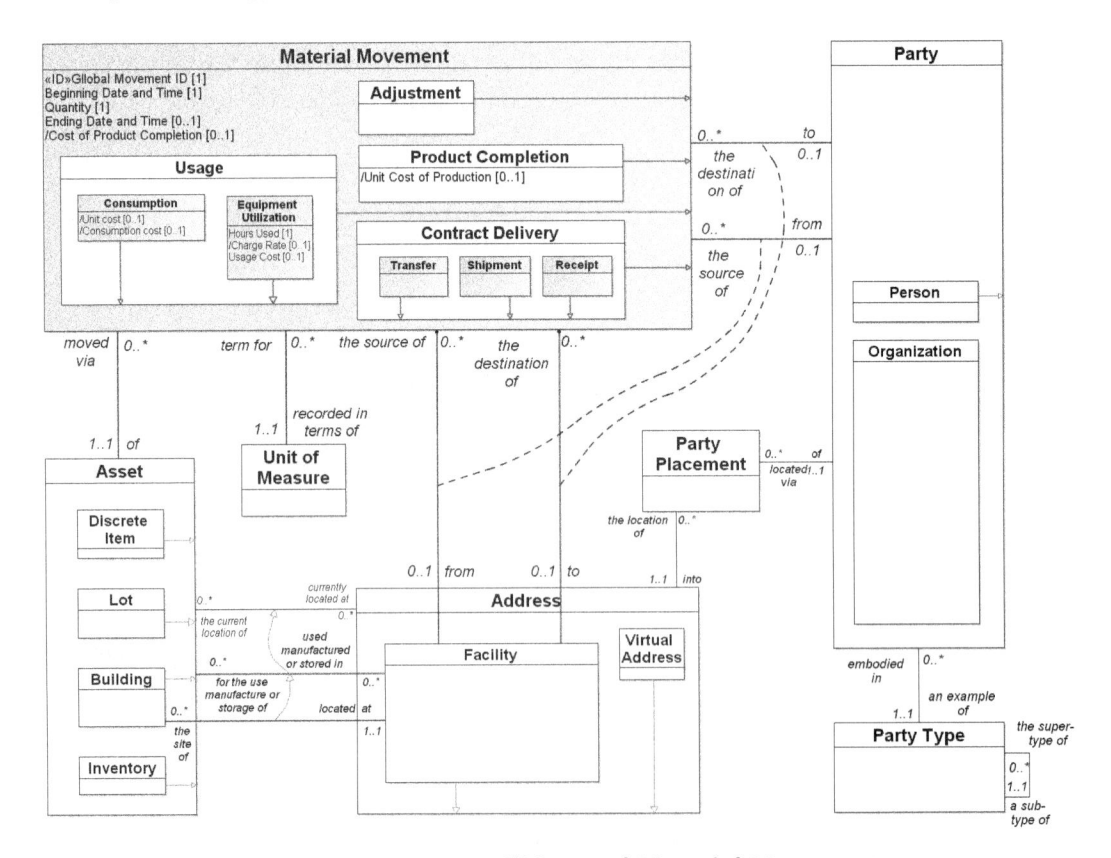

Figure 12-7: Assets, Facilities, and Material Movements

Here, the entity class **Material Movement** is the transfer of an **Asset** from one place to another. The definition of "one place" and "another" is a little tricky here: it depends on the nature of the movement. There are two major categories of **Material Movement** in most commercial enterprises:

- Those **Material Movements** associated with *manufacturing*. Here you have:

    - The actual creation (**Production Completion**) *of* materials, which involve moving it *from* a **Facility**, such as a **Work Center** to another **Facility**, such as either another **Work Center** or a **Warehouse**.

    - The **Consumption** *of* an **Asset**, either from **Inventory** (in the case of raw materials or spare parts) or as a **Discrete Item** (such as a sub-assembly).

    - The **Actual Utilization** *of* time on a piece of production equipment (a **Discrete Item**).

- Those **Material Movements** associated with buying or selling products. These entail **Delivery** of an **Asset**, in one of the following three forms. Specifically:

    - **Receipt** *of* an **Asset** *from* a (vendor) **Party**, consigning it *to* a **Facility** such as a **Warehouse**.

    - **Shipment** *of* an **Asset** *to* a (customer) **Party**, *from* a **Facility** such as a **Warehouse**.

    - **Transfer** *of* an **Asset** *from* one **Facility** *to* another **Facility**.

- Virtual **Material Movements** that constitute **Adjustments** in the known quantity of an **Asset**, which involves its virtual movement, either *from* the ether[*] *to* a **Facility** (a positive adjustment), or *from* a **Facility** *to* the ether (a negative adjustment).

Because this cannot be an exhaustive list, there is also the possibility of an **Other Material Movement**.

All of these permutations result in the relationships surrounding **Material Movement** to resolve into the following assertions:

- Each **Material Movement** may be *from* either one **Party** (a vendor), or *from* one **Facility**, or not *from* anywhere at all (a positive **Adjustment**).

- Each **Material Movement** may be *to* either one **Party** (a customer), or *to* one **Facility**, or not *to* anywhere at all (a negative **Adjustment**).

Note that in all cases, there is a **Quantity** being moved, even if it is "1". For this reason, each **Material Movement** must be *in terms of* one **Unit of Measure**.

---

[*] "the upper regions of space." – Merriam-Webster OnLine. 2010.

Asset Types and Specification Locations

Where above we moved **Assets** from **Facility** to **Facility**, in Figure 12-8 an **Asset Specification Location** specifies a constraint on what *kind of* **Assets** can be placed in what *kind of* **Facilities**.

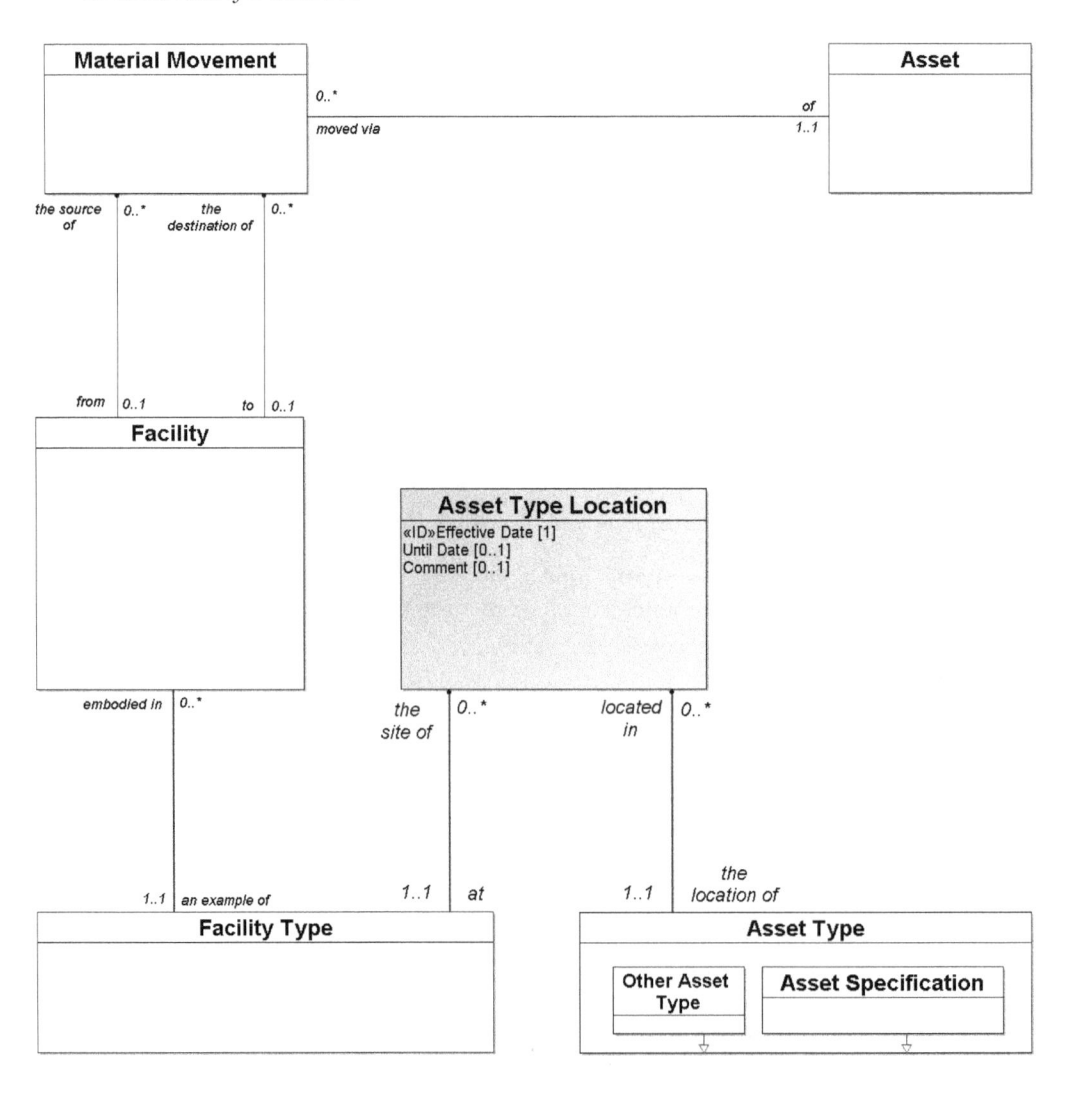

Figure 12-8: Asset Types and Facility Types

Business Rule

- An **Asset Type** may only be *moved via* a **Material Movement** *to* a **Facility** that is *an example of* a **Facility Type** that is *the site of* an **Asset Type Location** that is either *described by* a particular **Asset Specification** or is *an example of* that **Asset Type**. *(Translation:* An **Asset** may only be moved to a **Facility** that is appropriate for that kind of **Asset**. For example, an **Asset Type** "compressor" can be moved to a "Plant", but not to a "Home". A "Bridge Superstructure Unit" can be moved to a "Bridging", but pretty much not anywhere else.[♣])

Summary

"Facility" is one of those words that has very different meanings, depending on the industry that is using it. In banking, for example, a "Facility" is money set aside to loan to a preferred customer, even thought the lone hasn't yet been created.

That's not the sense in which it is used in this chapter. Here, **Facility** is a synonym for ***Physical Address***. From the point of view of "facilities management", it is "a place with a purpose", as distinguished from **Geographic Location**, which is simply "a place". That is, it is "a place identified as being in a **Geographic Location**, where **Parties** use (physical) **Assets** to perform **Activities**".

But one purpose it has in the overall scheme of things is as a means to locate **Persons**, **Assets**, **Activities**, and other things of interest to the enterprise.

It is, in fact, but one of two sub-types of the more general concept, **Address**. This includes the other sub-type, **Virtual Address**. This is, indeed, anything that can be used to locate **Persons**, **Assets**, **Activities**, and other things of interest to the enterprise. The latter is used to locate (mostly **Parties**) in cyberspace—that is, on electronic networks, such as the telephone system, the Internet, and corporate networks. A **Virtual Address** can be a **Telephone Address**[52], a **Web Address**, an **E-Mail** address, or an **Other Virtual Address** that hasn't been invented yet.

[♣] See Chapter 22 on "Highway Maintenance", below for details.
[52] What in ancient times (anytime before 1990 CE) was known as a "telephone number".

CHAPTER 13

Human Resources

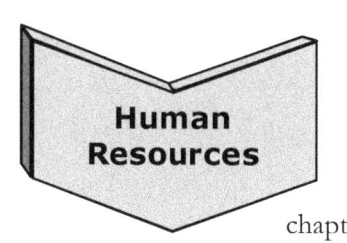

In order to support the production and sales of products and services, it is necessary for the enterprise to employ *people*. If the company is of any size whatsoever, managing the employment of all those people can turn out to be a very large job. This chapter describes some of the issues involved.

Employment

It is common in starting models to create the entity class **Employee**. This is a classic example of the flaw in data modeling that confuses the *nature* of a thing with the *role* that it plays. Employees are fundamentally *people*. The entity class of interest, then, must be **Person**, which we've already described in detail in Chapter 4. Clearly a person is not born an employee. Indeed, over the course of h'[*] life, 'e may well play the role of being an employee in more than one company.

We need a different approach.

In fact, the ***Role*** of being an ***employee***, as played by a **Person** for a **Company** is itself a thing of significance—albeit an abstract one. In Figure 13-1, this is shown by the entity class **Employment**, which is defined as "the fact that a particular **Person** is employed *with* a particular **Organization**". That is, each **Employment** must be *of* one and only one **Person**, and *with* one and only one **Organization**. This is a kind of **Party Relationship**.

---

[*]   Remember the "new" modern convention: This means "his or her". And *'e* means "he or she".

263

264 Enterprise Model Patterns

There is some disagreement about where the attribute **Social Security Number** should be placed. Many would make it an attribute of **Person**, or at least an instance of **Party Identifier Type**, as shown in Chapter 4. Since it was intended only to be shared with employers and the U.S. Internal Revenue Service, it is possible to make it an attribute of **Employment**, as shown here. Since it was not originally intended to be used as a universal identifier, the final location for it must be determined by consensus within your organization, and could be in any of several places.

If it is not an attribute of **Employment**, probably something like Employment Identifier should suffice.

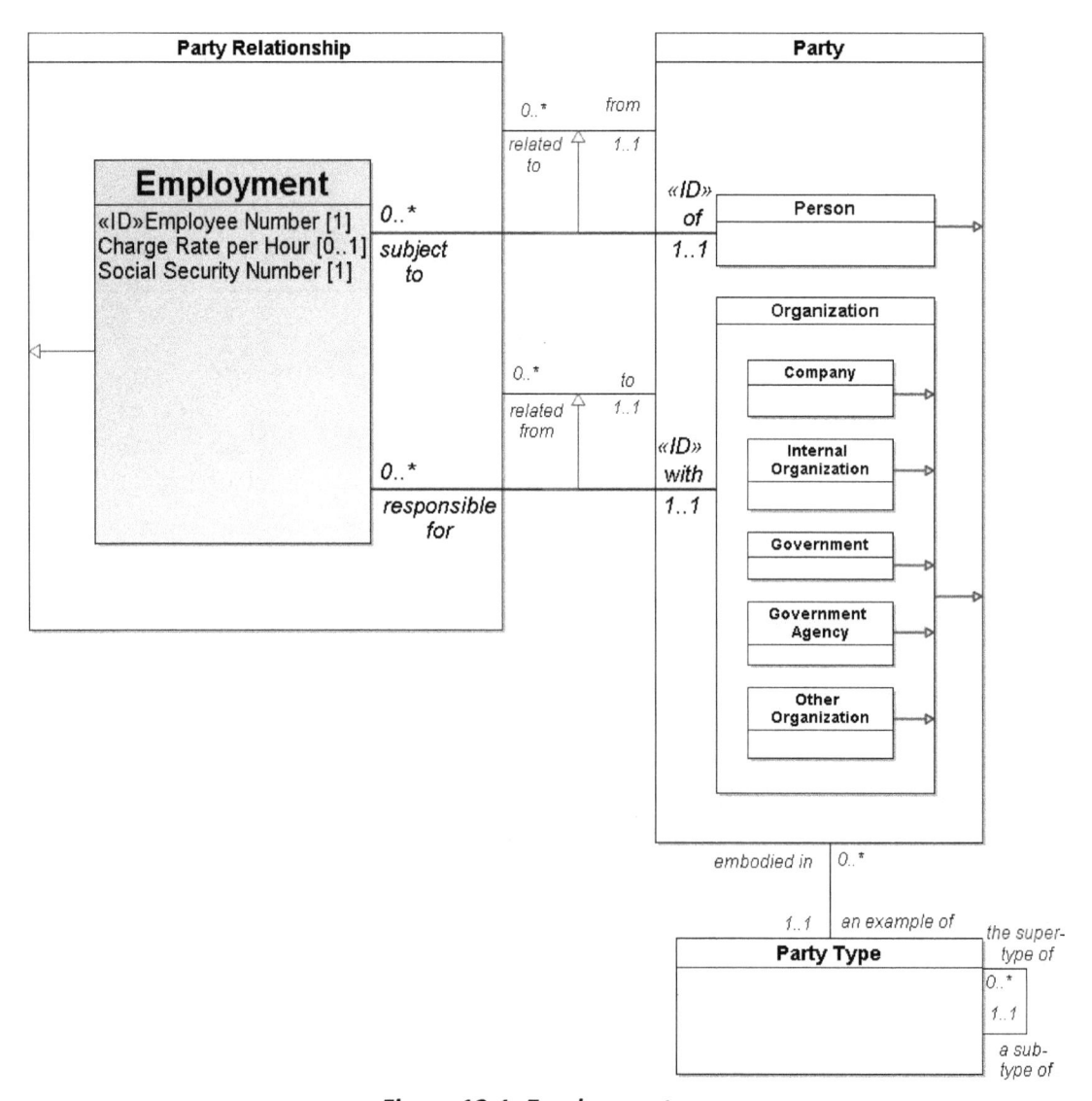

Figure 13-1: Employments

Note that, since **Employment** is a sub-type of **Party Relationship**, the latter's relationships *from* one **Party** and *to* another **Party** must apply. Because the meaning of *by* and *with* are more specific, it is reasonable to show them as well.

This is another example of relationship sub-types. The relationship "each **Employment** must be *of* one and only one **Person**" is in fact a *sub-type* of the relationship, "each **Party Relationship** must be *from* one and only one **Party**". Similarly, the relationship "Each **Employment** must be *with* one and only one **Organization**" is a sub-type of the relationship "Each **Party Relationship** must be *to* one and only one **Party**".

While available entity/relationship notations do not represent this structure, UML, in fact, does. It represents ***generalization*** (the UML word for a sub-type super-type combination) with the same arrow it uses to show that an entity class is a super-type of another entity class. These arrows are shown in Figure 13-1.

Position Assignments

Typically, a **Person** subjects h'self to **Employment** in order to do a particular job—to hold a **Position**—a defined role in a company. Figure 13-2 shows **Position Assignment** as the fact that a particular **Person** employed by an **Organization** (that is, *subject to* an **Employment**) is (for a period of time at least) assigned to exactly one **Position**.

Specifically, each **Position Assignment** must be *based on* one and only one **Employment** and must be *to* one and only one **Position**. Each **Position**, then, must be *an example of* one and only one **Position Type**.

Note that the **Position Type** itself must be *the responsibility of* one and only one **Organization**.

For example, a **Position Type**, defined by the Conglomerate Corporation's Human Resources Department, could be "Database Administrator". The Finance Department of the Conglomerate Corporation, for example, might have its own version of Database Administrator, called "Finance Database Administrator". This would be an instance of **Position** that is *the responsibility of* the "Finance Department".

266 Enterprise Model Patterns

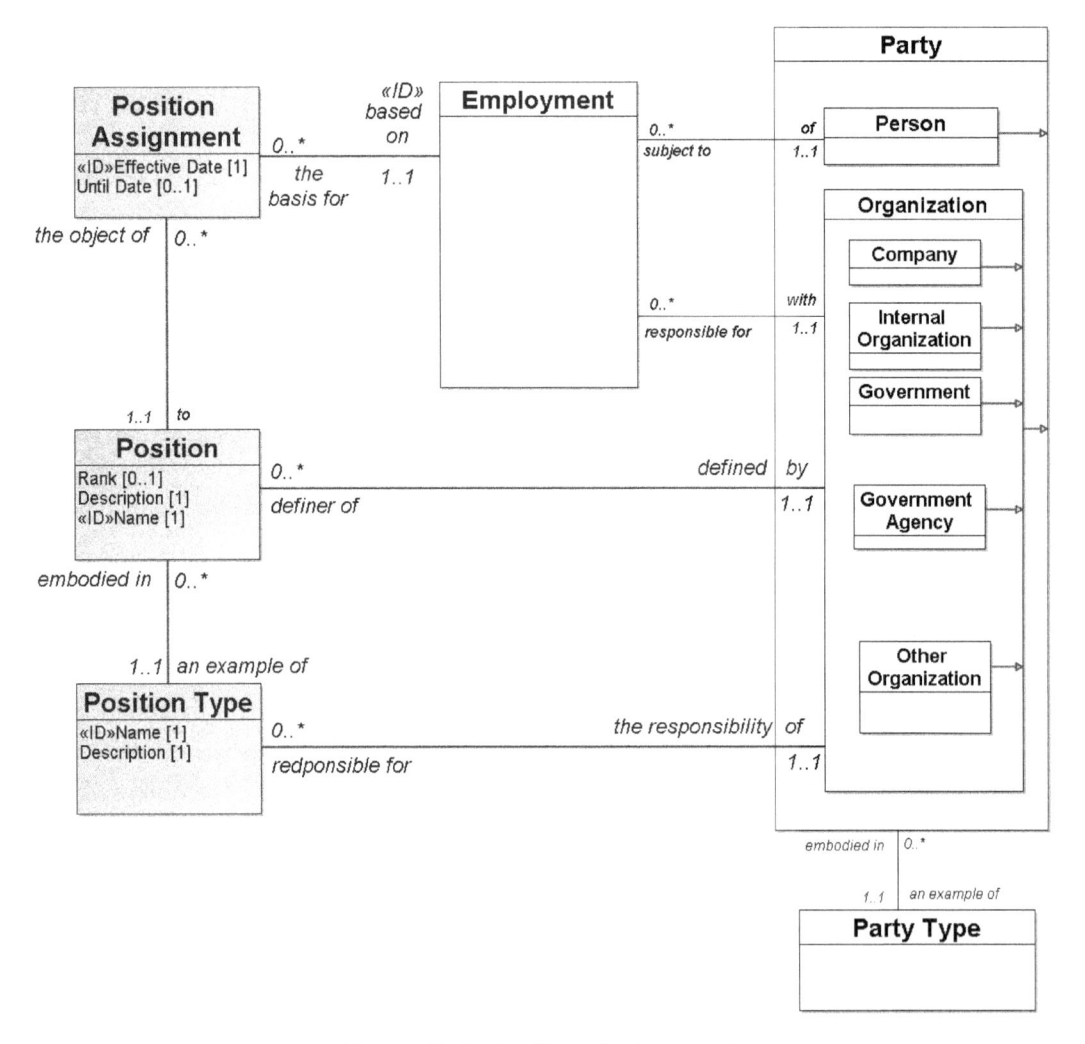

Figure 13-2: Position Assignments

"Rebecca Jenkins", who is subject *to* **Employment** *with* the "Information Technology Department" of "The Conglomerate Corporation", has been given a **Position Assignment** *to* the **Position** of "Finance Database Administrator" for the "Finance Department".

As our British colleagues would say, "Rebecca", who is employed by the "Information Technology Department", has been *seconded* to the "Finance Department".

Note that this can lead to a trap for the people using a data warehouse built on this model and asking the question, "How many people work for me?"

Let us assume that all the proper portals and query languages are available so that our executive can sit down, ask the question, and get back the number "42".

But what does that number mean? Is it the number of people who are *subject to* **Employment** *with* the Finance Department? Or the number of people who hold **Position Assignments** *to* **Positions** that are *the responsibility of* the Finance Department.

Very often, even a simple question requires subtlety in understanding the answer to that question.

To obtain a position it is normally expected that the person has a relevant set of skills and/or experiences. Figure 13-3 shows that either a particular **Position** or a **Position Type** may be *subject to* one or more **Position Requirements**, each of which must be either *for the ability to perform* one **Activity Specification**, or *for knowledge of* one **Domain of Knowledge**, such as a **Skill** or a **Language**. (**Other Domains of Knowledge** might be more specialized, such as `"Forensics"`, or `"Ancient Greek Literature"`♣.)

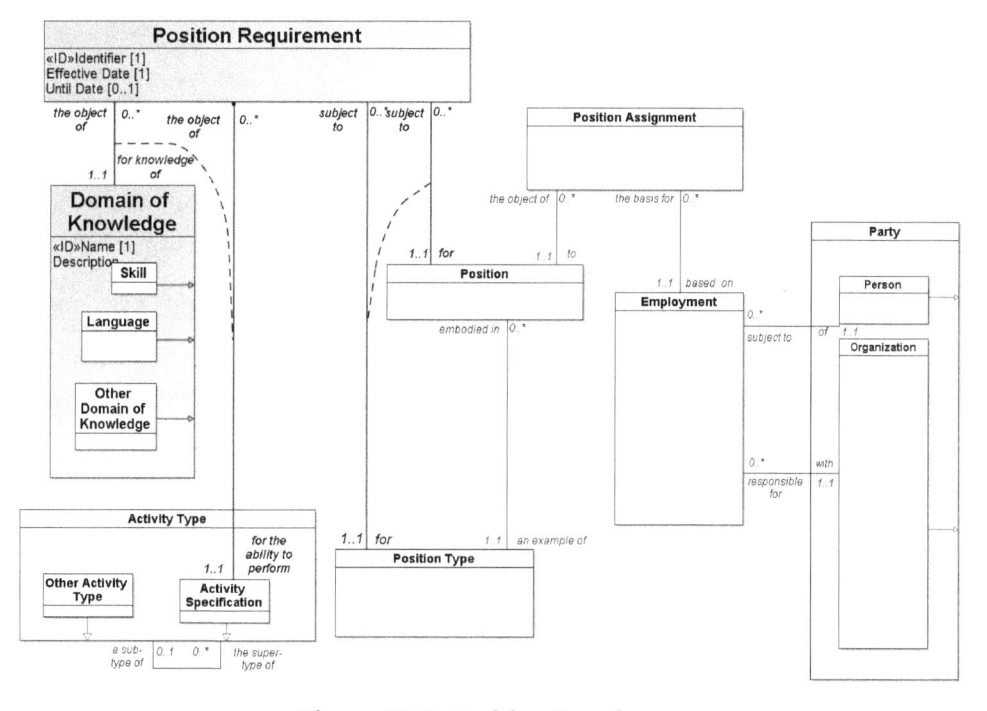

Figure 13-3: Position Requirements

♣   Ancient Greek Literature? You never know. We have to accommodate all possibilities.

For example, to hold the **Position Type** "Database Administrator", in general requires th*e ability to perform* the **Activity Specification** of "database design", but the **Position** of "Database Administrator for Finance" would also require knowledge of the **Domain of Knowledge** that is "Finance".

Oh, and if that department is in Paris, the **Position** also would require knowledge of the **Language**, "French".

Each of these requirements is described by a separate **Position Requirement**.

Once the requirements *for* the **Position** or **Position Type** have been identified, it remains to describe what responsibilities the job itself will entail. Specifically, it may be the case that anyone holding a **Position** may be *holder of* one or more specified **Responsibilities**. Each **Responsibility** must be *for the ability to perform* a particular **Activity Specification** or *to understand and use* a particular **Domain of Knowledge**. This is shown in Figure 13-4. It may be the case that this **Responsibility** is *assigned to* a particular **Person**, by virtue of h' **Employment** *with* an **Organization**. It may also be the case that a **Responsibility** is *assigned to* an employed person only for as long as 'e holds a particular **Position Assignment**.

Or it may be the case that a **Responsibility** is *assigned to* a particular **Position**, regardless of who holds it.

All of which is to say that each **Responsibility** must be <u>either</u> *assigned to* an **Employment** (*of* a **Person** *with* an **Organization**), <u>or</u> *assigned to* a **Person** solely by virtue of h' holding a particular **Position Assignment**, or *assigned to* anyone in a particular **Position**. (Note that the dashed line represents a comprehensive "exclusive or" constraint: even though UML definition is that it is only constraining 2 relationships at a time, a **Responsibility** may not, in fact, be assigned to more than one of any of the identified entity classes. [♣]

[♣] …so, in this case, a single **Responsibility** could be both *assigned to* a **Position** and an **Employment**, but we're saying here that, in fact, it couldn't be.

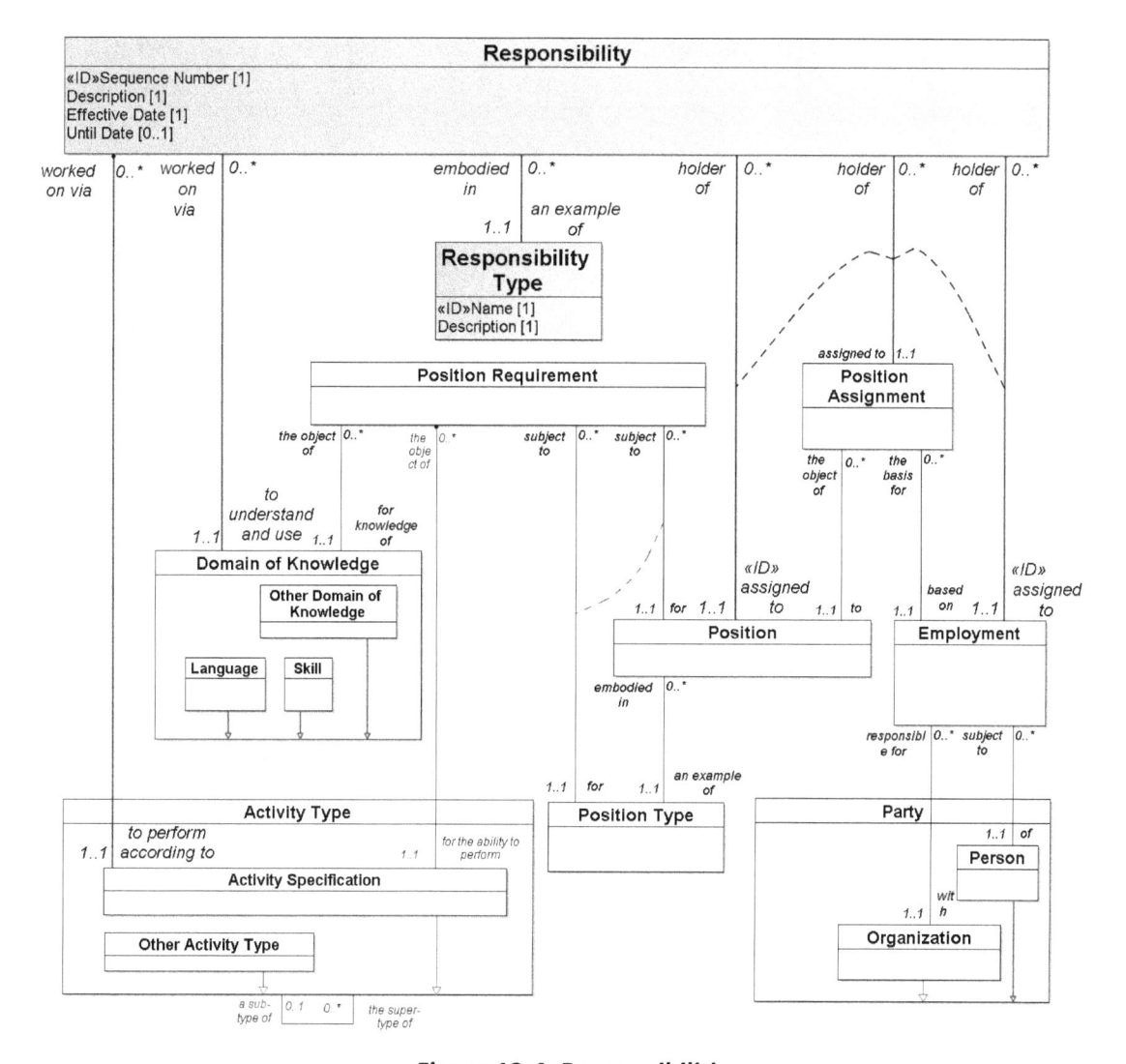

Figure 13-4: Responsibilities

Hiring

Ok, we have identified the skills required to do a job and the responsibilities that the employee will hold. The next task is to determine if a candidate does, in fact, have the necessary capabilities. Figure 13-5 shows that each **Person** may be *holder of* one or more **Capabilities**, each of which must be *in* either an **Activity Specification** or a **Domain of Knowledge**. That is, a **Capability** is the fact of a **Person's** being able to do something—either demonstrating acquaintance with a **Body of Knowledge** or performing a **Specified Activity** (that is, an **Activity Specification**).

270 Enterprise Model Patterns

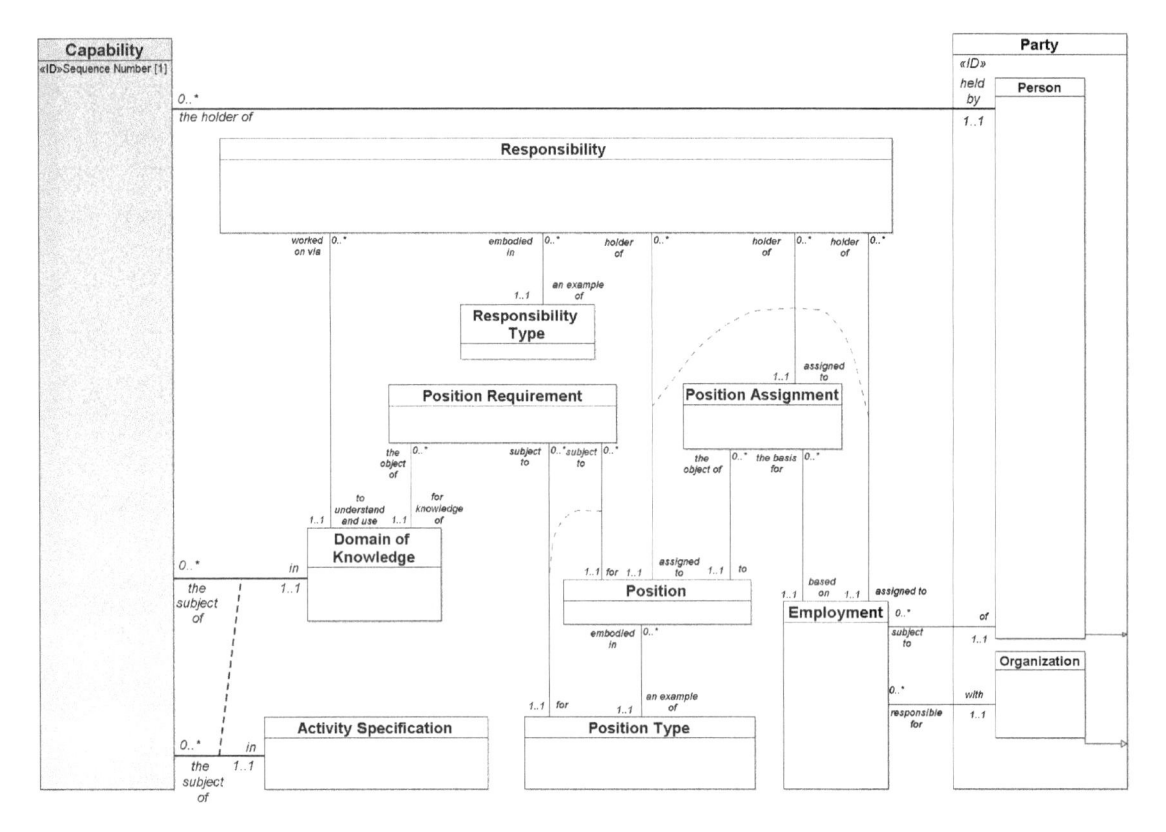

Figure 13-5: Capabilities

So, for example, Rebecca in the Information Technology Department may be assigned to make her *holder of* **Responsibility** *for* the **Activity Specification** "database tuning", simply because she's known to be good at it. (That is, she is *holder of* a **Capability** in the **Activity Specification** "database tuning". Or, she may be assigned that **Responsibility** by virtue of being in the **Position** of "Database Administrator for Finance", without regard for any **Capabilities** she may or may not hold.

Education and Certification

One way to acquire those **Capabilities**, of course, is to go through appropriate education or training. That this education may simply be derived from a lifetime of experiences will be shown, below. In addition, tests may be taken to certify one's knowledge, in order to acquire particular certification or license.

Certification Requirements

We'll begin with Figure 13-6 and **License**—a recognition of one's ability to perform a specified set of **Activity Specifications**. This may be a **Certificate** that simply asserts one is *qualified* to perform specified activities (that is, **Activity Specifications**), or it may be an **Other License** (such as a `"Driver's License"`) that actually grants permission to perform such activities. Each **License** must be *issued by* one **Organization** (or an authorized component of same).

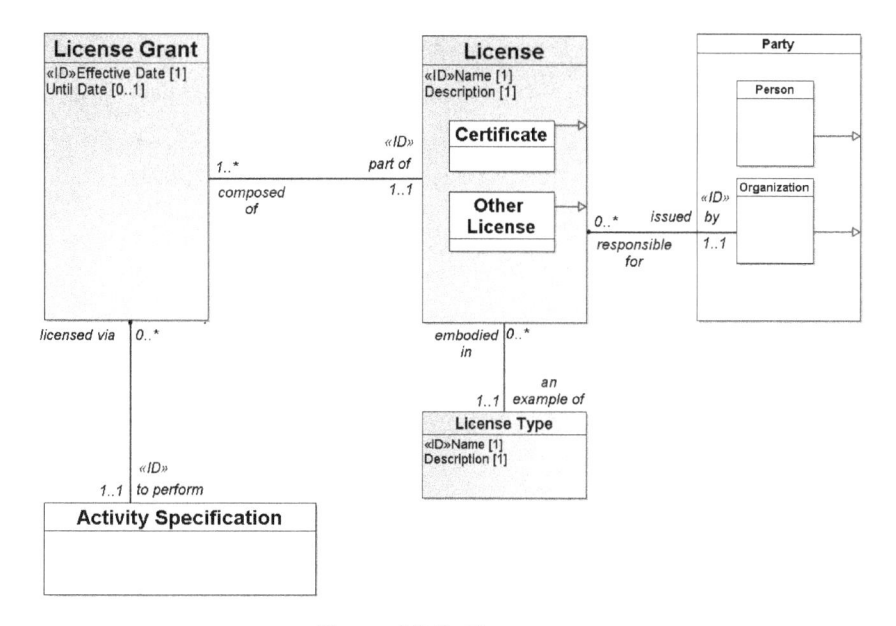

Figure 13-6: Licenses

For example, two **Certificates** that are *examples of* **License Type** `"Certified Data Management Professional (CDMP)"` are defined by the **Organization**, `"Data Management International"` (also known as `"DAMA International"`). These are `"CDMP Practitioner"` and `"CDMP Master"`, designating two levels of accomplishment in the performance of various **Services** related to data management

A **License Grant** is the fact that a particular **License** represents one's qualification *to perform* a particular **Activity Specification**. That is, each **License** must be *composed of* one or more **License Grants**, each of which must be *to perform* one **Activity Specification**. Alternatively, each **Activity Specification** may be *licensed or certified via* one or more **License Grants**, each of which must be *part of* one **License**.

272 Enterprise Model Patterns

As shown in Figure 13-7, each **License** may be *acquired via* one or more **License Requirement**, each of which must be *for* a particular **Educational Element**. That is, a **License Requirement** is the fact that a particular **License** can only be issued upon completion of a particular **Education Element**. A **License** may be *acquired via* one or more of these **License Requirements**.

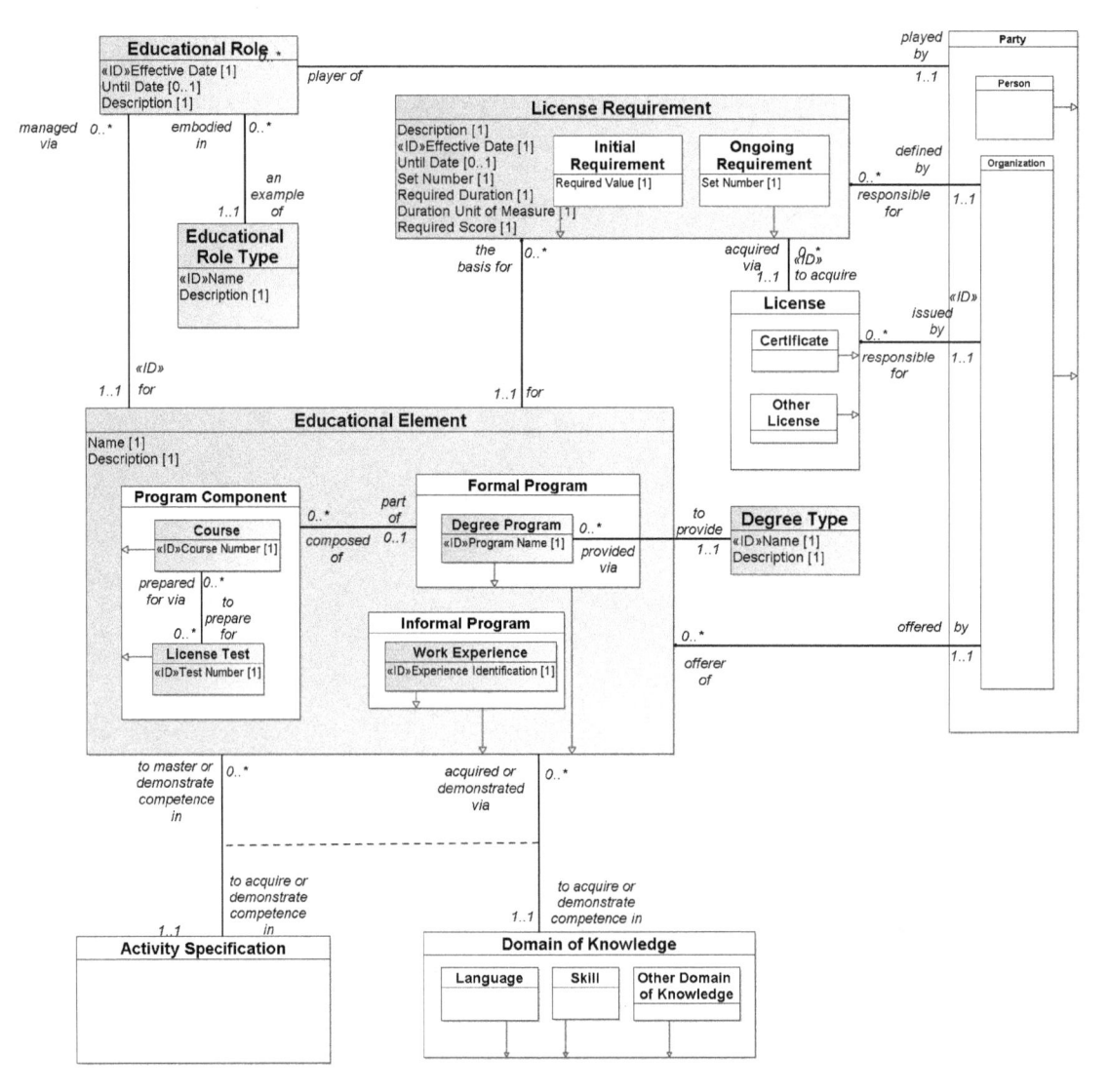

Figure 13-7: Courses and Licenses

An **Education Element** is a defined process that can be used *to acquire or demonstrate competence in* an **Activity Specification** or to *acquire or demonstrate competence in* a **Domain of Knowledge**. This must be either a **Formal Program**, a *part of* a **Formal** program (including **Course** or **License Test**), or an **Informal Program** (typically **Work Experience**). Among the available **Formal Program Components** that might be part of a **Formal Program**, a **Course** presents a particular subject, like "`Statistics 101`". A collection of **Courses** are *part of* a **Degree Program** *to provide* a **Degree Type** (such as a "`Masters of Business Administration`").

A **License Test** is a kind of formal examination covering a body of knowledge (such as a state Bar exam for lawyers, or a professional society's certification test, or a Driver's license written test). Each **Course** may be *to prepare for* one or more **License Tests**. Each **Formal Program** must be *offered by* one **Organization**, such as a university or a professional society.

In the DAMA case referred to above, the petitioner for either DAMA "`CDMP`" **Certificate** may be *acquired via* one or more specified **License Requirements**.[*] Specifically, the petitioner must pass at least three **License Tests** and have between 2 and 4 years of **Work Experience**. Up to 2 years experience may be waived in exchange for obtaining a college degree (from a **Degree Program**) of **Degree Type** ("`Bachelor's`" or "`Master's`") in the appropriate major. To obtain a "`CDMP Practitioner`" **Certificate**, all tests taken must be passed with at least 50% and the applicant must have at least 2 years experience. To obtain a "`CDMP Master`" **Certificate**, all tests must be passed with at least 70%, and the applicant must have at least 4 years experience.

The optional alternatives are addressed by the **License Requirement** attributes **Required Score** and **Set Number** in the **License Requirement**. For example, two tables are shown below that could be derived from the entity class **License Requirement** for the two DAMA **Certificates**. The **License Requirement** "`CDMP Practitioner`" is shown as Table 13-1. Immediately following this, Table 13-2 shows the requirements to become a DAMA "`CDMP Master`". In each case, the **License Requirements** that share a "`Set Number`" represent required alternatives. At least one member of each set is required.

For example, as shown in Table 13-1, to obtain a "`CDMP Practitioner`" **Certificate**, you must score at least 50% in the Core test. You must also score 50% in either Data Management or Data Modeling. The same requirement applies to the

---

[*] Any reader interested in becoming a "Certified Data Management Professional (CDMP)" may find out more at *http://dama.org/i4a/pages/index.cfm?pageid=3399*. (And it is a good place to validate this model.)

274 Enterprise Model Patterns

tests in Data Operations and Security. You also must have a Bachelor's Degree, a Master's Degree, or 2 years experience in Data Management.

Table 13-1: DAMA Certification Example - Practitioner

Certificate	Test	Degree Type	Work Experience / Activity Type	Value	Set
Practitioner	Core			50%	1
Practitioner	Data Management			50%	2
Practitioner	Data Modeling			50%	2
Practitioner	Data Operations			50%	3
Practitioner	Security			50%	3
Practitioner		Master's			4
Practitioner		Bachelor's			4
Practitioner			Data Management	2 (years)	4

Requirements to obtain a "CDMP Master" certificate, shown in Table 13-2, are structurally the same, but you need to score at least 70% on the tests and need an additional 2 years' experience.

Table 13-2: DAMA Certification Example - Master

Certificate	Test	Degree Type	Work Experience / Activity Type	Value	Set
Master	Core			70%	5
Master	Data Management			70%	6
Master	Data Modeling			70%	6
Master	Data Operations			70%	7
Master	Security			70%	7
Master		Master's			8
Master		Bachelor's			8
Master			Data Management	2 (years)	8

An **Educational Role** is the fact that a **Party** is somehow involved with an **Education Program**. The nature of that involvement is described by its **Educational Role Type**, such as teacher, administrator, and so forth.

The preceding steps described the **Initial Requirement** to achieve the `Certified Data Management Professional` designation. Every two years, it must be renewed by again meeting a different specific list of requirements.

Obtaining Certification

The fact of a person's actually taking the requisite courses and/or the appropriate tests to achieve the required **Capabilities** is shown in Figure 13-8. Here a particular **Course** may be *offered as* one or more **Course Offerings**, just as each **License Test** may be *conducted as* one or more **Test Offerings**. Together **Course Offering** and **License Test** constitute a set of **Education Program Offerings**. This is the fact that a **Course** is being made available at a particular time and place (a **Course Offering**), or the fact that a **License Test** is being offered on a particular **Date**, *at* a particular place.

Each **Education Program Enrollment** may be *to acquire* one or more **Capability Endorsements**, each of which must be *to acknowledge the holding of* a **Capability**.

Each **Course Offering** is scheduled with a **Start Date** and an **End Date**. If it is in the context of a university, it is further identified as to its year, semester, and section. Each **Test Offering** is scheduled via a **Test Date**. In either case, the "place" where it is offered is a **Facility** suitable for the purpose.

The Figure 13-8 also shows that a **Person** may be *the recipient of* one or more **Education Program Enrollments**, the fact that a **Person** has enrolled *in* either an **Education Offering** or a **Degree Program**. Presumably, a person is first enrolled in the **Degree Program**, and then is subsequently enrolled in each of the required **Course Offerings**. In many cases, these both would precede being enrolled *in a* **Test Offering**.

Each **Education Program Enrollment**, in turn, may be *for the acquisition of* one or more **Capability Endorsements** that are each *to achieve* a **Capability** *in* either an **Activity Specification** or *in* a **Domain of Knowledge**. That is, a **Capability Endorsement** is the fact that a particular **Education Program Enrollment** (*by* a **Person**) resulted in confirmation of the extent to which the **Person** has attained the **Capability**.

276 Enterprise Model Patterns

Benefits

Once someone has been hired and is on the job, in exchange for work to be performed, the company's responsibility is to provide **Compensation** and other **Benefits**. Figure 13-9 shows a **Benefit** to be something of financial value paid to a **Person** in the course of an **Employment** with the **Company**.

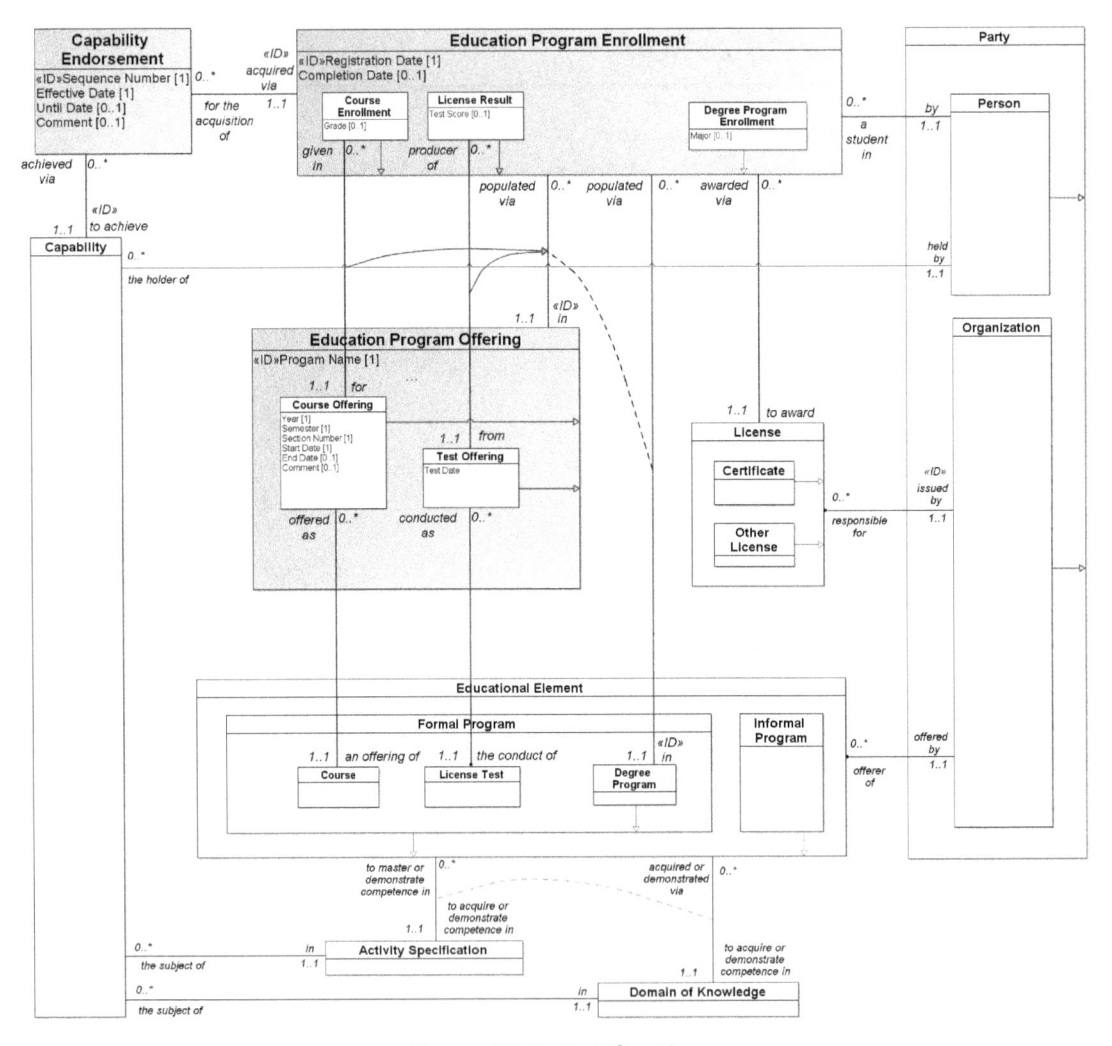

Figure 13-8: Certification

The most significant **Benefit**, of course, is financial **Compensation**, typically in the form of a **Salary**. If the work is done on commission, however, it could be **Incentive Compensation**, instead. People working under such circumstances often can take a **Draw** against future earnings.

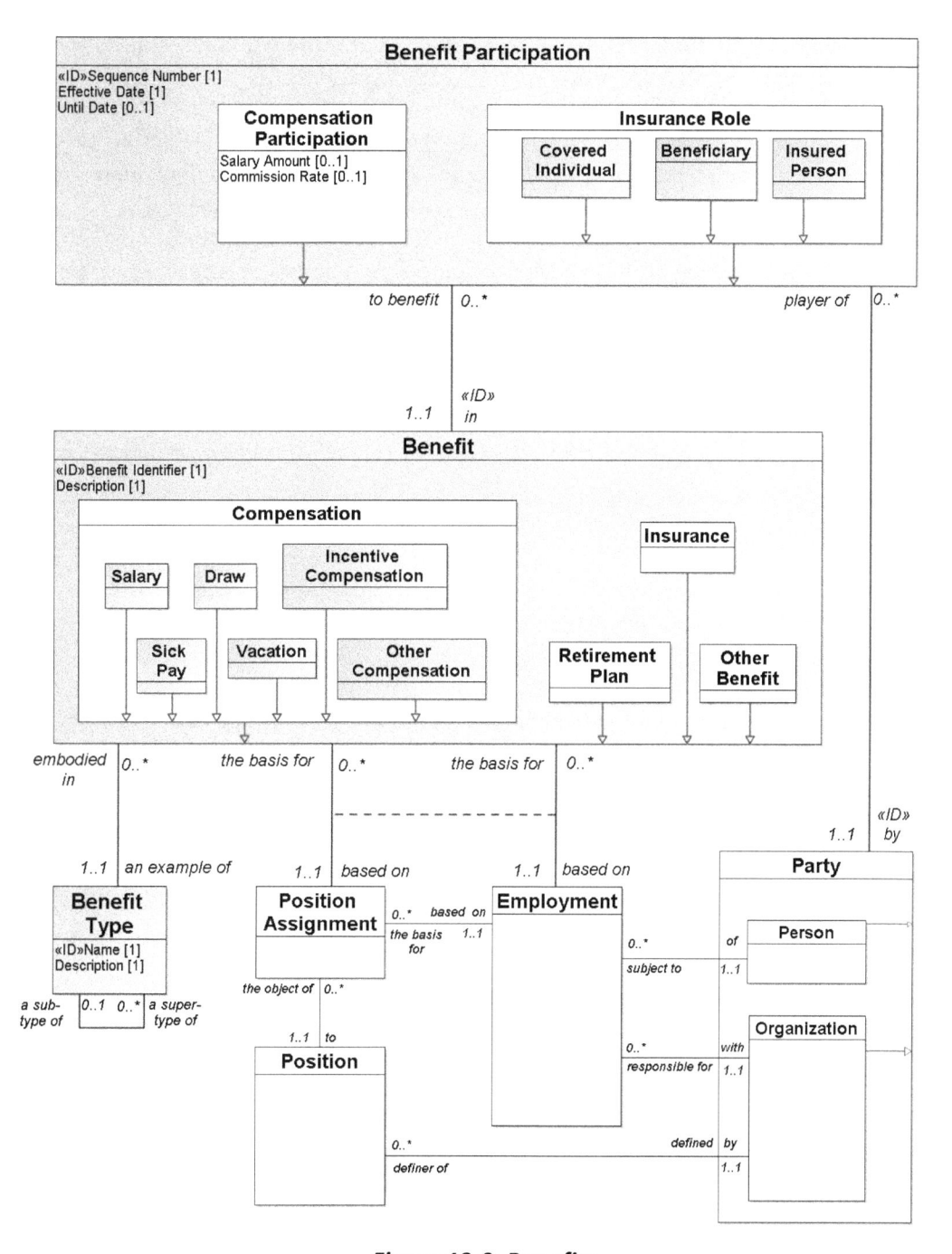

Figure 13-9: Benefits

In addition to normal paychecks, the company often offers **Sick Pay**, to continue salary payments if the person becomes too ill to work. And of course, there is **Vacation**—paid-for time off for recreation. There may also be instances of **Other Compensation** as well. The employer may also offer **Insurance Coverage** (either life insurance or health insurance, or both), and a **Retirement Plan** of some sort. There may also be **Other Benefits**.

The nature of the **Benefit** is defined by its **Benefit Type**, which again, at least reproduces the sub-type structure for **Benefit**—Insurance, Retirement Plan, or Compensation, with Compensation being *a super-type of* (among others) **Salary**.

A **Benefit** is something promised by the employer. An employee's actually receiving a **Benefit** is a **Benefit Participation** *in* a **Benefit** *by* a **Person** (either the employee or a designated other **Person**.) Primary among these, of course, is **Compensation Participation**, which records, for example, a Salary Amount or a Commission Rate. An instance of **Compensation Participation** would specify an **Effective Date** and, optionally an **Until Date**, as well as, for example, a **Salary Amount**. It would be *for* an instance of **Salary** and be a role played by the **Person** who is the employee.

Benefits accrue to more than just the employee. Various family members are *players of* one or more **Insurance Roles**. An **Insurance Role** must be one of the following:

- **Covered Individual** - An **Insurance Role** *in* an **Insurance Coverage** that is *played by* the **Person** who would receive proceeds if a claim were filed and approved. This would be either the employee or a family member receiving health insurance coverage, or the employee for a life insurance policy.

- **Beneficiary** – An **Insurance Role** in a life insurance policy *played by* the spouse or other family member who would be paid if the employee died.

- **Insured Person** – An **Insurance Role** that is *played by* the person in whose name the policy is taken out.

There may be a complex set of rules and policies around the question of who is allowed to participate in a **Benefit**. This fact is illustrated in Figure 13-10. Each **Benefit Rule** must be *a constraint upon* a particular **Benefit Type**, and it must be *an example of* a particular **Benefit Rule Type**. In this model, the detailed content of a **Benefit Rule** is not diagrammed, but the fact that it exists as *a constraint upon* a **Benefit Type** is important.

Given these **Benefit Rules**, each **Benefit Participation** *may be constrained by* one or more **Benefit Rules**, via the intersect entity class, **Benefit Rule Application**. That is, each **Benefit Rule Application** must be *constrained by* a **Benefit Participation** and the application *of* one **Benefit Rule**.

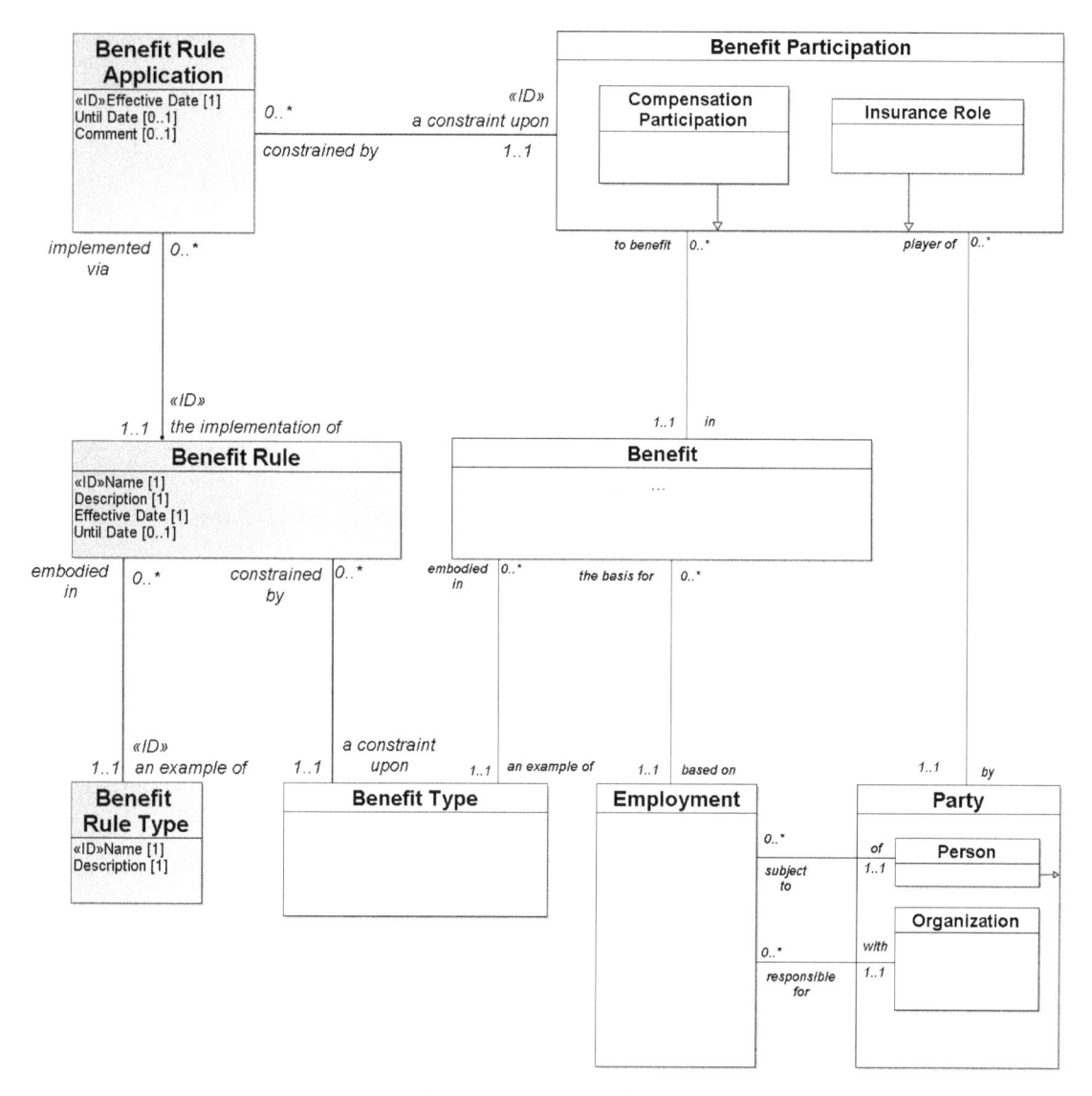

Figure 13-10: Benefit Rules

Payday!

A **Compensation Payment**, as shown in Figure 13-11, is a check or transfer *from* one **Party** *to* another **Party**.[*] Each **Compensation Payment** must be *based on* a

---

[*] For this section, your author is indebted to Ed Kaminski, CPA, who served as the accountant for his company Essential Strategies, Inc. for many years. Mr. Kaminski is

Covered Individual that is *entitled to* a **Benefit**. It may be a **Salary**, a **Draw**, or an **Incentive Compensation**. A **Compensation Payment** records the fact that a particular amount of money is being paid out by the company to either the employee h'self or to another company or agency involved in providing a particular **Benefit**, such as insurance or retirement savings.

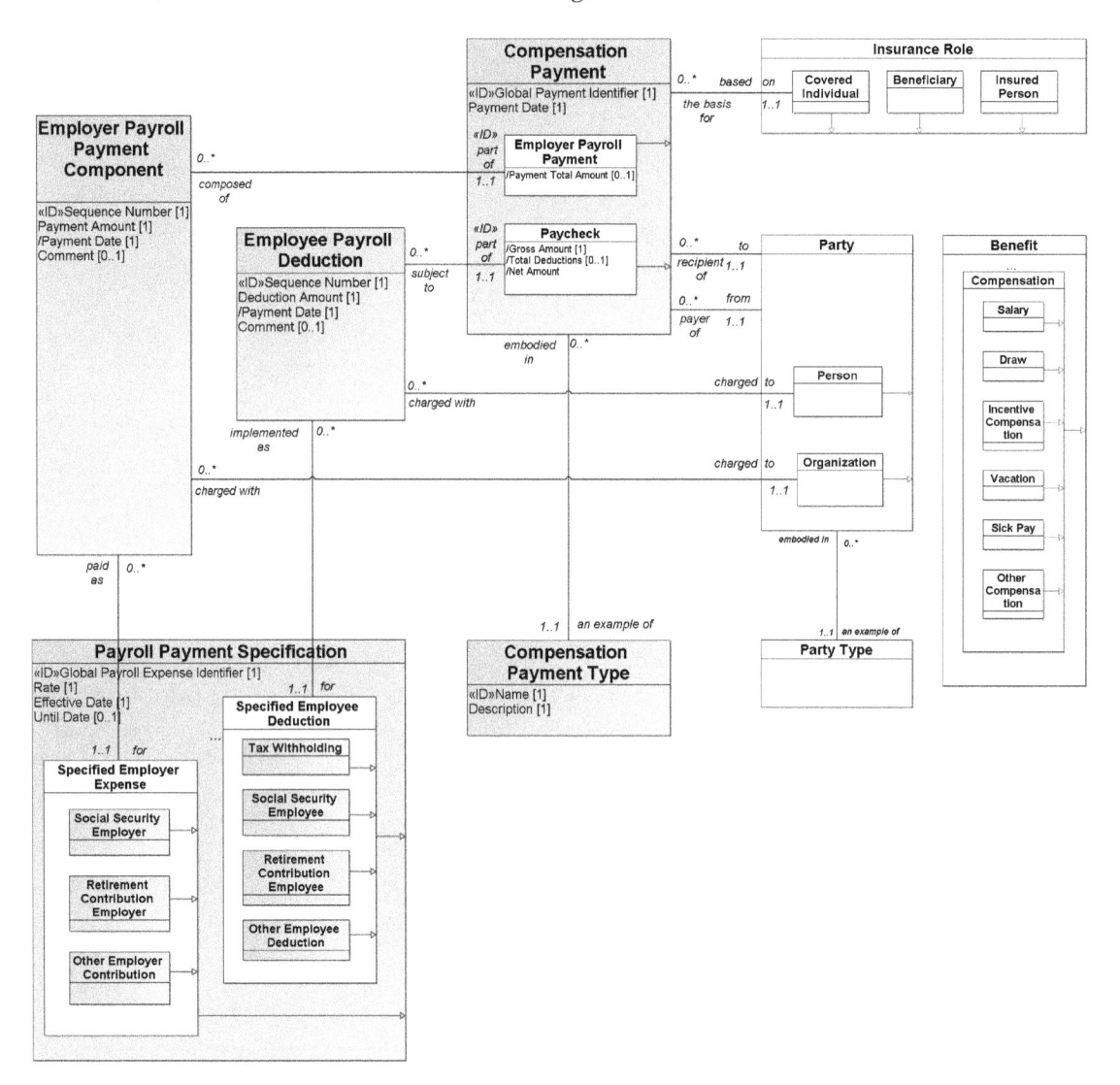

Figure 13-11: Benefit Payments

---

the man who taught your author how to set up the payments described here. He was also most helpful when all had to be reconciled for each new tax year.

Specifically, there are two kinds of **Compensation Payments:** 1) A payment to the employee, which covers the gross salary for the period, less any deductions; (In the model, this is a **Paycheck**.) 2) Payments to other agencies and companies on behalf of the employee (In the model, this is an **Employer Payroll Payment**).

In the United States, the **Net Amount** of a **Paycheck** paid to an employee (a **Covered Individual**) *for* a **Salary** is calculated as the **Gross Amount**, less **Total Deductions**. The **Gross Amount**, in turn, is derived by inferring the **Gross Salary** for the **Covered Individual** being paid. The **Total Deductions** is calculated by summing up the "**Payment Amount**" for all **Employee Payment Deductions** that are *part of* this **Paycheck**.

Each of these **Employee Payroll Deductions** must be *for* one and only one **Specified Employee Deductions**. A **Specified Employee Deduction** defines an item to be withheld from an employee's paychecks—for example, **US Government Withholding** (for Income Taxes), the **Employee's** contribution to **Social Security**[∇], and any **Retirement Contribution** paid for by the **Employee**.

The second category of **Compensation Payment** consists of **Employer Payroll Expense Payments**. These are *for* **Specified Employer Expenses**—specifically, the employer's contribution to **Social Security**, as well as the **Retirement Contribution** paid for by the employer. These are the **Specified Employer Expenses** that are *paid for* by the **Organization** that is the **Person's** employer, just as each **Specified Employee Deduction** must be *paid for by* the **Person** who is the employee in question.

The **Employer Payroll Payment** and **Paycheck** described here are not the only **Compensation Payments** for a payday. To be sure, described here are some of the **Compensation Payment Types** that these **Compensation Payments** are *an example of*. But there are others.

[∇] In the United States, Social Security is the government-sponsored pension program. In fact, there two parts, with deductions for each: 1) the "Federal Insurance Contributions Act" (FICA)—the original "Social Security"—is the pension part, established in the late 1930s, and 2) Medicare, added in 1965, which provides medical insurance for those of retirement age.

In other countries, the deductions and checks required will be different—and either more or less complex. For simplicity in this exercise, the Medicare and FICA payments are treated together as "social security" payments.

Business Rules

- Each **Employee Payroll Deduction** must be *charged to* the **Person** who is *the recipient of* the **Compensation Payment**.

- Each **Employer Payroll Expense** must be charged to the **Organization** that is *the payer of* the **Compensation Payment**.

Table 13-3 describes the components of a sample paycheck.

First, the lines below **Gross Salary** are the **Employee Payroll Deductions**, each of which will subsequently be sent to the appropriate taxing authorities. In the United States, all go to the Internal Revenue Service (known to Americans simply as "The IRS"), which then forwards the appropriate amounts to the Social Security Administration. Associated with this paycheck are the contributions by the employer to the Social Security programs (including "Medicare"), plus a contribution to the employee's retirement fund.

Table 13-3-a: Paycheck Elements

Payroll Payment Specification	Payroll Payment Specification (Detail)	Paycheck	Specified Employee Expense	Specified Employer Expense
Gross Salary		$1,000.00		1000
Employee Payroll Deductions	Federal W/H		-$15.45	
	Social Security		-$62.00	
	(Rate) 0.06200			
	Medicare		-$14.50	
	(Rate) 0.01450			
Net pay		$908.05		
Due the IRS (Employee)			91.95	

Thus, the processing of a paycheck includes, in this example, not only the check to the employee, but also checks to the Internal Revenue Service and the bank handling the employee's retirement fund.

Human Resources 283

Table 13-3-b: Paycheck Elements

Payroll Payment Specification	Payroll Payment Specification (Detail)	Paycheck	Specified Employee Expense	Specified Employer Expense
Employer Payroll Payments	Social Security			$62.00
	Medicare			$14.50
Due IRS (Employer)				$76.50
(Total IRS Payment)				($168.45)
Retirement Program (Employer)				$150.00
Total cost to employer of Payday				$1,226.50

Accounting Implications

So far, the model has represented the real-world phenomena of **Benefits**, **Compensation Payments**, and the like. Now we have to link this to the accounting system, described in Chapter 11. This is shown in Figure 13-12.

As we've seen, a paycheck transaction has four components:

1. The gross amount, less deductions, that produces a net amount paid to the employee. (In the Table 13-3, that's $908.05.)

2. Deductions collected by the employer and passed to either the government (for Social Security in the United States) or to a fund for the employee's retirement. (In the example, the portion collected from the employee is $91.05)

3. Amounts paid by the employer, either to the government (again for Social Security in the United States). (In the example, $76.56 is for employer payment, plus the $91.05 withheld from the employee's paycheck, for a total of $168.45.)

4. Amounts paid to the employee's financial institution for 'e retirement program. (In this case, there was no employee deduction, so the total is the amount of the employer's contribution is $150.00.)

This results in the cutting of three checks:

1. The paycheck to the employee. ($908.05).

284 Enterprise Model Patterns

2. A payment to the Internal Revenue Service. ($168.45)

3. A payment to the employee's financial institution for the retirement account. ($150)

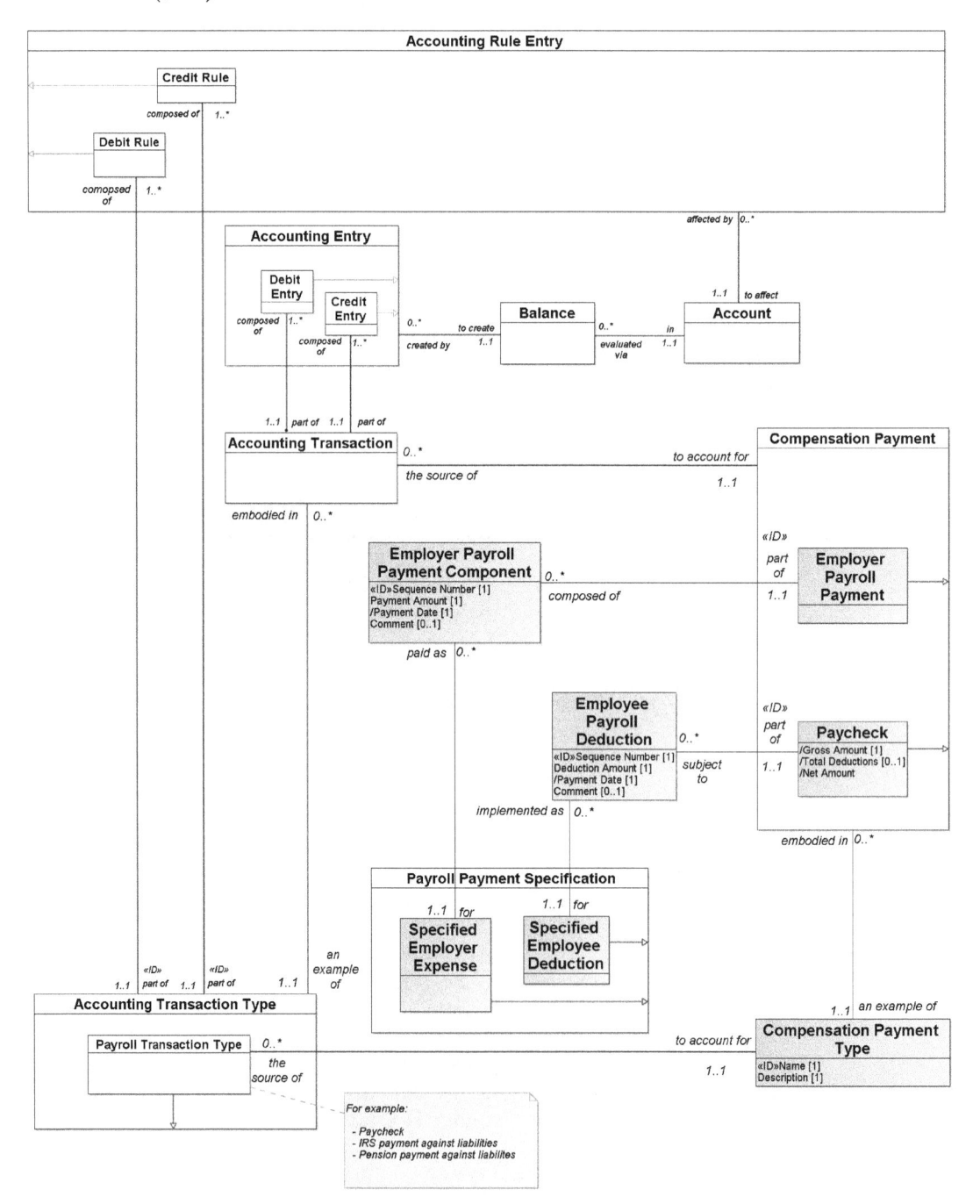

Figure 13-12: Payroll Accounting Transactions

Each of these triggers a journal entry (an **Accounting Transaction**) to account for it in the company's books.

As we saw in Chapter 11, the *structure* of each **Accounting Transaction** (which accounts are debited and which are credited) is determined by rules defined for the **Accounting Transaction Type** it is *an example of*. Figure 13-12 includes that part of the model reproduced here, with **Accounting Rule Entries**. Recall that each **Accounting Transaction Type** may be composed of one or more **Accounting Rule Entries** (specifically one or more **Credit Rules** and one or more **Debit Rules**).

Business Rule

- An Accounting Transaction that is *to account for* a Compensation Payment must be *an example of* an Accounting Transaction Type that is *to account for* the Compensation Payment Type that the Compensation Payment is *an example of*. (**Translation**: The Accounting Transaction that is for a Compensation Payment must correspond to the Accounting Transaction Type that is for the corresponding Compensation Type.)

Each of these, in turn, specifies which **Account**'s **Balances** are to be *created by* the **Account Transaction** that the **Account Transaction Type** is *embodied in*.

According to the **Accounting Rule Entries**, the following **Account Entries** are required for the **Accounting Transaction Type** `"Paycheck"`:

- One **Debit Entry** `"Entry Value"` is *subtracted from* the previous **Balance** `"Balance Value"` *in* the **Equity Account** `"Payroll Expense"`, to create a new one.
- One **Credit Entry** `"Entry Value"` is *added to* each previous **Balance** `"Balance Value"` *in* the **Liability Accounts** `"Tax Withholding Liability"` and `"Employee's Social Security Liability"`, to create new ones.
- One **Credit Entry** `"Entry Value"` is *subtracted from* the previous **Balance** `"Balance Value"` *in* the **Asset Account** `"Cash"`, to create a new one.

Table 13-4 shows an example of the **Accounting Entries** for the **Accounting Transactions** that are *an example of* **Accounting Transaction Type** `"Paycheck"`. The `"Payroll Expense"` is subtracted from equity, while the withholding, social security and Medicare are added back to liabilities, and the difference is deducted from the asset "Cash". Total credits equal total debits.

Table 13-4: Payroll Accounting Transactions – Sample Paycheck

No.	Transaction	Credit	+ -	Amount	Debit	+ -	Amount
1	Paycheck	Cash (asset)	-	$908.05	Payroll expense♣	-	$1000
		IRS Withholding (liability)	+	$15.45			
		Social Security (liability)	+	$76.50			
1	(TOTAL)			$1000			$1000

Table 13-5 shows examples of the **Accounting Entries** for the **Accounting Transactions** that are *examples of* **Accounting Transaction Types** "IRS Payment" and "Retirement Payment". In each case, the appropriate amount is both deducted from the asset cash and the liabilities. One check can address all three liabilities, as long as the value of the check is equal to the sum of the deductions from liabilities.

Table 13-5: Payroll Accounting Transactions – IRS and Retirement Payments

No.	Transaction	Credit	+ -	Amount	Debit	+ -	Amount
2	IRS Payment	Cash	-	168.45	IRS Withholding (liability)	-	$15.45
					Social Security - Employee (liability)	-	$76.50
					Social Security – Employer (expense)	-	$76.50
2	(TOTAL)			168.45			168.45
3	Retirement Payment	Cash	-	150	Retirement Expense	-	150
3	(TOTAL)			150.00			150

♣ Recall from Chapter 11 that expenses are subtractions from equity.

CHAPTER 14

Marketing and Communications

Marketing is one of the most important functions carried out by many companies. Indeed, for some companies, it is at the center of what the company is all about. Perhaps because of that, the part of the model specific to marketing is deeply imbedded in the Level 1 model already described in Chapter Two.

A significant part of a company's marketing activities, for example, concern managing customer data. From a data modeling perspective, this much is entirely the domain of the **Party** model described in Chapter Two.

What this leaves, then, is *communications* between the company and those customers.

About Communications

A company communicates with customers, prospects, and the public at large through various media: advertising, telephone calls, e-mails, mass mailings, and so forth. All of these media share an important characteristic: they all carry out **Communication**.

Figure 14-1 shows the entity class **Communication**. A **Communication** is defined as the passing of information among two or more parties.

Communications fall into three major categories: the first category, **Personal Communication**, is initiated by an individual and is directed to either one person or a relatively small number of people. This includes as sub-types:

- **Mailing of Letter** – A **Personal Communication** that involves writing a message on a physical medium and sending it to someone via a postal service.

288 Enterprise Model Patterns

- **Face to Face Meeting** – A **Personal Communication** whereby two or more people are together in the same room, or are sharing a video conference of some sort.

- **Placement of a Telephone Call** – A **Personal Communication** in which one person uses a telephone network to enable speaking to someone in a different location. This is an audio-only communication.

- **Sending of an E-Mail Message** – A **Personal Communication** in which a person composes text, which is then sent electronically to one or more other people via the Internet or a corporate data network.

- **Sending of a Facsimile** – A **Personal Communication** in which one person uses scanning equipment and the telephone network to send an image (a facsimile, typically of a document) to one or more other people.

- **Other Personal Communication** – A **Personal Communication** that is not one of the above.

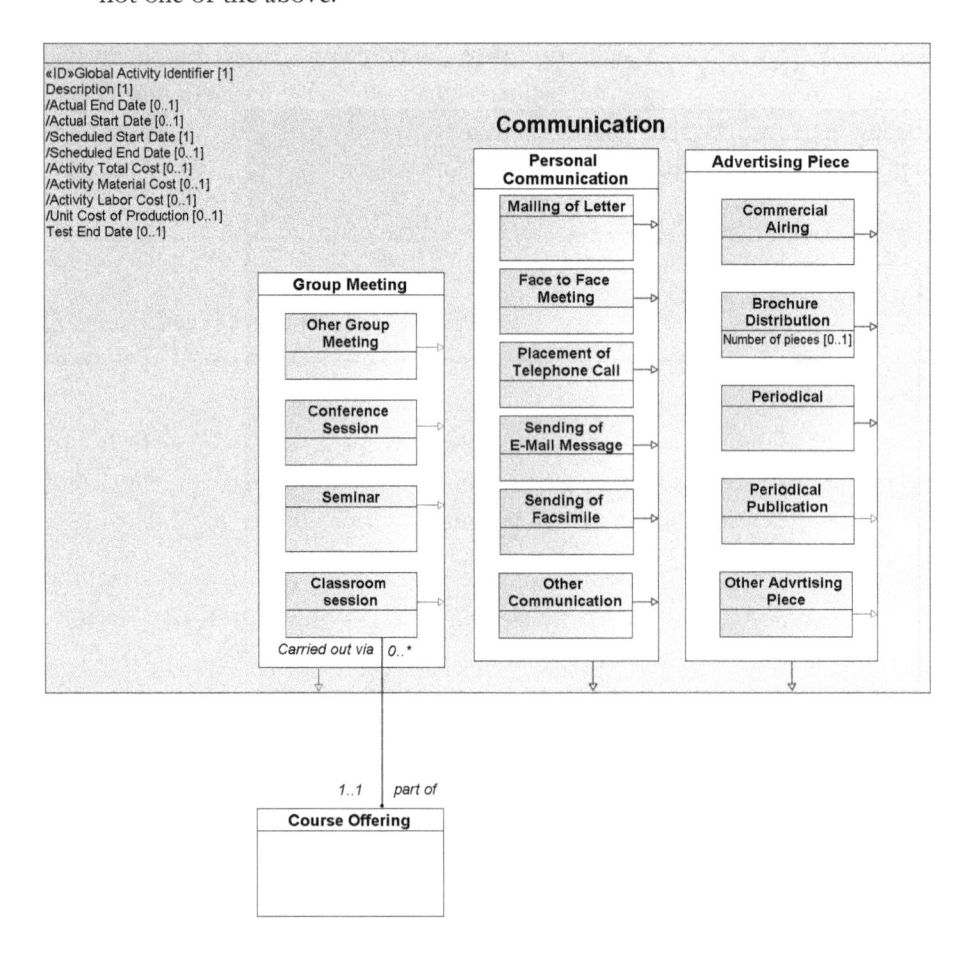

Figure 14-1: Communications Among Parties

Marketing and Communications

A second category is **Group Meetings**, in which a collection of people are brought together, either for education or the discussion of issues. These might include:

- **Conference Session** – A **Group Meeting** in which multiple people interested in a specific topic gather to discuss it as part of a larger meeting to address a more general topic of which the **Conference Session** topic is a part.

- **Seminar** (either electronic or in person) – A relatively informal **Group Meeting** (or a set of **Group Meetings**) in which one person or group of people present a body of information to an audience of one or more people.

- **Classroom Session** – A formal **Group Meeting** for the purpose of having a person or set of people present a formal body of knowledge, as *part of* a **Course Offering**. (See page 275 for details.)

- **Other Group Meeting** – A **Group Meeting** that is not a **Conference Session**, a **Seminar**, or a **Course**.

The third category is **Advertising Piece**—a formally published package of materials to be distributed to a relatively large number of people—most commonly to promote products or services for sale. This can be:

- **Commercial Airing** – An **Advertising Piece** that consists of running a television or radio (or internet) commercial on one or more stations.

- **Brochure Distribution** – An **Advertising Piece** that consists of distributing a printed brochure, typically via a postal service, but it could also be handed out by representatives in a public place.

- **Periodical Publication** – The printing and distribution of a magazine, newspaper, or newsletter to a set of subscribers.

- **Other Advertising Piece** – An **Advertising Piece** that is not one of the above.

Note that several kinds of **Communication** (for example, **Telephone Call** and **Group Meeting**) may also be for advertising purposes.

Communication Role

In a simple model, two relationships between **Communication** and **Party** would be sufficient, showing that each **Communication** must be *from* one **Party** and *to* one **Party**. Because the **Communication** could be anything from a conference call to a seminar, however, this isn't adequate. So instead, Figure 14-1 shows that each **Communication** must be *conducted via* one or more (actually two or more) **Communication Roles**, where each must be *played by* a **Party**.

290 Enterprise Model Patterns

A **Communication Role** is the fact that a particular **Party** is somehow involved with a **Communication**, either as an **Originator**, **Recipient**, another kind of **Participant**, or in an **Other Communication Role**. This is represented in Figure 14-2. Each **Communication Role**, then, must be either an **Originator Role**, a **Recipient Role** (in the case of, for example, `"simple marketing telephone calls"`), a **Participant Role** (in the case of `"conference calls"`, `"webcasts"`, and `"focus groups"`), or an **Other Communication Role**. The sub-type structure shows that, but so also does the relationship line asserting that each **Communication Role** must be *an example of* one and only one **Communication Role Type**. Again, as with **Party** and **Party Type**, as well as other examples we've seen in this book, **Communication Role Type** recapitulates the sub-types shown for **Communication Role** (Originator Role, Recipient Role, et cetera). The existence of the **Communication Role Type** entity class permits specifying more detailed **Communications Roles** than would necessarily show up as sub-types in the drawing.

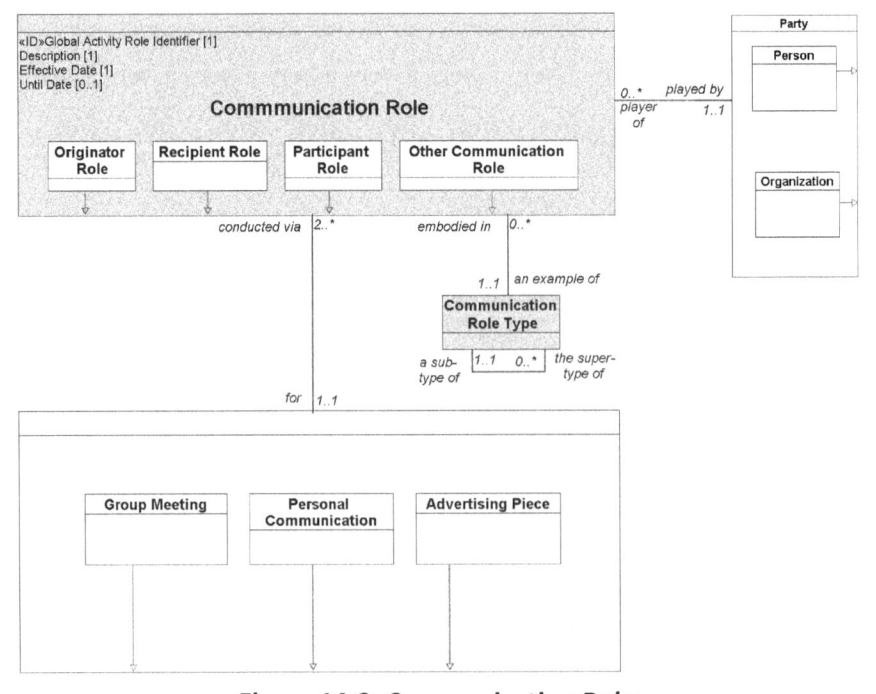

Figure 14-2: Communication Roles

There are many different kinds of **Communication**. Some **Communications** are via **Group Meetings**, but **Personal Communications** may also be to sets of named individuals. In these cases, one **Communications Role** can represent a particular **Party's** playing the **Originator Role**, and others can represent each **Party's** playing the **Recipient Role**. In other cases, such as **Advertising**

Marketing and Communications

Communications, many of the **Communications Role** instances will simply be examples of **Participant**.

Communications Among Sites

In some cases, such as telephone conversations, e-mail, or snail mail, the **Communication Role** is not just *played by* a **Party**, but it is *played by* a **Party** at a particular **Address**. In Figure 14-3, this is shown by an additional relationship, where each **Communication Role** may be *played by* a **Party Placement**—that is, a **Party** being located at a particular **Address**.

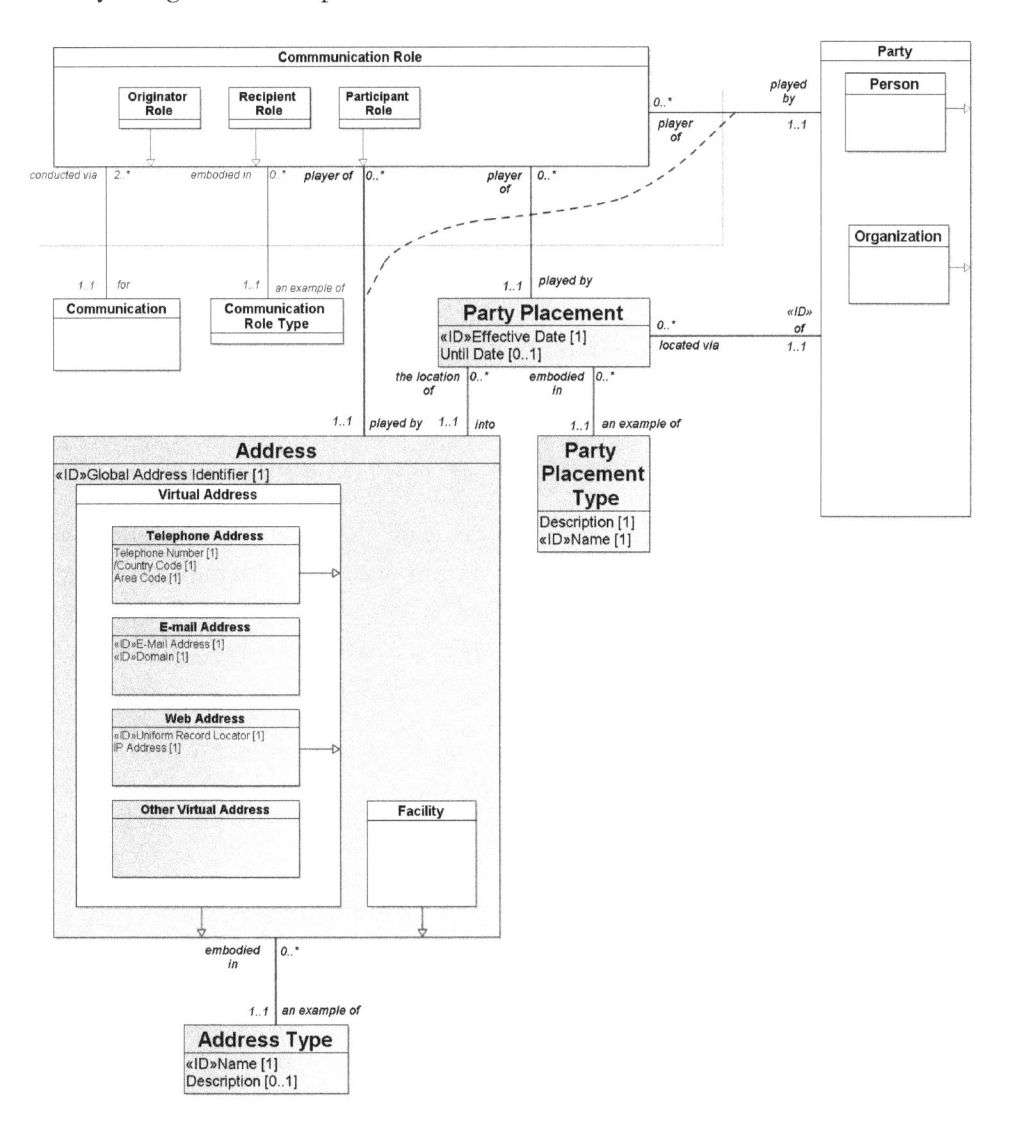

Figure 14-3: Communications Among Sites

Alternatively, a mailing can go out, or a marketing call may be made, without knowing who the recipient is. In that case, all that is known is that a **Communication Role** is *directed toward* an **Address**, whether it is a physical address (a **Facility**), an **E-Mail Address**, or a **Telephone Address**. Each occupant, for example, is recorded as simply being a **Communication Role** *played by* a particular physical **Address**.

In other cases, the **Communication** may be in the form of a web site, so in that case, the **Originator Role** could be *played by* the **Web Address** involved, while each **Participant Role** would be *played by* the individual's **E-Mail Address**.

Thus, each **Communication Role** must be *played by* one and only one **Party**, *played by* one and only one **Party Placement**, or *played by* one and only one **Address**. (This is represented on the drawing by the arc drawn across those relationships.♣)

Communications are activities that take place at a particular time, as specified by the attributes **Actual Start Date**, **Actual Start Time**, **Actual End Date**, and **Actual End Time**.

Communication Procedures

The definition of the nature, contents, medium, et cetera. of the **Communication** is described by **Communication Procedure**, as shown in Figure 14-4.

Communication Procedure has what appears to be the same set of sub-types as **Communication**, but here this is distinguishing between the *Procedures* that go into creating an advertisement or making a telephone call, while **Communication** describes the actual placement of an advertisement or the making of a telephone call.

Figure 14-4 elaborates on **Communication Procedure**, showing sub-types:

- **Mass Market Procedure**, the effort required to create and place advertising. This includes:
    - **Commercial Production**, to air commercials on television or radio.

♣ Note that, as stated before, each "arc" in UML is intended to mean an "exclusive or" relationship between only two of the relationships at a time. The complete expression of mutual exclusivity therefore would require three arcs to represent all possible combinations. For the sake of graphic simplicity it is assumed here that mutual exclusivity is transitive.

Marketing and Communications

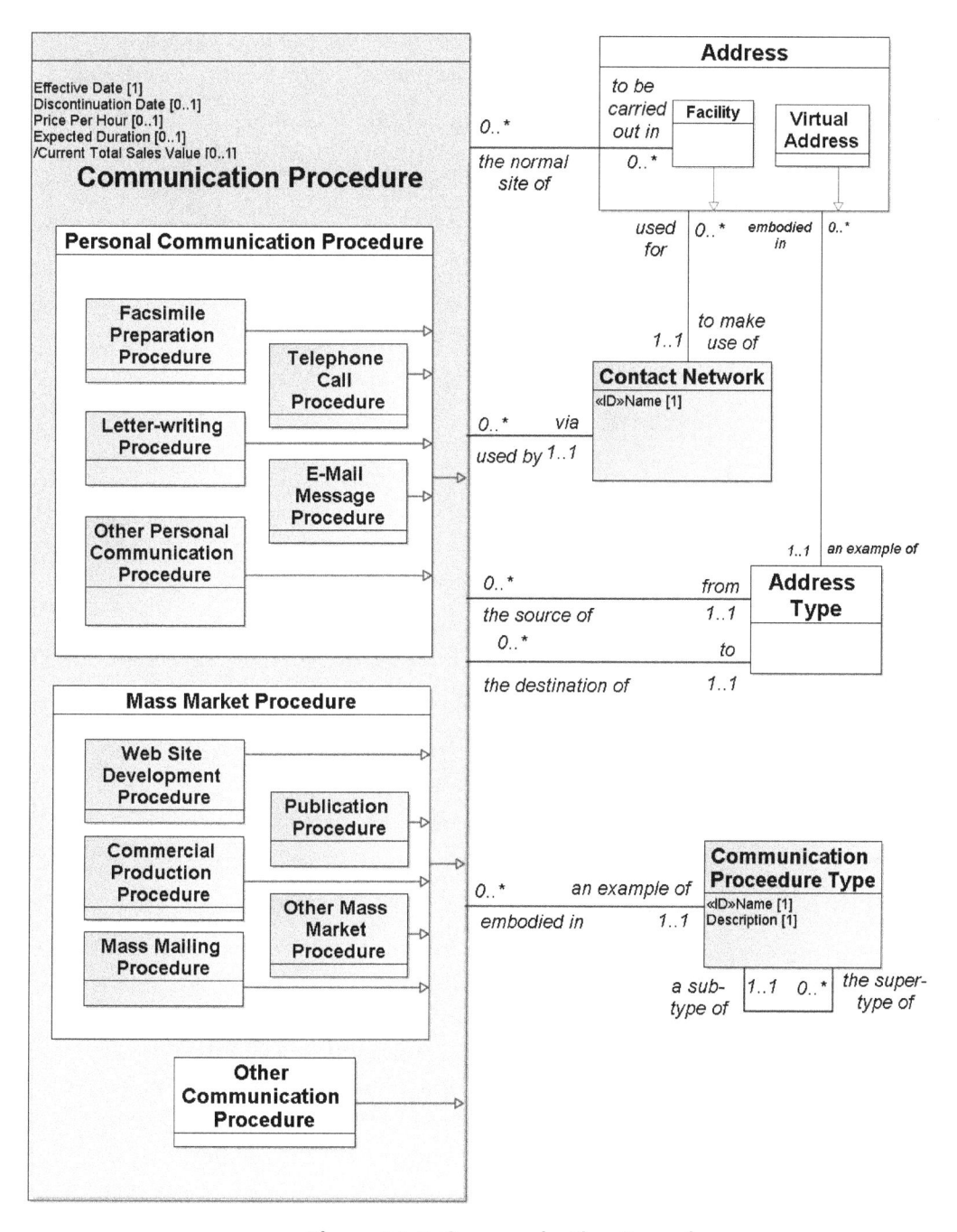

Figure 14-4: Communication Procedures

- **Mass Mailing Procedure**, of materials to a large audience.
- The **Publication Procedure**, creating **Information Resources**, will be discussed shortly.

- **Web Site Development Procedure**, that sets up **Web Addresses** containing information about the enterprise.

- **Other Mass Market Procedures**, which is anything to do with advertising that is not **Commercial Production**, **Mass Mailing**, the **Publication Process**, or **Web Site Production**.

• **Personal Communication Procedure**, including:

- **Telephone Call Procedure**.
- **E-mail Message Procedure**.
- **Facsimile Preparation**.
- **Letter-writing Procedure**
- **Other Personal Communication Procedure**

• **Other Communication Procedure**. any **Communication Procedure** that is not one of the above.

Where **Communications** are between individuals at their **Addresses**, the specification of a kind of **Communication Procedure** determines the **Address Types** involved. Specifically, each **Communication Procedure** must be *from* one **Address Type** and *to* the same or a different **Address Type**. Note that an **Address** may be *to make use of* a **Contact Network**, such as a telephone or data network. The **Communication Procedure** may be *via* a specified **Contact Network**.

Again, **Communication Procedure Type** recapitulates the sub-types shown for **Communication Procedure**.

For example, a **Telephone Call Procedure** that describes a conference call to a group of prospects may be *embodied in* a **Telephone Call** from the company's **Telephone Address** to a set of **Telephone Addresses** at prospects' offices. This would use the **Contact Network** "Telephone System", where a **Contact Network** is a collection of **Addresses** (usually **Virtual Addresses**) that are linked together. As another example, a **Website Procedure** can be defined to be *via* the **Contact Network**, "Internet Conferencing Service". Thus, **Communications** that are *examples of* this **Communication Procedure** would be between the company representative's **Web Address IP Address** and the **Web Address IP Addresses** of prospects who log into the Internet Conferencing Service.

As a further example, a **Communication Procedure** for a mass mailing campaign could be designed to be *from* an example of the **Address Type** "office", to an example of the **Address Type** "home". The **Contact Network** would be "U.S.

`Postal Service"`. An actual piece of mail, then, would be a **Communication** from the **Party Placement** that is the company located in a particular office, to numerous examples of <u>either</u> an addressed recipient that is a **Party Placement**, putting that recipient **Party** in a particular physical address (**Facility**), <u>or</u> to "occupant" at that physical **Address**.

Not shown on the model is the fact that **Communication Procedure** may be *intended for people with* a particular **Legal Party Category Value** (such as those in the **Party Category** `"Income Range"`, with the value `"Greater Than $200,000.00"`).

Advertising and Information Resource

Advertising is a significant kind of communication done by marketing organizations (including Government Agencies, by the way). This may use any of various kinds of media. The media have changed over time, but the basic structure and objectives have not. Originally, (for several centuries) it was newspapers and magazines. In the twentieth century, radio—and ultimately television—completely changed the dynamics of advertisements. Then, in the last twenty years, the World-wide Web has done so yet again.

A `"mass mailing"`, a `"television commercial"`, or for that matter, a `"PowerPoint™ presentation in a seminar"` is, in fact, an **Information Resource**, as described in Chapter 10. That is, these are examples of tangible expressions of a person's ideas and concepts. This is something to be managed by a company as its intellectual property.

Figure 14-1 adds **Information Resource** (both **Instance** and **Definition**) from Chapter 10 to the model being developed in this chapter.

The link between the two is **Communications Vehicle**, which represents the fact that a particular **Information Resource Instance** is used in a particular **Communication**. Each of the items mentioned—a television commercial or a PowerPoint™ presentation in a webcast—is an example of an **Information Resource Instance** being *content in* a **Communications Medium** that is being *used as* a **Communication**.

In Chapter 10, **Information Resources** were described in general. In this context, we are only concerned with **Information Resource Instances** that are used for communicating with the world that is our marketplace, along with the **Information Resource Definitions** that describe them. As previously described, an

Information Resource Instance can be either a **Physical Copy** or a **Virtual Copy**. In the case of marketing communications, a **Physical Copy** can be a **Brochure** or a **Print Advertisement** in a newspaper or magazine. It could also be a physical **Photograph**. These are elaborated on as **Document** and **Image** respectively in **Information Resource Definition**.

The **Moving Image** shown in the model as an **Information Resource Definition** may be *embodied in* a **TV Commercial**. Similarly, a **Document** may be *embodied in* a **Print Advertisement**".

The act of creating either the original work or the copy is done by someone playing an **Authorship Role** (a kind of **Information Resource Role**). Often (in this context), this role may be taken on in response to a **Communication Role** being carried out for the **Communication Procedure**. That is, a **Communication Role** may be *the source of* one or more **Authorship Roles**.

Figure 14-5 showed that a **Communication** could *be the use of* one or more **Communication Vehicles**, each of which must be *the use of* either one and only one **Information Resource Instance** or one and only one **Information Resource Definition**. It is therefore the case that an **Information Resource Instance** may also be *content in* one or more **Communication Media**, each *used for* one **Communication**.

For example, a **Brochure Distribution** may be *the user of* a **Communication Medium** that is, in turn, *the use of* a **Brochure**. Alternatively, a **Brochure** may be the *content in* one or more **Communication Vehicle** that is *used for* a **Brochure Distribution**. Similarly, a **TV Commercial** may be *content in* a **Communication Vehicle** that are each *used in* a particular **Commercial Airing**.

Communication in Context

As the reader has already probably figured out, the structure of **Communication** makes it clear that it is, in fact, a kind of *Activity*. This is now revealed officially in Figure 14-6. That is, **Communication** is a sub-type of **Activity**, just as **Communication Procedure** is a sub-type of **Activity Specification**.

It therefore follows that **Communications Role** is but a sub-type of **Activity Role**, and **Authorship** is *a sub-type of* **Information Resource Role**.

And of course, brochure design, commercial video, and commercial photograph, can now take their place as sub-types of information resource definition.

Marketing and Communications 297

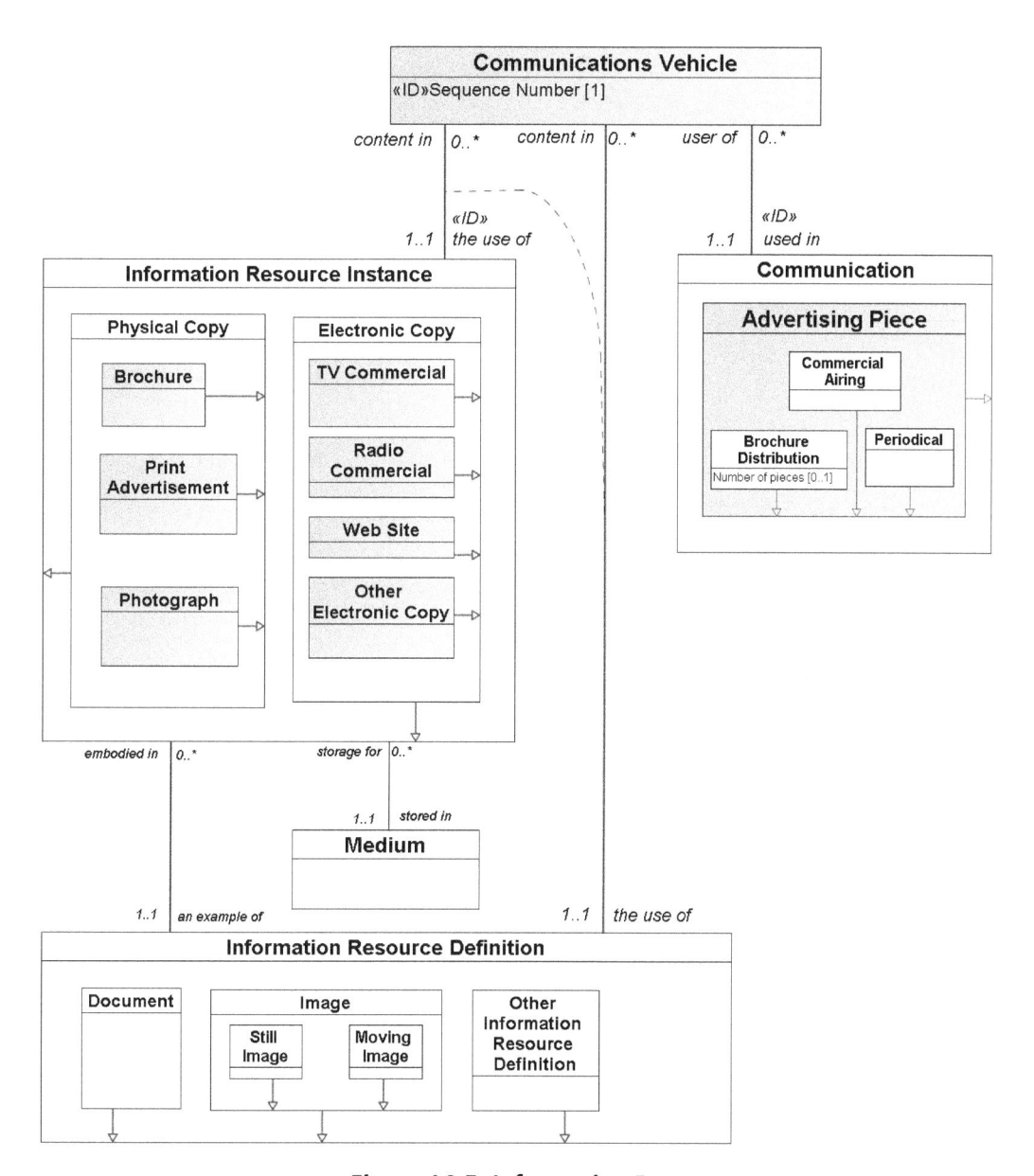

Figure 14-5: Information Resources

298 Enterprise Model Patterns

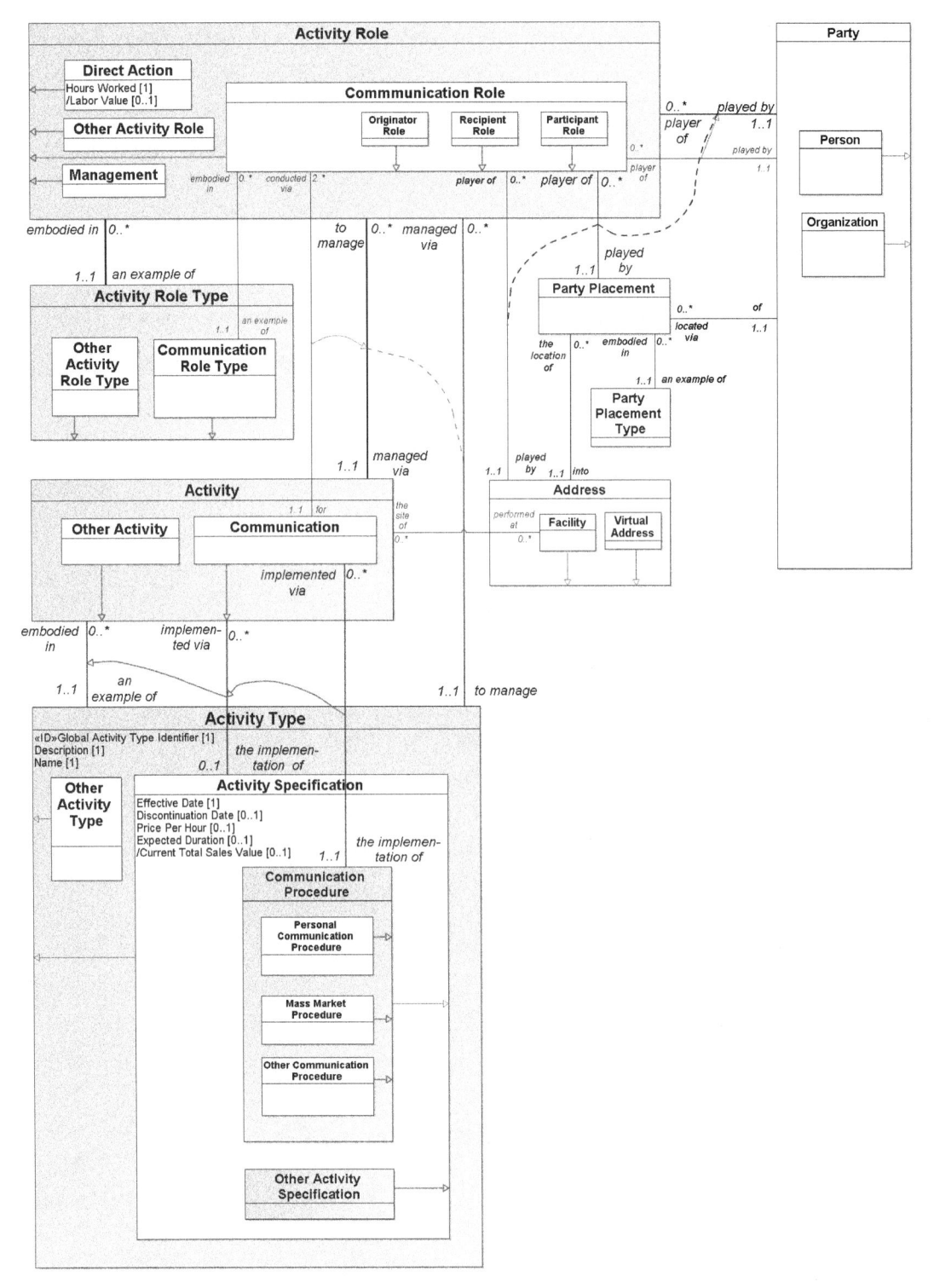

Figure 14-6: Communications and the Enterprise Model

Marketing and Communications 299

Events

Now that we've recognized that **Communication** is but a special kind of **Activity**, the model for **Events** comes into play. The model of events from Chapter 7 is updated in Figure 14-7. This time, however, it is a **Communication** that may be *the cause of* an (**Internal**) **Event**, which in turn, may be *the cause of* one or more **Triggers** that are *the cause of* other **Communications**.

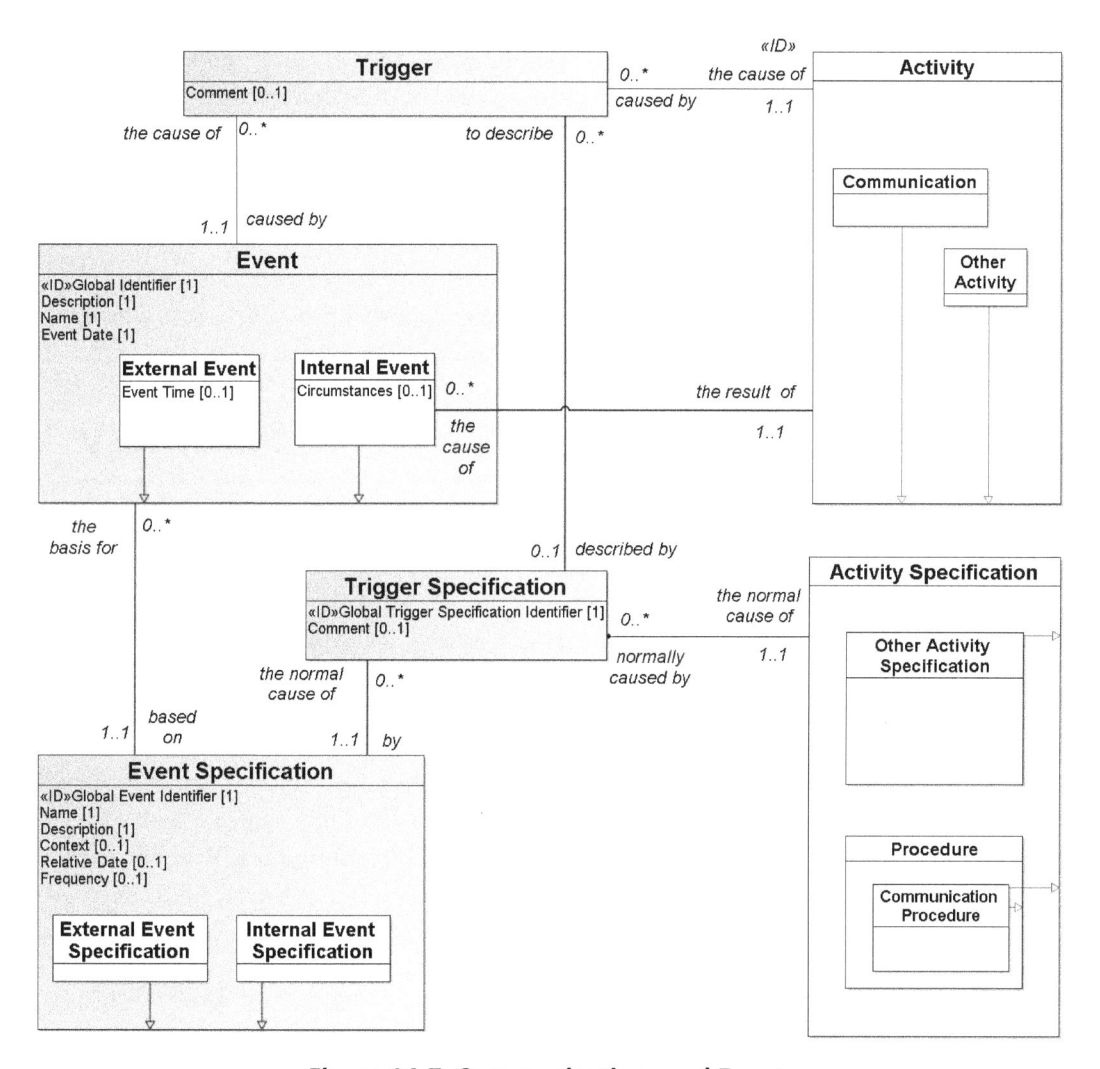

Figure 14-7: Communications and Events

On the other hand, a customer's desire to place an order is an example of an **External Event**. It then may be *the cause of* one or more **Triggers** *of* an **Activity**

Instance—specifically, a **Communication** that is the customer's placing of a **Telephone Call**. This, in turn, will be *the cause of* one or more **Triggers**, each of which is *of* a particular **Activity Instance**, where an **Activity Instance** is a task done by the company to fill the order. Many of these **Activities** will simply be **Communications** from one part of the enterprise to another—or to a supplying company.

Note that an **External Event** may in fact be a **Temporal Event**. It may be that every Monday, a manager calls a department conference call. The *specification* of that call is an example of an **Activity Specification** that is a **Telephone Call Procedure**. An **External (Temporal) Event Specification** with a `"Frequency"` of `"Every Monday"` is the *normal cause of* a **Trigger Specification** that is *the normal cause of* a **Communication Procedure** that is `"Weekly department conference call"`.

Thus, when Monday, January 11, 2010 rolls around, a business rule engine, based on the **Event Specification** and the **Trigger Specification** described above, initiates the conference call telephone number for each Department member to call.

Summary

A **Communication** is a critically important kind of **Activity** in a company or government agency. In this chapter, we discussed primarily the kinds of **Communication** that are involved in interacting with potential and actual customers. The structures described, however can apply to any kind of **Communication**.

If **Communication** was the act of interacting between two or more **Parties** (both **Persons** and **Organizations**) then the characteristics and features of such **Communications** are specified in their respective **Communication Procedures**. If the former is a sub-type of **Activity**, then the latter is a sub-type of **Activity Specification**.

A **Communication** may be both the producer of and the user of **Information Resources**, both **Instances** and **Definitions**.

As with any other **Activity**, a **Communication** may be *caused by* a **Trigger** that was, in turn, *caused by* an **Event**. It may also be *the cause of* an **Internal Event** that triggers another **Activity** (a **Communication** or something else).

CHAPTER 15

Contracts

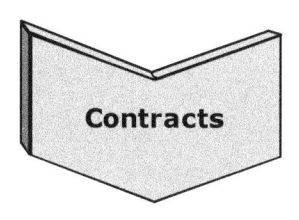

One place modelers often start is by modeling a **Sales Order**, typically producing a model such as the one shown in Figure 15-1. A **Sales Order** is a request *from* a **Customer** for a specified list of products (here **Asset Specifications**) and/or services (here **Activity Specifications**). That is, each **Sales Order** must be *from* one and only one **Customer**, and it may be *composed of* one or more **Line Items**, each of which must be either *for* one and only one **Activity Specification**, or *for* one and only one **Asset Specification**. Here the entity class **Activity Specification** is taken from Chapter 7. Here the entity class **Asset Specification** is taken from Chapter 6 of this book.

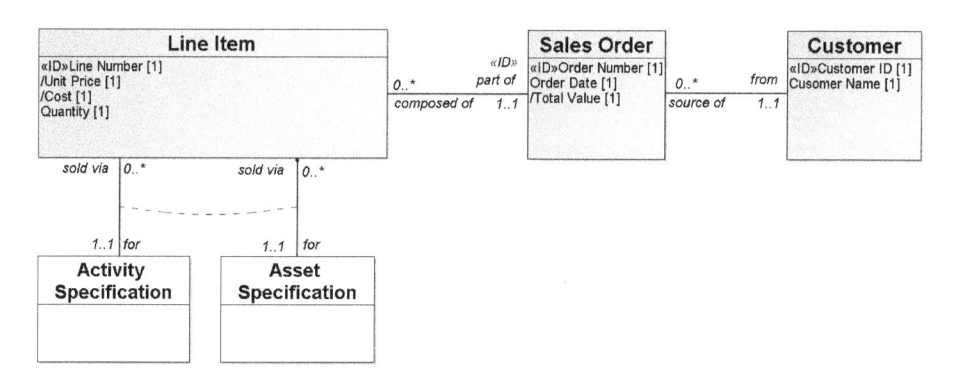

Figure 15-1: Sales Orders

That is, each **Sales Order** must be *from* one and only one **Customer**, and it may be *composed of* one or more **Line Items**, where a **Line Item** is an entry specifying a single **Asset Specification** or **Activity Specification** to be supplied to *the customers in* a **Contract**.

Each **Line Item**, then, must be either *for* one and only one **Activity Specification**, or *for* one and only one **Asset Specifications**.

That is, each **Sales Order** must be *to* one and only one **Customer**, and it may be *composed of* one or more **Line Items**, each of which must be either *for* one and only one **Activity Specification**, or *for* one and only one **Asset Specifications**.

This model would be produced for a marketing or sales organization. In another part of the **Organization**, the Procurement Department is looking for a model of **Purchase Orders**, so the modeler typically produces a model such as the one shown in Figure 15-2. This model of course is completely different from the **Sales Order** model shown earlier. In this one—a **Purchase Order**—an authorization is *to* a **Vendor** to supply a specified list of products (again, **Asset Specifications**) and/or services (**Activity Specifications**).

That is, each **Purchase Order** must be *to* one and only one **Vendor**, and it may be *composed of* one or more **Line Items**, each of which must be either *for* one and only one **Activity Specification**, or *for* one and only one **Asset Specifications**.

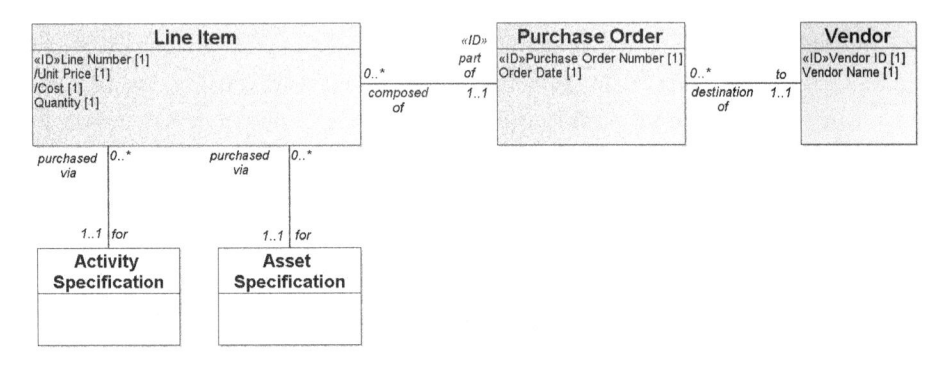

Figure 15-2: Purchase Orders

Contracts

Do you see a pattern here? Even though these models serve different departments in the enterprise, they in fact model exactly the same thing—a sales transaction. The only difference is that in one case *we* are the *vendor*, and in the other case *we* are the *customer*. The structure of both transactions is the same.

Note that the terms "customer" and "vendor" do not represent fundamental "things of significance" to the enterprise. Rather they describe roles. The underlying reality is the **Person** or **Organization** that is doing the buying or selling.

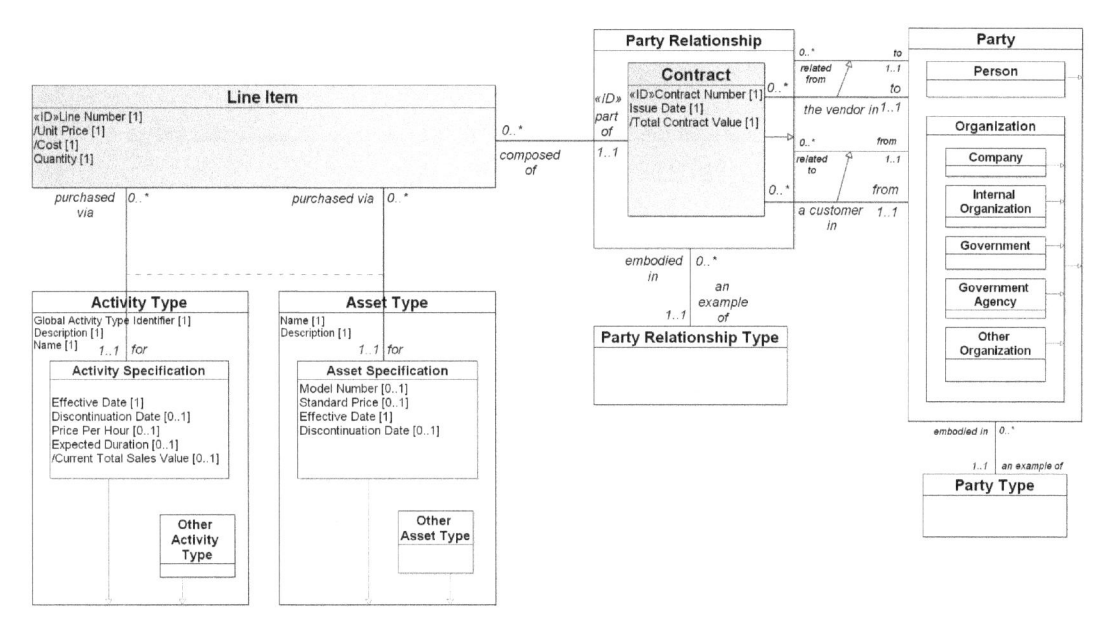

Figure 15-3: Contracts

In other words, a **Person** or an **Organization** is not inherently a customer or a vendor. He/she/they are only so by virtue of their playing a *role* in sales or purchase orders. The appropriate entity class in both cases is **Party** (first described in Chapter 4), and which encompasses both **Person** and **Organization**. The **Purchase Order** and the **Sales Order**, then, are but two different views of the underlying entity class, **Contract**, shown in Figure 15-3, with two relationships to **Party**.

That is, the "customer-ness" of the first role is conveyed not by it as an entity class, but as the role that each **Party** may be *a customer in* one or more **Contracts**. Similarly, the "vendor-ness" of the second role is conveyed not by it as an entity class, but as the role that each **Party** may be *a vendor in* one or more **Contracts**.

According to Merriam-Webster, a **Contract** is "a binding agreement between two or more persons or parties; *especially*: one legally enforceable".[53]

Note that this approach requires the company being addressed in the model to explicitly identify itself as a **Party**, as well. This makes it possible, among other things, to make explicit just which department (**Internal Organization**) is doing the buying or selling.

---

[53] Merriam-Webster. 2010. "contract". *The Merriam-Webster Online Dictionary* Retrieved 11/19/2010 at *http://www.merriam-webster.com/dictionary/contract*.

A **Party** (including us) can be either in the role of *customer in* or in the role of *vendor in*.

Business Rule

- A **Party** may not be both *the seller in* and *the buyer in* a single **Contract**.

Note, by the way, that what is here called a "contract" can be one of the most difficult entity classes to name in a real company or government agency. A bank will call it an "Agreement", although this also encompasses "Instrument" (as you will see in Chapter 20, below). We could extend our example and simply call it "Order". Moreover, more specialized terms, such as "lease" and "future" are also possible.

The point is that the name of this entity class, more than most others, must be determined by the company commissioning the model. Think of the word "Contract" as a placeholder until you decide the most appropriate word for your organization.

In Figure 15-3, **Contract** is shown as being an example of the more general concept, **Party Relationship**, already described in Chapter 4. A **Contract** is, after all, an example of a relationship between two (or more—more about that later) **Parties**.

This, among other things, provides yet another example of a UML innovation described previously: being able to portray relationships as sub-types of other relationships. There are two examples of this here:

- The relationship "each **Party** may be a *customer in* one or more **Contracts**" is a sub-type of the relationship "each **Party** may be *related from* one or more **Party Relationships**".
- Similarly, the relationship "each **Party** may be a *vendor in* one or more **Contracts**" is a sub-type of the relationship "each **Party** may be *related to* one or more **Party Relationships**".

As will be shown when we get to some of the industry specific models, the combinations of "parties" to the contract can get much more complex than this, but this will do for our initial pattern.

Attributes of **Contract** typically consist of a **Contract Number** and an **Issue Date**. A computed field, such as the total value of the contract is also shown in the Figure. The formula is described on page 305, below.

Additional attributes could include both **Expected** and **Actual Completion** dates.

As with **Purchase Orders** and **Sales Orders**, each **Contract** may be *composed of* one or more **Line Items**, each referring to something being bought or sold. That is, each **Line Item** must be for <u>either</u> one **Activity Specification** or one **Asset Specification**. These are ...**Specifications**, not instances of **Activity** or **Asset**, since the **Contract** begins its life being about something requested, not what is actually delivered. Contract delivery is described fully on the pages below, beginning with page 307.

In this context, "contract" refers to the fact of the agreement. Any documents produced would be recorded as instances of **Information Resource**. That is not covered here.

Contract Costs

Note that the **Contract** is the basis for a company's finances, since that is the principle vehicle for money coming into and going out of the company. The financial implications of a **Contract** are represented by several attributes in the entity classes shown. Indeed, many of the attributes are calculated from others in the model. By convention, these are shown here preceded by the "forward slash" (/).[*]

To begin with, each instance of **Activity Specification** is expected to have a value for **Price Per Hour**. Purchasers of each **Activity Specification** will be charged this rate for the hours required to carry it out. Similarly, each **Asset Specification** should have a value for **Standard Price**. The **Line Item**, then is an order for a specific **Quantity** of the **Activity** or **Asset**. It may be that for this order, a different **Cost** was specified other than the quoted **Cost** of the **Asset** or **Activity**. In that case, the amount is specified here. If not, it can be computed as follows:

1. **Line Item /Unit Price =**

    Either

---

[*] This is the UML notation approach. This is another area where UML can express concepts that cannot be shown in an entity/relationship model. Your author used parentheses to indicate derived attributes, but these have no semantic meaning in the tool.

> INFER-THROUGH *(for,* **Asset Specification,** **Standard Cost**) *(...if for an asset)*
>
> or
>
> INFER-THROUGH *(for,* **Activity Specification,** **Price Per Hour**) *(...if for an activity)*

Given the "Unit Price", it is now possible to compute the /Cost of the **Line Item** thus:

2. **Line Item** /Cost =

   Line Item Quantity *times* **Line Item** /Unit Price.

The "Value" of each **Line Item** that is *part of* a **Contract** can then be used in the calculation of the "Total Value" of the **Contract**, thus:

3. **Contract Total Contract Value** =

   SUM-THROUGH *(composed of,* **Line Item,** /Cost) [*]

Each of these financial values can then become values in an accounting transaction, to be recorded in the books of the company. (See Chapter Five's discussion of Accounting.)

The particular terms of a **Contract** can be anything—payment timing, quality of products and/or services, et cetera. These can be incredibly complex—requiring a separate data modeling exercise in itself—but, for this simpler example, it is possible for a company simply to define a set of **Standard Contract Terms**, as shown in Figure 15-4. In this case, a **Standard Contract Term** is just a piece of text referring to a constraint on either the delivery or the payment specified under the **Contract**. **Term Value** is the fact that a particular **Standard Contract Term** has been applied to a **Contract**. This may include a **Default Value** and/or a **Description** of that application.

---

[*] "SUM-THROUGH is a function for obtaining the total of multiple instances of an attribute through a "one-to-many" relationship. The arguments for the function are <role name>, <entity class summed through>, <attribute being summed>. The idea is that the "Value" of the set of **Line Items** that are *part of* a **Contract** can be added together to get a value for the "Total Value" of the **Contract**.

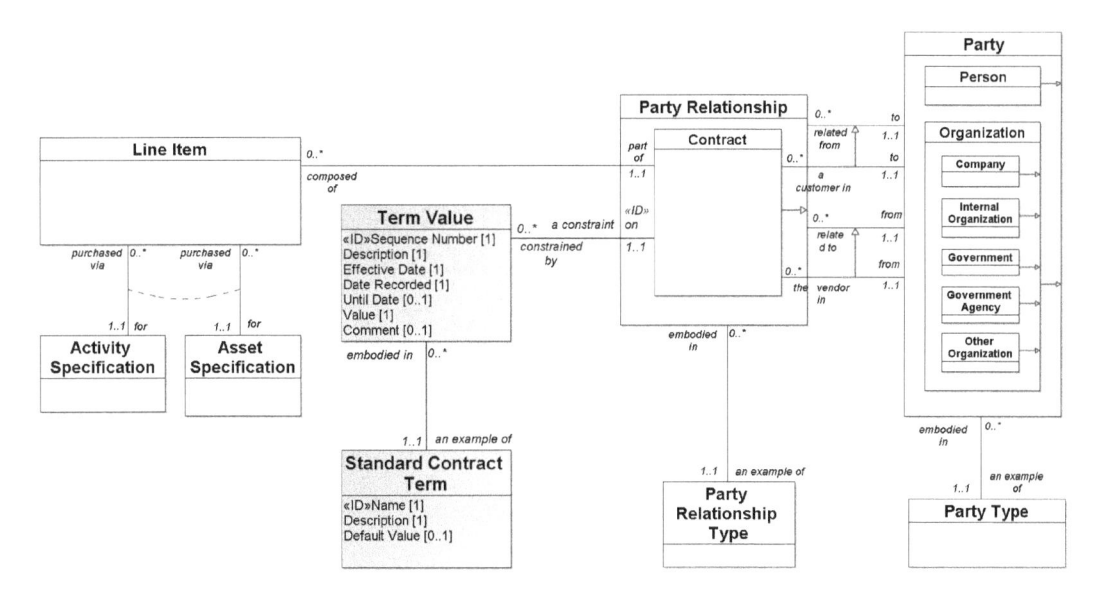

Figure 15-4: Contract Terms

Employment as a Contract

In addition to its use as a vehicle for buying and selling products and services, a **Contract** can be used to employ people. The **Employment** discussed in Chapter 13 is, in fact, a **Contract**. This is shown in Figure 15-5 Of course, calling a **Position Assignment** a sub-type of **Line Item** may seem to be pushing the point, but a **Line Item** is the fact that something is being ordered and supplied in the **Contract**. Normally, this is an **Activity Specification** or a physical **Asset**, but using it here to also be delivery of the services that constitute a **Position** is not that far off. While it could be argued that a **Position Assignment** is not the same thing as a **Line Item**, it is clear that they have parallel structures. It is definitely the case, however, that an **Employment** really is a **Contract**.

Delivering Against a Contract

Chapter 12 (specifically, page 258) described how a **Material Movement** portrays **Assets** being moved between **Parties** and **Facilities**. A modified version of that diagram is reproduced as Figure 15-6. Here, note that a **Contract Delivery** may be *to fulfill* a **Line Item** that is *part of* a **Contract**, if that **Contract** is *for* an **Asset Specification**.. If it is a **Receipt**, it is usually associated with a purchase order, and if it is a **Shipment**, it is usually associated with a sales order—but returns can be recorded against either, as well. A **Transfer** is usually not associated with a **Contract**, per se, but an authorization for the **Transfer** might play that role.

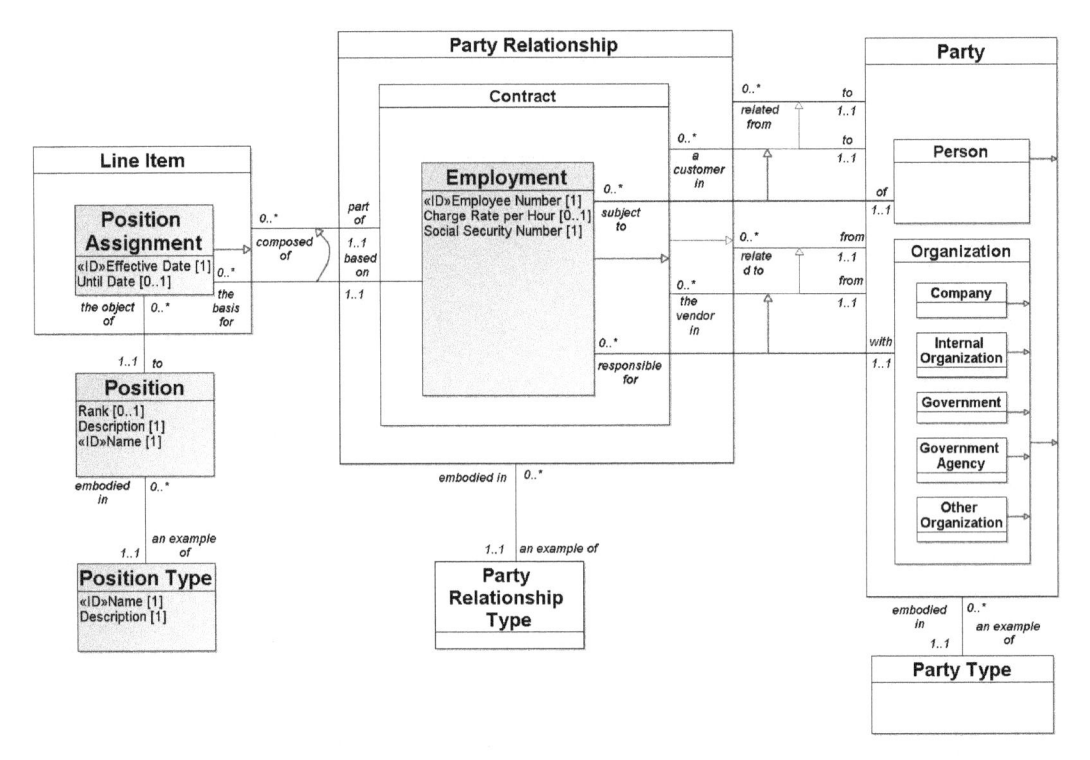

Figure 15-5: Employment as Contract Delivery

In Figure 15-6, each **Contract Delivery** must be *to fulfill* one and only one **Line Item** that is *part of* a **Contract**. Any **Material Movement** must be *of* one and only one **Asset**. The principal attribute of **Material Movement** is the Quantity being moved. The **Material Movement** may be either *to* a **Party** (if it is a **Shipment** to a customer) or *to* a **Facility** (such as a warehouse, if it is a **Receipt** from a vendor). Similarly, it may be either *from* a **Party** (if it is a **Receipt** from a vendor) or *from* a **Facility** (such as a warehouse, if it is a **Shipment** to a customer). That is, a purchase order **Line Item** *is fulfilled by* a **Material Movement** *from* a vendor **Party** and *to* a warehouse **Facility**. A sales order **Line Item** *is fulfilled by* a **Material Movement** *to* a customer **Party** and *from* a warehouse **Facility**.

Note the use of "may be" (0..1) in describing both the source and destination of the **Material Movement**. This is because another sub-type of **Material Movement** is **Adjustment**. An **Adjustment** occurs when inventory is checked and material has either been moved *to* the **Facility** *from*, say, the mysterious ether, or has disappeared *from* the **Facility** *to* the same mysterious ether.

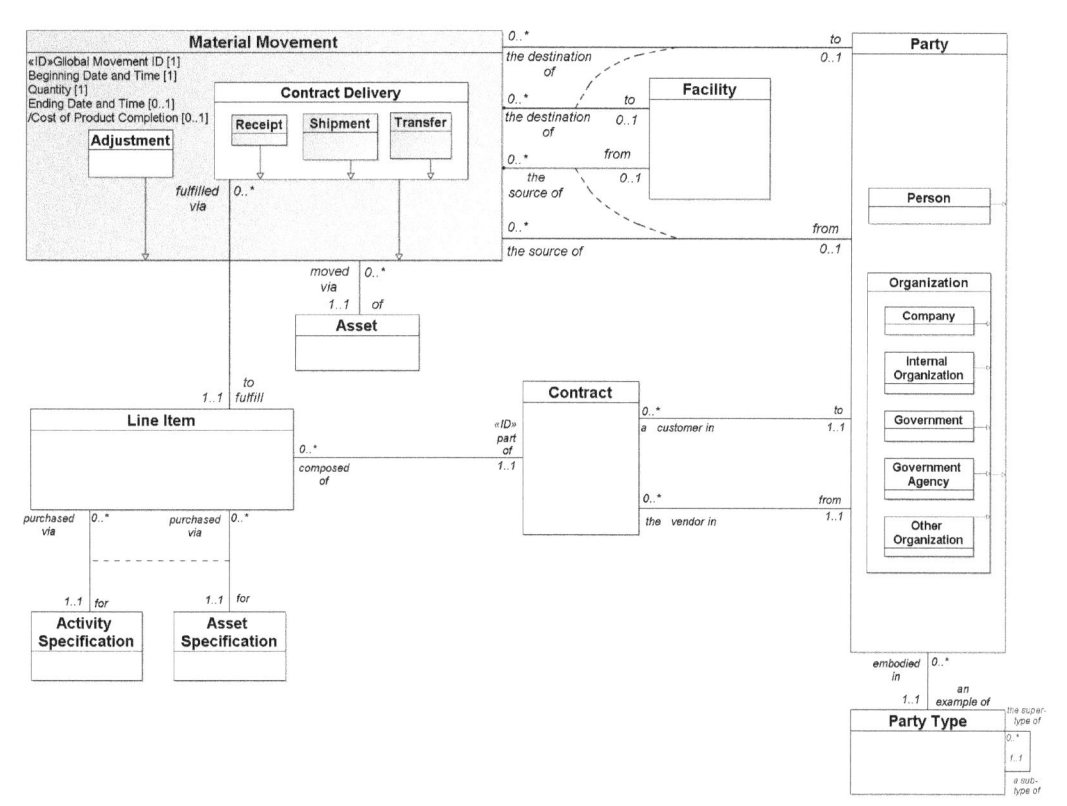

Figure 15-6: Supplying Assets

If the **Contract** contained **Line Items** *for* **Activity Specifications** (services), these **Line Items** would be *fulfilled via* actual **Activities**, as shown in Figure 15-7.

Each **Line Item** that is *for* a **Service** may be *fulfilled via* either one or more **Activities** or by one or more **Projects**, or both. In fact, a **Project** is defined to be a very large collection of **Activities**, so it is more likely that a single **Project** is *to fulfill* a single **Line Item**. In that case, it might be the trigger for multiple contracts. That is a more complex scenario than is being addressed in this pattern, however.

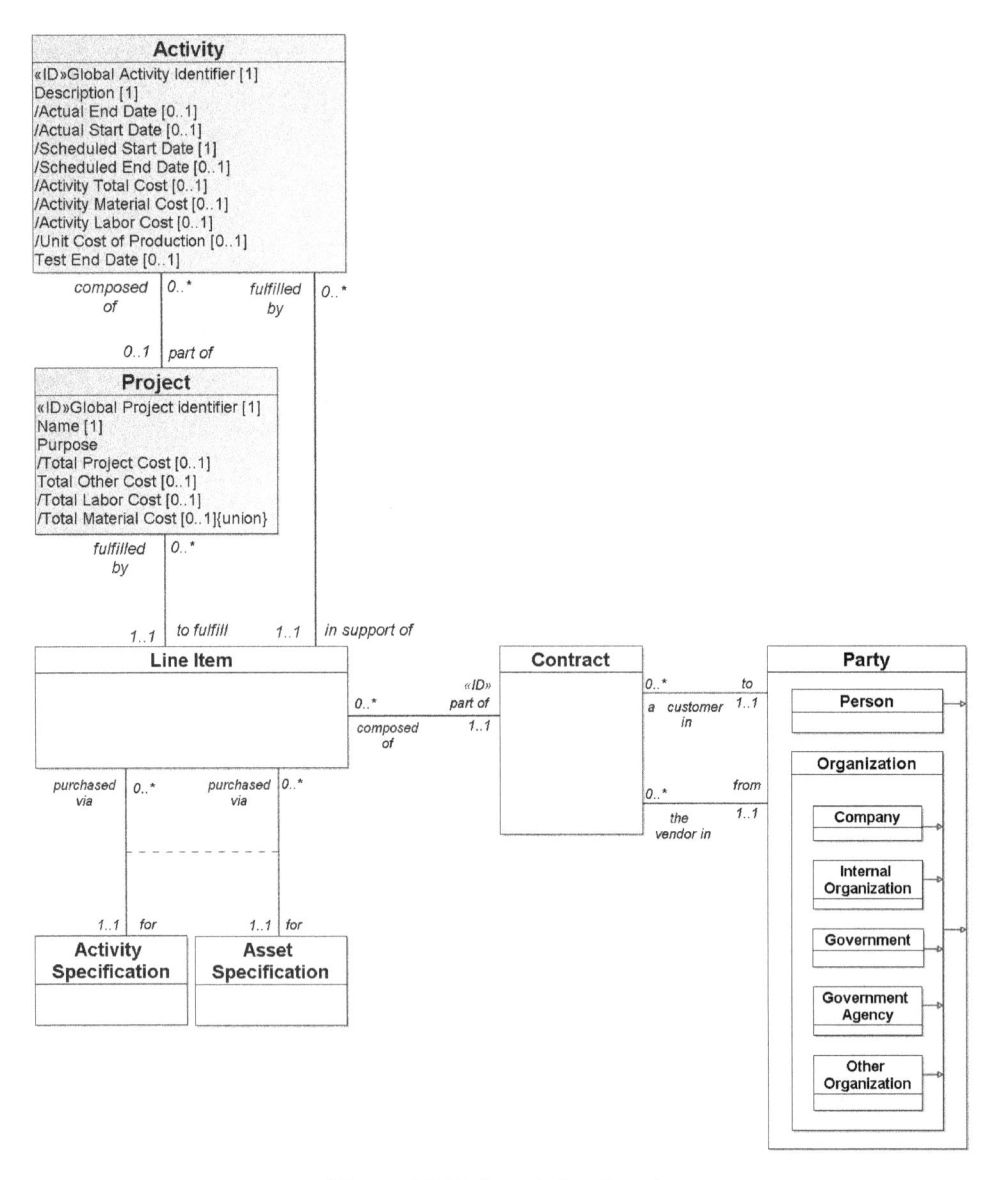

Figure 15-7: Supplying Services

Contract Roles

Contracts can have many more roles than just *customer in* and *vendor in*. A **Party** could be responsible for delivery, payment, support, or one of many other possible **Contract Roles**. Indeed, in addition to being *for* the **Contract** directly, it could be *for* an **Asset Movement** *to fulfill* a **Line Item** that is *part of* the **Contract**. It could be *for* an **Activity** that is *to fulfill* a **Line Item** on the **Contract**. Or it could be specific to the **Line Item** itself. This is shown in Figure 15-8.

Contracts 311

In many cases the roles *customer in* and *vendor in* are required, so they are shown as explicit relationships and are not included as instances of **Contract Role**. In some enterprises, however, even these are not that well defined. (See Chapter 20 on banking. In these cases we had to simply define sub-types for "Customerness" and "Vendorness". This approximates the concepts, but realizes that all roles—even these—are optional.

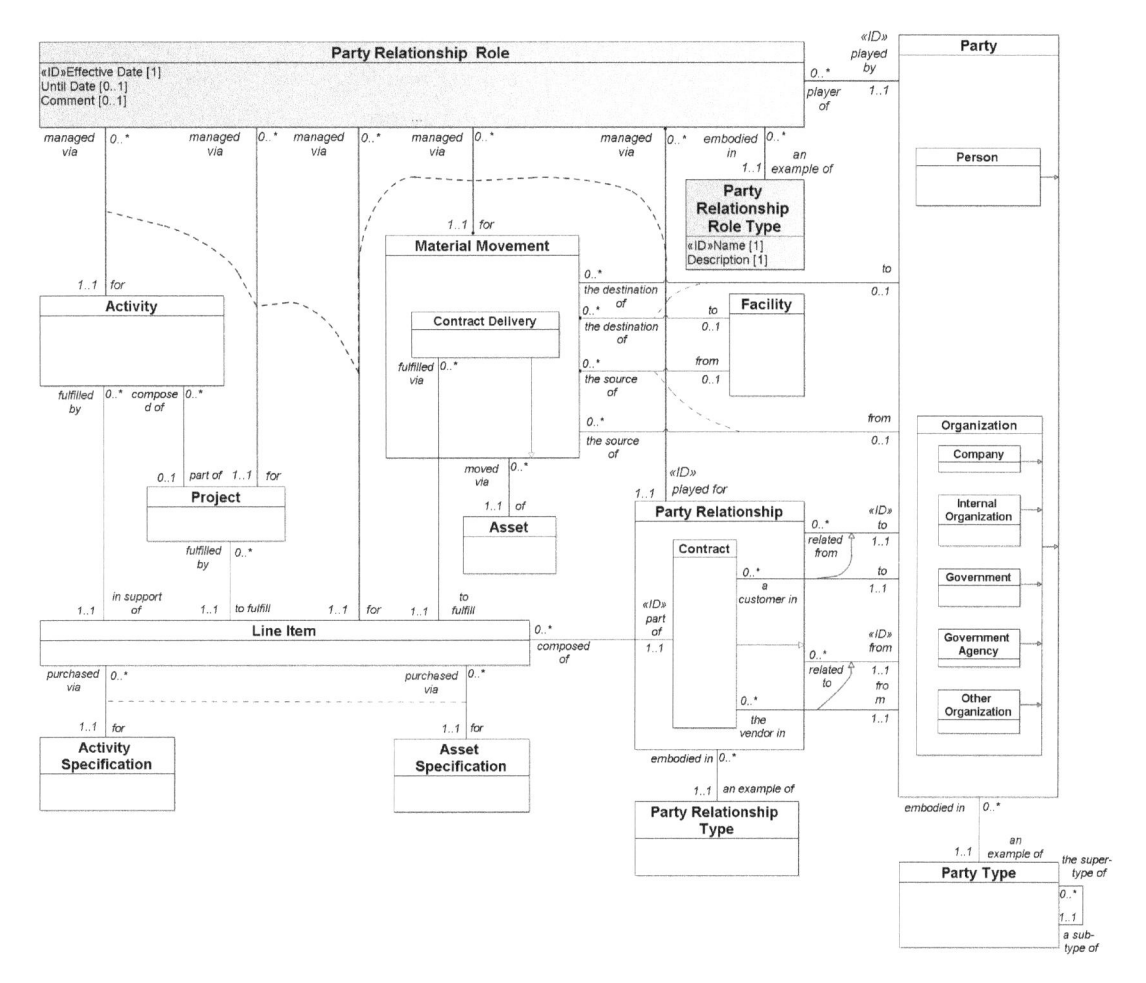

Figure 15-8: Contract Roles

Summary

While it is convenient for the respective departments to be concerned solely with purchase orders or sales orders, the fact of the matter is that, from the point of view of the organization, these are both examples of **Contracts**. A contract is a "binding agreement between two or more persons or parties; *especially* one legally enforceable.[54] In sales orders, we are being obligated to provide a service or product to someone else. In purchase orders, we are obligating someone else to provide a product or service to us. The only difference is the role we play.

Contracts (also called "agreements", "orders", and more specific names as well) itemize what is to be delivered and the terms (usually payment terms) to be followed. This is via **Line Items** that, for a **Contract** each point to one of the products or services being purchased, as well as via **Contract Term Values** describing constraints on the **Contract**.

At the time of the order being placed, the products and services are listed as specifications (either **Asset Specifications** or **Activity Specifications**). Delivery against the contract consists of supplying actual (instances of) **Assets** or performances of actual **Activities**.

Note that the banking industry has a very distinctive approach to contracts, which is why that industry is featured in Part Five on specific industry models. See Chapter 20.

Payment of or receipt of the amount of money due from the transaction results in a particular set of **Accounting Transaction Types**. These were used as examples in Chapter 11 on Accounting.

---

[54] Merriam-Webster. 2010. "contract". *The Merriam-Webster Online Dictionary* Retrieved 11/19/2010 at *http://www.merriam-webster.com/dictionary/contract*.

CHAPTER 16

Manufacturing

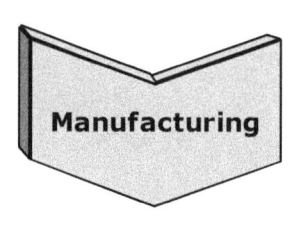

Manufacturing was covered in more detail in *Data Model Patterns: Conventions of Thought*. That book included process manufacturing and materials planning, which will not be described here. But the basic principles of the manufacturing model are significant enough and applicable widely enough to be worth restating here.

The Manufacturing Process

This first section is concerned with laying out the organization of a manufacturing plant and the organization of work around **Work Orders**.

Routing Steps

Planning for the manufacture of a particular product (described by an **Asset Specification**) begins by defining the set of steps required. That is, a **Routing Step** is the fact that a particular **Work Center** is *the site of* a set of one or more **Production Procedures** *for the production of* a particular **Asset Specification**. This is shown in Figure 16-1.

Routing Step describes an overall effort at a **Work Center**, while **Production Procedure** is the definition of a more detailed task. This leads to the following business rule:

314 Enterprise Model Patterns

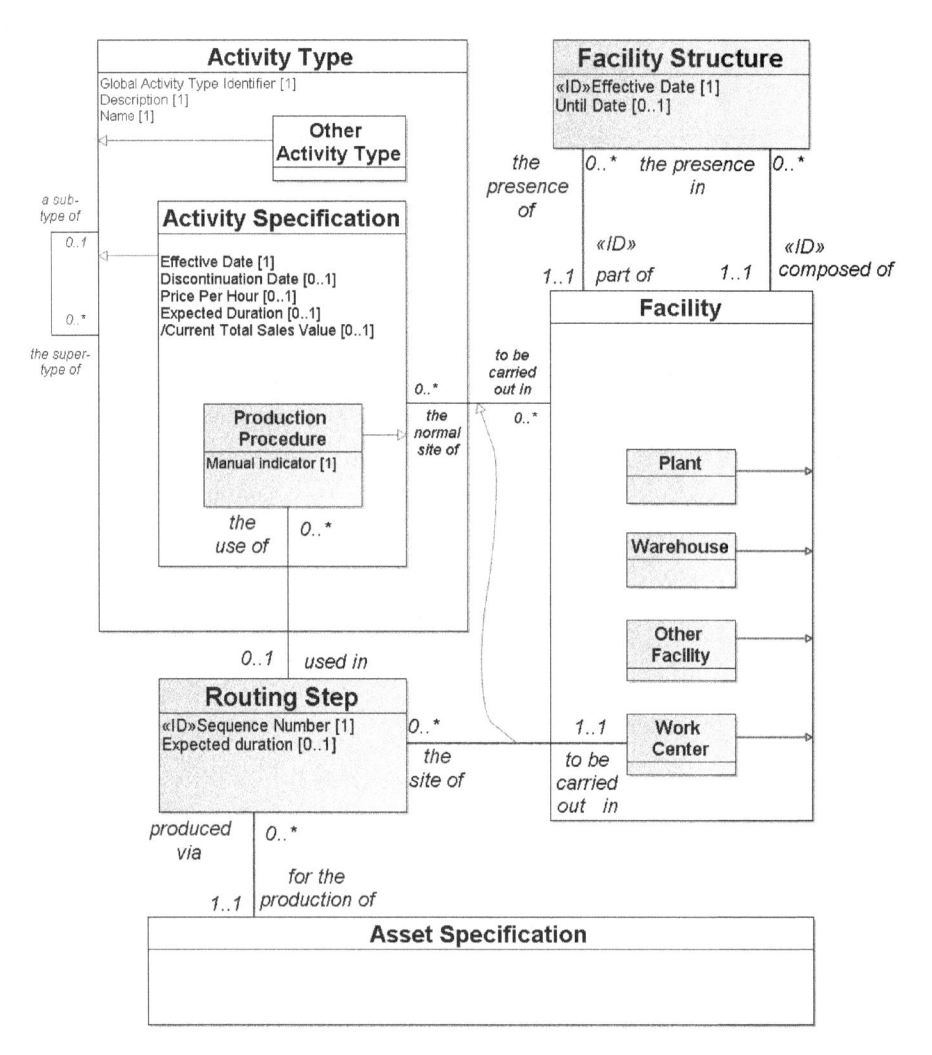

Figure 16-1: Routing Steps

Note that, in addition to **Expected Duration** that is an attribute of **Activity Type**, the **Expected Duration** is also shown as an attribute of **Routing Step**. (See the discussion of "Dependence" below for a description of the overlap of **Activity Type** and **Routing Step**.)

Here **Work Center** is shown as a kind of **Facility**. It is specifically, a **Facility** where manufacturing tasks take place. **Facility** was described in more abstract terms as "a place with a purpose" in Chapter 12. A **Work Center** may be *part of* a larger **Facility**, which can be either another **Work Center** or a **Plant**. A **Plant** is a very large, stand alone, facility, such as a factory or a refinery, which is where families of products are made.

Business Rule

- Each **Production Procedure** *used in* a **Routing Step** must be *to be carried out in* the same **Facility** as the **Routing Step** is *to be carried out in*.

Note that the Figure shows the **Warehouse** as is a sub-type of **Facility**. A **Warehouse** is a **Facility** usually consisting of a large **Building** for the purpose of storing **Assets**.

Because in some companies a **Work Center** can be moved from one **Plant** or larger **Work Center** to another over time, and because it is difficult to predict exactly what sort of configurations of **Facilities** might occur, Figure 16-1 expands on the model of addresses in Chapter 12 to define a **Facility Structure** as the fact that one **Facility** is part of another. That is, each **Facility Structure** must be *the presence of* one **Facility** *in* another **Facility**. Thus, each **Facility** may be *composed of* one or more other **Facilities**, and each **Facility** (over time, at least) may be *part of* one or more other **Facilities**.

An alternative would be to replace **Facility Structure** with a simple "pig's ear" showing a many-to-one recursive relationship: each **Facility** may be composed of one or more **Facilities;** in this case, each **Facility** would be constrained to be *part of* no more than one and only one **Facility**.

The "correct" approach depends on the particular circumstances being described by the model. Is it necessary to be able to say that a **Facility** can be *part of* more than one other **Facility**?

Work Orders

A **Work Order** is an official authorization to perform a specified set of work. If it is for manufacturing, it is a **Production Work Order**; while for plant maintenance, it is a **Maintenance Work Order**.

Production Work Orders

The actual production of a product or material to specification (that is, *to produce* something according to an **Asset Specification**) is *authorized by* a **Production Work Order**. That is, each **Production Work Order** may be *to authorize* one or more

Production Steps, each of which must be *the implementation of* a **Production Procedure** that is *used in* a **Routing Step**. (This is shown in Figure 16-2.)

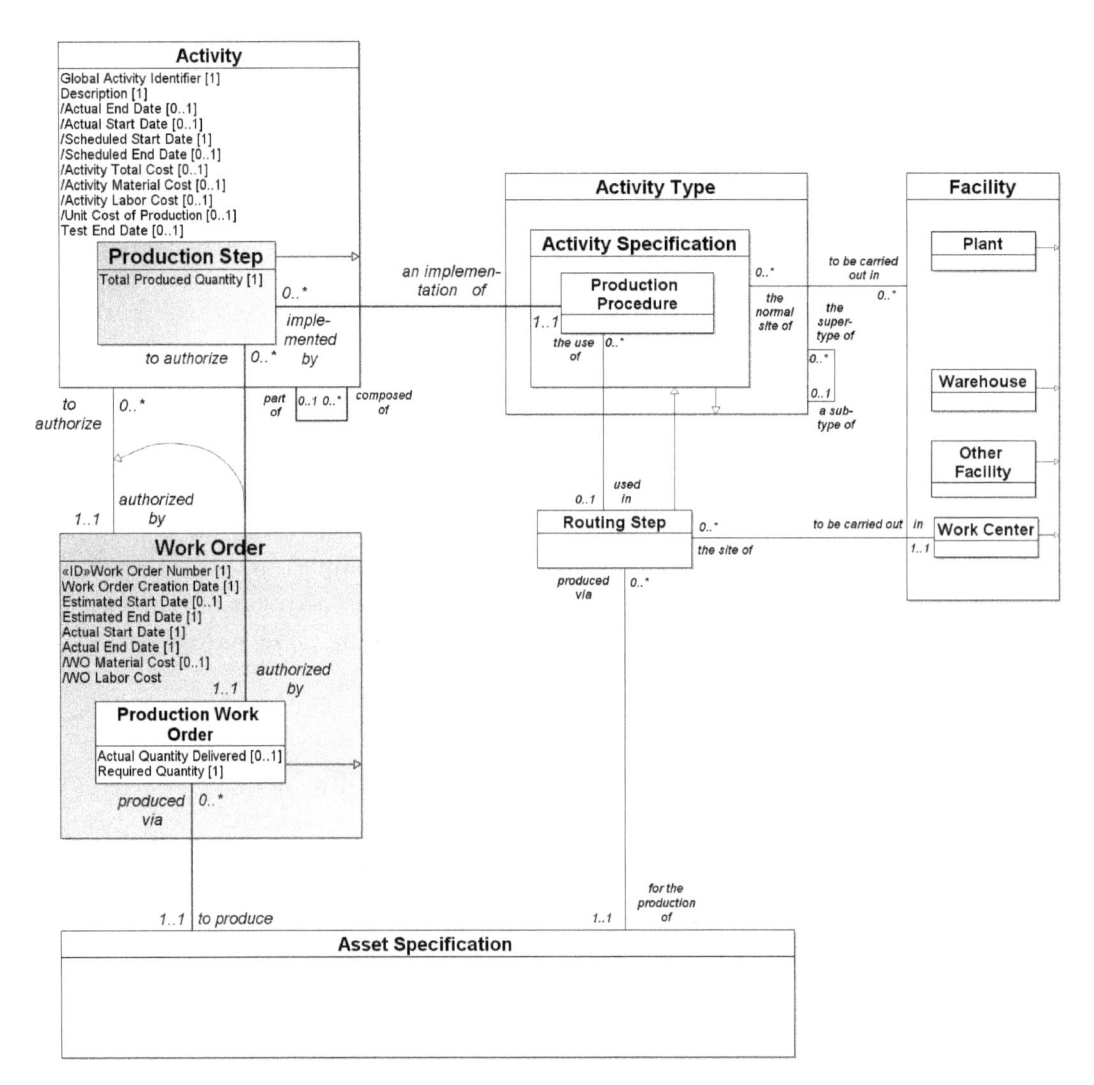

Figure 16-2: Production Work Orders

In other words, the set of **Production Steps** that are required *to make* an **Asset Specification** are *authorized by* a **Production Work Order**.

Business Rule

- Each **Production Step** that is *authorized by* a **Production Work Order** must be *the implementation of* a **Production Procedure** that is *used in* a **Routing Step** *for the production of* the **Asset Specification** that the **Production Work Order** is *to produce*. *(Translation:* **Routing Steps** and their component **Production Procedures** control the **Production Steps** undertaken to produce a particular **Asset Specification**.)

Where a **Production Procedure** (inheriting attributes from **Activity Specification**) describes its **Estimated Duration**, the actual **Production Step** (**Activity**) that is *an implementation of* that **Production Procedure**—is placed in time with **Scheduled Start Date, Scheduled End Date, Actual Start Date,** and **Actual End Date.** The set of actual dates for all the **Production Steps** within a **Work Order** must be within the actual dates of the **Work Order**. That is, the following business rules apply:

Business Rules

- The Actual Start Date of the first **Production Step** must be no earlier than the Actual Start Date of the **Production Work Order** that was to authorize the **Production Step**.

- The Actual End Date of the last **Production Step** must be no later than the Actual End Date of the **Production Work Order** that was *to authorize* the **Production Step**. *(Translation:* **Production Steps** have to happen within the timeframe specified by their authorization **Work Order**.)

Dependence

As described in Chapter 7, **Activities**, either at the specification level or at the instance level, often depend on each other. For example, it may be that one activity cannot begin before another ends. Figure 16-3 shows this as **Activity Dependence** and **Activity Specification Dependence**—kinds of **Activity Structure** and **Activity Specification Structure**, respectively.

318 Enterprise Model Patterns

Each instance of either kind of **Activity Dependence** must be *an example of* one **Activity Dependence Type**. **Activity Dependence Type** describes the nature of the **Activity Dependence**. It may be either:

- "End-to-start" (ES) – the *on* **Activity** (or **Activity Specification**) must complete before the *of* **Activity** (or **Activity Specification**) can begin.

- "Start-to-start" (SS) – the two **Activities** (or **Activity Specifications**) must begin at the same time.

- "End to end" (EE) – the two Activities (or Activity Specifications) must end at the same time.

- "Offset" (Of) – one **Activity** (or **Activity Specification)** begins after a specified **Overlap** (with its **Overlap Unit**) such as "2.5" and "hours".

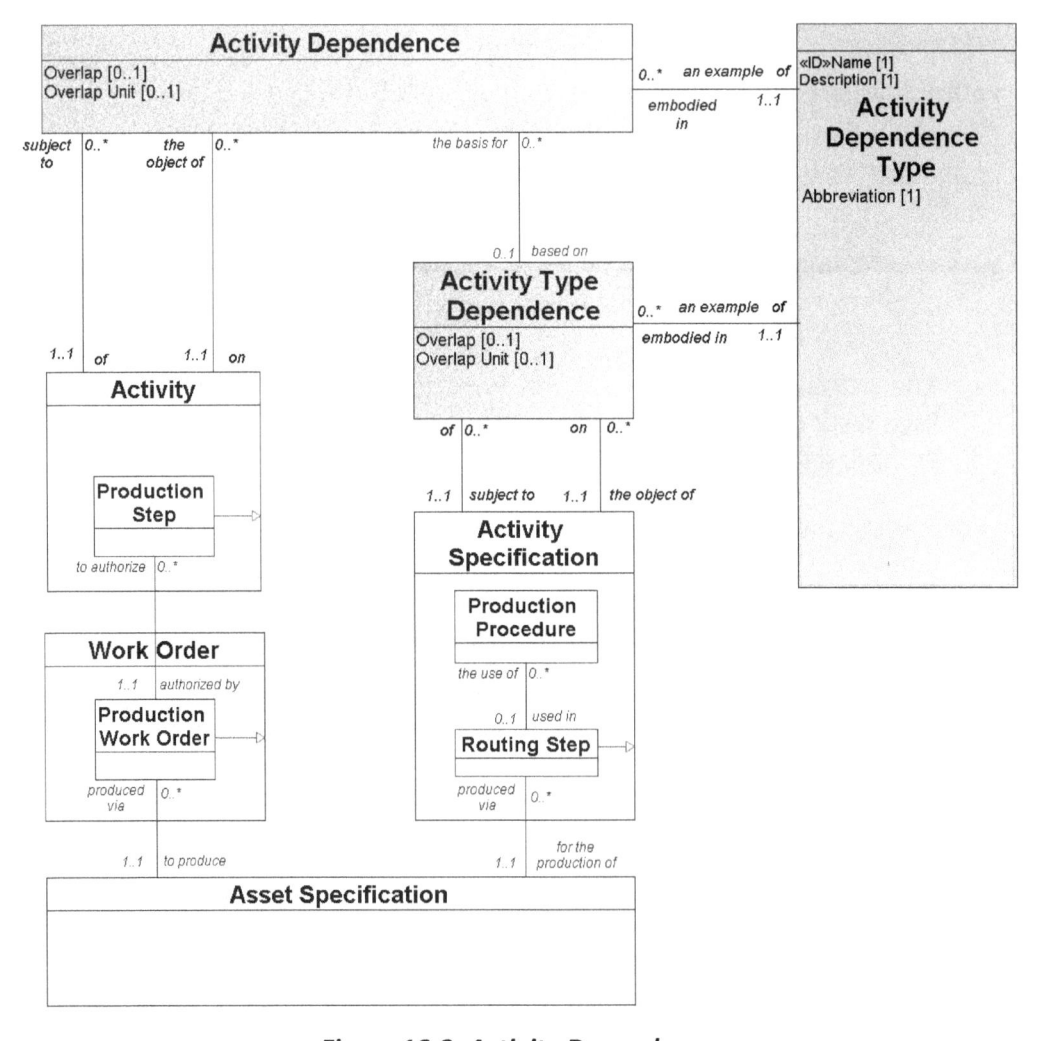

Figure 16-3: Activity Dependence

Activity Specification Dependence covers the official dependencies that are defined for the **Production Procedures** to be executed. The actual Activity Dependence that is defined for actual **Production Steps** is defined (again for all kinds of **Activities**) as **Activity Dependence**. This **Activity Dependence** should be *based on* the **Activity Specification Dependence** that controls the **Production Procedures** that the associated **Production Steps** are *an example of*.

The **Routing Steps** of the **Activity Dependence Type** with the **Name** `"End-to-start"` are all dependent on each other in sequence. That is `"Create glass sheets"` must complete before `"Cut glass sheets can begin"`.

Business Rules, Part I

- If an **Activity** is *subject to* an **Activity Dependence** *on* another **Activity**, and the Name of the **Activity Dependence Type** that it is *an example of* is "End-to-start", then neither the first **Activity's** Scheduled Start Date nor its Actual Start Date may be <u>before</u> the Scheduled End Date nor the Actual End Date (respectively) of the second **Activity**. *(Translation:* Any **Activity** that has an "end-to-start" dependency on another **Activity** cannot be scheduled to begin until the other **Activity** has finished.)

- If an **Activity** is *subject to* an **Activity Dependence** *on* another **Activity**, and the Name of the **Activity Dependence Type** that it is *an example of* is "Start-to-start", then both the Scheduled Start Date of the first **Activity** must be the same as the Scheduled Start Date of the second **Activity** and the Actual Start Date of the first **Activity** must be the same as the Actual Start Date of the second **Activity**. *(Translation:* Any **Activity** that has a "start-to-start" dependency on another **Activity** must be scheduled to begin when the other **Activity** begins.)

Business Rules, Part I-a

- If an **Activity** is *subject to* an **Activity Dependence** *on* another **Activity**, and the Name of the **Activity Dependence Type** that it is *an example of* "End-to-end", then both the Scheduled End Date of the first **Activity** must be the same as the Scheduled End Date of the second **Activity** and the Actual End Date of the first **Activity** must be the same as the Actual End Date of the second **Activity**. *(Translation:* Any **Activity** that has an "end-to-end" dependency on another **Activity** must have a scheduled end date that is the same as the scheduled end date of the other **Activity**.)

- If an **Activity** is *subject to* an **Activity Dependence** *on* another **Activity**, and the Name of the **Activity Dependence Type** that it is *an example of* is "Overlap", then the first **Activity's** Scheduled Start Date must be the Overlap Amount (in the specified "unit") after the Scheduled Start Date nor the Actual Start Date (respectively) of the second **Activity**. *(Translation:* Any **Activity** that has an "overlap" dependency on another **Activity** must schedule its end date to begin a designated period of time (the Overlap Amount) after the other **Activity** is scheduled to begin.)

Business Rules, Part II

- If an **Activity Specification** is *subject to* an **Activity Specification Dependence** *on* another **Activity Specification**, and the Name of the **Activity Dependence Type** that it is *an example of* "End-to-start", then neither the Scheduled Start Date nor the Actual Start Date of any **Activity** that is *the implementation of* this **Activity Specification** may be <u>before</u> the Scheduled End Date nor the Actual End Date (respectively) of any **Activity** that is *an implementation of* the second **Activity Specification**.

- If an **Activity Specification** is *subject to* an **Activity Specification Dependence** *on* another **Activity Specification**, and the Name of the **Activity Dependence Type** that it is *an example of* is "Start-to-start", then both the Scheduled Start Date of any **Activity** that is *the implementation of* the first **Activity Specification** must be the same as the Scheduled Start Date of any **Activity** that is *the implementation of* the second **Activity Specification**.

Business Rules, Part II-a

- If an **Activity Specification** is *subject to* an **Activity Specification Dependence** *on* another **Activity Specification**, and the Name of the **Activity Dependence Type** that it is *an example of* its "End-to-end", then both the Scheduled End Date of any **Activity** that is *the implementation of* the first **Activity Specification** must be the same as the Scheduled End Date of any **Activity** that is *the implementation of* the second **Activity Specification**.

- If an **Activity Specification** is *subject to* an **Activity Specification Dependence** *on* another **Activity Specification**, and the Name of the **Activity Dependence Type** that it is *an example of* its "End-to-end", then both the Scheduled End Date of any **Activity** that is *the implementation of* the first **Activity Specification** must be the same as the Scheduled End Date of any **Activity** that is *the implementation of* the second **Activity Specification**. (***Translation***: The dependence described for two **Activity Specifications** must translate into corresponding dependencies for **Activities** that are *the implementation of* corresponding **Activity Specifications**.)

Business Rule, Part III

- If an **Activity Specification** is *subject to* an **Activity Dependence** *on* another **Activity**, and the Name of the **Activity Dependence Type** that it is *an example of* is "Overlap", then the first **Activity Specification's** Scheduled Start Date nor the Actual Start Date must be the Overlap Amount (in the specified "unit") after the Scheduled Start Date nor the Actual Start Date (respectively) of the second **Activity**. (***Translation***: The **Activity Dependence Type** constrains the estimated and actual start date and end date of each dependent Activity Specifications.)

For example, to manufacture a windshield, **Routing Steps** include:

```
1. Create glass sheets.

2. Cut glass sheets.

3. Combine sheets with inner layer and form into
windshields.
```

322 Enterprise Model Patterns

```
4. Add hardware.
```

Within each of these steps are a series of **Production Procedures**, many of which may overlap. For example, "Create glass sheets" involves Production Procedures to "Heat the sand until it melts", "Add minerals", "Pour the glass onto a smooth surface", and so forth. The "Add minerals" could begin 15 minutes after "Heat the sand until it melts".♣

Figure 16-4 shows that each flavor of **Activity ... Dependence** is a sub-type of the more generic **Activity ... Structure** entity classes, described in Chapter 7, above. Hence the relationships with each of the **Activity ... Dependences** are sub-types to the relationships with corresponding **Activity ... Structures**.

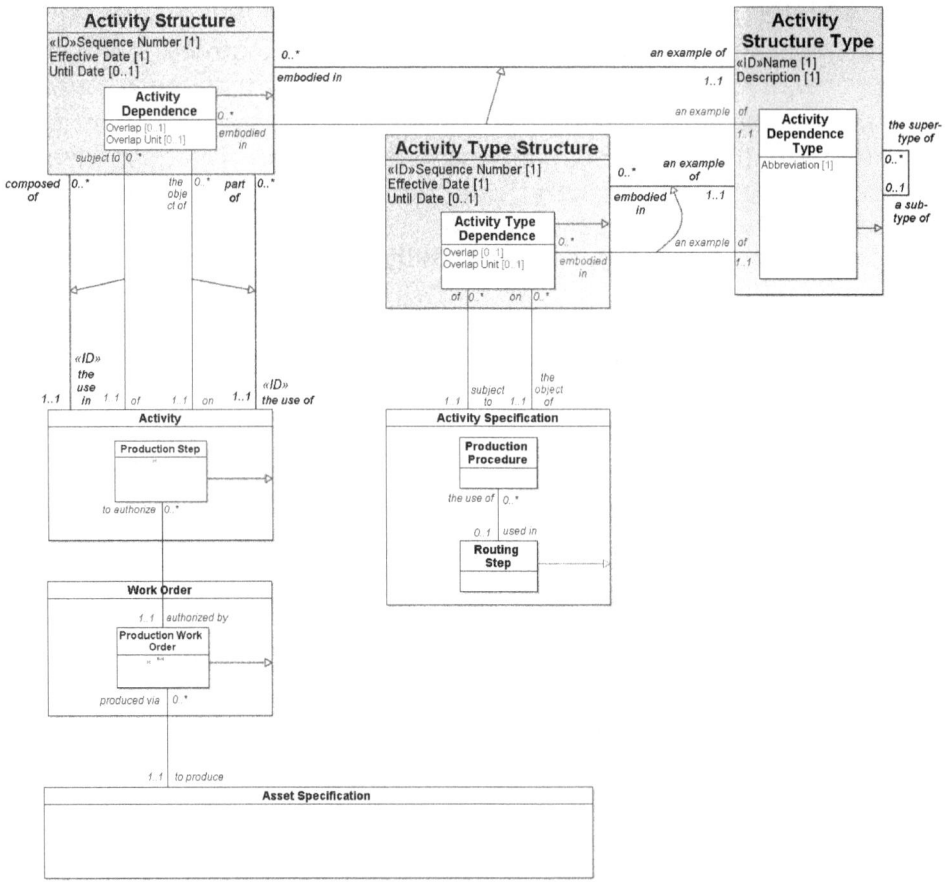

Figure 16-4: Activity Dependence as Activity Structure

♣ Please understand that this is a purely fictional example. Any similarity between this example and any real windshield factory is purely coincidental.

Manufacturing

Maintenance Work Orders

The structure of **Maintenance Work Orders** is very similar to that of **Production Work Orders**. Indeed, the super-type, **Work Order** covers a lot of the same conceptual ground for both, as shown in Figure 16-5. Similarly, **Maintenance Task**, a sub-type of **Activity**, encompasses both **Production Step**, already discussed, and **Maintenance Task**.

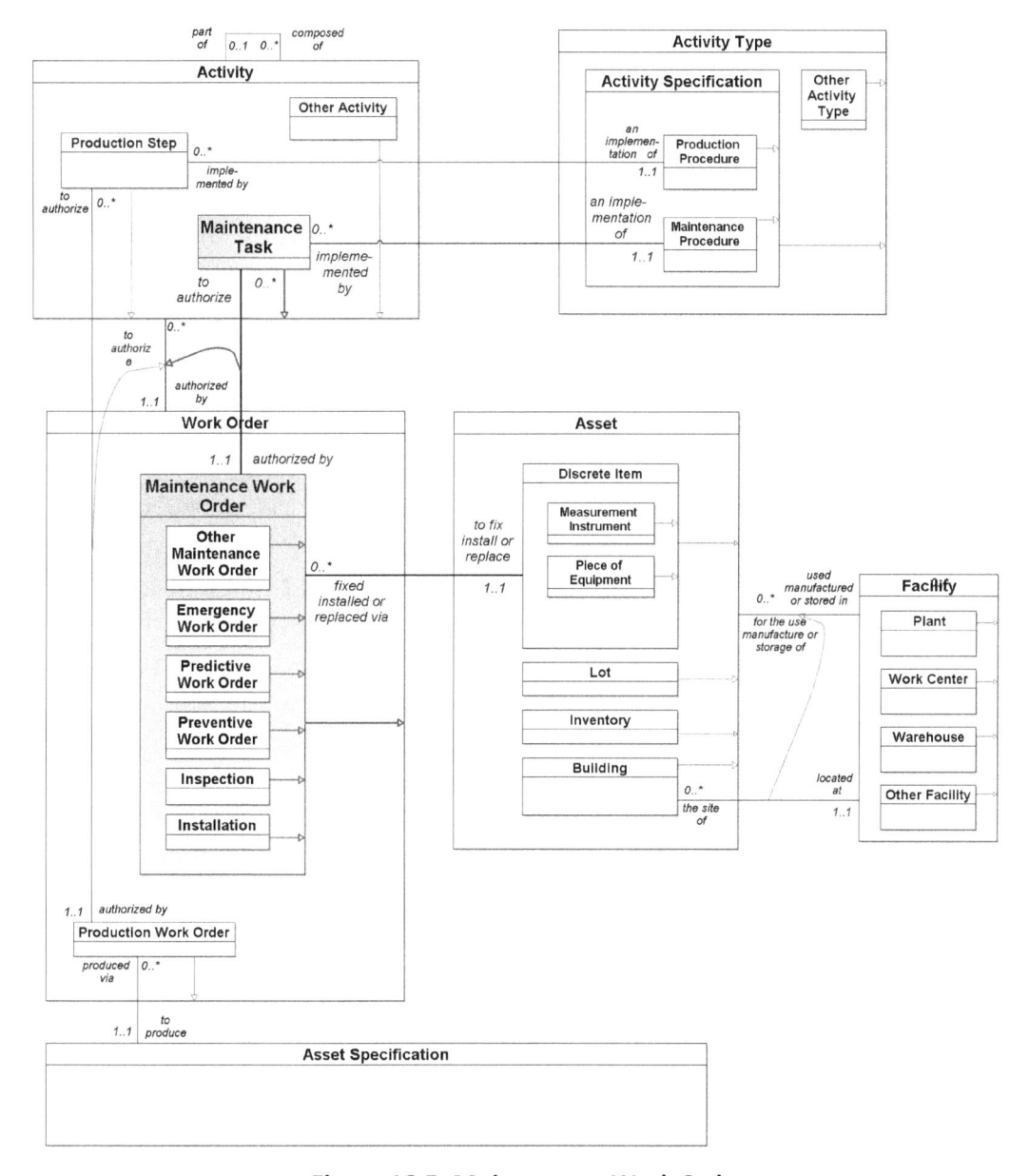

Figure 16-5: Maintenance Work Orders

That is, just as each **Production Work Order** may be *to authorize* one or more **Production Steps**—then each **Maintenance Work Order** may be *to authorize* one or more **Maintenance Tasks**.

Note that where each **Production Work Order** must be *to produce* one and only one **Asset Specification**, each **Maintenance Work Order** must be *to fix, install, or replace* one (instance of a) **Discrete Item**, such as a piece of **Production Equipment** or an **Instrument**, among others.

Where **Production Steps** are usually *the implementation of* **Routing Steps** and **Production Procedures**, for the most part, each **Maintenance Task** is *the implementation of* a **Maintenance Procedure**.

Where a **Discrete Item** is *fixed, installed, or replaced via* a **Maintenance Work Order**, it may be composed of (via an **Asset Structure**) other **Discrete Items**. These may be separately *fixed, installed, or replaced via* **Maintenance Tasks**. Thus, each **Maintenance Task** must be *to fix, install, or replace* one component **Discrete Item**.

There are basically five kinds of **Maintenance Work Orders**, along with others not described here:

- **Emergency Work Order** – Something broke and it has to be fixed as quickly as possible.

- **Preventive Work Order** – Maintenance on a **Piece of Equipment** or a **Building** to keep parts in good order so that they won't fail.

- **Predictive Work Order** – Similar to a **Preventive Work Order**, but on parts that have shown symptoms that typically precede a particular kind of failure.

- **Inspection** - This means examination of a **Discrete Item** to see if there are any signs of wear, calling, perhaps, for a **Predictive** or **Preventive Work Order**.

- **Installation** – The placement of a **Discrete Item** into its proper location in a **Facility**.

- **Other Maintenance Work Order** – A **Maintenance Work Order** that is not an **Emergency Work Order**, a **Preventive Work Order**, a **Predictive Work Order**, an **Inspection**, or an **Installation**.

Material Usage

Up to this point, we have seen the nature and environment of manufacturing. Now we come to the resources consumed whenever something is manufactured—materials and labor. This section describes the consumption of materials; the following section will describe the consumption of labor. In each case, we see both the planned and actual consumption of the resource.

Asset Specification Structure

Chapter 6 presented the concepts of **Asset** and **Asset Specification Structure**. This is the fact that a particular **Asset** (either an instance or a **Specification**) is a component in another **Asset** (instance or **Specification**). Figure 16-6 shows the **Asset Specification** part of this. Here, an **Asset Specification Structure** describes what is supposed to be the (specified) composition of an **Asset Specification**. That is, a particular **Asset Specification Structure** is *the use of* one **Asset Specification** *in* another **Asset Specification**.

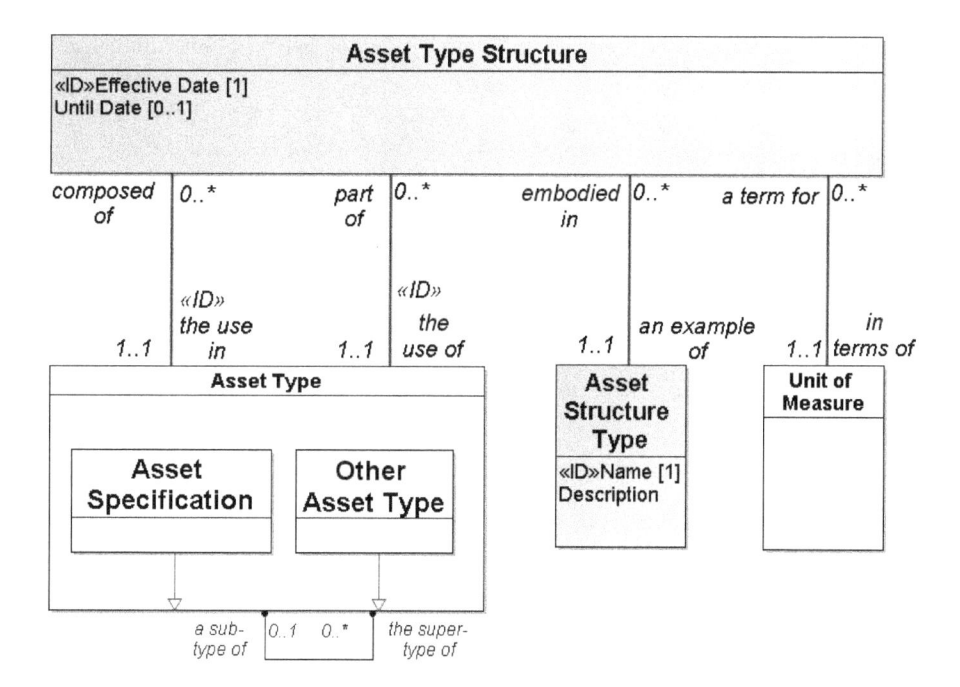

Figure 16-6: Asset Specification Structure

326 Enterprise Model Patterns

For example, as specified in a catalogue, a `"Lenovo T41 Laptop Personal Computer"` might be composed of a `"Model K-41 keyboard"`[*], a `"Model C-41 Chassis"`, a `"Model D-41 Display screen"`, and so forth. It could have as a component *either* a `"Model U-134-50 50 gigabyte disk drive"`, or a `"U-134-80 80 gigabyte disk drive"`. Each of these components would be described by one **Asset Specification Structure**, each of which would be *the use of* one component **Asset Specification** and *the use in* one parent **Asset Specification**. Moreover, each **Asset Specification Structure** would be *an example of* a particular **Asset Structure Type**. Each of the first components described above could be assumed to be *examples* of **Asset Specification Structure Types** with the **Name** of `"Required"`. The disk drives would be described by **Asset Specification Structures** that are *examples of* **Asset Specification Structure Types** with the **Name** of `"Primary Option"`. Anti-glare treatment of the screen could be described by an **Asset Specification Structure** that is *an example of* an **Asset Specification Structure Type** with the **Name** of `"Secondary Option"`.

Material Usage Costs

Determining material costs involves following the movement of material into the manufacturing process.

Material Movement

Figure 16-7 shows that in the manufacturing process, there are two principal kinds of **Material Movement** concerned with manufacturing:

- **Consumption** – the use *of* an **Asset**, such as **Inventory**, a **Lot**, or a **Discrete Item**, or *of* an **Asset Specification**, such as `"water"`, or `"natural gas"`. This is *charged to* an **Activity**.

- **Product Completion** – the production of an **Asset**, *by* either a particular **Production Step** or *by* the set of steps *authorized by a* **Production Work Order**.

Both of these sub-types inherit the attribute **Quantity** from their super-type **Material Movement**. In the case of **Consumption**, this is the quantity of material (either physical **Asset** or **Asset Specification**) used in the manufacturing process.

---

[*] Model numbers in this example are purely imaginary.

In the case of **Product Completion**, this is the quantity of the **Asset** completed by the **Activity** or **Work Order**.

Note the number of derived attributes in the various entity classes. These describe an example of how to calculate the cost of materials in the manufacturing process. The actual method in your plant may vary, but the basic components should be as shown here.

First of all, each **Asset Specification** is given a **Standard Price**, to be used for calculating the costs. This can be a corporate decision, average of purchases, or from some other source. For purposes of this exercise, each **Asset** also has the attribute **Unit Cost**, which could be inherited from the appropriate **Asset Specification** if it is a raw material or component. In that case, the formula is:

1. **Asset /Unit Cost =**

    INFER-THROUGH (*specified by*, **Asset Specification**, **Standard Price**)

If it is a manufactured product, it must be derived by extending the process being described here. Assume, for the sake of argument, that **Asset /Unit Cost** exists for a raw material or component.

The entity class **Consumption** inherits the **Quantity** consumed from **Material Movement**. It also can make use of **Asset /Unit Cost** via the formula:

2. **Consumption /Unit Cost =**

    INFER-THROUGH (of, **Asset**, **/Unit Cost**)

    (or)

    INFER-THROUGH (of, **Asset Specification**, **Standard Price**)

The attribute **/Consumption Cost** can then be calculated thus:

3. **Consumption /Consumption Cost =**

    Material Movement Quantity times **Consumption /Unit Cost**

The total material cost for each **Activity** is represented by the attribute **/Activity Material Cost** in **Activity**. This is calculated via the formula:

4. **Activity /Activity Material Cost =**

328 Enterprise Model Patterns

SUM-THROUGH (*charged with*, **Consumption**, Consumption Cost)

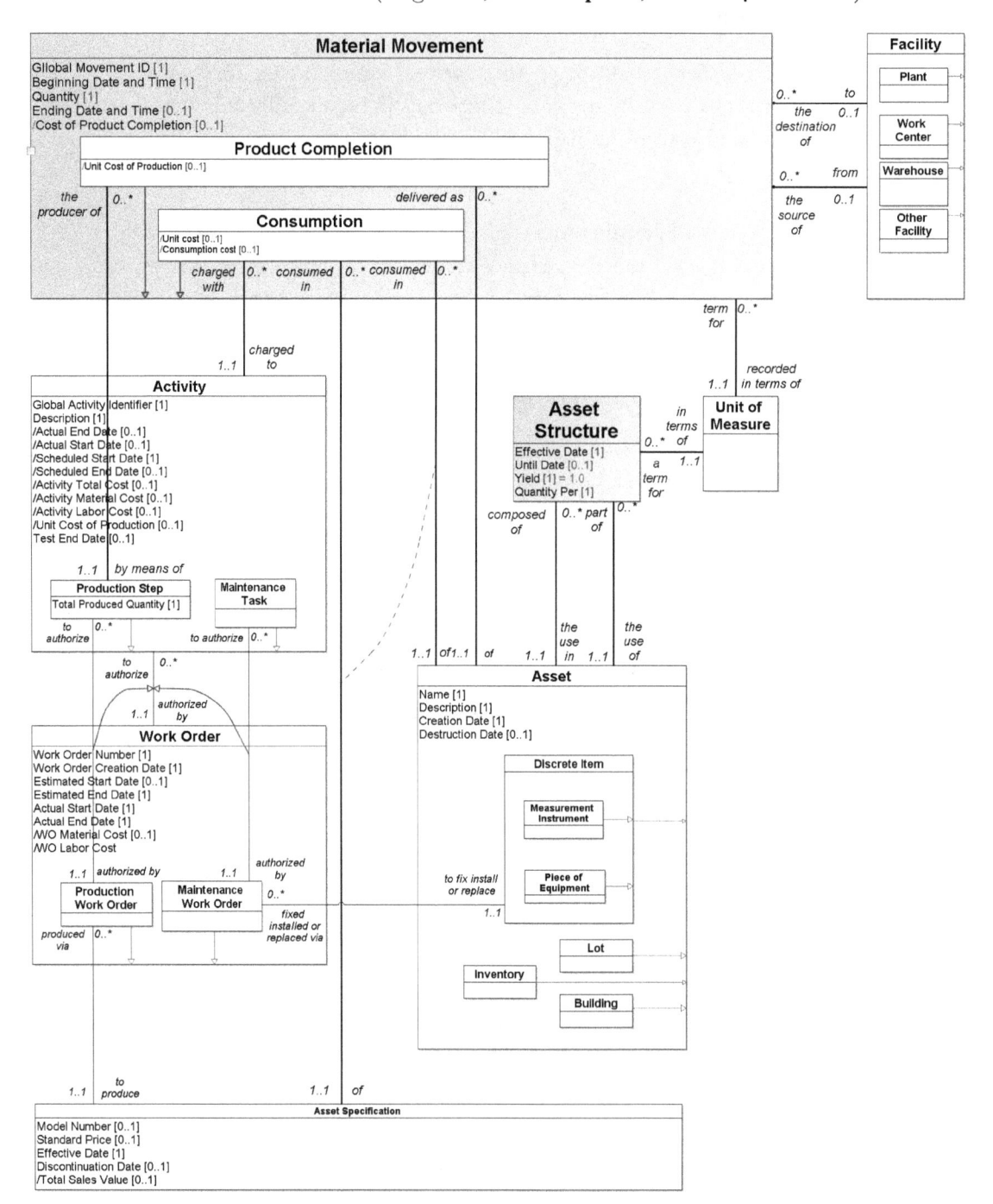

Figure 16-7: Material Movements

The cost can then be summarized for all **Activities** that are *authorized by* each **Work Order** into the **Work Order** attribute /WO Material Cost. This is calculated from the formula:

5. **Work Order** /WO Material Cost =

    SUM-THROUGH (*to authorize*, **Activity**, /Activity Material Cost)

In the next section, we'll see how the cost of labor is added to the final cost of production.

Asset Structure

Figure 16-7 also shows an alternative way of describing the conversion of raw materials or parts into finished products. **Asset Structure** is the fact that a particular **Asset** is a component in another **Asset**. In this case, one instance links the component with the assembled product. This is different from the **Material Movement** representation, because that shows that **Consumption** and **Product Completion** are separate instances, linked only by the fact that they are for either the same **Production Step** or the same **Production Work Order**.

The **Material Movement** approach allows us to describe a **Work Order** that would require 9 instances to combine, say, 5 components to produce 4 different finished products. The **Asset Structure** approach would require 20 instances, and would not be able to relate them to each other.

Utilizing Equipment

Figure 16-8 shows two additional kinds of **Material Movement** relevant to manufacturing. The first is **Equipment Utilization**.

Here, instead of a quantity of material consumed, the Quantity inherited from **Material Movement** is interpreted to mean Hours Used of a **Discrete Item**. This can be multiplied by the Charge Rate of the appropriate **Discrete Item** to determine the cost of that usage. This then is *charged to* an **Activity** that accumulates a set of **Actual Utilizations** into /Activity Equipment Usage in a manner analogous to the way /Activity Material Usage was calculated above.

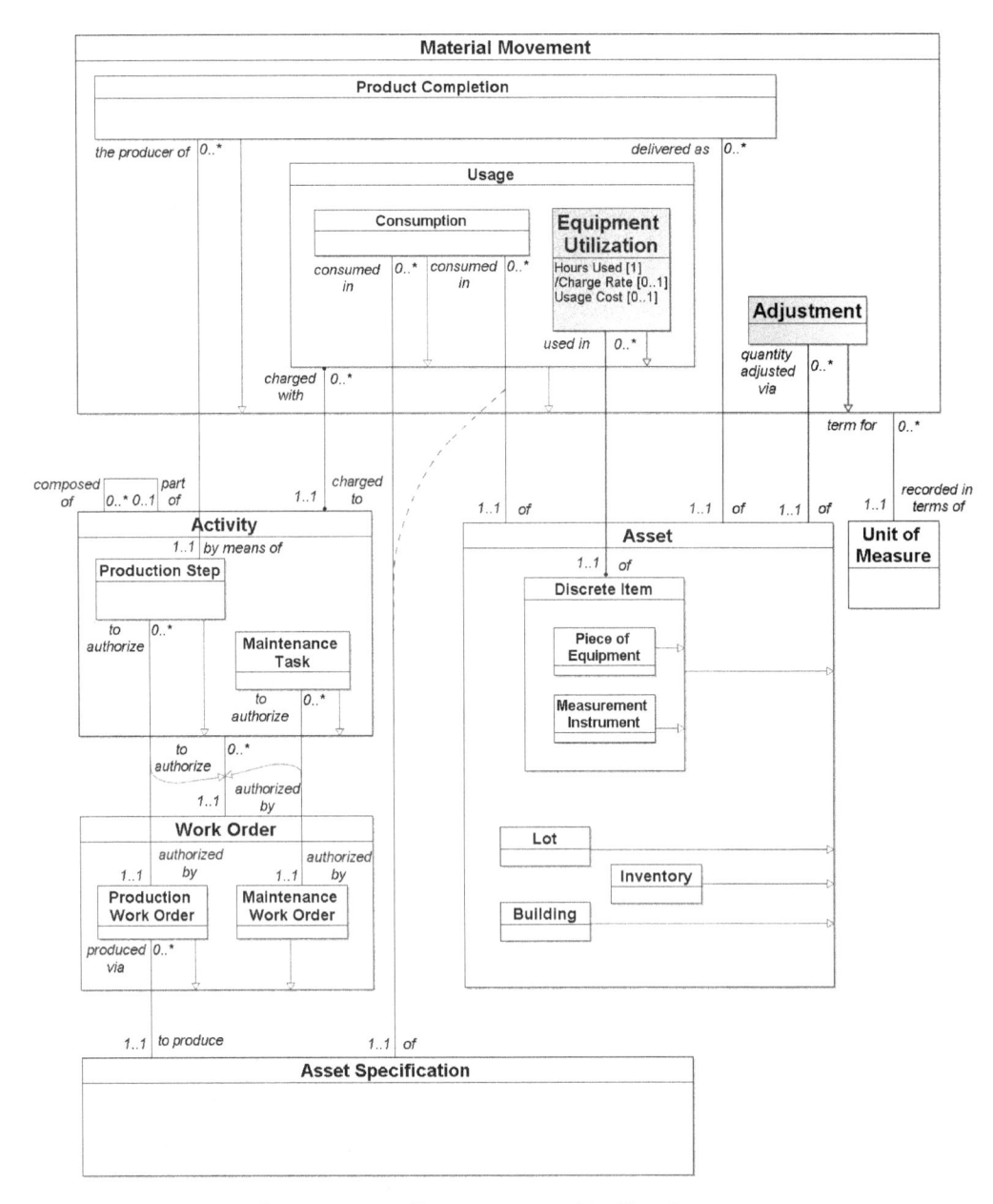

Figure 16-8: Adjustments and Utilization

Adjustments

The third kind of **Material Movement** added to Figure 16-8 is **Adjustment**. This is the same **Adjustment** we saw in the context of **Contracts** in Chapter 15. The idea is the same, but instead of **Adjustments** to inventory of purchased or sold items, we are concerned here with raw materials and sub-assemblies.

Note in the Figure that each **Asset Movement** only may be *from* and *to* a **Facility**. When an inventory evaluation is done, often materials are found to have moved *from* (for example) the **Warehouse**, *to* the ether somewhere. The *destination* of the **Movement** is unknown. Alternatively, they may have suddenly appeared, having been moved *to* the **Warehouse**, but their *source* is unknown.

Labor Usage

The third component of cost for manufacturing, after material and equipment processing cost is the cost of labor. As with material costs, labor costs can be viewed both in terms of expected standard labor cost and actual labor cost.

Standard Labor Cost

As with standard material cost, standard labor cost is determined for an **Activity Specification**, not for the actual **Activity**. Figure 16-9 shows that the labor expected to be required to carry out **Activities** *described by* an **Activity Specification** is its **Standard Labor Requirement**—the fact that a particular number of hours of labor are required to complete any **Activity** that is *an example of* a particular **Activity Specification**. Specifically required are **People** who possess a particular **Skill**, or who have appropriate values for a particular **Party Characteristic**.

That is, each **Standard Labor Requirement** must be *for* an **Activity Specification**, and must be either *for the delivery of* a **Skill** (such as `"woodworking"` or `"project management"`), or *for having a required value of* a particular **Party Characteristic** (such as having a `"weight"` of `"over 200 pounds"`).

This calls for determining which **Persons** either are *holder of* a **Capability** *in* a required **Skill**, or are *described by* a **Party Characteristic Value** Characteristic Value *of* a **Party Characteristic** that is within the bounds of the **Standard Labor Requirement's** Minimum Value and Maximum Value.

For example, the **Required Value** of the **Standard Labor Usage** might say either that a candidate must have at least a `"First Class"` rating for the **Skill** of `"metal-working"`, or must have less than `"200 pounds"` as the value of the **Party Characteristic**, `"weight"`.

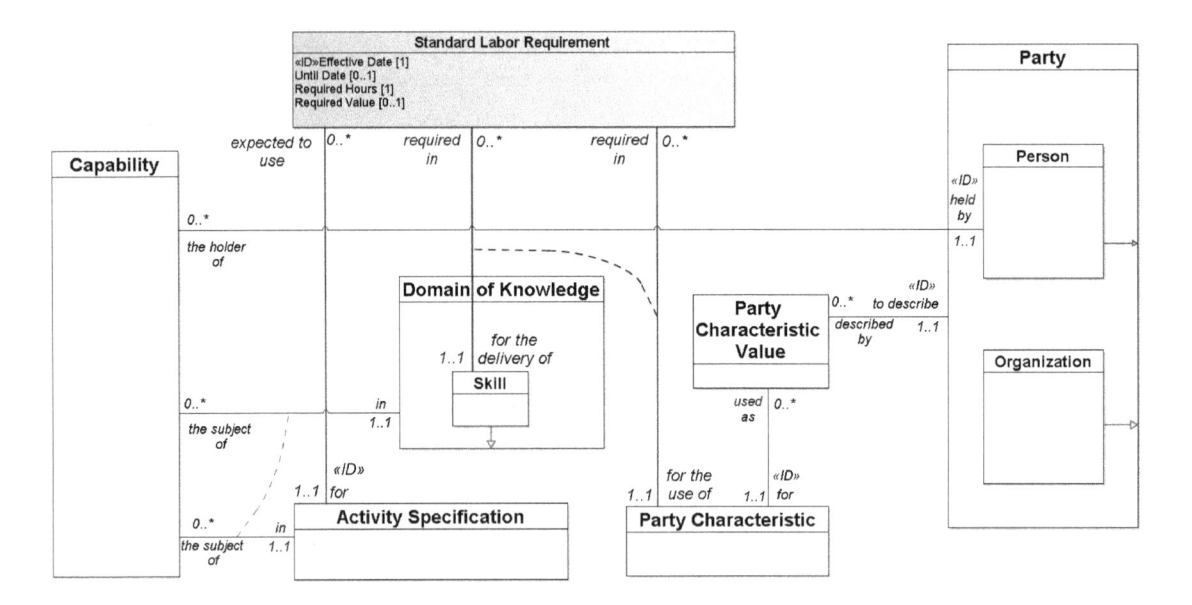

Figure 16-9: Labor Requirement

Business Rule

- If a **Standard Labor Requirement** must be *for having a required value for* a **Party Characteristic**, then for a **Party** to meet that requirement, the **Characteristic Value**—of the **Party Characteristic Value** *for* that **Party Characteristic** and *to describe* that **Party**—must be greater than the **Standard Labor Requirement's** Minimum Required Value, or less than its Maximum Required Value. Which is used is determined by the **Standard Labor Requirement** attribute Minimum Indicator (Minimum Required Value if it is "True", or Maximum Required Value if it is "False"). *(Translation:* A **Standard Labor Requirement** is a requirement for people whose **Labor Characteristic Values** fall within required value ranges.)

Actual Labor Cost

The actual cost of labor entails evaluating the number of hours spent by real people on real tasks. In this model, the **Persons** involved are presumed to be *holders of* **Employment** (that is, employees). Specifically, the model in Figure 16-10 asserts that each **Labor Usage** (that is something like a time-sheet entry) must be *of* one

Manufacturing 333

and only **Employment** (that is, a **Person** that is *a holder of* **Employment** *with* an **Organization**. If this is not the case, then the relationship could be generalized to say that each **Labor Usage** must be *of* one and only one **Person**.

Just as material costs were calculated based on the quantity of material used, the cost of labor is based on the **Hours Worked** *of* an **Employment** (that is, *by* an employee), *charged to* an **Activity**. In an approach similar to calculating material cost, the **/Labor Value** is derived from the **Labor Usage's Hours Worked** and the **Person's Charge Rate**, as captured in his or her **Employment**. Specifically, the formula is:

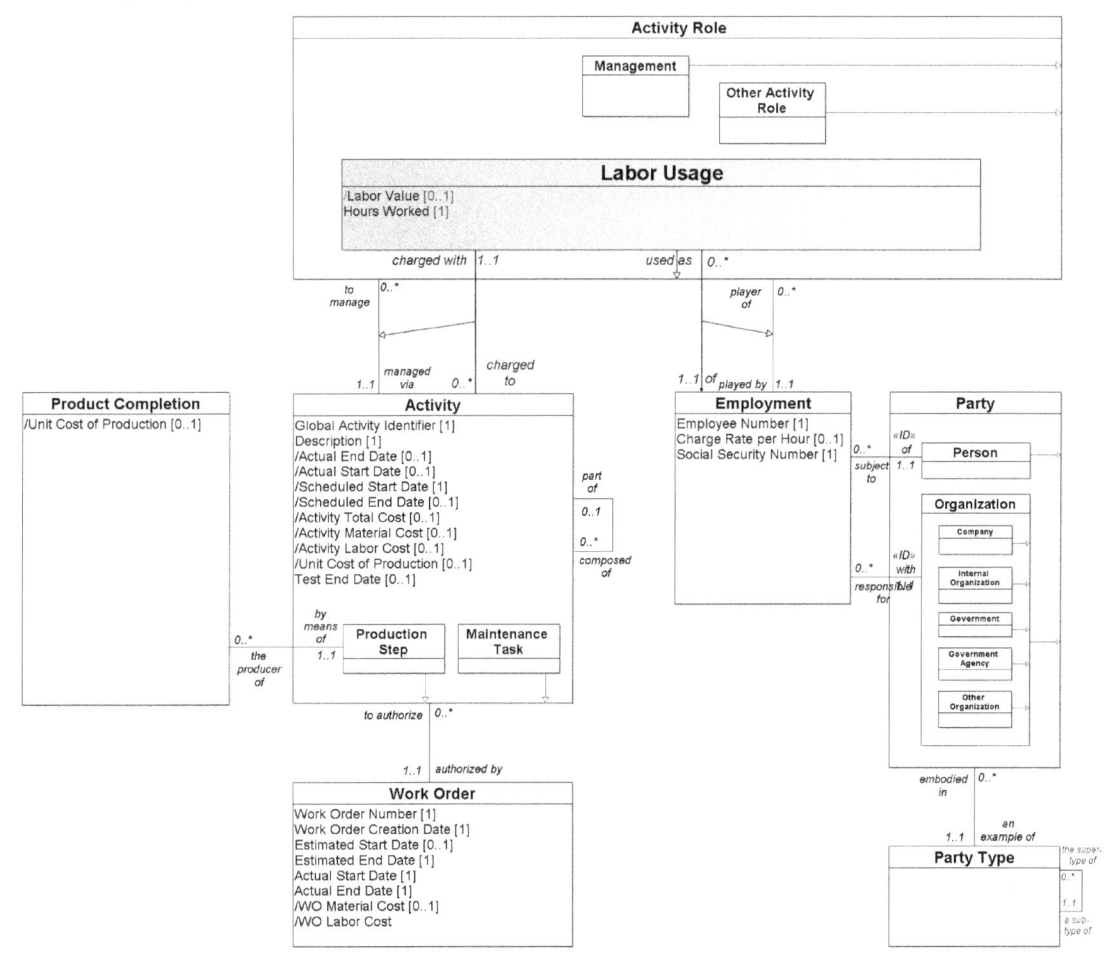

Figure 16-10: Actual Labor Usage

6. **Labor Usage /Labor Value** =

    Hours Worked times INFER-THROUGH (*of*, **Employment**, **Charge Rate per Hour**).

As with materials, the /Activity Labor Cost summarizing all of the Labor Usages that were *charged to* an Activity is calculated as:

7. Activity /Activity Labor Cost =

    SUM-THROUGH (*charged with*, Labor Usage, /Labor Value).

The total cost for the Work Order (/WO Labor Cost) is similarly summarized across Activities as:

8. Work Order /WO Labor Cost =

    SUM-THROUGH (*to authorize*, Maintenance Task, Activity Labor Cost))

Note that all of these costs are calculated the same way, whether the Work Order is for Production Steps or Maintenance Tasks.

Accounting for Manufacturing Costs

Figure 16-11 shows the financial activities associated with manufacturing. Specifically, a Labor Usage (a kind of Activity Role) shows how much time a Person spent performing an Activity. The Person has a Charge Rate that can be multiplied by the Hours Worked to arrive at the computed attribute Labor Value. This then can be the Total Value Each Side for an Accounting Transaction that is *an example of* the Accounting Transaction Type Labor Usage Charge.

Similarly, the Consumption of an Asset or an Asset Specification incurs a /Consumption Cost, derived from the price of the Physical Asset Specification and the Quantity Used. Again, this will trigger an Accounting Transaction, probably *an example of* an Accounting Transaction Type such as `"Material Consumption Charge"`.

Manufacturing

Accounting Entry
Sequence Number [1]
Entry Value [1]

Debit Entry
Credit Entry

Balance
Sequence Number [1]
/Balance Value [1]
Effective Date [1]

Account
Account Number [1]
Name [1]
Description [1]

Specifically:
- *"Labor Usage charge"*
- *"Material consumption charge"*
- *"Equipment usage charge"*

Account Type
Name [1]
Description [1]

Cost Center
Cost Center Code [1]
Name [1]
Description [1]

Accounting Transaction
«ID»Transaction Number [1]
Transaction Date [1]
Purpose [1]
/Total Value Each Side [1]

Accounting Transaction Type
«ID»Name [1]
Description [1]

Activity Role
Global Activity Role Identifier [1]
Description [1]
Effective Date [1]
Until Date [0..1]

Labor Usage
/Labor Value [0..1]
Hours Worked [1]

Material Movement
Gllobal Movement ID [1]
Beginning Date and Time [1]
Quantity [1]
Ending Date and Time [0..1]
/Cost of Product Completion [0..1]

Product Completion
/Unit Cost of Production [0..1]

Usage

Consumption
/Unit cost [0..1]
/Consumption cost [0..1]

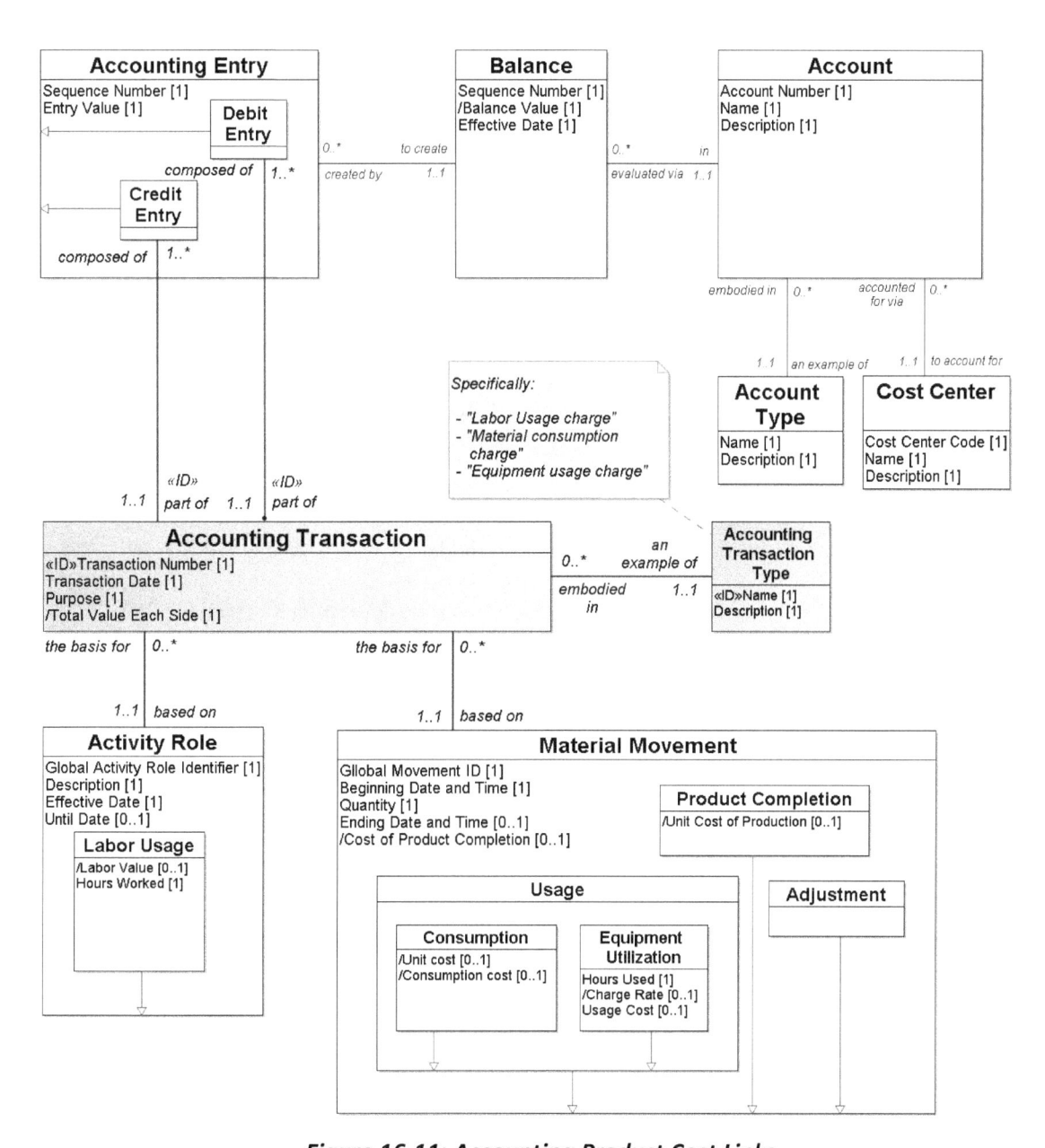

Equipment Utilization
Hours Used [1]
/Charge Rate [0..1]
Usage Cost [0..1]

Adjustment

Figure 16-11: Accounting Product Cost Links

Summary

This chapter described the model for *Discrete Manufacturing*—that is, the manufacturing of products (**Discrete Items**) that can be counted.

This is as opposed to *Process Manufacturing*, which produces chemicals. That is described more fully in *Data Model Patterns: Conventions of Thought*.

Here we learned about the **Routing Elements** that describe the structure of the manufacturing process and the **Work Orders** that drive it. As it happens, the structure of the manufacturing effort is very similar to that for maintaining the equipment involved. Indeed, your author had the opportunity to study a nuclear power plant and discovered that no one there produced electricity. They were entirely devoted to maintaining (ok, and operating) the equipment that produced the electricity. Issues of inventory control, scheduling procurement, and installing equipment were right out of the manufacturing model.

Naturally, much of this model is based on the **Asset** model, since its objective, after all, is to consume and produce **Assets**.

CHAPTER 17

The Laboratory

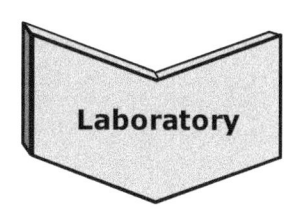

Many companies and government agencies make use of sampling and laboratory testing. Manufacturers evaluate both finished product quality and the effectiveness of the production processes. Various government agencies do laboratory testing to identify pollution conditions, to perform forensic analyses, and for many other reasons. Hospitals, clinics, and doctor's offices perform laboratory tests to help diagnose health problems.

This chapter describes the characteristics of sampling and laboratory analysis across a broad range of purposes.

Samples

The starting point for any laboratory exercise is the taking of **Samples**. The data involved are described in the model fragment that is Figure 17-1. A **Sample** is a relatively small amount of material extracted for the purpose of evaluating its quality or content. This may be, for example, to support a manufacturing process, basic research, a pharmaceutical clinical trial, a forensic analysis, or an environmental study. In the part of the model shown in Figure 17-1, each **Sample** must be *taken during* exactly one **Sampling Activity**.

In the context of a manufacturing plant, each **Sampling Activity** must be *taken from* one of the following:

- A **Work Center** processing materials.
- A **Storage Location**, a designated area within a **Warehouse** or **Plant**—such as a specific shelf or cabinet.
- An identified **Inventory** of material.

337

338 Enterprise Model Patterns

- A specified **Lot** of material.
- A **Piece of Equipment** such as a machine used in the manufacturing process.

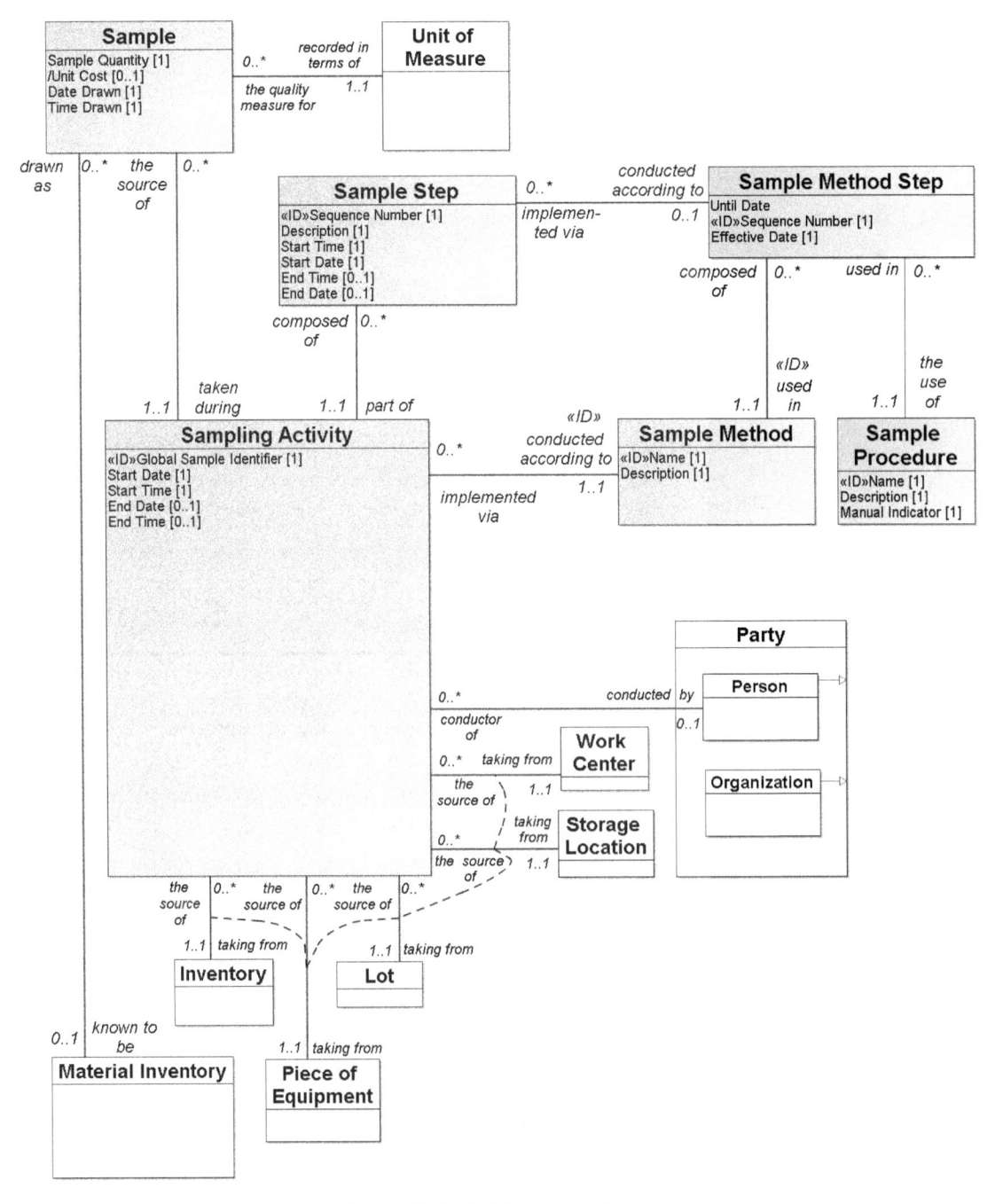

Figure 17-1: Taking Samples

In different settings, the choice of sources could be different. For example, in a hospital, it could be a sample of blood drawn from a patient; in a national forest, it could be drawn from an environmental monitoring station of some sort.

In the examples shown here, it is assumed that the identity of the material being sampled and tested is known, as would be the case in a manufacturing plant. In other settings, however, that may not be the case. For example, detecting the presence of pollutants in the air, while identifying the identity of the material involved, based on laboratory tests, is an extension of this model and not described here.

The model describes as much as can be said now, by asserting that "each **Sample** *may be known to be* a **Specified Material**. In a different context, this might be *is hypothesized to be* a **Specified Material**. In either case, the identity of the material would be determined by one or more **Observations**. (See page 347, below.)

Each **Sample** must be *taken during* a **Sampling Activity**. Each of these, in turn, must be *composed of* one or more **Sample Steps**, each *conducted according to* one pre-defined **Sample Method**. The **Sample Method** prescribes the steps (**Sample Method Steps**) to be followed to carry it out properly. That is, the process to be followed is documented as a serial numbered set of **Sample Method Steps**. Note that each **Sample Step** must be *conducted according to* one **Sample Method**, but it may also be more specifically *conducted according to* a **Sample Method Step**, and by implication, *according to* a **Sample Method**.

Each **Sample Method Step**, in turn, must be *implemented via* a set of **Sample Procedures**. That is, a **Sample Method Step** is defined to be the fact that a **Sample Procedure** is used to carry out a **Sample Method**.

Business Rules

- If a **Sample Step** is specifically *conducting according to* a **Sample Method Step**, then that **Sample Method Step** must be *part of* the **Sample Method** that is *implemented via* the **Sampling Activity** that the **Sample Step** is *part of*. *(Translation:* If a **Sampling Activity** must be *conducted according to* a **Sample Method**, then any component **Sample Steps** must be *conducted according to* **Sample Method Steps** that are part of the same **Sample Method**.*)*

- A **Sample Step** may be *conducted according to* a **Sample Method** without specifying a more detailed **Sample Method Step**.

Note that each **Sampling Activity** may be either manual or automated. If manual, the **Sampling Activity Manual Indicator** is "True". If automated, the **Sampling Activity Manual Indicator** is "False".

For example, the **Sample** may be drawn automatically as part of the process, it may be drawn by someone's turning on a spigot, or it could be taken by inserting a strip of sensitive material into a tank.

Each **Sample** must be *recorded in terms of* one **Unit of Measure**, such as "ounce", "kilogram", et cetera. As first described in Chapter 4, for reporting purposes, the **Unit of Measure** may be *converted to* one or more other **Units of Measure** *via* a **Unit of Measure Conversion**. (Because it is shown in Chapter 4, it is not repeated here.) Unless it is captured via an automated process, good laboratory practices require that each **Sampling Activity** also be recorded as being *conducted by* a particular **Person**.

Laboratory Tests

Once **Samples** have been drawn, they may be subject to one or more **Laboratory Tests**. A **Laboratory Test** is a collection of **Laboratory Test Steps** to determine a numerical value of one or more **Asset Characteristics** of a **Sample**. material.

Figure 17-2 shows that each **Laboratory Test** must be *conducted on* one and only one **Sample**. It must be *conducted according to* a pre-defined **Test Method**—which is, in turn, composed of a set of **Test Method Steps**. Each of the latter is itself *an example of* a **Test Procedure Specification**. That is, a **Test Method Step** is the fact that a particular **Test Procedure Specification** is part of a particular **Test Method**.

Business Rule

- Each **Laboratory Test Step** that is *part of* a **Laboratory Test** may only be *conducted according to* a **Test Method Step** that is *part of* the **Test Method** that is *conducted as* the specified **Laboratory Test**. *(Translation:* Only **Laboratory Test Steps** may be *part of* a **Laboratory Test** if they correspond to **Test Method Steps** that are *part of* the corresponding **Test Method**.)

A **Laboratory Test Step** is the actual taking of a measurement describing the **Sample**. It must be *conducted according to* one **Test Method Step** that is *part of* a **Test Procedure Specification**.

That is, a **Test Method** may be *conducted as* one or more actual **Laboratory Tests**, each of which is given at a point in time and is itself *composed of* one or more **Laboratory Test Steps**, each of which is *conducted according to* one of the **Test Method Steps** that is *part of* the **Test Method**.

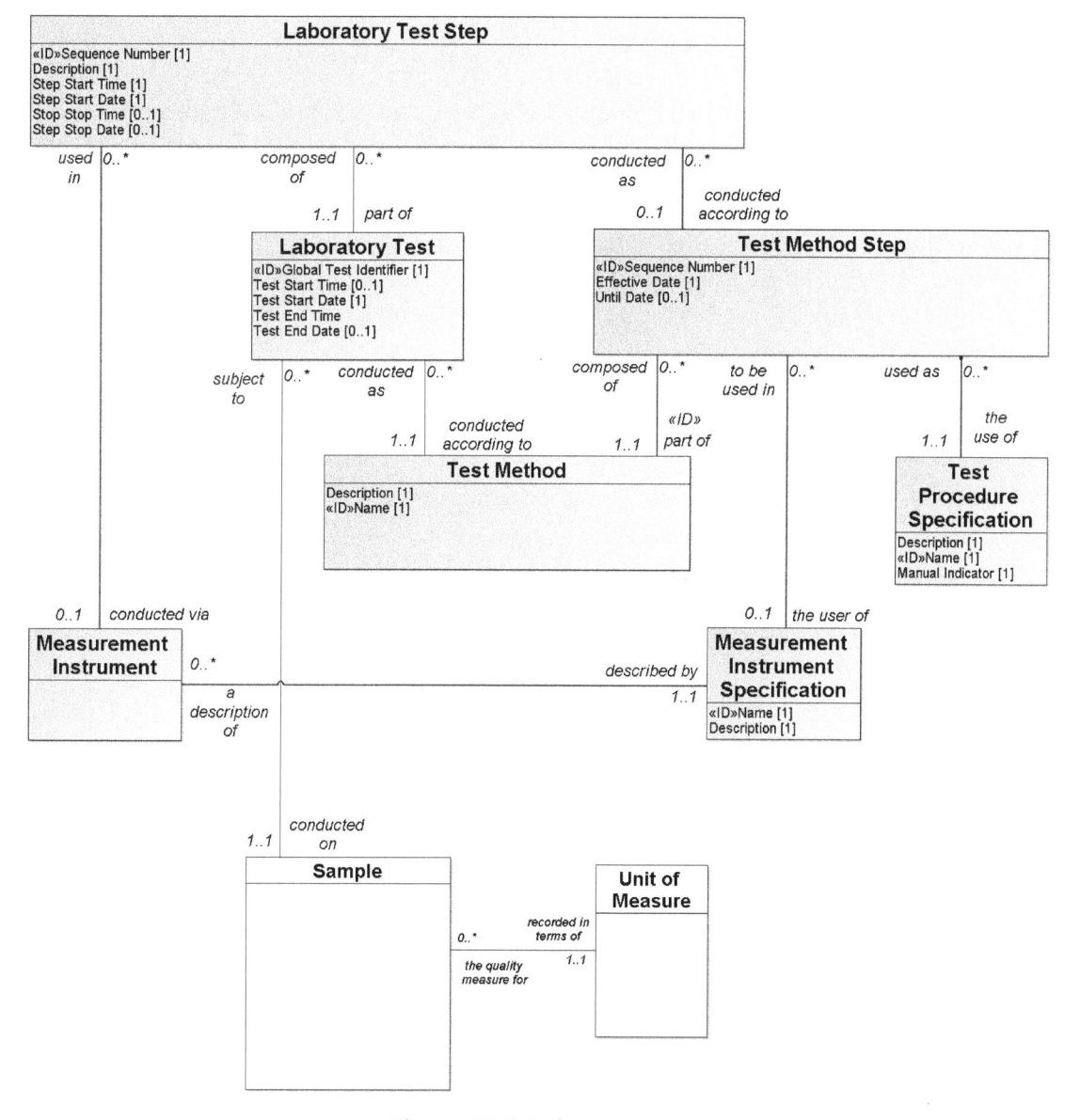

Figure 17-2: Laboratory Tests

A **Laboratory Test** could, for example, be conducted to detect a component chemical, identify the pH, or evaluate physical characteristics, such as viscosity. For example, **Test Procedure Specifications** required for the **Test Method** "Determine pH manually" would include

1. Transfer a small portion of the Sample into a beaker;
2. Obtain pH test strip;
3. Insert pH test strip into beaker;
4. Use color of strip to estimate pH value.

Note that each pre-defined **Test Method Step** may be *to make use of a* (Pre-defined) **Measurement Instrument Specification**, while each actual **Laboratory Test Step** may be *conducted via* an actual **Measurement Instrument**.

Some tests, however, such as checking for pH values—which can be done with test strips—do not require a **Measurement Instrument**. Hence Figure 17-2 shows that each **Laboratory Test Step** may be *conducted on* no more than one (1..1) **Instrument**.

Note that a single **Laboratory Test** takes place at a particular time (as captured in values of the attributes **Test Start Date, Test Start Time, Test End Date,** and **Test End Date Time**.) In some cases, the test may be instantaneous, so the **Test Start Date Time** and **Test End Date Time** have the same value. In other cases, an elapsed period of time is involved.

The actual conduct of the **Laboratory Test** for pH described above, beginning at 3:00 pm on November 22, 2010, involved recording four **Laboratory Test Steps** that each (via a **Test Method Step**) in succession invoked one of the four **Test Procedure Specifications** just listed.

The same sample could be tested for pH at different times, using two methods— the manual one just described, and an automated one, revealing the value as a digital display. Both could be conducted on the same **Sample**, but each is a separate **Laboratory Test Step**, *conducted according to* its respective **Test Method**.

Sampling in Context

Figure 17-3 shows that the entity classes we've just been describing are special cases of the **Assets, Activities, Activity Types, Asset Specification Structures**, and **Facilities**—described in the enterprise model in Section Two.

Since a **Sample** is a physical material, it is a sub-type of **Asset**, as are the **Inventory** or **Lot** that it may be drawn from. It may also be extracted from the **Asset** that is a **Piece of Equipment**, such as a pump or other part of the manufacturing machinery. Or, without identifying the **Piece of Equipment**, it can be simply taken from a particular **Work Center** (or **Storage Location**)—that is, a **Facility**. In something other than the manufacturing context, it could be taken from an **Other Facility**, such as an air quality measuring station.

Figure 17-3 adds **Storage Location** as a sub-type of **Facility**. This is, after all, an address inside a **Warehouse** or **Plant**. Note that instead of the more generic **Facility Structure**, for purposes of this model, a simple recursive relationship between **Facilities** is sufficient. That is, each **Facility** may be *composed of* one or more (other) **Facilities**, but each **Facility** may only be *a part of* one and only one (other) **Facility**.

This diagram again shows examples of how UML can describe relationships as sub-types of other relationships. Entity/relationship notation does not have the ability to make that explicit, but UML does. That relationships can be sub-types of other relationships is a useful concept here.

For example, the relationship…

- Each **Sampling Activity** must be *conducted according to* one and only one **Sample Method**

…must be a sub-type of…

- Each **Activity** must be *the implementation* of one and only one **Activity Specification**,

…which, in turn, must be a sub-type of

- Each **Activity** must be *an example of* one and only one **Activity Type**.

Similarly…

- Each **Sample Method Step** must be *used in* one and only one **Sample Method**

…must be a sub-type of…

- Each **Activity Specification Structure** must be *the use in* one and only one **Activity Specification**,

…and…

344 Enterprise Model Patterns

- Each **Sample method Step** must be *the use of* one and only one **Sample Procedure**

…must be a sub-type of…

Each **Activity Specification Structure** must be *the use of* one and only one **Activity Specification**.

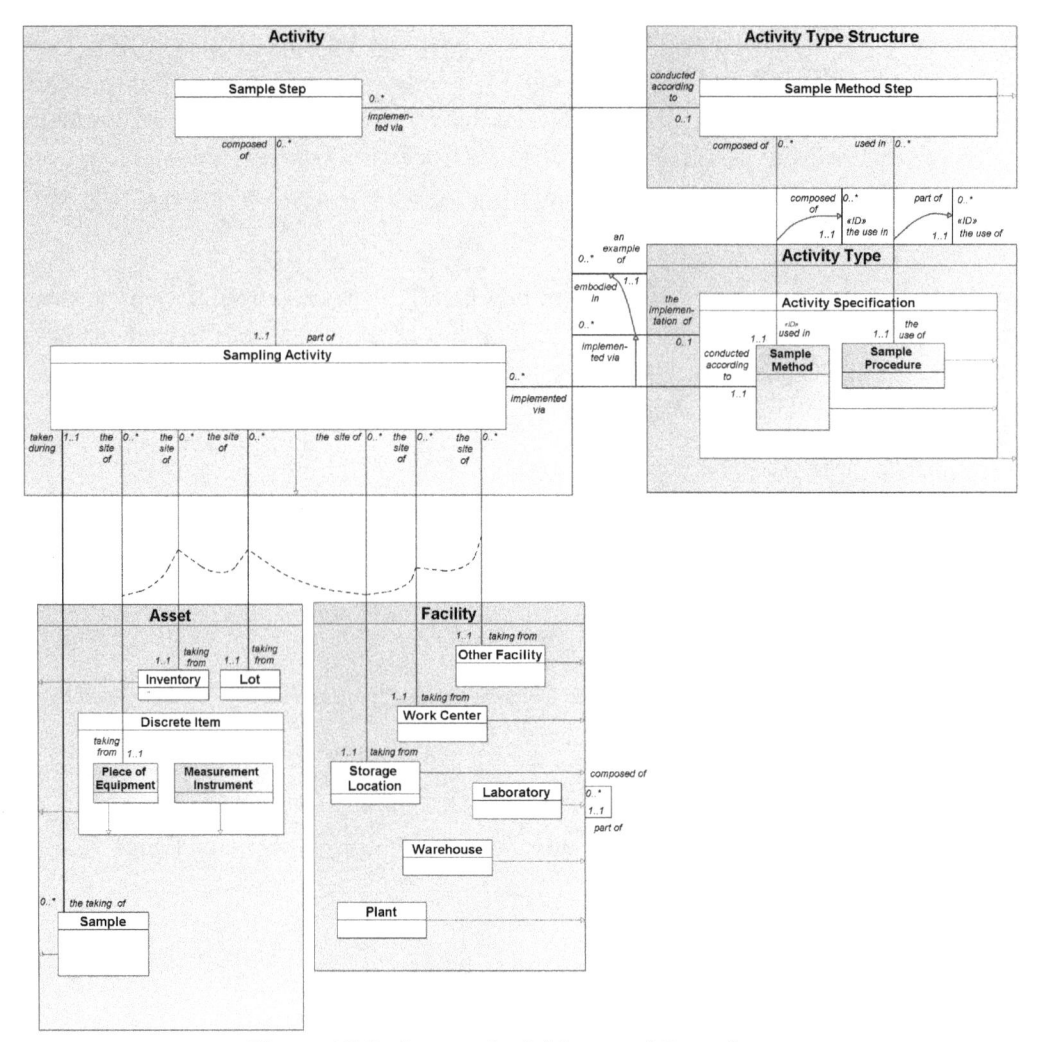

Figure 17-3: Assets, Activities, and Samples

The Laboratory Model in Context

Just as the **Sampling Activity** and **Sample Step** are kinds of **Activity**, so too are the **Laboratory Test** and the **Laboratory Test Step**, as shown in Figure 17-4. **Test Method** and **Test Procedure** are both **Activity Specifications**. As with **Sample Method Step**, since **Test Method Step** is *part of* an **Activity Type** that is a **Test Method**, and is *the use of* an **Activity Type** that is a **Test Method Procedure**, **Test Method Step** is clearly a sub-type of **Activity Specification Structure**.

And of course, the detailed relationships are sub-types of the more general relationships as well.

For example, the relationship...

- Each **Laboratory Test** must be *conducted according to* one and only one **Test Method**

...must be a sub-type of...

- Each **Activity** must be *the implementation* of one and only one **Activity Specification,**

...which, in turn, must be a sub-type of

- Each **Activity** must be *an example of* one and only one **Activity Type.**

Similarly...

- Each **Test Method Step** must be *part of* one and only one **Test Method**

...must be a sub-type of...

- Each **Activity Specification Structure** must be *the use in* one and only one **Activity Specification,**

...which, in turn, must be a sub-type of:

- Each **Activity** must be *the use in* one **Activity Type**.

...and...

- Each **Test method Step** must be *the use of* one and only one **Test Procedure**

...must be a sub-type of...

346 Enterprise Model Patterns

- Each **Activity Specification Structure** must be *the use of* one and only one **Activity Specification**.

...which, in turn, must be a sub-type of:

- Each **Activity** must be *the use of* one **Activity Type**.

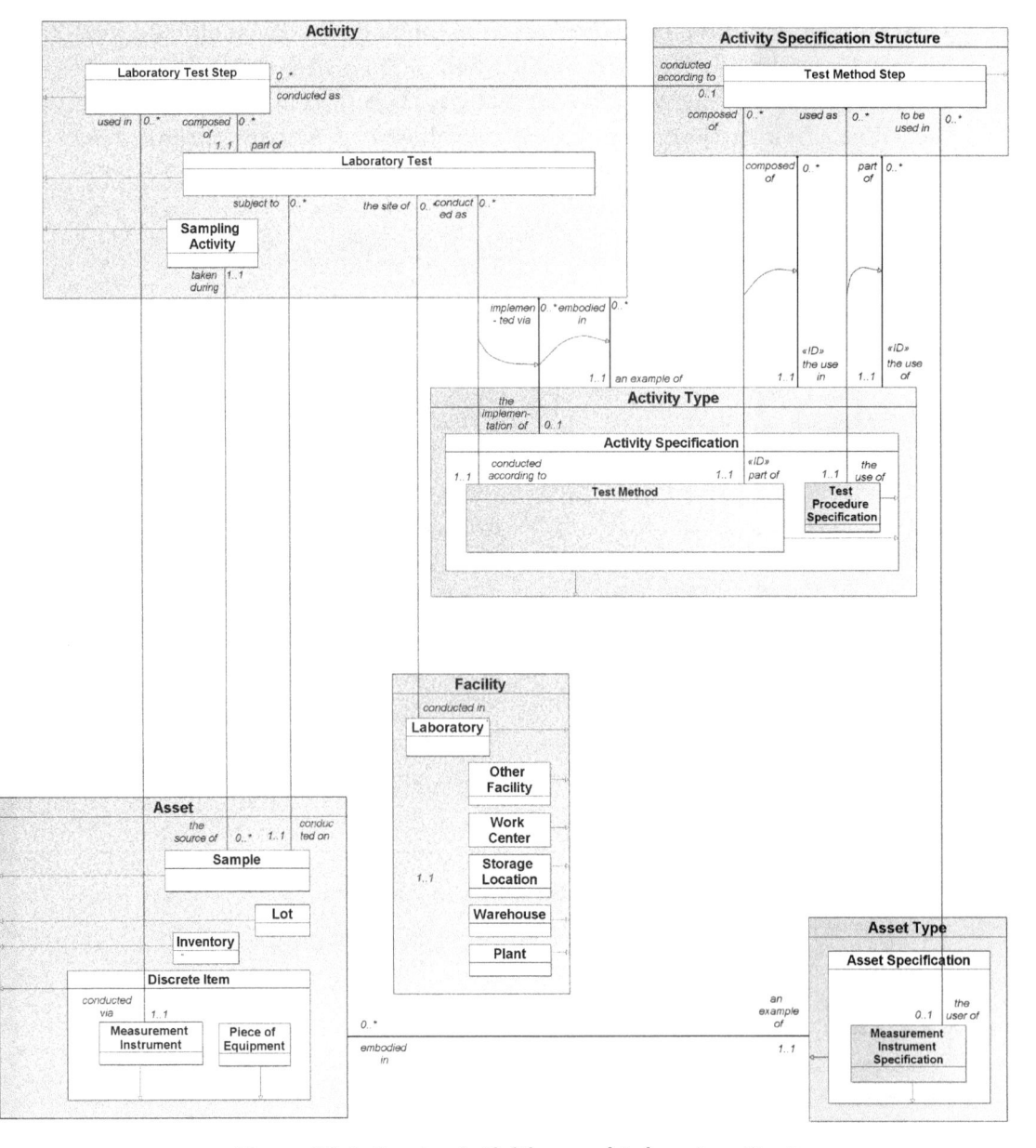

Figure 17-4: Assets, Activities, and Laboratory Tests

Observations

The purpose of the laboratory assignment is to produce *data* about a **Sample**, and evaluate them in terms of standard values expected from the same **Laboratory Test**. An **Observation**, then, is the fact that data have been captured to describe a **Sample**. To meet the purpose of the assignment, you must collect both *Actual Observations* and *Standard Observations*.

Actual Observations

The goal of the **Laboratory Test** is to produce actual *data* about a **Sample** of real material.

The numbers that come from a **Laboratory Test** are represented in Figure 17-5 as **Direct Measurements** *from* a **Laboratory Test**. That is, each instance of **Direct Measurement** must be *from* one **Laboratory Test**, and it provides a value for the attribute, **Value Quantity**.

Alternatively, a person may simply look at the **Sample** and observe things like "color", "cloudiness", and other visible characteristics. This second approach is recorded as a second kind of **Observation**—a **Physical Observation**.

In either case, the **Observation** must be *of* a single **Parameter**. A **Parameter** is "an(especially measurable or quantifiable) characteristic or feature"[55] That is, it is what is being measured.

Each instance of **Parameter** will, of course, be described by values of the attributes **Name** and **Description**. The **Parameter** may have a **Default Value**, and it may be a **Parameter** that is *derived via* one or more **Parameter Derivation Elements**, as is described later. (See page 353, below.)

The primary attribute of a **Direct Measurement**, of course, is **Value Quantity**, such as "6.5".

Of course the **Direct Measurement** of "6.5" is not meaningful unless we know what it is a measure *of*. That is, what is the **Parameter** being measured? In this case it could be "pH". Or it could be "carbon particles present".

---

[55] DK Illustrated Oxford Dictionary. 1998. (Oxford, UK: Oxford University Press): 591.

348 Enterprise Model Patterns

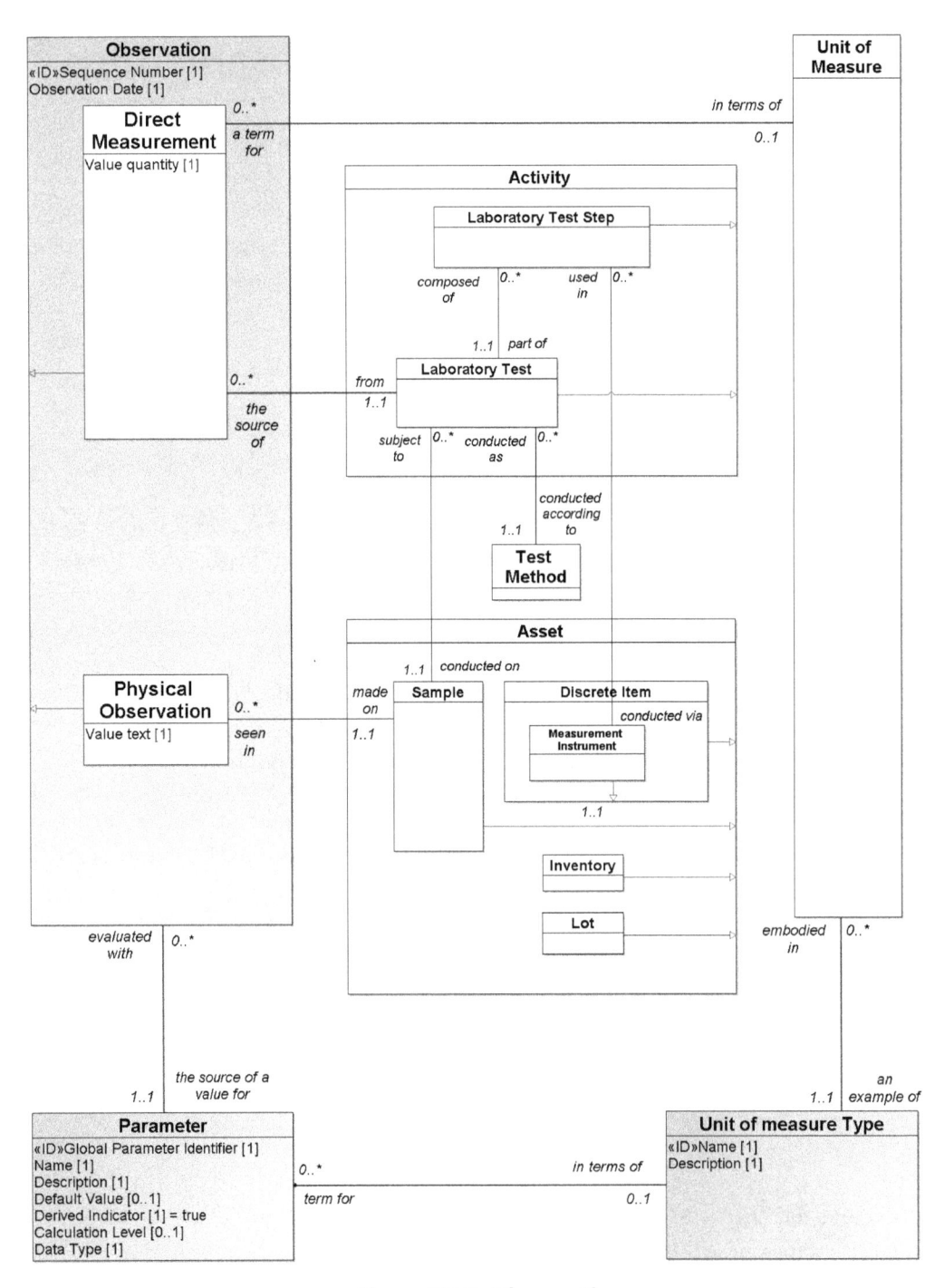

Figure 17-5: Observations

As it happens, the **Parameter** "pH" is unusual, in that it does not have a unit of measure. In most cases, however, a **Direct Measurement** is *in terms of* one **Unit of Measure**. A **Unit of Measure** is "is a definite magnitude of a physical quantity, defined and adopted by convention and/or by law, that is used as a standard for measurement of the same physical quantity."[56]

Each **Unit of Measure**, in turn, must be *an example of* one **Unit of Measure Type**. It is the **Parameter** being observed that determines what **Units of Measure** are available for capturing the **Direct Measurement**. The **Unit of Measure** selected is one of a pre-defined list of those that *are examples of* the **Unit of Measure Type**.

For example, one **Parameter** that is *normally in terms of* the **Unit of Measure Type** whose **Name** is "mass per volume" described above, could be "presence of cadmium". Available **Units of Measure** that are *examples of* that **Unit of Measure Type** are "micrograms per liter", and "parts per billion". If the **Parameter** involved is "presence of cadmium", current environmental laws only recognize those two **Units of Measure**, although others are possible.

Expected Observations

The secret to evaluating the implications of an **Observation** is to compare it with what was expected. That is, the actual **Value Quantity** for a **Direct Measurement** *from* a **Laboratory Test** *on* a **Sample**, may only be meaningful if it is compared with the **Maximum Allowable Value** and **Minimum Allowable Value** for an **Expected Observation** (as shown in Figure 17-6).

In fact, it is the set of **Expected Observations** that constitute the definition of a particular **Test Method** or **Test Method Step**. That is, in each case, the **Test Method** or the **Test Method Step** must be *defined in terms of* a set of one or more **Expected Observations**.

For example, the amount of cadmium contamination described in the previous section can, in principle, be determined via a **Test Method**, which is expected to return values for "presence of cadmium". That is, an **Expected Observation** would be *on* an **Asset Specification** for, say, "drinking water", and would be in terms of the **Parameter**, "presence of cadmium".

---

[56] *International Vocabulary of Metrology – Basic and General Concepts and Associated Terms (VIM)* (8th ed.), Joint Committee for Guides in Metrology, 2008, pp. 6–7, http://www.bipm.org/utils/common/documents/jcgm/JCGM_200_2008.pdf.

350 Enterprise Model Patterns

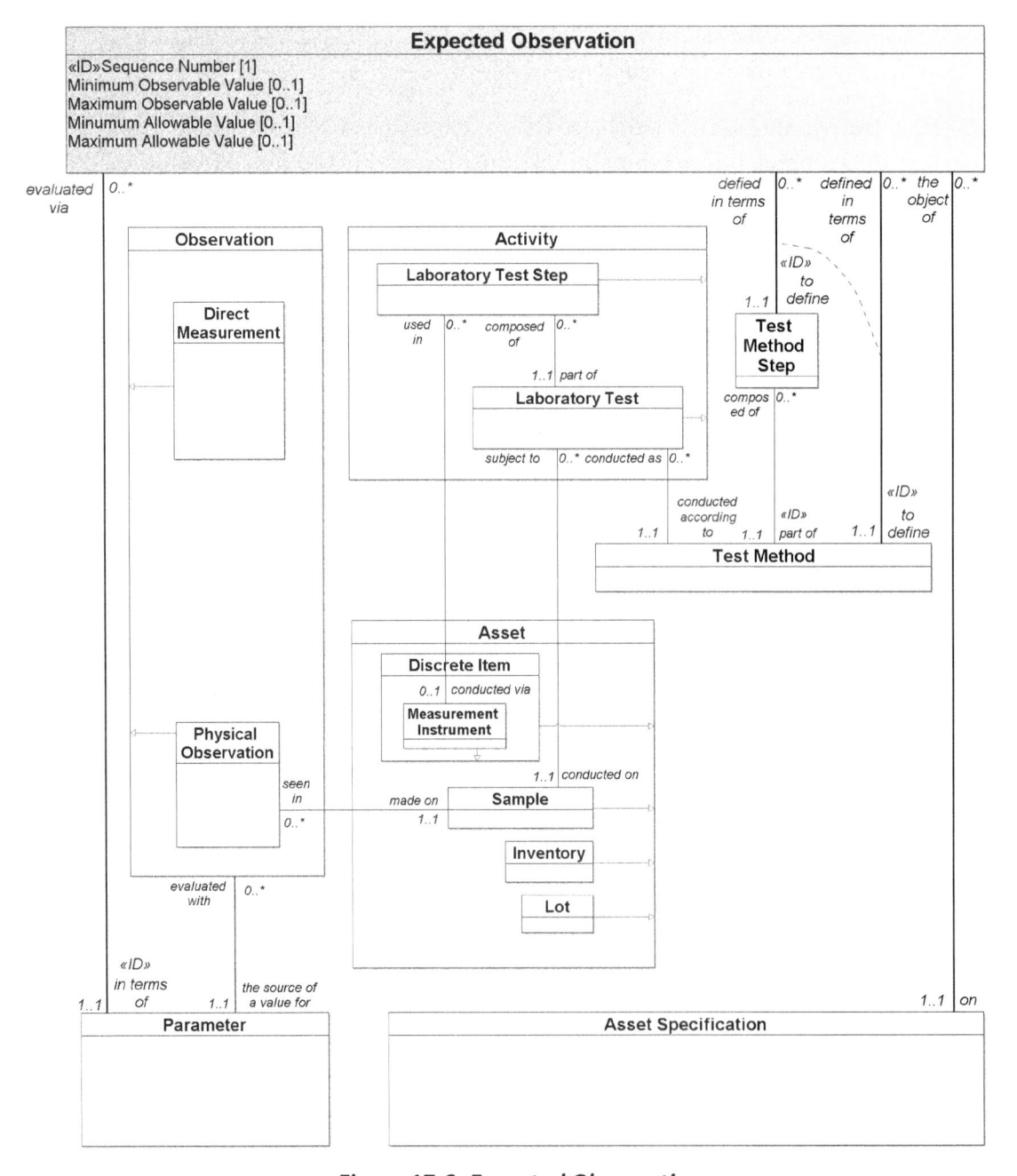

Figure 17-6: Expected Observations

An **Expected Observation** may be constrained in capturing data by its **Minimum and Maximum Observable Value**, as well as its **Minimum and Maximum Allowable Value**. In the first case, the limits are assigned by physics. A value outside those values is clearly in error. In the second case, these constraints represent business rules: "Thou shall not have more than the maximum amount of (for example) cadmium in the drinking water."

Here, the U.S. Environmental Protection Agency has determined that the minimum allowable quantity of `"presence of cadmium"` is `"zero (0)"`, and the maximum allowable in drinking water is `".005"` (`"mg/L"`).[57]

Note that this example only gives a flavor of what business rules surrounding the results of observations might look like. The model of business rules required to describe constraints (on cadmium contamination, for example) can be quite complex—but that complex model should fit inside this one.

Parameters and Characteristics

Previously, both in the Abstraction Level 0 model and in each of the Abstraction Level 1 models, we saw the concept of a **Characteristic** that was given values for particular objects (**Party**, **Activity**, **Asset**, and **Geography**). The idea was that each of these could be described by values assigned in the course of collecting data about the respective objects. In each case, the **...Characteristic Value** *of* a **...Characteristic** was both *for* a particular object (a **Party**, an **Activity**, an **Asset**, or a **Geographic Location**), and *given by* a **Party**. Depending on the category, **Characteristic** could be `"number of employees"` (for a **Company**), `"height"` (for a **Person**), `"duration"` (for an **Activity**), `"width"` (for an **Asset**), and so forth.♥

Figure 17-7 shows several significant things about the relationship between the laboratory and general data collection about an enterprise's environment.

First of all, notice that all the **Characteristics** described in previous chapters are, in fact, instances of **Parameters** in the sense of each being the name of something being measured or identified. According to the Merriam-Webster On-line dictionary, a "characteristic" is "a distinguishing trait, quality, or property."[58] A

---

[57] Environmental Protection Agency. 1992. "Basic Information about Cadmium in Drinking Water". Retrieved 1/25/2012 from http://water.epa.gov/drink/contaminants/basicinformation/cadmium.cfm#four.

♥ Of course "width" is typically *not* recorded for a **Person**…

[58] Merriam-Webster, "Characteristic". *The Merriam-Webster Online. http://www.merriam-webster.com/dictionary/characteristic.*

"parameter", on the other hand, is "any of a set of physical properties whose values determine the characteristics or behavior of something."[59]

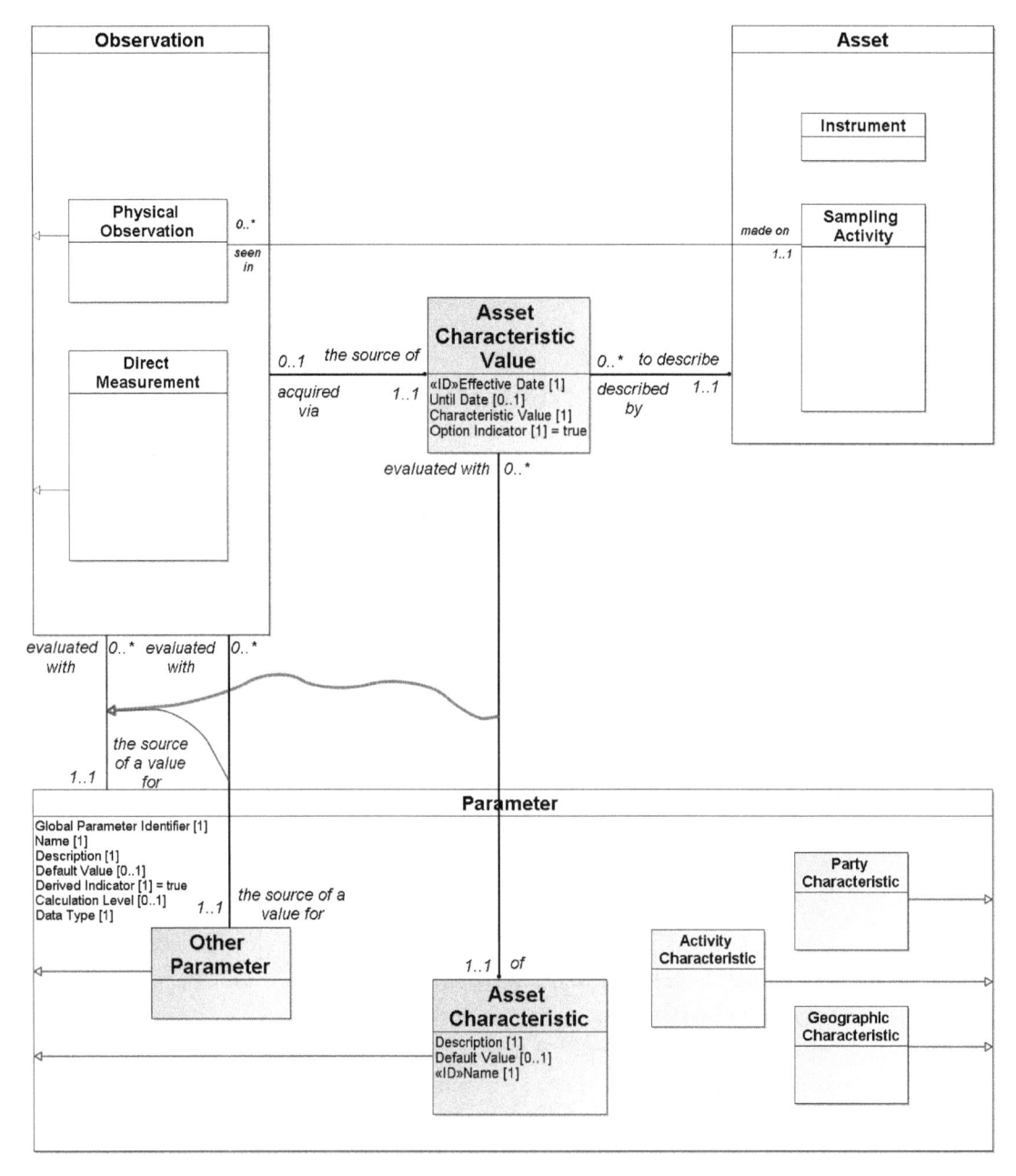

Figure 17-7: Parameters

---

[59] Merriam-Webster, "Parameter". *The Merriam-Webster Online*. Retreived 2010 from *http://www.merriamwebster.com/dictionary/parameter* .

Thus, each **Parameter** turns out to be a measurable **Party Characteristic**, **Activity Characteristic**, **Asset Characteristic**, or **Geographic Characteristic**. Since there may be **Parameters** that are not specific to any of these objects, you also have a sub-type to describe **Other Parameter**.

Because of the nature of the laboratory, however, of all these **Characteristics**, only **Asset Characteristics** can be captured and reported via **Samples**, **Laboratory Tests**, and **Observations**. By definition, the laboratory only measures **Characteristics** of physical objects and materials. Other kinds of **Characteristic Values** (**Activity**, **Party**, and **Geographic**) cannot be captured in this way—at least not directly. Some may be derived from **Asset Characteristics**, however, as described below.

Indeed, some kinds of **Asset Characteristic Values** cannot be captured this way, either.

Note that the UML notation is being bent a little a bit here. The relationship "each **Observation** must be *the source of a value for* one **Other Parameter**", is a sub-type of the relationship, "each **Observation** must be *the source of a value for* one **Parameter**. More significantly, however, the pair of relationships:

- Each **Observation** must be *the source of* one **Asset Characteristic Value**, plus
- Each **Asset Characteristic Value** must be *of* one **Asset Characteristic**

together also represent a sub-type of the relationship, "each **Observation** must be *the source of* one **Asset Characteristic**". (This is shown on the diagram with a wavy inheritance line.[*])

Derived Parameters

While data are primarily collected to describe the **Assets** of the physical world, some **Parameters** (of all kinds) *can* be derived mathematically from those thus collected. We have already seen that within each model area, when we saw **Party Characteristic Derivation Element**, **Asset Characteristic Derivation Element**, and **Activity Derivation Element**.

Each of these is shown in Figure 17-8 as a sub-type of the more generic **Parameter Derivation Element**.

---

[*] No, the authorities at the Object Management Group don't know about this...

354 Enterprise Model Patterns

One slight liberty has been taken here, that is a discrepancy between this model and the detailed models shown in Section Four: In each of those cases, it is only a **Continuous Characteristic** that is being derived. For the sake of graphic simplicity, here, it appears that any **Parameter** may be derived. The constraint at the **Characteristic** level, however, can still be assumed as an underlying business rule.

What is significant about this part of the model is that now calculations can be made *across areas of interest*. Any kind of **Parameter** can be derived from any other kind of **Parameter**.

Thus, in Figure 17-7, for example, any **Parameter** (such as a **Party Characteristic**) may be *derived from* one or more **Parameter Derivation Element** that is each *the use of* either a **Parameter** that is an **Asset Characteristic** (or a **System Variable** or a Constant), to derive the value of another **Parameter** (which could be any kind of **Characteristic**).

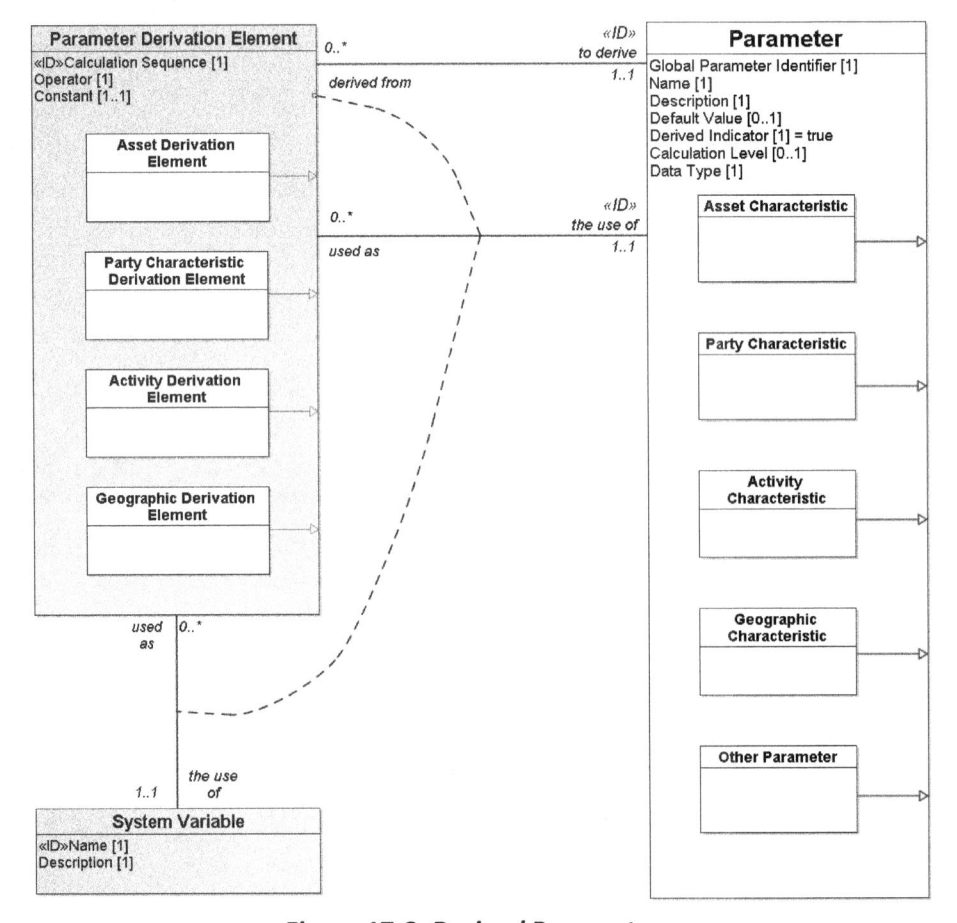

Figure 17-8: Derived Parameters

For example, in a manufacturing setting, the parameters being measured from samples are indeed characteristics of **Assets**. That is, the resulting **Observations** are *the source of* **Asset Characteristic Values**. Many of the **Asset Characteristics** thus evaluated may, in turn, be used to determine characteristics of the manufacturing **Activities**.

In other fields, other **Characteristics** may be derived from the **Asset Characteristics** captured in the sampling and laboratory processes. In a medical setting, for example, the presence of a particular amino acid could mean that a **Person** has a value for "`presence of cancer`" of "`positive`". In a forensic laboratory, some of the measurements captured from a tissue **Sample** actually can be used to draw conclusions about the **Characteristics** of the **Party** whose body is being examined. In the world of environmental protection, a **Sample** of the **Asset** "`soil`" may be tested to determine characteristics of the **Geographic Location** from which it was taken.

Summary

The model of the laboratory is somewhat specialized and probably outside the interests of most readers. On the other hand, in this day of television shows featuring forensic laboratories, the audience may be greater than one would expect. The topic should be of interest to data modelers, however, in what it shows us about how data can be captured and manipulated. Every business, along with other intellectual endeavors, as well, is confronted with the task of gathering information not just to carry out transactions, but to increase its understanding of the nature of the world with which it deals. It is to be hoped that this chapter provided some insights about accomplishing that.

PART FIVE

ABSTRACTION LEVEL 3: SOME INDUSTRY-SPECIFIC EXAMPLES

We began this book with a reasonably abstract and truly generic model of an enterprise, covering the fundamental questions of "who?" (people and organizations), "where?" (geographic areas), "what?" (physical assets), and "how?" (activities and events). We also addressed "when?", but time is, after all, in a different dimension, so it required special treatment. This was Abstraction Level 1. We then backed up to look at Abstraction Level 0, which was both a template for the first four parts of the Level 1 model, plus two "meta" models covering information resources and accounting.

Level 2, then, addressed the question of "why?" The reason enterprises (and government agencies) are in business is to provide products and/or services to the public. This entails more complex structures to address managing facilities, managing employees, marketing, negotiating contracts (sales), manufacturing, and a laboratory. Modeling each of these areas meant bringing together the entity classes from the Level 1 model in more complex and concrete ways.

Collectively, the models presented so far should address some 90% of the modeling needs of any enterprise or government agency.

"Yes, but we're different!" you say. The <fill in blank here> industry has some very special kinds of complex data that don't fit into any of the patterns presented so far.

Banking and pharmaceutical research and oil field production (for example) all have very specialized data requirements.

This is, of course, true. The patterns presented so far are indeed just that—patterns. They represent overall structures that are a good place to begin when setting out to model a particular business or agency. Even in the areas presented so far, you are expected to elaborate on them to meet your particular requirements. The particular areas that are genuinely unique in your industry, however, and indeed in areas unique in your company, require special attention. But understand the following:

- This is indeed addressing only the last 10% of the requirements of your company.
- Even this 10% makes use of structures found in the more abstract models.
- Within this 10%, a large part is, in fact, standard for your industry, so "patterns" still apply, even if they are only industry level patterns.

That is, yes, we can develop a set of semantic patterns for each industry. Indeed, Len Silverston set out in the second edition of his book to do just that.[60] This book is not quite that ambitious. Rather than attempting to model many industries comprehensively, this part of the book will use examples of specific industry-level problems to demonstrate how to apply the more abstract patterns to meet the more concrete requirements.

Note that while in some cases the underlying structure is fundamentally different from the Enterprise (Level 1) model, other examples are really just the Enterprise model with more detailed sub-types and additional structures. Yet others simply require different names.

The Examples

The next five chapters of this book will present examples of these, under the following topics:

- **Criminal Justice** – The model presented here is based on the "Global Justice XML Data Model" (GJXDM), developed for the United States Department of Justice in 2007. That model (and its successor, the National

---

[60] Len Silverston. 2001b. The Data Model Resource Book, Volume 2: A library of Universal Data Models by Industry Types. (New York: John Wiley & Sons).

Enterprise Information Model) were developed using XML. That notation is ideal for data communication, but has no ability to capture the semantics of the terms it is communicating. This model was derived from the documentation of GJXDM. It looks suspiciously like the Enterprise (Level 1) Model, although one would never suspect that, looking at the XML code of its original rendering.

- **Microbiology** – The more interesting parts of this model are the property of the client from which this excerpt was taken—so they're not here. But the part of the model shown here does demonstrate what you can do when you pursue the nature of physical reality far enough. It pursues the subtypes of **Asset** all the way to amino acids and DNA.
- **Banking** – Much of the model of a bank is very similar to the Enterprise Model in Level 1. The definition of what constitutes a product, however, is definitely an interesting (which is to say challenging) bit of modeling. The model presented here is the result of working for four different banks—and then adding some thought to come up with something different from what is currently in any of them. It requires some fundamental changes to the Enterprise (Level 1) model.
- **Oil Field Production** – This model is about "upstream" processing of petroleum products. In particular, it describes a prototypical oil well, its configuration, and much of the hardware that makes it work. It presents an example of taking the Level 1 and 2 concepts and elaborating on and renaming them to produce a very specific model of a very specific kind of facility. Indeed, it was a project to address oil production that refined the meaning of "facility" described in Chapter 12.
- **Highways** – The model here is derived from a project in a Canadian Provincial Highway Department, and addresses the question "what is a 'road'?" It turns out that it can be a *line* that you follow on a map to get from point A to point B, an *area*, if you are planning right-of-way, or a *solid*, if you are building it. This uses extensive parts of the **Facility** model and the **Asset** model, but with a great deal more intricacy.

Figure Five-1 shows these models in the context of the overall effort.

A Word of Advice—and an Invitation

All of these models are derived from the Enterprise and Functional Model already presented in this book. Where your author contends that the Level 0 and Level 1 models are substantively true as a representation of the fundamental structure of any organization, the particular models shown for both Levels 2 and 3 may be different from what you understand of those areas. These are not presented as the absolutely true final answer. Instead they are presented as examples of how to go about creating a model that does meet your needs. Each assertion in this model that causes the reader to say, "Hey! That's not right!"—has met your author's objective of stimulating thought on modeling issues. He would only request that you note down your disagreement and forward it to him (*modeling@essentialstrategies.com*). The first 10 responses will receive a free copy of *UML and Data Modeling: A Reconciliation*.

As a modeler, you are ultimately expected to produce a model that accurately and powerfully represents the business being modeled. But neither the industry model fragments in Part Five, nor the functional model fragments in Part Four are the final correct answers. What they are intended to do is to provide insights into the process required to come up with that definitive model, using the patterns of Levels 1 and 2. As for all of the other industry-specific models in your experience: Consider them your homework assignment.

Copyright © 2008 Essential Strategies, Inc.

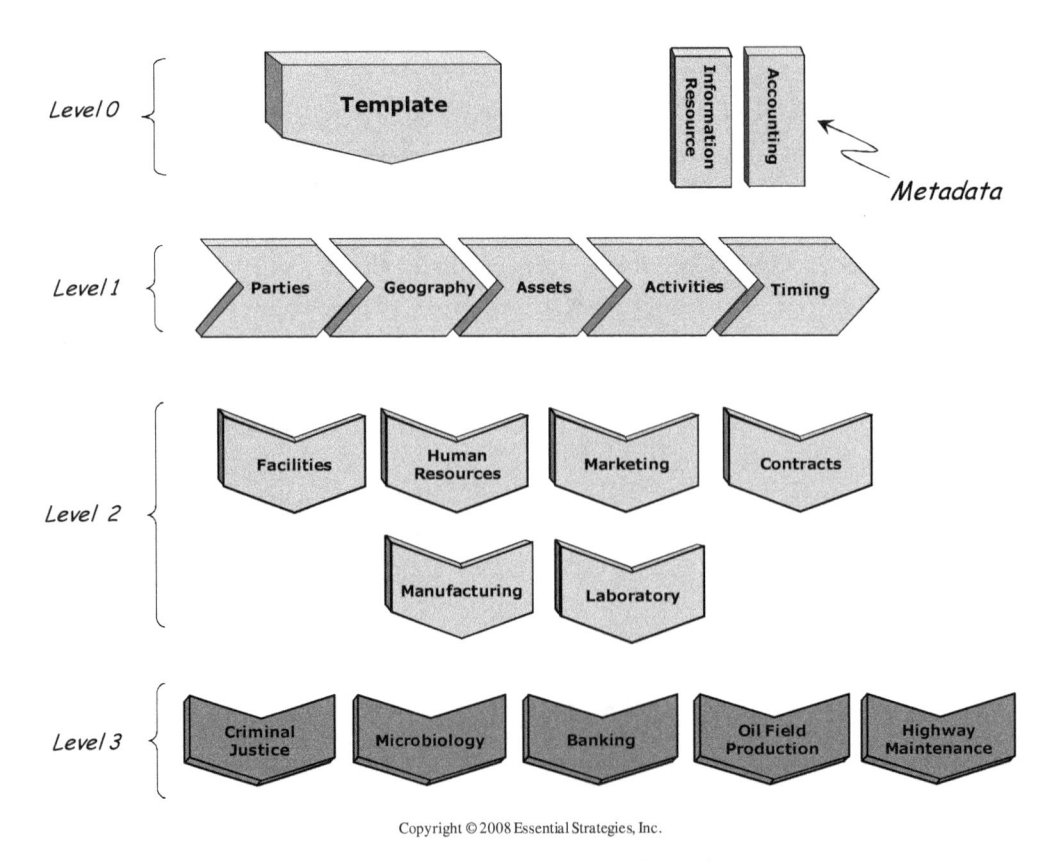

Figure Five-1: Elements of Level 3

CHAPTER 18

Criminal Justice

The model presented here is based on something called the "Global Justice XML Data Model" (GJXDM)—developed in XML by the United States Department of Justice. Since the objective of that "model" was to address inter-communications among departments, XML was chosen for its strength in creating communications structures. Unfortunately, XML is not as good at helping people understand what's behind those communications. The model created here is an attempt to reveal more graphically the semantic structure of GJXDM. It was done as an exercise, so it has not yet been blessed by anyone in the justice community. There is no consensus about the "truth" of the model. Your author contends, however, that data modeling is a much better vehicle for acquiring such a consensus than is XML. The result presented here is derived from the documentation of the Global Justice XML Data Model and it does seem a reasonable "layman's view" of the criminal justice system.

After the Global Justice XML Data Model was completed, the Justice Department teamed up with the Department of Homeland Security to create the "National Information Exchange Model" (NIEM). This entails a more sophisticated approach to XML to make it a bit more constrained, and therefore a bit more readable - at least to the relational database community. It has also been extended beyond the realm of Justice Department concerns to be more available to other agencies in other fields. It is to be hoped that at some point, a more graphic version of the NIEM model will be available to allow for validation by the non-technical community that it must serve.

You will note, by the way, that while the language of the model shown here is mostly specific to the justice community, the underlying structure is very similar to the Enterprise Model of Level 1.

The model is in two primary parts: one describes cases, and the other describes the people and organizations involved in pursuing them.

Cases

Figure 18-1 shows our old friend **Activity** (from Chapter 7 of this book) as a component of something known in the criminal justice community as a **Case**. A case is the set of **Activities** expended to solve a particular crime or other malfeasance. The term also encompasses the court case that follows an arrest. Examples could include one with **Case Number** `"98743"` and the **Description**: `"Investigation of the murder discovered June 23, 2008 at 24738 Mulholland Drive"`. Once a suspect(s) has been arrested and brought to trial, the prosecution and trial have a separate **Case Number**, with a description such as `"Prosecution of John Smith for the murder of Mary Smith"`.

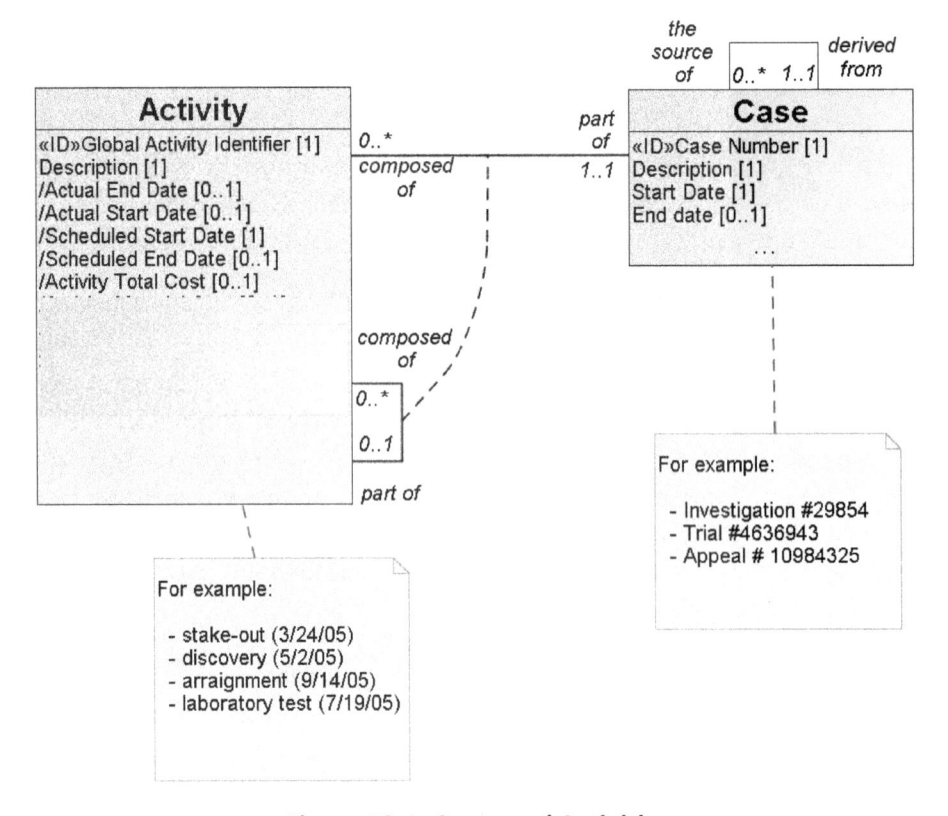

Figure 18-1: Cases and Activities

Each **Case** is usually *composed of* one or more **Activities**, which, during an investigation, can include such things as `"stake-out"`, `"interview suspect"`, and one or more `"laboratory tests"` to identify the contents of material found on the victim's clothes. During a trial, this includes the conduct of the trial itself, plus all the preparation activities done by both the prosecution and the defense. Upon conviction, it entails all the **Activities** associated with appeals, incarceration, parole, and so forth.

Each **Case** may be *the source of* one or more other **Cases**. Similarly, each **Case** may be derived from one and only one other **Case**.

Note that each **Activity** may be *composed of* one or more other **Activities**, which means that an **Activity** must be either *part of* a **Case** or *part of* another **Activity**.

Figure 18-2 adds to the model the concepts of **Case Type** and **Activity Type**. A **Case Type** is the definition of a *fundamental* category of **Cases**, such as "Investigation", "Trial", "Appeal", and so forth. An **Activity Type**, similarly, is the definition of a *fundamental* category of **Activities**, such as "Arraignment", "Stake out", "Discovery", "Hearing", et cetera. Each **Case**, then, must be *an example of* one and only one **Case Type**, while each **Activity** must be *an example of* one and only one **Activity Type**. (From the other direction, each **Activity Type** may be *embodied in* one or more **Activities**, and each **Case Type** may be *embodied in* one or more **Cases**.) Note that these are only the definition of categories. Instances of **Case** and **Activity** are things that actually happen.

For example, a **Case** might be defined with the **Case Number** of "ea-4567324", the **Description** of "Robbery of Chase Bank Branch on 432 Mulberry Street August 8, 2005". This could be *an example of* the **Case Type** whose description is "Robbery Investigation".

Note that certain **Activity Types** are only appropriate for certain **Cases**. For example, instances of the **Case Type** "Trial" would be composed of instances of **Activity Types** "Arraignment", "Discovery", "Trial day", "Verdict", et cetera. Instances of such a **Case Type** presumably would not be *composed of* instances of the **Activity Type** "Stake out". **Case Activity Rule**, then, is the fact that instances of a particular **Activity Type** are appropriate for instances of a particular **Case Type**. In other words, each **Activity** must obey the following business rule:

Enterprise Model Patterns

Business Rule

- Each **Activity** can only be *an example of* an **Activity Type** that is *part of* a **Case Activity Rule** that is *the presence of* a **Case Type** that is *embodied in* the **Case** that the **Activity** in question is *part of*. *(Translation:* **Case Activity Rule** assures that only **Activities** can be specified that are appropriate for the **Case** they are *part of*.)

Activity 0..* *part of* / *composed of* 1..1 **Case**

embodied in 0..* — *embodied in* 0..*

Case Activity Rule
«ID»Sequence Number [1]
Comment [0..1]{nonunique}

part of 0..* / *composed of* 0..*

an example of 1..1 — *the presence of* 1..1 — *the presence in* 1..1 — *an example of* 1..1

Activity Type
«ID»Global Activity Type Identifier [1]
Description [1]
Name [1]

Case Type
«ID»Name [1]
Description [1]

For example:
- Arraignment
- Discovery
- Laboratory Test

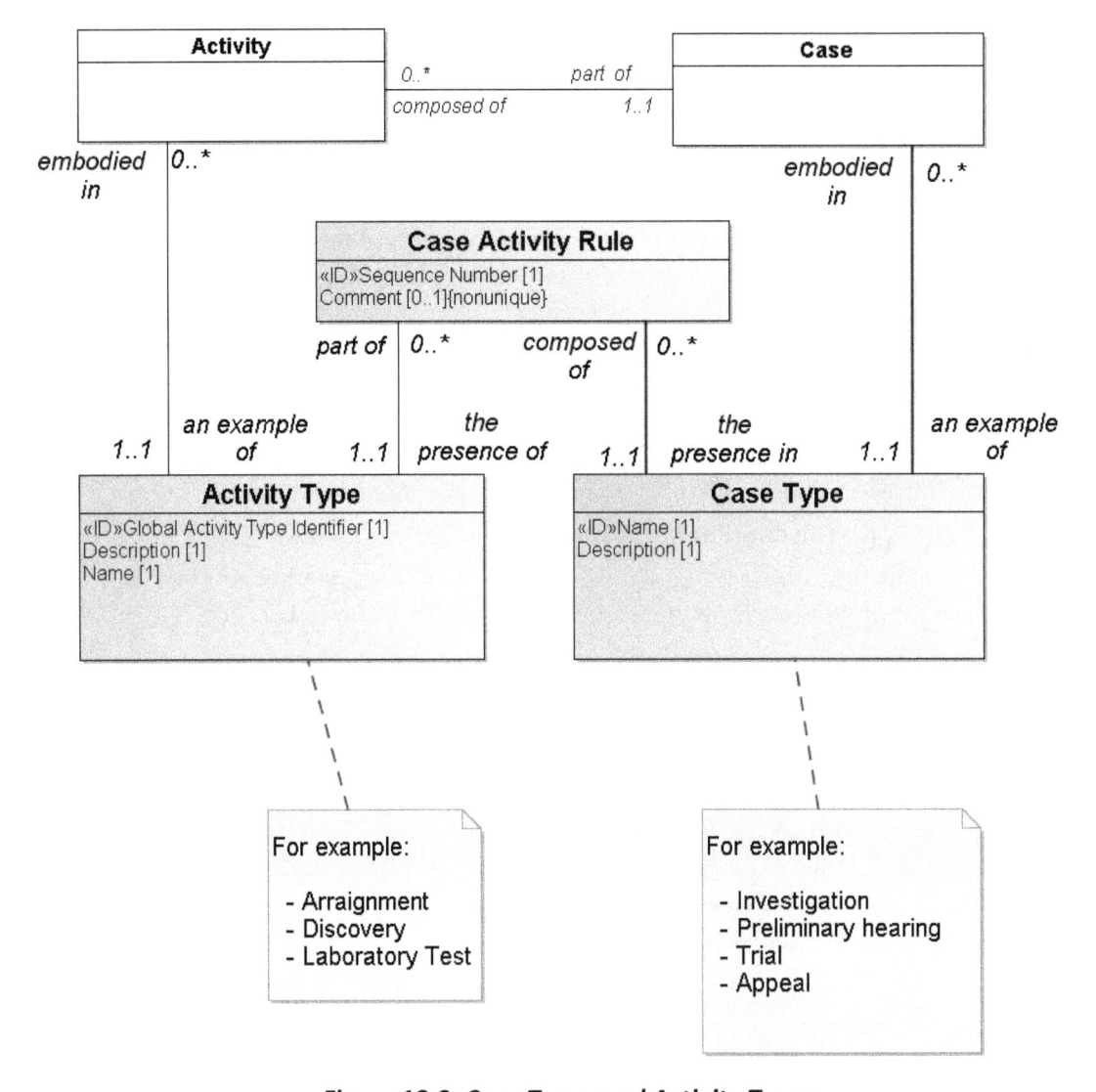

For example:
- Investigation
- Preliminary hearing
- Trial
- Appeal

Figure 18-2: Case Types and Activity Types

Evidence and Status

Figure 18-3 adds the concepts of evidence and status to the model. A piece of **Evidence** is any document, hair fragment, DNA sample, or other substance or object that may have relevance to a **Case**. To be **Evidence**, it must be *submitted to* a **Case**. Each (piece of) **Evidence** must be *an example of* one and only one **Evidence Type**, such as "Document" or "Image".

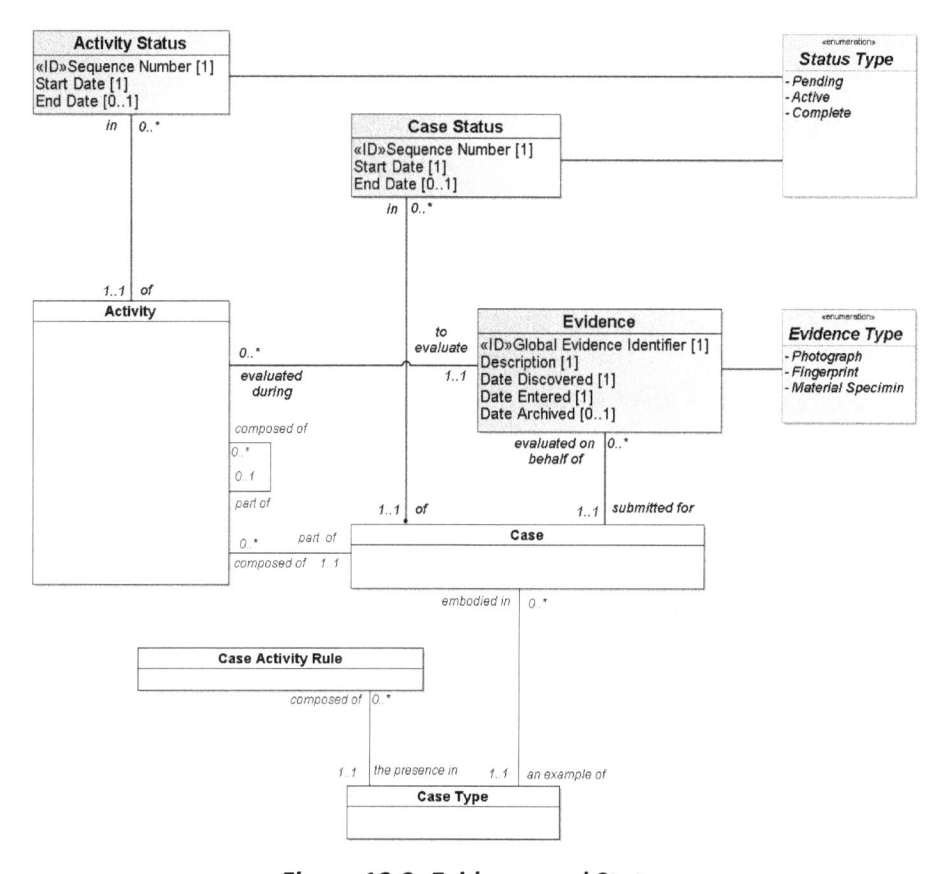

Figure 18-3: Evidence and Status

In addition, both **Activities** and **Cases** are managed in terms of their status. That is, each **Case** may be in one or more **Case Stati** in the course of its life. Similarly, each **Activity** may be in one or more **Activity Stati**. Each **Case Status** or **Activity Status** must be *an example of* one **Status Type**. **Status Types**, in their simplest form, could be "Pending", "Scheduled", "Active", or "Complete", but of course they can be defined to be anything, depending on the agency's project management practices. Some **Status Types** may be only appropriate to either **Activity Status** or **Case Status**, but not both.

Note that in Figure 18-3, **Status Type** and **Evidence Type** are both shown with the annotation "<<enumeration>>".

This is a UML feature that allows us to list sample values, instead of listing the attributes of the **Status Type** and **Evidence Type** entity classes. (The attributes in all cases are simply **Name** and **Description**, so it is not really necessary to repeat them.) This is a bit neater than attaching annotations with sample values, as was done in Figure 18-2. Later, we will encounter type entity classes that are themselves part of more complex structures, so this won't work for them. But it is useful here.

Linking to the Enterprise Model

The reader should have already figured out that **Case** looks suspiciously like **Project** from the **Activity** model in Chapter 7. Indeed, it is a logical sub-type of **Project**, as shown in Figure 18-4. This means, among other things, that the relationship from **Case** to **Activity** is, in fact, a sub-type of the relationship between **Project** and **Activity**.

The constraint that asserted that "each **Activity** must be *part of* either one **Case** or one other **Activity** actually was inherited (via the sub-type relationship) from the assertion that each **Activity** must be either *part of* one ***Project*** or one other **Activity**.

A second connection to the Enterprise Model is the recognition that **Evidence** consists of something—either a **Sample** that is a physical **Asset** or an **Information Resource Instance** such as an e-mail message, a map, or someone's notes on the back of an envelope. Thus, in Figure 18-4, each piece of **Evidence** must be either *the use of* a **Sample** that may or may not be *known to be* a particular **Specified Material**, or *the use of* a particular **Information Resource Instance**. The **Information Resource** is either a **Document** or an **Image**.

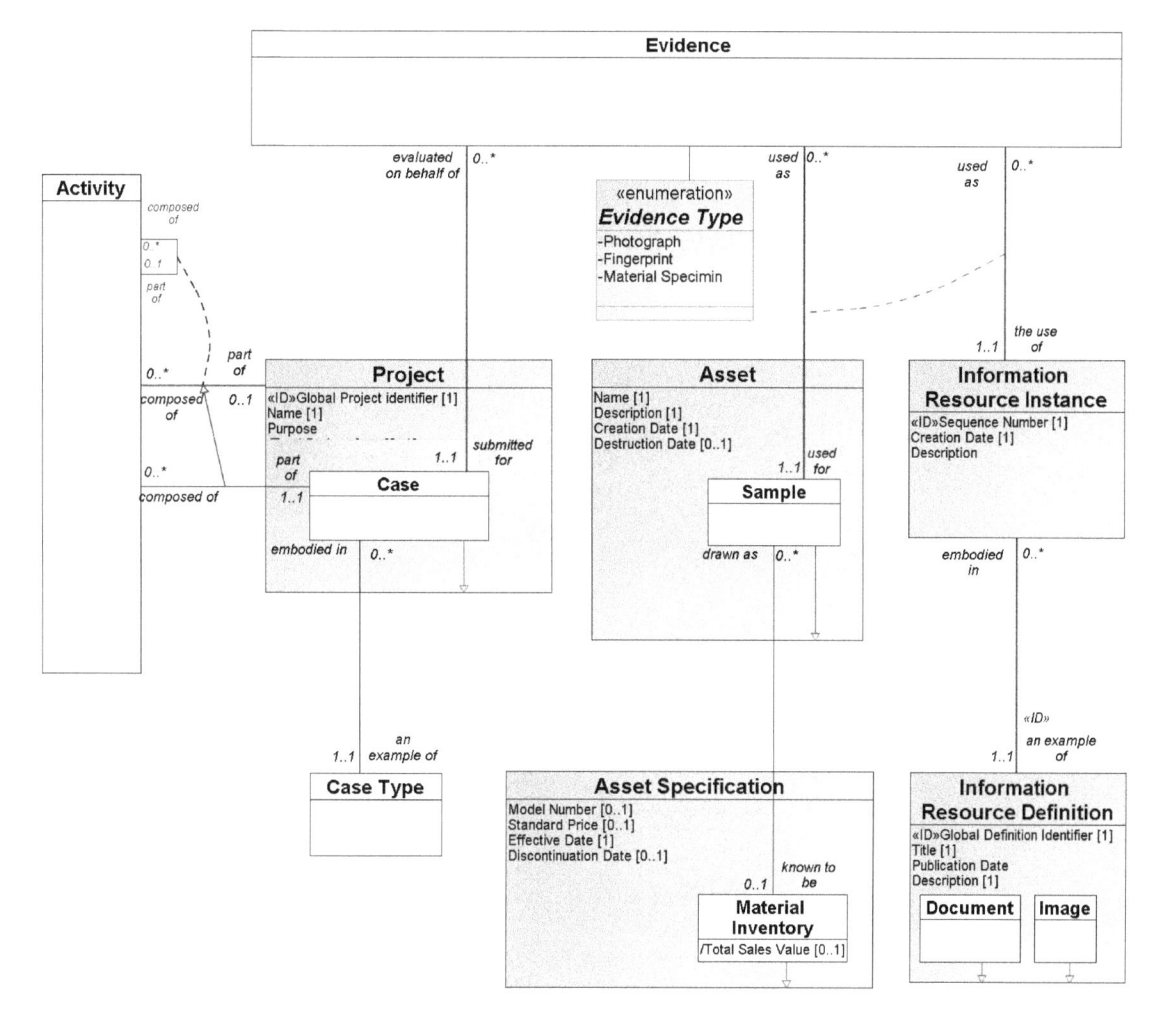

Figure 18-4: Linking to the Enterprise Model

Events

The story of a **Case** is told through its **Events**. Each **Activity** may be *triggered by* one or more **Events**, each of which must be *an example of* exactly one **Event Type**, such as "Occurrence of a crime", "Suspect decides to confess", et cetera. Each **Event** must be *the trigger of exactly one* **Activity** (which of course could be an umbrella for a set of other **Activities)**, and it must be *during* one and only one **Case**. This is all represented in Figure 18-5. An **Event** must be either an **External Event**, outside the control of the agency, or an **Internal Event**, under the control of the agency—typically the completion of an **Activity**.

368 Enterprise Model Patterns

An **Event** is recorded because it is *the trigger of* an **Activity**. "Commission of a crime" is an **External Event** that triggers an **Activity**. For example, the occurrence of a "bank robbery" is *the trigger of* an **Activity**, such as when a bystander sets out to "call the police". Some **External Events** may be recorded, however, even if they are not the immediate *trigger of* an **Activity**. Hence the model simply asserts that each **Event** <u>may</u> be *trigger of* one **Activity**.

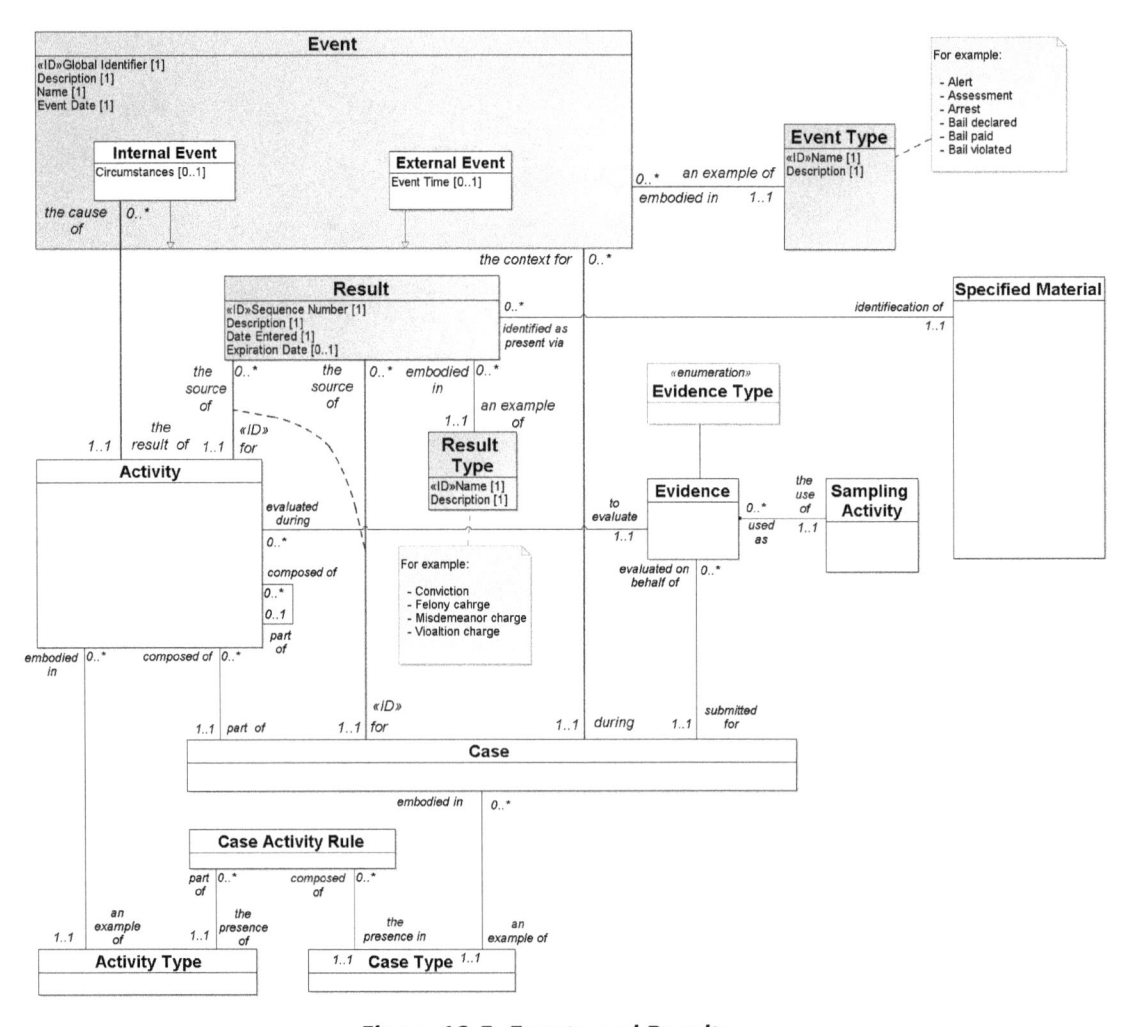

Figure 18-5: Events and Results

An **Activity**, in turn, may be *the cause of* another **Internal Event** that, in turn, is *the trigger of* another **Activity**. That is, an **External Event**, such as the aforementioned occurrence of a "bank robbery" is *the trigger of* an **Activity**, such as a bystander "calling the police". This **Activity**, in turn, is *the cause of* an **Internal Event**, that, in turn, is *the trigger of* the **Activity** "initiation of Case #34564". Each **Activity**, in sequence, then (via an **Internal Event**) triggers the next one or several other **Activities**, such as `"Dispatch officers to the scene"`, and so forth.

Both **Cases** and **Activities** may be *the source of* one or more **Results**, each of which must be *an example of* one **Result Type**, such as `"Charge"`, or `"Incarceration"`. Each **Result Type** may further be *a super-type of* one or more other **Result Types**. So, for example, a `"Charge"` may be either as a `"Felony"`, `"Misdemeanor"`, et cetera.

Again, in the notation, the dashed line connecting relationships means an "exclusive or". So here, each **Result** must be either *for* one **Activity**, or *for* one **Case**.

People and Organizations

The second half of the Criminal Justice model makes extensive use of the **Party** entity class described in Chapter 4 of this book. Indeed, the structure is identical, but the population of the supporting entity classes describes this arena more specifically.

Figure 18-6 repeats the representation of **Party**, as described more extensively in Chapter 4. The reader may recall that the sub-types of **Party** are **Person** and **Organization**. As with the earlier example, an **Organization** may be any of the following sub-types:

- **Company** – a commercial organization, such as a corporation, partnership, or sole proprietorship.
- **Government Agency** – a component of a national government that performs a specified function, such as the FBI, Federal Communications Commission, Federal Drug Administration, et cetera.
- **Government** – the organization with jurisdiction and control for a **Geopolitical Area**.
- **Other Organization** – which could include professional societies, terrorist organizations, labor unions, et cetera.

Here, however, the original **Internal Organization** is separated into **Company Department** and **Government Internal Organization**. Because the domain is fundamentally a government function, it is reasonable to give **Government Internal Organization** special status. Also new is the concept of a **Political Organization**, such as a political party, `"Greenpeace"`, or a `"Non-Governmental Organization"`.

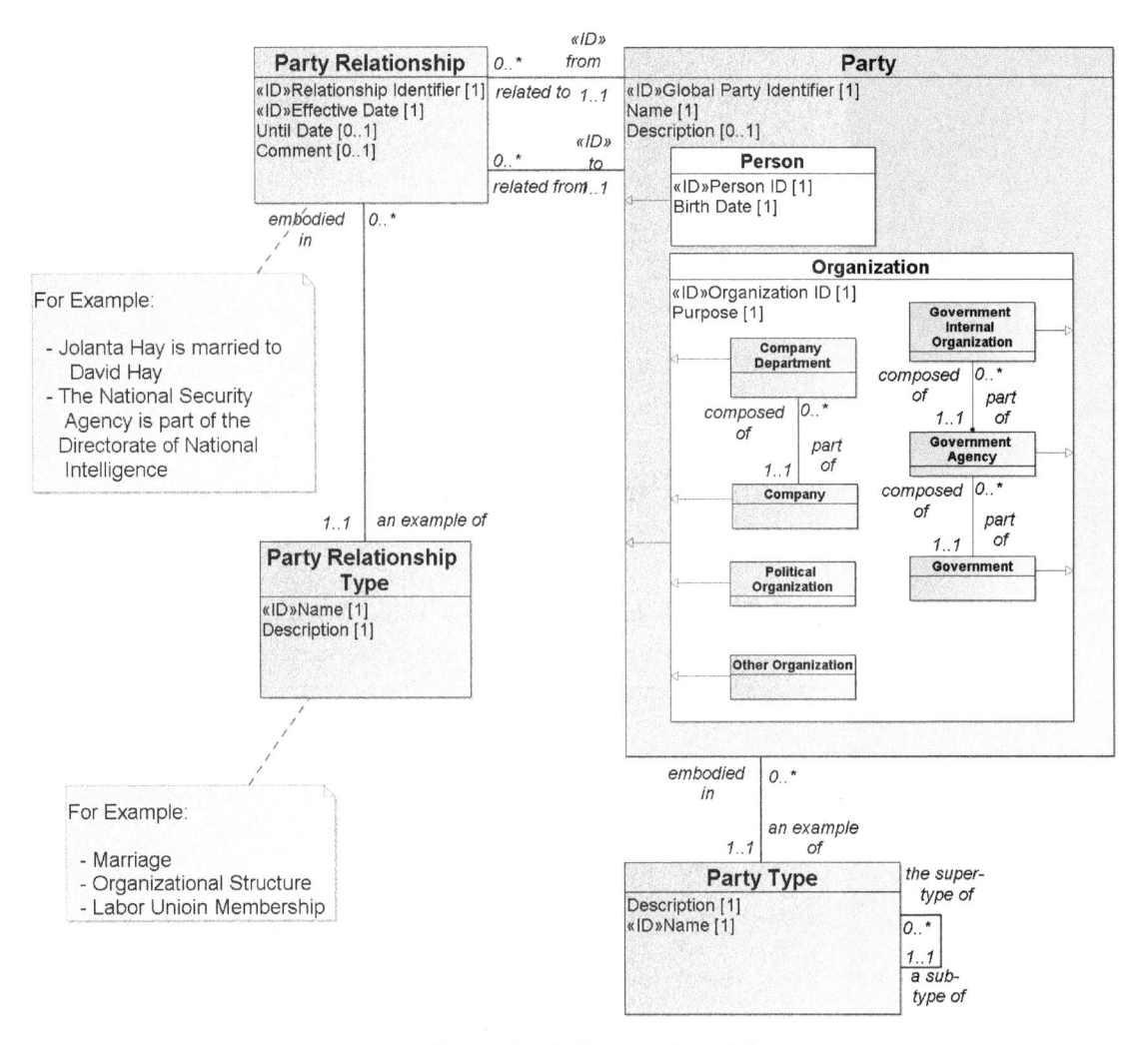

Figure 18-6: Parties (Again)

Figure 18-6 also repeats **Party Relationship** and **Party Relationship Type** from Chapter 4. In addition, however, the model includes explicit relationships between pairs of **Party** sub-types.

Specifically:

- Each **Company Department** must be *part of* one and only one **Company**.
- Each **Company** may be *composed of* one or more **Company Departments**.
- Each **Government Internal Organization** must be *part of* one and only one **Government Agency**.
- Each **Government Agency** may be *composed of* one or more **Government Internal Organizations**.

- Each **Government Agency** must be *part of* one and only one **Government**.
- Each **Government** may be *composed of* one or more **Government Agencies**.

In addition to `Organizational Structure`, examples of Party Relationship Type could include `Marriage`, `Union Membership`, et cetera.

Characteristics and Categories

The model for Criminal Justice (continued in Figure 18-7) relies heavily on the **Party Characteristic** entity class, first described in Chapter 4. Here, however, instead of making **Party Category** a sub-type of **Party Characteristic** (along with **Continuous Party Characteristic**), **Party Characteristic** and **Party Category** are separated. This makes no difference in the logic of the model. The figure does add the concept of **Category Scheme**, however, which groups categories together.

A **Characteristic** is a parameter or attribute that can accept a continuous value, such as a real number or a date. (This is equivalent to **Continuous Party Characteristic** in Chapter 4.) Examples include, for **Person**, `Height`, `Weight`, and so forth. For **Company** or **Government Agency**, it might include `Number of Employees`. **Party Characteristic Value** specifies a particular Characteristic Value for the **Party Characteristic**, *to describe* a particular **Party**.

For those parameters that take discrete values, such as `Baptist`, `$50,000 to $75,000`, or `blonde`, the entity class **Party Category** actually contains each possible value for the **Party Category Scheme**. The entity class **Party Classification** simply asserts that a particular **Party** is classified *into* a particular **Party Category**. In this case, the **Party Categories** specified would each be *part of* a **Party Category Scheme**—in these cases, religion, income range, and hair color.

The fact that a particular **Party** falls into a particular **Party Category** is an instance of **Party Classification**. In this case, there is no **Value**, since the **Party** simply *is* in the **Party Category**. **Effective Date** and **Until Date** do apply here, though.

In the example shown on the drawing, the **Party Category Scheme** `Scars, Marks, and Tattoos`, contains the **Party Categories** `ART ARM` (`Arm, non specific, artificial`), `ART BRST` (`Breast, nonspecific artificial`), and so forth. **Party Classification** *of* a

372 Enterprise Model Patterns

Person *into* one of these categories is the assertion that that **Person**, in fact, has one of those scars, marks, and/or tattoos, such as an "Arm, non-specific, artificial" tattoo.

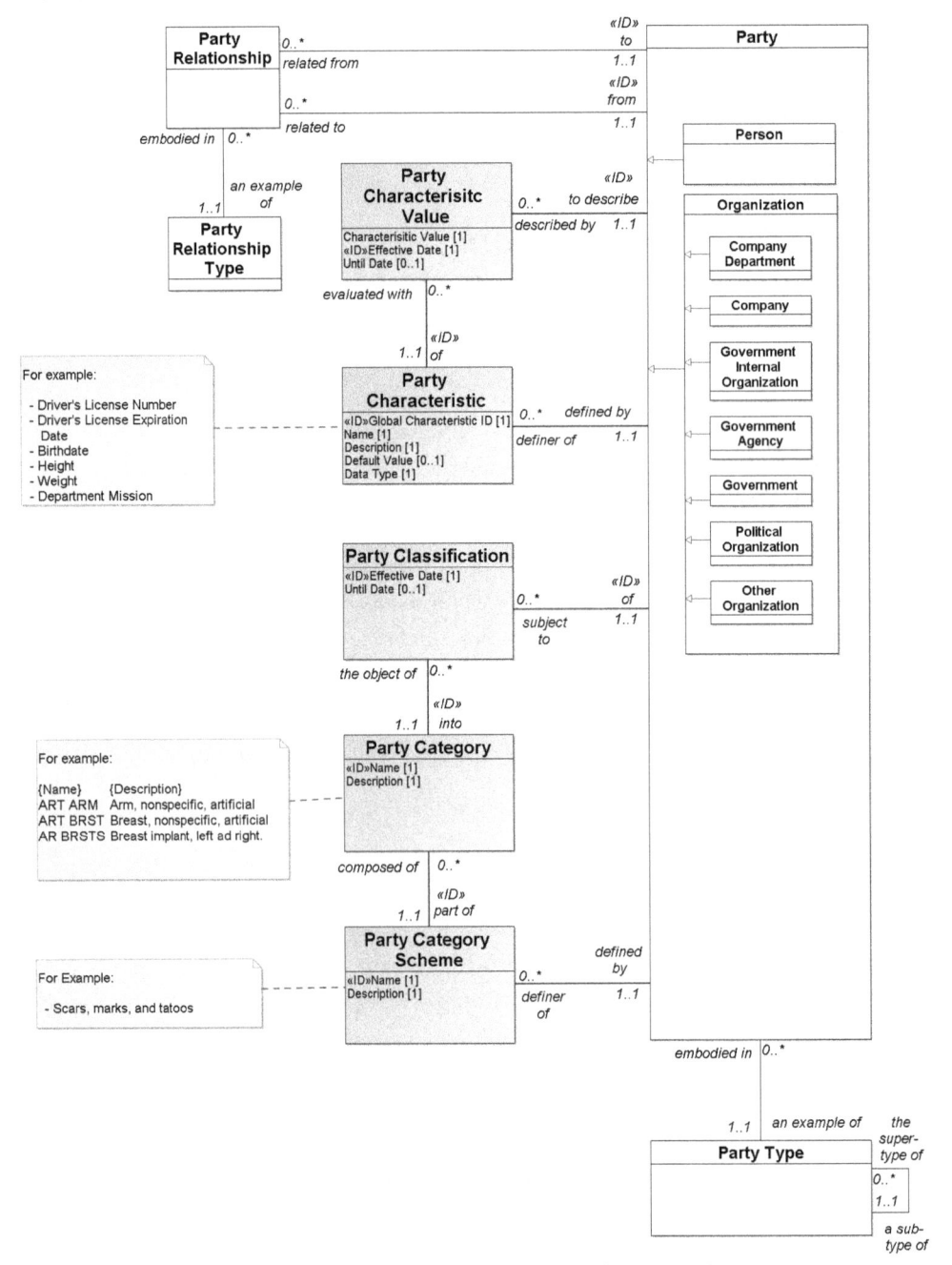

Figure 18-7: Characteristics and Categories

Note that this is an alternative to the approach taken in Chapter 4, where a **Party Category** was shown as a sub-type of **Party Characteristic**, and was *constrained to* a set of **Legal Party Category Values**. The entity class **Party Characteristic Value** would then provide a Characteristic Value, and an external business rule required that value to be equivalent to one of the **Legal Party Category Values**. In effect, the **Party Category** in the Chapter 4 version is equivalent to the **Party Category Scheme** shown here. The **Party Category Legal Value** in Chapter 4 is the **Party Category** shown here.

The Chapter 4 version is more abstract and a bit more compact intellectually, showing that categories are in the same category (if you'll pardon the expression) as characteristics. The version shown here is a bit more direct and easier to see and explain.

Employment

The employment model shown in Chapter 13 applies directly here. In this case, we are looking at **Position Types** such as "Police Officer", "Detective", "District Attorney", and so forth. This provides for actual **Positions** in Houston (Harris County), Texas to be "Houston Police Officer", "Harris County Judge", "Harris County District Attorney", and so forth. This is shown in Figure 18-8.

Roles

Figure 18-9 finally links the **Person** and **Organization** part of the model to the **Cases** part of the model shown previously. In it, we see that **Persons** and **Organizations** play multiple roles in carrying out both **Cases** and **Activities**. Specifically, a **Case Role** is the fact that a particular **Person** or **Organization** has something to do with a **Case**. What that something might be is shown by the **Case Role Type**. That is, each **Case Role** must be *played by* one **Party**, *for* a **Case**, and it must be *an example of* one **Case Role Type**. For example, "Edward Nottingham" played the **Case Role** (an example of the **Case Role Type** "Presiding Judge") over a **Case** that consisted of a trial conducted from "January 23rd, 2004" (**Effective Date**) through "January 29th, 2004" (**Until Date**).

Similarly, an **Activity Role** is the fact that a particular **Person** or **Organization** has something to do with an **Activity**. Again, that is determined by the **Activity Role Type** that the **Activity Role** is *an example of*. For example, if the **Activity** is an example of the **Activity Type** "Laboratory Test", an appropriate **Activity Role Type** might be "Performer of the test". This would be performed

374 Enterprise Model Patterns

by "Sarah Schofield", who has the **Position** of "Laboratory Analyst, level 2".

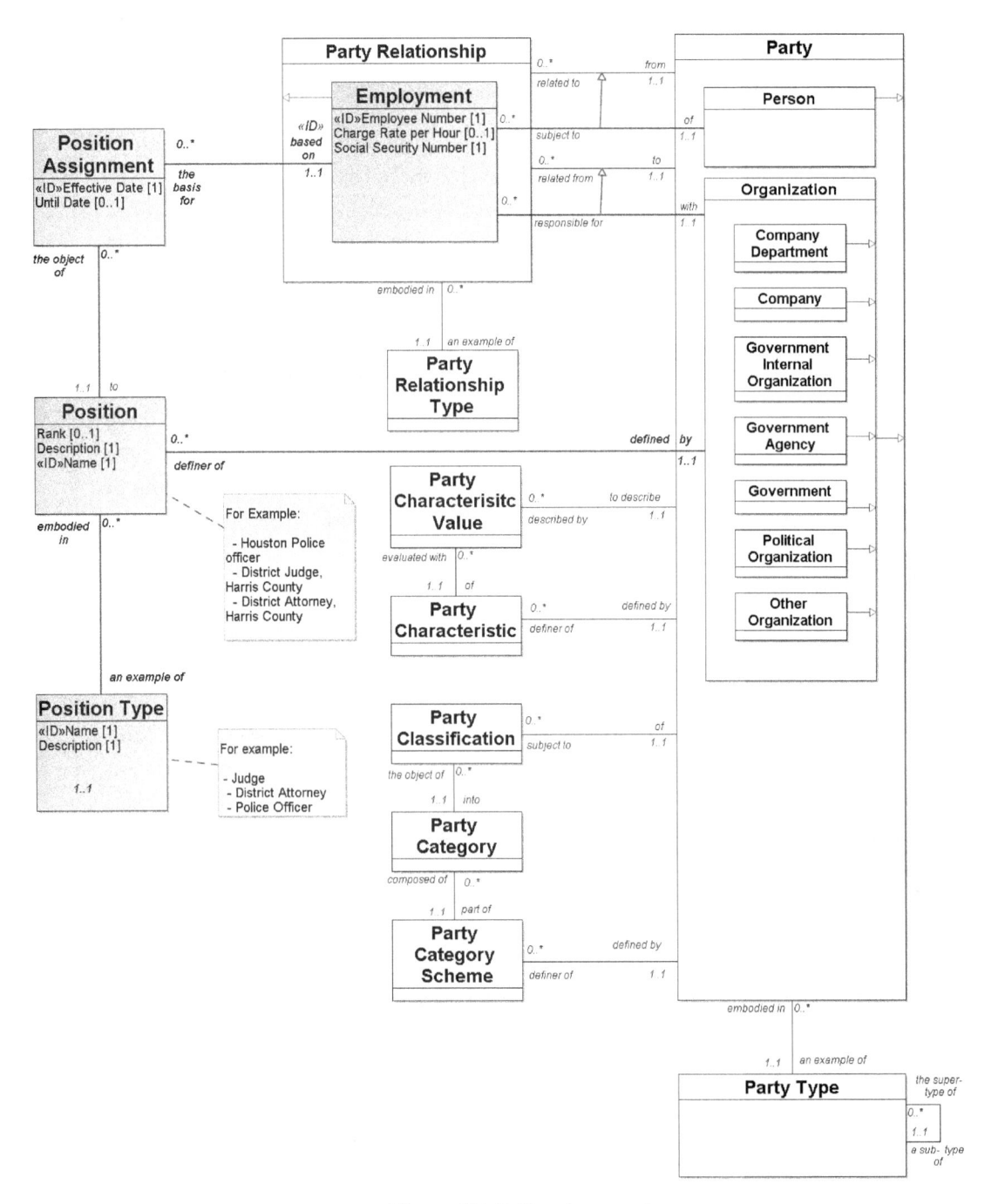

Figure 18-8: Employment

It is in the definition of specific **Case Roles** and **Activity Roles** that this model is tailored to a particular criminal justice organization. Typical roles could be `"The Accused"`, `"Judge"`, `"Defense Attorney"`, and so forth.

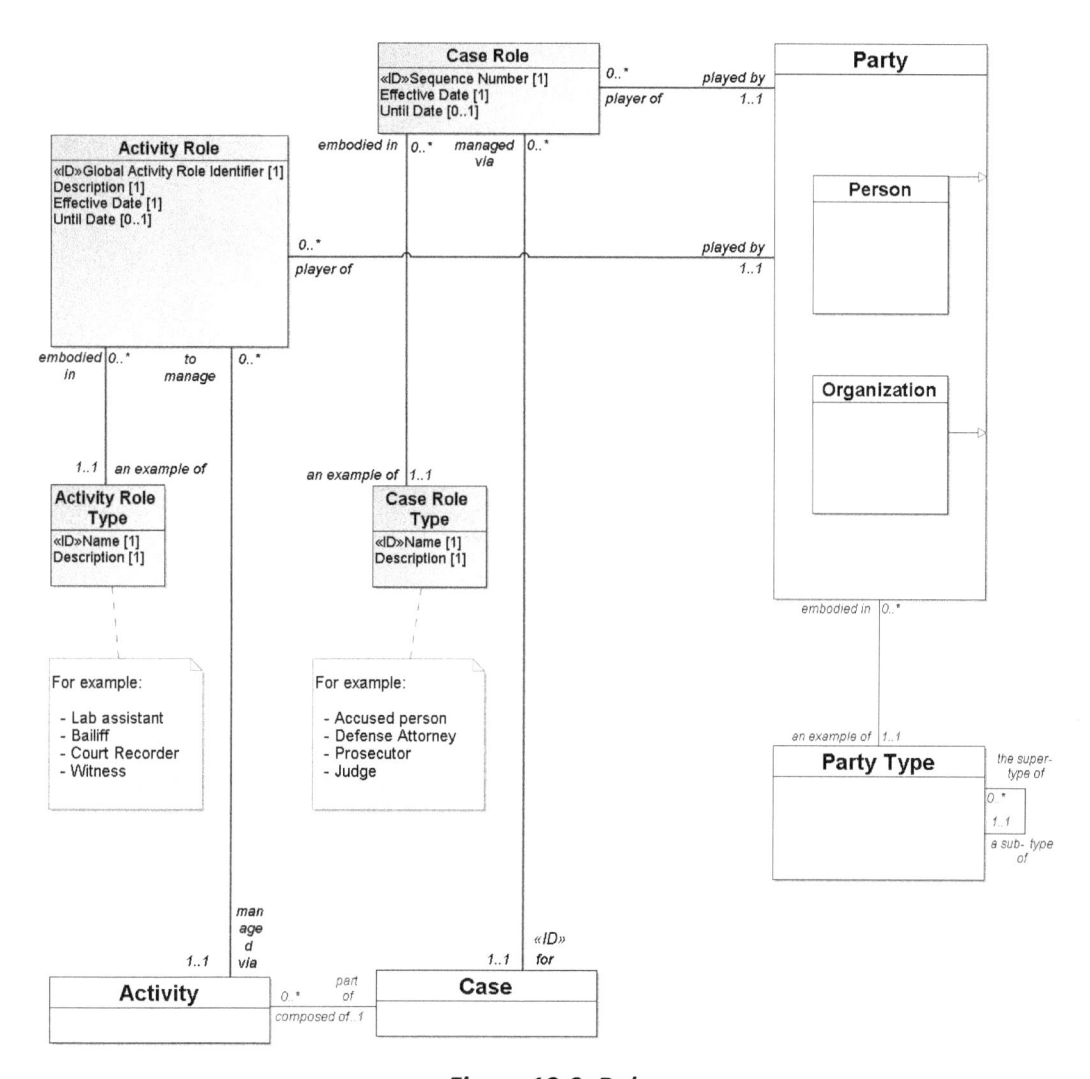

Figure 18-9: Roles

Figure 18-10 shows how roles can be defined in advance. Essentially, the figure asserts that a given **Position** (no matter who holds it) may be *authorized to perform* either an **Activity Role Type** or a **Case Role Type** (or both—note the absence of an exclusive or constraint between the two relationships), and each of these must be *played for*, respectively, an **Activity Type** or a **Case Type**.

Thus, an `"FBI Agent"` is *authorized to play* the **Activity Role Type** `"Arresting officer"`, for the **Activity Type** `"Arrest"`. A `"Houston

Police Officer"` would also be so authorized. A `"Harris County Judge"` would be authorized to play the **Case Role Type** of `"Presiding Judge"` for a **Case Type** `"Criminal Trial"`.

In this example, where Edward Nottingham played the **Case Role** (an example of the **Case Role Type** `"Presiding Judge"`) over a **Case** that consisted of a trial conducted from January 23rd through January 29th, 2004, presumably, Edward Nottingham held the **Position** of `"Harris County Judge"`.

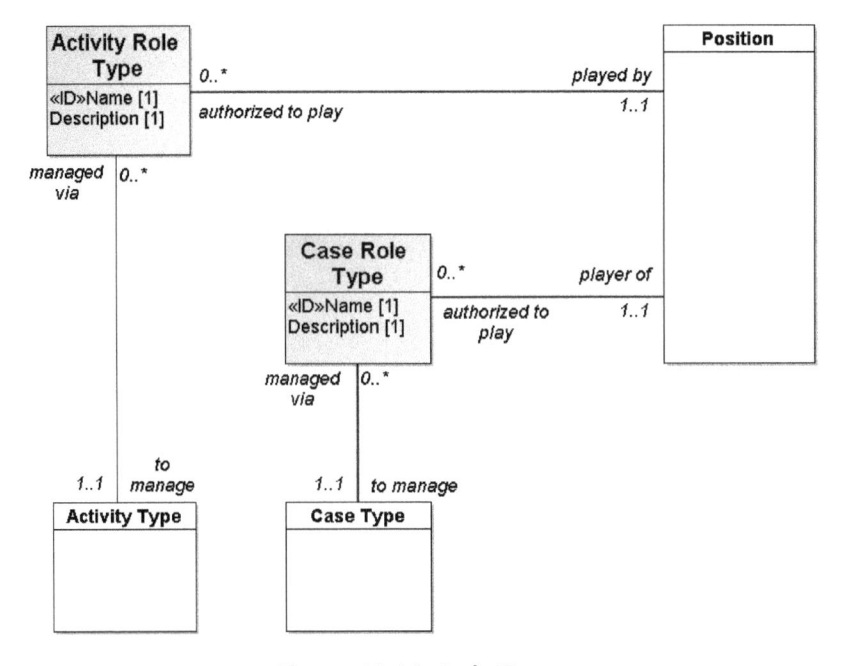

Figure 18-10: Role Types

Summary

This first detailed industry model is in fact little more than the Level 1 model with extensive renaming. It is an elaboration on the **Activities Model** of Chapter 7 and the **People and Organizations** model of Chapter 4. **Evidence** is the only significant addition. **Status** is also an addition, but this has general applicability.

Note that to use this model more generally, it is necessary to rename **Case** to something like **Project** and to update the *contents* of the various **...Type** entity classes.

The next industry-specific models will diverge more from the Level 1 and 2 models.

CHAPTER 19

Microbiology

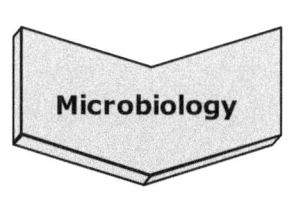

Data modeling provides an excellent vehicle for understanding all kinds of domains of discourse, not just in the business or technology field. A project with a client active in biotechnology gave your author an opportunity to relearn some of his high school chemistry and add to that a body of knowledge that has grown considerably since his high school days. A large part of the model developed for that client is proprietary, but it has given permission to reveal the basic model of microbiology, presented here.

Interestingly enough, this is not a departure from the Enterprise Model presented earlier. Instead, it takes a couple of that model's premises and drives them into considerably more detail.

Basic Chemistry

Figure 19-1 shows the three kinds of matter that we all learned about in high school chemistry class: elements (here **Chemical Elements**), compounds (here **Chemical Compounds**), and mixtures (here **Chemical Formulations**).[*]

Chemical Elements are the basic substances that everything else is made up of. A quantity of a **Chemical Element** consists of identical atoms, each consisting of a nucleus consisting of protons and neutrons, plus a number of electrons orbiting the nucleus. This is the simplified explanation. The reality is vastly more subtle and complex than this, but this is enough knowledge of atomic physics for our purposes here.

---

[*] You did take chemistry in high school, yes? Ok, if not, have some patience as we teach you what you might have missed.

378 Enterprise Model Patterns

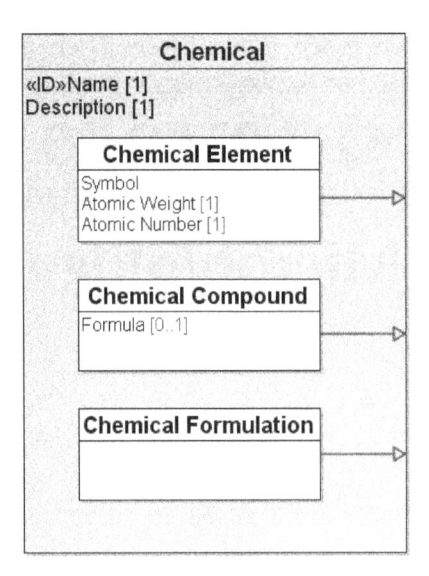

Figure 19-1: Chemicals

The set of 122 known **Chemical Elements** are typically organized by Atomic Number (the number of protons in its nucleus). The first 92 **Chemical Elements** are naturally occurring. Between 1940 and 2009, an additional 20 "transuranic" elements have been created in minute quantities.[61]

A **Chemical Compound** is an assembly of **Chemical Elements** that are bound together at the atomic level. It consists of identical molecules, each of which is a collection of atoms physically linked together in a way that makes them difficult to separate. Water, for example, is a compound, with each of its molecules consisting of two hydrogen atoms tightly linked to one oxygen atom. The combination of atoms that is possible for a particular set of atoms is constrained by each atom's structure. Each **Chemical Compound** is described uniquely by a formula capturing the number of atoms of each kind in the compound. The formula for water, for example is H2O, signifying the two hydrogen ("H") atoms and one oxygen ("O") atom involved. Fragments of atomic structures that can appear in multiple kinds of molecules are called radicals. For example, the amino radical has the formula –NH2, and the carboxyl radical has the formula –COOH. Showing the oxygen atoms strung out like that between the carbon and hydrogen atoms, instead of simply saying CO2H, indicates something about the radical's physical structure.

---

[61] Wikipedia. 2010a. "Recently Discovered Elements".
http://en.wikipedia.org/wiki/Chemical_element#Recently_discovered_elements (accessed June 14, 2010).

A mixture (a **Chemical Formulation**) is any collection of elements and/or compounds whose atoms are not chemically bound together. That chocolate cake consisting of flour, shortening, cocoa, and sugar, is a mixture because none of the ingredients are chemically bound together at the molecular level.

Biochemistry[*]

The world we live in is made up of elements, compounds, and mixtures. There is a select number of **Chemical Compounds** (called **Organic Compounds**) that make up the living parts of our world. These are the basic building blocks of life, and are shown in Figure 19-2. They fall into two major groups, as defined in the following sections.

What Life is Made of

Every cell of every living organism consists of **Proteins** that are composed of compounds called **Amino Acids**. Here are the definitions of these:

- **Amino Acid** – "A group of nitrogenous organic compounds that serve as units of structure of the proteins and are essential to human metabolism."[62] "Any of a group of organic compounds containing both the carboxyl and amino groups, forming the basic constituents of proteins."[63]

- **Amino** – "Of the monovalent group (-NH2)."[64]

- **Carboxyl** – "The univalent acid radical (-COOH), present in most organic acids."[65]

---

[*] It is impossible to find definitions of these terms that don't require at least a basic knowledge of chemistry and the nature of life. To describe these more fully would require a college text book. The interested reader is referred to a good example of such a textbook, *Molecular Biology of the Cell*, written in 1994 by Bruce Alberts Dennis Bray, Julian Lewis, Martin Raff, Keith Roberts, and James D. Watson (New York: Garland Publishing). But be warned: You have to be *really* interested in microbiology to read that one. It is an excellent, well written text, but it is *very* comprehensive.

[62] "Amino Acid". 1964. *Webster's New World Dictionary of the American Language*. (Cleveland: World Publishing Company): 48.

[63] "Amino Acid". 1998. *DK Illustrated Oxford Dictionary*. (New York: Oxford University Press): 37.

[64] "Amino". 1998. *DK Illustrated Oxford Dictionary*. (New York: Oxford University Press): 37.

380 Enterprise Model Patterns

- **Protein** – "Any of a group of organic compounds composed of one or more chains of amino acids and forming an essential part of all living organisms"[66]

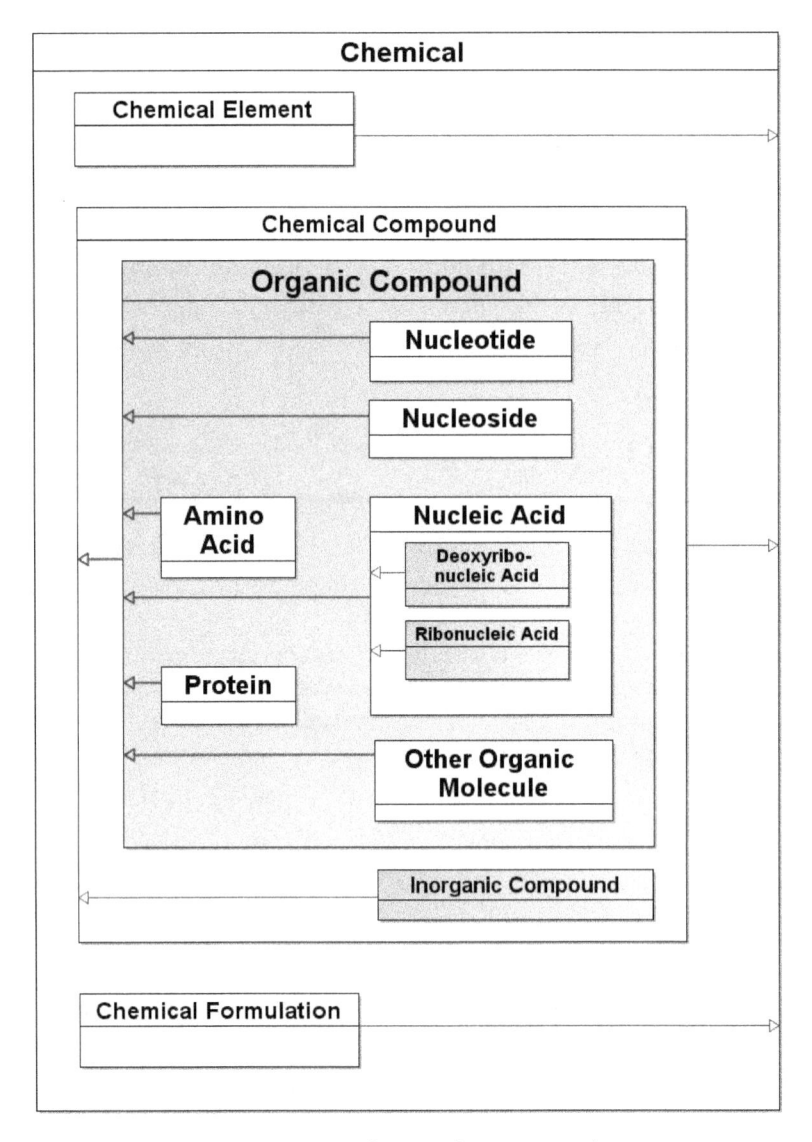

Figure 19-2: Chemical Compounds

---

[65] "Carboxyl". 1998. *DK Illustrated Oxford Dictionary*. (New York: Oxford University Press): 126.

[66] "Protein". 1998. *DK Illustrated Oxford Dictionary*. (New York: Oxford University Press): 656.

How Life is Organized

The amino acids and proteins comprise cells that are each specialized to carry out different functions in any living organism. The "roadmap" that determines what a particular cell does in this scheme is encoded in each cell's deoxyribonucleic acid (DNA). Here is the chemistry behind that:

- **Nucleic Acid** – "Either of two complex organic molecules (DNA and RNA), consisting of many nucleotides linked in a long chain, and present in all living cells."[67] "The molecule consists of linked units called nucleotides, each containing a 5 carbon sugar (ribose for RNA, deoxyribose for DNA), a purine or pyrimidine base (adenine, guanine, cytosine, thymine, or uracil), and phosphoric acid."[68]

- **Deoxyribonucleic Acid (DNA)** – "A self-replicating material present in nearly all living organisms. Esp. as a constituent of chromosomes... A DNA molecule consists of two strands that spiral around each other to form a double helix held together by sub-units called bases [adenine, guanine, cytosine, or thymine], which always pair in specific ways: adenine with thymine and cytosine with guanine."[69]

- **Ribonucleic Acid (RNA)** – "A nucleic acid present in living cells, esp. in robosomes where it is involved in protein synthesis." [Oxford, 1998, p. 705] "Nucleic acid that promotes the synthesis of proteins in the cell and in some viruses is the genetic material. The molecule consists of a single strand of nucleotides, each containing the sugar ribose, phosphoric acid, and one of four bases: adenine, guanine, cytosine, or thymine. Messenger RNA carries the information for protein synthesis from DNA in the nucleus [of the cell] to the ribosomes in the cytoplasm. Each amino acid to be formed is specified by a sequence of three bases in messenger RNA. Transfer RNA brings the amino acids to their correct position on the messenger RNA."[70]

---

[67] "Nucleic Acid". 1998. *DK Illustrated Oxford Dictionary.* (New York: Oxford University Press): 561.

[68] "Nucleic Acid". 1977. *The Random House Encyclopedia.* (New York: Random House, Inc.): 2447.

[69] "Deoxyribonucleic Acid". *1998. DK Illustrated Oxford Dictionary.* (New York: Oxford University Press): 249.

[70] "Ribonucleic Acid". 1977. *The Random House Encyclopedia.* (New York: Random House, Inc.): 2579.

- **Nucleoside** – "An organic compound consisting of a purine or pyrimidine base linked to a sugar."[71]

- **Nucleotide** – "An organic compound consisting of a nucleoside linked to a phosphate group."[72] These are linked together to form **Nucleic Acid**.

And of course, as you can imagine, this is by no means an exhaustive list of the **Organic Compounds** that have been identified. In addition, many of the client pharmaceutical company's products are themselves **Other Organic Compounds** not known previously, as well as **Non-organic Compounds**.

Composition

You may have noticed in the definition of **Protein** that it is "composed of one or more chains of amino acids", and **Nucleic Acid** is defined as "consisting of many nucleotides". A **Nucleotide** is "consisting of a nucleoside". All of these relationships, plus the more comprehensive relationship among **Chemical Elements**, **Chemical Compounds**, and **Chemical Formulations**, are shown in Figure 19-3. Note that the cardinality of these relationships is the reverse of what you normally would find. Where normally a parent object only <u>may be</u> *composed of* one or more children objects, here it is required. A **Protein** <u>must be</u> composed of at least one **Amino Acid**, or it does not exist. Similarly, a **Nucleic Acid** doesn't exist if it isn't *composed of* at least one (actually many) **Nucleotide**. And that **Nucleotide** doesn't exist if it isn't *composed of* one **Nucleoside**.

Along the same lines, each **Chemical Compound** must be *composed of* at least 2 instances of **Chemical Element**.

The most significant examples of **Chemical Formulation** are the company's products for sale. These are created by combining **Other Organic Molecules** (that they have invented), along with both **Chemical Elements** and **Inorganic Compounds** to provide bulk and additional desirable characteristics. Thus, a **Chemical Formulation** is constructed from both **Chemical Elements** and **Chemical Compounds**.

---

[71] "Nucleoside". *1998. DK Illustrated Oxford Dictionary.* (New York: Oxford University Press): 561.

[72] "Nucleotide". *1998. DK Illustrated Oxford Dictionary.* (New York: Oxford University Press): 561.

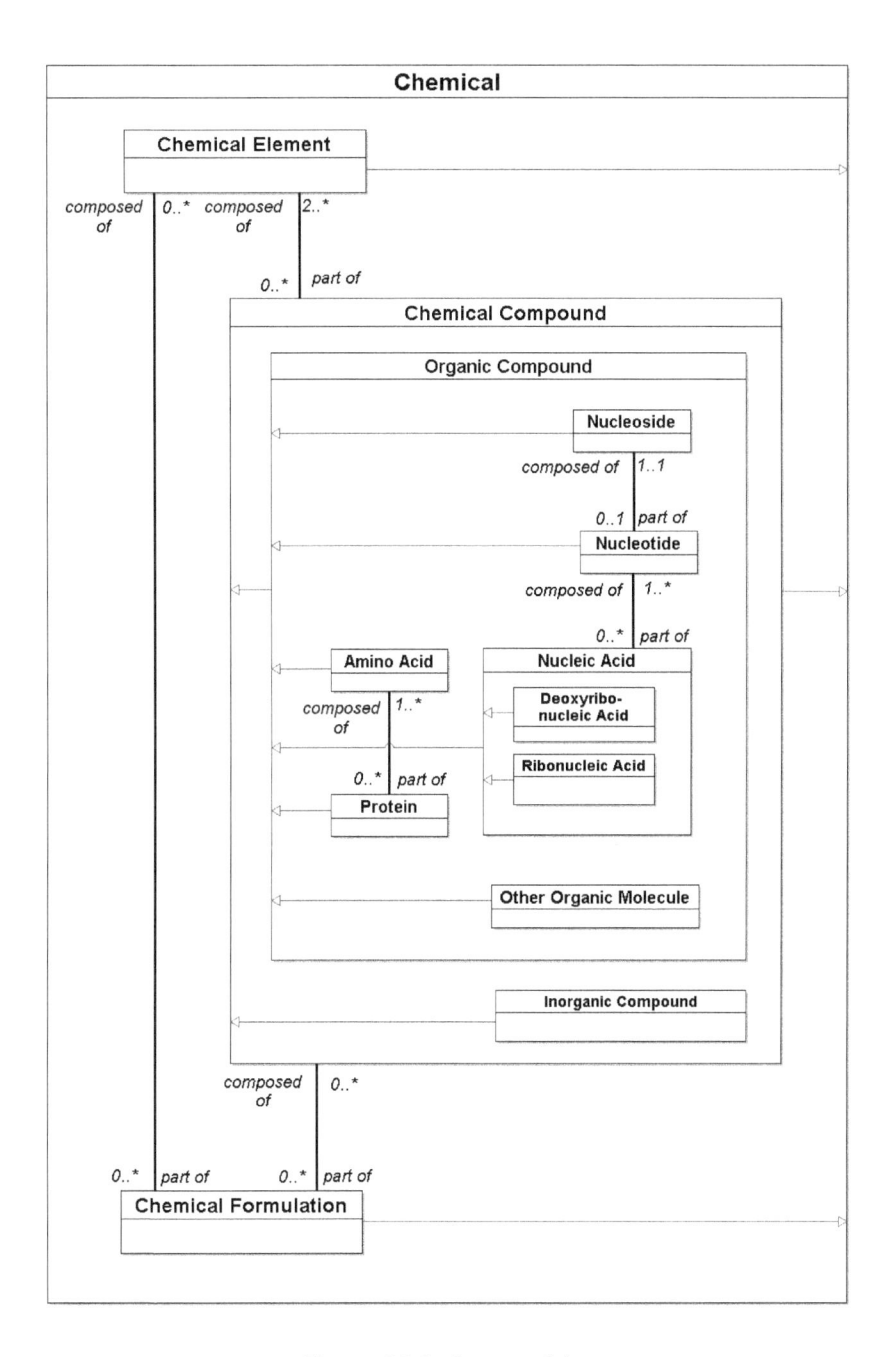

Figure 19-3: Composition

384 Enterprise Model Patterns

It cannot be shown in the drawing, but it is therefore true that:

Business Rule

- Each **Chemical Formulation** must be composed of 2 or more of either **Chemical Elements** or **Chemical Compounds**, or both. *(Translation:* Every component of a **Chemical Formulation** must be *composed of* elements and/or compounds.)

Physical Structures

Figure 19-1 shows that so far, we have *not* been talking about actual proteins and amino assets. We have been describing the specification of hypothetical **Chemicals**. Linking this back to the Enterprise Model at Level 1, it is clear that what we have been talking about are sub-types of **Asset Type**. That is, from our definition in Chapter 6, an **Asset** is "an item of value owned"[73] that has physical presence in the world. An **Asset Type** is a categorization of **Assets**. Here we are going to bend Merriam-Webster's definition of "Asset" to include parts of the physical world that are *not* owned.♣

Note that these are **Other Asset Types**, not **Asset Specifications** (as shown in Figure 19-4). This is a fundamental scheme for categorizing the physical world, with an **Asset Type** being one of those categories. There is no concern yet for how the chemicals described might be represented as products for sale.

So far we have been dealing only with the specification of assets in the pharmaceutical world. The attributes **Name**, and **Description** apply to all of the **Chemicals** we have described so far.

More significantly, note that many of the relationships just described were "many to many". By rights, this would require a separate intersect entity class for each

---

[73] Merriam-Webster. "The Merriam-Webster Online Dictionary." http://www.merriam-webster.com/dictionary/asset (accessed October 22, 2008).

♣ Naming this entity class is problematic at best. "Product", "Material", "Thing", "Stuff"—none of these really capture the full meaning of this entity class. Asset seemed good, partly because it seemed to have little in the way of unfortunate associations. Indeed, there is the concept of ownership in the word, so it may not be right for our physical compounds, but it's the best your author has come up with, so far.

occurrence of the relationships shown. In addition, there is no assurance that this includes all that should be included.

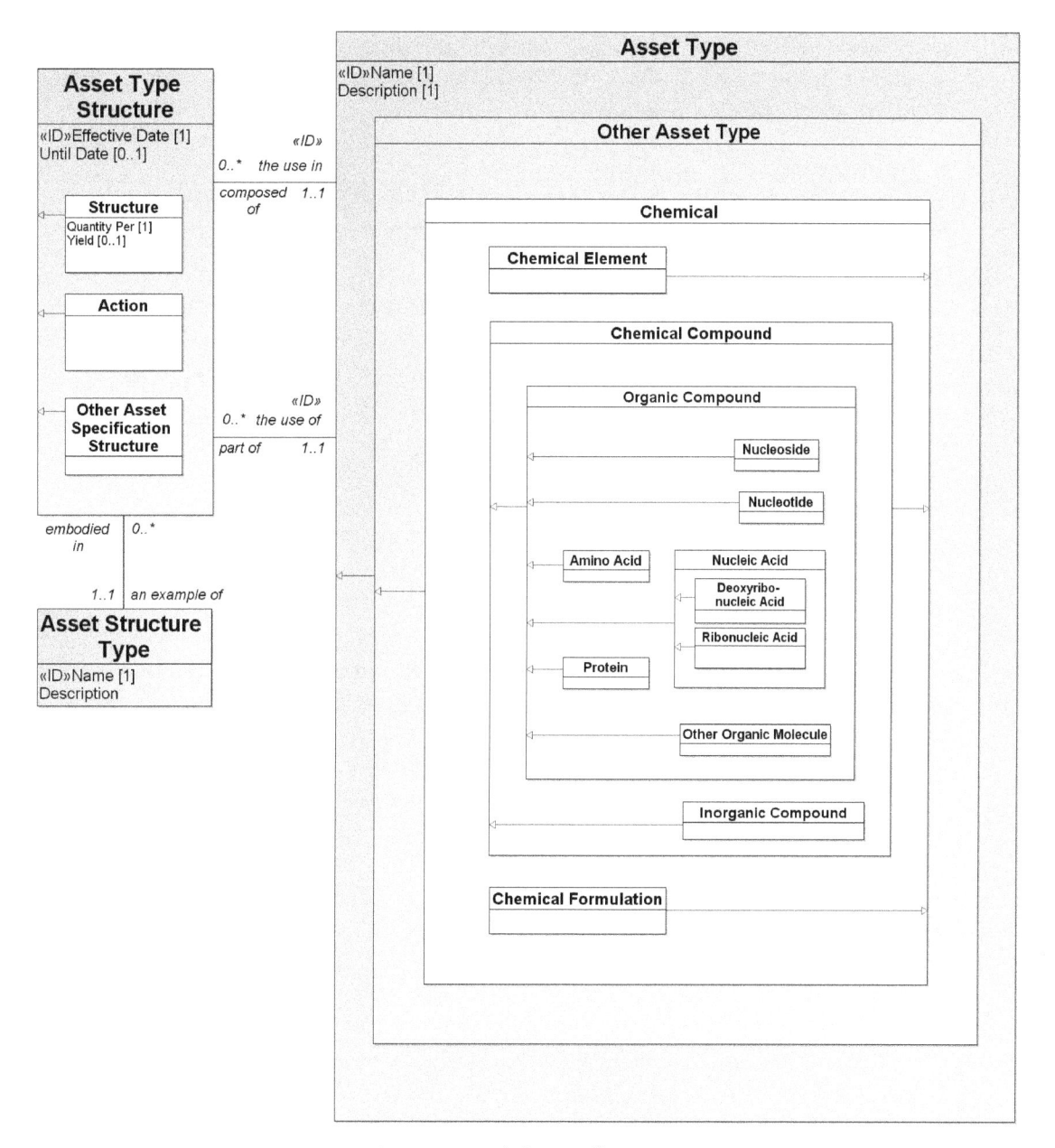

Figure 19-4: (Physical) Assets

The Enterprise Model comes to the rescue. We have already posited the existence of **Asset Type Structure**—the fact that any **Asset Type** may be *part of* one or more other **Asset Type**. That is, each **Asset Type Structure** must be *the use of* one **Asset Type** and its *use in* another **Asset Type**.

Because of the Chemistry involved, an **Asset Type Structure** encompasses not simply **Structure** in the physical sense of one thing's being physically part of another thing, but also **Action**, in the sense that a particular **Chemical** can be expected to act in a particular way on another **Chemical**. This is particularly significant in the world of **Organic Compounds**, with their **Amino Acids** and **Proteins** carrying out the body's work.

Packaged Products

Ok, if the company has invented a medicine that will cure cancer, it must ultimately be packaged for sale. Figure 19-5 shows that this includes not only the definition of an appropriate **Chemical Formulation**, but also a **Specified Packaged Product** available for sale.

Packaging actually happens in two steps. The first is to determine the physical **Product Form** of the product—tablets, capsules, or liquid. Thus, as shown in Figure 19-5, each **Packaged Product** must be *in* one and only one **Product Form**. In addition, each **Packaged Product** is designated as being intended to be *administered via* a **Route of Administration**. This describes the means for making the medicine available to the body: oral, intravenous injection, intramuscular injection, et cetera. Thus, the product in a specified **Product Form**, with a specified **Route of Administration** is the first level of a **Packaged Product**.

The physical medicine is then put into bottles, ampoules, vials, et cetera. That is, this initial **Packaged Product** is then, *part of* a more complex **Packaged Product**. The result, in addition to being composed of a **Chemical Formulation** with the constraints described by its **Product Form** and **Route of Administration**, is also *composed of* one or more **Specified Packaging Items**, such as a **Label**, a **Specified Container**, and, as necessary, **Other Specified Packaging**. The latter includes the insert required to describe the dosing instructions, potential side-effects, and so forth.

Note that the elements associated with converting a **Chemical** into a product for sale constitute **Asset Specifications**. Here you don't have a "model number" as would an electronics manufacturer, but a Product Code.

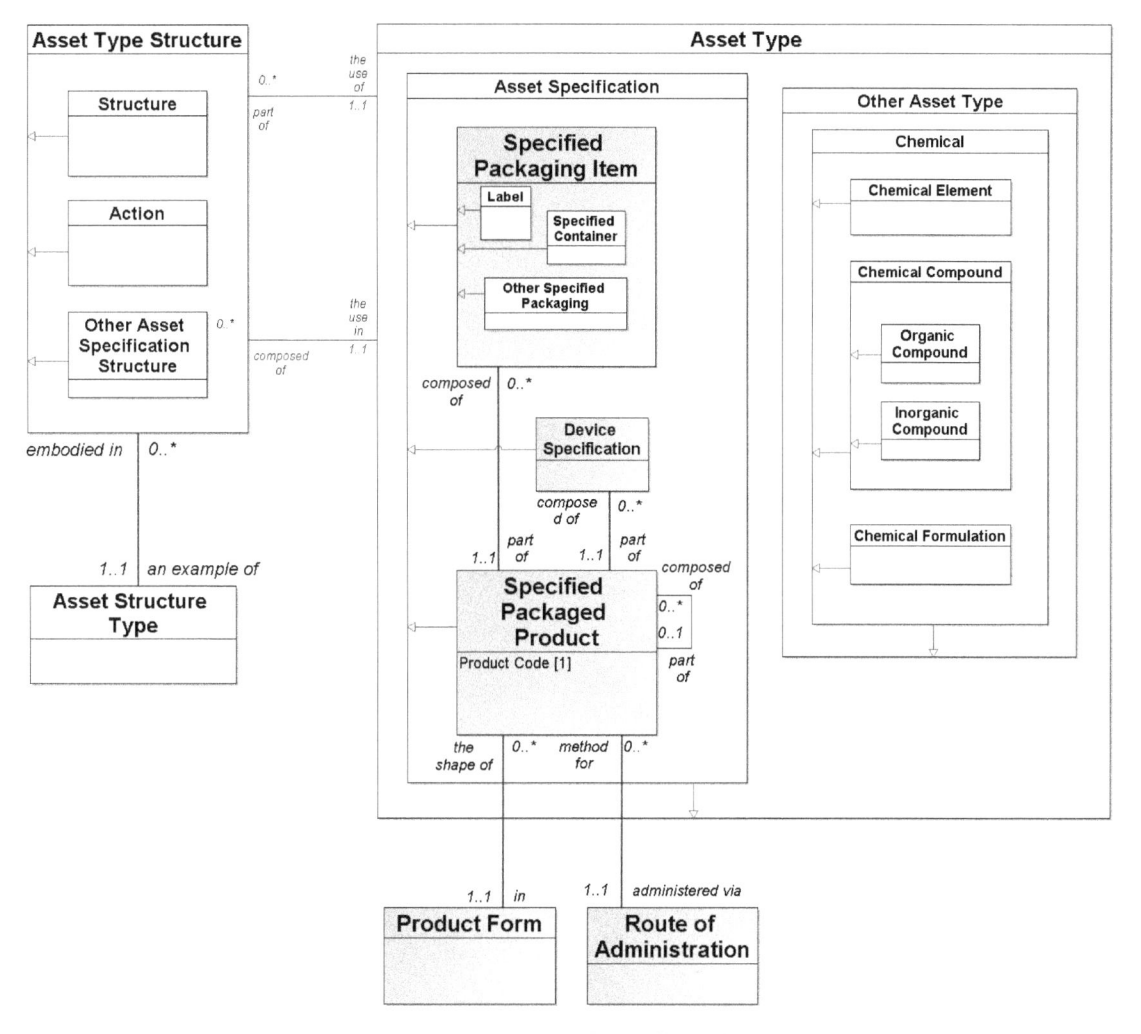

Figure 19-5: Packaged Products

Summary

This example of making a model more concrete for a particular company consists of simply breaking the standard **Asset** into progressively greater detail as sub-types. Note that, as with many real projects, we didn't start with the standard pattern. We started by talking about something of significance to the pharmaceutical company—chemicals. Only after we had come to understand the nature of the model did we recognize that these are indeed instances of an important part of the Level 1 model pattern.

Ok, if you have these patterns firmly planted in your brain, you recognized the fit right away. But it is important to take clients from the business community through the process of analyzing their terms and gradually extracting the patterns—keeping it clear that however much it may look like other people's models, this is *their* personal model.

CHAPTER 20

Banking

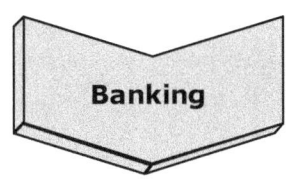

This chapter is based on the models your author developed for four different banks. As a consequence, it isn't exactly like any of them, but it is to be hoped that it includes the best features of all.

Doing a data model of banking presents a particular challenge: The "product" of a bank is fundamentally *intangible*. This has several implications:

- To the bankers, in one sense it is treated like a product in any other business. It is categorized, bought, and sold. The entity classes describing instances and specifications have some of the same structure as the entity classes describing physical products.
- Defining and categorizing a list of banking products is more difficult, however. There is an ISO standard of product names that runs several hundred entries. Getting a particular bank to align itself even with that standard is hard, since each bank is creative in the way it defines products.
- A "product" in banking is really a set of defined "services", assembled for marketing purposes. In fact, the list of available services is more finite and more consistently understood across the industry.
- In the standard contract model, a contract is the mechanism by which physical products and services are bought and sold. A **Contract** is an order for one or more (physical) **Asset Specifications**, and it is then filled by delivery of instances of a real **Asset**. Even when a conventional contract is for **Services**, delivery is in the form of **Activities** that execute those services. For a bank, however, while it also buys and sells product specifications, delivery of the product (the instance of it) is in fact *the **Contract** itself*.

Instruments and Instrument Specifications

In banking, the product being sold is a *financial instrument*. This is a specialized, formal, legal document that specifies a legal arrangement whereby a bank either holds a customer's money in trust, or lends the customer money. Also included in each case is a set of services provided by the bank to support these roles. Figure 20-1 shows that each **Instrument** must be *managed by* one or more **Parties**, and *acquired by* one or more **Parties**. In most cases, there is only one *banker for* an **Instrument** and only one *customer for* it. But there can be more complex instruments with more than one **Party** on either side of the transaction. In these cases the situation is more completely represented through the use of **Instrument Role**, to be described in a following section.

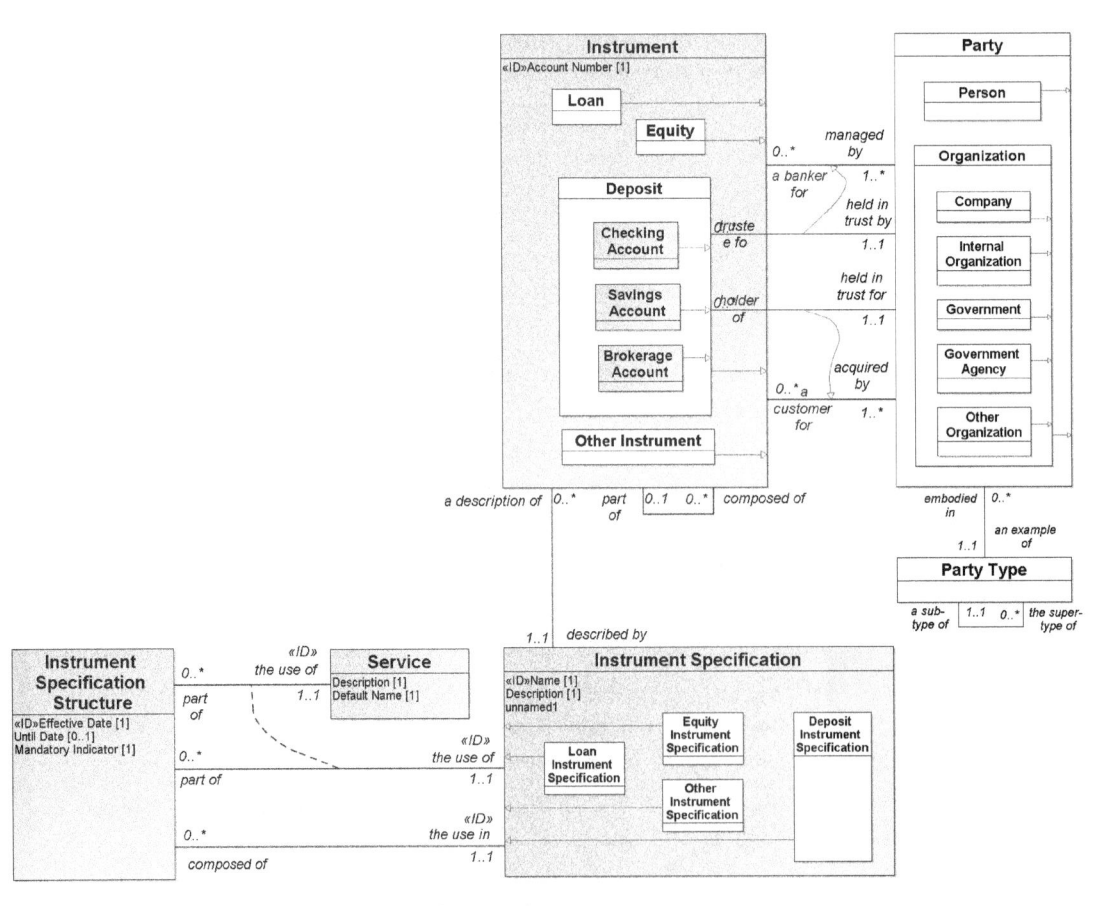

Figure 20-1: Instruments

About Financial Instruments

As mentioned earlier, the possible catalogue of different kinds of **Instruments** can be quite extensive. Even so, they all come down to the three main categories shown in Figure 20-1: **Loan**, **Deposit**, and **Equity**. (There are **Other Instrument** categories, but these typically are combinations of the main three.) Of particular interest here are three primary sub-types of **Deposit**: the **Checking Account**, the **Savings Account**, and the **Brokerage Account**. As all should know, the **Savings Account** and **Checking Account** are arrangements whereby the bank holds the customer's money safely.

The **Checking Account** provides mechanisms for easy access (checks and automated teller machines, for example), and may pay a nominal interest on it. The **Savings Account** does not have the mechanisms for easy access, but generally pays a higher interest rate.

Also included as **Instruments** available are **Loan** and **Equity**. A **Loan** is an instance of an **Instrument** whereby a *banker* **Party** makes money available to a *customer* **Party**. An **Equity** is an **Instrument** whereby one **Party** acquires ownership of part of a **Company**.

The bank invests the money received in **Checking** and **Savings Accounts** in mortgages and other (**Loan**) **Instruments**, but it is responsible for returning the money deposited and paying any interest agreed to. The bank (and in the United States, the Federal Government) assumes the risk for any investments it makes. In a **Brokerage Account**, the customer also entrusts money to the bank, but either the customer directly determines how the money will be invested, or the customer hires the broker to manage the investments.

In either case, the customer bears all the risk from such investments. It is a **Brokerage Account** that serves as a vehicle for the customer's buying other **Instruments**, such as **Equities**. This will be described shortly.

An example of an **Instrument** might a **Checking Account** acquired by Mark MacHogan at the Montrose Branch (Houston) of Conglomerate Bank. That is, the money is *held in trust for* **Person** `"Mark MacHogan"`, and it is *held by* the **Organization** `"Montrose Branch of Conglomerate Bank"`. (Note that the relationship "each **Deposit** must be *held in trust for* one and only one **Party**" is a sub-type of the relationship "each **Instrument** must be *acquired by* one **Party**".)

An **Instrument** may be composed of one or more other **Instruments**. This is shown in Figure 20-1 as a simple relationship, "each **Instrument** may be *composed of* one or more other **Instruments**".

For example, *Mark MacHogan*'s `"Executive Account"` with Conglomeration Bank may be composed of `"Executive Checking"` and an `"Auto Transfer Savings Account"`.

A bank defines the **Instruments** it will market to the public by coming up with **Instrument Specifications** in advance. An **Instrument Specification** describes the services, characteristics, and terms of each **Instrument** to be marketed by the bank. An individual **Instrument** held by a customer is then *described by* one of these **Instrument Specifications**.

The sub-types of Instrument Specification correspond to those for Instrument: **Loan Instrument Specification**, **Deposit Instrument Specification**, and **Equity Instrument Specification** (plus, of course, **Other Instrument Specification**).

An **Instrument** may be *composed of* one or more other **Instruments**, as shown by the looped line attached to **Instrument** in Figure 20-1. Because these are actual **Instruments**, an **Instrument** cannot be *part of* more than one other **Instrument**, so the "recursive" relationship is sufficient. In the case of **Instrument Specifications**, however, one can easily be specified to be *part of* more than one other **Instrument Specification**. For this reason, Figure 20-1 shows that each **Instrument Specification** may be *composed of* one or more **Instrument Specification Structures**, each of which must be either *the use of* another **Instrument Specification**, or *the use of* a **Service**. That is, **Instrument Specification Structure** is the fact that a particular **Instrument Specification** or a particular **Service** is part of the **Specification** of an **Instrument**.

Thus the product `"Executive Checking"` offered by Conglomerate Bank is specified to always include the product `"Ordinary Checking"` plus the product `"Auto-transfer Savings Account"`. As `"Executive Checking"`, it also might include the **Service**, `"Automatic savings roll-over"`, `"Executive Summary Statement"`, and so forth. Each of the component **Instrument Specifications** (`"Executive Checking"` and `"Auto-Transfer Savings Account"`) would have its own set of **Services** attached, such as `"Overdraft Protection"`, `"Automated Teller Machine access"`, `"Teller access"`, et cetera.

Note that at the bottom of the hierarchy, an **Instrument Specification** may be only *composed of* **Services**.

Services for a savings account would include such basic things as `"Holding money"`, `"Receiving money"`, and `"Paying money"`, but they can also be expanded to cover `"Use of a Teller"`, `"Use of an automatic teller machine"`, `"Overdraft protection"`, and so forth.

Note that, in this pattern, an instance of **Instrument** is identified by an Account Number, and an instance of **Instrument Specification** is identified by its (presumably unique) Name. An instance of **Instrument Specification Structure**, on the other hand, is identified by a combination of the *use of* relationship, *the use in* relationship, and the attribute Effective Date. These are part of this pattern, but for any real database, the decisions that go into this should be re-visited, and the identification structure revised, if necessary.

Instrument Characteristics

All the way back to Level 0 of abstraction, we have seen how types of things can be defined in terms of the ... **Characteristics** that describe them, and then actual things are described by values for those ... **Characteristics**. Your author's opportunity to "invent" that configuration came from his first consulting experience with Oracle Corporation. The client was a bank trying to address the problem of different kinds of banking products all being described by different kinds of parameters. Some had "Interest rate", for example, while others might have "Minimum balance", "Term", and so forth. This could be addressed by defining different sub-types for each product, but that is clumsy, and as the client put it, the marketing department "likes to be creative", coming up with new products every few weeks. Clearly something different was needed. Figure 20-2 shows the original solution to that problem.[*]

Starting at the bottom, Figure 20-2 shows how each **Instrument Specification** may be *defined by* one or more **Instrument Characteristic Assignments**, each of which must be *of* one **Instrument Characteristic**.

For example, a **Checking Account** might be *defined by* the **Instrument Characteristics** `"Minimum balance"`, `"Monthly fee"`, and so forth. A **Certificate of Deposit**, on the other hand, is defined by the characteristics `"Interest Rate"`, `"Term"`, and so forth. One **Instrument Characteristic**

---

[*] Your author was chagrined to discover later that he was not the only person to have invented this solution. Apparently, the proper term is not "invented" but "discovered". He would like to think he discovered it first, though, back in November of 1986.

Assignment is *the use of* one **Instrument Characteristic** *to define* one **Instrument Specification**.

Note that each **Instrument Characteristic**, as defined here, may optionally be described by the attribute **Default Value**, as well as attributes **Minimum Value**, **Maximum Value**, or both.

In **Instrument Characteristic Assignment**, the **Instrument Characteristic** values for **Default Value**, **Minimum Value**, and **Maximum Value** may be overridden. That is, **Instrument Characteristic** provides basic constraints that apply to all instances of it as used by different **Instruments**.

If a particular **Instrument Characteristic Assignment** has values specified for the same attributes, however, these values override those in the associated **Instrument Characteristic**.

For example, the **Maximum Value** for `"Overdraft fee"` may, by corporate standard, be `"$100.00"`, but as this **Instrument Characteristic** is assigned to a particular **Instrument Specification**, the **Maximum Value** for the **Instrument Characteristic Assignment** is only `"$10.00"`.

The following rules apply:

Business Rules

- If present, the Minimum Value of an instance of **Instrument Characteristic Assignment** must be <u>greater than</u> the Minimum Value of the **Instrument Characteristic** that it is *of*.

- If present, the Maximum Value of an instance of **Instrument Characteristic Assignment** must be <u>less than</u> the Maximum Value of the **Instrument Characteristic** that it is *of*. *(**Translation**: If an **Instrument Characteristic Assignment** specifies a minimum and/or maximum value, these have to be "inside" any minimum or maximum value specified for the **Characteristic** itself.)*

- The Default Value of any **Instrument Characteristic Assignment** (if present) always overrides any Default Value recorded for the **Instrument Characteristic** that the **Instrument Characteristic Assignment** is *of*.

Banking **395**

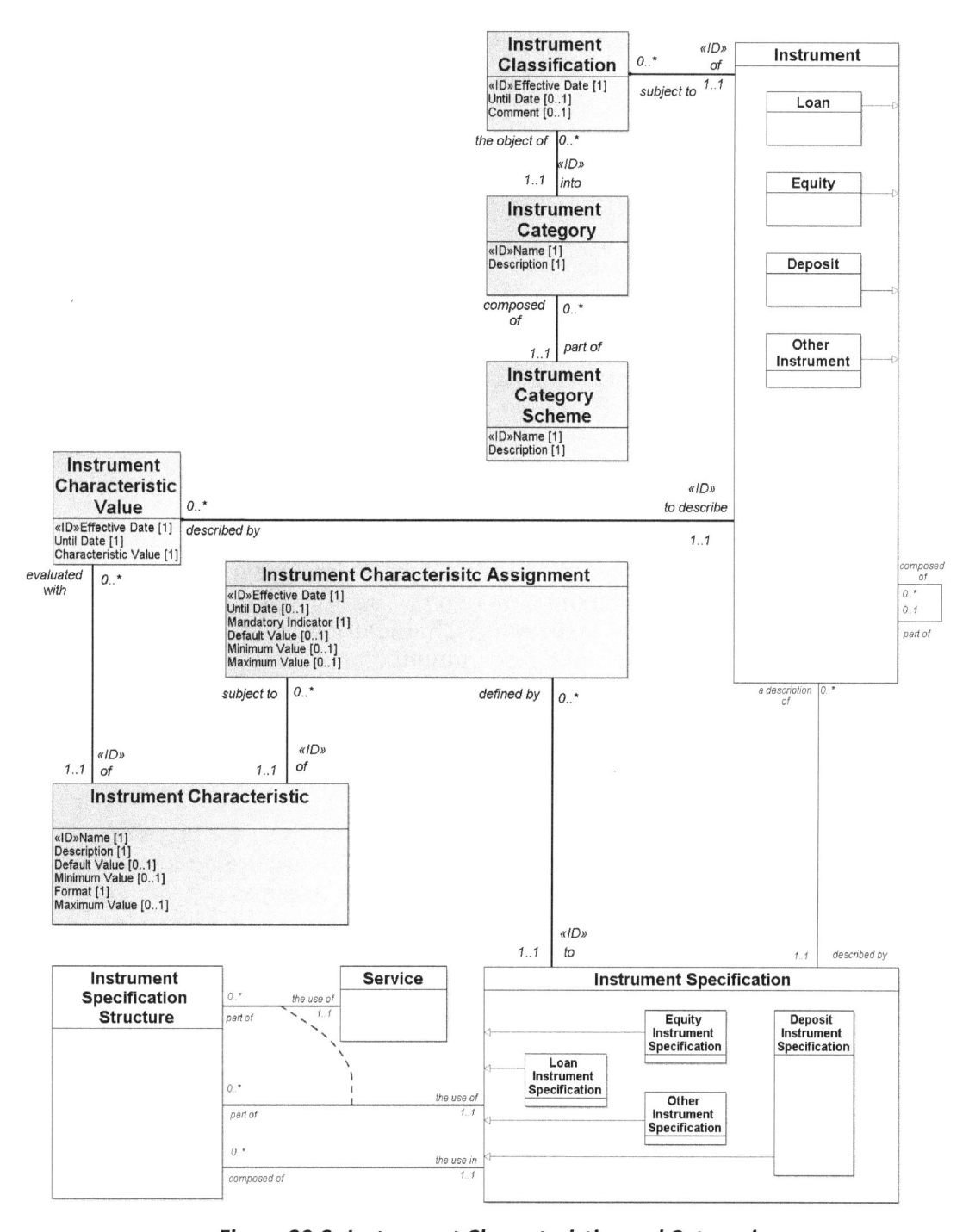

Figure 20-2: Instrument Characteristics and Categories

Instrument Characteristics and **Instrument Characteristic Assignments**, along with the **Instrument Specification**, are the domain of the people in the bank that create products. When a customer comes into the bank and wants to open a checking account, however, this involves capturing actual values for the **Instrument** purchased. What is required is to give each **Instrument Characteristic Value** an actual Characteristic Value that is *of* a specified **Instrument Characteristic** and *for* the **Instrument** being established.

Each **Instrument Characteristic Value**, then, must be *of* an **Instrument Characteristic**, *to describe* one **Instrument**.

Business Rules

- If a customer wants to buy an **Instrument**, the **Instrument Specification** that it is *an example of* must be identified.

- The **Instrument Characteristic Value** Characteristic Value *to describe* the **Instrument** may only be *of* an **Instrument Characteristic** if that **Instrument Characteristic** is *subject to* an **Instrument Characteristic Assignment** that is *to* the **Instrument Specification** that is referred to in the first rule here. *(Translation:* **Instrument Characteristic Assignment** assures that a particular **Instrument Characteristic** is appropriate to describe **Instruments** of a particular **Instrument Type**.)

- An **Instrument** must be *described by* an **Instrument Characteristic Value** for each **Instrument Characteristic** that is both *subject to* an **Instrument Characteristic Assignment** that is *to* the **Instrument Specification** that is referred to in the first rule here, and whose Mandatory Indicator is "True". *(Translation:* If an **Instrument Characteristic** is assigned to an **Instrument Type** via an **Instrument Characteristic Assignment** that has a Mandatory Indicator with the value "True", then there must be an **Instrument Characteristic Value** *of* that **Instrument Characteristic** *to describe* that **Instrument**.)

Characteristic Values

It is possible to imagine a computer portal being used by the bank's officer opening an account for a customer. The portal would begin by having the officer enter all of the **Party's** information (**Name**, **Address**, et cetera). Then it would call up the desired **Instrument Specification**. The computer would then display **Instrument**

Characteristics that have been assigned to that **Instrument Specification**, and request values for them.

Instrument Categories

Also in Figure 20-2 are the entity classes, **Instrument Category** and **Instrument Category Scheme**. As we saw in the Criminal Justice model (Chapter 18), this is an alternative to the way categories and characteristics are described in the Level 1 Enterprise Model. In these more concrete contexts, the notion of categorization is sufficiently different from the notion of describing things in terms of their **Characteristics**, that a separate treatment is called for.

An **Instrument Category** is a grouping of **Instruments** according to common characteristics. **Instrument Classification** is the fact that a particular **Instrument** falls into a particular **Instrument Category** at a particular time (between its **Effective Date** and its **Until Date**)

Here, an **Instrument Category Scheme** could be, for example, "Account Values", *composed of* **Instrument Categories**, "Less than $5,000", "Between $5,000 and $100,000", "$100,000 to $5,000,000", and so forth. Alternatively, an **Instrument Category Scheme** could be "Investment Goals", composed of **Instrument Categories** "Growth", "Income", "Safety", et cetera. **Instrument Categories** can be used to classify **Instruments**, **Instrument Specifications**, or both. For example, the **Instrument Category Scheme** "Account Values" would probably most appropriately apply only to **Instruments**. The **Instrument Category Scheme**, "Investment Goals", on the other hand, could apply to both, with slightly different meanings: In the case of **Instrument Specifications**, "Investment Goals" would describe the objectives of the **Instrument Specification** as intended by the bank. In the case of **Instruments**, this **Instrument Category** would describe the goals for that particular investment.

Marketing Relationships

While each **Instrument** has been identified as to who the customer and bank department are, it is common for a customer to have multiple accounts (**Instruments**) with the bank. Thus, a **Marketing Relationship** may be formed between the bank and each prospect or customer, as shown in Figure 20-3, Each **Marketing Relationship** is the fact that a **Party** (the *prospect*) has entered into a formal or informal arrangement with another **Party** (the *account manager*).

398 Enterprise Model Patterns

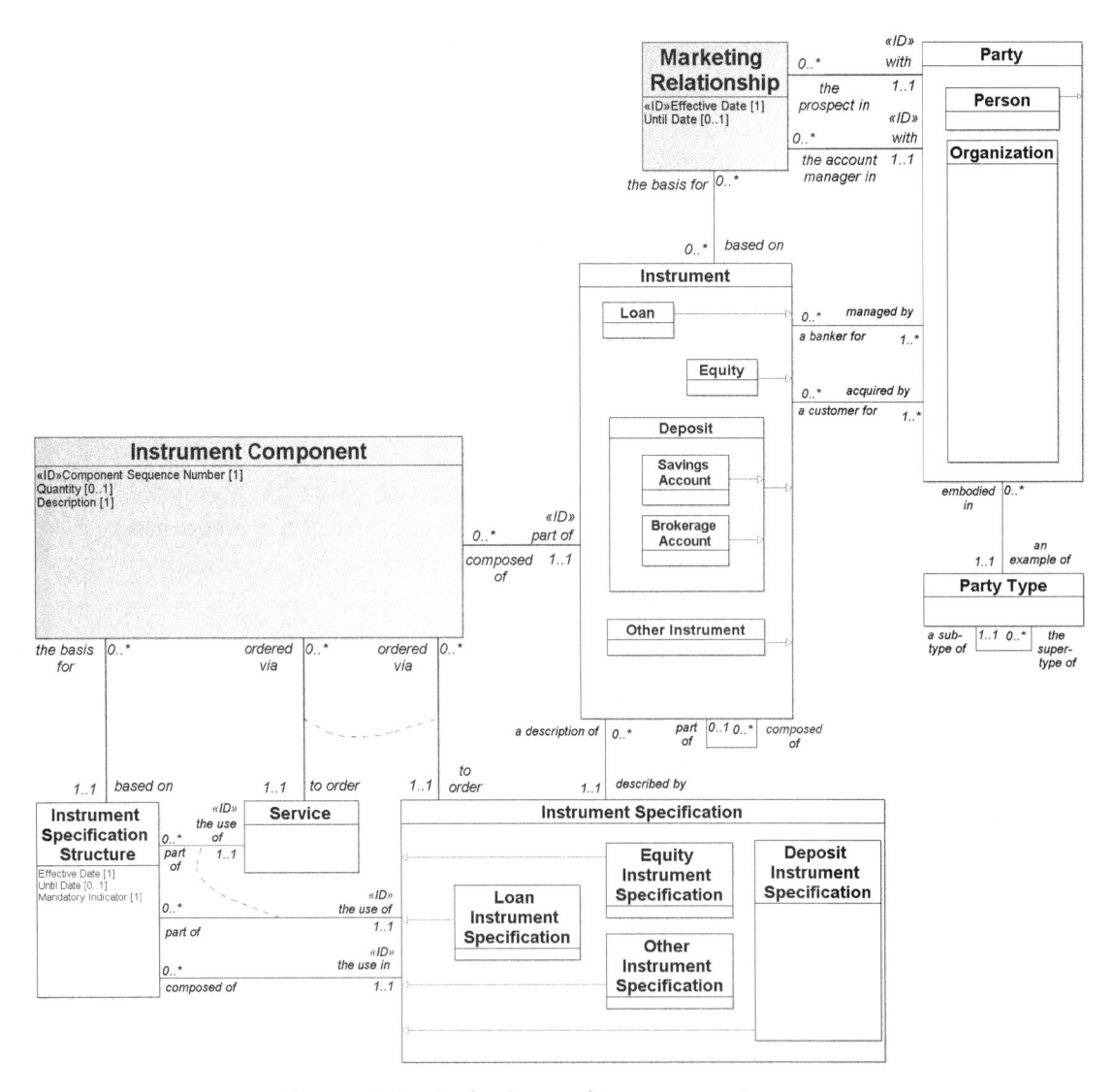

Figure 20-3: Marketing and Instrument Components

How precise the banking side is described (a **Person**, an **Internal Organization**, or the bank itself (a **Company**) is up to the modeler and the bank being addressed. Each **Marketing Relationship** may be *the basis for* one or more **Instruments**. Each **Instrument** may be *based on*, typically, one and only one **Marketing Relationship**, although it could be based on more than one.

Instrument Components

Where the **Instrument Specification Structure** described the **Services** that are defined to be part of an **Instrument Specification**, the actual features of a real **Instrument** are specified through a set of **Instrument Components**. Each

Instrument may be *composed of* one or more **Instrument Components**, each of which must be *to order* either one **Service** or one **Instrument Specification**.

Some of the components (primarily **Services**) described for an **Instrument Specification** through its **Instrument Specification Structure** instances are *optional*. These are designated by the attribute of **Instrument Specification Structure**, **Mandatory Indicator**. Where some services are optional for the **Instrument Characteristic**, the entity class **Instrument Component** describes which ones actually apply to a particular **Instrument**.

Business rules will assert that the component **Instrument Specifications** and **Services** should correspond to the structure already defined for the **Instrument Specification**. Specifically:

Business Rules

- Each **Instrument** <u>must be</u> *composed of* one **Instrument Component** that is *to order* each **Instrument Specification** or **Service** that is *part of* an **Instrument Specification Structure** whose Mandatory Indicator is "True", and that is *the use in* the **Instrument Specification** that is *embodied in* the **Instrument** in question. *(Translation:* If a (parent) **Instrument Specification** <u>must be</u> *composed of* a particular other (child) **Instrument Specification** or **Service**, then any **Instrument** that is *the embodiment of* the parent **Instrument Specification** <u>must have</u> that child **Instrument Specification** or **Service**.)

- Each **Instrument** <u>may be</u> *composed of* one **Instrument Component** *to order* each **Instrument Specification** or **Service** that is *part of* an **Instrument Specification Structure** whose Mandatory Indicator is "False", and that is *the use in* the **Instrument Specification** that is *embodied in* the **Instrument** in question. *(Translation:* If a (parent) **Instrument Specification** <u>may be</u> *composed of* a particular other (child) **Instrument Specification** or **Service**, then any **Instrument** that is *the embodiment of* the parent **Instrument Specification** <u>may or may not have</u> that child **Instrument Specification** or **Service**.)

Note that these rules are constrained, as are all Business Rules presented thus far, by the logic of the situation. Given the definitions of **Instrument Component** and **Instrument Specification Structure**, these rules must apply independent of any business policy. They can be enforced with the confidence that they are true because they are logically consistent.

400 Enterprise Model Patterns

Other business rules carry out business policy. For the most part, the data modeler may not be aware of them, or if 'e is, 'e must confirm them with management of the firm. The following is an example of this. It is not required to be so, based on the logic of the model. Management is responsible for defining this (or its opposite) and for enforcing it.

Business Rule

- Each **Instrument** <u>may be</u> *composed of* an **Instrument Component** *to order* any **Instrument Specification** or **Service** that is <u>not</u> *part of* an **Instrument Specification Structure** that is *the use in* the **Instrument Specification** that is *embodied in* the **Instrument** in question. *(Translation:* Even if an **Instrument Specification** or **Service** is not *part of* a standard **Instrument Specification Structure**, an **Instrument** may still order that **Instrument Specification** or **Service** via a **Component**.)

In other words, if an **Instrument** is specified that calls for a non-standard component, it is the bank that must determine what the policy is. The rule here happens to assert that an **Instrument** may have an **Instrument Component Service** or **Instrument Specification**, even if that hadn't been recognized as a component before. Your bank's policies may be different.

Agreements

Figure 20-4 shows a super-type of **Instrument** and **Marketing Relationship**, that of **Agreement**. This includes financial **Instrument** and **Marketing Relationship**, as well as **Other Agreement**.

Note that this extends the concept enough to include **Other Agreements**, such as ordinary sales and purchase orders for non-financial services and supplies. The relationships between the two sub-type entities and **Party** become sub-types of the relationships between **Agreement** and **Party**:

Banking 401

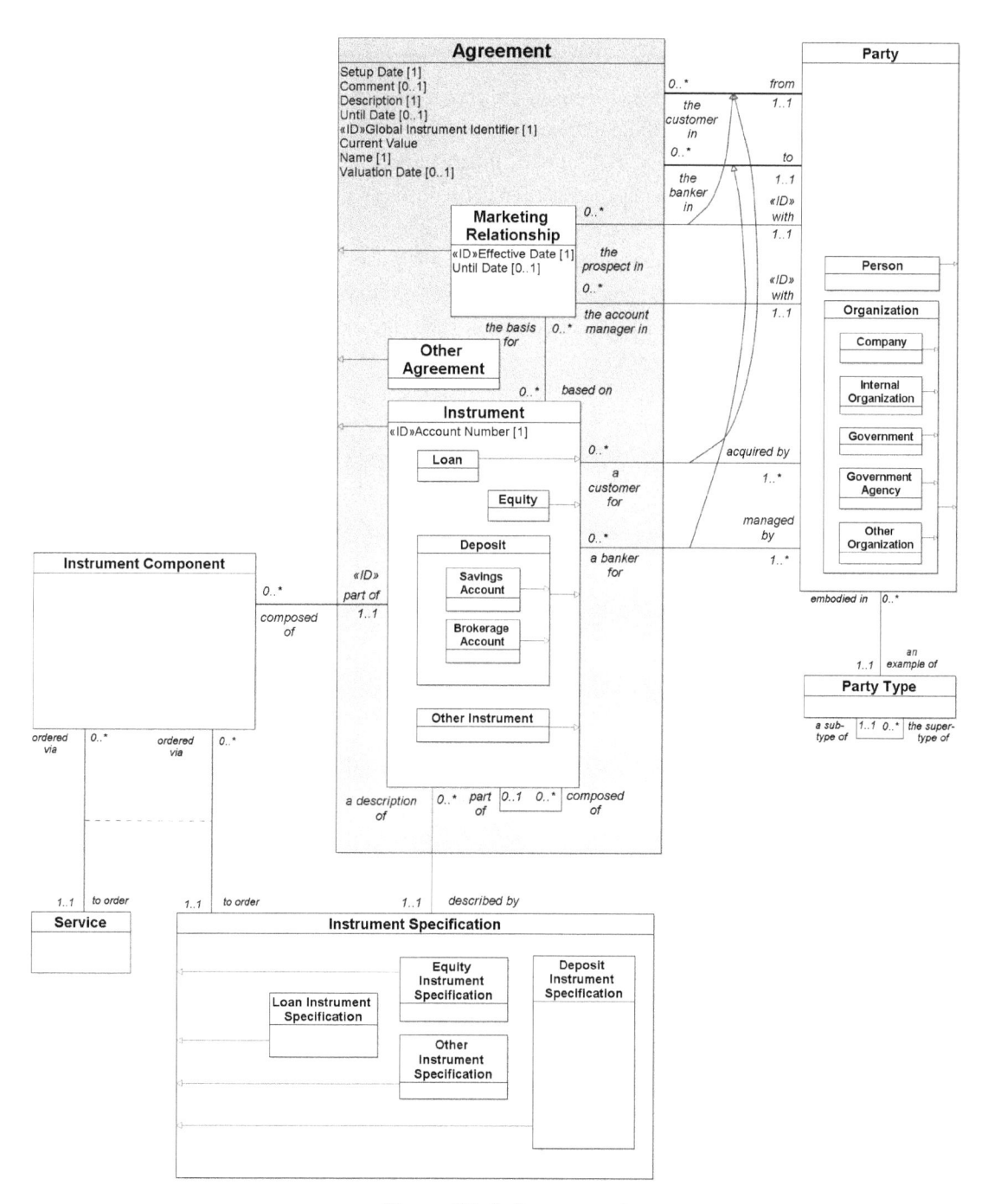

Figure 20-4: Agreements

Roles

The original two relationships between **Instrument** and **Party** were adequate to explain the basic structure of **Instrument**. It quickly became apparent, though, that there could be more than one *banker in* and more than one *customer in* an **Agreement**, so the relationship is really "many-to-many", requiring, in each case, an "intersect entity class" to describe each occurrence of one **Party** (for example) being *the banker in* one **Instrument**. Rather than a separate intersect entity class for each kind of relationship, Figure 20-5 shows a single **Banking Role** as a sub-type of the more general concept **Agreement Role**. This allows an unlimited number of **Parties** to play roles in an unlimited number of **Agreements**. Specifically, an **Agreement Role** is the fact that one **Party** is involved in some way with one **Agreement**. That is, each instance of **Agreement Role** must be *played by* one and only one **Party**, and it must be *played for* either one and only one **Instrument** or one and only one **Instrument Specification**.

Different banks have different ways to organize roles, two of which are shown in the Figure 20-5.

In addition to **Management Role**, which distinguishes between the banker and the customer, **Money Role** describes the role a **Party** plays with respect to the money involved in the **Instrument**:

- **Provider** – this is the *provider of money in* an **Agreement**. For a deposit account, this is the customer. For a loan, this is the bank.
- **Holder** – this is the *holder of money in* an **Agreement**. For a deposit account, this is the bank. For a loan, this is the customer.
- **Other Money Role** – this is anyone playing any other **Instrument Role**, with respect to money, *for* an **Agreement**.

A **Management Role** is one of the following:

- **Banking Role** – a role played by a department or an officer of the bank in either issuing debt or accepting deposits.
- **Customer Role** – a role played by a **Person** or **Organization** outside the bank that is doing business with the bank.
- **Third Party Role** – a role played by someone who is neither affiliated with the bank nor a customer in this Instrument.

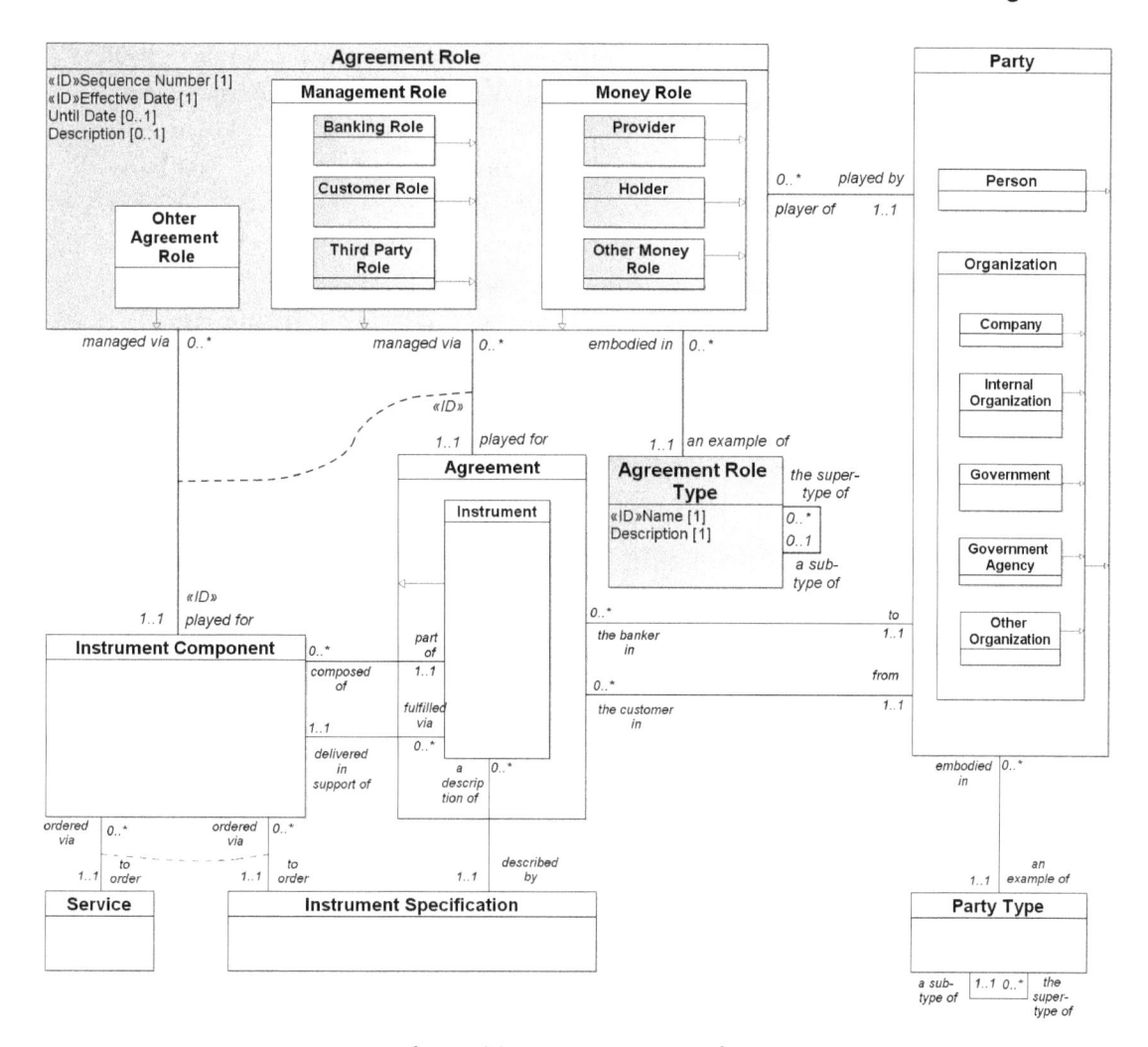

Figure 20-5: Agreement Roles

As in other parts of the model, instances of **Agreement Role Type** correspond to the sub-types shown in the drawing (**Management Role**, **Holder**, **Customer Role**, et cetera). It also includes the ability to assert that one **Agreement Role Type** (such as **Banking Role**) is a *sub-type of* another **Agreement Role Type** (in this case **Management Role**). Thus, other **Agreement Role Types** may be specified to describe possible kinds of **Instrument Roles** in more detail than can be done with visible sub-types. The only constraint is that, with the existing instances, each of these new ones may only be *a sub-type of* one other **Instrument Role Type**.

Where a **Brokerage Account** entails the purchase of stock, the stock itself has various **Money Roles**. The company whose equity is involved is called the "issuer". That is a **Holder Role** (of the money) for the original initial public offering (known in the industry as an "IPO"). An *initial public offering* is the official making of stock in a company available to the public. It is what is also known as "taking a company public". Another role played for the **Instrument** is the **Underwriter** (*a sub-type o*f **Other Money Role**) who conducts and administers the sale. The **Party** playing the "underwriter" role could be an investment bank or an **Other Organization** called a "Syndicate", assembled from a group of investment banks. And of course, there are all the **Persons** and **Organizations** that purchased shares in the initial public offering. These are **Providers** of funds for the **Instrument**.

As described earlier, in a **Brokerage Account**, shares of stock are bought and sold repeatedly after the initial public offering. In each case, an **Instrument** is bought by a **Provider** of funds and sold to a **Holder** of funds.

An alternative way of looking at how to organize roles is **Management Role**, otherwise known as "Legal Vehicle Role". Here the concept of role is coupled with the nature of the **Party** playing it.

- A **Banking Role** is a bank legal entity (**Company**) that is engaging in business with a customer. (This is also known as a *"legal vehicle role".*)
- A **Customer Role** is any non-bank **Party** that does business with the bank. (This is also known as a *"counterparty".*)
- A **Third Party Role** is a **Party** that uses its credit in support of the credit offered to another **Party**. (This is also known as a *"supporter".*)

Delivering Against Instruments

As originally contracted, an **Instrument** is ultimately an order for services (purchased as a product), although it may be an order for other **Instruments**. So, how do we record delivery of instances of these services?

An **Instrument** is unique as a kind of **Contract**, in that fundamentally, delivery of an instance of the ordered **Instrument Specification** is often either the **Instrument** itself or another **Instrument**. You set up a checking account. This is basically an order for a checking account. By definition you have received what was ordered. In addition, if the **Instrument** (for example `"Executive Account #30893790"`, held by Mark MacHogan) is *composed of* an **Instrument Component** that is *to order* another **Instrument Specification** (such as the product, `"Executive Checking"`). the **Instrument Component** is *fulfilled via* another **Instrument** *acquired by* Mark MacHogan as `"Executive Checking, Acct 24072"`.

Thus, in Figure 20-6, one way an **Instrument Component** may be *fulfilled* is *via* an **Instrument**.

Think about this: In the chapter on **Contracts** (Chapter 14), if you ordered an **Asset Type** that was *delivered via* a **Material Movement**, this was *of* an **Asset**. In banking, on the other hand, delivery of an ordered **Instrument Specification** is the **Instrument** that is the **Contract** itself! This is what makes banking unique.

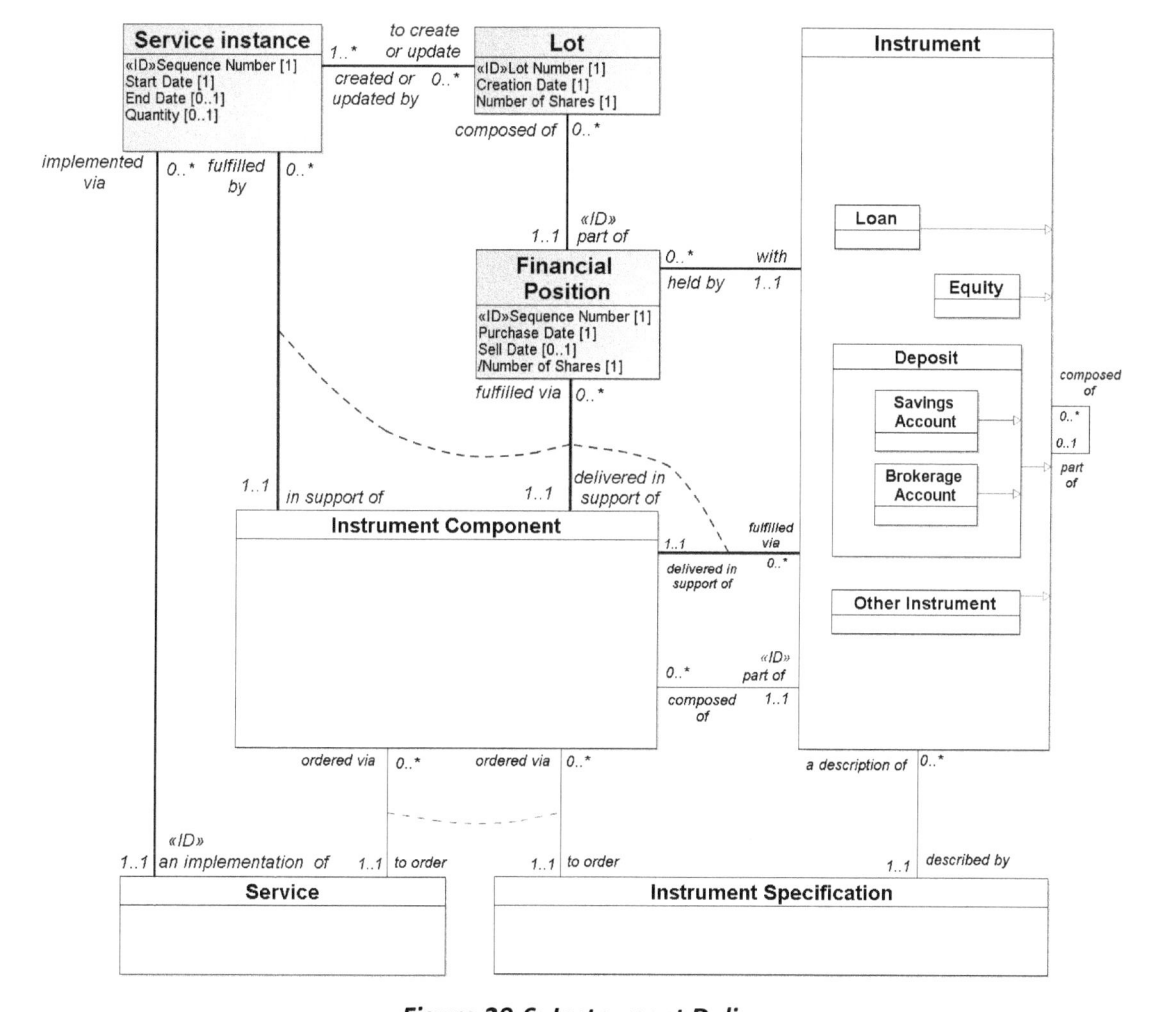

Figure 20-6: Instrument Delivery

Each of the **Services** ordered, on the other hand, may be *implemented via* one or more **Service Instances**. A **Service Instance** is an instance of a **Service** actually occurring at a point in time, in support of an **Instrument Component**. (This is more like the **Contract** model.) These are, among other things, the transactions conducted (via teller or Automated Teller Machines), special reports sent to the customer, wire transactions, and so forth. Thus, another way an **Instrument Component** may be *filled* is *via* a **Service Instance**.

Where the **Instrument** is a **Brokerage Account**, at least two **Instrument Components** will be created for each purchase or sale transaction:

- One will be *to order* a **Service**, which is the conduct of the transaction.
- The other will be *to order* an **Instrument Specification** for something like `"Shares of stock in Google Corporation"`.

Fulfilling these components, then, requires:

- Performing the **Service Instance** that carries out the transaction, recording the **Start Date** and **End Date**, delivering a **Quantity** of shares.
- Creating an **Instrument** that is *an instance of* the **Instrument Specification** that was ordered (for example `"Google Corporation Stock"`, as sold to Mark MacHogan), along with a **Financial Position** recording that, as a result of this transaction, plus those that went before, there exist `"25 shares of Google Corporation Stock, held by Mark MacHogan"` *in support of* the **Instrument Component** that ordered them.

A **Financial Position** is the fact that a certain number of shares of a particular company were held for a specified period of time, in support of a particular **Instrument Component**. The total amount of a **Financial Position** must be composed of one or more **Lots**, where a **Lot** is a quantity of shares obtained at one time. That is, each transaction involves the purchase or sale of a **Lot**. The **Service**, then, `"Buy or sell stock"` may be *implemented via* a **Service Instance** *to create or update* one or more **Lots**. For example, *Mark MacHogan* might purchase 100 shares of Google Corporation on 14 January 2010, and another 100 shares of Google Corporation on 3 May, 2010. Each purchase generates a **Service Instance** to buy a **Lot**, recording the **Number of Shares** and the **Creation Date** involved. The derived attribute **/Number of Shares** in

the **Financial Position** that is with the **Instrument** `"Google Corporation Stock, (acquired by Mark MacHogan)"` stands at `"200"`.[*] Subsequently, 50 shares may be sold via a **Service Instance** *to update* two **Lots**, subtracting 25 shares from the first and 25 shares from the second. The **Number**

---

[*] …computed as SUM-THROUGH (*composed of*, **Lot**, "Number of Shares").

of Shares in each Lot is then reduced by that amount—as is the total /Number of Shares for the entire Financial Position.

Thus, in this case, an Instrument Component is *filled via* a Financial Position.

Note that an Instrument (such as a mortgage Loan) that originally is a transaction between the bank and a customer can itself be sold to someone else. That is, a collection of mortgages or other Loans could be packaged up into a separate Other Instrument. The money (including part of the interest) expected to be paid by the *customers in* each of these Loans would then pass to the purchaser. This collection of mortgages would then be *an example of* an Instrument called a *collateralized debt obligation*. That is, "a type of structured asset-backed security (ABS) whose value and payments are derived from a portfolio of fixed-income underlying assets."[74]

This phenomenon became an issue in 2008 and 2009, when banks would package sets of mortgages and sell them. The problem was that a large number of the mortgage holders couldn't pay them back. Thus the Instruments lost considerable value.

Geography and Currency

Figure 20-7 shows some additional elements in the banking model.

First, because the monetary value of Instruments changes constantly, the entity class Valuation has been added to keep track of the Value over time of a Financial Position, an Instrument, or an Instrument Component. That is, each instance of Valuation provides a Value *for* a Financial Position, an Instrument Component, or an Instrument at a particular time (between the Effective Date and the Until Date). The *source of* the Valuation is shown via the relationship to Organization, and the Currency it was *recorded in terms of* is also shown.

Currency provides a unit of measure for describing that Valuation. It is *recorded in terms of* one Currency, such as "US Dollar", "British Pound", "Euro", et cetera. Both the name (e.g., "US Dollar") and the official abbreviation (e.g., "USD") can be recorded for each. Each Currency must be *established for* one Country.

---

[74] Wikipedia. "Collateralized debt obligation" (accessed June 25, 2010).

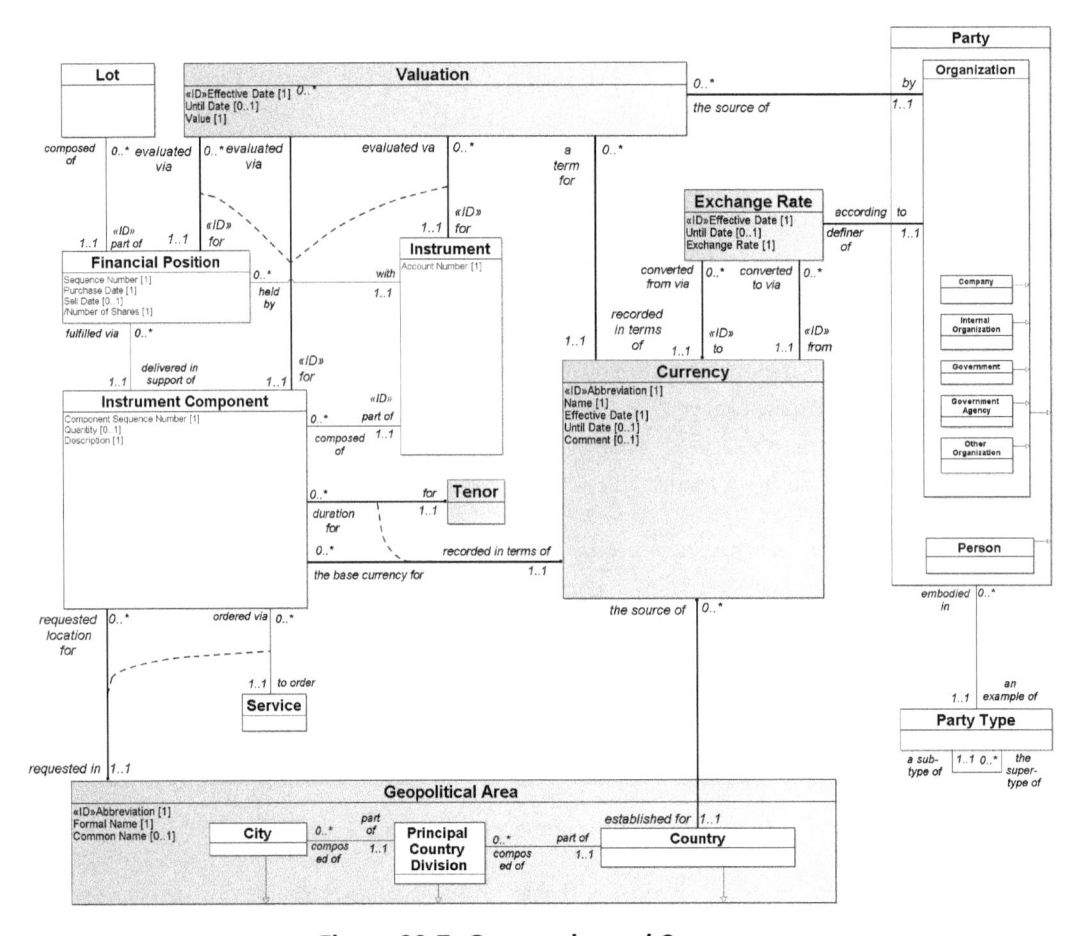

Figure 20-7: Geography and Currency

Once information has been recorded in terms of one **Currency**, it can be retrieved in terms of any other **Currency**, thanks to **Exchange Rate**. Each **Exchange Rate** must be *from* one **Currency** *to* another. So on June 23, 2010, to convert an **Instrument** balance from "USD" to "GBP", the **Exchange Rate** Exchange Rate can be multiplied by an **Instrument** Balance, or an **Instrument Component** Value to report the same numbers in terms of a different **Currency**. Thus, the **Exchange Rate** Rate can be multiplied by the Value of the **Valuation** to see how it would be expressed in a different currency from the one it was recorded in.

Exchange Rates change daily. Important attributes, then, are **Effective Date** and **Until Date**. It's not shown in this model, but it is recommended that **Effective Time** and **Until Time** be included as well. Moreover, it is important to know which **Party** is the *supplier of* the rate. For example, according to the **Party** "X-rates.com", on 23 June, 2010, you could change any quantity of British Pounds into Dollars by multiplying the quantity by 1.49119. A day later it was 1.49271. A year before, on 23 June 1009, the rate was 1.6037. The British Pound has gotten less expensive.

Currency provides a unit of measure for describing that **Valuation**. It is *recorded in terms of* one **Currency**, such as "US Dollar", "British Pound", "Euro", et cetera (Both the **Name** (e.g., "Dollar") and the official **Abbreviation** (e.g., "USD") can be recorded for each. Each **Currency** must be *established for* one **Country**.

It may seem overkill to include the attributes **Effective Date** and **Until Date** in **Currency** itself. It seems that most country's currency has been around forever. Well, except the Euro, of course. And on 1 January, 1995, 10,000 "old" Polish Zloty could buy 1 "new" Polish Zloty.[75] These turn out to be important (if not very dynamic, over time) attributes of **Currency**. So, yes, these dates are relevant to **Currency**.

Figure 20-7 also shows an expanded definition of **Instrument Component**. In addition to the **Instrument Specifications** and **Services** that are linked to an **Instrument** via this entity class, instances of it can also be used to specify other characteristics of the **Instrument**. In addition to having an **Instrument Component** for each **Instrument Specification** and/or each **Service** *ordered*, additional **Instrument Components** can be used to request a particular **Geopolitical Area** to be served, the **Currency** to be applied to the whole **Instrument**.

Included in the Figure is **Tenor**, the time required for a bill of exchange or promissory note to become due for payment.[76] The structure of an **Instrument Component** means that the time period involved is itself a component of the **Instrument**, not an attribute value as might be expected.

Guidance Facility

Sometimes a bank sets aside money for a customer to be sure it is available when the customer actually applies for a loan. This reserve, called a **Guidance Facility**,

---

[75] Wikipedia. http://en.wikipedia.org/wiki/ Polish Zloty (accessed June 24, 2010).

[76] "The Free Dictionary by Farlex." http://www.thefreedictionary.com/tenor *(accessed August 18, 2010)*.

410 Enterprise Model Patterns

or simply "Facility", is normally not communicated to the customer. The concept is shown in Figure 20-8 as a sub-type of **Agreement**. Each **Guidance Facility** must be *based on* a prior **Marketing Relationship** between the bank and the customer. Eventually, a **Guidance Facility** may be *implemented via* one or more **Guidance Lines of Credit**, or it may be *implemented via* another kind of **Loan**.

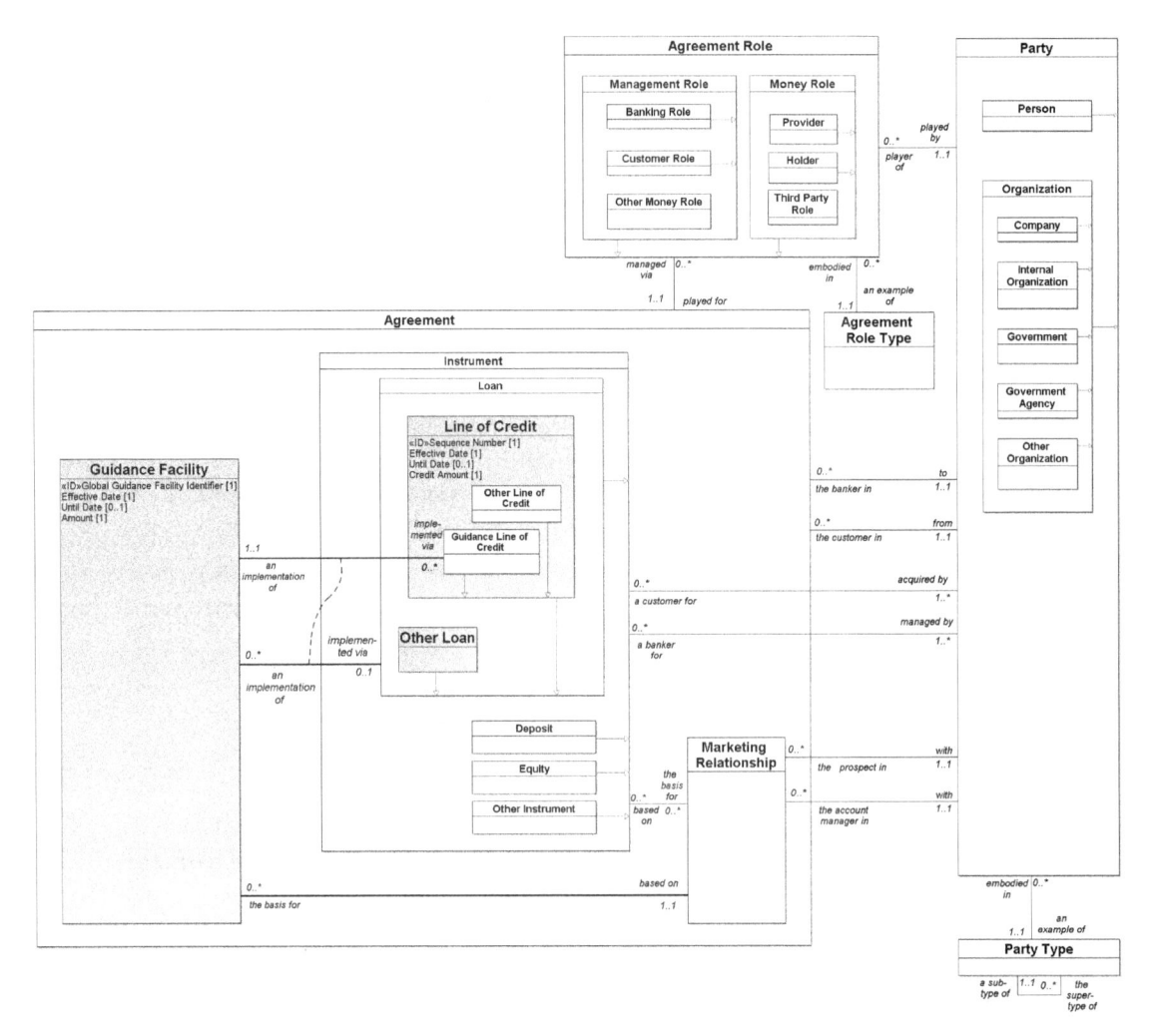

Figure 20-8: Guidance Facility

A **Line of Credit** is an agreed upon amount of money to be loaned to the customer, but not paid all at once. Rather it is a fund that the customer can draw upon, as necessary. Even though the **Guidance Facility** is not known to the customer ahead of time, it can be *the basis of* a **Guidance Line of Credit** that the customer not only knows about but actively manages.

Other Lines of Credit are also possible, without reference to a **Guidance Facility**.

Banking and the Enterprise Model

As stated previously, fitting the banking model into the Enterprise Model (Abstraction Level 1) structures is a little difficult, but as always, most of it fits.

Agreements and Asset Types

Figure 20-9 shows the beginning of this reconciliation. Clearly, **Agreement** is a sub-type of **Party Relationship**.

The relationships between each of the **Agreement** Sub-types and **Party** are clearly sub-types of the relationships between **Party Relationship** and **Party**. Specifically, the two relationships between **Instrument** and **Party** and the two relationships between **Marketing Relationship** and **Party** are respectively sub-types of corresponding two relationships between **Agreement** and **Party**. These relationships are, in turn, sub-types of the two relationships between **Party Relationship** and **Party.**

These are detailed in Table 20-1.

Table 20-1: Agreement Sub-types

Sub-type Entity Class	*relationship*	Entity Class	Super-type Entity Class	*relationship*	Entity Class
Instrument Party	*acquired by a customer in*	Party Instrument	Agreement Party	*from a customer in*	Party Agreement
Agreement	*from*	Party	Party Relationship	*from*	Party
Party	*related to*	Agreement	Party	*related to*	Party Relationship
Instrument Party	*managed by a banker for*	Party Instrument	Agreement Party	*to the banker in*	Party Agreement
Agreement	*to*	Party	Party Relationship	*to*	Party
Party	*the banker in*	Agreement	Party	*related from*	Party Relationship

412 Enterprise Model Patterns

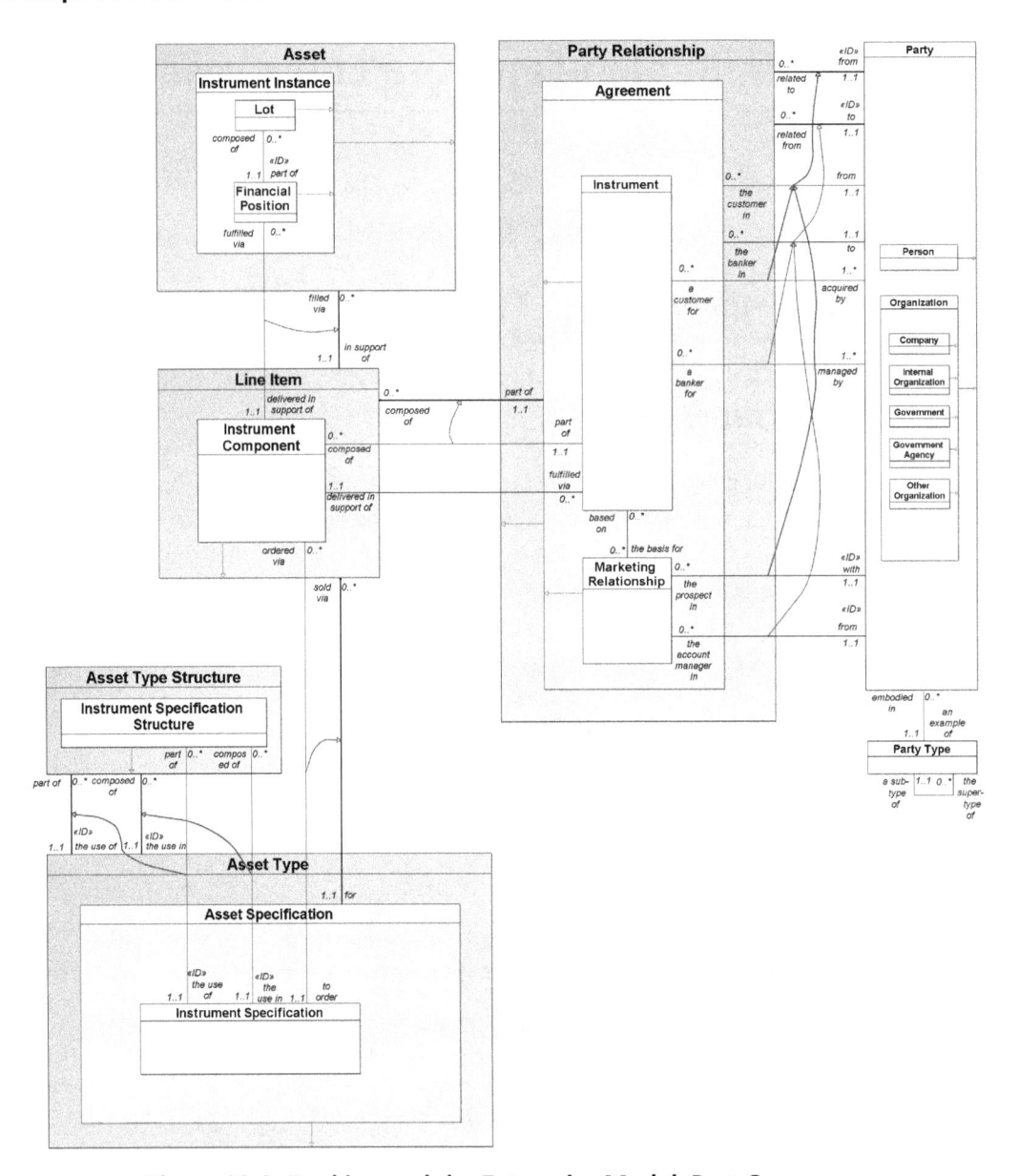

Figure 20-9: Banking and the Enterprise Model, Part One

Continuing with the process of mapping the Banking Model to the Enterprise Model, Figure 20-9 shows how:

- **Instrument Specification** is a sub-type of **Product Model**, which is a sub-type of **Asset Specification**, which in turn is a sub-type of **Asset Type**.
- **Instrument Specification Structure** is a sub-type of **Asset Type Structure**.

- **Instrument Component** is a sub-type of **Line Item.**
- **Instrument Instance**, in the form of **Financial Position** or **Lot**, is a sub-type of **Asset**.

The relationships to the sub-types in this configuration are also sub-types of the relationships between the super-types. There are two relationships between **Instrument Specification** and **Instrument Specification Structure**, one between **Asset Type** and **Line Item**, and one between **Line Item** and **Asset**. Table 20-2 shows the sub-type relationships for these in detail.

Table 20-2: Asset Structure Sub-types

Sub-type Entity Class	relationship	Entity Class	Super-type Entity Class	relationship	Entity Class
Instrument Specification	part of	Instrument Specification Structure	Asset Type	part of	Asset Type Structure
Instrument Specification Structure	the use of	Instrument Specification	Asset Type Structure	the use of	Asset Type
Instrument Specification	composed of	Instrument Specification Structure	Asset Type	composed of	Asset Type Structure
Instrument Specification Structure	the use in	Instrument Specification	Asset Type Structure	the use in	Asset Type
Instrument Specification	ordered via	Instrument Component	Asset Specification	sold via	Line Item
Instrument Component	to order	Instrument Specification	Line Item	for	Asset Specification
Instrument	composed of	Instrument Component	Agreement	composed of	Line Item
Instrument Component	part of	Instrument	Line Item	part of	Agreement
Instrument Component	fulfilled via	Financial Position	Line Item	filled via	Asset
Financial Position	delivered in support of	Instrument Component	Asset	in support of	Line Item

Roles and Activities

In the **Party** section of the Enterprise Model, as presented in Chapter 4, there was no need to define **Party Relationship Role**. But if it had been included, it would have looked like the entity class by that name in Figure 20-10. It is a perfect super-type to show how **Agreement Role** fits into the Enterprise Model. The relationship between **Party Relationship Role** and various other entity classes

414 Enterprise Model Patterns

(**Party**, **Agreement**, and **Instrument Component**) is a neat super-type for the relationships between **Agreement Role** and **Party**.

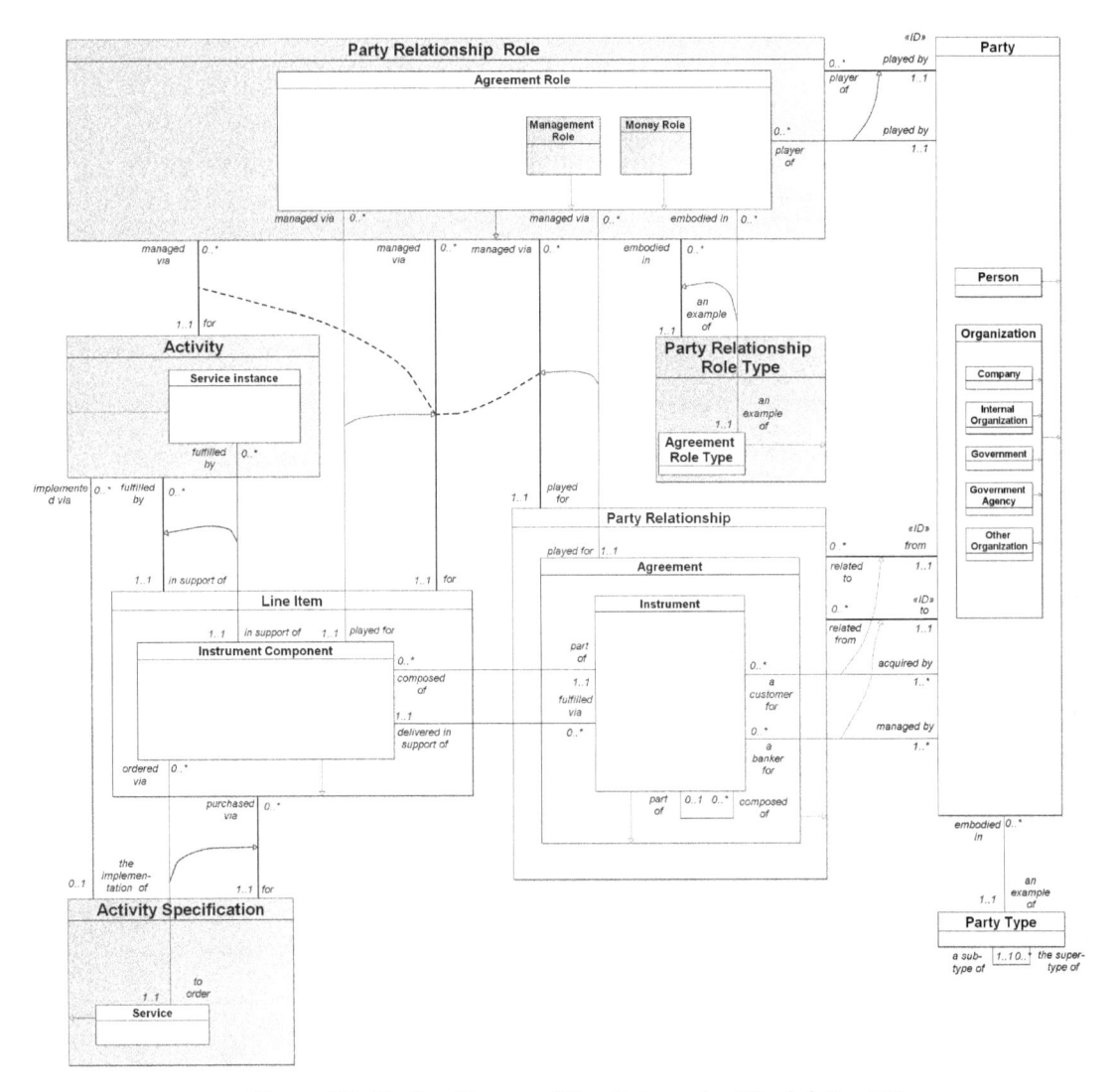

Figure 20-10: Banking and the Enterprise Model, Part Two

+Similarly, the relationship between **Party Relationship Role** and **Party Relationship Role Type** neatly encompass the relationship between **Agreement Role** and **Agreement Role Type**.

Also in the diagram is the fact that **Service** is a sub-type of **Activity Specification** and **Service Instance** is a sub-type of **Activity**. As we've already seen, **Instrument Component** is a sub-type of **Line Item**. Both **Activity** and **Activity Specification** have relationships with **Line Item**, so the relationships between their sub-types and **Instrument Component** are sub-types of these relationships.

This is shown in detail in Table 20-3.

Table 20-3: Agreement Role Relationship Sub-types

Sub-type Entity Class	*relationship*	Entity Class	Super-type Entity Class	*relationship*	Entity Class
Agreement Role	*played for*	Agreement	Party Relationship Role	*played for*	Party Relationship
Agreement	*managed via*	Agreement Role	Party Relationship	*managed via*	Party Relationship Role
Agreement Role	*an example of*	Agreement Role Type	Party Relationship Role	*an example of*	Party Relationship Role Type
Agreement Role Type	*embodied in*	Agreement Role	Party Relationship Role Type	*embodied in*	Party Relationship Role
Agreement Role	*played by*	Party	Party Relationship Role	*played by*	Party
Party	*player of*	Agreement Role	Party	*played by*	Party Relationship Role
Agreement Role	*played for*	Instrument Component	Party Relationship Role	*for*	Line Item
Instrument Component	*managed via*	Agreement Role	Line Item	*managed via*	Party Relationship Role
Instrument Component	*fulfilled by*	Service Instance	Line Item	*fulfilled by*	Activity
Service Instance	*in support of*	Instrument Component	Activity	*in support of*	Line Item
Instrument Component	*to order*	Service	Line Item	*for*	Activity Specification
Service	*ordered via*	Instrument Component	Activity Specification	*purchased via*	Line Item

Summary – An Issue

There remains an important issue with one assertion on this figure: an **Instrument Specification** is a kind of **Asset Specification**, as it was defined in the Enterprise Model. There, it was convenient to constrain the term to mean ***physical assets*** only. But an **Instrument** is not a physical asset. The concept of "virtual" assets was basically covered by Chapter 8, on **Information Resources**. This concept covered everything from documents to computer software, but it did not, in fact, address financial **Instruments** directly. Somehow calling an **Instrument** simply an **Information Resource** doesn't convey what is going on.

Just as **Accounting** is fundamentally different from the rest of the Enterprise Model (since it is, after all, describing the same enterprise that the Enterprise Model does—albeit in a very different way), so are financial products fundamentally different from physical products—even as they are the same.

Physical assets have value, as do information assets. This value can be carried on the accountant's books as value. Financial assets, on the other hand *are* value. They also are carried on the books in the same terms. But out in the world, where they would otherwise be shipped from place to place, stored, and "worn out", their intangible qualities make them very different.

Even so, as we have seen, the data that we have captured about **Instruments**, as they are bought and sold, is very much the same kind of data captured when buying and selling **Products** and other **Assets**. Of course, there is the problem that an instance of an **Instrument** is the same as the **Agreement** that was involved in ordering it. That is a strange wrinkle.

So, Figures 20-9 and 20-10 represent the best that your author can do to represent the kind of mapping that shows how banking fits into the other structures in the business. The point is that this book is about patterns and how to use them to explore the concepts that underlie your business. The Enterprise Model has been tested and found to be a pretty sound basis for creating more detailed models from it. In some cases, this is easier than others.

But these are patterns only—intended to stimulate thinking and to align that thinking with fundamental structures. It is not intended that they exactly follow the requirements of any particular bank. Knowing that the structure of bank products is similar to the structure of physical products is useful in modeling banks. But recognizing that does not diminish the fact that banks really are different.

Banking is inherently complex. If we have succeeded in extracting any underlying simplicity from such a complex topic, this is not a trivial accomplishment. Your author will be satisfied with that.

Chapter 21

Oil Field Production

The oil industry is divided into two principle parts: ***Upstream*** processing makes use of "equipment, facilities or systems located in the wellbore or production train above the surface choke or Christmas tree."[77]♣ and ***Downstream*** processing takes the crude oil from that point to the refinery, turns it into products, and then distributes and sells those products.

This chapter is about the upstream processing (also called oil "production"), and describes in some detail just what an oil well is and how it is constructed.

Facilities

Where Chapter 19 elaborated on the structure of the physical (albeit living) world with extensive sub-types of **Asset**, this chapter describes the oil production (drilling) industry in terms of the intricacies with which it describes **Facilities**. Specifically, it lays out the difference between ***surface facilities*** and ***sub-surface facilities***. The distinction between a **Facility** and the hardware **Assets** required to make it work is particularly noteworthy in this example.

You'll remember from Chapter 12 that a **Facility** is a place with a purpose. That is, it is a **Geographic Location** where **Persons** and **Organizations** (**Parties**) make

---

[77] Schlumberger, Inc. *Oilfield Glossary*. "Upstream". *http://www.glossary.oilfield.slb.com* (accessed July, 2010).

♣ A ***choke*** is "A device incorporating an orifice that is used to control fluid flow rate or downstream system pressure". [Schlumberger. "choke" (accessed June 27, 2010).] A ***christmas tree*** is "an assembly of valves, spools, pressure gauges and chokes fitted to the wellhead of a completed well to control production". [Schlumberger. "christmas tree" (accessed June 27, 2010).]

use of **Assets** to perform **Activities**. An oil well is a good example of one of those. Note that it is common to confuse the physical equipment with the **Facility**. But every single piece of equipment could be replaced (indeed this could be a frequent occurrence) and the **Facility** would still retain its identity. This chapter will focus on the relationships between a particular kind of **Asset** and the **Facility** that is a typical oil well.

Surface Facilities

Figure 21-1 shows the architectural model for **Facility**, as understood by the oil industry. The basic sub-types in this world are **Surface Facility** and **Sub-surface Facility**. As the name suggests, a **Surface Facility** is implemented via a collection of equipment for doing the preliminary processing of crude oil and gas, once it is removed from the ground.

The primary sub-type shown here is a **Manifold**, although there are certainly many **Other** kinds of **Facility**, as well. For those of you not in this industry, a **Manifold** is "An arrangement of piping or valves designed to control, distribute, and often monitor fluid flow."[78] This is the collection of pipes at the top of the well that directs fluids in the various directions required.

Attributes of **Manifold** include:

- **On SKADA Indicator** – "Supervisory control and data acquisition (SCADA) is the system that connects to the production facilities' controllers and data sources and collects the measured data and stores them in a database."[79] The value of this attribute for an instance of **Manifold** determines whether or not an instance of **Manifold** is monitored this way.

- **Leak Test Enabled Indicator** – Is the instance of **Manifold** able to detect leaks automatically?

- **Valves Quantity** – The number of valves that are part of an instance of **Manifold**.

- **Ports Quantity** – The number of connections that link an instance of **Manifold** with the set of pipes that constitute the distribution network.

---

[78] Schlumberger, Inc. *Oilfield Glossary*. "Manifold". *http://www.glossary.oilfield.slb.com* (accessed June 27, 2010).

[79] Society of Petroleum Engineers. 2006. "Automated Production Surveillance." *http://www.slb.com/resources/technical_papers/software/96645.aspx*.

Oil Field Production 419

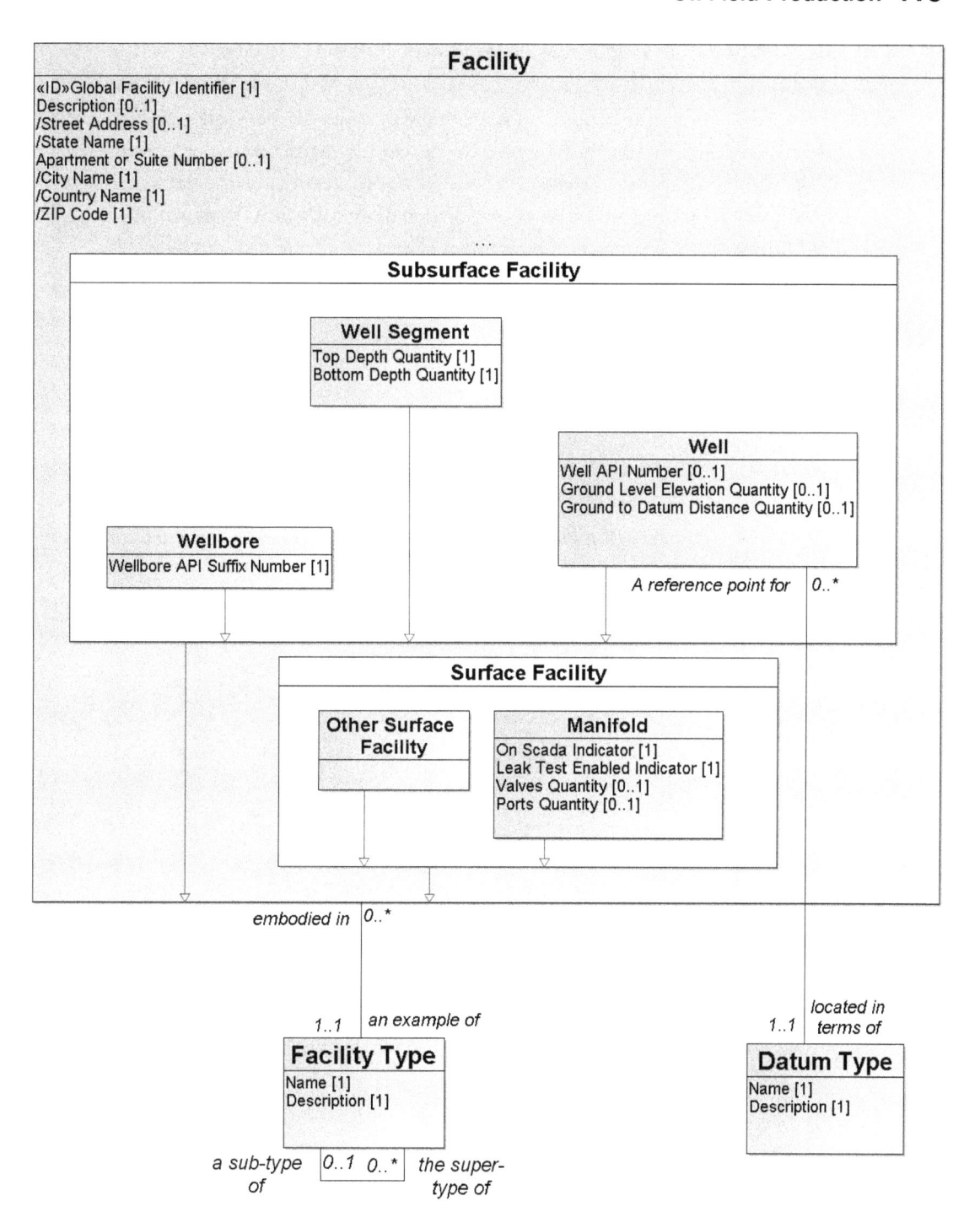

Figure 21-1: Facilities

The **Subsurface Facility** of primary interest here is the oil well hole itself (the **Well**), as implemented by various pieces of pipe casing and other equipment. A

420 Enterprise Model Patterns

Well is a **Facility** that is a collection of **Wellbores** (holes in the ground) used to retrieve liquid and gaseous hydrocarbons from below the ground. The **Well** actually begins a few feet[*] above the ground with a point described as the **Well's** *datum*. This is the "zero point" used as a reference for describing depths of various points in the **Well**. The ground level of the Earth is usually a few feet below the datum. In Figure 21-1, each **Well** must be *located in terms of* exactly one **Datum Type**. In most cases, the **Datum Type** is a piece of equipment at the top of the well piping called a "Kelly Bushing".

Well is shown with numerous attributes that locate it on the Earth:

- **Ground Level Elevation** describes the overall height, above sea level, of the point on the ground where the opening of the **Well** is placed.

- **Ground Level to Datum Distance Quantity** tells how far from the physical surface of the earth the datum, or "Kelly Bushing", is located.

Figure 21-2 shows a drawing of a physical **Well** which, for purposes of this exercise, has the fictional **Well API Number** of "0504060807".

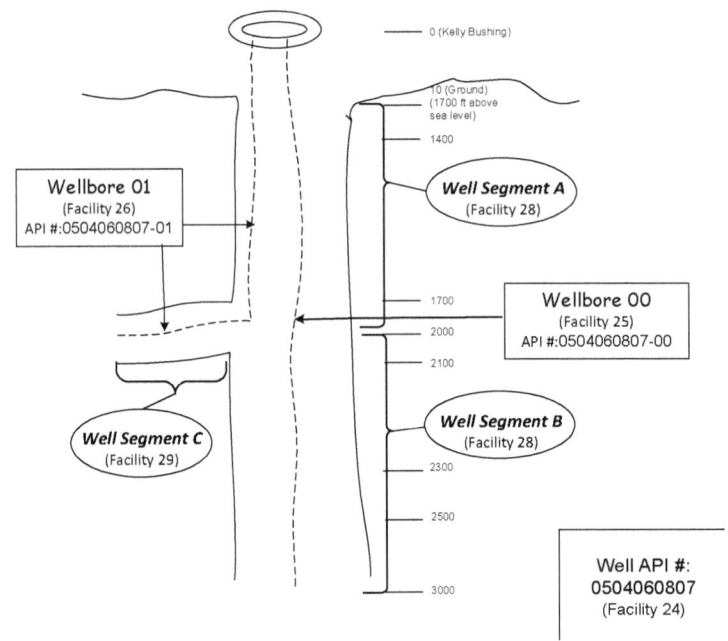

Figure 21-2: Diagram of Wellbores

---

[*] The example is from an oil company's U.S. field, so the unit of measure is assumed to be feet. Adding the logic to address variable units of measure would be exactly the same as was done for **Assets** in Chapter 6.

Oil Field Production   421

The **Global Facility Identifier** for all **Facilities** (henceforth referred to here simply as "Facility ID") in this example is `"24"`. The **Datum Type** of this example is a `"Kelly Bushing"` that is 10 feet above the ground surface. That is, the **Ground to Datum Distance Quantity** for the **Well** shown is `"10"` (feet). In the example diagrammed, the **Ground to Datum Distance Quantity** is indeed shown as being 10 feet below the "top" of the well.

In this case, the Ground Level Elevation Quantity is 1700 feet above sea level. The Ground to Datum Distance Quantity is 10 feet, which puts the Kelly Bushing at 1710 feet above sea level.

This **Well** has two **Wellbores**. A **Wellbore** is a single path from the surface to the lowest point in the **Well**.

In the Figure, the two **Wellbores** are:

- **Wellbore** `"00"` (**Facility** `"25"`) goes from the top of the well straight down to the lowest point, some 3000 feet below. This **Wellbore** has an API prefix of the **Well** number `"0504060807"`, identifying the **Wellbore** more fully as **Wellbore** `"0504060807-00"`.

- **Wellbore** `"01"` (**Facility** `"26"`) goes down about 1700 feet and turns approximately 90º. In the diagram, it isn't shown going any lower than 2100 feet, but in its full representation, it could go even deeper than **Wellbore** `"00"`. This **Wellbore** has an API Prefix of the **Well** number `"0504060807"`, identifying the **Wellbore** more fully as **Wellbore** `"0504060807-01"`.

Each **Well** is divided into **Well Segments**. Each **Well Segment** is a portion of a **Wellbore** that does not cross a point of intersection and has a consistent diameter. In Figure 21-2, there are three **Well Segments**:

- **Well Segment** `"A"` (**Facility** `"27"`) extends from a Top Depth Quantity of `"0"` (that is, 10 feet above the ground) to a Bottom Depth Quantity of `"1800"` feet below the Kelly Bushing.

- **Well Segment** `"B"` (**Facility** `"28"`) extends from a Top Depth Quantity of `"1800"` feet below the Kelly Bushing to a Bottom Depth Quantity of `"3000"` feet below the Kelly Bushing.

- **Well Segment** `"C"` (**Facility** `"29"`) extends horizontally from the bottom of **Well Segment** `"A"`, but only its vertical depth is shown. In this exercise, the actual length of **Well Segment** `"C"` is not shown. It extends vertically from a Top Depth Quantity of "1800" feet below the Kelly Bushing to a Bottom Depth Quantity of "2100" feet (at least for the portion showing on the diagram).

Well, **Wellbore**, and **Well Segment** are shown in the model drawing that is Figure 21-1 as sub-types of **Subsurface Facility**.

Completions

Figure 21-3 shows physical casings added to the sample **Well**. Note that there is an outer casing that goes to about 2300 feet in **Wellbore** "00". At about that level, a smaller casing overlaps the larger one with a ring sealing the intersection. This second casing contains perforations that permit petroleum products to be drawn into the **Well**. This creates a single path from the holes at the bottom to the top of the well. This path is called a **Completion** (specifically **Completion** "X"). There is a third casing attached to the first that goes into **Well Segment** "C". There are perforations in the first casing between 1400 feet and 1500 feet, as well as in the casing that is in well segment C. A solid casing inside the first one, with a plug below the Well Segment C intersection produces a second path to the surface, isolated from the first one. This second path is a second **Completion** (**Completion** "Y").

We are not yet concerned with the physical casings themselves yet, however. Instead we are concerned with the fact that they define two specific routes for oil and gas to get from their reservoirs to the surface.

A **Completion**, then, is "the assembly of down hole tubulars[*] and equipment required to enable safe and efficient production from an oil or gas well".[80] A **Well** may have more than one **Completion** if they are mechanically isolated to prevent hydraulic communication with each other. That is, there are two **Completions** shown in Figure 21-3:

- **Completion** "X" (**Facility** "31") draws fluids from depths of between 2400 and 2800 feet (**Well Segment** "B"), and passes them directly to the surface.

---

[*] A "tubular" is "any type of oilfield pipe, such as drill pipe, drill collars, pup joints, casing, production tubing and pipeline." [Schlumberger. 27 June, 2010. "Tubular"]

[80] Schlumberger, Inc. "Oilfield Glossary. "completion"." *http://www.glossary.oilfield.slb.com* (accessed June 27, 2010).

- **Completion** "Y" (**Facility** "35") draws fluids from both **Well Segment** "C" and **Well Segment** "A", and the two sets of fluids combine as they come to the surface.

Again, note that these are the **Facilities** by which oil and gas are delivered to the surface. ▽ We have not yet described the physical pipes or other equipment.

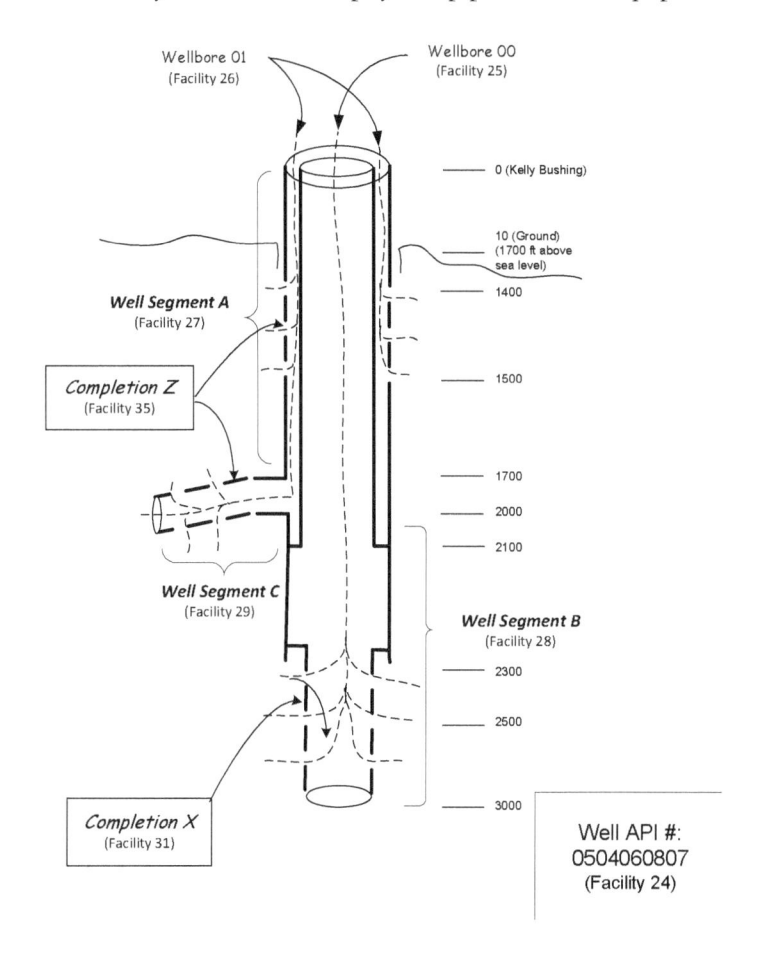

Figure 21-3: Completions

In the latest well drawing, Figure 21-3, **Well Segment** "A" hosts two **Wellbores** ("00" and "01"). **Wellbore** "00" transverses two **Well Segments** ("A" and "B"), however. The four permutations involved are shown in Table 21-1.

▽   Note also that the same **Facility** that is for pumping oil and gas from underground reservoirs may also be used to inject steam into the reservoir to provide pressure to make the oil and gas rise through adjacent oil wells.

A **Completion** may extend over more than one **Well Segment**. In the example shown in Figure 21-3, **Completion** "Z" extends over **Well Segments** "A" and "C", while **Completion** "X" is only in **Well Segment** "B". Remember that the "completion" part is only that where fluids are coming into the well.

Table 21-1: Well Segment Wellbore Placement

Well (Facility ID)	Well Segment (Facility ID)	Wellbore (Facility ID)	Well Segment (Top Depth)	Well Segment (Bottom Depth)
0504060807 (24)	A (27)	00 (25)	0 (feet)	2000
0504060807 (24)	A (27)	01 (26)	0	2000
0504060807 (24)	B (28)	00 (25)	2000	3000
0504060807 (24)	C(29)	01 (26)	2000	2100

Figure 21-4 shows the architectural model for this. In this case, a separate entity class has been specified for each combination of two **Facility** sub-types:

- Each **Well Segment Wellbore Placement** must be *of* one **Well Segment** *in* one **Wellbore**.

- Each **Completion Well Segment Placement** must be *of* one **Completion** *in* one **Well Segment**.

- Note that the remaining combination, **Completions** and **Wellbores** can be inferred from the first two, as shown in the "de-normalized" table that is Table 21-2.

Table 21-2: Completion Well Segment Placement

Well (Facility ID)	Completion (Facility ID)	Well Segment (Facility ID)	Wellbore (Facility ID)	Well Segment (Top Depth)	Well Segment (Bottom Depth)
0504060807 (24)	Z (35)	A (27)	01 (26)	0 (feet)	2000
0504060807 (24)	Z (35)	C(29)	01 (26)	2000	2100
0504060807 (24)	X (31)	A (27)	00 (25)	0	2000
0504060807 (24)	X (31)	B (28)	00 (25)	2000	3000

Oil Field Production

- On the assumption that there might be **Other Sub-surface Facilities** as well as **Other Surface Facilities**, the more general approach to linking them together is shown in Figure 21-5. Here, each **Facility Structure** must be *the presence of* any **Facility** and *the presence in* any other **Facility**.

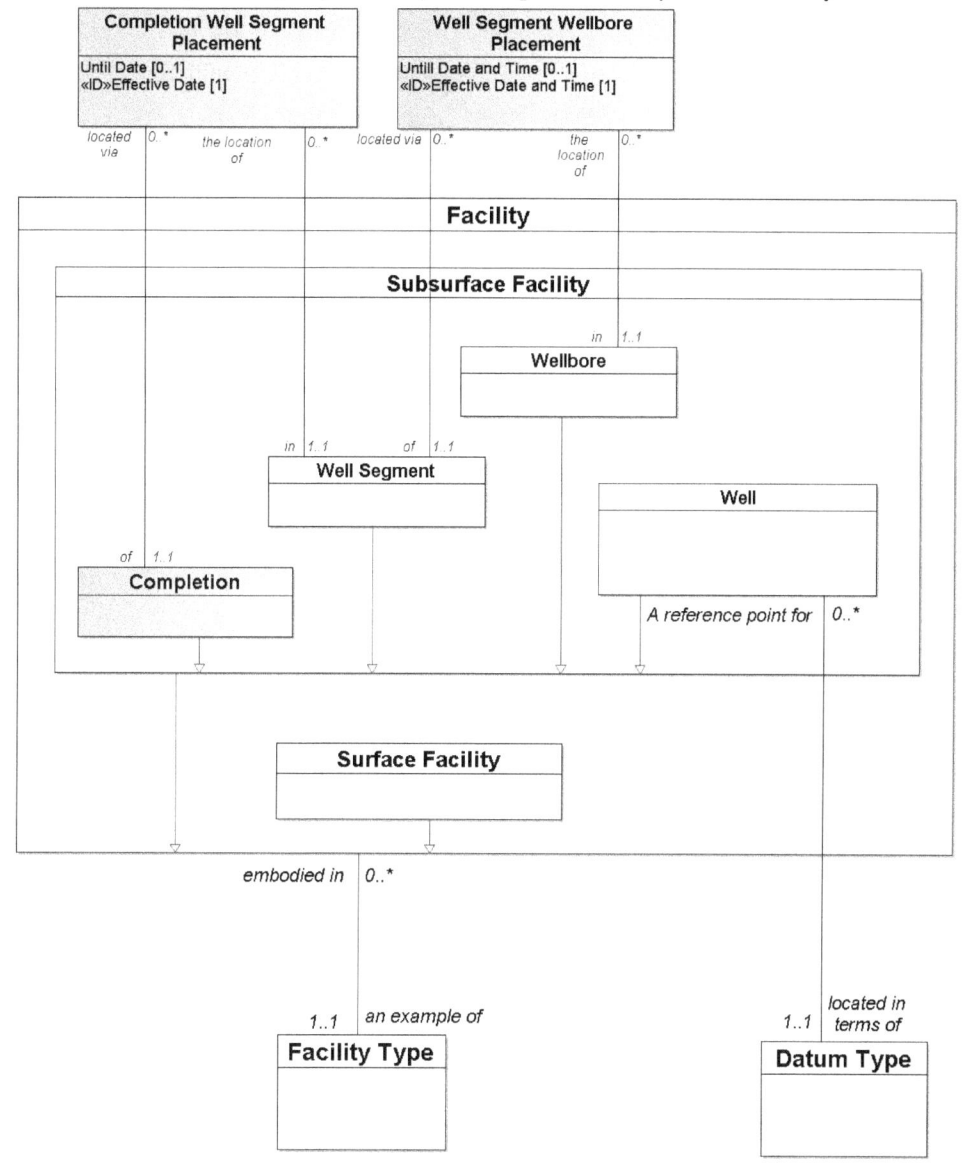

Figure 21-4: Completions

Purposes and Products

Figure 21-6 provides some context for the **Facility** that we are building. Each **Completion** (path from the surface to a point underground) has, as its

426 Enterprise Model Patterns

Completion Primary Purpose, *either* the extraction of crude oil or natural gas, *or* the injection of steam into the reservoir to provide pressure to make the oil and gas rise through adjacent wells. While each **Completion** will be *intended to accomplish* more than one **Completion Primary Purpose** over time, at any one point in time each **Completion** is *intended to accomplish* one **Completion Primary Purpose** that is *an example of* a **Completion Purpose Type**. That is, between a specified **Start Date and Time** and its **Termination Date and Time** it is primarily *intended to accomplish* either `"Production"` or `"Injection"` (of steam).

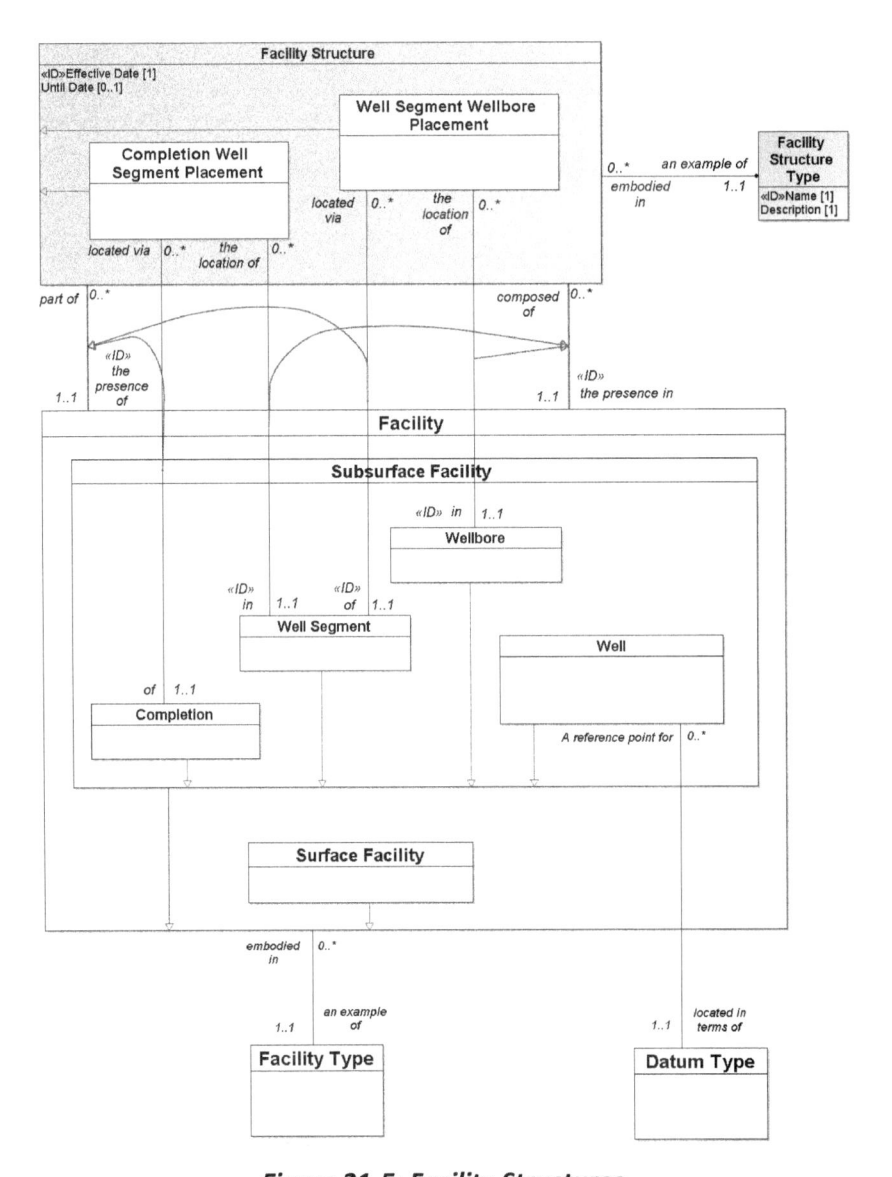

Figure 21-5: Facility Structures

Oil Field Production 427

Even if a **Wellbore** has no **Completions**, a **Wellbore Purpose** can be specified. This is usually *an example of* `"data acquisition"`.

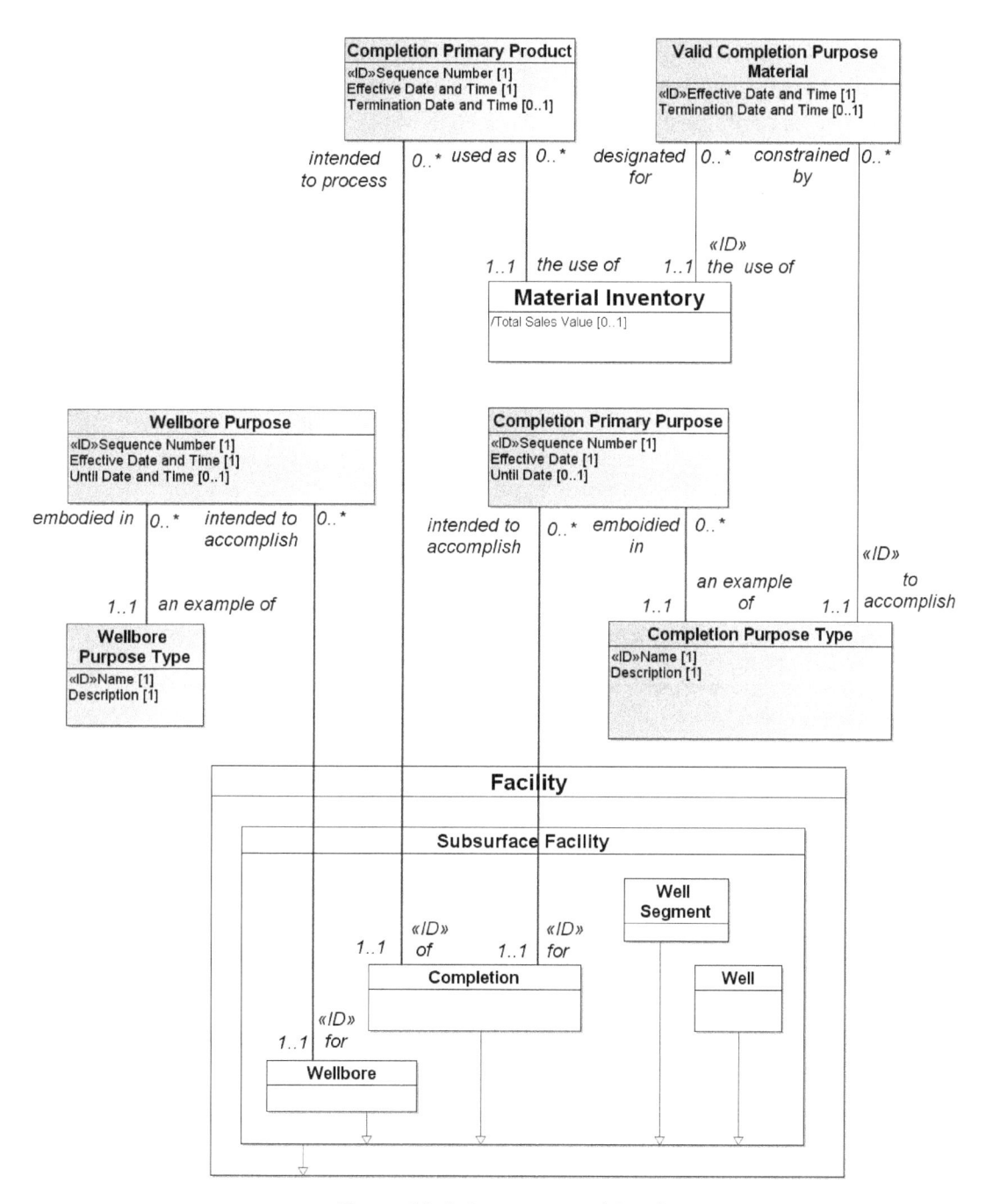

Figure 21-6: Purposes and Products

Ultimately, a **Completion** only meets its **Completion Primary Purpose** if the **Specified Material** *designated for* its **Completion Purpose Type** is *used as* a **Completion Primary Product** *of* that **Completion**. Typically this would be either oil emulsion or steam.[≈] Note that at the time a **Completion Primary Purpose** is "Production", it is expected that the **Specified Material** involved will be "Oil Emulsion". If it is "Injection" the **Specified Material** involved would be "Steam".

The entity class **Valid Completion Purpose Material** specifies legal combinations of **Completion Purpose Type** and **Material Type**. Thus the constraints:

Business Rule

- During the time that the **Completion Primary Purpose** for a **Completion** is an example of a particular **Completion Purpose Type**, the **Completion Primary Product** of that **Completion** must be the use of a **Material Type** that is designated for a **Valid Completion Purpose Material** that is to accomplish that **Completion Purpose Type**. *(Translation:* If the **Completion Primary Purpose Type** is "Extraction", then one **Valid Completion Purpose Material** might be *the use of* "Crude oil". Another **Valid Completion Purpose Material** might be *the use of* "natural gas".

Well Assemblies

Thus far we've described the functional characteristics of an oil **Well**. These are the **Facilities**. What most people see, though, are not those, but the assembly of pipes, valves, and pumps that implement the **Well**. Figure 21-7 shows our example with clusters of hardware specifically labeled as **Well Assemblies**. Each **Well Assembly** is the piping with a single diameter (and other equipment) that implements a section of the **Well** (between intersections). In the example, four **Well Assemblies** are shown:

≈ Ok, or concrete.

- The **Well Assembly** "45" is the outer pipe that runs from the Kelly Bushing almost to the bottom of the well, ending at 2300 feet.

- The **Well Assembly** "46" is a smaller piece of pipe (perforated, so fluids can enter) overlapping Well Assembly 45, with a plug to prevent leakage, and running to the bottom of the well, 3000 feet down.

- The **Well Assembly** "47" intersects Well Assembly 45, and runs laterally.

- The **Well Assembly** "48" runs inside **Well Assembly** 45 from the Kelly Bushing to 2100 feet. Plugs at the bottom create a second chamber, separating **Completion** Z from **Completion** X.

While each **Well** is "custom made", the **Well Assembly Specification** still must be drawn up to define exactly the components and configuration of the finally built **Well Assembly**. As with other **Asset Specifications**, a **Well Assembly Specification** is the definition of the configuration, composition, and characteristics of one or more instances of a **Well Assembly**.

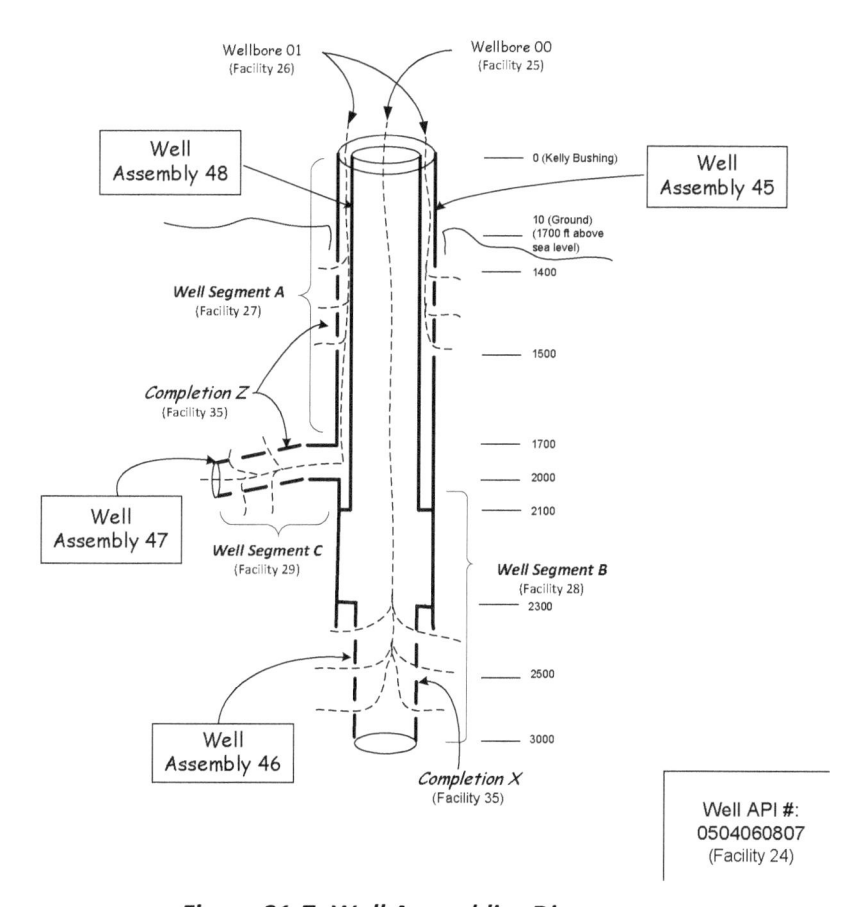

Figure 21-7: Well Assemblies Diagram

430 Enterprise Model Patterns

Since these **Well Assemblies** are the hardware that make an oil well work, now it is appropriate to examine the model of **Assets** that constitute these **Well Assemblies**. Figure 21-8 shows the appropriate sub-types of **Asset**, **Asset Specification**, and **Asset Type** that are called on in this situation—as described originally in Chapter 6, the Chapter describing **Assets**. To begin with, all of these are ultimately *examples of* the **Asset Type** that are **Discrete Item**. (See Figure 6-2 and Table 6-1 on pages 132-133.)

As will be seen below, **Well Assemblies** are constructed from **Pieces of Equipment**.

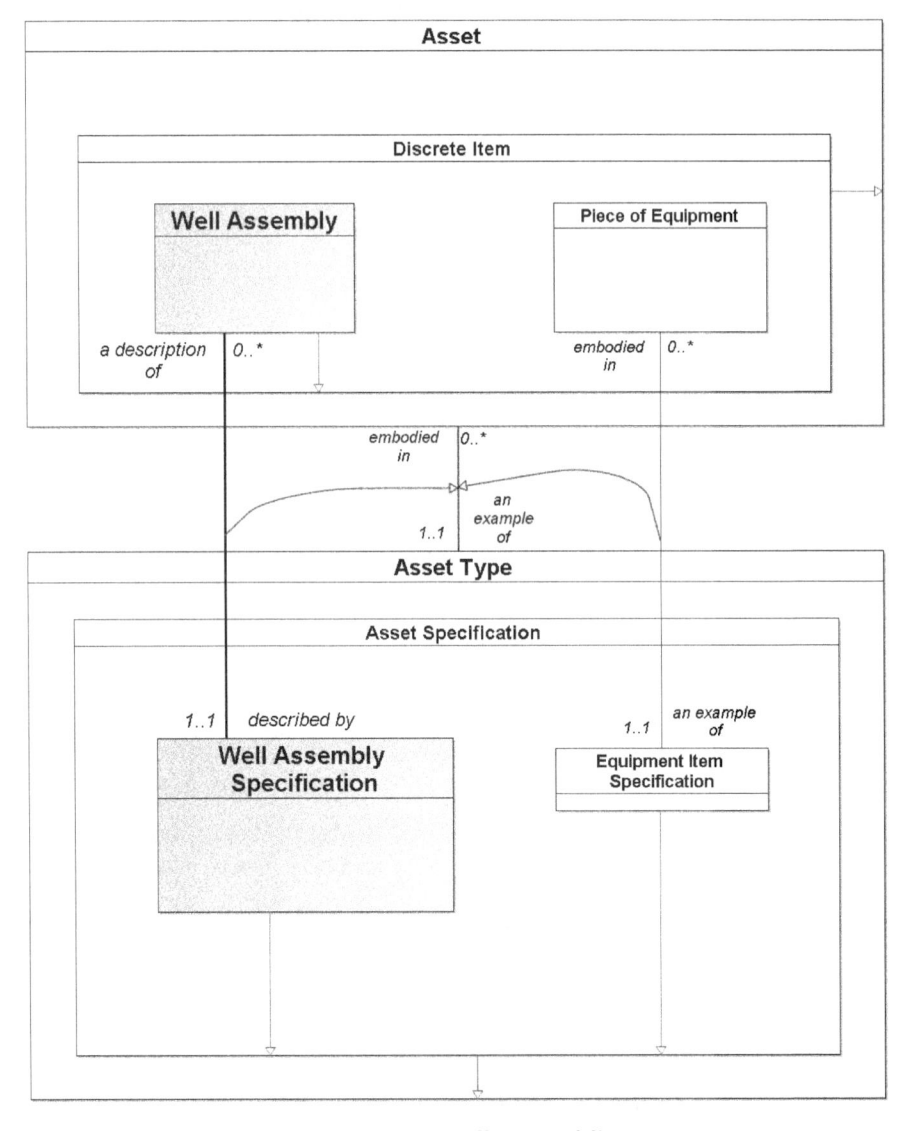

Figure 21-8: Well Assemblies

Well Assemblies in Facilities

The fact that a **Well Assembly** is actually installed in the **Facility** that is a **Well** is shown in Figure 21-9. Here, each **Well Assembly** must be *placed via* exactly one **Installation** *into* a **Well**. Since **Well Assembly Placement** is a sub-type of **Material Movement**, it implies the action of doing the **Installation**. Note that in the case of an **Installation** it must be *into* one **Facility**, but there is no reference to its being *from* another **Facility**. As with any **Material Movement**, it takes place at a particular Beginning Date and Time and an optional Ending Date and Time describing the elapsed time of the installation process. This implies that at some time there may also be a **Removal** of the **Well Assembly** as well. This is a different instance of **Material Movement**. It will have a different Beginning Date and Time and Ending Date and Time. This time there will be the reference to the **Facility** it is moved *from*, but not the one moved *to*. This is why the model asserts that each **Well Facility** must be *placed via* <u>one or more</u> **Well Assembly Placements**. There must be one initially, and there may be a second when the **Well Assembly** is removed.

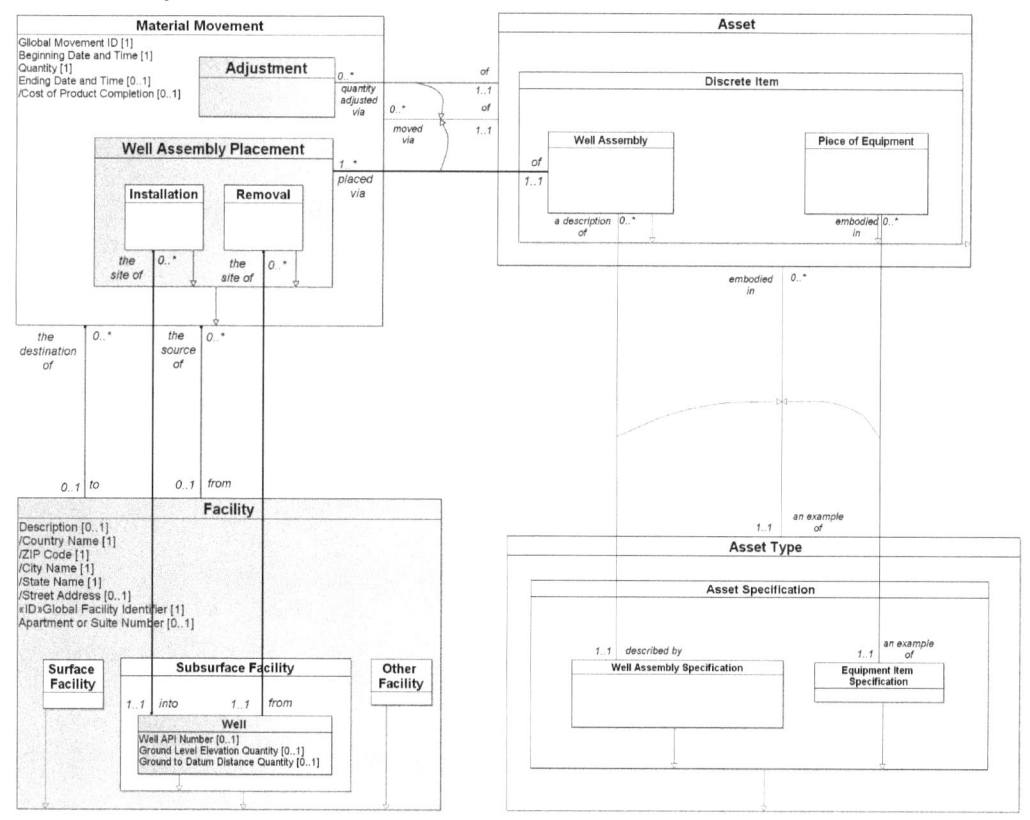

Figure 21-9: Well Assemblies in Facilities

Well Assembly Structure

Each **Well Assembly** is composed of assorted pipes, valves, and other attachments. To describe the composition of the **Asset** that is a **Well Assembly**, we'll again borrow a portion of the model from the **Asset** presentation in Chapter 6. Specifically, in Figure 21-10, **Well Assembly Structure** is shown as a sub-type of **Asset Structure**. In this case, though, each **Well Assembly Structure** must be *the use of* a **Piece of Equipment** and *the use in* a **Well Assembly**. This is because the relationships from **Well Assembly** to either **Piece of Equipment** or **Equipment Specification** must be sub-types of the corresponding relationships to **Asset Structure**.[*]

An alternative to this representation would be to use the model of **Manufacturing** from Chapter 16 to show the actual consumption of hardware time in the building of the **Well Assembly**. The reader is invited to explore that approach.

Table 21-3 shows the physical components of the **Well Assemblies** that were first described in Figure 21-7. There are four **Well Assemblies** described:

- **Well Assembly** "45" – The outer pipe, combined with a slotted pipe that runs from ground level to about 2100 feet down. This includes a section of solid pipe, a section of grooved pipe, and a section of solid pipe, all welded together.

- **Well Assembly** "46" – At the bottom of **Well Assembly** "45", a narrower, slotted tube is added, with a plug at the top to prevent fluids from leaking out.

- **Well Assembly** "47" is a slotted pipe attached at right angles to **Well Assembly** "45", about 2000 feet underground.

- **Well Assembly** "48" is a solid pipe that fits inside the one of **Well Assembly** "45". With the plug added at the bottom, just below the intersection with **Well Assembly** "47", this separates **Completion** "X" from **Completion** "Z".

---

[*] This is a rare example of the more specific semantic model requiring changes to the nice tidy Enterprise Model. It happens.

Oil Field Production 433

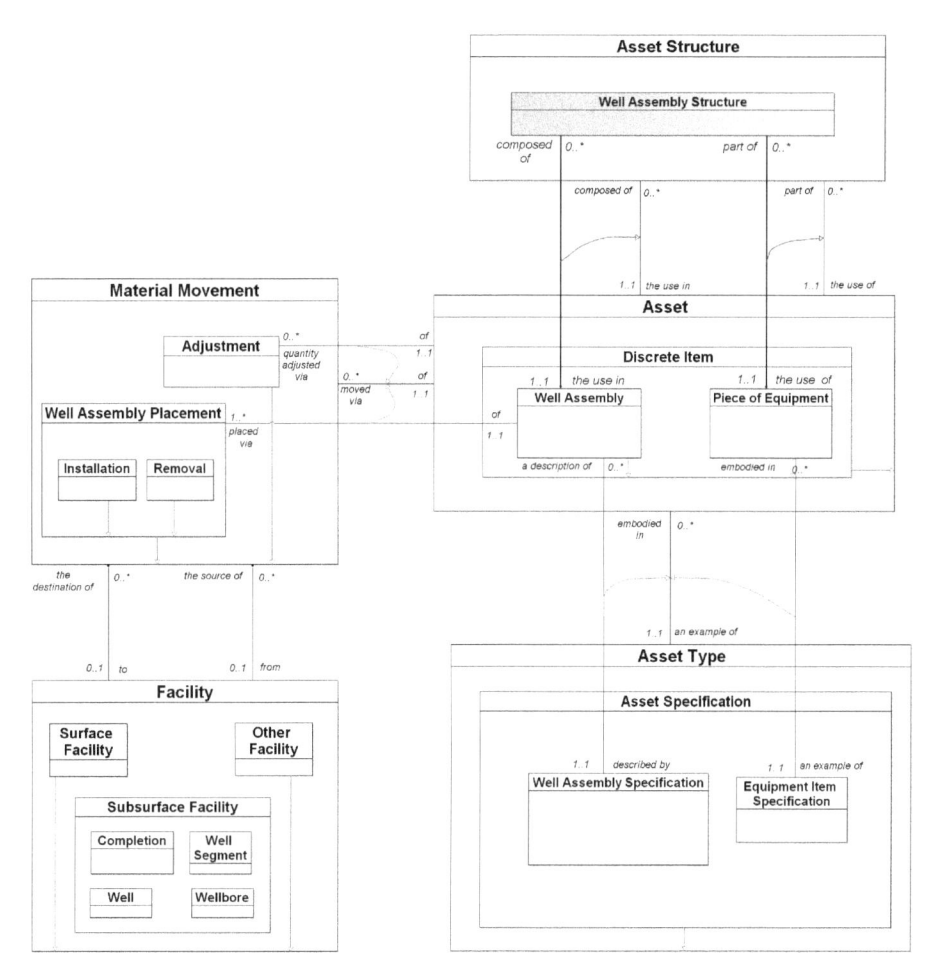

Figure 21-10: Well Assembly Structure

Table 21-3: Well Assembly Components

Well Assembly (ID)	Equipment Specification (Desc.)	Equipment (Desc.)	Seq. No.	Length	Top Depth	Bottom Depth
45	12" Pipe	14	1	2300	0	1400
	12" Slotted Pipe	53	2	100	1400	1500
	12" Pipe	14	3	800	1500	2300
46	Packer (S/N: 1432522)	45	1	-	2300	2300
	10" Slotted Pipe	52	2	700	2300	3000
47	10" Slotted Pipe	54	1	1000	1700	200
48	11" Pipe	32	1	2150	0	2150
	Packer (S/N: 20984733)	45	2	-	2150	2150

434 Enterprise Model Patterns

The original **Well Assembly** configuration diagram (Figure 21-7) is repeated and annotated differently in Figure 21-11. Each of the structures described in Table 21-3 is annotated in this diagram.

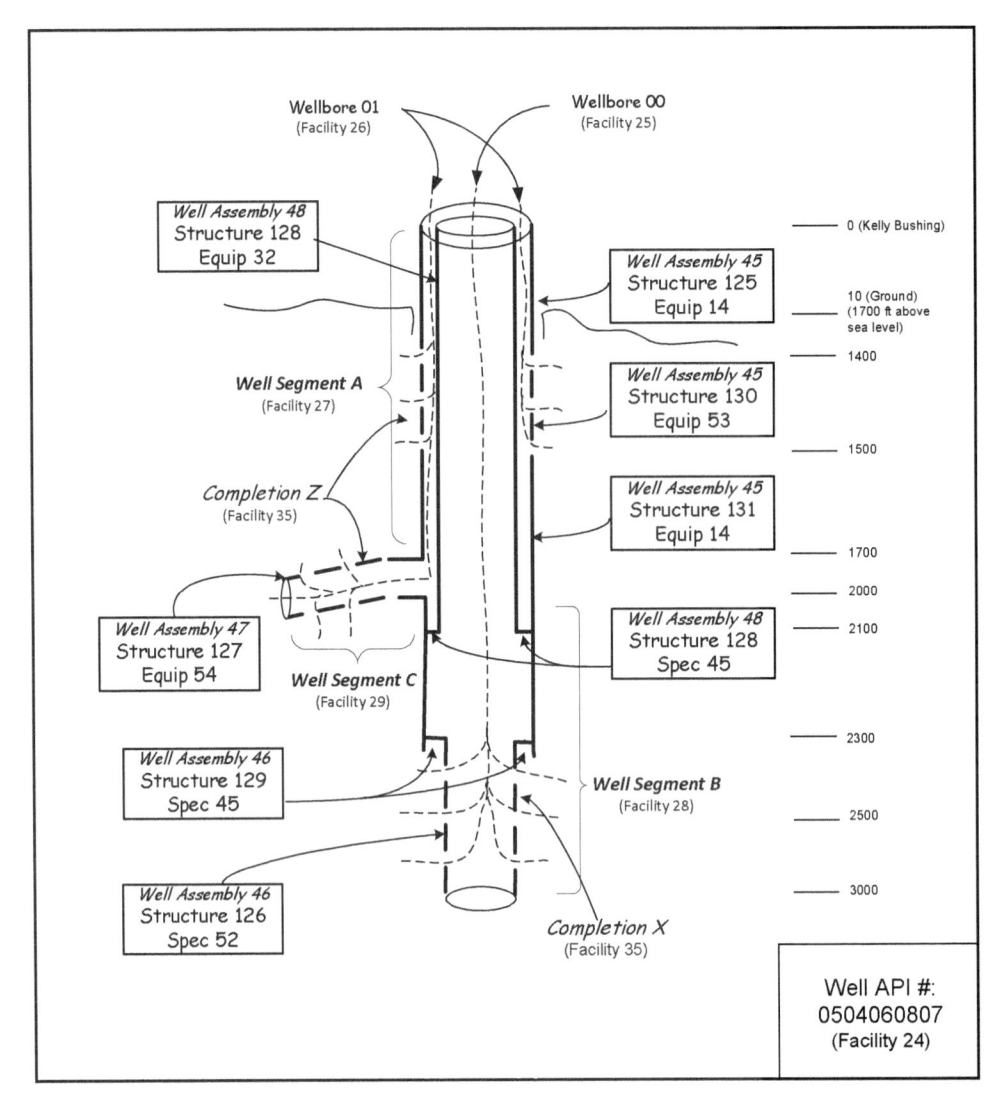

Figure 21-11: Well Assembly Components Diagram

Well Assembly Characteristics

Since each **Well Assembly** is custom-made to fit in a particular **Well**, the concept of a **Well Assembly Specification** differs from that of a **Product Model**, in that the latter describes a mass-produced product, like a computer, while the former is a design for a **Well**—to be built only once. The specification for a **Well Assembly** is *described by* a unique set of **Asset Characteristic Values** *of* appropriate **Characteristics**. Figure 21-12 shows first how each **Well Assembly Specification** (among others) may be *described by* one or more **Asset Specification Characteristic Value**, each of which must be *of* one **Asset Characteristic**.

Note that each actual **Well Assembly** also may be *described by* one or more **Asset Characteristic Values** *of* **Asset Characteristics**. If this is the same **Asset Characteristic** that was *evaluated with* an **Asset Specification Characteristic Assignment** that is *to describe* the **Well Assembly Specification** that the **Well Assembly** being *described* is *an example of*, then the two values are expected to be close. That is, the **Asset Characteristic Value** is expected to be *based on* the corresponding **Asset Specification Value**.

For example, an **Asset Assembly Characteristic Assignment** *of* the **Asset Characteristic** "Notional Diameter" *to describe* **Well Assembly Specification** "A-235" may have a **Standard Value** of "14" (inches), with a **Tolerance** of ".1" (inch). The **Well Assembly** "45" is *an example of* **Well Assembly Specification** "A-235". Therefore, the **Asset Characteristic Value Characteristic Value** *of* "Notional Diameter" *to describe* **Well Assembly** "45"—is expected to be within appropriate tolerance of "14" inches. So "14.05" inches may be acceptable, but "14.2" inches is not.

Thus, in Figure 21-12, each **Asset Characteristic Value** must be *based on* one and only one **Asset Specification Characteristic Value**.

436 Enterprise Model Patterns

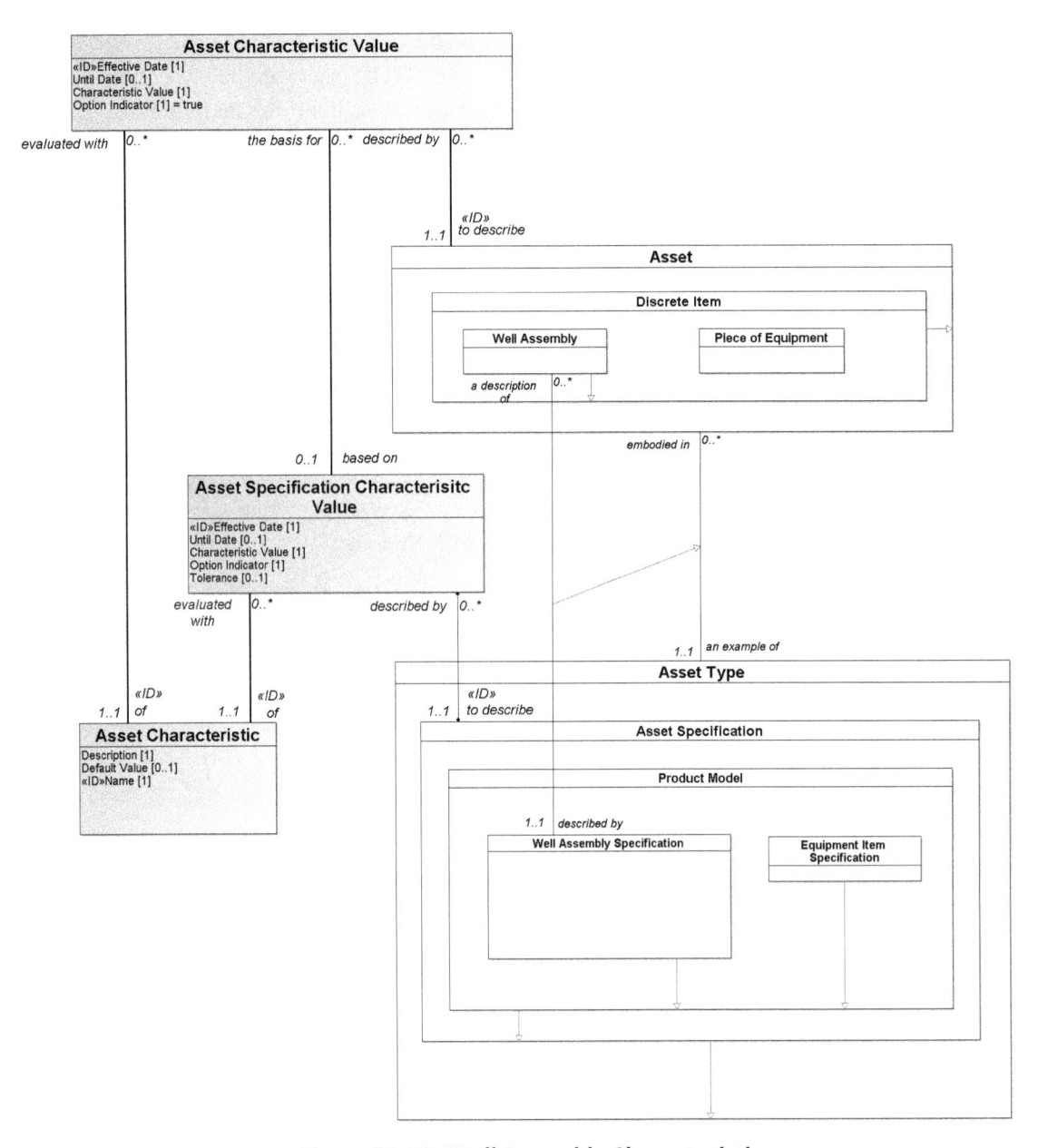

Figure 21-12: Well Assembly Characteristics

CHAPTER 22

Highway Maintenance

One of the most interesting aspects of the consulting business is that in every company or government agency, there is inevitably one word that is the most central to the enterprise's business. This, however, is the word whose definition cannot be agreed to. It is viewed differently by everyone in the business. In the case of a Canadian Provincial agency concerned with highway maintenance, the word was *road*.

To the driver trying to find h' way from the airport to a hotel, a road is a collection of *lines* and intersections to be navigated. A map is useful to the extent that it accurately describes that route. The thickness of the lines may say something about the suitability of a particular segment, but that is secondary to the information about its "connectedness".

To the part of the agency concerned with planning roads and highways, the land required to build them, along with the right-of-way required, are geographic *areas*.

To the department responsible for building and maintaining the roads and highways, these are carefully shaped *solids*, with a particular profile, constructed of cement, asphalt, or other compounds.

So, the bit of the Enterprise Architectural Model unique to the highway department is all about the roads that are its responsibility in all three forms: lines, areas, and solids.

Paths

The first view of the highway system is of a network of lines. To get from the airport to the hotel in the center of the city, a tourist map may show the principle roads into the city. That may be adequate, however, only to get the driver to the neighborhood. Getting to the actual entrance of the hotel may require a more intricate series of twists and turns.

The driver is not concerned in this case (except in the most general terms), with the condition of the road, its construction, or any of the other characteristics that may be of interest to, say, a highway construction crew.

To the driver, ultimately the road is simply a network of links with intersections connecting them together. "Take Highway 50 to 6th Street and turn right. Then go to Elm Drive and turn left". From this point of view, a highway system is simply a set of **Paths** connecting pairs of **Nodes**. That is, a **Path** is simply a route from one point (intersection) to another. Figure 22-1 shows the entity class **Path**, connecting *from* one **Node** *to* another **Node**.

The kinds of **Paths** shown include:

- **Main Roadway Path** – as it sounds, a piece of a national or provincial highway, managed by a provincial agency.
- **Non-inventoried Path** – farm or other country roads, not maintained by a provincial agency.
- **Ramp** – a roadway other than a main highway. Typically, this is part of a freeway interchange.
- **Frontage Roadway Path** – a roadway that runs parallel to an expressway, to provide access to the homes and stores along side of it.
- **Approach Driveway** – The portion of a driveway that intersects a street that is part of the street right-of-way.
- **Collector Distributor Roadway Path** – A roadway that leads from a surface street to an expressway, including either an entrance or an exit ramp.

This particular agency is not concerned with city streets, except to the extent that they are part of provincial or national roads. If desired, however, **Street** can be added.

A **Node** is any coming together of two or more **Paths**. The Highway Department is primarily concerned with two principle kinds (plus of course **Other Node**):

- **Grade Crossing** – This is a point where two (or more) highways intersect on the same level. It is possible to turn left or right from one to the other.
- **Alignment Node** – When a road is curved, it is rendered in plans as a succession of relatively short, straight, line segments (**Paths**). The link between any two of these is called an "Alignment Node". Note that in the

model, it is shown that each **Alignment Node** may be identified as *prior to* another **Alignment Node**. Going in the other direction, the second **Alignment Node** is, of course, *subsequent to* the first one.

A **Path's Bi-directional Indicator** is "`false`" if the traffic can only go from the *from* **Node** to the *to* **Node**. It is "`true`" if traffic can go in both directions.

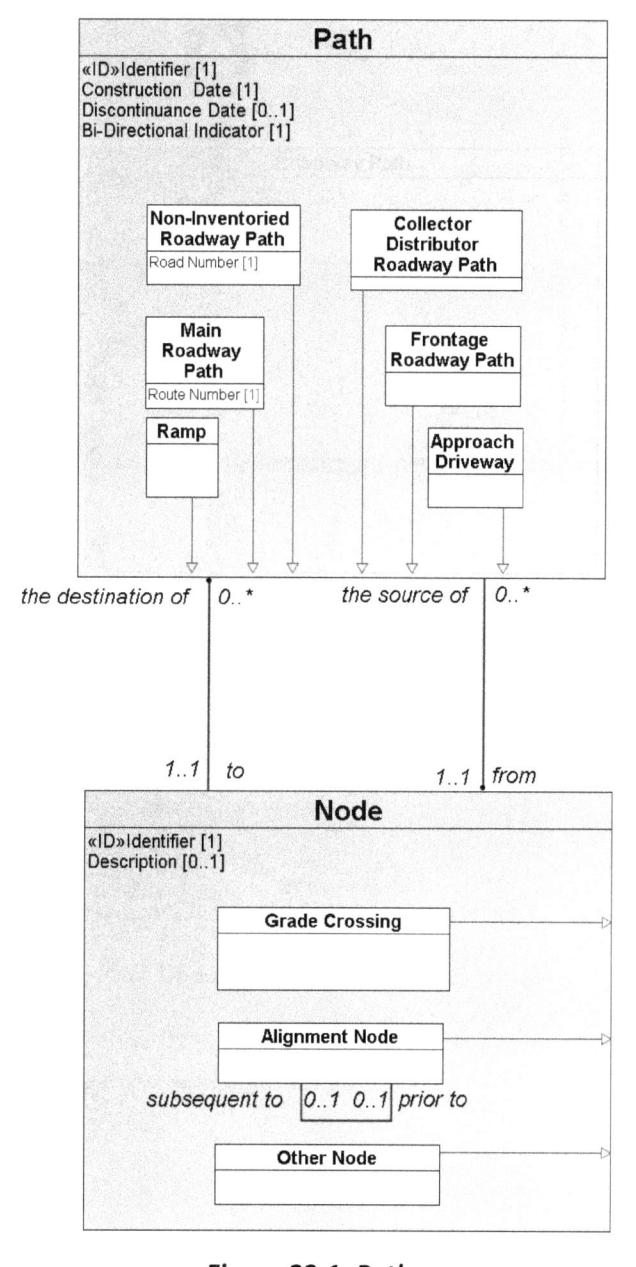

Figure 22-1: Paths

440 Enterprise Model Patterns

Figure 22-2 shows a schematic drawing of two fictional Provincial Core Highways (2 and 14) and two equally fictional local highways (522 and 753), plus two unlabeled roads. In the drawing, a **Path** exists between **Grade Crossings** "1054-1" and "1054-3". Another is the overpass from **Grade Crossing** "1054-3" to **Grade Crossing** "1054-2". A third **Path** goes between **Grade Crossings** "1054-3" and "1054-7".

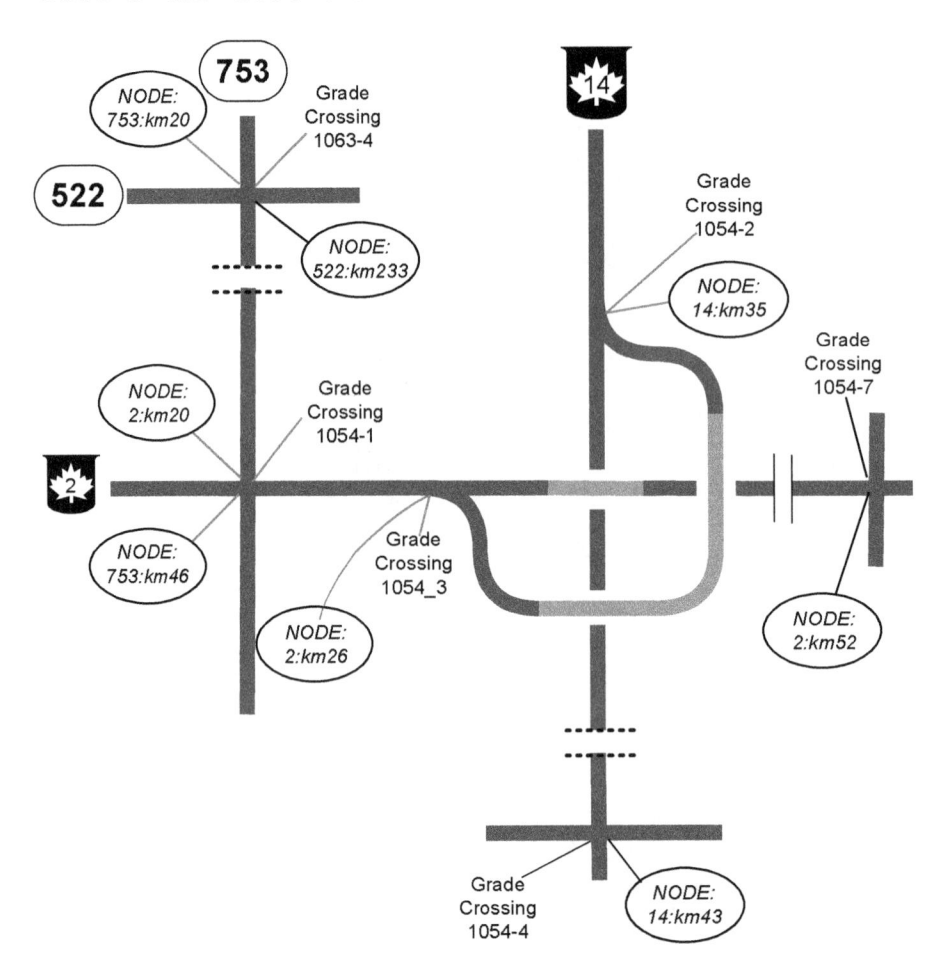

Figure 22-2: Grade Crossings and Nodes

Notice that the intersection between core highway "2" and core Highway "14" is *not* a **Grade Crossing**. That is a "Grade *Separated* Crossing", to be described shortly.*

---

* Note that the highway numbers are completely fictional. If you happen to live in the Province of Alberta and are looking for these intersections, you are unlikely to find

Note that in this example, each **Grade Crossing** is described by two **Nodes**. Each **Node** is described in terms of the number of one of the highways involved, plus its place on that highway. Hence, the **Grade Crossing** "1054-1" is described in two ways: "2:km20" is a point 20 kilometers from the point of origin of Highway 2, and "753:km46" is a point 46 kilometers from the point of origin of Highway 753. Thus the **Grade Crossing** that is "1054-1" is called "2:km20" on Highway 2 and is also "753:km46" on Highway 753. The intersection is a single **Grade Crossing**, with two names.

(Similarly, **Nodes** "2:km26" and "2:km52" are also on Highway 2, but they are at kilometers 26 and 52, respectively.)

For this reason, in Figure 22-3, **Path Placement** is recognized as a separate entity class, where each **Path Placement** must be *of* exactly one **Node** and *on* exactly one **Path**. (For purposes of this exercise, we will assume that the **Unit of Measure** that the **Path Placement** is *in terms of* is "kilometers".) That is, **Path Placement** is the fact that a particular **Grade Crossing** appears on a particular **Path** and is identified in terms of its placement on that **Path**. A given **Grade Crossing** must be *located on* at least one but possibly more paths. Thus the Distance attribute describes where in the underlying highway the **Node** (in this case a **Grade Crossing**) falls. In the example, this is the kilometer number. In this entity class, the attribute **Node Name** in **Path Placement** is derived from the **Path Identifier** (which is itself an inference from **Path Identifier** in **Path**), and the **Distance** of the specified **Grade Crossing** from the beginning point of the **Path** (its *from* **Node**).

Hence, from the point of view of the **Path** that is a section of Canadian Highway 2, the **Node** that is **Grade Crossing** "1054-1" is at a **Distance** of "20" (km) from the starting point of that highway. Hence, **Path Placement Name** is derived to be "2km20".

Note that each **Grade Crossing** must be *located in* one **Grade Crossing Site**. As a physical site (described above in Chapter 12) a **Grade Crossing Site** includes not only the two (or more) roads intersecting, but also the land around the intersection, the presence of traffic lights and/or stop signs, and the like. This is but one kind of

---

them. But the system in Alberta for identifying grade crossings, nodes, bridges, and grade separated crossings is being reflected here. It is a particularly rational system, and is well to be emulated. Other states and provinces may have their own schemes, of course, which should still fit in this model.

442 Enterprise Model Patterns

the more general idea of **Intersection Site**. **Intersection Site** is also a super-type of **Interchange**, described below.

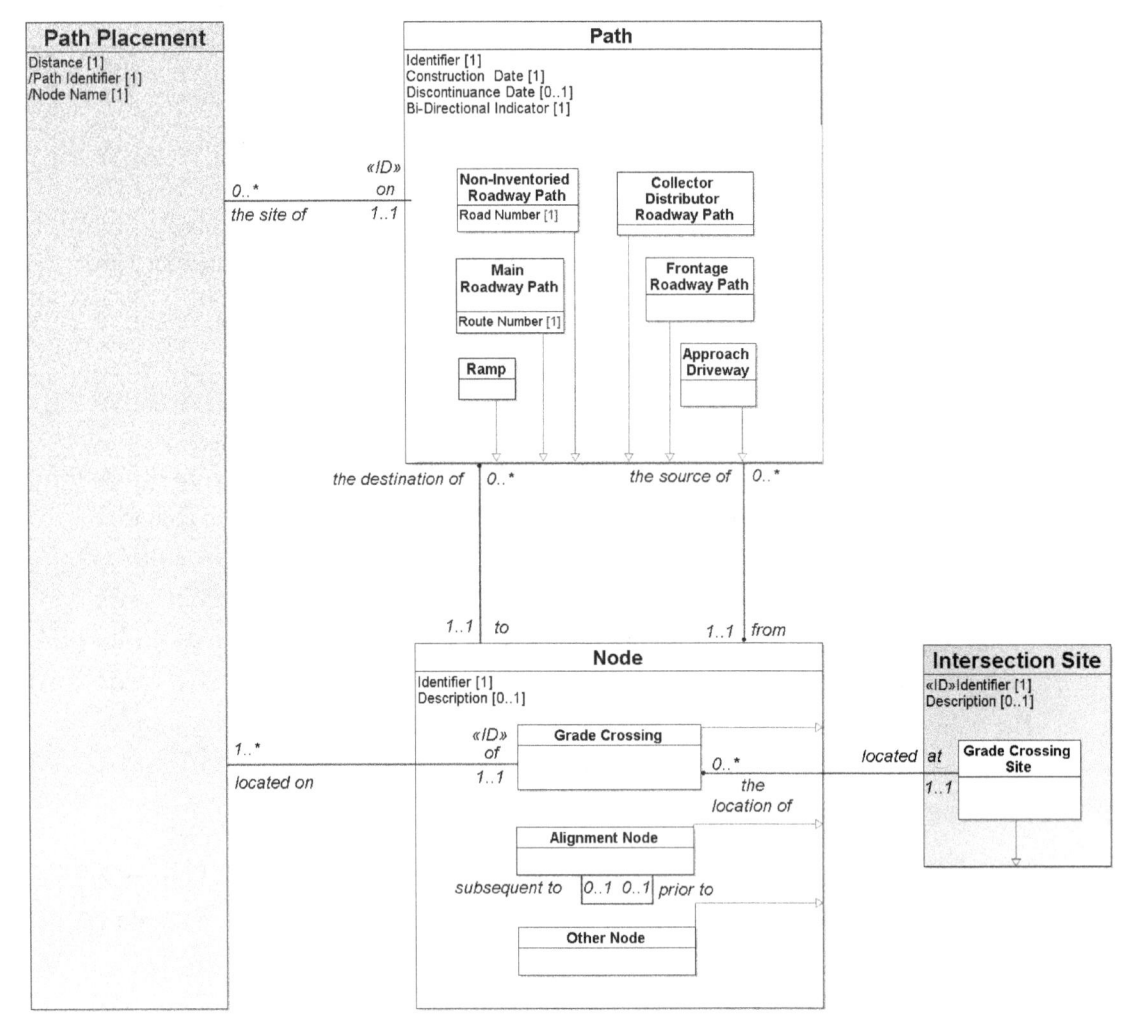

Figure 22-3: Path Placements and Intersection Sites

The sub-types shown in Figure 22-1, showing the kinds of **Paths** available, only apply to **Roadway Paths**. Figure 22-4 extends the concept of **Path** to include **Non-roadway Paths**. These are other kinds of networks of concern to the highway agency, including:

- **Utility** (such as a **Water Line**, **Gas Line**, **Power Line**, or **Other Utility**) – Each of these are important to the highway agency, because they have to be accommodated when a roadway is built, or when significant maintenance is done.

- **Railroad Track Segment** – The highways must intersect railroads, so the railroad routes must be taken into account.
- **Canal** – This is a man-made channel for the purpose of transporting water from where it is plentiful to where it is needed—usually for irrigation purposes.
- **Natural Feature** – Describes the route of a natural phenomenon, such as a **River** or a **Ridge** of a hill.

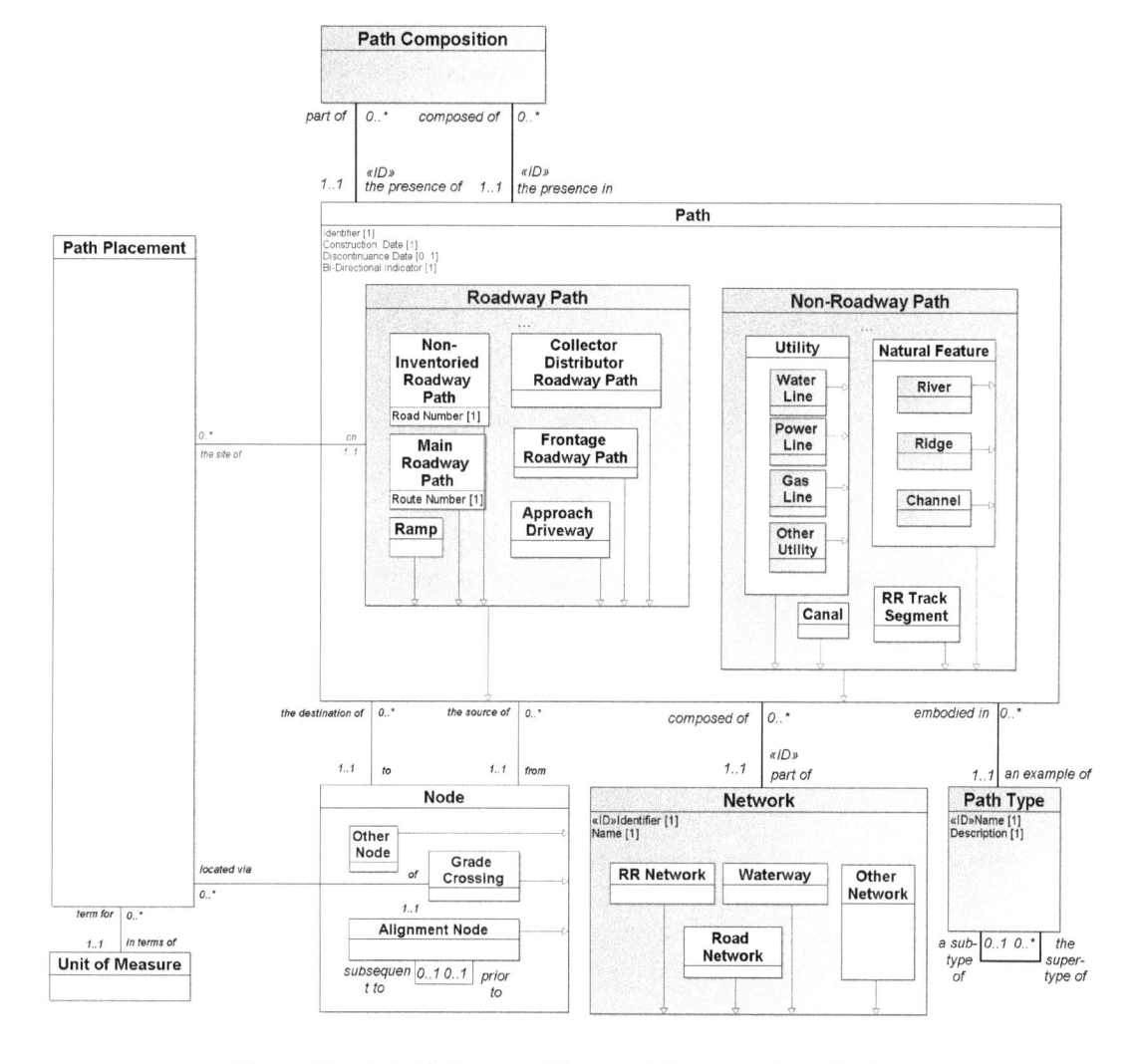

Figure 22-4: Path Composition and Non-Roadway Paths

Note that each **Path** must be *an example of* one and only one **Path Type**. This structure is the same as has been seen elsewhere in this book, whereby **Path Type** simply reproduces, as entity class instances, the concepts shown also as entity classes that are sub-types of **Path**. Instances of **Path Type** include "`Roadway Path`", "`Canal`", "`Water Line`", "`Approach Driveway`", and so forth. There is also the ability to say such things as Main Roadway Path is *a sub-type of* **Roadway Path**.

Additional **Path Types** can be added if each is *a sub-type of* an existing **Path Type**.

Complex Paths

Also in Figure 22-4 is the entity class **Path Composition**. This is the fact that a (shorter) **Path** may be *a component in* one or more other (longer) **Paths**. This allows us to recognize that the **Path** from the airport to the hotel is made up of many component **Paths**. This allows for the complete description of a longer route, seen from a high level, to be decomposed into as much detail as necessary to fully describe it.

It is also how a **Roadway Path** may be assembled from a set of **Alignment Nodes** and the **Roadway Paths** linking them together.

A second way to collect multiple **Paths** together is to aggregate them into **Networks**. Where a single string of **Paths** can connect to create a larger **Path** through a set of **Path Compositions**, (the set of all Provincial Core Highways in the Province of Saskatchewan, for example) is considered a **Network**—specifically, a **Road Network**. Among other **Networks** represented in the Figure are **Railroad Networks** (consisting of all **Railroad Track Segments** in a given area), and **Waterway Networks** (consisting of all **Channels**, **Canals**, and **Rivers** in a given area).

Locating Nodes Geographically

Figure 22-5 shows how the **Nodes** (and by implication, the **Paths** and **Networks** linking them) are placed on the Earth. From Chapter 5, the figure shows **Geographic Point**, a singular point in three dimensional space. Each **Node** is identified as being *at* exactly one **Geographic Point**.

Describing the **Geographic Point** can be done various ways, depending on the **Reference System** involved.

This could be the "`Geographic Coordinate System`" (latitude and longitude), a "`Cartesian System`" (X, Y, and Z coordinates), or the "`Linear Reference System`" *(LRS)*—a system where features (points or

Highway Maintenance 445

segments) are localized by a measure along a linear element.[81]. Other **Reference Systems** could also be used.

Each **Reference System** is *defined in terms of* a particular set of **Identification Components**. For example, the default "Geographic Coordinates" approach is in terms of "latitude", "longitude", and "elevation". The "Cartesian" approach is in terms of "X", "Y", and "Z", relative to a **Geographic Point** that is its "datum". The "Linear Reference System" is in terms of "linear distance", again from a **Geographic Point** that is its "datum".

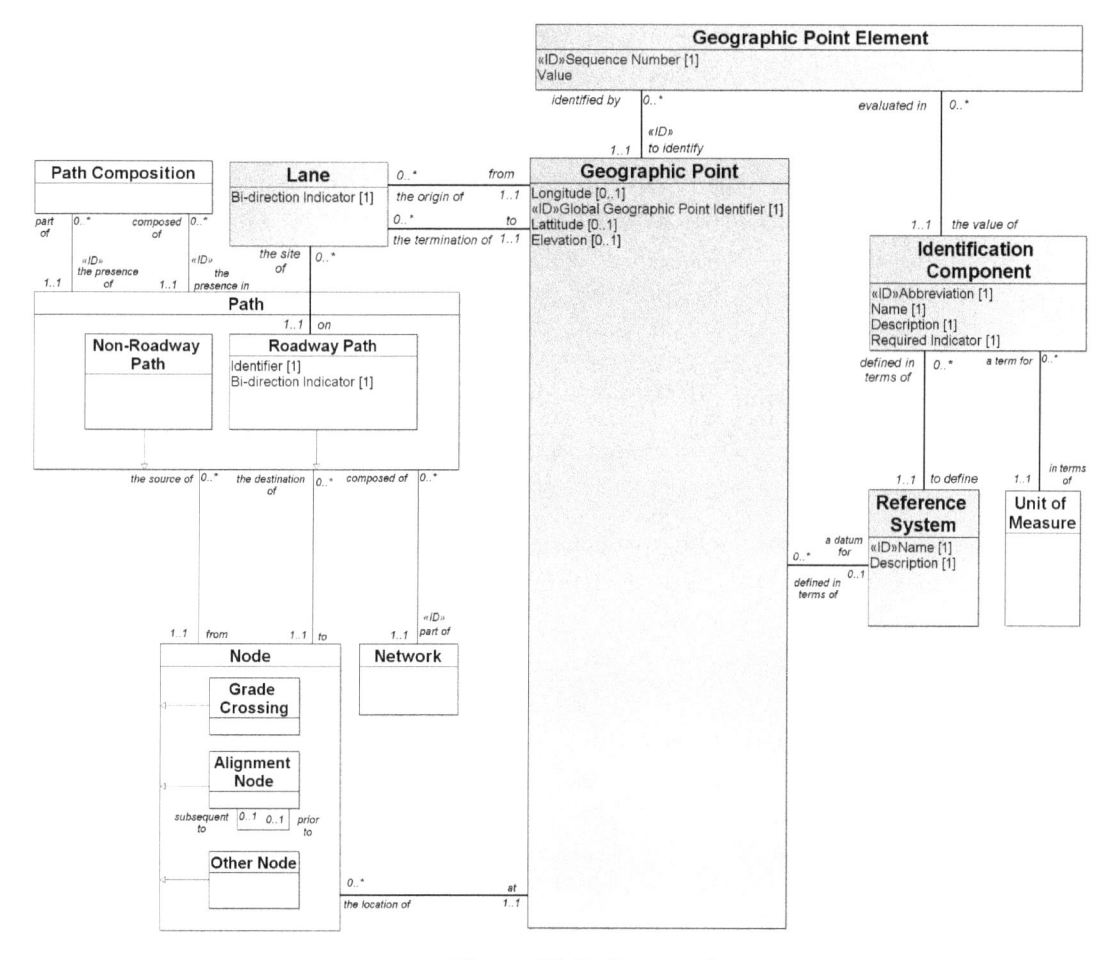

Figure 22-5: Geography

---

[81] Blazek. R. 2004. "Introducing the Linear Reference System in GRASS, *Bangkok, GRASS User Conf. Proc*".(Page 1, http://gisws.media.osaka-cu.ac.jp/grass04/viewpaper.php?id=50.

Each **Geographic Point**, then, may be *identified by* one or more **Geographic Point Elements**, each of which must be *the value of* a single **Identification Component**. If the default `"Geographic Coordinates"` **Reference System** is not used, it is expected that the **Geographic Point Element** used *to identify* a particular **Geographic Point** in terms of a particular **Reference System** must be *the value of* an **Identification Component** *to define* that **Reference System**. It is possible, however, for one **Geographic Point** to be described in terms of more than one **Reference System**, if it has values for all the **Identification Components** in each **Reference System**.

Business Rule

- To define a **Geographic Point** in terms of a particular **Reference System**, a **Geographic Point Element Value** is required for each **Identification Component** that is required *to define* that **Reference System**. The **Identification Component** attribute Required Indicator is "true" if it is required. *(Translation:* A **Reference System** is defined in terms of **Identification components**. To define a point in terms of that **Reference System**, the point has to be described in terms of at least the required components. There may be optional components that could be specified as well.*)*

Because it is the most commonly used, the **Identification Components** of the `"Geographic Coordinates"` **Reference System** are specified as attributes of **Geographic Point**: **Latitude**, **Longitude**, and **Elevation**. This does not preclude using other **Reference Systems**, as well, although it is necessary to provide the datum for locating either the LRS or the Cartesian **Reference Systems**. Table 22-1 shows two points described using two different reference systems. Note that to use the Cartesian Coordinates, the first point had to be identified as a **datum**.

Figure 22-5 also shows that a **Roadway Path** may be *the site of* one or more **Lanes**. A **Lane** is a portion of a **Roadway Path** where traffic flows. Where the **Roadway Path** is a road being a line, **Lanes** begin to provide some area. In fact, though, **Roadway Paths** are still concerned with describing the conduct of traffic in a particular direction.

Highway Maintenance

Table 22-1: Describing a Geographic Point

Geographic Point Global ... Identifier	Reference System Name	Identification Component Name	Geographic Point Element Value	Unit of Measure Abbreviation
State Capital Steps, Denver, Colorado	Geographic Coordinates	Latitude	35.739154	Degrees North
		Longitude	104.984703	Degrees West
		Elevation	5,280	Feet above mean sea level"
City Hall, Denver, Colorado	Cartesian Coordinates	Datum	State Capital Steps, Denver, Colorado	
		X	1035	Feet West
		Y	200	Feet South
		Z	-74	Feet

Business Rules

- If the **Path's** Bi-direction Indicator is set to "False", then any **Lanes** that are *on* that **Path**, by definition, are going in the direction of the **Path**—that is, from the *from* **Node**, and to the *to* **Node**. The Bi-direction Indicator of each **Lane** is moot. *(Translation:* If the **Path** is not two-way (**Path** Bi-direction Indicator="False"), then all lanes must be going the same direction as the **Path**.)

- If the **Path's** Bi-direction Indicator is set to "True", and if a **Lane's** Bi-direction indicator is "True", then the **Lane's** direction is from the **Path's** *from* **Node** to its *to* **Node**. If it is "False", then the **Lane's** direction goes the other way—from the **Path's** *to* **Node** to its *from* **Node**. *(Translation:* If a **Path** is two-way (**Path** Bi-direction indicator="True"), then each **Lane** must be designated as going in the same direction (**Lane** Bi-direction Indicator = "True"), or the opposite direction (**Lane** Bi-direction Indicator = "False") from the **Path**.

- A **Lane** must be between two **Geographic Points** that are inside the two **Geographic Points** that are *the location of* the two **Nodes** that define the **Path** that the **Lane** is *on*. *(Translation:* Each **Lane** must be shorter than the **Path** it is on.)

Grade Separated Crossings

Figure 22-6 shows our example enhanced by annotations describing the highway interchange. Here a **Grade Separated Crossing** consists of two **Paths** that cross but do not communicate directly with each other. In the example, it would not be possible to simply turn left from Highway 2 in order to get to Highway 14. It is necessary to take a **Ramp**.

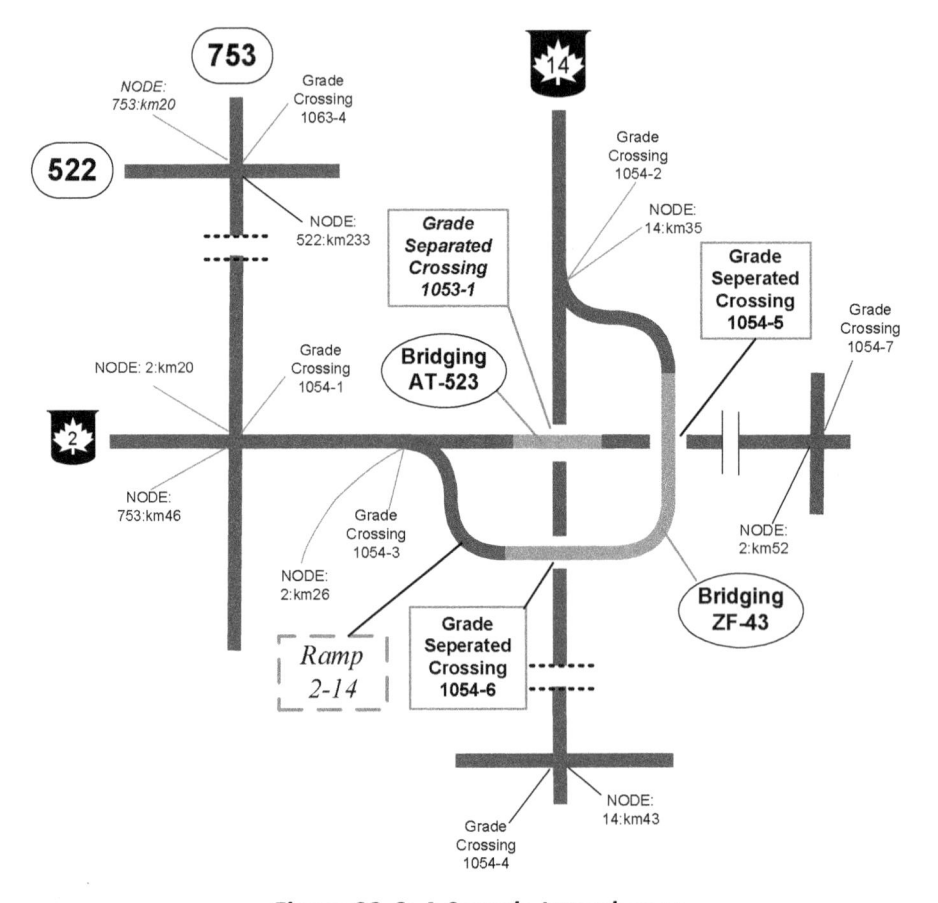

Figure 22-6: A Sample Interchange

The **Ramp** is a **Roadway Path** that begins at **Grade Crossing** `"1054-3"` and ends at **Grade Crossing** `"1054-2"`. Since it is not a single highway, here the **Ramp** is simply labeled **Ramp** `"2-14"`. The value of its **Bi-directional Indicator** is clearly `"False"`—traffic will only be able to go in one direction. The **Path** is *on* a giant **Bridging**—the fact that a **Path** is in the air, crossing over other **Paths** without communicating with them. In the example, **Bridging** `"ZF-43"`

Highway Maintenance 449

crosses two **Roadway Paths**, without communicating directly with either. These constitute two **Grade Separated Crossings**, (`"1054-6"` and `"1054-5"`). The **Bridging** at ground level on Highway 2, over Highway 14 (**Bridging** `"AT-523"`), also constitutes a **Grade Separated Crossing**.

Figure 22-7 shows the portion of our semantic model that is concerned with **Bridges** and **Grade Separated Crossings**.

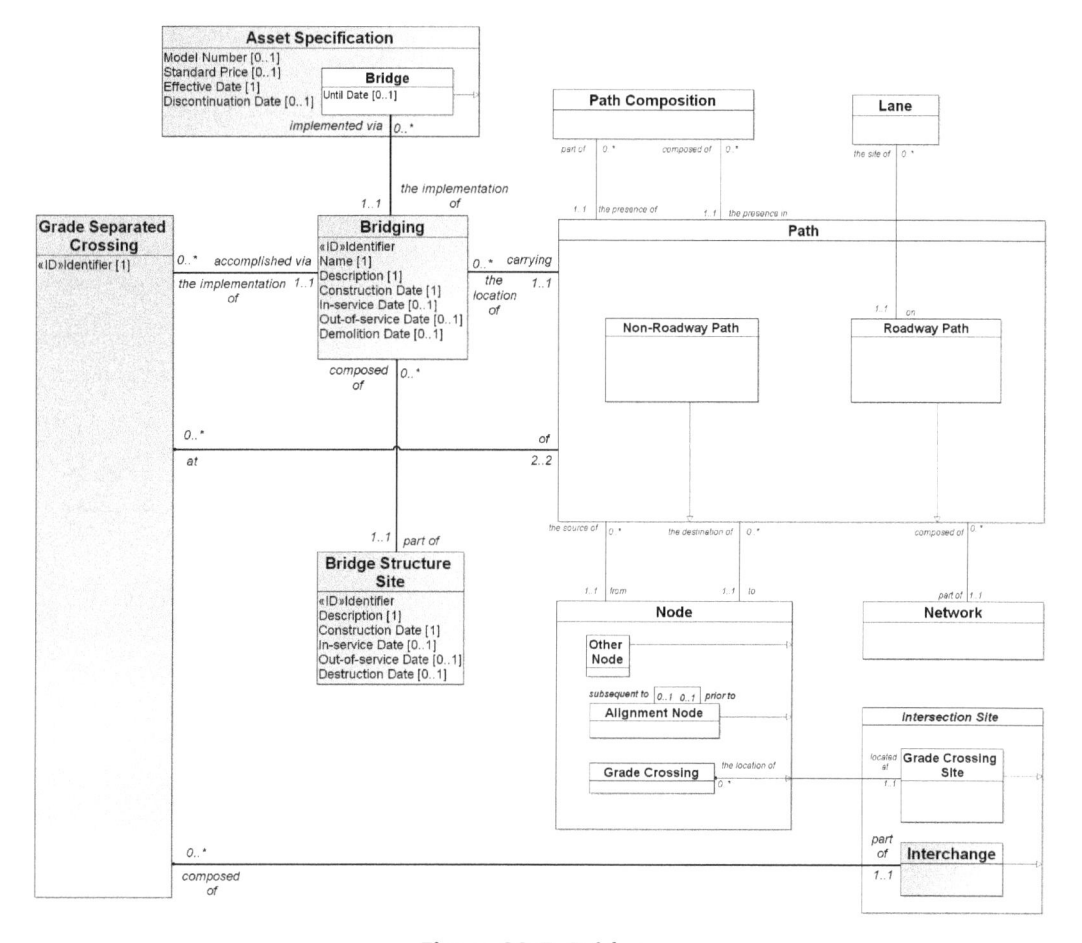

Figure 22-7: Bridges

First, it shows **Bridging**, which is the *part of* a **Bridge Structure Site**. The **Bridge Structure Site** may in turn be *composed of* one or more **Bridgings**, as well as the moorings on each side, plus assorted approach-ways, and other necessary elements.

As shown, each **Bridging** must be *carrying* one and only one **Path**. So, in the example, **Bridging** "AT-523" is carrying **Main Roadway Path** "Route 2". The **Bridging** labeled "ZF-43" is *carrying* **Ramp** "2-14".

In the model, each **Bridging** may be *the implementation of* one or more **Grade Separated Crossings**. Continuing our example, **Bridging** "ZF-43" is *the implementation of* the **Grade Separated Crossings** "1054-4" and "1054-5".

Each **Grade Separated Crossing**, in addition to being *accomplished via* one **Bridging**, must be *of* exactly two **Paths**. It also must be *part of* one **Interchange**. An **Interchange** is an intersection of at least two **Paths** with at least one **Grade Separated Crossing** involved.

Recall from Figure 22-1 that each **Grade Crossing** was *part of* a **Grade Crossing Site**. Here, in Figure 22-7, **Grade Crossing Site** is but a sub-type of **Intersection Site**. The other sub-type is **Interchange**. Here is another place where a component of a road is an area.

Flows

The reason that there are **Paths** is to carry **Flows**. In the case of **Roadway Paths**, the flow is of traffic—a number of vehicles per hour; in the case of **Rivers** or **Canals**, the flow is water; in the case of **Power Lines** the flow is of electricity.

In Figure 22-8, **Flow** is defined as a quantity of material (or energy) that passes through a **Path** during a specified period of time. Attributes of **Flow** include **Start Date [and Time]**, **End Date [and Time]** and **Quantity**. The **Quantity** is *in terms of* a **Unit of Measure**.

Because there are many kinds of **Flows** that can pass through even the same kind of **Path**, **Flow Type** describes the kind of flow. It could be "all vehicles", "cars only", "semi-trailer trucks", "rail cars", and so forth. The **Unit of Measure** can be "number of vehicles", "kilowatt hours", "number of railcars", and so forth, depending on both the **Flow Type** and the **Path Type**.

Highway Maintenance 451

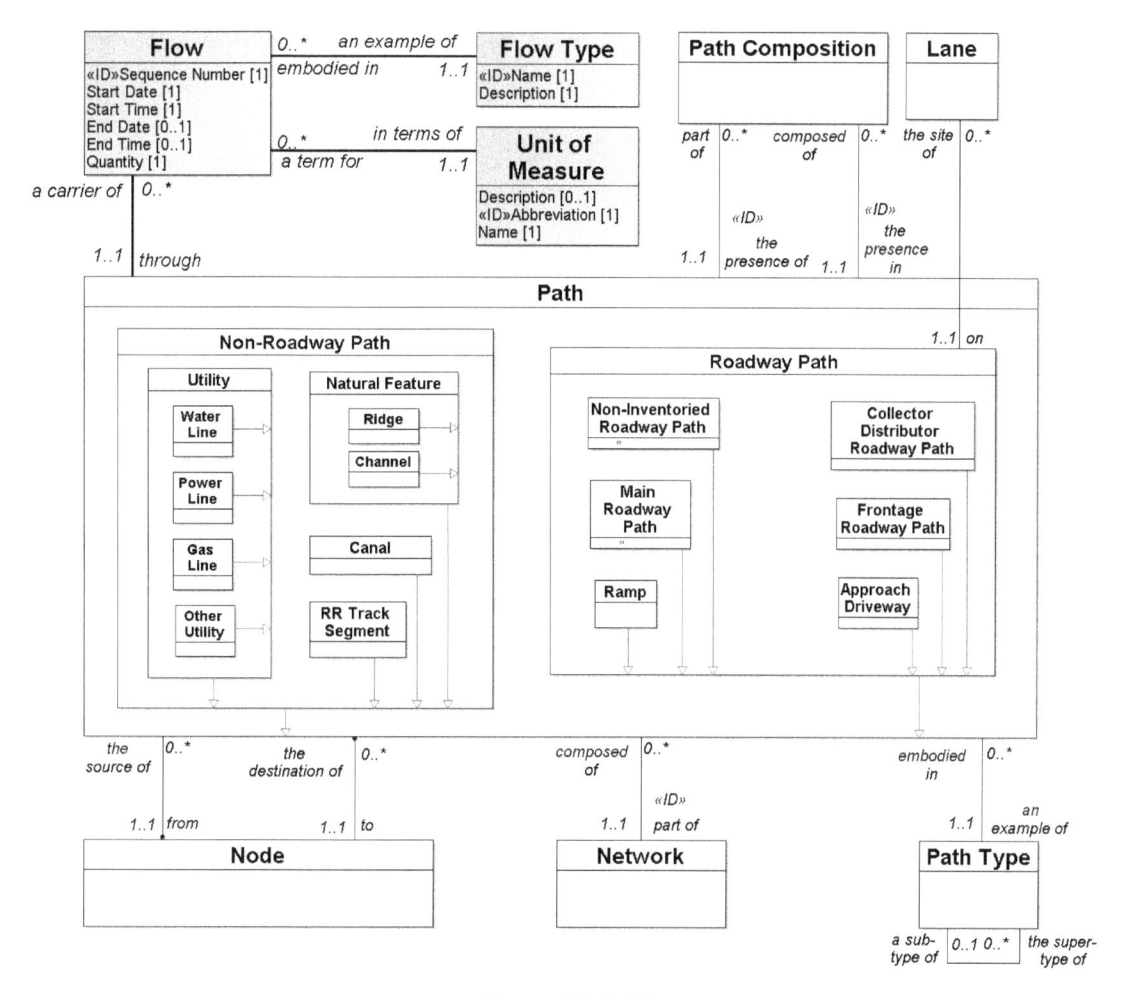

Figure 22-8: Flows

As in the last few chapters, Figure 22-9 shows how the concepts we have been describing so far, fit into the Enterprise Model. Well, into the **Facilities** model, anyway. In this case, most of the entity classes we've seen so far are, in fact, subtypes of **Facility**. The **Geographic Point** and its associated entity classes are not, since they are **Geographic Locations** and are only used to place selected **Facilities** on the Earth. Also, **Flow** is what the **Facilities** are used for. A **Flow** is not itself a site of any kind.

Otherwise, **Path**, **Node**, **Intersection**, **Network**, **Bridging**, and **Grade Separated Crossings** are all kinds of **Facilities**.

Facility Structure is an entity class that links two **Facilities** together, so the **Path Composition** as shown in Figure 22-9 is, in fact, a sub-type of **Facility Structure**, as shown. Another kind of **Facility Structure** is **Adjacency** for recording, for example, that a **Roadside Facility** is adjacent to a particular **Roadway Path** that is a piece of a highway.

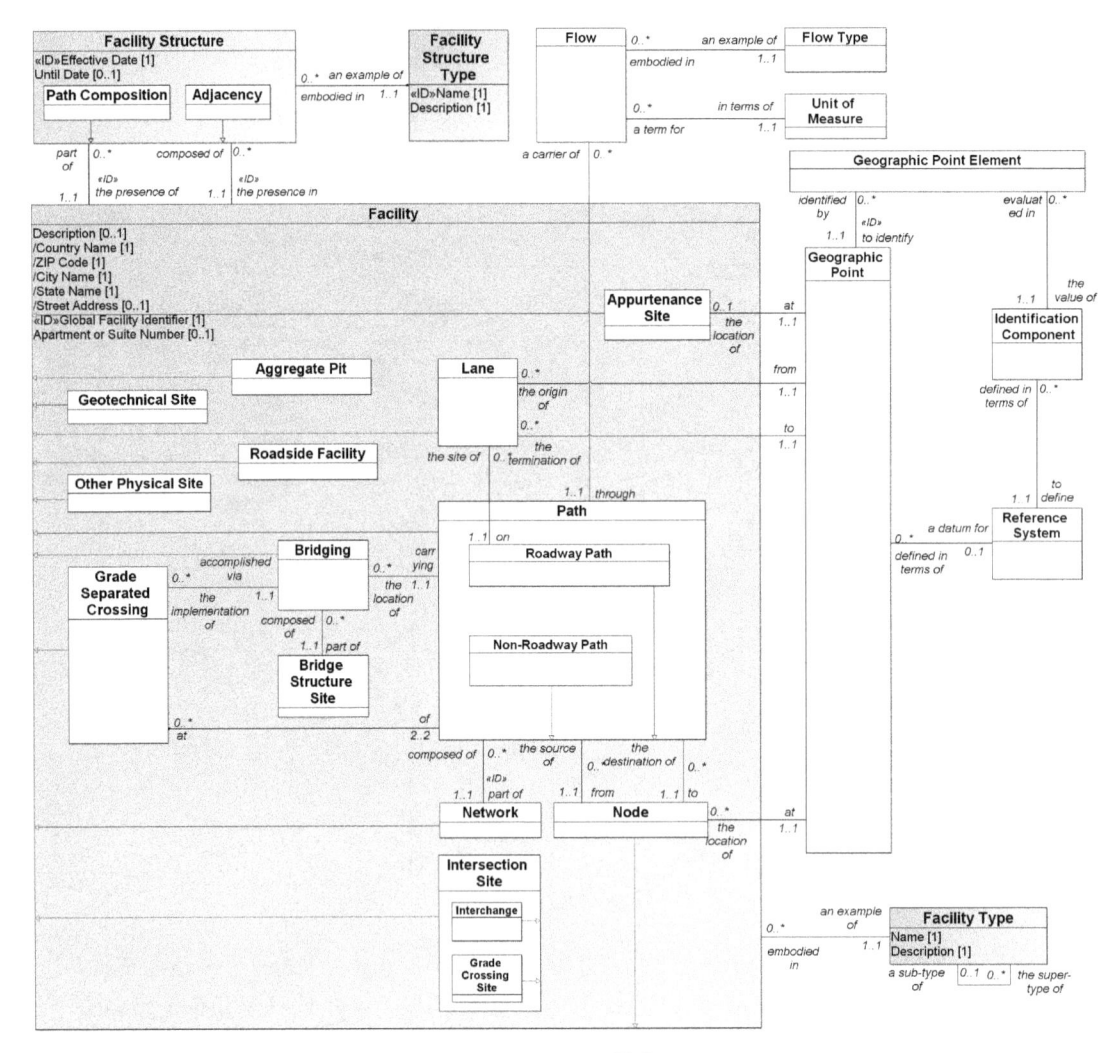

Figure 22-9: Facilities

Note that we have added a few **Facilities** not previously discussed. These are not part of the complex structure of the other sites, but they are important, nonetheless:

- **Aggregate Pit** – a place where gravel and other materials used for paving are mined.
- **Geotechnical Site** – a place recognized as a site where geotechnical phenomena (principally earthquakes) occur. (Important for planning roads.)

- **Roadside Facility** – a rest area, with parking, bathrooms and trash cans provided by the Province, and optionally, gasoline and food provided by private companies.
- **Appurtenance Site** – the site of a sign or other thing sticking up out of the roadway.

The attributes of **Facility** are ones that we have been showing for the sub-type sites all along. Indeed in each case, these would be inherited from **Facility**:

- In-service Date
- Out-of-service Date

The first is required, but of course all the others will be filled in as they happen.

Physical Assets

If all we have seen so far are the **Facilities** associated with the highway system, what about the asphalt and concrete, beams and girders, and all the other physical **Assets** that make up the real, physical highways? Figure 22-10 elaborates on the **Asset Specification** entity class we've already seen several times. Based on the primary categories first introduced in the Chapter 6 discussion of **Assets**, the primary sub-types remain **Product Model**, for a model of a discrete piece of equipment or other manufactured item, and **Specified Material** for something that is measured in volume or weight.

Under the category of **Product Model**, you have all the various things that go into the building and maintenance of roads and bridges. First, of course is the physical **Roadway** that is the expression of the **Roadway** navigated as a **Facility**. When it comes to implementing **Bridgings**, at the small end, you have **Bridge Culvert**, a large pipe that goes under a road to direct a stream. Supporting the **Bridging** more fully, you have the basic **Bridge**, which is made up of at least **Girders** and **Abutments**. There are also **Piers** which are the intermediate supports for the adjacent ends of spans in multiple span truss bridges. A larger **Bridge** is assembled as a **Bridge Super-structure Unit**. Sub-types of this include:

- **Girder Superstructure** – for a **Bridge** segment that is assembled from steel girders.
- **Suspension Superstructure** – for a suspension bridge.
- **Truss Super-structure** – for a **Bridge** made of girders organized in triangles and assembled into units to cross between piers.

454 Enterprise Model Patterns

- **Rigid Frame Superstructure** – for a **Bridge** intended to carry weight with a simple frame of concrete and steel.
- **Flat Slab Superstructure** – for a **Bridge** that is simply a piece of reinforced concrete.
- **Arch Superstructure** – for a Bridge of arch design.

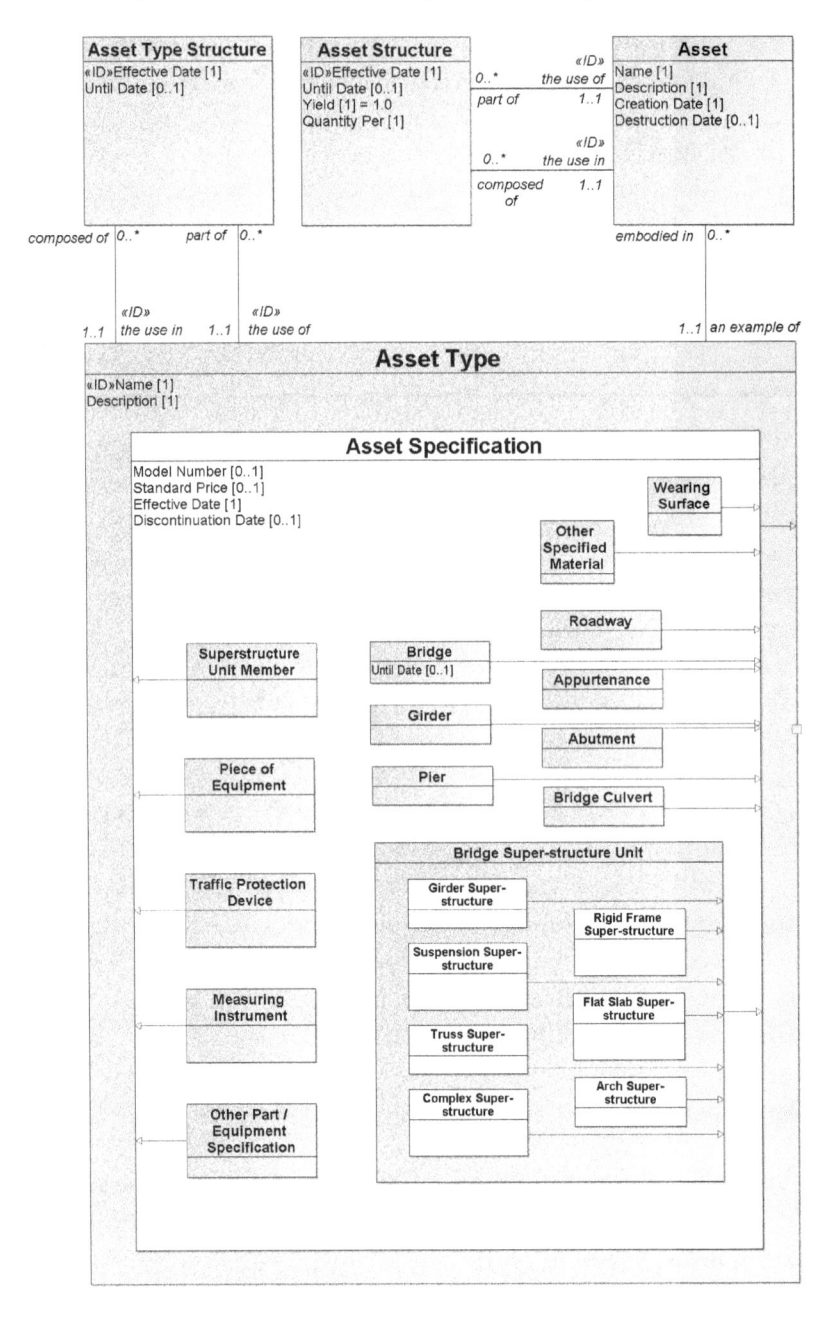

Figure 22-10: Asset Specifications

Highway Maintenance 455

In each of these cases, an instance of the entity class is the entire super-structure. It is made up of components called **Super-structure Unit Member**. These, in turn, are composed of **Girders** and **Pieces of Equipment**.

In the highway maintenance business, the primary **Specified Material** is called the **Wearing Surface**. This is used for pavement, whether it is asphalt, concrete, or some other material.

In addition, there are **Traffic Protection Devices** (such as stoplights) and **Measuring Equipment**. The latter is used primarily for measuring the flow of traffic past a particular point.

The complex structure of sub-types for **Asset Specifications** implies that the structure of actual **Assets** will be equally complex. In Figure 22-10 you have **Asset Specification Structure** and **Asset Structure**. Each **Asset Structure** is the fact that a particular **Asset** is *part of* one other **Asset**. Similarly, each **Asset Specification Structure** is the fact that a particular **Asset Specification** is *part of* another **Asset Specification**. Since most highway construction is assembled "to order", the significant structure here is **Asset Structure**, which describes how the roadway, bridge, et cetera was *actually* constructed. This is as opposed to **Asset Specification Structure**, which is what the blueprints proposed.

As mentioned, **Facility** is a synonym for **Physical Site**, and in several chapters, we've discussed how to get **Physical Assets** to and from **Facilities**. Borrowed from the Contracts and Manufacturing chapters (Chapters 15 and 16, respectively), Figure 22-11 shows **Material Movement**. In this case, it is describing nothing other than the fact that a particular **Asset** was (or will be) moved *from* one **Facility** *to* another **Facility**. Principle sub-types include:

- **Installation** - *from* an inventory location of some sort, *to* a **Roadway Site**, **Path**, **Interchange**, or what have you.
- **Removal** – *from* a **Roadway Site** to either scrap inventory, or to destruction. (That is, there is no *to* relationship instance.
- **Adjustment** – as the result of an inventory measurement, this is either the appearance of an **Asset** *to* an inventory, but with no identifiable *from* location, or the disappearance of an **Asset** *from* an inventory, but with no identifiable *to* location.

456 Enterprise Model Patterns

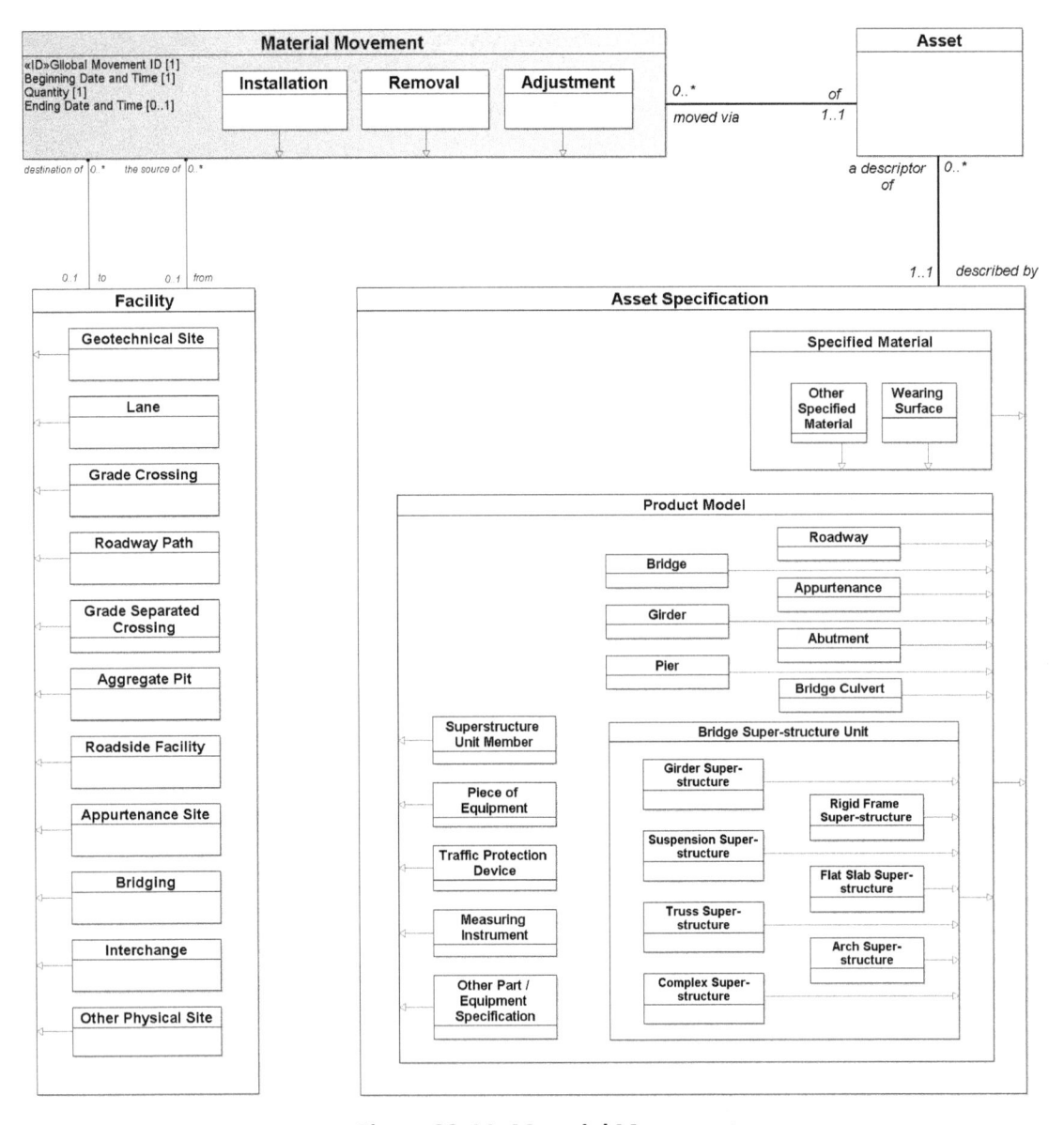

Figure 22-11: Material Movements

For planning purposes, Figure 22-12 shows **Asset Specification Location**, the fact that a particular **Asset Specification** or a kind of **Asset Specification** may be expected to be *in* a **Facility** that is *an example of* a particular **Facility Type**.

Here you can see that **Bridging** is the fact that a roadway crosses something over the air (a **Facility**), but a **Bridge** is the set of girders and other physical materials (a physical **Asset**) that are *the implementation of* the **Bridging**.

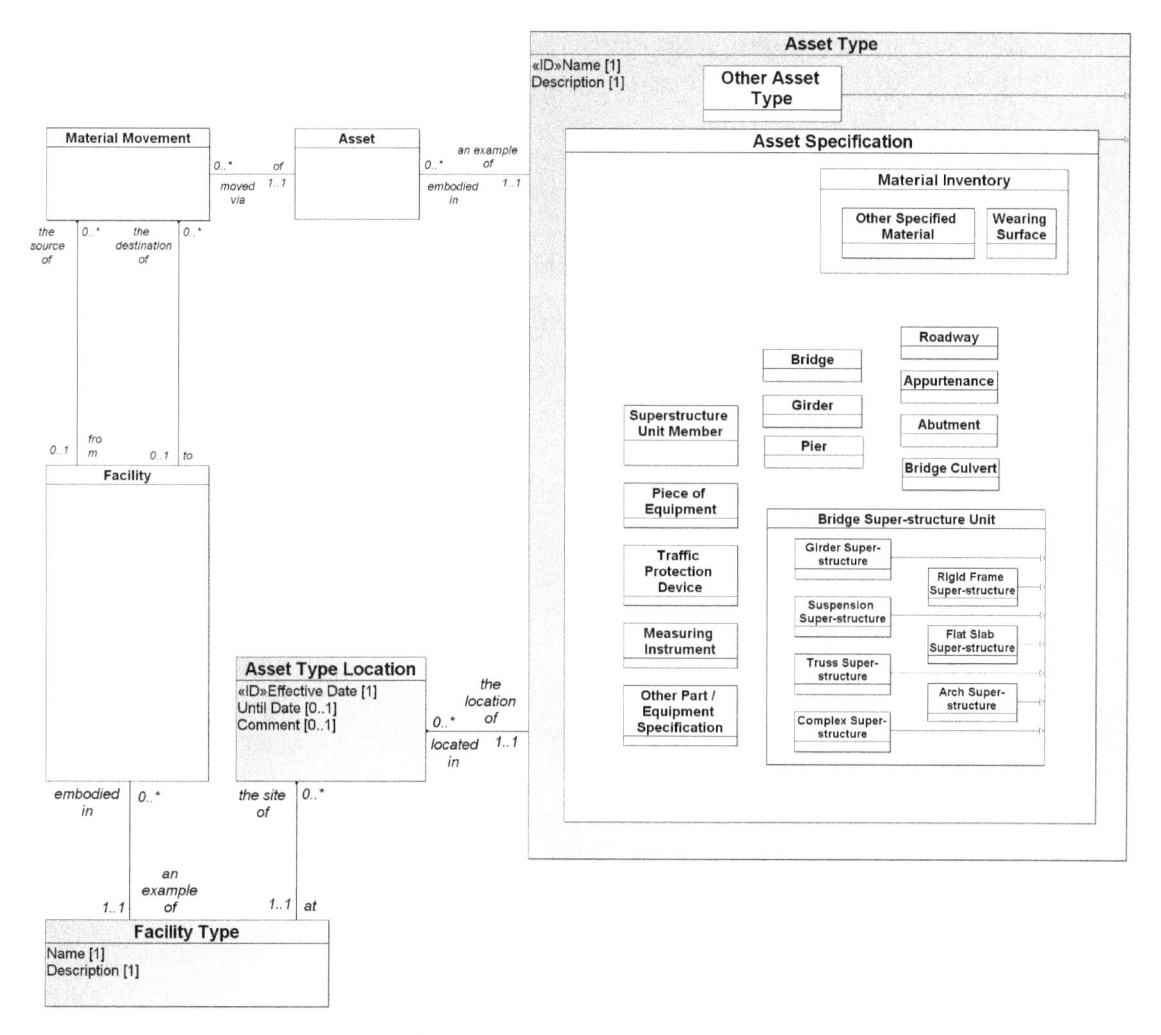

Figure 22-12: Asset Placements

For example, the cantilevered **Truss Super-structure** that is the Forth Railway Bridge, was installed (a **Material Movement** that is an **Installation**) in a **Bridging** site across the Firth of Forth in Scotland on 4 March 1890.

This establishes conclusively what the **Asset Specification Location** instance would assert: a **Truss Super-structure** may be built in a **Bridging Facility**.

A Final Word About Identifiers

There is a bit of chicanery going on here with respect to unique identifiers. By the time a system is to be built, the analysts will have to address the problem of uniquely identifying **Facilities** (for example), along with all of the other elements described in this book.

The easiest way to do it of course would be to have a **Global Site Identifier** that applies to all physical sites. But many sites, like bridges and highways and oil wells, have identifiers already, issued according to a scheme that is very old. In other cases, however, identification has not really been addressed.

This is a book about model patterns. It is intended as a starting point. In each case, your author surmised an identification scheme that seemed to approximate a reasonable approach. It is in no way represented as being the definitive solution. An important part of any project to implement these patterns will be to sit down and ask the question, how do we know which of these things we are looking at?

Summary

The specialized models in Parts Four and Five of this book are just that—specialized. On the face of it, each of them doesn't seem to apply to many of the readers of this book. But they are presented not just as potential solutions to the problems that some of you encounter. More significantly, they are intended to broaden the views of all. This is in two ways:

First of all, buried in each example are modeling techniques that can be borrowed and applied to other areas. The modeling problems addressed are often unique, to be sure, but the intellectual exercise of pursuing the solutions is quite universal.

Second, and perhaps most important, they provide an opportunity to learn about areas in our world that you otherwise would know nothing about. What other books would introduce you to forensic science, oil drilling, and highway construction—not to mention microbiology?

One of the great things about data modeling is that it is a wonderful way to learn about the world. You can think of it as dilettante heaven! It is a great way to pick apart the true nature of any field of study.

In each case here, your author's education was greatly increased as he had to deal with things that were otherwise alien to him. He has been grateful for the experience, and hopes that you will be as well.

Glossary

This glossary contains definitions for all entity classes, plus other terms deemed to be of interest.

Unless otherwise noted, the definitions are those of your author.

Term	Definition	Chap
(Chemical) Action	The fact that one Chemical (usually a Chemical Compound or Chemical Element) reacts with another Chemical Compound or Chemical Element in a specified way.	19
(Chemical) Structure	The fact that one Asset Specification is *part of* another Asset Specification.	19
(Instrument) Lot	A quantity of shares obtained at one time.	20
?Other?	A representation of the fact that a Cost Center Assignment may be *to* pretty much anything else in the model.	11
<<Id>>	A UML *stereotype* that identifies an attribute or a role as part of the unique identifier for an *entity class*. That is, each instance of the *entity class* is uniquely identified by a concatenation of the values of the labeled attributes and roles.	2
Abutment	The part of a bridge resting on the ground, providing support.	22
Account	"A place in which to record particular kinds of effects of the firm's transactions."[82]	11
Account Balance	The value of the money described for a particular Account for a designated period of time.	11
Account Categorization	The fact that, at a particular time, an Account is considered to be a member of a particular Account Category.	11
Account Category	A dynamic classification of Accounts. An Account can be *subject to* many Account Categorizations *into* Account Categories at the same time and over time.	11
Account Category Scheme	A collection of Account Categories that constitute a set.	11

---

[82] M. J. Gordon, Gordon Shillinglaw. 1969. *Accounting: A Management Approach. Forth Edition.* (Homewood, Illinois: Richard D. Irwin, Inc.): 28.

Term	Definition	Chap
Account Rollup Structure	The fact that the money in one Account is part of the total money in another Account. Note that each Account Rollup Structure must also be *part of* one and only one Roll-up Scheme.	11
Account Type	A fundamental classification of Accounts. As with other parts of the model, the first instances of Account Type reproduce the sub-types shown in the figure: Asset Account", "Liability Account", and "Equity Account". *Sub-types of* "Equity Account" include "Revenue Account", "Expense Account" and "Other Equity Account". Other Account Types can be added, so long as each is *a sub-type of* one and only one other Account Type.	11
Accounting Entry	A component of an Accounting Transaction that describes the effect of a quantity of money on a single Account. This must be either a Debit Entry or a Credit Entry.	11
Accounting Rule Entry	A component of an Accounting Transaction Type that determines what Accounts should be updated by Accounting Transactions that are *examples of* that Accounting Transaction Type—and whether it should be an addition or subtraction to the account. This must be either a Debit Rule or a Credit Rule.	11
Accounting Transaction	A collection of Account Entries to affect the *Chart of Accounts* to reflect a business event.	11
Accounting Transaction Type	A fundamental classification category of Accounting Transactions. These include "issue invoice", "make sale", "receive payment for sale", et cetera.	11
Activity	An instance of an action taken, a procedure followed, or a service rendered.	7
Activity /Activity Labor Cost	SUM-THROUGH (*charged with*, Labor Usage, /Labor Value).	16
Activity /Activity Material Cost	SUM-THROUGH (*charged with*, Consumption, Consumption Cost).	16
Activity Characteristic	A distinguishing trait, quality, or property that can be given a value for either an Activity or an Activity Specification.	7
Activity Characteristic Assignment	The fact that a particular Activity Characteristic is only appropriate for a particular Activity Type or a particular Activity Specification.	7

Glossary

Term	Definition	Chap
Activity Characteristic Value	The fact that, at a particular time duration, a particular Activity or Activity Specification took a particular Characteristic Value *of* an Activity Characteristic.	7
Activity Dependence	The fact that, as scheduled, one Activity must be completed, started, or overlapping a specified amount another Activity.	7
Activity Dependence	The fact that starting one Activity is dependent upon the completion of another Activity. Whether the other activity must be completed, must be a specified amount of time in, or whatever the constraint is, is determined by the Activity Dependence Type that the Activity Dependence is *an example of*.	16
Activity Dependence Type	The definition of a kind of Activity Dependence. Specifically: • "End-to-start" (ES) – the on Activity (or Activity Specification) must complete before the off Activity (or Activity Specification) can begin. • "Start-to-start" (SS) – the two Activities (or Activity Specifications) must begin at the same time. • "End to end" (EE) – the two Activities (or Activity Specifications) must end at the same time. • "Offset" (Of) – one Activity (or Activity Specification) begins after a specified Overlap (with its Overlap Unit) such as "2.5" and "hours".	16
Activity Derivation Element	The fact that a Continuous Activity Characteristic is at least partly *derived via* another Activity Characteristic, a Constant, or a System Variable.	7
Activity Identifier	A characteristic of Activities and/or Activity Specifications that can be used for identifying individual instances of either.	7
Activity Identifier Assignment	The fact that an Activity Identifier, that is *an example of* a particular Activity Identifier Type, may be applied to Activities or Activity Specifications that are (directly or indirectly) *examples of* a specified Activity Type.	7
Activity Identifier Type	The definition of a fundamental category of Activity Identifier, such as "Corporate Official Name", "Nickname", and so forth.	7

Term	Definition	Chap
Activity Name	A piece of text labeling either an Activity or an Activity Specification.	7
Activity Name Assignment	The fact that an Activity Name, that is *an example of* a particular Activity Name Type, may be applied to Activities or Activity Specifications that are (directly or indirectly) *examples of* a specified Activity Type.	7
Activity Name Type	The definition of a fundamental category of Activity Name, such as "Corporate Official Name", "Nickname", and so forth.	7
Activity Placement	The fact that a particular Activity, Activity Specification, Event, or Event Specification is *in* a particular Address.	12
Activity Role	The fact that a particular Party has something to do with the performance of an Activity.	7
Activity Role Type	The definition of a fundamental type of Activity Role. It consist of at least three instances: "Direct Action", "Communications Role", and "Management". Other Activity Role Types may be added if each is *a sub-type of* an existing Activity Role Type.	7
Activity Specification	An Activity Type that specifically describes an Activity sufficiently to offer it for sale.	7
Activity Specification Dependence	The fact that, as designed, one Activity must be completed, started, or overlapping a specified amount another Activity.	7
Activity Specification Dependence	The definition of a constraint that controls all the Activities that are *examples of* a particular Activity Specification. Specifically it controls.	16
Activity Specification Step	A component of an Activity Specification that describes how part of the Activity Specification is to be carried out.	7
Activity Specification Structure	The fact that any one Activity Specification is associated with another Activity Specification. Two principal sub-types are Work Breakdown Specification Structure (as an alternative to explicitly specifying Activity Step and Project), and Activity Specification Dependency. Other Activity Structures may also be specified.	7
Activity Status	As an Activity progresses to completion, it goes through multiple states, as defined by its Status Type. Activity Status is the fact that a particular Case is in one of those states.	18

Glossary

Term	Definition	Chap
Activity Step	A subdivision of an Activity that is the execution of a particular task.	7
Activity Structure	The fact that any one Activity is associated with another Activity. Two principal sub-types are Work Breakdown Structure (as an alternative to explicitly specifying Activity Step and Project), and Activity Dependency. Other Activity Structures may also be specified.	7
Activity Structure Type	The definition of a kind of Activity Structure. By definition, at least six instances exist: "Work Breakdown Structure". "Activity Dependency", "Other Activity Structure", "Work Breakdown Specification Structure", "Activity Specification Dependence", and "Other Activity Specification Structure". Other Activity Structure Types may be specified, each of which would be *a sub-type of* one other Architecture Structure Type.	7
Activity Type	The definition of a fundamental category of an Activity. The first instances are, by definition "Service" and "Procedure". These can be sub-divided further.	7
Actual Account Balance	An Account Balance that describes the actual state of the Account for a current or past period of time.	11
Address	A means for locating a Party, an Asset, or an Activity. Must be either a Physical Address that has a physical location, or a Virtual Address, a node on an electronic network.	12
Adjustment	A virtual Material Movement that constitutes a modification of the known quantity of an Asset. This involves a virtual movement, either *from* the ether *to* a Facility (a positive adjustment), or *from* a Facility *to* the ether (a negative adjustment).	12
Advertising Piece	A Communication that consists of publication by the company of Printed material or video content to promote an enterprise's products or services.	14
Aesthetic Conventions	A set of modeling standards that concern the overall appearance and organization of a drawing. This includes such things as relative positions of different categories of entity classes on the page, use of lines, and general graphic design principles. These have traditionally not been addressed in the literature.	1
Aggregate Pit	A place where gravel and other materials used for paving are mined.	22

Term	Definition	Chap
Agreement	A super-type of Instrument and Marketing Relationship, that of Agreement. This includes not only financial Instruments and Marketing Relationships, as well as Other Agreements. This extends the concept enough to include ordinary sales and purchase orders for non-financial services and supplies. The relationships between the two sub-type entities and Party become sub-types of the relationships between Agreement and Party.	20
Agreement Role		
Alignment Node	When a road is curved, it is rendered in plans as a succession of relatively short, straight, line segments (Paths). The link between any two of these is called an "Alignment Node". Note that, in the model, it is shown that each Alignment Node may be identified as *prior to* another Alignment Node. Going in the other direction, the second Alignment Node is, of course, *subsequent to* the first one.	22
Amino	Of the mononovalent group (-NH$_2$).[83]	19
Amino Acid	A group of nitrogenous organic compounds that serve as units of structure of the proteins and are essential to human metabolism."[84] "Any of a group of organic compounds containing both the carboxyl and amino groups, forming the basic constituents of proteins.[85]	19
Approach Driveway	The portion of a driveway that intersects a street that is part of the street right-of-way.	22
Appurtenance	Something that sticks out in a roadway, such as a sign.	22
Appurtenance Site	the site of a sign or other thing sticking up out of the roadway.	22
Arch Super-Structure	A Bridge Superstructure Unit that is for a Bridge of arch design.	22

---

[83] *DK Illustrated Oxford Dictionary.* 1998. (New York: Oxford University Press.) Page 37.

[84] Webster's New World Dictionary of the American Language. 1964. (Cleveland: World Publishing Company.) Page 48.

[85] *DK Illustrated Oxford Dictionary.* 1998. (New York: Oxford University Press.) Page 37.

Glossary

Term	Definition	Chap
Architect's View	In David Hay's version of John Zachman's *Architecture Framework*[86], the perspective of the person who distills a wide range of business owners views (and the corresponding semantics) of the business to arrive at a single view of the underlying nature of the enterprise. Each box in the model of this view ("entity class") represents the definition of something of fundamental significance to the enterprise. Annotated lines between the boxes represent one-to-many relationships between entity classes. Attributes are collected and available, although they may or may not be displayed.	1
Architectural Conventions	A set of modeling standards that concern the grouping of entity classes according to their meaning. (In *Data Model Patterns: Conventions of Thought*, these were called "semantic conventions").	1
Architecture Framework	This is David Hay's version[87] of John Zachman's "Framework for Information Architecture"[88][89], which describes the complete set of terms of reference for understanding an enterprise. It is organized in terms of 6 "views" (*Planner's View, Business Owner's View, Architect's View, Designer's View, Builder's View,* and *Functioning System View*) of the enterprise, with 6 "dimensions" (*Data, Activities, People, Timing, Events,* and *Motivation*) for each view.	1
Archiving	A Disposition Action that entails placing an Information Resource Instance in special long-term storage.	10

---

[86] Hay, D.C. 2003. *Requirements Analysis: From Business Views to Architecture.* (Upper Saddle River, NJ: Prentice Hall PTR.) Pages 5-6.

[87] Hay, D.C. 2003. *Requirements Analysis: From Business Views to Architecture.* (Upper Saddle River, NJ: Prentice Hall PTR.) Pages 5-6.

[88] Zachman, John. 1987. "A framework for information systems architecture", *IBM Systems Journal,* Vol. 26, No. 3. (IBM Publication G321-5298.)

[89] Sowa, John. F., and John A. Zachman. 1992. "Extending and Formalizing the Framework for Information Systems Architecture", *IBM Systems Journal,* vol 31, No 3. (IBM Publication G321-5488.)

Term	Definition	Chap
Asset	A physical thing that has presence in the world. This can be a building, computer, office supply, and the like. Assets include the products made and consumed, the equipment used to make and transport those things, the raw materials that are required to make them, and the buildings and other structures that house them and their construction activities.	6
Asset /Unit Cost	INFER-THROUGH (*specified by*, Asset Specification, Standard Price).	16
Asset Account	"any [set of] rights which has value to its owner."[90]	11
Asset Category	An Asset Characteristic that can only take one of a discrete list of values. This could be the "Color" of a car, or the "left-handedness" of a wrench. This is as opposed to a Continuous Asset Category that can take as a value any real number or a piece of text.	6
Asset Characteristic	A distinguishing trait, quality, or property that can be given a value for either an Asset or an Asset Specification.	6
Asset Characteristic Assignment	The fact that a particular Asset Characteristic is part of the definition of either an Asset Type or an Asset Specification.	6
Asset Characteristic Value	The fact that a particular Asset or a particular Asset Specification takes a particular Characteristic Value *of* a particular Asset Characteristic.	6
Asset Derivation Element	The fact that a Continuous Asset Characteristic can be derived, at least in part, by another Asset Characteristic.	6
Asset Identifier	The definition of a characteristic that can be used to uniquely identify an Asset.	6
Asset Identifier Assignment	The fact that Assets of a particular Asset Type can assume an Asset Identifier Value that is *an example of* a particular Asset Name Type.	6
Asset Identifier Value	The text or number that uniquely identifies a particular instance of an Asset.	6
Asset Legal Category Value	One of the values that is legal for an Asset Category to take.	6
Asset Name	Text describing or identifying a particular Asset.	6

---

[90] *Ibid.*, p. 22.

Glossary

Term	Definition	Chap
Asset Name Assignment	The fact that Assets of a particular Asset Type can assume an Asset Name that is *an example of* a particular Asset Name Type.	6
Asset Name Type	The definition of a category of Asset Name.	6
Asset Role	The fact that a Party play can be involved in the manufacture, disposition, or management of a particular Asset or Asset Specification.	6
Asset Role Type	The definition of a kind of Asset Role. The first instances of this must be "Manufacturer", "Wholesaler", "Retailer", and "Other Asset Role". Others may be defined, each as a *sub-type of* one of these.	6
Asset Specification	An Asset Type that describes an Asset sufficiently to offer it for sale. Instances are typically identified by a Model Number.	6
Asset Specification Location	The fact that a particular Asset Type can be used in a particular Facility. For example, a Bridge Superstructure Unit can be used for a Bridging, but not in an Aggregate Pit.	12, 22
Asset Specification Structure	The fact that of one Asset Specification is a component of another Asset Specification. This could be, for example, the fact that a particular model of Dell computer is designed to contain a particular model of disk drive.	6
Asset Structure	The fact that of one Asset is a component of another Asset. This could be, for example, the fact that a particular Dell laptop computer (with a particular serial number) contains a particular disk drive (with a particular serial number). It might also be the fact that a specified Lot of a particular pharmaceutical contains a specified Lot of a particular active ingredient.	6
Asset Structure Type	The definition of a kind of either Asset Specification Structure or Asset Structure.	6
Asset Type	The definition of a fundamental category of Asset.	6
Association	(See relationship.)	1
Attribute	A discrete, atomic piece of information that identifies, describes, classifies, or measures an entity class The *values* of a set of attributes of an entity class describe instances of that entity class. If an entity class is the definition of a thing of significance about which an enterprise wishes to hold information, then an attribute defines one kind of information held.	1

Enterprise Model Patterns

Term	Definition	Chap
Attribute	A descriptor of a kind of information captured about an Entity Class.	10
Authorship Role	The fact that a Person is one of the creators of an Information Resource.	10
Authorship Role	A Communication Role that is the act of creating either the original work or the copy.	14
Balance Sheet	A representation of the *Chart of Accounts* that describes the *value of* the organization at a given point in time, and how much of that value is either owned by the stockholders or owed to others.	11
Banking Role	A Management Role played by a department or an officer of the bank in either issuing debt or accepting deposits.	20
Barker / Ellis Notation	A *Notation Convention* developed by Harry Ellis and Richard Barker in the early 1980s, which emphasizes the semantic aspects of the model. This makes it particularly appropriate for architectural data models.	1
Beneficiary	An Insurance Role in a life insurance policy by the spouse or other family member who would be paid if the employee died.	13
Benefit	Something of financial value paid to a Person in the course of an Employment with the Company.	13
Benefit Participation	The fact that a Person is receiving a Benefit.	13
Benefit Rule	*A constraint on* a how a particular Benefit Type may be implemented.	13
Benefit Rule Application	The fact that a particular Benefit Rule is in fact constraining a Benefit Participation *by* an employee.	13
Benefit Rule Type	The definition of a kind of Benefit Rule.	13
Benefit Type	The definition of a fundamental kind of Benefit.	13
Bridge	is the set of girders and other physical materials (a physical Asset) *that the implementation of* the Bridging.	22
Bridge Culvert	A large pipe that goes under a road to direct a stream.	22
Bridge Structure Site	A Facility that encompasses the entire area required for a Bridging.	22
Bridge Superstructure Unit	An assembly of components of a Bridge. This could be a Girder Superstructure, an Arch Superstructure, et cetera.	22
Bridging	The fact that a Path is in the air, crossing over other Paths without communicating with them.	22

Term	Definition	Chap
Brochure	A Physical Copy or an Information Resource Instance that in a page or two describe some aspect of the enterprise.	14
Brochure Distribution	An Advertising Piece that consists of distributing a printed brochure, typically via a postal service, but it could also be handed out by representatives in a public place.	14
Brokerage Account	An instance of an Instrument whereby the customer entrusts money to the bank, but either the customer directly determines how the money will be invested, or the customer hires the broker to manage the investments. The customer bears all the risk associated any investments made.	20
Builder's View	In David Hay's version of John Zachman's *Architecture Framework*[91], the perspective of the person well versed in the technology involved, with the job of implementing the Designer's designs. In the data domain, the Builder's View is not so much of a data model as of a schematic of how data are physically stored in a database. This is in terms of disk drives, "tablespaces", and the like.	1
Building	A permanent enclosure, such as a house, an office building, a factory, or a warehouse.	6

---

[91] Hay, D.C. 2003. *Requirements Analysis: From Business Views to Architecture.* (Upper Saddle River, NJ: Prentice Hall PTR.) Pages 5-6.

Term	Definition	Chap
Business Owner's View	In David Hay's version of John Zachman's *Architecture Framework*[92], the perspective of the people who run the day-to-day activities of the enterprise. The important thing to capture here is the *semantics* of the enterprise. Since this is about *language*, there is no modeling notation per se, although the conceptual notations described for the *architect's view* can be used. Because it is *linguistic*, it is more often represented in structured text of various forms. Traditionally, this has included simple compilation of a glossary, but more recently, the *semantic languages* of the *Resource Description Framework (RDF)* and the *Web Ontology Language (OWL)* have appeared in an attempt to capture an organization's use of language.[93] [94] It is also addressed by techniques described in the Object Management Group's "Semantics of Business Vocabulary and Business Rules.[95]	1
Business Term	The use of a particular Expression to describe a particular Concept.	10
Canal	A segment of a man-made Non-Roadway Path that is for the purpose of transporting water from where it is plentiful to where it is needed—usually for irrigation purposes.	22
Capability	The fact of a Person's being able to do something—either demonstrates acquaintance with a Body of Knowledge or perform a specified activity (that is, an Activity Specification).	13
Capability Endorsement	The fact that a particular Education Program Enrollment (*by* a Person) resulted in the issuance of a Grade or Score confirming the extent to which the Person has attained the Capability.	13

---

[92] Hay, D.C. 2003. *Requirements Analysis: From Business Views to Architecture.* (Upper Saddle River, NJ: Prentice Hall PTR.) Pages 5-6.

[93] Allemang, D., Jim Hendler. 2009. Semantic Web for the Working Ontologist: Effective Modeling in RDFS and OWL. (Boston: Morgan Kaufmann.)

[94] Hay, D.C. 2008. "Semantics, Ontology, and Data Modeling", *Cutter Report on Business Intelligence, Vol. 6, No. 7.* June 1, 2008.

[95] Object Management Group. 2008. *Semantics of Business Vocabulary and Business Rules.* OMG Available Specification formal/2008-01-02. Available at: *http://www.omg.org/spec/SBVR/1.0/.*

Term	Definition	Chap
Carboxyl	The uniavalent acid radical (-COOH), present in most organic acids.[96]	19
Cardinality	A constraint on the number of instances of a property can be associated with a class. This must be either *minimum cardinality* or *maximum cardinality*.	1
Cartesian System	A Reference System that uses "X", "Y", and "Z", distances relative to a single "Geographic Point" that is its "datum".	22
Case	A set of Activities required to solve or prosecute a particular crime or malfeasance.	18
Case Activity Rule	The fact that an Activity that is *an example of* a particular Activity Type can be *part of* any Case that is *an example of* a particular Case Type/.	18
Case Status	As a Case progresses to completion, it goes through multiple states, as defined by its Status Type. A Case Status is the fact that a particular Case is in one of those states.	18
Case Type	The definition of a fundamental type of case, such as "Investigation", "arraignment", "trial", and "appeal".	18
Certificate	A License asserting that one is *qualified* to perform specified activities (that is, Activity Specifications).	13
Channel	A Natural Feature that is segment of an indentation in the land (smaller than a river), where water flows.	22
Characteristic	"a distinguishing trait, quality, or property."[97]	4
Chart Of Accounts	A listing of all the accounts in the general ledger, each account accompanied by a reference number. A form of an enterprise's *General Ledger*, organizing quantities of money held or owed by the company. This is in terms of things that the enterprise deals with, such as products or personnel. The basic rules and transactions for recording changes to the financial quantities are well-defined.	11
Checking Account	An instance of a Deposit that provides mechanisms for easy access (checks and automated teller machines, for example). It may or may not pay a nominal rate of interest.	20
Chemical	The material that constitutes all physical things.	19

---

[96] *DK Illustrated Oxford Dictionary.* 1998. (New York: Oxford University Press.) Page 126.

[97] Merriam-Webster. (Viewed 2010) *Merriam-Webster OnLine Dictionary.* "Characteristic".

Term	Definition	Chap
Chemical Compound	An assembly of Chemical Elements that are bound together at the atomic level. It consists of identical molecules, each of which is a collection of atoms physically linked together in a way that makes them difficult to separate. Water, for example, is a compound, with each of its molecules consisting of two hydrogen atoms tightly linked to one oxygen atom. The combination of atoms that is possible for a particular set of atoms is constrained by each atom's structure.	19
Chemical Element	A Chemical that consists of identical atoms, each consisting of a nucleus consisting of *protons* and *neutrons*, plus a number of electrons orbiting the nucleus. This is the simplified explanation. The reality is vastly more subtle and complex than this, but this is enough knowledge of atomic physics for our purposes here.	19
Chemical Formulation	Any collection of elements and/or compounds whose atoms are not chemically bound together. That chocolate cake consisting of flour, shortening, cocoa, and sugar, is a mixture because none of the ingredients are chemically bound together at the molecular level.	19
City	A Geopolitical Area that is recognized as a municipality.	5
City /Country Name	INFER-THROUGH (*part of*, State, /Country Name).	12
City /State Name	INFER-THROUGH (*part of*, Principal Country Division, Default Name).	12
Class	A collection of things (*objects*) that share one or more characteristics (*attributes*).	1
Class Model	In UML, this is a representation of classes (sets) of things of interest. The modeling language has no limitations as to what can be a class. In this book, we are concerned solely with *entity classes*, which are sets of things of significance to the enterprise, government agency, or domain of interest that is the subject of the model.	1
Cleaning Activity	The removal of dirt or debris from a Facility.	7

Glossary

Term	Definition	Chap
Collateralized Debt Obligation	A type of structured asset-backed security (ABS) whose value and payments are derived from a portfolio of fixed-income underlying assets.[98]	20
Collector Distributor Roadway Path	A roadway that leads from a surface street to an expressway, including either an entrance or an exit ramp.	22
Commercial Airing	An Advertising Piece that consists of running a television or radio (or internet) commercial on one or more stations.	14
Commercial Production	A Mass Market Procedure that is to prepare commercials on television or radio.	14
Communication	An Activity that is the transmission of information between one or more representatives of the enterprise with representatives of other organizations.	14
Communication Medium	The fact that a particular Information Resource Instance is *used in* a particular Communication.	14
Communication Procedure	An Activity Specification that defines how a particular kind of Communication will be carried out. This is either a Personal Communication Procedure, a Mass Market Procedure, or an Other Communication Procedure.	14
Communication Procedure Type	The definition of a fundamental category of Communication Procedure. The first instances must correspond to the sub-types of Communication Procedure, such as "Personal Communication Procedure", "Prepare a Facsimile", et cetera. Any Communication Procedure Type added must be *a sub-type of* an existing Communication Procedure Type.	14
Communication Role	The fact that a particular Party is somehow involved with a Communication, either as an Originator, Recipient, or other kind of Participant.	14
Communication Role Type	The definition of a fundamental kind of Communication Role. The first instances must be "Originator Role", "Recipient Role", "Participant Role", and "Other Communication Role. Additional Communication Role Types may be added if each is *a sub-type of* one of those already there.	14

---

[98] Wikipedia. Viewed June 25, 2010. "Collateralized debt obligation".

Enterprise Model Patterns

Term	Definition	Chap
Communications Role	The fact that a Party participated in a Communication. (See Chapter 16 for more information.)	7
Company Department	An Organization that is a subdivision of a Company.	18
Compensation	An amount of money to be paid to an *employee*. This is *an example of* various kinds of Compensation Type, both shown as sub-types and as instances of Benefit Type that are *sub-types of* "Compensation".	13
Compensation Participation	The fact that an employee is actually eligible to receive a Compensation.	13
Compensation Payment	A check or transfer *from* one Party *to* another Party.	13
Compensation Payment Type	The definition of a kind of payment associated with an employee's paycheck. Principle instances are "Employer Payroll Payment" and "Paycheck".	13
Completion	"the assembly of down hole tubulars[*] and equipment required to enable safe and efficient production from an oil or gas well".[99]	21
Completion Primary Product	The fact that a Specified Material passes through a particular Completion during a specified period of time.	21
Completion Primary Purpose	At a point in time, this is the Completion Primary Purpose Type that the Completion is intended *to accomplish*—specifically, "production" (of hydrocarbons) or "injection" (of steam).	21
Completion Primary Purpose Type	The definition of a Completion Primary Purpose. This is usually only either "production" (of hydrocarbons) or "injection" (of steam) Each Completion Purpose Type, then, may be *constrained by* one or more Valid Completion Purpose which is *the acceptable use of* a Specified Material, such as "crude oil", "natural gas', or (depending on the Completion Purpose Type) "steam".	21
Complex Super-Structure	A Bridge Superstructure Unit that is a complex mixture of bridge types.	22
Compound	(See Chemical Compound).	19

---

[*] A "tubular" is "any type of oilfield pipe, such as drill pipe, drill collars, pup joints, casing, production tubing and pipeline." [Schlumberger. 27 June, 2010. "Tubular"]

[99] Schlumberger, Inc. Viewed June 27, 2010. *Oilfield Glossary.* "completion". Available at: *http://www.glossary.oilfield.slb.com*.

Glossary

Term	Definition	Chap
Computer / Communications Equipment Item	A Piece of Equipment that carries out information processing functions, either in one place, or over an information processing network.	6
Concept	Something that understood to exist or to be the case.	10
Conference Session	A Group Meeting in which multiple people interested in a specific topic gather to discuss it as part of a larger meeting to address a more general topic of which the Conference Session topic is a part.	14
Consumption	A Usage that is the Consumption *of* an Asset, either from Inventory (in the case of raw materials or spare parts) or as a Discrete Item (such as a sub-assembly).	12
Consumption	The use *of* an Asset, such as Inventory, a Lot, or a Discrete Item, or *of* an Asset Specification, such as "water", or "natural gas". This is *charged to* either a specific Maintenance Task, or a total Work Order.	16
Consumption /Consumption Cost	Material Movement Quantity times Consumption /Unit Cost.	16
Consumption /Unit Cost	INFER-THROUGH (of, Asset, /Unit Cost) (or) INFER-THROUGH (of, Asset Specification, Standard Price).	16
Contact Delivery	A category of Material Movement that is associated with buying or selling products. This is either Receipt of Assets from a vendor, Shipment of Assets to a customer, or Transfer of Assets from one place to another within the company.	12
Contact Network	A collection of Addresses (usually Virtual Addresses) that are linked together, *used by* one or more Communication Procedures.	14
Context Model	An overview of a business domain. In data modeling, this is a sketch of the primary things of concern to an enterprise. In a data flow diagram, this represents the business domain as a single process and itemizes the principle external entities that provide data to it or get data from it.	1
Continuous Asset Characteristic	An Asset Characteristic that can take as a value any real number or a piece of text. This is as opposed to an Asset Category that can only take one of a discrete list of values.	6
Continuous Party Characteristic	A Party Characteristic that is evaluated as a real number, date, or piece of text.	4

476 Enterprise Model Patterns

Term	Definition	Chap
Continuous Thing Characteristic	A Thing Characteristic that can take as a value any real numeric value, text, or a date.	9
Contract	"a binding agreement between two or more persons or parties; *especially*: one legally enforceable".[100]	15
Contract "Total Value"	SUM-THROUGH (*composed of*, Line Item, "/Value)").	`15
Contract Delivery	A Material Movement which is associated with a Contract. This includes Receipt and Shipment.	15
Cost Center	An element of the organization (usually a department), or other Internal Organization that is being accounted for.	11
Cost Center Assignment	The fact that a particular Cost Center is defined for the purpose of accounting for a particular Internal Organization, an Activity or Project, an Asset, or something else (represented on the model as ??Other??).	11
Counterparty	An Instrument Role where a non-bank Party does business with the bank. (This is an example of a Customer Role.)	20
Country	A Geopolitical Area that is a nation.	5
Course	A Program Component that is a scheduled set of encounters between a teacher and one or more students, wherein the teacher is expected to impart knowledge about a particular subject.	13
Course	A formal set of Group Meetings for the purpose of having a person or set of people present a formal body of knowledge.	14
Course Enrollment	An Education Program Enrollment that is the fact that a Course was held, resulting in a Grade and *for the acquisition of* a Capability Endorsement.	13
Course Offering	The fact that a Course is being offered on a particular Date, *at* a particular place (a Facility set up for that purpose.).	13

---

[100] Merriam-Webster (viewed 2010) "The Merriam-Webster OnLine Dictionary". "contract".

Glossary

Term	Definition	Chap
Covered Individual	An Insurance Role *in* an Insurance Coverage that is *by* the Person who would receive proceeds if a claim were filed and approved. This would be either the employee or a family member receiving health insurance coverage. Or the employee for a life insurance policy.	13
Creation Date	For an Asset, an attribute that represents date the Asset came into existence.	9
Credit Entry	An Accounting Entry that subtracts from the Account Balance of an Asset Account, adds to the Account Balance of a Liability Account, or adds to the Account Balance of an Equity Account.	11
Credit Rule	An Accounting Rule Entry that specifies which Asset Account to be subtracted from, which Liability Account to be added to, or which Equity Account to be added to.	11
Currency	The money in general use in a country.[101] Specifically, the unit of value, as defined in a country. This is a kind of Unit of Measure.	20
Customer	A Party that plays the role of being *the customer in* a Contract.	15
Customer Role	A Management Role played by a Person or Organization outside the bank that is doing business with the bank.	20
Data Type	The format of an attribute – numeric, character string, Boolean, et cetera.	1
Date (Data Type)	A *data type* describing a point in time positioned on the calendar.	1
Debit Entry	An Accounting Entry that adds to the Account Balance of an Asset Account, subtracts from the Account Balance of a Liability Account, or subtracts from the Account Balance of an Equity Account.	11
Debit Rule	An Accounting Rule Entry that specifies which Asset Account to be added to, which Liability Account to be subtracted from, or which Equity Account to be subtracted from.	11
Default Name	An attribute for entity classes, such as Party and Asset, that are in fact named via other entity classes. this is a *Name* that can be used for convenience.	9

---

[101] *DK Illustrated Oxford Dictionary.* 1998. (New York: Oxford University Press.) "Currency".

Term	Definition	Chap
Degree Program	A Formal Program in a college or university that results in the student's obtaining a degree of a specified Degree Type.	13
Degree Type	A formal kind of degree, such as "Bachelor's", "Master's", et cetera.	13
Deoxyribonucleic Acid	A self-replicating material [an Organic Compound] present in nearly all living organisms. Esp. as a constituent of chromosomes… A DNA molecule consists of two strands that spiral around each other to form a double helix held together by sub-units called bases [adenine, guanine, cytosine, or thymine], which always pair in specific ways: adenine with thymine and cytosine with guanine.[102]	19
Deposit	An instance of an Instrument whereby a bank holds a customer's money safely, and invests it conservatively. The bank pledges to protect the amount invested. It bears all the risk from any investments made.	20
Deposit Instrument Specification	An Instrument Specification describing a Deposit account offered by the bank.	20
Description	An attribute of most entity classes, that describes at some length each instance of that class.	9
Designer's View	In David Hay's version of John Zachman's *Architecture Framework*[103] the perspective of the person who applies technology to address the issues, problem, et cetera, in terms of the architecture represented by the conceptual model. This model is organized in terms required for manipulation by a particular data management technology. This includes relational tables and columns, XML Schema tags, object-oriented classes, and so forth. It should reflect the structures of the conceptual model, but it is constrained by the technology involved.	1
Destruction	A Disposition Action that entails permanently destroying an Information Resource Instance.	10

---

[102] *DK Illustrated Oxford Dictionary*. 1998. (New York: Oxford University Press.) Page 249.

[103] Hay, D.C. 2003. *Requirements Analysis: From Business Views to Architecture*. (Upper Saddle River, NJ: Prentice Hall PTR.) Pages 5-6.

Glossary

Term	Definition	Chap
Destruction Date	For an Asset, an attribute that represents date the Asset ceased to exist.	9
Device Specification	A piece of hardware, such as a syringe, that is included in a Specified Packaged Product.	19
Direct Action	An Activity Role wherein the Party (usually a Person) is directly involved in completing the Activity. It includes an attribute Hours Worked for the hours spent on the Activity between the Effective (start) Date and the Until (end) Date. (See Chapter 15	7
Direct Measurement	An Observation that is taken by performing a Laboratory Test on a Sample, as opposed to a Physical Observation which obtains data solely by a person's examining the Sample.	17
Discrete Item	An Asset that is a single physical item that is uniquely identifiable. Your author's laptop computer, with **Serial number "3245-A"** is an example of this.	6
Disposition	In response to (*triggered by*) an actual Event, *the carrying out of* a Disposition Action *of* one Information Resource Instance, on a particular Disposition Date. The Disposition must be *based on* a Disposition Rule.	10
Disposition Action	This is something that could be done to an Information Resource Instance, such as "Destruction", "Archiving", et cetera.	10
Disposition Event	Something that happens to trigger a Disposition Rule. Typically, this is the passage of a specified period of time.	10
Disposition Rule	A set of conditions and requirements for archiving or deleting Information Resource Instances that are *examples of* a particular Information Resource Definition.	10
Disposition Rule Element	A particular component of a Disposition Rule. This Disposition Rule Element must be *to take* one Disposition Action, typically in response to a Specified Event. (Such as the elapse of one year since its creation.)	10
Distribution	The fact that a particular Information Resource Instance (copy) was sent or will be sent to a particular Party.	10
Document	An Information Resource Definition that is text-based.	10

480 Enterprise Model Patterns

Term	Definition	Chap
Domain Name	An identification label that defines a realm of administrative autonomy, authority, or control on the Internet, based on the Domain Name System (DNS). Domain names are used in various networking contexts and application-specific naming and addressing purposes.[104]	12
Domain Of Knowledge	A collection of information that comprehensively describes a particular subject. For example, this could be embodied in a Skill, or it could be a Language. (Other Domains of Knowledge might be more specialized, such as "Forensics", or "Ancient Greek Literature"[♣].)	13
Double-Entry Bookkeeping	A set of processes and rules for dealing with transaction to the Chart of Accounts.	11
Downstream Processing	Processing that takes crude oil and gas from the surface choke or Christmas tree to the refinery, turns it into products, and then distributes and sells those products.	21
Draw	Compensation paid in anticipation of Incentive Pay to be earned.	13
Education Program Enrollment	The fact that a Person has enrolled *in* either an Education Program Offering or a Degree Program.	13
Education Program Offering	The fact that a Course is being made available at a particular time and place (a Course Offering), or the fact that a License Test is being offered on a particular Date, *at* a particular place. In either case, the "place" is a Facility suitable for the purpose. Each Education Program Enrollment may be *to acquire* one or more Capacity Endorsements, each of which must be *to acknowledge the holding of* a Capability.	13
Educational Element	A defined process that can be used *to acquire or, demonstrate competence in* an Activity Specification or to acquire or demonstrate competence in a Domain of Knowledge. This must be either a Formal Program, a *part of* a Formal program (including Course or License Test), or an Informal Program (typically Life Experiences).	13

---

[104] Wikipedia. (Viewed 2010.) Available at http://en.wikipedia.org/wiki/Domain_name.

♣ Ancient Greek Literature? You never know. We have to accommodate all possibilities.

Glossary

Term	Definition	Chap
Educational Role	The fact that a particular Person has something to do with the carrying out of an Educational Element.	13
Educational Role Type	The definition of a kind of Educational Role, such as "Teacher", "Administrator", et cetera.	13
Effective Date	An attribute that represents the beginning of a period when a transaction will be in effect.	9
Electron	A stable elementary particle with a charge of negative electricity, found in all atoms and acting as the primary carrier of electricity in solids.[105]	19
Electronic Copy (Of An Information Resource)	An Information Resource Instance that has been captured in electronic form. This could be a digital file, e-mail, cable, or some such.	10
Element	(See Chemical Element.)	19
E-Mail Address	A label for a node on a communications network (usually *the Internet*, but private networks can also have E-Mail Addresses) where someone can receive messages from others. The label consists of a specific name concatenated with a *domain name* that describes a portion of the network, where the address is located.	12
E-Mail Message Procedure	How to send an E-mail.	14
Emergency Work Order	Something broke and it has to be fixed as quickly as possible.	16
Employee	A Person *subject to* an Employment *with* an Organization for a specified period of time.	13
Employee Payroll Deduction	An amount of money withheld from a Paycheck to pay *for* a Specified Employee Deduction.	13
Employee Payroll Payment Component	An amount of money paid by the employer *for* a Specified Employer Expense.	13
Employer Payroll Payment	Payments to other agencies and companies on behalf of the employee.	13
Employer Payroll Payment Component	A payment to another agency or companies on behalf of the employee.	13
Employment	The fact that a particular Person is employed *with* a particular Organization.	13

---

[105] *DK Illustrated Oxford Dictionary*. 1998. (New York: Oxford University Press): 264.

Term	Definition	Chap
Enterprise Data Model	An *entity / relationship model* whose domain is the architecture of an entire business or government agency. Specifically, it incorporates models at least for people and organizations, geographic locations, physical assets and information resources, activities and events, and accounting. In addition will contain more complex models of specific functional areas.	1
Entity Class	A *class* that is specifically the definition of a thing of significance about which the organization wishes to hold (which is to say, collect, maintain, and use) information. This may be a tangible thing like a product or customer, or it may be an intangible thing like a transaction or a role.	1
Entity Class	A group of entities that are described by the same set of attributes.	10
Equipment Utilization	A Usage that is the Actual consumption *of* time on a piece of production equipment (a Discrete Item) during a manufacturing process.	12
Equipment Utilization	This records the fact that a particular Building or Discrete Item (Piece of Equipment or Instrument) was used in the manufacturing process.	16
Equity	An Instrument whereby one Party acquires ownership of part of a Company.	20
Equity Account	The amount of the company's assets contributed or earned by the company's owners. This is usually either "owner-held stock" or "retained earnings". Among the equity accounts are two sub-categories of accounts that have special significance.	11
Equity Instrument Specification	An Instrument Specification describing an Equity instrument. This is often equivalent to a "prospectus".	20
Exchange Rate	A means for translating Valuations from the Currency in which they were recorded to another Currency for reporting purposes.	20
Expected Observation	Constitutes the definition of a particular Test Method or Test Method Step. That is, in each case, the Test Method or the Test Method Step must be *defined in terms of* a set of one or more Expected Observations.	17
Expense Account	The assets spent by the company to acquire goods and services. This is the money spent for "hotel", "airfare", "purchase of equipment", et cetera. Each dollar of expense represents *a decrease in* the organization's equity.	11

Glossary

Term	Definition	Chap
Expiry Date	Canadian for *Until Date*.	9
Expression	A collection of Words, Phrases, or Sentences intended to represent meaning. By definition, each of these Expressions must be *expressed in* one and only one Language.	10
Expression Structure	The fact that a particular Expression is a component in another Expression. A Sentence is composed of Phrases, that are composed of Words.	10
Face To Face Meeting	A Personal Communication whereby two or more people are together in the same room, or are sharing a video conference of some kind.	14
Facility	A place with a purpose. A synonym for Physical Address. Not to be confused with Geographic Location, which is simply "a place on the Earth".	12
Facility /City Name (Direct Version)	INFER-THROUGH (*located in*, City, Default Name≈)	12
Facility /City Name (Indirect Version)	INFER-THROUGH (*described by*, Geographic Placement, /City Name)	12
Facility /Country Name	INFER-THROUGH (*located in*, City, /Country Name)	12
Facility /State	INFER-THROUGH (*located in*, City, /State Name)	12
Facility /Street Address	INFER-THROUGH♣ (*located in*, Other Surveyed Area, Street Address).	12
Facility /Zip Code (Direct Version)	INFER-THROUGH (*located in*, Postal Area, Postal Code).	12
Facility /Zip Code (Indirect Version)	INFER-THROUGH (*described by*, Geographic Placement, Default Name, *defined by*, Postal Area).	12
Facility Structure	The fact that one Facility is *part of* another at a given time.	12

≈ "Default Name" is inherited from the super-type **Geographic Area**.

♣ Think of this as an imaginary attribute derivation language. Functions have been created as necessary. "INFER-THROUGH" is one of those. More will appear as the book goes on. In this case, INFER-THROUGH recognizes that all attributes in a "parent" (on the "one" side of a "one-to-many" relationship) entity class are available to the child entity class. In this case, "Street Address" in **Other Surveyed Area** can be considered an attribute of **Facility** via this function. Here the resulting attribute has the same name as its source but it doesn't have to.

484 Enterprise Model Patterns

Term	Definition	Chap
Facsimile Preparation	How to send a FAX.	14
Financial Instrument	A specialized formal legal document that specifies a legal arrangement whereby a bank either holds a customer's money in trust, or lends the customer money.	20
Financial Position	The fact that a certain number of shares of a particular company were held for a specified period of time, in support of a particular Instrument Component.	20
Flat Slab Super-Structure	A Bridge Superstructure Unit that is for a Bridge that is simply a piece of reinforced concrete.	22
Flow	As a quantity of material (or energy) that passes through a Path during a specified period of time.	22
Flow Type	A fundamental classification of Flow. This could be "all vehicles", "cars only", "semi-trailer trucks", "rail cars", and so forth. The Unit of Measure can be "number of vehicles", "kilowatt hours", "number of railcars", and so forth.	22
Formal Program	A set of classes and degrees specifically organized to deliver a specific body of knowledge (Domain of Knowledge) or competence in carrying out an Activity Specification.	13
Frontage Roadway Path	A roadway that runs parallel to an expressway, to provide access to the homes and stores along side it.	22
Functioning System View	In David Hay's version of John Zachman's *Architecture Framework*[106],this is both the beginning and the end of the system development process. Analysis begins by understanding the nature of the current system, and implementation ends with people, systems, databases, and procedures in place. This is not the subject of a model, *per se*.	1
Gas Line	A Utility that is a segment of the flow of natural gas.	22
General Ledger	A record of a company's assets and liabilities, and of the flow of money into or out of the company. A collection of the firm's accounts.[107]	11

---

[106] Hay, D.C. 2003. *Requirements Analysis: From Business Views to Architecture*. Upper Saddle River, NJ: Prentice Hall PTR: 5-6.

[107] Internet Center for Management and Business Administration, Inc. (Obtained) 2010. *NetMBA Business Knowledge Center*. (Available at: *http://www.netmba.com/*).

Glossary

Term	Definition	Chap
Geographic Area	A Geographic Location in (spherical) two dimensions with identified boundaries.	5
Geographic Category	A Geographic Characteristic that is constrained to take as a Characteristic Value one of a list of Legal Geographic Category Values.	5
Geographic Characteristic	A distinguishing trait, quality, or property that can be given a value for a Geographic Location.	5
Geographic Characteristic Assignment	The fact that a particular Geographic Location Characteristic may be specified for a Geographic Location Type. That is, a Geographic Location Characteristic Value *for* a particular Geographic Location cannot be assigned unless the Geographic Location Type that is *embodied in* that Geographic Location, is *defined in terms of* one or more Geographic Characteristic Assignments that are *of* the Geographic Location Characteristic that the Geographic Location Value is *of*.	5
Geographic Characteristic Value	The fact that a particular Geographic Characteristic has a particular Characteristic Value for a particular Geographic Location.	5
Geographic Continuous Characteristic	A Geographic Characteristic that takes as Characteristic Values for Geographic Characteristic Value either a real number, a piece of text, or a date.	5
Geographic Coordinates System	A Reference System that makes use of latitude, longitude, and elevation to place Geographic Points on the Earth's surface.	22
Geographic Definition	A Geographic Relationship wherein a Geographic Point is used to define the boundaries of either a Geographic Area, a Geographic Line, or a Geographic Solid.	5
Geographic Derivation Element	The fact that a Continuous Geographic Location Characteristic is at least in part derived from another Geographic Characteristic.	5
Geographic Identifier Assignment	The fact that a Geographic Location Corporate Identifier Type can be *embodied in* Geographic Location Names that are *for* Geographic Locations that are *examples of* a specified Geographic Location Type.	5
Geographic Line	A one dimensional Geographic Location, representing a linear feature, such as a railroad or highway route.	5
Geographic Location	A place on the Earth	5

Term	Definition	Chap
Geographic Location Corporate Name Type	The definition of a kind of Geographic Location Name that is *issued by* the Organization that is the site of the modeling effort.	5
Geographic Location Identifier	A characteristic of a Geographic Location (not stored as an attribute) whose value can be used to determine uniquely each instance of Geographic Location.	5
Geographic Location Identifier Value	The fact that a particular Geographic Location Identifier has been used to specify a particular Geographic Location.	5
Geographic Location Name	The fact that a particular Geographic Location is *labeled with* a *Name Value* that is *an example of* a particular Geographic Location Name Type.	5
Geographic Location Type	The definition of a kind of Geographic Location. Instances include the equivalent of the sub-types of Geographic Location. That is "Geopolitical Location", "City", "Other Surveyed Area", and so forth. Others are possible, but each must be *a sub-type of* one of these or one of its sub-types.	5
Geographic Name Assignment	The fact that a Geographic Location Corporate Name Type can be *embodied in* Geographic Location Names that are *for* Geographic Locations that are *examples of* a specified Geographic Location Type.	5
Geographic Name Standard	A standard, developed by a particular Organization, which has been accepted to specify official names for Geopolitical Areas. An example is the International Standards Organization's (ISO) standard.	5
Geographic Overlap	A Geographic Relationship wherein a Geographic Area is not entirely contained within another, but part of the two areas is in common.	5
Geographic Placement	The fact that a particular Facility is *located in* a particular Geographic Location that is *defined by* a particular Geographic Location Type. The unique identifiers for Geographic Placement guarantee that each Address may be *located in* only one Geographic Location *defined by* particular Geographic Location Type.	12
Geographic Placement, /City Name (Indirect Version)	INFER-THROUGH (*in*, Geographic Location Default Name (WHERE (*defined by*, Geographic Location, Name="City")).	12

Glossary

Term	Definition	Chap
Geographic Point	A dimensionless Geographic Location, identified typically by its latitude, longitude, and elevation.	5
Geographic Point Element	The fact that a particular Identification Component (a latitude, or an "X" value, for example) is part of a definition of a Geographic Point.	22
Geographic Relationship	The fact that one Geographic Location is somehow associated with another. This must be either a Geographic Structure, a Geographic Definition, or a Geographic Overlap.	5
Geographic Relationship Type	The definition of a kind of Geographic Relationship. At least three instances must be "Geographic Structure", "Geographic Definition", and "Geographic Overlap". Others are possible, but each must be *a sub-type of* one of these or one of its sub-types.	5
Geographic Role	The fact that a Party is somehow involved in the management of a particular Geographic Location.	5
Geographic Role Type	The definition of a kind of Geographic Role. One instance of Geographic Role Type must be "Jurisdiction", corresponding to the primary sub-type of Geographic Role.	5
Geographic Solid	A three-dimensional Geographic Location, used for among other things describing oil reservoirs and areas in space transversed by satellites.	5
Geographic Structure	A Geographic Relationship where one Geographic Area is entirely contained within another.	5
Geopolitical Area	A Geographic Area whose boundaries are established by law or treaty.	5
Geotechnical Site	a place recognized as a site where geotechnical phenomena (principally earthquakes) occur. (Important for planning roads.)	22
Girder	A piece of steel which provides structural strength to a Bridge.	22
Girder Super-Structure	for a Bridge segment that is assembled from steel girders.	22
Global Identifier	An attribute of master data entity classes that defines a surrogate identifier. That is, values are generated automatically by a computer program. It is "global" in that it ensures that all instances of the entity class being so identified, are unique in the organization (or in the world?).	9

488 Enterprise Model Patterns

Term	Definition	Chap
Government Internal Organization	An Organization that is a subdivision of a Government Agency.	18
Grade Crossing	A point where two (or more) highways intersect on the same level. It is possible to turn left or right from one to the other.	22
Grade Crossing Site	An Intersection Site that is the location of a Grade Crossing.	22
Grade Separated Crossing	An *intersection* that consists of two Paths that cross but do not communicate directly with each other.	22
Group Meeting	A Communication among three or more people, either in person or via video conferencing technology.	14
Guidance Facility	An amount of money set aside by a bank for a customer, to be sure it is available when the customer actually applies for a loan. Existence of this reserve is normally not communicated to the customer.	20
Hierarchical Structure	A network configuration constrained such that each node can have only one higher level node. This is sometimes referred to metaphorically, as a tree structure. This is as opposed to a *network structure* that has no such constraint.	6
Holder	A Money Role describing the *holder of money in* an Instrument.	20
Holding	A Disposition Action that entails continuing to hold an Information Resource Instance until further notice.	10
Home	A Facility (Physical Address) where people live.	12
Identification Component	One of the variables that constitutes a Reference System. For example "X coordinate", "latitude", and so forth.	22
Image	An Information Resource Definition that is "a visual representation of something: as (1) : a likeness of an object produced on a photographic material (2) : a picture produced on an electronic display (as a television or computer screen)".	10
IMM	(See Information Management Metamodel)	1
Incentive Compensation	Compensation paid based not on time worked but as commissions on revenue brought into the company.	13
Income Account	(See Revenue Account)	11

Glossary

Term	Definition	Chap
Income Statement	The Revenue Accounts and Expense Accounts, gathered together to describe the *flow* of money into and out of the firm.	11
Infer-Thru	A function in an imaginary language used to describe inference by one entity class of data in another entity class that it is dependent on. Specifically: INFER-THROUGH(<*role name*>, <object entity class name>, <attribute name>) WHERE(<*role name*>, <object entity class name>, <attribute name>=<value>>) –	12
	This recognizes that the attributes of a "parent" entity class (the "one" end of a "many-to-one" relationship) are available to the "child" entity. For example, in Formula 1, below, the value for an instance of Street Address in Other Surveyed Area is information that can be used to describe any instance of Facility that is located in that instance of Other Surveyed Area.	
	The parameters of this function are: *Role name* – the name of the role used to navigate from the subject entity class to the object entity class. *Entity class name* – the name of the object entity class that holds the inferred attribute. Attribute name – the name of the attribute being inferred. WHERE clause – required for the more complex navigation that will be required when describing the more abstract approach in the next section.	
Informal Program	An Education Element that is not derived from formal class work or testing.	13
Information Engineering	A comprehensive approach to system development developed by James Martin and Clive Finkelstein, and published in 1981.[108] It both introduced a particular notation for modeling data, plus the *System Development Life Cycle*.	1

---

[108] James Martin and Clive Finkelstein. 1981. "Information Engineering", Technical Report, two volumes, (Lancs, UK : Savant Institute, Carnforth.) Nov 1981.

Term	Definition	Chap
Information Management Metamodel	A project by the Object Management Group to define a comprehensive metamodel of modeling languages, to enable models in one modeling language to be translated to another modeling language.	1
Information Reference	The fact that one Information Resource Definition refers to another. Typically this is in a footnote or an endnote, although it could be a more informal reference as well.	10
Information Resource	Any collection of concepts expressed in a form that can be communicated to others.	10
Information Resource Content	The fact that a Business Term (Word, Phrase, or Sentence) is used by an Information Resource Definition.	10
Information Resource Definition	The definition of the meaning and/or content of an Information Resource. A set of articulated concepts.	10
Information Resource Description	The fact that an Information Resource Definition is *the use of* one Business Term to describe it.	10
Information Resource Element	The fact that a particular Information Resource Definition makes use of a Business Term in one of several specified ways. This could be as an Information Resource Description, as Information Resource Content, or as an Information Resource Topic.	10
Information Resource Instance	A physical or electronic instance of an Information Resource.	10
Information Resource Relationship	The fact that one Information Resource Definition is formally associated with at least one other Information Resource Definition.	10
Information Resource Role	The fact that a particular Party participates in some way in the creation, destruction, or management either *for* an Information Resource Definition (for example, in an Authorship Role), or *for* an Information Resource Instance.	10
Information Resource Topic	The fact that a particular Business Term may be used to locate a particular Information Resource Definition.	10
Information Structure	The fact that one Information Resource Instance is *composed of* at least one other Information Resource Instance.	10

Glossary

Term	Definition	Chap
Inheritance	The fact that *attributes* and *relationships* that are *properties* of a *super-type* class are also *properties* of all of its *sub-type* classes.	1
Initial License Requirement	A License Requirement that describes an Education Element required the first time a License is to be granted.	13
Initial Public Offering	The official making available to the public of stock in a company.	20
Inorganic Compound	Any Chemical Compound that does not contain carbon.	19
Inspection	Examination of a Discrete Item to see if there are any signs of wear, calling perhaps for a predictive or Preventive Work Order.	16
Installation	The putting of a Discrete into its proper place in a facility.	16
Installation	A Well Assembly Placement that is the fact that a particular Well Assembly was made part of a particular Oil Production Facility at a particular date and time.	21
Instrument	A Discrete Item that is a device for measuring some characteristic of (in the case of a laboratory) a Sample material. An Instrument may also be used to measure various aspects of the production process for material content, product quality, and so forth.	6, 17
Instrument	In banking, an instance of a *financial instrument*. A specialized formal legal document that specifies a legal arrangement whereby a bank either holds a customer's money in trust, or lends the customer money.	20
Instrument Category	A group of Instruments that can be identified by common characteristics or characteristic values. This is not as rigorous as the set of sub-types for classifying Instruments. An Instrument can be in one or more Categories and this could change over time.	20
Instrument Characteristic	A variable, attribute, or parameter whose values would describe instance of Instrument.	20
Instrument Characteristic Assignment	The fact that a particular Instrument Specification is at least partially defined in terms of a particular Instrument Characteristic.	20
Instrument Characteristic Value	A Characteristic Value *of* an Instrument Characteristic, *to describe* a particular Instrument.	20

Term	Definition	Chap
Instrument Classification	The fact that a particular Instrument falls into a particular Instrument Category at a particular time (between its Effective Date and its Until Date).	20
Instrument Component	A *part of* an Instrument that specifies a particular actual feature (typically a Service) to be provided to support the Instrument. Where an Instrument Specification lists a particular Instrument or Service as being optional, this links an actual Instrument to the particular Service or Instrument selected.	20
Instrument Role	The involvement a Party has in the purchase, sale, or management of an Instrument.	20
Instrument Role Type	The definition of a fundamental classification of Instrument Role. The first instances of this recapitulate the sub-types already shown for Instrument Role.	20
Instrument Specification	The kind of Instrument, defined before any instances of it are sold. This determines the Services it will consist of, as well as the Instrument Characteristics that will be used to describe it.	20
Instrument Specification Structure	The fact that an Instrument Specification has as a component either another Instrument Specification or a Service.	20
Insurance	Compensation in the form of a contract whereby one party agrees to pay the employee or 'e beneficiaries for loss by a specified contingency or peril.	13
Insurance Role	A Benefit Participation that is the fact that a particular Person participates in the holding of Insurance.	13
Insured Person	An Insurance Role that is *played by* the person in whose name the policy is taken out.	13
Integer (Data Type)	A *data type* describing a number without a fractional part, such as 42.	1
Interchange	An Intersection Site that is the entire area required for a Grade Separated Crossing.	22
Internet Protocol Address	An identifier for a location on the Internet.	12
Intersection Site	A Facility that encompasses the entire area required for a Grade Crossing or a Grade Separated Crossing. This includes not only the two (or more) roads intersecting, but also the land around the intersection, the presence of lights and/or stop signs, and the like.	22

Term	Definition	Chap
Inventory	A collection or a quantity of an Asset that can only identified in bulk. Nuts and bolts and gasoline exist in this form. For example, in one location (more about locations shortly), you could have an Inventory of gasoline with a "Quantity" of 300 gallons. Alternatively, you might have an Inventory of 4000 #10 Envelopes.	6
IP Address	A numerical label that is assigned to devices participating in a computer network that uses the Internet Protocol for communication between its nodes.[109]	12
Label	A Specified Packaging Item that is printed material describing both the indications and the counter-indications of the Specified Packaged Product that it applies to.	19
Knowledge	What people *know and act upon*. As opposed to *data* that are collections of symbols, and *information* that consists of a collection of data that have meaning that is based on their context.	10
Knowledge Management	Recognition that it is that *knowledge* is an important asset to an organization.	10
Labor Usage	The fact that, during a specified time period (between an Effective Date and an Until Date), a particular *Employee* had a specified number of Hours Worked, *charged to* a particular Activity.	16
Labor Usage /Labor Value	Hours Worked times INFER-THROUGH (*of*, Employment, Charge Rate).	16
Laboratory Test	A collection of Laboratory Procedures that is the use of a Measuring Instrument to determine a numerical value of an Asset Characteristic of a Sample. material.	17
Lane	A portion of a Roadway where traffic flows. Where the Roadway Path is a road being a line, Lanes begin to provide some area. In fact, though, Roadway Lanes are still concerned with describing the conduct of traffic in a particular direction.	22

---

[109] RFC 760, "DOD Standard Internet Protocol". *DARPA Request For Comments.* Internet Engineering Task Force. January 1980. http://www.ietf.org/rfc/rfc0760.txt. Retrieved 2008-07-08.

Term	Definition	Chap
Language	The words, their pronunciation, and the methods of combining them used and understood by a community.[110]	5
Language	the words, their pronunciation, and the methods of combining them used and understood by a community.[111]	13
Legal Activity Characteristic Value	One of the list of Category Values that an Activity Category may be *constrained by*. Each Activity Characteristic Value Characteristic Value, if it if *of* an Asset Category, must be equal to the Category Value of one of the Legal Characteristic Values that it is *a constraint on*.	7
Legal Geographic Category Value	A value that a Geographic Location Category can assume, as *embodied in* a Geographic Location Characteristic Value. That is, the characteristic value of a Geographic Location Characteristic must be the same as the allowed value of one of the Legal Geographic Category Values that are *constraints on* the Party Name Component Type that the Party name Component is an *example of*.	5
Legal Party Category Value	One of the values a Party Category may assume.	4
Legal Vehicle Role	An Instrument Role where a bank legal entity (Company) engages in business with a customer. (This an example of a Banking Role.)	20
Level Of Abstraction	The degree to which a model represents concrete things in the world (less abstract) and general concepts that the concrete things are examples of (more abstract).	1
Liability Account	any amount owed to another party. Examples of this might be "credit cards", "notes payable", or "employee withholding'.	11
License	Recognition by a recognized authority of one's ability to perform a specified set of Activity Specifications.	13

---

[110] Merriam Webster. 2010. Merriam-Webster Online. Available at http://merriam-webster.com.

[111] Merriam Webster. (Viewed 2010.) *Merriam-Webster Online*. (Available at: http://www.merriam-webster.com/dictionary/language.)

Glossary

Term	Definition	Chap
License Grant	The fact that a particular License represents one's qualification *to perform* a particular Activity Specification.	13
License Requirement	The fact that a particular License can only be issued upon completion of a particular Education Element. A License may be *acquired via* one or more of these License Requirements.	13
License Result	An Education Program Enrollment that is the fact that a Test Offering was held, resulting in a Score and *for the acquisition of* a Capability Endorsement.	13
License Test	A Program Component that is an examination of a Person's knowledge of a particular Body of Knowledge (such as "Data Management") or Activity Specification (such as driving).	13
Line Item	An entry specifying a single Asset Specification or Activity Specification to be supplied by *the vendors* to *the customers in* a Contract.	15
Line Item "/Cost"	Either INFER-THROUGH (*for*, Asset Specification, "Standard cost")♥ (*…if for an asset*) or INFER-THROUGH (*for*, Activity Specification, "Price per hour") (*…if for an activity*)	15
Line Item "Value"	Line Item "Quantity" *times* Line Item "/Cost".	15
Line Of Credit	An agreed to amount of money to be loaned to the customer but not paid all at once. Rather it is a fund that the customer can draw upon as necessary.	20
Linear Reference System	A Reference System that is in terms of "linear distance", from a Geographic Point that is its "datum".	22
Loan	An instance of an Instrument whereby a *banker* Party makes money available to a *customer* Party.	20
Loan Instrument Specification	An Instrument Specification describing a kind of Loan that can be offered by the bank.	20

♥ As described earlier (page **Error! Bookmark not defined.**), "INFER-THROUGH" is a function for obtaining a value of an attribute in an entity class related to this entity class via a "many-to-one" relationship. The arguments for the function are <role name>, <entity class inferred through>, <attribute being inferred>. The idea is that if each **Line Item** must be *for* exactly one **Activity Specification**, for example then all attributes of **Activity Specification** must be, by implication, attributes of **Line Item**.

Term	Definition	Chap
Lot	A quantity of inventory that is uniquely identified with a "Lot Number". In pharmaceutical and chemical manufacturing, typically the output of each production run is given a lot number, which is kept track of as the quantity of material is then subdivided to be used or sold.	6
Mailing Of A Letter	A Personal Communication that involves writing a message on a physical medium and sending it to someone via a postal service.	14
Main Roadway Path	A piece of a national or provincial highway, managed by a provincial agency.	22
Maintenance Task	An Activity *authorized by* a Maintenance Work Order *to fix, install, or replace* a Discrete Item, such as a Piece of Equipment.	16
Maintenance Work Order	A Work Order that is *to authorize* one or more Maintenance Tasks, *to fix, install, or replace* one and only one Discrete Item (along with any components also needing attention).	16
Management Area	A Geographic Area whose boundaries are defined by an enterprise.	5
Management Role	An Activity Role that describes a Party's participation in the management of an Activity.	7
Management Role	An Instrument Role that is the role a Party plays with respect to the money involved in the Instrument.	20
Manifold	An arrangement of piping or valves designed to control, distribute and often monitor fluid flow.[112]	21
Manufacturer	An Asset Role, in which a Party is responsible for physically creating an Asset Specification, or who has already created specified Assets.	6
Manufacturing Equipment Item	A Piece of Equipment that is used in a production process.	6
Many-To-Many Relationship	An association between two classes in which each instance of one may be associated with one or more instances of the other.	1
Marketing Relationship	The fact that a particular (customer) Party is about to do, is doing, or has done business with the bank. There may be one or more Instruments based on each Marketing Relationship.	20

---

[112] Schlumberger, Inc. Viewed June 27, 2010. *Oilfield Glossary*. "manifold". Available at: http://www.glossary.oilfield.slb.com.

Glossary

Term	Definition	Chap
Mass Mailing	A Mass Market Procedure that is the sending of materials to a large audience.	14
Mass Market Procedure	A Communication Procedure that is the effort required to create and place advertising.	14
Material Movement	The transfer of an Asset from one place to another. The definition of "one place" and "another" is a little tricky here: it depends on the nature of the movement. Each Material Movement may be *from* either one Party (a vendor), or *from* one Facility, or not *from* anywhere at all (a positive Adjustment). Each Material Movement may be *to* either one Party (a customer), or *to* one Facility, or not *to* anywhere at all (a negative Adjustment).	12
Maximum Cardinality	The greatest number of instances of a *property* allowed for a class. Usually this is either "1" or "*". If the *property* is a *relationship*, "1" means that no more than one *class* may be associated with this *class*. If it is an *attribute*, this means that no more than one value is allowed for the *attribute*. In a relational environment, the *maximum cardinality* of an *attribute* can never be more than 1. If the *property* is a *relationship*, "*" means that any number of instances of the second *class* can be associated through this *relationship* with the first *class*.	1
Measurement Instrument	A Discrete Item used in a laboratory to determine values for characteristics of materials.	6
Measuring Instrument	A Piece of Equipment with sensors that displays a value representing a physical phenomenon perceived by the sensors. For example, this might be used for measuring the flow of traffic past a particular point.	22
Medium	" a means of effecting or conveying something: as … a substance regarded as the means of transmission of a force or effect ."[113]	10
Metadata (Also "Meta Data" And "Meta-Data".	The data that describe the structure and workings of an organization's use of information, and which describe the systems it uses to manage that information.[114]	1

---

[113] Merriam Webster. 2010. "Medium". *The Merriam Webster OnLine Dictionary*. Retrieved 11/16/2010 from *http://www.merriam-webster.com/dictionary/medium*.

[114] Hay, D.C. 2006. *Data Model Patterns: A Metadata Map*. (Boston: Morgan Kaufmann).

Term	Definition	Chap
Mixture	(See Chemical Formulation)	19
Minimum Cardinality	The lowest number of instances of a *property* allowed for a class. This must be either "1" or "0". If it is "1" either the relationship or the attribute involved is mandatory. If it is "0" either the relationship or the attribute involved is optional. (This is also called the *optionality indicator*.	1
Modeled Concept	A Concept structure that can appear in an entity/relationship model.	10
Money Role	An Instrument Role that specifically is the role a Party plays with respect to the money involved in the Instrument.	20
Moving Image	An Information Resource Definition that is a rapid succession of Images providing the sensation of the movement of objects within it.	10
Name	An attribute of a *reference entity classes* that briefly describes or identifies instances of that class.	9
Natural Area	A Geographic Area whose boundaries reflect some natural phenomenon. This could be as specific as a continent or a lake, or more nebulous as a wildlife habitat.	5
Natural Feature	A Non-Roadway Path that describes a segment of the route of a natural phenomenon, such as a River or a Ridge of a hill.	22
Network	A collection of Paths, connected to create a larger Path through a set of Pat Compositions, (the set of all Provincial Core Highways in the Province of Saskatchewan, for example).	22
Network Structure	A collection of nodes arranged so that a node may have more than one higher level node. This is opposed to a *hierarchical structure*, where a node can have only one higher level node.	22
Neutron	An elementary particle with about the same mass as a *neutron*, but without a charge.[115]	19
Node	An intersection point where two or more Paths come together.	22
Non-Inventoried Roadway Path	A farm or other country roads, not maintained by a provincial agency.	22

---

[115] *DK Illustrated Oxford Dictionary*. 1998. (New York: Oxford University Press.) Page 551.

Glossary

Term	Definition	Chap
Normalization	A process, originally articulated by Dr. E.F. Codd in his *relational theory*, for organizing data to reduce redundancy to the minimum possible.[116] It involves guaranteeing that each attribute in a "relation" (*table* or *entity class*) is truly an attribute of that relation and none other.	1
Notational Convention	A set of modeling standards to define the symbols used in the models (they're *syntax*). In data modeling, the symbols include at least those portraying the classes of things significant to the enterprise (*entity classes*), and those for the relationships among them. Relationship symbols include those for *cardinality* (the "one" and "many" in a "one-to-many" relationship) and **optionality** (whether or not an occurrence of one entity class must have an occurrence of the other entity class). These conventions may also include the structure of phrases used to name relationships and entity classes. Syntactic conventions are the subject of most data modeling books.	1
Nucleic Acid	Either of two complex organic molecules (DNA and RNA), consisting of many nucleotides linked in a long chain, and present in all living cells.[117] The molecule consists of linked units called nucleotides, each containing a 5 carbon sugar (ribose for RNA, deoxyribose for DNA), a purine or pyrimidine base (adenine, guanine, cytosine, thymine, or uracil), and phosphoric acid.[118]	19
Nucleoside	An organic compound consisting of a purine or pyrimidine base linked to a sugar."[119]	19
Nucleotide	An organic compound consisting of a nucleoside linked to a phosphate group."[120] These are linked together to form Nucleic Acid.	19
Number	A *data type* describing a real number, such as 3542.35.	1

---

[116] Edward F. Codd. 1970. "A Relational Model of Data for Large Shared Data Banks". *Communications of the ACM* 13, No. 6 (June).

[117] *DK Illustrated Oxford Dictionary*. 1998. (New York: Oxford University Press.) Page 561.

[118] *The Random House Encyclopedia*. 1977. (New York: Random House, Inc.) Page 2447.

[119] *DK Illustrated Oxford Dictionary*. 1998. (New York: Oxford University Press.) Page 561.

[120] *DK Illustrated Oxford Dictionary*. 1998. (New York: Oxford University Press.) Page 561.

Term	Definition	Chap
Object	A thing of interest. In the context of a data model, an instance of a class.	1
Object Identifier	In an object-oriented environment, this is a *surrogate identifier* assigned to all objects. Also called an *OID*.	1
Observation	The fact that data have been captured to describe a Sample.	17
Office	A building or part of a building where people carry out their business.	12
OID	See object identifier.	1
Oil Production Facility	A Facility involved in the production of petroleum products. It is either a Surface Facility or a Sub-surface Facility.	21
One-To-Many Relationship	An association between two entity classes in which each instance of one may be associated with one or more instances of the other, but each instance of the second one may only be associated with no more than one instance of the first.	1
Ongoing License Requirement	A License Requirement that describes an Education Element required if a previously granted License is to be renewed.	13
Optionality Indicator	(See minimum cardinality.)	1
Organic Compound	A Chemical Compound that contains carbon. These make up the living parts of our world. Organic Compounds are the basic building blocks of life.	19
Organization	A collection of Persons, brought together physically or virtually to accomplish a purpose.	4
Originator Role	A Communication Role in which the Party involved initiated the Communication.	14
Other License	A License that actually grants permission to perform specified activities (that is, Activity Specifications).	13
Other Surveyed Area	Any Geographic Area (other than a Geopolitical Area, Management Area, or Natural Area, This includes land surveyed for a house, a road, a shopping mall, and the like.	5
Other Surveyed Area /Country Name	INFER-THROUGH(*part of*, Principal Country Division, /Country Name).	12
Other Surveyed Area /Principal Country Division Name	INFER-THROUGH(*part of*, Principal Country Division, Default Name).	12
OWL	See Web Ontology Language	1

Glossary

Term	Definition	Chap
Parameter	"An (especially measurable or quantifiable) characteristic or feature".[121] "Any of a set of physical properties whose values determine the characteristics or behavior of something."[122]	17
Parameter Derivation Element	*the use of* either a Parameter that is an Asset Characteristic (or a System Variable or a Constant), to derive the value of another Parameter (which could be any kind of Characteristic).	17
Participant Role	A Communication Role in which the Party involved was a member of a group in a Group Communication.	14
Party	A Person or Organization of interest.	4
Party Category	The definition of a set of Parties that share one or more attribute values.	4
Party Characteristic	A distinguishing trait, quality, or property that can be given a value for a Party.	4
Party Characteristic Assignment	The fact that a particular Characteristic may assume Characteristic Values *for* one or more Parties that are *examples of* a particular Party Type.	4
Party Characteristic Derivation Element	The fact that the value of a Continuous Party Characteristic is at least partly derived from another Party Characteristic.	4
Party Characteristic Value	The fact that a particular Party Characteristic has a particular Value for a particular Party.	4
Party Identifier	The definition of a characteristic that can be used to identify instances of a Party. For example, an "Employee ID", "Employer Identification Number", and so forth.	4

---

[121] DK Illustrated Oxford Dictionary. 1998. (Oxford, UK: Oxford University Press.) p. 591.

[122] *Ibid*. "Parameter"

Term	Definition	Chap
Party Identifier Assignment	The fact that a particular Party Identifier can be used to identify Parties that are *examples of* a particular Party Type. Specifically, the fact that a particular Party Identifier may be *evaluated in* one or more Party Identifier Values *assigned to* Parties that are *examples of* a specified Party Type.	4
Party Identifier Value	The value *for* a particular Party Identifier *assigned to* a particular Party.	4
Party Legal Name Component Value	A value that a Party Name Type can assume, as *embodied in* a Party Name Component. That is, the component name of a Party Name Component must be the same as the component value of one of the Party Legal Name Component Values, that are *constraints on* the Party Name Component Type that the Party name Component is an *example of*.	4
Party Name	Text identifying a particular Party that is *an example of* a Party Name Type.	4
Party Name Component	*Part of* a Party Name.	4
Party Name Type Assignment	The fact that a particular Party Name Type can be used in to describe Parties that are *examples of* a particular Party Type. Specifically, the fact that a Party that is *an example of* a particular Party Type may be *labeled by* a Party Name that is *an example of* a specified Party Name Type.	4
Party Placement	The fact that a Party is located at a particular Address.	12
Party Placement Type	The definition of a kind of Party Placement, such as "home address", "shipping address", or "office address".	12
Party Relationship	The fact that one Party has a defined association with another Party, The nature of the relationship is defined by the Party Relationship Type that the Party Relationship is *an example of*.	4
Party Relationship Type	The definition of a kind of Party Relationship, such as "marriage", "corporate structure", "union membership", and so forth.	4
Party Type	The definition of a kind of Party. The set of Party Types must at least include the sub-types of Party, such as "Person", "Organization", "Company", and so forth.	4

Glossary

Term	Definition	Chap
Path	A defined way to travel from one Node to another.	22
Path Composition	The fact that one longer Path contains, as a component, another, shorter Path.	22
Path Placement	The fact that exactly one Node is connected to exactly one Path. It is named by a combination of the highway number involved plus the number of kilometers from the highway's starting point.	22
Path Type	The definition of a fundamental classification of Path. The first instances of this must correspond to the sub-types of Path: "Roadway Path", "Frontage Roadway Path", "River", and so forth. The sub-type relationships in the Path entity class are described by the relationship, "each Path Type may be *a sub-type of* one and only one other Path Type. Additional Path Types can be added if each is *a sub-type of* an existing Path Type.	22
Paycheck	A payment to the employee, which covers the gross salary for the period, less any deductions.	13
Person	A human being of interest.	4
Personal Communication	A Communication initiated by an individual and directed to either one person or a relatively small number of people.	14
PERT Chart	(See Program Evaluation and Review Technique Chart.)	7
Personal Communication Procedure	A Communication Procedure that supports one person's communicating with one or several others.	14
Phrase	"A group of words forming a conceptual unit, but not a sentence."[123]	10
Physical Address	(See Facility)	12
Physical Copy (Of An Information Resource)	An Information Resource Instance that is manifest as a physical document, letter, book, et cetera.	10
Physical Observation	An Observation that obtains data solely by a person's examining a Sample, as opposed to a Direct Measurement that is taken by performing a Laboratory Test on the Sample,	17

---

[123] *DK Illustrated Oxford Dictionary.* 1998. (New York: Oxford University Press.) P. 614.

Term	Definition	Chap
Piece Of Equipment	A manufactured device that is either manufactured or used by the organization. This might be either on a production line, or in another context, such as an air conditioner.	6
Pier	The intermediate support for the adjacent ends of spans in multiple span truss bridges.	22
Placement Of A Telephone Call	A Personal Communication in which one person uses the telephone network to enable speaking to someone in a different location.	14
Planner's View	In David Hay's version of John Zachman's *Architecture Framework*[124], this is the view of the CEO and other top executives. It is concerned with what the enterprise is about. At this level is typically drawn a *context model*. This is a sketch of the primary things of concern to an enterprise. It consists of pairs of major categories (represented as *entity classes*), connected by *many-to-many relationships*. This is also called by some "conceptual", "subject", or "environmental" model.	1
Plant	A collection of buildings and other structures for the purpose of manufacturing or other processing.	12
Plant	a very large facility, such as a factory or a refinery which is where families of products are made.	16
Political Organization	An Organization whose purpose is carrying out political objectives.	18
Position	A defined role in a company.	13
Position Assignment	the fact that a particular Person employed by an Organization (that is, *subject to* an Employment) is (for a period of time at least) assigned to exactly one Position.	13
Position Requirement	The fact that a particular Position or Position Type, in order to be carried out satisfactorily, requires *the ability to perform* a particular Activity Specification, or *knowledge of* one Domain of Knowledge.	13
Position Type	The definition of a formal category of Position.	13
Postal Area	A Management Area whose boundaries are determined by the national postal service.	5

---

[124] Hay, D.C. 2003. *Requirements Analysis: From Business Views to Architecture*. (Upper Saddle River, NJ: Prentice Hall PTR): 5-6.

Glossary

Term	Definition	Chap
Power Line	A Utility that is a segment of the flow of electric power.	22
Predictive Work Order	Similar to a Preventive Work Order, but on parts that have shown symptoms that typically precede a particular kind of failure.	16
Preventive Work Order	Maintenance on a Piece of Equipment or a Building to keep parts in good order so that they won't fail.	16
Principal Country Division	A Geopolitical Area the set of which completely defines the area of a Country. In the United States and Mexico, this is a *state*, In Canada, France, and other countries, this is a ***province***. Other countries use these and other terms.	5
Principal Country Division /Country Name	INFER-THROUGH (*part of*, Country, Default Name).	12
Procedure	An Activity Specification to be *implemented via* Activities.	7
Product Completion	A Material Movement that is an Asset's movement *from* a Facility, such as a Work Center to another Facility such as either another Work Center or a Warehouse.	12
Product Completion	The production of an Asset, *by* either a particular Production Step or *by* the set of steps *authorized by a* Production Work Order.	16
Product Form	The physical form of a Chemical Formulation that is *part of* a Specified Packaged Product. This might be a powder, a liquid, a suppository, et cetera.	19
Product Model	An Asset Specification of an item that can be counted or viewed individually. For example, this could be a model of a computer or a truck, or specifications for a piece of manufacturing equipment. This could also be something like a "Standard House Plan JX-364", describing a specification for a kind of mass-produced house.	6
Production Step	An Activity undertaken at a particular time to manufacture a quantity of an Asset . It is *the implementation of* a Procedure that is *used in* a Routing Step.	16
Production Work Order	Authorization for the actual production of a product or material to specification (that is, *to produce* something according to an Asset Specification).	16

Term	Definition	Chap
Profit/Loss Statement	(See Income Statement.)	11
Program Component	An Educational Element that is *part of* a Formal Program, such as a Degree Program	13
Program Evaluation And Review Technique (PERT) Chart	a network model that allows for randomness in activity completion times. PERT was developed in the late 1950's for the U.S. Navy's Polaris project having thousands of contractors. It has the potential to reduce both the time and cost required to complete a project.[125]	7
Project	A larger, more complex Activity. This may also be called a "Program". Alternatively, a "Program" could be composed of "Projects" that in turn were composed of "Activities.	7
Projected Account Balance	An Account Balance that describes the anticipated state of the Account for a future period of time.	11
Property	A characteristic of a *class*. This is either an *attribute* or a *role*.	1
Proposition Type	A Concept that is an assertion of the state of things. In logic, a statement consisting of subject and predicate that is subject to proof or disproof.[126] This is only the Concept of such an assertion. The actual assertion of a Proposition would be a kind of Business Term.	10
Protein	Any of a group of organic compounds composed of one or more chains of amino acids and forming an essential part of all living organisms.[127]	19
Proton	A stable elementary particle with a positive electric charge, equal in magnitude to that of an *electron*, and occurring in all atomic nuclei.[128]	19
Provider	A Money Role describing the *provider of money in* an Instrument.	20
Province	A kind of Principal Country Division. Provinces appear in Canada and France, among others.	5

---

[125] Internet Center for Management and Business Administration, Inc. (NetMBA). 2010. "PERT". Available on: *http://www.netmba.com/operations/project/pert/*.

[126] *DK Illustrated Oxford Dictionary.* 1998. (New York: Oxford University Press.) P. 655.

[127] *DK Illustrated Oxford Dictionary.* 1998. (New York: Oxford University Press.) Page 656.

[128] *DK Illustrated Oxford Dictionary.* 1998. (New York: Oxford University Press.) Page 656.

Glossary

Term	Definition	Chap
Publication Process	A Mass Market Procedure that is the creation Information Resources to be made available to a large number of people.	14
Purchase Order	A Contract in which "we" play the role of being *the customer in* it.	15
Radical	An element or atom or a group of these normally forming part of a compound and remaining unaltered during the compound's ordinary chemical changes.[129]	19
Railroad Network	A Network consisting of all Railroad Track Segments in a given area.	22
Railroad Track Segment	A segment of the Railroad Network . The highways must intersect railroads, so the railroad routes must be taken into account.	22
Ramp	A roadway other than a main highway. Typically, this is part of a freeway interchange.	22
RDF	See Resource Description Framework.	1
Receipt	A Contract Delivery *of* an Asset that is *from* a (vendor) Party, consigning it *to* a Facility such as a Warehouse.	12
Receipt	A Contract Delivery in which a Quantity of an Asset has moved *from* a Party (the vendor) *to* one Facility.	15
Recipient Role	A Communication Role in which the Party involved received the telephone call, materials, et cetera that constituted the Communication.	14
Recursive Relationship	A relationship between instances of the same entity. For instance, one organization can report to another organization.	1
Reference System	A scheme for describing points on the Earth. Several exist, including *Geographic Coordinates*, which uses latitude and longitude, and *Cartesian* which uses "X", "Y", and "Z" coordinates, plus a reference point "datum".	22

---

[129] *DK Illustrated Oxford Dictionary*. 1998. (New York: Oxford University Press.) Page 672.

Term	Definition	Chap
Relational Theory	A technique for organizing data into simple sets of rows and columns.[130]	1
	Specifically, a table was called a *relation* consisting of *rows* described by a fixed set of *attributes* as columns. There was no logical relationship (and no sequence implied) between rows, nor between attributes. This offered considerable advantage by reducing the complexity of the resulting data structures. Among other things, it also introduced the discipline of *normalization* that allowed one to take large quantities of data and infer structures from them.	
Relationship	An *association* between two or more *entity classes*. In this book, all relationships are binary—between only two entity classes.	1
	In UML, this is called an *association*.	
Removal	A Well Assembly Placement that is the fact that a particular Well Assembly no longer part of a particular Oil Production Facility as of a particular date and time.	21
Resource Description Framework	An infrastructure that enables the encoding, exchange and reuse of structured metadata. RDF is an application of XML that imposes needed structural constraints to provide unambiguous methods of expressing semantics. RDF additionally provides a means for publishing both human-readable and machine-processable vocabularies designed to encourage the reuse and extension of metadata semantics among disparate information communities. The structural constraints RDF imposes to support the consistent encoding and exchange of standardized metadata provides for the interchangeability of separate packages of metadata defined by different resource description communities.[131]	1

---

[130] Edward F. Codd. 1970. "A Relational Model of Data for Large Shared Data Banks". *Communications of the ACM* 13, No. 6 (June).

[131] Eric Miller. 1998. "An Introduction to the Resource Development Framework". D-Lib Magazine, May, 1998. Retrieved from *http://www.dlib.org/dlib/may98/miller/05miller.html*, 2010.

Glossary

Term	Definition	Chap
Responsibility	The fact that *knowledge of* a particular Domain of Knowledge or *the ability to perform* a particular Activity Specification is required for a job.	13
	In particular, the Responsibility may be *assigned to* an Employment (*of* a Person *with* an Organization), or *assigned to* a Person holding a particular Position Assignment, or *assigned to* anyone I a particular Position.	
Responsibility Type	The definition of a fundamental kind of Responsibility.	13
Retailer	An Asset Role, in which a Party is either responsible for selling an Asset Specification to end customers, or has already sold actual Assets to end customers.	6
Retirement Contribution Employee	The Employee's contribution to e' retirement plan.	13
Retirement Contribution Employer	The employer's contribution to a fund for the employee's eventual retirement.	13
Retirement Plan	Compensation in the form of money set aside to pay the employee for the period after 'e has stopped working.	13
Revenue Account	the amount of the company's assets contributed or earned by the company's owners. This is usually either "owner-held stock" or "retained earnings". Among the equity accounts are two sub-categories of accounts that have special significance.	11
Reverse Polish Notation	A representation of a formula as a collection of statements. Each contains a variable and an operator. The operators are executed in sequence, with the result being used in conjunction with the next variable by the next operator.	6

Term	Definition	Chap
Ribonucleic Acid	A nucleic acid present in living cells, esp. in robosomes where it is involved in protein synthesis." [Oxford, 1998, p. 705] "Nucleic acid that promotes the synthesis of proteins in the cell and in some viruses is the genetic material. The molecule consists of a single strand of nucleotides, each containing the sugar ribose, phosphoric acid, and one of four bases: adenine, guanine, cytosine, or thymine. Messenger RNA carries the information for protein synthesis from DNA in the nucleus [of the cell] to the ribosomes in the cytoplasm. Each amino acid to be formed is specified by a sequence of three bases in messenger RNA. Transfer RNA brings the amino acids to their correct position on the messenger RNA.[132]	19
Ridge	A Natural Feature that Is a segment of the line that describes the highest points along a series of hills.	22
Rigid Frame Super-Structure	A Bridge Superstructure Unit that is for a Bridge intended to carry weight with a simple frame of concrete and steel.	22
River	A Natural Feature that is a segment of the route of water from the mountains to the sea.	22
Road	1. A paved network of links to be used to get from one place to another. 2. A portion of land that is paved in order to achieve definition. 3. A solid body of concrete, asphalt, or other material that is the physical embodiment of definition.	22
Road Network	A Network consisting of all Roadway Paths in a given area.	22
Roadside Facility	a rest area, with parking, bathrooms and trash cans provided by the Province, and optionally, gasoline and food provided by private companies.	22
Roadway	The physical solid that is a road.	22
Roadway Path	Farm or other country roads, not maintained by a provincial agency.	22

---

[132] *The Random House Encyclopedia.* 1977 (New York: Random House, Inc.) Page 2579.

Glossary

Term	Definition	Chap
Role	*UML:* One of the directions of a *relationship*. That is, each *relationship* consists of the *role* played by one class with respect to the other, plus the *role* played by the other class with respect to the first one. *A Model:* The fact that a Party has a defined responsibility with respect to something being managed by the organization. For example, a Contract Role is the fact that a particular Party has a defined part to play in the management or execution of a Contract.	1
Role (Relationship End)	A property of a subject Entity Class that asserts a specific association with another Entity Class.	10
Rollup Scheme	A Rollup Scheme is a collection of Accounts and Rollup Structure instance that collectively represent the financial state of the enterprise. Business rules ensure that it is coherent and that no expense or revenue is double counted. In particular, note that each Account Rollup Structure is uniquely identified by the combination of relationships to both *the use of* Account and *part of* an Account Rollup Structure. For any given Rollup Structure, an Account can only be *part of* a parent Account once.	11
Route Of Administration	The means by which a Chemical Formulation that is *part of a* Specified Packaged Product makes medicine available to the body. This could be "oral", "intravenous injection", "intramuscular injection", et cetera.	19
Routing Step	The fact that a particular Work Center is *the site of* one or more Procedures *for the production of* a particular Asset Specification.	16
Salary	Compensation that is a fixed amount of money paid periodically.	13
Sales Order	A Contract in which "we" play the role of being *the vendor in* it.	15
Sample	A relatively small amount of material extracted for purpose of evaluating its quality or content. This may be, for example, to support a manufacturing process, basic research, a pharmaceutical clinical trial, or an environmental study.	17
Sample Method	Prescribes the steps to be followed to carry out a sampling process properly. In each case, the process to be followed is documented as a serial numbered set of Sample Method Steps.	17

Term	Definition	Chap
Sample Method Step	The fact that a Procedure is used to carry out a Sample Method.	17
Savings Account	An instance of a Deposit that pays an interest rate, generally higher than what would be paid for a Checking Account.	20
Second	(Brit.) temporarily assign someone to work in a department.	4
Seminar	A relatively informal Group Meeting (or a set of Group Meetings) in which one person or group of people present a body of information to an audience of one or more people.	14
Sending Of A Facsimile	A Personal Communication in which one person uses scanning equipment and the telephone network to send an image (a facsimile, (typically of a document) to one or more other people.	14
Sending Of An E-Mail Message	A Personal Communication in which a person composes text which is then sent electronically to one or more other people via the Internet or a corporate data network.	14
Sentence	"A set of words complete in itself as the expression of a thought, containing or implying a subject and predicate and conveying a statement, question, exclamation, or command."[133]	10
Service	An Activity Specification to be *implemented via* Activities to be offered for sale to customers.	7
Service Instance	An instance of a Service actually occurring at a point in time, in support of an Instrument Component. Where the Instrument is a Brokerage Account, one Instrument Component will be created *to order* a Service which is the conduct of the transaction. Subsequently, a Service Instance carries out the transaction, recording the Start Date and End Date, delivering a Quantity of shares.	20
Shipment	A Contract Delivery *of* an Asset that is *to* a (customer) Party, *from* a Facility *to a* Warehouse.	12
Shipment	A Contract Delivery in which a Quantity of an Asset is moved *from* a Facility *to* a Party (the customer).	15
Sick Pay	Compensation that is paid for time lost due to illness.	13
SKADA	(See Supervisory control and data acquisition.)	21

---

[133] *DK Illustrated Oxford Dictionary.* 1998. (New York: Oxford University Press.) P. 751.

Glossary 513

Term	Definition	Chap
SKADA Indicator	An attribute of Manifold that determines whether or not it is monitored using the *Supervisory control and data acquisition* system.	21
Skill	A learned power of doing something competently : a developed aptitude or ability.[134]	13
Social Security Employee	An employee contribution to either (in the United States) the "Federal Insurance Contributions Act" (FICA), or to Medicare.	13
Social Security Employer	The employer's contribution to the "Federal Insurance Contributions Act (FICA)" fund, as well as to the "Medicare" fund.	13
Specified Container	A Specified Packaging Item that holds the Chemical Formulation that is *part of* a Specified Packaged Product. This could be a bottle, a vial, or an ampoule, or something else.	19
Specified Employee Deduction	A deduction from the employee's paycheck to pay taxes, social security, retirement, and/or something else.	13
Specified Employer Expense	The definition of a kind of expense the employer is obligated to pay, Major types of these (in the United States) include Social Security Employer, and Retirement Contribution Employer. There may be Other Employer Contributions specified as well.	13
Specified Material	An Asset Specification that is a liquid, powdered, or gaseous substance, which can only be described in terms of weight or volume. As an Asset Specification, This could describe a particular grade of sand, or a grade of crude oil. The characteristics that constitute this specification will be described below.	6
Specified Packaging Item	The definition of a component of a Packaged Product other than the medicine involved. This could be a Label, a Specified Container, or some Other Specified Packaging Item.	19
Standard Contract Term	One of a list of available constraints that might be applied to a Contract, to control either the *customer's* or the *vendor's* behavior.	15

---

[134] Merriam-Webster. Obtained 2010. *Merriam-Webster OnLine*. (Available at: *http://www.merriam-webster.com/dictionary/skill*.)

Term	Definition	Chap
Standard Labor Requirement	The fact that a particular number of hours of labor are required to complete any Activity that is *an example of* a particular Activity Specification. Specifically required are people possess a particular Skill, or who have appropriate values for a particular Party Characteristic.	16
Starry Skies Positional Convention	A way of arranging entity class boxes on a diagram so that the end of each relationship that points to many instances of an entity class ("..0") is toward the left or top of the model. This has the effect of putting entity classes representing tangible objects (such as Party) in the lower right area of the diagram, and putting those representing the less tangible roles, interactions, and transactions (such as Observation) in the upper left.	2
State	A kind of Principal Country Division. States appear in the United States and Mexico, among others.	5
Stereotype	A way of adding to the notation has made it possible to use the notation in areas for which it was not originally intended. Each is a property of an element on the model, marked with "<<" and ">>". The only stereotype of interest in this book is the one for "participant in a unique identifier ("<<id>>").	1
Still Image	A single Image, such as a photograph.	10
Storage Location	A Facility that is usually inside a Plant or Warehouse for the purpose of storing materials. Its address is smaller than the entire Warehouse, designated by a row and/or shelf, for example.	17
String (Data Type)	A *data type* describing alphanumeric text.	1
Subject Matter Expert (SME)	A person with significant experience and knowledge of a given topic or function.	1
Subsurface Facility	The oil well hole itself (the Well), as implemented by various pieces of pipe casing and other equipment.	21
Sub-Type	A class whose members are also members of a larger class (its *super-type*).	1

Term	Definition	Chap
Sum-Through	A function in an imaginary language used to describe accumulation by one entity class of values in a dependent entity class. Specifically: SUM-THROUGH (<*role name)*, <object entity class name>, <attribute name>) – This will be used in a later chapter to allow a summary attribute in a "parent" entity class instance to obtain a sum of the values of all the "child" instances related to that parent. For example, if an Order may be *composed of* one or more Line Items. The Order attribute /Total cost is computed as the sum of the values of the Line Item Cost for all the instances of Line Item that are related to this instance of Order.	12
Super-Type	A class, some of whose members are also members of another class (a *sub-type*).	1
Supervisory Control And Data Acquisition	The system that connects to the production facilities' controllers and data sources and collects the measured data and stores them in a database."[135]	21
Supplier	(See *Vendor*)	15
Supporter	An Instrument Role where a Party uses its credit in support of the credit offered to another Party. (This is an example of a Third Party Role.)	20
Surface Facility	A Facility that implemented via a collection of equipment for doing the preliminary processing of crude oil and gas, once it is removed from the ground.	21
Surrogate Identifier	An artificial attribute for a entity class whose value uniquely identifies instances of that class. Values have no intrinsic meaning and are usually assigned automatically, sequentially.	1
Suspension Super-Structure	A Bridge Superstructure Unit that is for a suspension bridge.	22

---

[135] Society of Petroleum Engineers. 2006. "Automated Production Surveillance" Available at Schlumberger Web site: *http://www.slb.com/resources/technical_papers/software/96645.aspx*.

Term	Definition	Chap
System Development Life Cycle	An approach to developing systems that was developed by James Martin and Clive Finkelstein in 1981.[136] This is an approach that begins with strategic planning and then proceeds through design, construction, transition, and implementation.	1
System Variable	A characteristic of the environment, such as today's date.	4
Tax Withholding	A deduction to be made available for the payment of taxes at the end of the year.	13
Telephone Address	A number on the international telephone network. (That is, a telephone number.)	12
Telephone Address/Country Code	INFER-THROUGH (*registered in*, Country, Country Telephone Code).	12
Telephone Call Procedure	How to make a telephone call.	14
Tenor	The time required for a bill of exchange or promissory note to become due for payment.[137]	20
Term Value	The fact that a particular Standard Contract Term has been applied to a Contract. This may include a value and/or a description of that application.	`15
Test Method	a collection of Procedures that are used to analyze the physical characteristics and/or content of a Sample material.	17
Test Method Step	The fact that a particular Procedure is part of a particular Test Method.	17
Test Offering	The fact that a License Test is being offered on a particular Date, *at* a particular place (a Facility set up for that purpose.).	13

---

[136] James Martin and Clive Finkelstein. 1981. "Information Engineering", Technical Report, two volumes, Lancs, (UK : Savant Institute, Carnforth.) Nov 1981.

[137] The Free Dictionary by Farlex. (Viewed August 18, 2010.) "Tenor". Available at *http://www.thefreedictionary.com/tenor*.

Glossary

Term	Definition	Chap
The Internet	A global system of interconnected computer networks that use the standard *Internet Protocol* Suite (TCP/IP) to serve billions of users worldwide. It is a *network of networks* that consists of millions of private, public, academic, business, and government networks of local to global scope that are linked by a broad array of electronic and optical networking technologies.[138]	12
The World-Wide Web	A system of interlinked hypertext documents accessed via *the Internet*.[139]	12
Thing	A separate and distinct individual quality, fact, idea, or usually entity.	9
Thing Association	The fact that an actual Thing is somehow associated with another actual Thing. This could be as a component, as in an Asset Structure, a functional relationship, as in an Activity Dependency, or another kind of association altogether. At this level, it is the fact that such an association *actually exist*s.	9
Thing Category	The definition of a way of classifying Things. The classification may change over time, and the same Thing can be classified into more than one Thing Category.	9
Thing Category Legal Value	One of the possible values of Thing Category that may be applied for a Thing.	9
Thing Characteristic	A variable, attribute, or parameter whose values would describe instances of Thing or Thing Specification.	9
Thing Characteristic Assignment	The fact that Thing Characteristic Values *for* a particular Thing Characteristic may be *to describe* Things that are either *described by* a particular Thing Specification or (directly or indirectly) *an example of* a particular Thing Specification. It also can describe the fact that Thing Characteristic Values *for* a particular Thing Characteristic may be *to describe* Thing Specifications that are *an example of* a particular Thing Specification.	9

---

[138] Wikipedia. (Viewed 2010.) (Available at: http://en.wikipedia.org/wiki/The_Internet.)

[139] Wikipedia. (Viewed 2010.) (Available at: http://en.wikipedia.org/wiki/World_Wide_Web.)

Term	Definition	Chap
Thing Characteristic Value	The actual number, text, date, et cetera that is the value *for* a Thing Characteristic *to describe* either a Thing or a Thing Specification.	9
Thing Derivation Element	The fact that a Continuous Thing Characteristic may be derived from a particular other Thing Characteristic.	9
Thing Identifier	The definition of one of several possible short combinations of numbers and characters used to identify a Thing.	9
Thing Identifier Assignment	The fact that Thing Names that are *examples of* a particular Thing Name Type can be used *to describe* Things that are either *examples of* a particular Thing Type or *described by* a particular Thing Specification.	9
Thing Identifier Type	The definition of a fundamental kind of Thing Identifier. This could be an "Employer Tax Id", "Model Name", et cetera.	9
Thing Name	One of several possible short pieces of text to briefly describe or identify a Thing.	9
Thing Name Type	The definition of a fundamental kind of Thing Name. This could be "Maiden Name", "Corporate Name", "Trade Name", et cetera.	9
Thing Role	The fact that a Party is somehow involved with the production, consumption, or management of a particular Thing.	9
Thing Role Type	The definition of a fundamental category of Thing Roles.	9
Thing Specification	A Thing Type that describes a Thing sufficiently to offer it for sale.	9
Thing Specification Structure	A Thing Specification Structure is the fact that a Thing is specified as having an association with another specified Thing as part of its definition. At this level, it is the fact that such an association *can exist*. Both Thing Relationship and Thing Specification Structure are each an *example of* a Thing Relationship Type.	9
Thing Structure Type	The definition of a fundamental rationale or a kind of Thing Structure or Thing Specification Structure.	9
Thing Type	A fundamental, unchanging category of Things.	9
Third Party Role	A Management Role played by someone who is neither affiliated with the bank or a customer in this Instrument.	20

Glossary

Term	Definition	Chap
Traffic Protection Device	A Piece of Equipment (Asset Specification) designed to control traffic, such as a stoplight or a stop sign.	22
Transfer	A Contract Delivery *of* an Asset that is *from* one Facility *to* another Facility.	12
Transfer	A Contract Delivery in which a Quantity of an Asset is moved *from* one Facility *to* another Facility.	15
Truss Super-Structure	A Bridge Superstructure Unit that is for a Bridge made of girders organized in triangles and assembled into units to cross between piers.	22
UML	(See Unified Modeling Language.)	1
Unified Modeling Language	A standardized general-purpose modeling language in the field of software engineering. The standard is managed, and was created by, the Object Management Group. The entire language contains numerous models. The one that is of interest in this book is the *class model*.	1
Uniform Record Locator	A meaningful label for a Web Address. (also known as its *URL*.)	12
Unique Identifier	A combination of *attributes* and *roles*, the values of which can be used to uniquely identify instances of an *entity class*. In a relational database, this is implemented by a primary key.	1
Unit Of Measure	A definite magnitude of a physical quantity, defined and adopted by convention and/or by law, that is used as a standard for measurement of the same physical quantity.[140]	4
Unit Of Measure	A definite magnitude of a physical quantity, defined and adopted by convention and/or by law, that is used as a standard for measurement of the same physical quantity.[141]	9
Unit Of Measure Conversion	The fact that quantities expressed in a particular Unit of Measure can be expressed rigorously in a different Unit of Measure.	4

---

[140] "measurement unit", in *International Vocabulary of Metrology – Basic and General Concepts and Associated Terms (VIM)* (8th ed.), Joint Committee for Guides in Metrology, 2008, pp. 6–7. May be seen at: http://www.bipm.org/utils/common/documents/jcgm/JCGM_200_2008.pdf.

[141] "measurement unit", in *International Vocabulary of Metrology – Basic and General Concepts and Associated Terms (VIM)* (8th ed.), Joint Committee for Guides in Metrology, 2008, pp. 6–7. May be seen at: http://www.bipm.org/utils/common/documents/jcgm/JCGM_200_2008.pdf.

Term	Definition	Chap
Unit Of Measure Conversion	The fact that quantities expressed in a particular Unit of Measure can be expressed rigorously in a different Unit of Measure.	9
Until Date	An attribute that represents the end of a period when a transaction will be in effect.	9
Upstream Processing	Processing of petroleum products that makes use of "equipment, facilities or systems located in the wellbore or production train above the surface choke or Christmas tree."[142]	21
URL	(See Uniform Record Locator.)	12
Usage	A Material Movement that describes the fact that an Asset was made use of during a manufacturing process. This must be either Consumption or Equipment Utilization.	12
Utility	A Non-Roadway Path that describes a segment of a utility such as a Water Line, Gas Line, Power Line, or Other Utility.	22
Vacation	Compensation paid for a specified period of time taken off from work for recreation.	13
Valid Material Completion Purpose	The fact that a particular Completion Purpose Type is *the acceptable use of* a particular Specified Material.	21
Valuation	The amount of money represented by a Financial Position, an Instrument Component, or an Instrument, *recorded in terms of* a particular Currency. Each Valuation is effective between its Effective Date and its Until Date.	20
Vehicle	A Piece of Equipment that is a device for transporting people and goods from one place to another.	6
Vendor	A Party that plays the role of being *the vendor in* a Contract. (Also, *Supplier*)	'15
Virtual Address	An Address that is a node on an electronic network.	12
Warehouse	A building for the purpose of storing products or materials.	12
Warehouse	A Facility, usually consisting of a large Building for the purpose of storing Assets.	16
Water Line	A Utility that is a segment of the flow of potable water.	22

---

[142] Schlumberger, Inc. Viewed July, 2010. *Oilfield Glossary*. "Upstream". Available at: http://www.glossary.oilfield.slb.com.

Glossary

Term	Definition	Chap
Waterway	A Network consisting of all Channels, Canals, and Rivers in a given area.	22
Web Address	A node on the view of *the Internet* that is the World-Wide Web. It is labeled by a "Uniform Record Locator (URL)" but is identified by an "Internet Protocol (IP)" number.	12
Web Ontology Language	A family of knowledge representation languages for authoring *ontologies*. The languages are characterized by formal semantics and RDF/XML-based serializations for the Semantic Web.	1
Web Site Development	A Mass Market Procedure that sets up Web Addresses containing information about the enterprise.	14
Well	A Facility that is a collection of wellbores (holes in the ground) used to retrieve liquid and gaseous hydrocarbons from below the ground.	21
Well Assembly	A Discrete Item that is the assembly of pipes, valves, and pumps that implement the well.	21
Well Assembly Placement	A Material Movement that describes either the Installation *into* or the Removal *from* a Surface Facility or a Sub-surface Facility.	21
Well Assembly Specification	As with other Asset Specifications, a Well Assembly Specification is the definition of the configuration, composition, and characteristics of one or more instances of a Well Assembly.	21
Well Segment	a portion of a wellbore that does not cross a point of intersection and has a consistent diameter.	21
Wellbore	A single path from the surface to the lowest point in the well.	21
Wellbore Purpose	Only specified if there are not Completion Primary Purposes specified. Usually *an example of* the Wellbore Purpose Type, "data collection".	21
Wholesaler	An Asset Role, in which a Party is either responsible for selling an Asset Specification to other Parties that in turn sell it to other Wholesalers or end customers, or has already sold actual Assets to such Parties.	6
Word	A meaningful element of speech, usually shown with a space on either side of it when written or printed.[143]	10

---

[143] *DK Illustrated Oxford Dictionary.* 1998. (New York: Oxford University Press.) P. 959.

Term	Definition	Chap
Work Breakdown Specification Structure	As an alternative to explicitly specifying Activity Specification Step the fact that one Activity Specification is a component of another Activity Specification.	7
Work Breakdown Structure	The division of a Project or an Activity into smaller Activities.	7
Work Breakdown Structure	As an alternative to explicitly specifying Activity Step and Project the fact that one Activity is a component of another Activity.	7
Work Center	A part of a plant where specific manufacturing steps take place.	12
Work Center	A Facility where production Activities take place.	16
World Wide Web	A system of interlinked hypertext documents accessed via the Internet. With a web browser, one can view web pages that may contain text, images, videos, and other multimedia and navigate between them via hyperlinks.[144]	12
Work Experience	An Informal Program that consists of recognizing the work someone has already done in a particular area of interest.	13
Work Order	an official authorization to perform a specified set of work. If it is for manufacturing, it is a Production Work Order, while for plant maintenance, it is a Maintenance Work Order.	16
Work Order /WO Material Cost	SUM-THROUGH (*to authorize*, Activity, /Activity Material Cost).	16
Work Order	SUM-THROUGH (*to authorize*, Maintenance Task, Step Labor Cost)).	16

---

[144] Wikipedia. "World Wide Web". *Wikipedia*. Retrieved 11/18/2010 from http://en.wikipedia.org/wiki/World-wide_web.

Bibliography

"If I have seen farther, it is by standing on the shoulders of giants."

Isaac Newton
Letter to Robert Hooke, 1676

Aber, J.S. 2008. "Brief History of Maps and Cartography". Emporia State University. Available at: http://academic.emporia.edu/aberjame/map/h_map/h_map.htm.

Adams, D. 1982. *The Restaurant at the End of the Universe*. New York: Pocket Books, pp. 37–38.

Ahlfinger, R. 2004. "Longitude at Sea." *Connexions*. Houston: Rice University http://cnx.org/content/m11963/latest/.

Alberts, Bruce, Dennis Bray, Julian Lewis, Martin Raff, Keith Roberts, and James D. Watson. 1994. *Molecular Biology of the Cell*. New York: Garland Publishing.

Allemang, D., and Jim Hendler. 2009. *Semantic Web for the Working Ontologist: Effective Modeling in RDFS and OWL*. Boston: Morgan Kaufmann.

American National Standards Institute (ANSI). 1975. "ANSI/X3/SPARC Study Group on Data Base Management Systems; Interim Report". FDT(Bulletin of ACM SIGMOD) 7:2.

Barker, R. 1990. *CASE*Method: Entity Relationship Modeling*. Wokingham, England: Addison-Wesley.

Bell, A.E. 2004. "Death by UML Fever", *ACMQueue*. Association for Computing Machinery. Available at: http://queue.acm.org/detail.cfm?id=984495.

Blazek,R. 2004. "Introducing the Linear Reference System in GRASS". Bangkok, GRASS User Conf. Proc. See at: http://gisws.media.osaka-cu.ac.jp/grass04/viewpaper.php?id=50

Booch, G., James Rumbaugh, and Ivar Jacobson. 1999. *The Unified Modeling Language User Guide*. Reading, MA: Addison-Wesley.

Bruce, T. 1992. *Designing Quality Databases with IDEF1X Information Models*. New York: Dorset House.

523

Business Rules Team (BRT). Unpublished. 2005. "Semantics of Business Vocabulary and Business Rules". A submission to The Object Management Group.

Chen, P. 1976. "The Entity-Relationship Approach to Logical Data Base Design". *The Q.E.D. Monograph Series: Data Management.* Wellesley, MA: Q.E.D. Information Sciences, Inc. This is based on his article, "The Entity-Relationship Model: Towards a Unified View of Data", ACM Transactions on Database Systems, Vol. 1, No 1, (March 1976), pages 9-36.

_____ . 1977. "The Entity-Relationship Model: A Basis for the Enterprise View of Data", *AFIPS Conference Proceedings,* Vol. 46, AFIPS Press, N.J., (1977 National Computer Conference), pages 77-84.

Codd, E. F. 1970. "A Relational Model of Data for Large Shared Data Banks". *Communications of the ACM* 13, No. 6 (June).

Cribbet, Johnson, Findley, and Smith. 2002, *Property, Cases and Materials*, 8th ed. Foundation Press. (From Wikipedia. 2010. "Metes and Bounds").

DAMA International, 2009. Data Management Body of Knowledge (DAMA-DMBOK), New Jersey: Technics Publications, LLC.

DK Illustrated Oxford Dictionary. 1998. New York: Oxford University Press.

Eva, Malcolm. 1994. *SSADM Version 4: A User's Guide Second Edition.* London: McGraw-Hill Book Company.

Finkelstein, C. 1989. *An Introduction to Information Engineering : From Strategic Planning to Information Systems.* Sydney: Addison-Wesley.

Fowler, M. 1997. *Analysis Patterns.* Reading, MA: Addison-Wesley.

"The Free Dictionary by Farlex." *http://www.thefreedictionary.com*

Gamma, E., Richard Helm, Ralph Johnson, and John Vlissides. 1995. *Design Patterns: Elements of Reusable Object-Oriented Software.* Reading, MA: Addison-Wesley Publishing Company.

Gordon, M.J., and Gordon Shillinglaw. 1969. *Accounting: A Management Approach. Fourth Edition.* Homewood, Illinois: Richard D. Irwin, Inc.

Hay, D. C. 1995. *Data Model Patterns: Conventions of Thought.* New York: Dorset House.

_____. 1999a. "There is no Object-oriented Analysis" *Data to Knowledge Newsletter.* January 15, 1999. Available at: *http://articles.davehay.com/public_pages/article_library/7?article_id=92*

_____. 1999b. "UML Misses the Boat". *ECO 99*. East Coast Oracle User's Group. April 1, 1999. Available at *http://articles.davehay.com/public_pages/article_library/7?article_id=85*

_____. 2003. *Requirements Analysis: From Business Views to Architecture*. Upper Saddle River, NJ: Prentice Hall PTR.

_____. 2006. *Data Model Patterns: A Metadata Map*. Boston: Morgan Kaufmann.

_____. 2008. "Semantics, Ontology, and Data Modeling", *Cutter Report on Business Intelligence, Vol. 6, No. 7*. June 1, 2008

_____. 2010. "Prepositions, Not Verbs or Nouns". *The Data Administration Newsletter*. May 1, 2010.

International Standards Organization. 2006. "Codes for the representation of names of countries and their subdivisions -- Part 1: Country codes.",*ISO 3166-1*. *http://www.commondatahub.com/live/geography/country/iso_3166_country_codes?gclid=CNOHjr7mi6MCFdVb2godeUMXew*.

Internet Center for Management and Business Administration, *NetMBA PERT*. Seen May 16, 2010 at http://www.netmba.com/operations/project/pert/.

Johnson, Samuel. 1755. Dictionary of the English Language.

Kemerling, Garth, 2002. *Philosophy Pages*. 18 October 2006.

Lo, Lawrence. (Viewed 5/11/2010). http://www.ancientscripts.com/cuneiform.html.

Mattessich, Richard. 1998. "Recent insights into Mesopotamian accounting of the 3rd millennium B.C.-successor to token accounting". *The Accounting Historian's Journal*. (Available at: http://findarticles.com/p/articles/mi_qa3657/is_199806/ai_n8798263/.)

Martin, J., and Carma McClure. 1985. *Diagramming Techniques for Analysts and Programmers*. Englewood Cliffs, NJ: Prentice Hall.

Martin, J., and Clive Finkelstein. Nov 1981. "Information Engineering", *Technical Report*, two volumes, Lancs, UK : Savant Institute, Carnforth.

McGilvray, D. 2008. "Data Model Comparison" in McGilvray, D., *Executing Data Quality Projects: Ten Steps to Quality Data and Trusted Information*. Boston: Morgan Kaufmann Publishers.

Menzies, G. 2002. *1421: The Year China Discovered America*. New York: Harper Collins.

_____. 2008. *1434: The Year a Magnificent Chinese Fleet Sailed to Italy and Ignited the Renaissance.* New York: Harper Collins.

Merriam Webster. 2010. *Merriam-Webster Online.* Available at http://merriam-webster.com.

Miller, G. A. 1956. "The Magical Number Seven, Plus or Minus Two: Some Limits on Our Capacity for Processing Information," *The Psychological Review,* 63:2 (March 1956), pages 81–97.

Mitchell, J., Editor. 1977. *The Random House Encyclopedia.* New York: Random House.

Movable Type, Ltd. 2010. *Information Design and Management.* Web Site. Latitude/Longitude distance retrieved May 17, 2010 from http://www.movable-type.co.uk/scripts/latlong-vincenty.html.

NETMBA. *NETMBA Business Knowledge Center.* Internet Center for Management of Business Administration. Available at http://Netmba.com.

Object Management Group (OMG). 2003. *UML 2.0 Infrastructure Specification.* OMG Adopted Specification ptc/03-09-15.

_____. 2008. *Semantics of Business Vocabulary and Business Rules.* OMG Available Specification formal/2008-01-02.

Page-Jones, Meiler. 2000. *Fundamentals of Object-Oriented Design in UML.* Reading, MA: Addison-Wesley.

The Random House Encyclopedia. 1977. New York: Random House, Inc.

Ross, Ronald. 1994. *The Business Rule Book: Classifying, Defining, and Modeling Rules, First Edition.* Boston: Database Research Group.

_____. 1997. *The Business Rule Book: Classifying, Defining, and Modeling Rules, Second Edition.* Boston: Database Research Group.

Rumbaugh, James, Ivar Jacobson, and Grady Booch. 1999. *The Unified Modeling Language Reference Manual.* Reading, MA: Addison-Wesley.

Schlumberger, Inc. 2010. *Oilfield Glossary.* http://www.glossary.oilfield.slb.com/search.cfm.

Silverston, L., Inmon, W.H, Graziano, K. 1997. *The Data Model Resource Book: A Library of Logical Data Models and Data Warehouse Designs.* New York: John Wiley & Sons.

Silverston, L.,. 2001a. *The Data Model Resource Book, Volume 1: A library of Universal Data Models for All Enterprises.* New York: John Wiley & Sons.

_____. 2001b. *The Data Model Resource Book, Volume 2: A library of Universal Data Models by Industry Types.* New York: John Wiley & Sons.

_____, Paul Agnew. 2009. *The Data Model Resource Book, Volume 3.* Indianapolis, IN: Wiley Publishing, Inc.

Simsion, Graeme. 2007. *Data Modeling Theory and Practice.* Bradley Beach, NJ: Technics Publications.

Sobel, David. 1995. *Longitude: The True Story of a Lone Genius Who Solved the Greatest Scientific Problem of His Time.* New York: Penguin Books.

Society of Petroleum Engineers. "Automated Production Surveillance" 2006. Schlumberger Web site: http://www.slb.com/resources/technical_papers/software/96645.aspx

Sowa, John. F., and John A. Zachman. 1992. "Extending and Formalizing the Framework for Information Systems Architecture", *IBM Systems Journal*, Vol 31, No 3. IBM Publication G321-5488.

Vincenty, T. 1975. "Direct and Inverse Solutions of Geodesics on the Ellipsoid with Application of Nested Equations". *Survey Review*, Directorate of Overseas Surveys of the Ministry of Overseas Development. April, 1975. Retrieved May 17, 2010 from http://www.movable-type.co.uk/scripts/latlong-vincenty.html.

Waldseemüler, Martin. 1507 *Universalis cosmographia secundum Ptholomaei traditionem et Americi Vespucii alioru[m]que lustrationes.* In the collection of the Library of Congress Geography and Map Division Washington, D.C. Available at: http://www.loc.gov/rr/geogmap/waldexh.html

Webster's New World Dictionary of the American Language. 1964. Cleveland: World Publishing Company.

Wikipedia. 2010a. http://en.wikipedia.org/wiki/Main_Page

Zachman, John. 1987. "A framework for information systems architecture", *IBM Systems Journal,* Vol. 26, No. 3. (IBM Publication G321-5298)

Zachman, John and Stan Lock. *The Zachman Framework*™„ http://zachmaninternational.com/index.php/home-article/13#maincol.

Index

"starry skies" orientation, 56, 59–61, 514
abstract asset, 129
abstraction
   explanation of, 70–73
   Level 0, 24, 76, 79, 181, 182, 351, 357, 393
   Level 1, 24, 76, 78, 81, 82, 235, 237, 287, 351, 357, 359, 361, 376, 384, 387, 397, 411
   Level 2, 24, 77, 237, 238, 239, 357
   Level 3, 24, 77, 357, 360
   levels of, 24, 71, 72, 73, 74, 75, 79, 205
abutment, 459
account, 221–27, 459
accounting, v, 76, 182, 221–36, 221, 222, 236, 283–86, 306, 312, 334, 335, 416, 459, 460, 477, 524, 525
activity, 77, 82, 153–72, 255–57, 460
address, 243–46, 463
amino acid, 379, 464
Architect's View, 65, 465
Architecture Framework, 465
Aristotle, 17
asset, 81, 129–52, 466
association. *See* relationship
attribute, 49, 467
Bachman, Charles, 21
banking, 389–416
Barker, Richard, 15, 27, 42, 73, 468
Barker-Ellis Diagram, 23, 468
beneficiary, 468
benefits, 276–79
bridge, 468
Business Owner's View, 35, 65, 465, 470
cardinality, 41, 45, 49, 51, 54, 382, 471
case, 362–64, 471
catalogue item, 47, 49, 50, 51, 52, 54, 55
certification, 270–76
channel, 471
chart of accounts, 221, 222, 232, 233
chemical compound, 378, 382, 459, 472, 474, 491, 500
chemistry, 377–84
Chen Model, 22
Chen, Peter, 21, 24, 31, 44, 73
class, 47, 472
Codd, Edgar F., 21, 499, 508, 524
Columbus, Christopher, 18
communications and marketing, 77, 238, 287–300
compensation, 279–86
constraints, 95–97
contract, 77, 239, 301–12, 476
cost center, 233–34, 476
criminal justice, 361–76
currency, 477
data model
   aesthetic conventions, 41, 56–64, 73
   architectural conventions, 41, 64–73, 73
   notational conventions, 41, 42–55, 73
data modeler, 17, 24, 29, 51, 68, 128, 400
data modeling
   issues, 33–38
   purposes of, 33
data type, 50
database management system, 247
DBMS. *See* database management system
Deoxyribonucleic Acid, 78, 381, 478
Designer's View, 65, 465, 478
dimensional models, 173, 179
disposition, 216–19, 479
distribution, 215–16, 479
DNA. *See* Deoxyribonucleic Acid
documents. *See* information resources
double-entry bookkeeping, 76, 182, 221, 222, 236
education. *See* certification
Ellis, Harry, 27, 42, 73, 468

529

Employee Identification Number, 91, 92
enterprise data model, 40, 221, 234, 482
entity class, 35, 41, 44, 47, 482
equity, 482
events, 168–70
Executive Leader's View, 65
facility, 77, 238, 241–61, 417–28, 483
Framework for Enterprise Architecture. *See* Zachman Framework
Fusé, Tomako, 25
Galileo, 18
general ledger, 221, 471
generalization, 45, 86, 108, 126, 258, 265
geographic location, 81, 107–28
geography, 76
girder, 487
GJXDM. *See* Global Justice XML Data Model
Global Justice XML Data Model, 358, 361
government agency, 84, 85, 92, 184, 369, 370, 371, 488
Hay, David, 34, 215, 465, 469, 470, 478, 484, 504
Hay, Robert, 25
highway maintenance, 437–58
human resources, 77, 238, 263–86
IDS. *See* Integrated Data Store
IE. *See* Information Engineering
IMM. *See* Information Management Metamodel
information assets, 76
Information Engineering, 22, 23, 45, 48, 489, 516, 524, 525
IE Diagram, 23
Information Management Metamodel, 27, 43, 488, 490
information resources, 181, 207–19, 490
Initial Public Offering, 403, 404, 491
inspection, 491
instrument, 491
insurance, 492
Integrated Data Store, 21
International Standards Organization, 113, 117, 486, 525
inventory, 493
IPO. *See* initial public offering
ISO. *See* International Standards Organization
ISO 3116-1, 113
ISO 3166, 115, 117, 118, 119, 525
jurisdiction, 125, 126, 487
knowledge management, 208
labor usage, 331–35
laboratory, 77, 239, 337–55
laboratory test, 58, 59, 60, 62, 63, 154, 340, 341, 342, 345, 347, 349, 373, 479, 493, 503
level of abstraction. *See* abstraction, levels
manufacturing, 77, 239, 313–36
map makers, 17, 19
maps, 17, 18, 19, 21
 created by Babylonians, 17
 Google, 19, 20, 21, 25
 Waldseemüller, 17, 18
material usage, 325–31
McGilvray, Danette, 34
metadata, 76, 179
microbiology, 377–88
model patterns, 38, 71, 458
NAICS. *See* North American Industry Classification System
National Information Exchange Model, 361
network, 498
NIEM. *See* National Information Exchange Model
normalization, 21, 22, 24, 499, 508
North American Industry Classification System, 194
nucleic acid, 499
object, 47
Object Identifier, 54
object-oriented design, 39, 46
OID. *See* Object Identifier
oil field production, 417–36
oil well, 428–36
ontology, 36

optionality, 41, 45, 51, 54, 498, 499
origami, 25, 26, 29, 190
Orr, Ken, 16
OWL. *See* Web Ontology Language
Party. *See* people and organizations
people and organizations, 76, 81, 83–106, 369–71
PERT. *See* Program Evaluation and Review Technique
physical assets, 76, 129, 186, 191, 453, 455
product specification, 78
Program Evaluation and Review Technique, 161, 172, 503, 506
protein, 78, 379, 380, 382, 506
Purchase Order, 47, 49, 51, 52, 53, 55, 302, 303, 507
RDF. *See* Resource Description Framework
relational theory, 21, 74, 499
relationship, 46
Resource Description Framework, 35, 470, 507, 508
Reverse Polish Notation, 103, 122, 148, 166, 172, 201, 509
semantic conventions. *See* data model, architectural conventions
semantic languages, 35, 470
semantic model, 35, 36, 46, 432, 449
semantics, 35, 36, 41, 42, 43, 46, 47, 64, 65, 71, 359, 465, 470, 508, 521
Simsion, Graeme, 24, 72
Social Security Number, 89, 91, 92, 95, 194, 264
stereotype, 54, 55, 459, 514
sub-type, 48

super-type, 48
surrogate identifier, 515
thing
   describing, 193–204
   explanation of, 183–87, 517
   relationships to, 191–93
   subtypes of, 188–91
Time, 77, 82, 173–79
UML. *See* Unified Modeling Language
Unified Modeling Language, 15, 24, 27, 28, 31, 39, 42, 43, 44, 45, 46, 48, 49, 51, 53, 54, 73, 74, 89, 127, 134, 146, 186, 253, 257, 258, 265, 292, 305, 343, 366, 459, 472, 508, 511, 519, 523, 525, 526
Uniform Record Locator, 244
unique identifier, 54
Unit of Measure, 99, 101, 103, 120, 122, 139, 145, 165, 198, 259, 340, 348, 349, 441, 447, 450, 477, 484, 519, 520
United Nations, 113
United States Census Bureau, 113
URL. *See* Uniform Record Locator
Vespucci, Amerigo, 18
Waldseemüller. *See* maps, Waldseemüller
Web Ontology Language, 35, 470, 500, 521
work order, 313, 315–24
Zachman Framework, 34–37, 34, 38, 64, 65, 527
Zachman, John, 34, 64, 65, 465, 469, 470, 478, 484, 504

CPSIA information can be obtained
at www.ICGtesting.com
Printed in the USA
LVHW10s1004170818
587178LV00034BA/410/P